The Concise Encyclopedia of Western Philosophy

Encyclopedias and philosophers are rarely concise. This classic encyclopedia, now updated, combines philosophers and conciseness in a manner perfectly suited to students and other non-specialists. Readers will enjoy philosophy in action here.

Paul Moser, Loyola University of Chicago

Ever since its first appearance in 1960, this *Concise Encyclopedia* has been recognised as a classic, providing not only a guide to philosophy at its best, but some remarkable samples of it too. It is a treasury of brilliant philosophical writing: A. J. Ayer on Russell, Michael Dummett on Frege, R. M. Hare on Ethics, Gilbert Ryle on Categories, P. F. Strawson on Metaphysics and Bernard Williams on Descartes, not to mention Dorothy Emmet, J. N. Findlay, H. L. A. Hart, Walter Kaufmann, G. S. Kirk, Alasdair MacIntyre, P. H. Nowell-Smith, R. S. Peters, Richard Robinson, J. O. Urmson, G. J. Warnock and many others.

This new edition builds on the strengths of the first and brings it completely up to date, with entries on newly emerging philosophers and on themes as diverse as aesthetics, 'African philosophy', gender, translation and philosophy of mind. The *Concise Encyclopedia* offers a lively, readable, comprehensive and authoritative treatment of Western philosophy as a whole, incorporating scintillating articles by many leading philosophical authors. It serves not only as a convenient reference work, but also as an engaging introduction to philosophy.

Jonathan Rée is a freelance historian, journalist and philosopher. His books include *Descartes*, *Philosophy and its Past*, *Proletarian Philosophers*, *Philosophical Tales*, *Heidegger* and *I See a Voice*.

The late **J. O. Urmson**, who edited the first edition, was author of *Philosophical Analysis*, *The Emotive Theory of Ethics* and *The Greek Philosophical Vocabulary*. He was Emeritus Professor at Stanford and Emeritus Fellow of Corpus Christi College, Oxford.

The Concise Encyclopedia of
Western Philosophy

**Edited by
Jonathan Rée
and
J. O. Urmson**

Third Edition

Routledge
Taylor & Francis Group

LONDON AND NEW YORK

First published 1960 by
Unwin Hyman Ltd

Second edition 1975

Third edition published 2005 by
Routledge
2 Park Square, Milton Park, Abingdon, Oxon OX14 4RN

Simultaneously published in the USA and Canada
by Routledge
270 Madison Ave, New York, NY 10016

Routledge is an imprint of the Taylor & Francis Group

© 1960 George Rainbird Ltd
© 1989, 2005 Jonathan Rée

Typeset in Times by
Newgen Imaging Systems (P) Ltd, Chennai, India
Printed and bound in Great Britain by
Biddles Ltd, King's Lynn

British Library Cataloguing in Publication Data
A catalogue record for this book is available from the British Library

Library of Congress Cataloging in Publication Data
    The concise encyclopedia of western philosophy/
edited by J. O. Urmson and Jonathan Rée.—3rd ed.
      p. cm.
    1. Philosophy – Encyclopedias. 2. Philosophers – Biography –
Encyclopedias. I. Rée, Jonathan, 1948– II. Urmson, J. O.
B41.C66 2004
190'.3–dc22   2004004479

ISBN 0–415–32923–X (hbk)
ISBN 0–415–32924–8 (pbk)

Contributors to the original edition (1960)

J. L. Ackrill
H. B. Acton
A. Hilary Armstrong
A. J. Ayer
Errol Bedford
Karl Britton
Joseph G. Dawson
M. A. E. Dummett
Dorothy M. Emmet
A. C. Ewing
Marvin Farber
J. N. Findlay
Thomas Gilby
Roland Hall
R. M. Hare
Rom Harré
H. L. A. Hart
D. J. B. Hawkins
P. L. Heath
Ronald W. Hepburn
Edmund Hill
Walter Kaufmann
I. G. Kidd
G. S. Kirk

Stefan Körner
J. D. Mabbott
Alasdair MacIntyre
D. M. Mackinnon
D. O. C. MacNabb
Philip Merlan
Ernest Nagel
P. H. Nowell-Smith
James O'Connell
D. J. O'Connor
R. S. Peters
Anthony Quinton
Richard Robinson
Erwin I. J. Rosenthal
Gilbert Ryle
Ruth Lydia Saw
P. F. Strawson
F. A. Taylor
Ivo Thomas
J. O. Urmson
James Ward Smith
G. J. Warnock
Alan R. White
Bernard A. O. Williams

Additional contributors to the second edition (1989)

Christopher J. Arthur
Ted Benton
Robert L. Bernasconi
Jay M. Bernstein
Stephen R. L. Clark
Peter Dews
Colin Gordon
Ian Hacking
Alastair Hannay
Ross Harrison
Paulin Hountondji
Richard Kearney
Douglas M. Kellner
David Farrell Krell
Peter Lamarque
Jean-Jacques Lecercle

Genevieve Lloyd
David Macey
Michael Macnamara
Rudolf A. Makkreel
David Papineau
Nicholas Phillipson
Jonathan Powers
Jonathan Rée
David-Hillel Ruben
Peter Singer
Kate Soper
Charles Taylor
Mary Tiles
Jeremy Waldron
Elisabeth Young-Bruehl

Additional contributors to the third edition (2005)

David Archard
Bruce Kuklick
Peter Lamarque

Matthew Nudds
Jonathan Rée

Introduction to the second edition

The very idea of an encyclopedia of philosophy is a bit embarrassing. Some people may fancy, from time to time, that they have achieved an encyclopedic grasp of the problems of philosophy. But all you ever get from an actual encyclopedia is a little knowledge about the personalities and problems which make up the HISTORY OF PHILOSOPHY. And this little knowledge will be enough to convince most people of one thing: that philosophy is such a jumbled and controversial subject that encyclopedic philosophical ambitions are symptoms of megalomania rather than expressions of wisdom.

The first edition of this *Concise Encyclopedia of Western Philosophy and Philosophers* came out in 1960, and it soon won itself the status of a minor classic. Part of its attraction was that none of its large team of contributors disguised their individual voices for the sake of encyclopedic unison. Nevertheless, the majority of these forty-nine authors had a common philosophical allegiance: like their editor, J. O. Urmson, they were participants in what many would regard as the Golden Age of twentieth-century English philosophy – the 'linguistic' movement centred in Oxford in the 1950s, which was inspired by the later Wittgenstein, and advocated by Austin, Hare, Strawson and above all Ryle (see also ANALYTIC PHILOSOPHY). The main thing that united the Oxford philosophers was their ambivalence about the project of philosophical ANALYSIS, particularly as interpreted by LOGICAL POSITIVISM and its English advocate, A. J. Ayer. They admired its intellectual unsentimentality and its terse, hard-edged prose; but they rejected its cut-and-dried scientism and its faith in technicalities and formal logic, and they felt uneasy about its condescension towards the classics of philosophy. As one observer of Oxford in the 1950s put it, philosophy was 'the subject which now spends its time debating whether it was once correct to describe it as Logical Positivism'.

Whatever else one may think of this episode in the history of English philosophy, it was a good moment for compiling an encyclopedia. Urmson's editorial policy, as explained in his Introduction to the first edition, was based on the assumption that 'there are no authorities in philosophy', and that 'there is no set of agreed results'. So he made his Encyclopedia into an incitement to thinking as well as a store of information. Readers could consult the articles on rationalism and empiricism, for example, to get a straightforward guide to two schools whose disagreement is supposed to structure the whole field of philosophical debate; but if they turned to the magisterial article on epistemology they would be told that 'their tug-of-war lacks a rope'. With the second printing (1967), moreover, readers found initials at the end of each article identifying its author: in the case of Epistemology and several others, it was Ryle himself. Hare wrote on ETHICS; Strawson on METAPHYSICS; Ayer on Russell; Dummett on Frege;

Williams on Descartes – to cite only a few examples. And Urmson had extracted perfect miniature samples of their work from his celebrated authors: the result was a remarkable philosophical anthology, as well as an Encyclopedia. Teachers also found that it served well as a textbook for introducing new students to philosophy.

Another of Urmson's objectives was to 'range beyond the confines of British and American philosophical fashions'. Here too, he had some notable successes: Kaufmann's articles on Hegel and Nietzsche are classic sources for his famous if tendentious interpretations; in his article on Husserl, Findlay was able to air his views about 'the strange drop from Phenomenology to Existentialism', and Farber gave a characteristically eccentric interpretation of PHENOMENOLOGY.

This new edition reproduces most of Urmson's Encyclopedia, edited and updated where necessary. I have removed about one-tenth of the original articles, either because they are obsolete, or because they are preposterous (like Kaufmann's notorious piece on Heidegger, which concluded, without argument, that 'there are probably few philosophers to whose vogue Andersen's fairy tale *The Emperor's Clothes* is more applicable').

This venerable material from the original edition is now supplemented with 80 new articles* from 31 authors. Some of the additions concern things that have happened in philosophy in the past thirty years; others take account of new ideas about old topics; several deal with political or literary aspects of philosophy which might have seemed to the first editor to be of little importance; but most of them have to do with PSYCHO-ANALYSIS, Marxism and traditions in European continental philosophy which would not have been regarded as intellectually legitimate by English philosophers in the 1950s.

The initials at the end of each article can be decoded by reference to the lists of contributors on p. v. Initials enclosed in round brackets indicate that the article is a survivor from the first edition; those in square brackets indicate that it is new. So readers can easily tell whose point of view they are being offered, and whether it belongs to the 1950s or the 1980s.

My aim has been to collect the widest range of perspectives on Western Philosophy and Philosophers which could be explained to non-specialist readers and squeezed into a pocketable book. This Encyclopedia is not meant to resolve questions about the nature of philosophy and its encyclopedias though; in fact it will succeed only if it sharpens them.

Jonathan Rée
June 1988

---

* Adorno, 'African Philosophy', Alienation, Althusser, Analytic Philosophy, Anderson, Animals, Anscombe, Applied Ethics, Arendt, Atomism, Bachelard, de Beauvoir, Benjamin, Bentham, Bloch, Canguilhem, Chomsky, Davidson, Deleuze, Derrida, Dialectical Materialism, Dilthey, Duhem, Dummett, Feuerbach, Foot, Foucault, Frankfurt School, Gadamer, Gender, Gramsci, Habermas, Heidegger, Hermeneutics, History of Philosophy, Holism, Horkheimer, Humanism, Ideology, Intentionality, Kierkegaard, Kojève, Kripke, Kuhn, Lacan, Lenin, Levinas, Lukács, MacIntyre, Marcuse, Marx, Merleau-Ponty, Metaphor, Modernism, Modernity, Nozick, Philosophy of Mind, Philosophy of Science, Political Economy, Political Philosophy, Post-modernism, Psychoanalysis, Quantum Mechanics, Quine, Rawls, Realism, Relativism, Relativity, Religion, Ricoeur, Rorty, Sartre, Saussure, Schelling, Smith, Structuralism, Transcendental Arguments, Urmson, Weil.

Introduction to the third edition

A decade and a half later, the *Concise Encyclopedia* is still in good health. But discussions have moved on, fashions have changed and a number of mournful obituaries have had to be written. The field remains as controversial as ever, and no attempt has been made to conceal divergences not only between the subjects of this Encyclopedia but also between its authors. Meanwhile the gap between what professional philosophers want to write about and what students and general readers want to read shows no signs of narrowing. With thorough line-by-line updating, refurbishment and revision, and more than eighty new articles[**] (identifiable by curly brackets – {} – enclosing the initials of the author) this third edition will continue to bridge the gap.

Jonathan Rée
December 2003

[**] New articles for 2004 include Academy, Aesthetics, Berlin, Burke, Categorical Imperative, Cavell, Coleridge, Continental Philosophy, Darwin, Diogenes Laertius, Evil, Hackenschmidt, Jonas, Logical Atomism, Neurath, Newton, Personal Identity, Sellars, Substance, Translation, Virtue Ethics.

A

Abelard, Peter (c.1079–1142) The
details of the stormy life of the Breton
philosopher Peter Abelard are found in
the autobiographical letter known as the
Historia Calamitatum, which describes
the consequences of his seduction of
Héloise, niece of Canon Fulbert of Notre
Dame: when their child was born they
married secretly but Héloise's brothers
broke into Abelard's room at night and
castrated him; subsequently Héloise
became a nun and Abelard a monk.

In philosophy, Abelard is noted for his
skill as a DIALECTICIAN and his contribution to the problem of UNIVERSALS. He
studied LOGIC under Roscellinus, a
NOMINALIST, and later disputed with the
REALIST theologian William of Champeaux
in Paris. The details of this debate are
given in Abelard's logical treatises
Concerning Genera and Species and
Glosses on Porphyry. He stands by the
principle that only individuals exist and
that universal terms get their meaning
purely from the abstractive power of the
mind. The famous formula that the mind
may consider factors separately without
considering them as separate from one
another gave a convenient dialectical
answer to the problem as formulated by
BOETHIUS. Abelard also wrote an ethical
treatise, *Know Thyself*, which emphasizes the subjective element in human
conduct and the role of intention in moral
evaluation. (J.G.D.)

Academy In or around 385 BC, PLATO
set up in a park outside Athens a school
called the *akademeia*. The institution came
to be called the Academy, and remained in
more or less continuous existence for
more than 900 years, being associated
first with the mathematical and ethical
teachings of Plato and his pupils, and
later with a revival of the SCEPTICISM
attributed to SOCRATES. A fashion for
referring to all sorts of educational institutions as 'academic' was associated with
the burgeoning taste for Platonism in the
seventeenth-century Europe, and has
incongruously survived it. {J.R.}

Adorno, Theodor W. (1903–69) The
German philosopher Theodor Adorno
was, along with Max HORKHEIMER and
Herbert MARCUSE, a major architect of the
FRANKFURT SCHOOL of Critical Theory.
Besides his work in philosophy, Adorno
was also active as a sociologist, literary
theorist and musicologist (he was student
of Alban Berg, a composer of several
songs and chamber works and a defender
of Arnold Schoenberg).

Adorno's most important philosophical works are *Negative Dialectics* (1966)
and *Aesthetic Theory* (1970). In *Negative
Dialectics* he argues that dialectics needs
to be freed from the totalizing impulse of
HEGEL's system, because the 'whole' of
contemporary society is not a Hegelian
reconciliation of universal and particular,
but the domination of particularity by
the universality of subjective reason,
determined solely by the drive for self-
preservation. Subjective reason conceives
of knowing as the mastery of things by
concepts, where nothing is cognitively
significant except what different items
share, or what makes them the 'same'. The
rule of identity and sameness is realized
not only philosophically, in the systems of
German IDEALISM, but also materially, in

the capitalist system where use values (particulars) are dominated by exchange value (universality). Negative dialectics is dialectics without a final moment of unification. It operates for the sake of the object of cognition, and its goal is to reveal the non-identity between objects and the concepts under which they are usually 'identified'. For Adorno cognitive utopia would not be a unified science, but a use of concepts to unseal the non-conceptual without making it their equal.

In *Aesthetic Theory* Adorno argues that the kind of non-identity thinking aimed at by negative dialectics is, for the time being at least, adumbrated in modernist works of art. Successful works of art claim us beyond our ability to redeem their claims conceptually. They are particulars demanding acknowledgement while simultaneously resisting understanding or explanation: in fact it is their very unintelligibility which reveals the wounding duality between particularity and universality in modern rationality. Art is a prefiguration of a world which comprehends individuals without dominating them. For Adorno modernist art enacts a critique of subjective reason, and reveals the possibility of another form of reason. Other noteworthy philosophical works by Adorno are: *Dialectic of Enlightenment* (with Max Horkheimer, 1947); *Kierkegaard: The Construction of the Aesthetic* (1933); *Against Epistemology: A Metacritique* (1956) (on HUSSERL); *The Jargon of Authenticity* (1964) (on HEIDEGGER); *Three Studies on Hegel* (1963); and *Minima Moralia: Reflections from Damaged Life* (1951). See also AESTHETICS, PHILOSOPHY OF SCIENCE.   [J.M.B.]

Aenesidemus   See STOICS.

Aesthetics   Philosophical reflection on beauty and the arts goes back to classical Greek thought, which sought for a definition of beauty, introduced the important term 'mimesis' (imitation), and launched the first sustained inquiry into the moral status of poetry. But modern philosophical aesthetics (which owes its name to Alexander Baumgarten in 1735) took its impetus and many of its guiding principles from KANT's *Critique of Judgment* (1790) and various eighteenth-century writings on 'taste' by the Earl of SHAFTESBURY, HUTCHESON, HUME and BURKE. These authors highlighted the question as to how far judgements of beauty could attain objectivity and universality, often making comparisons between art and morality. But it was Kant's account of aesthetic judgement as based on disinterested attention to the appearance of an object that became the foundation for subsequent thinking about the aesthetic realm, eventually transmuting into versions of artistic formalism that made no reference to morality. Philosophical aesthetics has two broad centres of interest: first the nature of art, and second, the nature of aesthetic experience in general.

One leading question in the philosophy of art concerns the definition of art. The idea of 'fine arts' (*beaux arts*), covering diverse forms like music, poetry, painting, sculpture and dance, was introduced in the eighteenth century; but the explicit search for an essence of art – a set of distinctive properties shared by all forms of art – was first given prominence by analytical philosophers in the second half of the twentieth century. The search has proved inconclusive, but four broad tendencies can be distinguished. Some philosophers reject the very idea of defining art: Morris Weitz, in 1956, applied WITTGENSTEIN's notion of 'family resemblance' to art, arguing that it is an 'open concept' with no 'essence'. Others have sought a definition in terms of the functions of art: for example, to express emotions (R. G. COLLINGWOOD) or to provide aesthetic experiences (Monroe Beardsley). A third group has proposed 'institutional' definitions, where the defining properties are not intrinsic or functional but relational. On this view, objects are works of art not in virtue of what they look like or what purpose they fulfil but by having the status of art conferred upon them by the 'art world' (George Dickie). Finally, there are 'historical' definitions (Jerrold Levinson, Noël Carroll), whereby an object counts as art if it stands in an appropriate relation to objects previously accepted as art. None of these approaches has received universal assent although there is broad acceptance that some kinds of relational properties are involved in identifying art. Related debates concern whether the concept of 'art' is fundamentally evaluative or merely classificatory and what ontological category art works fall into – for example, particulars or types – and whether there is only one such category for all kinds of art.

The philosophy of art also addresses questions about meaning, truth and value in the arts. Debates about meaning ask, for example: whether the task of artistic interpretation is to recover the artist's mental processes, conscious or unconscious, as suggested by romantic or expressivist conceptions of art; whether interpretation allows for imaginative creativeness on the part of the interpreter; whether plural, even conflicting, interpretations are permissible; and whether a work's very identity changes under different interpretations. The relation between art and truth has also been contested. For some, art is closely bound up with ideology (ADORNO), or it 'unconceals' truth at the heart of being (HEIDEGGER) or it aspires to universal truth (ARISTOTLE); others are more sceptical, either because of suspicions about truth itself (NIETZSCHE, RORTY), or because they consider art to be radically

distinct from philosophy (PLATO). The value that art is taken to have will depend on what conception of art is adopted; mimetic theories commend art for holding up a 'mirror to nature' or more generally for its cognitive (truth bearing) potential; others locate artistic value in kinds of pleasure or experience (Monroe Beardsley), yet others in expressive or formal qualities (CROCE, Clive Bell); according to Marxist tradition, value judgements are grounded in ideology and matters of aesthetic taste merely expressions of social and historical conditions (Terry Eagleton, Pierre Bourdieu). In recent years, the philosophy of art has focused increasingly on particular art forms. For example, there is debate about how pictures represent objects: is it through conventional symbolism (Nelson GOODMAN), through 'seeing-in' (Richard Wollheim), through make-believe (Kendall Walton), through modes of resemblance (Malcolm Budd) or in other ways? Issues about pictorial representation have been extended to photography and film (Roger Scruton, Noël Carroll). There are also philosophical problems about music: what kind of entities musical works are, how music expresses emotion, whether music has meaning, and whether pure instrumental music is strictly art. Literature has long been a topic of interest in aesthetics: whether there is a distinctive kind of 'poetic truth' (famously debated by Plato and Aristotle), how fictionality is to be explained, and how literature can be defined.

Apart from these specific questions in the philosophy of art, there are issues about aesthetic experience in general. Some of these issues span all artefacts and natural objects, as well as art. One concerns the very nature of aesthetic appreciation: is there, as Kant thought, a distinctive kind of *aesthetic* attention – disinterested, non-conceptual, and removed from desire and utility? If so, is this associated with a particular kind of *experience* and does it reveal particular *qualities*? The idea of a specific 'aesthetic attitude' has come under attack: as an unsupported 'myth' (George Dickie) and, by feminist aestheticians, in relation to art, as overly detached and apolitical. Modern debates about aesthetic properties originate in the work of Frank Sibley, who distinguished aesthetic qualities, such as *unified, balanced, integrated, dynamic* or *delicate*, from non-aesthetic, physical or perceptual, qualities, arguing that the former are non-condition-governed, require 'taste' for their apprehension, and are 'emergent' from the latter. All these claims are debated, as are realism and anti-realism about aesthetic qualities, whether such qualities are irreducibly evaluative, and how aesthetic and non-aesthetic properties relate. Finally, there has been burgeoning interest in aesthetics applied to nature and the environment. How does the aesthetic appreciation of nature relate to that of art? How far should aesthetic judgements about nature be informed by background scientific knowledge (Allen Carlson)? And, returning to a Kantian theme, what does it mean for nature – its magnitude and its power – to evoke experiences of the sublime? {P.L.}

'African Philosophy' The concept of African Philosophy originated as a variant of the general idea of 'Primitive' Philosophy, which in its turn is part of the history of European attempts to understand the strange practices of 'other peoples'. In *Primitive Culture* (1871) the English anthropologist E. B. Tylor (1832–1917) postulated a childish but coherent world-picture called 'animism', which he took to be at the basis of 'primitive society'. Animism, for Tylor, was a rudimentary scientific theory which attempted to explain natural phenomena by attributing them to the voluntary acts of personal spirits; it was not an arbitrary invention, but a special if naïve application of the principle of causality. In this sense Tylor's approach was intellectualist: he went beyond purely emotional factors, such as fear, upon which previous analyses of 'primitive culture' had focused, in order to identify its conceptual foundations. This intellectualist approach did not necessarily involve a rehabilitation of 'primitive' culture or an affirmation of cultural equality. 'Primitives' were still primitive, 'savages' still savage. For Tylor's intellectualism was a form of evolutionist sociology, in which inequalities of development were seen against a background assumption of the ultimate identity of humanity as a whole. Thus it contrasts, on the right hand, with theories of absolute difference, which fragment the idea of 'the human race' into several different 'races'; and on the left, with the principled egalitarianism which regards actual inequalities of achievement as historical accidents, which do not detract in any way from the equal value of all cultures and peoples.

Tylor drew extensively on COMTE's theory that the history both of the individual and of humanity as a whole passes from a theological stage, through a metaphysical one, to a positive or scientific stage. Comte had regarded each of these three stages as based on a specific 'philosophy', and held that their historical succession exhibited a progressive acceptance of the limits of human understanding. Thus theology, for Comte, was the earliest and most ambitious form of philosophy. It too had developed in three stages: fetishism, polytheism and monotheism. Fetishism – the habit of treating inert objects as though they were alive – was thus the absolute beginning of reason. However, according to Comte every member of every society has to go through all the same stages, and moreover no society and no scientific system, however highly developed, could break completely with its origins. So Comte insisted on the functional value of fetishism, as the stage of the initial stirring of conceptual exploration, which left its mark on all subsequent ones.

Tylor, in contrast, saw fetishism (or animism, as he re-named it) as an absolutely backward mentality, present in primitive societies but completely overcome in civilized ones. However, even Tylor's intellectualism came to be criticized for being excessively generous towards primitive cultures. In *How Natives Think: Mental Functions in Inferior Societies* (1910), the French philosopher Lucien Lévy-Bruhl (1857–1939) complained that the idea of 'animism' made the unjustified assumption that 'savages' are capable of rudimentary logical thought, and hence that they are essentially the same as the 'civilized adult white man'. Lévy-Bruhl suggested that savages are pre-logical and separated from Europeans by a gulf as large as that between vertebrate and invertebrate animals.

The French writer Raoul Allier reached very similar conclusions, on the basis of reports and letters written by Protestant missionaries. In *The Psychology of Conversion amongst Uncivilised Peoples* (1925) and *The Uncivilised Peoples and Ourselves: Irreducible Difference or Basic Identity?* (1927), Allier also challenged the idea of a universal human nature, and described the intellectual methods of 'savages' as 'para-logical'. On this basis he argued that when uncivilized individuals were converted to Christianity they underwent a total crisis, which gave them access not only to a new faith, but to a new humanity.

There was then a reaction against both pre- and para-logicism, and a well-meaning revival of intellectualism. Thus in *Primitive Man as Philosopher* (1927) the American anthropologist Paul Radin (1883–1959) described the role played by intellectuals in 'primitive society' in order to discredit the myth that 'primitive man' is totally submerged in society, dominated by the thinking of the group, and lacking individual personality. The French ethnographer Marcel Griaule (1908–56) pursued a similar task with the Dogon of French Sudan (now Mali). He did his best to efface himself as a theorist, and to act as little more than a secretary, recording, transcribing and translating the statements of some 'master of the spoken word' (see, e.g. his *Conversations with Ogotemmêli*, 1948). With the discovery of 'oral literature', numerous other investigators, including many Africans, have taken the same approach as Griaule.

In this context, 'primitive philosophy' means an explicit set of doctrines, rather than the merely implicit animism postulated in Tylor's *Primitive Culture*. But the Dogon cosmogony which was expounded with elaborate beauty by Ogotemmêli is more like a magnificent poem than an exercise in abstract, systematic, critical analysis. It is not clear why it should be categorized as 'philosophy' as opposed to, for example, 'religion' or 'mythology'.

Some of the more ardent exponents of this approach therefore attempted to go behind the actual words of their informants in order to reconstruct another, more systematic and philosophical discourse upon which they could be taken to depend. Thus *Bantu Philosophy* (1945), by the Belgian missionary Placide Tempels, depicted a specifically Bantu ontology involving a dynamic conception of the universe based on the idea of a complex, stratified plurality of forces. This ontology, he said, contrasted with the static Aristotelian concept of Being which predominated in Europe; and he presented the doctrine in a systematic, deductive form which looks distinctly philosophical. Tempels also argued for the theological conclusion that God has always been present to Bantu thought in the guise of a supreme force. This had important implications for his 'missiology' (theory of missionary activity): it meant that Allier was mistaken in conceiving conversion as a total crisis and breakthrough into a new type of humanity; rather it was a return to the real meaning of authentic Bantu thought, peeling away historical accretions to discover an original revelation of the divine.

But Tempels' generous conception of Bantu philosophy could also be seen as an expression of colonialist condescension. He admitted that the Bantu people themselves were incapable of formulating 'Bantu philosophy', but claimed that when the ethnologist articulated it for them, they recognized it immediately as representing their own view. However, this suggested that their thought became philosophical only thanks to outside intervention. It is not surprising that in his *Discourse on Colonialism* (1950), Aimé Césaire denounced Tempels for inviting colonists to respect the philosophy of the Africans rather than their rights.

Nevertheless, a number of later authors, mostly Africans, have followed Tempels in trying to reconstitute 'African philosophy', or, more cautiously, the philosophy of some particular group of Africans, or 'African thought' generally. The theory of negritude developed by Léopold Senghor, from the word coined by Césaire, is closely related to this idea of 'African philosophy'; so too are the works of the Rwandan writer Alexis Kagamé (1912–81) (*The Bantu–Rwandan Philosophy of Being*, 1956, and *Comparative Bantu Philosophy*, 1976).

The trouble with all these investigations is that they are based on an antiquarian conception of philosophy, as something which belongs essentially to the past: they are uncritical attempts to restore a philosophy which is supposed to be already given, a collective world-view passively shared by a whole society. They are exercises in what has been called 'ethnophilosophy', rather than philosophy itself. Unfortunately, the positive, factual and historical assumptions of ethnophilosophy still dominate African philosophy; but happily they do not have a monopoly.

The alternative is to take the idea of African philosophy more literally, so that it means the contributions which African thinkers make to the sorts of critical and reflexive discussions in which philosophy has traditionally been taken to consist. Then the European history of African philosophy could be replaced by an African history of philosophy, with philosophy defined by its simple if subversive insistence on truth (which of course does not exclude, but on the contrary presupposes being rooted in a historical situation and responding to extra-philosophical problems). African philosophy in this sense has a long history – certainly longer than that of ethnophilosophy. More and more Africans are rejecting philosophical antiquarianism as a manipulative impoverishment of the past: they are refusing to reduce African culture to pure traditions emptied of movement and controversy. Knowledge of old African cultures is no longer the necessary starting point for African philosophy; and it is certainly not the last word. See also HISTORY OF PHILOSOPHY, RELIGION.　　　　[P.J.H.]

Albert the Great (1206–80)　Albert the Great (also known as Albertus Magnus, Albert of Lauingen and Albert of Cologne) was canonized in 1931. He was born in Swabia, and studied at Padua, where he joined the Dominicans; later he became Bishop of Ratisbon. He taught at Cologne and Paris. He was a traveller, administrator, theologian, but above all an indefatigable experimentalist, especially in botany and zoology, held in grudging respect by his contemporary, Roger BACON. He wrote of ARISTOTLE with great sympathy, and together with his pupil Thomas AQUINAS, he led the movement which introduced a new form of Aristotelianism into Christian thought. But he was a less synthetic and impersonal thinker than Aquinas: he commented on Aristotle in the older style of paraphrase and digression, and is closer to AVICENNA than to AVERROES. His sympathy for the NEOPLATONISM of Dionysius and Proclus descended through his disciples, Ulrich of Strasbourg and Dietrich of Freiburg, to Master Eckhart, John Tauler and the Dominican mystics of the Rhineland. (T.G.)

Alembert, Jean le Rond d' (1717–83) French mathematician, see ENCYCLO-PEDISTS.

Alexander, Samuel (1859–1938) Samuel Alexander was born in Australia but educated in Victorian Oxford in the IDEALIST tradition. But as Professor at Manchester University for many years he became one of the most noted REALIST metaphysicians of his time. His great work was *Space, Time and Deity* (1920), which argued that the basic stuff of the universe is space-time or pure motion, and that everything develops out of it by a process of emergent evolution. Things or substances are volumes of space-time with a determinate contour; matter is low in the scale of evolution, and gives rise to life and finally – so far as we are concerned – mind; but no one can say what will emerge later in the process. The universe is always striving towards a future stage, which for the time being is the deity; God is never actual but always in the making. (J.O.U.)

Alienation Strictly speaking, to alienate something is to separate it from oneself or disown it. But an extended concept of alienation gained wide currency in the twentieth-century philosophy and social theory. Under converging influences from EXISTENTIALISM, the FRANKFURT SCHOOL, HUMANISM and PSYCHOANALYSIS, the term 'alienation' has been used in numerous diagnoses of the maladies of 'the modern world'. All sorts of alleged symptoms of 'MODERNITY' – the dichotomies of civilization and barbarism, scientism and irrationalism, town and country, mental and manual labour, atheism and religiosity, individualization and massification, banal popular culture and unintelligible high culture, intellect and feeling, masculine and feminine etc. – have been encompassed within theories of alienation.

Superficially, alienation refers to a subjective feeling of unease, dissociation or exile. At a deeper level, it indicates a structure which prevents people from 'identifying' with the social and spiritual conditions of their existence. Ultimately it implies that modernity is the loss or disruption of an original unity, and may also suggest that a day of reconciliation in a 'higher unity' is about to dawn.

But alienation is not supposed to be a catastrophe striking humanity from outside; it is essentially a perverted, malign and self-destructive expression of human creativity itself. Alienation means that people are subject to an oppression which – though they may not recognize it – is of their own making. In this sense Mary Shelley's story of Frankenstein and his monster provides an exact allegory of alienation.

The concept of alienation achieved popularity as the basis for an alternative to DIALECTICAL MATERIALISM in the philosophical interpretation of Marxism. Humanistic Marxists such as MARCUSE, SARTRE and the psychoanalyst Erich Fromm (1900–80) used the term to translate the German words *Entfremdung* and *Entäusserung*, with particular reference to the young MARX and his philosophy of labour or *praxis*. In the *1844 Manuscripts* (published in 1932) Marx tried to explain capitalism, or rather 'the system of private property', as a form of 'alienated labour'. As Marx acknowledged, this explanation was indebted to FEUERBACH, who argued in *The Essence of Christianity* that 'religion is the dream of the human mind' and that the God that people worship is really nothing more than their own 'alienated self', inverted and unrecognized. According to the young Marx, the function of labour in modern society is just like that which Feuerbach attributed to worship in religion: it creates the power which confronts and overwhelms it. Hence 'the *alienation* of the worker in his product means not only that his labour becomes an object, an *outside* existence, but also that it exists *outside* him, independent and alien, and becomes a self-sufficient power over against him – that the life he has lent to the object confronts him, hostile and alien'. Moreover, in Marx's theory money itself plays the part of Feuerbach's humanly constructed God: 'it is the visible deity, the transformation of all human and natural qualities into their opposites'; thus, 'the *divine* power of money resides in its nature as the alienated, externalised and self-estranging *species-being* of humanity: it is the alienated *power* of human beings'.

Some Marxist commentators (notably ALTHUSSER) have argued that the theory of alienation is no more than a regrettable vestige of pre-Marxist ideology. Nevertheless numerous traces of it are to be found in Marx's *Capital*, for example in the doctrine of 'commodity fetishism' and criticisms of bourgeois theorists like J. S. MILL for 'the folly of identifying a specific *social relationship of production* with the thinglike qualities of articles'. LUKÁCS' *History and Class Consciousness* (1923) was the first work to interpret Marxism in terms of alienation or rather 'REIFICATION'. Later, Lukács followed the theme back to HEGEL, arguing in *The Young Hegel* that alienation is 'the central philosophical concept of the *Phenomenology of Spirit*' (see also KOJÈVE). The concept is also at work in ROUSSEAU's social theory, and may indeed be traced much further back: perhaps it can even be detected in the theology of NEOPLATONISM (see also PLOTINUS) and in PRE-SOCRATIC doctrines of creation. For the idea that humanity is at odds with itself, and adrift from its spiritual home, is probably co-extensive with religion in general; in which case 'modernity' must be considerably older than is commonly supposed.   [J.R.]

Althusser, Louis (1918–90) The French-Algerian philosopher Louis Althusser is best known for his writings from 1960 onwards, the main theme of which was a re-working of Marxist orthodoxy and an associated defence of the scientific status of HISTORICAL MATERIALISM. Using ideas derived from French historical PHILOSOPHY OF SCIENCE and from STRUCTURALISM, Althusser argued that Marx's early works, with their 'HUMANIST' and 'historicist' philosophical basis, should be regarded as 'pre-scientific'. Later writings such as *Capital* could then be read as containing the elements of a new 'scientific' theory of social formations and their transformations. Human individuals were to be understood not as the self-conscious sources of their social life, but rather as 'bearers' of a system of social relations which exists prior to and independently of their consciousness and activity. In opposition to economic reductionism, Althusser argued for a recognition of the relative autonomy of political, cultural and intellectual practices within a loosely defined 'determination in the last instance' by economic structures and practices.

This notion of 'relative autonomy', together with Althusser's insistence upon the irreducible complexity of social contradictions and struggles, made it possible for a new significance to be given to cultural analysis and to forms of resistance not directly attributable to 'class struggle'. However, Althusser's 'scientism', and his apparent denial of autonomous human agency led to a growing division between Althusser and his followers. Althusser's response was a spate of self-critical writings which appeared to put an end to what was distinctive in the school of Marxist philosophy which he had engendered. [T.B.]

American Philosophy Philosophy in what is now the United States is characterized by distinctive religious and practical concerns that go back to the beginning of the eighteenth century. At its origin, American philosophy was a three-way conversation, led by a number of New England parish ministers who wrote on problems in protestant philosophical theology, debating the moral responsibility of the solitary individual confronting a mysterious deity, in dialogue with thinkers in England, Scotland and later Germany. This group included Ralph Waldo EMERSON, who became celebrated as a sage and interpreter of the uniqueness of the American intellect. But its pioneer was Jonathan EDWARDS, whose extraordinary talents still command attention today. Edwards was indebted to both the Platonic

and the empiricist tradition in Britain, and his followers also assimilated Scottish Realism and then German IDEALISM. In *Freedom of the Will* (1754) he delineated ideas about the compatibility of freedom and determinism that are comparable to those of HOBBES and HUME, while his *Religious Affections* (1746) argued for a connection between belief and action that anticipates some twentieth-century views.

The second part of the conversation was located in divinity schools in the northeast, south and mid-west. Apart from law and medical schools, these were the only institutions in America offering post-graduate instruction. The theologians at Andover, Harvard, Princeton and especially Yale gradually took over intellectual leadership from the old parish ministers. Though writing in particular conformity to their understanding of the New Testament, they developed a distinctive PHILOSOPHY OF MIND in which feeling, will, and intellect had carefully defined roles, and in which the intellect's ability to grasp the reality of the external world was not compromised.

The third set of participants in the conversation held chairs in philosophy in American colleges, and were the only ones who actually called themselves philosophers. They concurred in the Protestant doctrines of the theologians, but they also engaged with questions of politics and the grounds of social order. Many of them served as presidents of their institutions, and had captive student audiences and easy access to publication. Noah Porter (1811–92) of Yale led a move away from the realistic epistemology of the past to one grounded in the TRANSCENDENTAL IDEALISM of KANT.

This entire tradition went into abeyance in the Revolutionary and Constitutional period (1776–87), but despite the preoccupation of the 'Founding Fathers' with politics, they never lost sight of larger theoretical issues. The *Federalist Papers* (1787–8 – published anonymously but mostly attributable to Alexander Hamilton, 1755/7–1804, and James Madison, 1751–1836), which commented on the proposed American Constitution, remain an extraordinary set of arguments for republican government based on history, political observation, and a prudent and realistic appraisal of human nature. The briefer reflections on the nature of democratic government by Abraham Lincoln (1809–65), which are still widely read, reflect back on the Constitutional period but also look towards the present.

After the Civil War, the influence of Charles DARWIN devastated the religious orientation of traditional American philosophy. At the same time, many colleges were transformed into internationally recognized centres of learning, while new universities commanded national attention. Students who a generation earlier would have sought graduate training in Germany, or in a theological college, would by 1900 attend an American university to study for the doctoral degree. Theologians and clergymen gave way to professional philosophers, and students sought in secular philosophy much of what their predecessors had found in a theological education.

The starting point for American university philosophers in the second half of the nineteenth century was German idealism. But idealism in America soon took the distinctive form of PRAGMATISM, which linked mind or spirit with practice or action, and found a new approach to traditional problems of knowledge by focusing on practices and processes of inquiry. Pragmatism was hospitable to the natural and social sciences and embraced an optimistic perspective on politics, based on the conviction that it is never impossible for human effort to make a difference. Knowledge of the world consisted not in our grasp of a pre-existing object but rather in our ability to accommodate ourselves to a potentially hostile environment. Applying Darwinism to philosophy, the pragmatists treated beliefs not as mental entities but as modes of action, which had to struggle for survival in the competitive world of experience; to call them true was not to attribute a mysterious metaphysical property to them, but simply to say that they had prevailed in competition with others. Pragmatists also emphasized the social dimension of inquiry, showing how ideas are propagated not so much within individual minds as among groups of investigators. Some forms of pragmatism might also reinstate religion at least in a chastened form: after all, if beliefs about spirituality prospered, then pragmatists were bound to call them true. But even non-religious pragmatists held that the world was what human beings collectively made of it, and pragmatism at its most influential was a form of COMMUNITARIAN idealism, not unlike that of T. H. GREEN in England.

There were two varieties of pragmatism. One was associated with the Harvard philosophers Charles PEIRCE, William JAMES and Josiah ROYCE. The Harvard pragmatists took mathematics, logic and the physical sciences as their model of inquiry, though William James sought to justify religion as well as science. The second variant of pragmatism was the 'instrumentalism' of John DEWEY, who took the social sciences as his exemplar of useful knowledge. Dewey taught at the University of Chicago in the 1890s, and shaped the intellectual life of New York City after he moved to Columbia University in 1904, stressing the ways in which the social sciences could be applied to the improvement of the cultural and social world. As well as writing in their own learned magazines, the pioneers of pragmatism contributed to a wider educated culture with works such as Peirce's essays in the *Popular Science Monthly* of 1877–8, James's *Pragmatism* (1907) and Dewey's *Quest for Certainty* (1929). Their mix of the professorial and the popular defined what has been called the 'Golden Age' of American philosophy. When the totalitarianism of the 1930s precipitated an influx of European intellectuals, LOGICAL POSITIVISM became influential, and the ANALYTIC PHILOSOPHY that came in its wake turned its back on socially engaged normative reasoning. In the middle years of the century, C. I. LEWIS, Nelson GOODMAN, and W. V. QUINE continued the Harvard tradition, while calling pragmatism into question. Lewis's *Mind and the World-Order* (1929) introduced the influential notion of alternative conceptual schemes that might, in various ways, interpret the given data of sense. However, Wilfrid SELLARS, of the University of Pittsburgh, rejected this sort of empiricism, insisting in 'Empiricism and the Philosophy of Mind' (1956) that science was the unique construct that explained the materialistic physical and biological world that human beings inhabited.

The 1960s accelerated the withdrawal of philosophy into the academic enclave. Lewis's ideas were taken up by Goodman and Quine, who presumed some form of materialism but also used the tools of symbolic logic to argue that diverse frameworks of human understanding might be justified. This 'pragmatic analysis' was carried forward by Hilary PUTNAM as well as Thomas KUHN, whose *Structure of Scientific Revolutions* (1962) opened the way for attacks on the absolute legitimacy of the sciences. Richard RORTY, in *Philosophy and the Mirror of Nature* (1979), tried to throw out the whole idea

of knowledge as a representation of facts, in a way that his many critics thought led to relativism. At the same time, many other scholars proclaimed that philosophy was no more than a rather pretentious branch of imaginative literature, and that it had no future as a distinct discipline. American philosophy entered the twenty-first century in a confused and fragile state. {B.K.}

Analysis The Greek word 'analysis' means the resolution of a complex whole into its parts, as opposed to 'synthesis', which means the construction of a whole out of parts. Philosophers have always had two main aims, the construction of systems of METAPHYSICS, LOGIC or ETHICS (synthesis) and the clarification of important ideas (analysis). These cannot always be sharply distinguished, since what is synthesis from one point of view is analysis from another. PLATO's *Republic*, for example, may be considered as the construction in thought of a perfectly just society or as the analysis of the idea of a just society. Large parts of ARISTOTLE's *Ethics* are concerned with the analysis of such important ideas as 'voluntary action', 'virtue and vice', 'pleasure' etc.

In modern times CONTINENTAL PHILOSOPHY has tended to be synthetic and British philosophy analytic. For DESCARTES the analysis of concepts was only a preparation for the construction of a system of knowledge based on certain 'clear and distinct ideas' obtained by analysis; and SPINOZA sought to construct a view of the world deduced from a small number of definitions and axioms. British philosophers, on the other hand, have tended to be suspicious of constructive metaphysics and more concerned with the analysis of thought and experience into their fundamental elements.

From the beginning of the twentieth century the view that analysis is the distinguishing feature of philosophy was widely accepted in English-speaking countries. Philosophers who follow this trend often have little in common with each other except the use of the word 'analysis' to describe their various activities. The most that can be said is that they take the function of philosophy to be, not the acquisition of new knowledge (which is the function of the special sciences), but the clarification and articulation of what we already know. Three main stands can be detected in the practice of analysis.

(1) G. E. MOORE questioned the assumption – common amongst the IDEALISTS who dominated British philosophy at the end of the nineteenth century – that we do not know the humdrum things about the world that we ordinarily claim to know. Some had said that these things are actually false; others, that we could not know them to be true. The world, as it appears to us, is mere appearance, and its reality is recondite, wholly unlike what we take it to be, and accessible only through profound researches conducted in some technical language. Against this, Moore held that such truisms as that he had a body, that he was born some years ago and that he had existed ever since, could be known for certain. Nevertheless he had no wish to assert that metaphysical theories which contradicted these assertions were merely outrageous falsehoods. They were certainly that; but they were also mistaken attempts to answer genuine and puzzling questions. Though we cannot seriously doubt the truth of such ordinary statements, we may not be able to state clearly and precisely what they mean. We do not, in his words, 'know their proper analysis'; and almost all his philosophical activity was devoted to the analysis of propositions whose truth is not in doubt.

To give the proper analysis of a concept or proposition is to replace the word or sentence which is normally used to express it by some other expression which is exactly equivalent, but less puzzling. An analysis, therefore, is a sort of definition, a kind of equation with the puzzling expression, the *analysandum*, on the left-hand side and the new expression, sometimes called the *analysis*, sometimes the *analysans*, on the right. It implies the splitting of a complex form, or replacing an expression that stood for a complex concept by a longer expression that lays bare its hidden complexity. Moore seems to have used this technique solely with the aim of clarifying concepts; he had no metaphysical theory and did not suppose that the things mentioned in the analysis were in any sense more real or fundamental than those mentioned in the analysandum. How, indeed, could they be, if the analysandum and the analysis were to refer, as they must, to exactly the same things?

(2) Bertrand RUSSELL practised the same sort of definitional analysis as Moore, but for very different reasons and with very different aims. Where Moore sought only clarity and never wished to depart from common-sense beliefs, Russell sought metaphysical truth and was quite willing to say, with the idealists, that common sense beliefs can be false and ordinary language wholly inadequate for discovering and expressing truth. The idealists had claimed that only reality as a whole (the absolute) was wholly real; particular things were abstractions from this totality and, as such, only partially real or not real at all. Russell's picture (known as LOGICAL ATOMISM) was the exact opposite – that of a world composed of 'atomic facts', each corresponding to a true 'atomic statement'.

Consider the statement 'it is either raining or snowing'. This is not made true by correspondence with a complex alternative fact, either-rain-or-snow. It is true if either of the atomic parts of which it is composed ('it is raining' and 'it is snowing') is true. Thus compound or 'molecular' statements do not correspond or fail to correspond to compound facts; they can be broken down into atomic statements which do, when true, correspond to atomic facts. The aim of analysis was to break down complex facts into their atomic components, the method was to analyse complex statements into theirs. Russell's conception of analysis was influenced by the fact that he came to metaphysics from the study of mathematics and formal logic. As a mathematician, he regarded all defined terms as theoretically superfluous. Thus if 'two' can be defined as 'one plus one' and 'three' as 'two plus one', it follows that arithmetical operations could be carried on with no numerals other than 'one'. Russell himself had claimed to 'eliminate' in this way even the notion of 'number', by defining it in terms belonging to logic. As a metaphysician, Russell held that if the word 'number' could be eliminated by being defined, then numbers were not among the ultimate constituents of the world which it was his aim to discover. These constituents, whatever they turned out to be, would be only such things as would be named in a language in which all defined terms had been replaced by ultimately indefinable ones.

Russell's study of logic also convinced him that the *grammar* of natural languages is radically misleading. 'Horses do not bellow' and 'chimaeras do not exist' have the same grammatical form; but while the first denies that certain objects (horses) have a certain property (bellowing), the second does not deny that chimaeras have the property of existing. Rather it says that nothing in the world has the property of being a chimaera. Russell's aim here was that of replacing expressions whose grammatical form was misleading by expressions in 'proper logical form', where grammatical structures would reflect the form of the facts they stated. Confronted by the statement, 'the average plumber earns ten pounds a week', one might ask 'who is this average plumber?' and fall into wild metaphysical speculation. The remedy was to see that the statement could be translated into 'the number of pounds earned each week by plumbers divided by the number of plumbers is ten', a statement from which 'the average plumber' has been eliminated. No one is likely to be bemused in such a simple case; but serious consequences, both theoretical and practical, had certainly followed in the case of objects such as 'the State' or 'Public Opinion'. It is clear that these are – like armies, governments, schools and other institutions – in some sense abstractions, and that to say something about them is to say something, though not the same thing, about the people who make them up. In technical language they were said to be 'logical constructions' out of the more concrete objects (people) who compose them. Russell and his followers had high hopes that analysis could be carried to yet deeper metaphysical levels by showing that the things, including people, that we normally treat as belonging on the 'ground-floor level' of experience, were logical constructions out of more fundamental entities.

(3) Russell's views on logic and analysis were taken up by the LOGICAL POSITIVISTS, but with a very different aim. Where Russell sought a true metaphysical theory, the positivists held that all metaphysics was nonsensical; they were mainly concerned to establish a sharp line

between metaphysics and natural science. Analysis was to be used first for the elimination of metaphysics, and second for the clarification of the language of science. Here the word 'elimination' had a much more straightforward sense than in connection with Russell. Russell had not claimed that the objects which his analytical method 'eliminated' did not exist; only that they were not metaphysically ultimate. The positivists, on the other hand, used analysis to argue that metaphysical theories were literally nonsensical.

Since all metaphysics, including Russell's atomism, was to be eliminated, a new aim had to be found for analysis. It had never been agreed just *what* was to be analysed. Was it to be concepts and propositions, as Moore said? Or facts, as Russell usually said? In practice this had made little difference, since the actual technique of analysis had always been the replacement of one *expression* (word, phrase or sentence) by another. The method itself was always linguistic, even if the aims were not. With the positivists, aim and method came closer together; both 'concepts' and 'facts' were dismissed as metaphysical, thought was identified with language, and the analysis of linguistic expressions became an end in itself.

The name 'linguistic analysis' is often used for an approach to philosophy which became widespread in the English-speaking world following the decline of positivism in the 1950s. Its practitioners differed widely among themselves, for example, in their degree of affection for metaphysics. Their method is certainly linguistic, since it involves paying careful, even minute attention to the actual usage of words, phrases and sentences in a living language; but it cannot strictly be called 'analysis'. What is common to all linguistic analysts is their belief that the first step towards solving a philosophical problem is to examine the key words in the area that generates the problem and to ask how they are in fact used. Thus problems of perception are to be solved, not by condemning ordinary language wholesale and inventing a new vocabulary ('impressions', 'sensations', 'sense-data', etc.), but by asking what precisely we are claiming when we claim to see something. This is the sort of question which Moore asked; but whereas Moore jumped, almost without argument, to the conclusion that the answer must be given in terms of 'sense-data', linguistic analysts try to answer it by exploring the locutions in which the verb 'to see' and kindred words actually occur. There is nothing here to which we can point as being 'analysis' as we can point to definitional substitution in Moore and Russell. Perhaps the survival of the name 'analysis' is only a just tribute which some philosophers have paid to those from whom their own work stems. See also ANALYTIC PHILOSOPHY.   (P.H.N.-S.)

Analytic   The terms 'analytic' and 'synthetic' were introduced into modern philosophy by KANT, who defined an analytic judgement as one in which the idea of the predicate is already contained in that of the subject and therefore adds nothing to it. Thus 'all bodies are extended in space' is analytic, since the idea of extension is contained in that of body. On the other hand 'all bodies have some weight' is synthetic since the idea of weight is not so contained. Kant's distinction has been criticized for being too metaphorical (it is not clear what is meant by saying that one idea is 'contained in' another) and for being insufficiently general (it applies only to propositions of subject–predicate form).

Various attempts have been made to make the distinction more precise. An analytic proposition is sometimes said to be one the denial of which is self-contradictory; or it is said to be a covert tautology, on the grounds that, if we define 'body', as 'extended thing', 'all bodies are extended' means 'all extended things are extended'. It should be noted that on this view the analyticity of a proposition depends on our choice of definitions – a matter which, according to some philosophers, is arbitrary. Thus if we define 'body' as 'that which has extension and weight', then 'all bodies have weight' would be analytic. In that case, it would be impossible to determine, on the basis of its form alone, whether a sentence expresses an analytic proposition; it would be necessary to appeal to what the speaker means by it. Clearly, if these or similar definitions of analyticity are adopted, it will be easy to extend the notion to propositions not of subject–predicate form.

Analytic propositions, though they may inform us of the meanings of words, can give no knowledge of matters of fact. The philosophy of LOGICAL POSITIVISM was based on a sharp distinction between analytic and synthetic and on the view that all A PRIORI propositions must be analytic. Many subsequent philosophers came to doubt whether this sharp distinction can be maintained: see especially QUINE's essay 'Two Dogmas of Empiricism' (1951) in *From a Logical Point of View.*   (P.H.N.-S.)

Analytic Philosophy 'Analytic philosophy' is a name for the dominant tradition in academic philosophy in the English-speaking world. It is difficult to define it precisely in terms of characteristic concerns or doctrines. The questions it asks, and even the answers it gives, often have close parallels in the CONTINENTAL philosophical tradition. It might be argued that it is distinguished by its respect for the findings of the natural sciences, but

there are exceptions to this rule. Perhaps the sharpest difference lies at the level of method: analytic philosophy relies heavily on logical and linguistic ANALYSIS – from which it derives its name.

We may do better to concentrate on tradition rather than definition. Like continental philosophy, analytic philosophy recognizes DESCARTES as the rationalist father of modern philosophy, followed by the empiricist triumvirate of LOCKE, BERKELEY and HUME, and then by KANT's attempt to synthesize RATIONALISM and EMPIRICISM at the end of the eighteenth century. After this, however, analytic philosophy's version of history diverges from the Continental one. HEGEL and NIETZSCHE have no place in the analytic pantheon, and such twentieth-century philosophical movements as PHENOMENOLOGY, HERMENEUTICS and STRUCTURALISM are regarded as philosophically unimportant.

For analytic philosophy, the first major philosopher after Kant is Gottlob FREGE, at the end of the nineteenth century. Frege's researches into the foundations of mathematics led to revolutionary advances in both logic and the philosophy of language. Bertrand RUSSELL and Ludwig WITTGENSTEIN developed Frege's work on logic and language, and in Russell it was allied to an empiricist EPISTEMOLOGY inherited from Hume. This mix of logical analysis and empiricism gave rise to LOGICAL POSITIVISM. The logical positivists aimed to analyse all propositions into their fundamental logical form, and to dismiss as meaningless any propositions whose fundamental constituents did not correspond to elements of sense experience.

The influence of logical positivism waned after the Second World War. Wittgenstein recanted some of his earlier doctrines, and emphasized the social role of language as opposed to its purely representational function. J. L. AUSTIN argued that the route to philosophical illumination lay in the sophisticated conceptual distinctions embodied in everyday language. The school of 'ordinary language philosophy', centred on Oxford University, sought to dissolve philosophical puzzles by attending to the structure of ordinary usage. Much of the work done under the banner of 'ordinary language philosophy' was philosophically shallow, and this particular school ceased to be of much importance in the 1960s. But in another sense the post-war analytic tradition remained committed to 'linguistic philosophy': nearly all analytic philosophers continued to place the analysis of language at the centre of the philosophical stage. Different analytic philosophers, however, drew different philosophical conclusions from it. Thus the American philosophers W. V. QUINE and Wilfrid SELLARS concurred with the later Wittgenstein in denying that words derive their meanings from sensory ideas in the minds of speakers; but rather than locating the source of linguistic authority in social practices, as Wittgenstein did, they turned to the developing frameworks of scientific theory instead. The influential British philosophers P. F. STRAWSON and Michael DUMMETT drew yet further philosophical morals from the theory of language: Strawson, harking back to Kant, argued that linguistic reference would be impossible if we did not live in a world of reidentifiable spatiotemporal objects; while Dummett argued against metaphysical realism on the grounds that it would be impossible to grasp the meanings of sentences about the world if the world in itself were different from the world as we find it to be.

In Dummett's view, Frege's crucial contribution to philosophy was to show that the theory of meaning is the foundation of all philosophical investigation.

However, while it is unquestionably true that the analysis of language was central to philosophy in the analytic tradition for most of the twentieth century, it started being displaced in the 1970s by PHILOSOPHY OF MIND.

Treatments of the relationship between mind and language have varied in the analytic tradition. For the founding fathers the function of words was simply to convey ideas from one mind to another, and something of this conception remained in force during the period of logical positivism. But when Sellars, Quine and the later Wittgenstein discredited the idea of a self-sufficient mental realm which breathed significance into words, most analytic philosophers came to regard linguistic practice as primary, and mental events as little more than dispositions to verbal behaviour. Since then, however, there has been something of a reversion to the earlier view that mind is more fundamental than language: a school of 'NATURALISM' has emerged, which, while rejecting the idea of the mind as a self-intimating mental realm, seeks to treat the mind as an independent constituent of the natural world.

In *Philosophy and the Mirror of Nature* (1980) Richard RORTY argued that, once the traditional conception of mind as a special self-knowing substance is abandoned, any substitute naturalistic conception of mind will be unable to carry the same philosophical weight. Indeed, Rorty argues that the whole analytic tradition is fated to collapse, because it is committed to a notion of philosophy as the 'queen of the sciences', offering epistemological evaluations of human judgement in general; and the idea of epistemological evaluation, so Rorty's argument goes, presupposes the traditional distinction between a mirroring non-natural mind and a mirrored natural world.

However, analytic philosophy proved rather more healthy and adaptable than Rorty predicted. For a start, while epistemological evaluation clearly requires some contrast between representer and represented, self-intimating mental states as traditionally conceived are not the only possible representers. On the naturalistic conception mentioned earlier, for instance, beliefs can be conceived as organizational states of the brain, and yet at the same time as open to epistemological evaluation as better or worse representations of their subject matters. Of course, there is a philosophical problem about physical brain states having representational powers; but the task of explaining representation is by no means peculiar to naturalism. It is also true that, on the naturalist conception, mental states are not self-intimating, and so cannot provide the kind of incorrigible foundations for epistemology which were provided by mental states as traditionally conceived: but then various nonfoundational approaches to epistemology are open to naturalism.

It would be wrong to suggest that analytic philosophy as a whole has taken a naturalistic turn. Many analytic philosophers remain suspicious of the naturalistic conception of mind, and doubt its ability to replace language as the focus of philosophical analysis. This anti-naturalistic tendency has affinities with Rorty's critique of epistemology: the continued emphasis on language tends to go with doubts about the possibility of a perspective from which judgement in general can be evaluated. But those analytic philosophers who have doubts about epistemology continue to articulate them within the analytic tradition, appealing to Wittgenstein and Dummett and Donald DAVIDSON, rather than to Martin HEIDEGGER and Jacques DERRIDA. Perhaps we are entering a period of increasing convergence between the analytic and Continental

approaches; but the sheer power of tradition is likely to keep the two schools distinct for some time to come.   [D.P.]

Analytical Marxism   An attempted synthesis of HISTORICAL MATERIALISM with ANALYTIC PHILOSOPHY and PHILOSOPHY OF SCIENCE, pioneered by G. A. Cohen in *Karl Marx's Theory of History: A Defence* (1978).

Anaxagoras   Anaxagoras of Clazomenae flourished *c*.450 BC. He was prosecuted for impiety (for describing the sun as a white hot lump of stone) while working in Athens. His *On Nature* was probably written later than EMPEDOCLES' work of the same name, and tries to overcome the ELEATIC dilemma in another way. In the beginning all natural SUBSTANCES (not merely a limited number of basic substances like Empedocles' roots) were mixed together; then Mind – 'finest of all things and purest' – started a rotation which brought the heavier parts to the centre, by vortex-action, to form the earth, while driving the lighter to the circumference. Anaxagoras' cosmogony was traditional and non-cyclical; the production of a plural cosmos did not destroy the initial unity, since there was still 'a portion of everything in everything, except Mind'. As in Empedocles, apparent coming-to-be was held to be caused by mixture: objects were made up of 'seeds', each containing a portion of every natural substance, but having the appearance of that substance whose portion predominated. Anaxagoras insisted that matter could theoretically be divided *ad infinitum*, and (in opposition to ZENO OF ELEA) that it is 'both great and small'. See also PRE-SOCRATICS.   (G.S.K.)

Anaximander   Anaximander of Miletus flourished *c*.560 BC. His scientific activities included making a famous map of the world. Like THALES he tried to identify a single SUBSTANCE from which the world originated: for him this was 'the indefinite', probably implying a material of indefinite extent to which no precise name could be given because it did not exist within the world as we know it. A nucleus was somehow separated off from the indefinite to produce fire and dark mist. At its centre this mist solidified into earth, while the surrounding flame burst to form the heavenly bodies – wheels of fire, each showing through a single aperture in a tegument of mist. The earth itself was cylindrical, and stayed still because it was equidistant from everything else. Physical change within the world occurred through the mutual encroachments and reactions of opposed materials like the hot and the cold, and ultimate regularity was assured because they had to 'pay penalty and retribution to each other for their injustice according to the assessment of time'. To parallel his cosmogony, Anaximander also developed a zoogony, in which the first living creatures were generated out of primeval slime by the heat of the sun, emerging out of prickly husks onto dry land, and the first humans originally grew up inside a kind of fish, since otherwise they could not have survived their long period of helplessness in childhood. See also PRE-SOCRATICS.   (G.S.K.)

Anaximenes   Anaximenes of Miletus, who flourished c.545 BC, reverted to THALES' idea of a definite world-component as originative material, but said this was *aer* – air or mist. He was the first philosopher to offer an account of how a single SUBSTANCE could develop into a diversified world: *aer* changed its appearance, he argued, according to its degree of concentration. Rarefied, it became fire; condensed, water and earth. This was an important new idea; and Anaximenes was unusually methodical in citing a specific indication that density can affect, for example, temperature – when the lips are compressed in exhalation. He seems to have chosen air or mist as the basic substance not only because of its apparent meteorological connexion with fire (in the sky) and with rain, but also because – being motive, directive and in some way divine – it appeared to fulfil in the world the function that soul, commonly envisaged as breath, has in living creatures. See also PRE-SOCRATICS.   (G.S.K.)

Anderson, John (1893–1962)   Scots philosopher who became Professor at the University of Sydney in 1927 and the dominant figure in twentieth-century Australian philosophy. He was noted for his materialistic and deterministic opinions, and also for his outspokenly aggressive attacks on Christianity, patriotism, censorship and communism, or anything else in which he detected timid intellectual conformism. He never published a book, but his principal articles are collected in *Studies in Empirical Philosophy* (1962).   [J.R.]

Animals   Biologically speaking, animals are mobile, sentient organisms, whose cellular structure is less rigid than that of plants, and which do not photosynthesize. The class includes amoebas, tapeworms, sea-urchins, frogs, cats, dogs and people. Any animal, including us, is more like any other animal than either is like a mushroom or a rose; any two animals, if evolutionary theory is correct, are more closely related than either is to anything not an animal. It is this last fact, of evolutionary relatedness, which makes the class of animals something more than a construct. 'Animals', unlike 'weeds', constitute a real biological taxon, even though (as for other such taxa) there may be or have been organisms at once 'animal' and 'non-animal'.

Most modern biologists would agree that we are members of an animal species, *Homo sapiens*, which is closely related to other primates. (Chimpanzees and people have more in common, from a biochemical point of view, than many varieties of fruit fly which are indistinguishable to lay observation.) But some still believe that people, chiefly in virtue of their linguistic and forward-looking capacities, are as different from any other animal as animals are from plants. Other animals may mimic what people do in making decisions, formulating theories, painting pictures, engaging in class-conflict and productive labour, but – so it is said – they are not 'really' doing these things, because not 'really' thinking about them. This distinction between the separate 'kingdoms' of plants, animals and people, and their different 'souls', goes back at least as far as ARISTOTLE and was mainstream opinion in the West for the next two thousand years. The even more radical claim put forward by DESCARTES, that 'animals' do not even have sense-experiences, and that they are more like plants than people, was anticipated – by way of a *reductio ad absurdum* of STOIC claims about the irrational nature of all animals except people – by Strato of Lampsacus (mentioned by PORPHYRY, in his work *On Abstinence from Meat-eating*): if they only behaved 'as if' they were reasoning, then it must be that they only behaved 'as if' they were feeling or desiring. Some commentators adopt this merely as a rule of method, warning against imputing to animals a mental state more complex or anthropomorphic than is strictly necessary; others believe that it is actually true that animals other than people do not have feelings. This doctrine is useful to experimentalists disinclined to take issues of animal welfare seriously.

Cartesians claim that beings which cannot speak cannot 'think' either, and so cannot ever 'be in pain' in anything like the subjective sense in which 'we' often are. It is easy, and natural, for us to 'project' our own feelings and plans into the animals we live with, and to think that pet dogs are glad to see us, that cats go hunting and veal calves miss their mothers. Sceptics insist that, lacking language, such creatures cannot say even to themselves what they are doing, or what would satisfy them. 'Pain' or 'pleasure' cannot be attributed to them except in purely behavioural senses, and without any implication that there is 'anyone there' who is subjectively in distress or joy, or who reckons her life worth living. On this view there is no real need to anaesthetize (rather than immobilize) animals undergoing surgery. Members of our own species who lack language, and who should by analogy be thought insensible too, are usually given the benefit of the doubt.

The alleged impossibility of understanding what 'animals' do or feel is not usually accepted by people who work with animals. The supposed incommensurability between 'dumb beasts' and 'talking people' also raises serious problems for evolutionary theory and for psychology. If we couldn't think until we could talk, how, as a species or as individuals, did we ever learn to talk? It seems more likely that Cartesians, and recent thinkers influenced by WITTGENSTEIN's aphorisms, have exaggerated the importance for experience of the capacity to articulate that experience in the sort of tensed, referential language that people employ. There are, nonetheless, real practical and philosophical problems for those who seek to understand animals 'from within', by empathetic identification, not least those posed by our traditional moral categories.

For 'animal', as well as its biological or folk-taxonomic meaning, carries moral significance. To treat people 'like animals' is to treat them without due regard for their preferences, or their status as free and equal partners in the human community. To behave 'like an animal' is to pay no regard to the normal inhibitions and ceremonies of that community. To be an animal (a non-human animal) is to be a creature that cannot really return our friendship, or make or keep bargains, or participate in distinctively 'human' practices. BENTHAM, J. S. MILL and other classical UTILITARIANS, who sought to take account of 'animal pains and pleasures', were naturally thought (e.g. by WHEWELL) to be blind to the higher values of humanity. Taking 'animals' seriously meant taking 'animal pains and pleasures' seriously in our own lives, and few were really prepared to do that.

The doctrine that animals lie outside the realm of justice – that there is no injustice in dispossessing, enslaving, hurting or killing them – was first articulated by Aristotle (and later Stoics), but it was not invented by them. It seems that all human cultures draw a distinction between their own kind and everything else – though it has been usual, historically speaking, for the class of non-people to include many whom we would regard as our conspecifics, and the class of people to include at least such honorary members of the community as cattle, horses, pigs or (in the West) dogs. That folk-taxonomic division between our own people and outsiders has been progressively modified, by philosophers and prophets, and most civilized peoples now accept that all human beings are at least potentially 'of our kind', and that they should if possible be treated with respect, as we would ourselves wish to be treated. Humans are, in KANT's phrase, 'ends in themselves', whereas animals, as irrational beings, are owed nothing 'as of right'.

Mainstream Western thought from Aristotle to Kant often qualified the dictum that one can never treat an animal unjustly, saying that even though animals have no rights, it is better not to treat them wickedly or uncharitably or inhumanely. Deliberate cruelty or callous negligence was a sign of a bad character that might lead to injustices towards one's fellow humans. Pain was a recognizable evil that the decent person did not wantonly increase. According to popular morality, one ought not to cause 'unnecessary pain' to animals, but one has no obligation not to kill, dispossess, imprison or deprive them. Strict utilitarians, concerned to increase the ratio of pleasure to pain, should add an obligation to increase animal pleasure where possible, but they are as likely as the rest of us to discount the pleasures experienced by animals against those that we derive from the exploitative use of animals.

The political programme of classical LIBERALISM lays it down that the law should be invoked only to protect rights, and not to enforce any particular moral code. It was for that reason that many liberals opposed the first animal welfare legislation. Such laws came between citizens and their lawfully acquired property. One solution was to insist that the law might be invoked to decrease suffering, regardless of who the victim was, because no one had a natural right to treat other creatures just as she willed. Another was to claim that animals – which usually meant vertebrates more closely related to us ('more evolutionarily advanced') than fishes – possessed 'natural rights' on the same terms as people. Insofar as they were beings with feelings and interests and an ability to take decisions and recognize their companions, they had all the capacities that were shared by those who uncontroversially 'have rights'. If imbeciles had rights (i.e. if they ought to be protected by law not merely against cruel treatment but against robbery, undue frustration of 'natural capacities', enslavement and killing), so also did chimpanzees, horses, dogs and whatever other animals turned out to have at least as much mental development as the imbecile. Some philosophers concluded that imbeciles did not 'have rights' after all, and that if they were protected, it was only in order to appease public sentiment.

The probability is that neither utilitarianism nor a theory of abstract 'natural right' is adequate to the task of grounding a reformist view of how 'animals' should be treated. A vegetarian way of life would decrease the amount of animal suffering, but at the cost of decreasing gastronomic pleasure amongst repentant carnivores and lessening employment prospects. Utilitarianism does not give an unequivocal answer to the questions 'should we eat meat, bait badgers, experiment on apes?' because how much happiness is produced by any particular policy will depend on how we already feel about the policies. If enough people are in fact distressed by badger baiting, the practice might be worth outlawing; if too few, then not; but this does not tell us whether or not to disapprove. A theory of abstract natural right must also grapple with the obvious fact that animals are injured, exploited and killed not only by humans but by other animals too. Their natural rights, if they had any, would be like those that HOBBES supposed to exist before the institution of the state – rights that imposed no duties of care or protection on anyone else.

Those of us who are concerned for the welfare of our fellow animals might do better to appeal to the experience of a shared community life, and the virtues of loyalty and concern for dependants and friends – assuming that, despite Aristotle, we can have friendships with 'non-rational' beings. Under many legal systems, the actual rights of animals are already more extensive than any 'natural rights'. Increased understanding of what 'animals' are like, how closely related they are to 'us', and how poorly they have been served by moralists, may lead to an extension of those protections. The bargains we implicitly make with our domestic animals are at least as real as the 'SOCIAL CONTRACT' on which political philosophers have laid such stress, and ought not to be so radically rewritten as to leave those animals no better off for their troubles, 'Wild' animals, similarly, should be given at least as much respect as the 'environment', which is to say the whole living world of which we are a part. 'Environmentalism' often stands opposed to the demands of 'animal rightists', but the latter are more likely to achieve their goals through environmentalist policies than through the advocacy of abstract rights, or utilitarian calculation.

[S.R.L.C.]

Anscombe, G. E. M. (1919–2001)

One of the most forceful English philosophical teachers of her generation, Elizabeth Anscombe was liable to tremendous dismay about philosophers whose bland fluency prevents thought 'about the stuff itself'. She spent the first half of her career at Oxford University, the second at Cambridge. She was deeply influenced by WITTGENSTEIN, and pioneered the translation of his works into English. Apart from two highly compressed books (*Intention*, 1957; *An Introduction to Wittgenstein's 'Tractatus'*, 1959), she published numerous brief papers, covering topics in the HISTORY OF PHILOSOPHY, METAPHYSICS, and EPISTEMOLOGY, and especially ETHICS and the PHILOSOPHY OF MIND, both of which she saw in terms of the topic of her first book; and in the philosophy of RELIGION, where she wrote explicitly as a Catholic.

Her *Collected Papers* in three volumes appeared in 1981.   [J.R.]

Anselm of Canterbury (1033–1109)

Anselm was born in Aosta, Italy, joined the Benedictine Abbey of Bec in Normandy, and subsequently became Archbishop of Canterbury, eventually being canonized in 1494. Apart from ERI-GENA, Anselm was the first systematic thinker of the Middle Ages. Meeting the difficulties occasioned by the DIALECTI-CIANS of his day with the celebrated formula 'a faith seeking understanding', he was not prepared to substitute dialectic for theology, but still he insisted upon a reasoned presentation of traditional Christian belief.

His philosophical writings were a response to a request by some of his monks for a meditation on the existence and nature of God based in reason rather than scriptural authority. In the *Monologion* he begins with our experience of differences in degrees of value, goodness and being in the objects around us. From this he argues to the necessary existence of an absolute standard, an absolute good, an absolute being on which the relative depends; this absolute, he claims, is what we call God. The argument follows a Platonic method already used by AUGUSTINE, and would later be elaborated by AQUINAS.

In the *Proslogion*, Anselm presents his famous ONTOLOGICAL ARGUMENT. We may, he says, start with no more than the commonly accepted idea of what we mean by the term God, namely a being than which no greater can be thought. This, he says, is a point of departure available even to the fool who, according to scripture, denies God's existence. Such a being, then, can be said to exist in the mind. But to exist actually is more perfect than to exist in the mind. To deny the actual existence of God, then, is to fall

into foolish contradiction. If God is the being than which nothing greater can be thought, he must exist in reality as well as in the mind.

The argument of the *Proslogion* at once aroused controversy and it has continued to divide philosophers to this day. The monk Gaunilo wrote a *Book on behalf of the Fool* attacking the validity of the conclusion and arguing that similar reasoning could be used to establish the 'existence' of anything whatever, for instance a most perfect island. In his reply, Anselm pointed out that the argument can work only in the unique case of the most excellent of all beings.

In the Middle Ages the Franciscans tended to accept the argument, though SCOTUS required that it be shown that the nature of God is not self-contradictory. Aquinas on the other hand rejected it. DESCARTES accepted the argument; LEI-BNIZ, like Scotus, required the possibility of God to be accounted for; and KANT rejected it.   (J.G.D.)

Antisthenes (c.444 to c.366 BC)

Commonly held to be one of the prototypes of the CYNICS, Antisthenes was a pupil of the rhetorician Gorgias, a close friend of SOCRATES, and critic of PLATO. From the few surviving fragments of his numerous writings, we see the intertwining of three threads: the SOPHISTIC, the Socratic, and what was later to become the Cynic. He held virtue to be sufficient for happiness. As knowledge necessitating moral action it could be taught, and once gained it was unshakeable. Education began with the study of the meaning of words. Words corresponded directly with reality, and a proposition was either true or meaningless, contradiction and false statement being impossible. But the stress was on practical ETHICS rather than theoretical learning. Although not an ascetic, Antisthenes condemned luxury. Virtue should be combined with exertion, without which real pleasure was impossible (Hercules was the ideal example). Established laws, convention, birth, sex, race, were unimportant in comparison with the law of virtue, by which the state should be governed. Although many of his views are clearly Socratic, the ancients asserted that his importance lay in giving the impulse, through DIOGENES, to the way of life later called Cynic, and it is likely that STOICISM too was influenced by his practical ethics. (I.G.K.)

A posteriori See A PRIORI.

Applied Ethics There is nothing new about philosophers seeking to apply their ethical ideas to the world in which they live. PLATO set out his view of the ideal republic, AQUINAS wrote on the justification for going to war, HUME defended suicide, and John Stuart MILL attacked the subjection of women. Yet from the early twentieth century until the 1960s, mainstream ANALYTIC PHILOSOPHY spurned practical questions. ETHICS was seen as limited to the analysis of moral language, and hence as neutral between different moral views. To enter into practical questions, as Bertrand RUSSELL did, was to remove one's philosophical hat and become a 'moralist', on a par with preachers and leader-writers.

The bar against serious study of applied ethics came under pressure in America during the 1960s, when first the struggle for racial equality, and then the resistance to the war in Vietnam, began to raise crucial questions which were clearly both practical and philosophical. The radicalization of the campuses, with mounting student demand for courses relevant to their present concerns, proved irresistible. Within a few years, an applied ethics course was available in almost every philosophy department in the English-speaking world. Such courses frequently attracted large enrolments, and this interest was reflected in new journals such as *Philosophy and Public Affairs*, and in a new, or revived, field of philosophical debate and writing.

Initially the most popular topics in applied ethics were equality, warfare and obedience to the state. With the end of the Vietnam war there was a hiatus in discussions of war, but they became more prominent again in the 1980s, in the context of concern over nuclear weapons: since traditional 'just war' doctrine condemns the deliberate killing of the innocent, and demands that the gains be worth the costs of fighting the war, could a nuclear war ever be just? Discussions of racial and sexual equality also underwent changes: there was widespread agreement on the issue of equality, but the more controversial positions, such as reverse discrimination, attracted considerable attention. Following the publication of John RAWLS' *A Theory of Justice*, there was a thorough discussion of inequalities of wealth within societies, though the far greater disparity in wealth between rich and poor nations received less attention.

Some areas of applied ethics have become virtual sub-specialities of their own, often linking up with other related disciplines. Questions about the environment, and about our relations with the entire non-human world, for example, have opened avenues of inquiry into the nature of intrinsic value, and into the application of principles of equality, rights and justice to those who are incapable of reciprocity, and in some cases are not even sentient. Until recently, most ethical thinking has been, explicitly or implicitly, human-centred. (UTILITARIANS were exceptions, looking to sentience, rather than humanity, as the basis of moral concern.) But this tendency came under strong attack, and an explicitly and exclusively human-centred ethic is now rarely defended. Sentient ANIMALS, at least, are widely accepted as being of direct moral concern, even if some would still defend the legitimacy of a preference for our own species. On the other hand, attempts to bestow intrinsic value on non-sentient objects like trees, rivers and forests are still highly controversial.

Perhaps the most important sub-speciality in applied ethics at the moment, however, is bioethics. Although this term was originally coined to refer to an ethical approach to the whole biosphere, it has come to be used much more narrowly, as a label for studies in ethical issues arising from medicine and the biological sciences. Philosophers began by contributing to discussions of abortion and euthanasia, and have gone on to write on the ethics of human experimentation, resource allocation, new developments in reproduction, and future prospects such as sex selection and genetic engineering. They have also played a prominent role in government inquiries and in interdisciplinary centres for bioethics. With the creation of the first 'bleeper philosophers' – philosophers attached to hospitals who carry a paging device in case they need to be consulted about the ethics of an emergency treatment – philosophy has come a long way from the earlier attitude that it has nothing to contribute to ethical decision-making. See also ANIMALS, POLITICAL PHILOSOPHY.

[P.S.]

A priori   'A priori' is a Latin phrase meaning 'from what comes before', contrasted with a posteriori, 'from what comes after'. The terms were introduced in the late scholastic period to translate two technical phrases in ARISTOTLE's theory of knowledge. An a posteriori argument was one which moved from observed effects to unknown causes; an a priori argument proceeded from causes to effects or from ground to consequent. A priori arguments were held to provide indubitable scientific knowledge as opposed to probable belief. Aristotle distinguished what is prior in the order of nature from what is prior in the order of knowledge or discovery. There are many truths, such as that fire burns or that water will not flow uphill, that we know from experience before we are able to explain them. Until we discover their causes our knowledge of such truths will be a posteriori or empirical and not truly scientific or a priori.

From the seventeenth century, for example in DESCARTES and LEIBNIZ, a priori came to mean 'universal, necessary and wholly independent of experience'. The term a posteriori fell into disuse and a priori was now usually contrasted with 'empirical' that is, depending on experience. The term a priori is now used of (1) arguments; (2) propositions and (3) ideas.

(1) An a priori argument is one in which the conclusion follows deductively from the premises, as for example in a mathematical proof. If the premises are true and the argument valid, no experience is needed to confirm the conclusion and no experience could refute it. By contrast, an argument from experience (empirical, inductive or probable argument) is one in which the conclusion, however strongly supported by the premises, is not necessitated by them. For example, if we argue that it will rain somewhere in England next January, on the grounds that no January has been known to pass without some rain, this argument, though weighty, is not conclusive. There might be a January without rain even though there never has been yet. Since HUME it has been generally believed

that natural science always contains an empirical element and therefore cannot be a priori.

(2) A proposition is a priori if it is known independent of experience, except in so far as experience is necessary for understanding its terms. Thus we know a priori that a whole is equal to the sum of its parts; for, once we understand the terms involved, we see that this is universally and necessarily true and that no experience could refute it.

(3) Empiricist philosophers – so called because they tend to emphasize the role of experience in knowledge as opposed to a priori elements – have sometimes held that all *ideas* are derived from experience. We can (they say) have no idea unless we have either come across an instance of it in experience – as in the case of 'red' or 'horse' – or fabricated it out of elements we have come across – as in the case of 'dragon'. There are, however, some ideas whose origin is difficult to explain in this way. Among them are ideas of great importance in philosophy, such as substance (thing), cause, existence, equality, likeness and difference. Of these it is claimed that, far from being derived from experience, they are necessary for it, and we could have no experience without them. This is not to say that we are born with them, but rather that they are presupposed by our being able to have any experience at all. (PLATO's *Meno* and LEIBNIZ's *New Essays on Human Understanding* are classic expositions of this view, sometimes called the doctrine of Innate Ideas. For the empiricist view see LOCKE and HUME.)

It is clear that all ANALYTIC propositions are a priori. If 'bachelor' means 'unmarried man' we need not investigate any particular cases to satisfy ourselves of the truth of the proposition 'No bachelor is married'. But the question whether any SYNTHETIC proposition can be known a priori is one of the most important and difficult in philosophy. The RATIONALISTS believed that the fundamental principles of science could, like those of logic and pure mathematics, be known a priori. Hume argued (in effect) that the principles of logic and pure mathematics were indeed a priori, but only because they were analytic. But all knowledge of matters of fact, both common sense and scientific, depended, he argued, on such causal principles as that every event must have a cause and that like causes must have like effects. He claimed that these principles could not be known a priori and had to be derived from experience.

KANT saw the force of Hume's argument, noting its sceptical tendency and devoting his most important book, the *Critique of Pure Reason*, to establishing the possibility and scope of a priori knowledge. He held that such knowledge was possible in mathematics (which he did not regard as analytic) and in physics. With regard to metaphysics he agreed substantially with Hume, but undertook to show why we are bound to continue to ask metaphysical questions even if it is impossible for us to answer them. In the twentieth century the LOGICAL POSITIVISTS and many philosophers influenced by them followed Hume in denying the possibility of synthetic a priori knowledge. This programme ran into difficulties, however, when doubts arose about the validity of the distinction between analytic and synthetic (see also ANALYSIS, ANALYTIC).   (P.H.N.-S.)

Aquinas, Thomas (c.1225–74)   Born at Roccasecca near Aquino on the northern border of the ancient Kingdom of Sicily, Aquinas proceeded from Monte Cassino to the University of Naples where he joined the Dominicans; he then studied under

ALBERT THE GREAT at Cologne, worked for nine years as adviser to the Papal Court, and taught in Paris. A large man, decided and calm, patrician yet modest, he enjoyed the affection even of his adversaries. There are ninety-eight items in the catalogue of his works, some running to several folios. Canonized in 1323, and proclaimed Doctor of the Church in 1567, he is the classical systematic theologian of Catholic Christianity. In 1879, Pope Leo XIII inaugurated a revival of Thomist philosophy, based on the early *Summa Contra Gentiles* as well as the later *Summa Theologica* (or *Theologiae*).

According to tradition Aquinas asked his colleague William of Moerbeke (1215–86) to make fresh Latin translations of ARISTOTLE, with a view to separating authentic Aristotelian doctrine from the contributions of Arab commentators, notably AVICENNA and AVERROES, and purifying it of NEOPLATONIST strains inherited from AUGUSTINE, Proclus, Dionysius and BOETHIUS. Aquinas's so-called baptism of Aristotle, however, was no mere surface reconciliation. Aquinas meant to follow Aristotle's arguments to their philosophical conclusions, rather than merely fitting them into an existing theological framework. He pressed the Aristotelian distinction between potentiality and actuality to the core of reality itself, and turned the old 'problem of the one and the many' into that of the creation of all existents. He showed that a universal and particular Providence followed from the nature of knowledge and love at their best, and defended immortality without denying that the soul is essentially embodied. If he borrowed from Aristotle he also made capital gains.

Aquinas called for careful interpretation of the relations between reason and faith. On the one hand, he was not a special pleader who treated rational investigation as ancillary to religious belief; on the other, he never countenanced a practical separation between them, indeed he fought against the celebrated 'double truth' theory associated with Siger of Brabant and the Latin Averroists. Aquinas' solution lay in the notion of subordination without subservience. The world was composed of real things acting as true causes, that is as principles and goals of activity rather than mere instruments or occasions. To be truly wise was to see them in the light of their 'first cause'. Creatures were real; moreover they interacted and depended on one another. By a judicious use of analogy – considered as a law of being rather than an artifice of logical classification or literary metaphor – the mind could range at large and discover truth beyond its experience.

But Aquinas never lost sight of individual and personal substance. This is particularly evident in his psychological and moral philosophy. The philosophical sciences differed from the particular sciences in that they did not stay with the proximate causes but sought reasons more universal, though not on that account more summary. He never fell into the philosophism which seeks to deduce facts from reasons or to treat the specialist sciences as mere applications of metaphysics. Aquinas was a poet and on occasion a writer of distinguished prose, but the general run of his expository style is curt and repetitive. Many of his works were dictated to or written up by secretaries, and the sparse vocabulary sometimes conceals the variety of his ideas and the delicacy of his distinctions. In his exposition of Boethius' *De Trinitate*, Aquinas mapped out the three basic philosophical disciplines: Logic, Theoretical Philosophy and Moral Philosophy.

(1) Logic comprised the study of scientific method and the rational constructions (*entia rationis*) which we impose on experience. In this field, Aquinas completed a commentary on Aristotle's *Posterior Analytics* and began one on the *De Interpretatione*. His academic discussions of logic fall into two sets, the *Quaestiones Disputatae*, which in the main follow the systematic exposition of a teaching-course, and the *Quaestiones Quodlibetales*, or questions for special occasions.

(2) Theoretical Philosophy, as Aquinas understood it, aims to isolate what is general and constant in the changing world of individual facts, and comprises three provinces: first, Natural Philosophy, which deals with objects which exist in material processes and cannot be understood without reference to them; second, Mathematical Philosophy, which considers the implications of quantity without reference to the sensible world; and third, Metaphysical Philosophy, which reaches beyond the sensible world because its objects are either non-material (for instance, God), or not of necessity material (for instance, substantial unity).

Aquinas' receptiveness to Aristotle's natural and metaphysical philosophy scandalized some of his contemporaries. Rejecting NEOPLATONISM he saw ideas as embodied here and now about us. The first two categories of the material world were 'substance', or whatever is able to exist in and of itself, and 'accidents', or secondary, inhering realities, such as being quantified, qualified or related. Material processes were shaped by the four causes – final, efficient, material and formal. A final cause was the immanent purpose or end (*finis*) of an activity; an efficient cause, *agens*, was the producer of an effect; the material cause was its basic potential subject, and the formal

cause, its actual determinant. All material substances were a combination of matter, *materia prima* and form, *forma substantialis*. Bare matter so conceived was not the ultimate atomic or infra-atomic point which can be calculated or recorded by scientific apparatus, but the substantial potentiality common to all material things which are formed differently in number, degree and kind under the action of secondary causes.

A tang of reality infuses Aquinas' psychology, which is less a study of consciousness than of human substance and activity. He applied the matter–form distinction uncompromisingly, describing the soul as the substantial form of the body. This implied that human beings are psychophysical unities, and that we are, by one and the same actuality, bodily, vegetative, sensitive and intellective beings – a conception which raises obvious difficulties for the doctrine of the immortality of the soul.

The celebrated five ways, *quinque viae*, sometimes called the proofs for the existence of God, focus on the general themes of change, dependence, contingency, limited perfection and utility. Aquinas argues that if these themes comprised the whole of reality they would be inexplicable, and that we are therefore bound to postulate an ulterior reality in the form of a changeless changer, uncaused cause, necessary being, complete perfection and ultimate end – notions which could be combined to make up the nominal definition of God. However, our classification of different sorts of being could not accommodate God, and we have to content ourselves with the *via negationis* – defining not what God is but what he is not. But Aquinas goes beyond traditional negative theology by showing that we can think positively when we are dealing with unmixed values: to say that God is good means more than that he is not evil, or that he is the cause of the goodness we see about us. Goodness is more properly his than ours, being taken to its highest strength, *via eminentia*.

(3) The chief science in the field of practice was Moral Philosophy, which included personal ethics, economics and politics. Aquinas' moral philosophy added little to the typology of the virtues set forth in Aristotle's *Nicomachean Ethics* on which he wrote a commentary, though he hinted at a heroic ideal of theological perfection and criticized the STOIC notion of passionless virtue.

Aquinas' social philosophy is dominated by his theory of Law. Law was rational ordinance, rather than a manifestation of might; it served the common good, or the communion of persons. In human communities it came from the ruler who was the representative but not the owner of the people. The Eternal Law in the mind of God was the exemplar of all law; it was impressed on human minds as NATURAL LAW, which is immutable in its principles though particular precepts can be variously developed according to region and period. In contrast, though not in contradiction, stands the Positive Law: its precepts may sometimes reinforce the Natural Law, but as such they are not conclusions from it but rather pragmatic supplements to make the good life easier or to safeguard public order. Aquinas was the first to depart from the traditional view, formed by the Stoics and Augustine, that the civil power, like private property, was only a remedy against our sinful anti-social appetites. He revived Aristotle's idea of the State as meeting the essential demands of human nature, which, he says, are both 'social' (concerned with the moral requirements of living together in community and society) and 'political' (concerned with specific constitutional

forms). Human legislation had its limits, and should not seek to cover the whole field of morality. (T.G.)

Arcesilaus of Pitane   See SCEPTICS.

Arendt, Hannah (1906–75)   The political theorist Hannah Arendt was born in Königsberg and educated chiefly at Marburg (with Martin HEIDEGGER) and Heidelberg (with Karl JASPERS). She fled Germany in 1933, lived in Paris and emigrated to America in 1941. Her first major work, *The Origins of Totalitarianism*, published in 1951, remains a classic historical study of Nazism and Stalinism as instances of a novel form a government, totalitarianism. Her next three books, *The Human Condition* (1958), *Between Past and Future* (1961) and *On Revolution* (1963), present basic political concepts and distinctions in challenging interpretations. For example, she analyses work, labour and action, public space and the private realm, history, freedom, authority, power and violence, emphasizing their historical evolution as concepts and their present meaning and political relevance. Arendt thought that the precondition for a 'new science of politics', neither traditionally liberal nor conservative, was a radical, critical re-examination of all political thought since the rise of the Greek city-states. In 1963, Arendt published *Eichmann in Jerusalem*, a controversial study of EVIL in the context of the Israeli trial of a leading Nazi functionary. The book posed questions about morality and politics that Arendt took up in her last (and unfinished) philosophical study of thinking, willing and judging, called *The Life of the Mind* (1978). [E.Y.B.]

Aristippus of Cyrene (c.435–356 BC)   A SOPHIST and friend of Socrates, Aristippus is regarded by tradition as the founder of the CYRENAIC school. His views are certainly in harmony with Cyrenaic tenets, but it is possible that they were first systematically formulated by his grandson, also named Aristippus. He made enjoyment of present pleasure the goal of his life, eschewing regret for the past and toil for the future. But happiness consisted in the prudent, intelligent control of such pleasure, not in slavery to it, or abstinence. Hence his famous remark on his expensive mistress Lais: 'I have Lais, not she me.' All acts were indifferent except in so far as they produced pleasure for the doer. Aristippus cultivated the art of adapting himself to place, time and person, especially at the court of Dionysius of Syracuse. It was said that he alone could play the dandy or go in rags. He had an extraordinary capacity for enjoyment combined with a great freedom from wants, and this combination was to pose a difficult choice of ideals for his successors.   (I.G.K.)

Aristotle (384–322 BC)   The son of a doctor from Stagira in northern Greece, Aristotle was a member of PLATO'S ACADEMY for twenty years, from 367. When Plato died and SPEUSIPPUS became head of the Academy, Aristotle left Athens and went first to Assos (on the coast of Asia Minor) and then to Lesbos. About 342 he was invited by King Philip of Macedonia to go there to supervise the education of the King's son, Alexander. A few years later he returned to Athens to found a new school, which became known as the Lyceum or Peripatos. The school flourished; but in 323 Aristotle left Athens for political reasons and retired to Euboea, where he died in 322.

Aristotle's early writings were mostly intended for a general public. Written in a polished style (some in dialogue form), they were largely Platonic in outlook. These works were well known in antiquity but only fragments survive. The works we possess are systematic treatises intended for serious students, and they had only a limited circulation until they were edited by Andronicus in the first century BC; our texts are based ultimately on this edition, as were all translations into Latin and Arabic. Aristotle's treatises have a rather peculiar character, for they are in essence notes of or for lectures. They were added to and altered over a period of years without ever receiving a final rewriting. Moreover what we count as a single treatise may really consist of several separate courses strung together by Andronicus or an earlier editor. All this makes it difficult to give an account of how Aristotle's thought changed or developed.

Aristotle's very name suggests to some people the idea of a dogmatic system of rigid doctrines. But in fact he was always reopening questions and admitting difficulties. He did not argue arrogantly from premises he laid down as self-evident, but gave careful consideration to ordinary opinions and to the views of his predecessors. He assumed that divergent views would all have some element of truth in them, seeking to clarify issues and qualify or refine the various inconsistent solutions on offer. The philosophical value of his work resides not in his conclusions (or 'doctrines') but in his skill in analysis and acuteness in argument. The following notes introduce some of the ideas which recur constantly in Aristotle.

1 *Categories.* Aristotle's categories classify reality: everything that exists falls under one of them – it is either a SUBSTANCE or a quality or a quantity or a relation etc. (Aristotle sometimes lists ten categories, usually fewer.) It is because items in different categories have irreducibly different sorts of being that terms like 'is' and 'one', which are

applicable in all categories, are in an important way ambiguous (compare the scholastic doctrine of *transcendentalia*). Inattention to this type of ambiguity and to categorical distinctions led, Aristotle argued, to philosophical paradoxes.

Substance is prior to the other categories because substances exist 'separately' while qualities, etc., exist only as their attributes. Individual substances (e.g. Socrates or this table) are the subjects to which predicates belong and are not themselves predicates of anything else. Aristotle places in the category of substance not only individual substances but also their species and genera (e.g. 'man', 'animal'). For to say that Socrates is a man is not to mention some quality which he has, but to say *what he is*. Moreover science, which studies reality and above all substance, defines and studies species rather than individuals, even though species do not exist separately as individuals do. There is a deep difficulty in Aristotle's thought here, which may be expressed by saying that his word *ousia* (literally 'being') does duty both for our 'substance' and for our 'essence' and 'species'.

2 *Form and matter.* A table is wood and glue put together in a certain way. Aristotle distinguishes as separate aspects of the table its matter (the wood and glue) and its form (how it is put together, its structure). Many central ideas (and puzzles) are connected with this distinction. (a) Form is *immanent*: the form of table exists only as the form of this table or that table, that is, as the form of certain matter. There is no separately existing Platonic Form of Table (or indeed of Man or Justice). (b) Form or structure is normally determined by function. It is because of what it has to do that a table has a flat top and four legs. Form may in fact be identified with function: to say what a

table does is to say what it is. (c) Matter is 'for the sake of' form, not *vice versa*. If you want an axe – something for cutting down trees – you must of course use iron to make it; but there can be iron without an axe. So to state something's form or function explains it far better than stating what it is made of; the form implies the appropriate matter but the matter does not imply the form. (d) Wood and glue, the matter of a table, are not matter in an absolute sense. In a piece of wood we can again draw a distinction between form and matter, since wood, like everything else, is made of earth, air, fire and water (or of some of these) combined in a certain way. Nor are these four elements pure matter. They can change into one another. This implies a persistent underlying stuff capable of receiving the form of earth, air, etc., which is what Aristotle calls *first* (or '*prime*') *matter*, a characterless substrate which never actually exists on its own but only in the form of earth, air etc. (e) Besides pressing the distinction of matter and form to the extreme concept of prime matter, Aristotle also applies it by analogy. Thus in the definition of a species he treats the genus as the matter and the differentia as the form: the genus is relatively indeterminate, the differentia gives its definite character to the species. This is typical of Aristotle's way of extending the application of key concepts, adding a certain unity to his thought at the cost of some obscurity. (f) Aristotle believes that there can be form without matter, but it is very different from a Platonic Form: *God* is form without matter.

3 *Actuality and Potentiality.* A block of wood is potentially a statue, an acorn potentially an oak; conversely, the completed statue and the mature oak are actualizations of those potentialities. (a) For Aristotle, there is a close

connection between the antithesis form–matter and the antithesis actuality–potentiality. Matter is what has the potentiality of receiving form; form is what actualizes the potentiality. So Aristotle sometimes uses the two antitheses interchangeably. (b) There are limits on the form any given material can take: an acorn *cannot* become an elm, wood *cannot* be made into an axe. But Aristotle does not think it adequate to say that every actual so-and-so comes from a potential so-and-so; what is required is a quite general philosophical analysis of the notions of growth and change. (c) Aristotle argues that actuality is always prior to potentiality. It is prior in definition, in that actuality has to be mentioned in the definition of a potentiality, but not *vice versa*. It is also prior in value, because actuality is the end for the sake of which potentiality exists. And it is prior in time: although an acorn exists before the oak it grows into, it is itself the product of an existing oak: 'for from the potentially existing the actually existing is always produced by an actually existing thing, for example, man from man, musician by musician; there is always a first mover, and the mover already exists actually'. (Of course a table is not produced by a table; but it is produced by someone who already has the *form* of a table 'in mind'.) (d) Since a potentiality implies the possibility of change to the actuality, which is better, there can be no element of potentiality in a perfect changeless being.

4 *The Four 'Causes'*. Aristotle holds that the full explanation of anything must say what it is made of (material cause), what it essentially is (formal cause), what brought it into being (efficient cause) and what its function or purpose is (final cause). The oddity of describing all these as *causes* is not to be held against

Aristotle; 'cause' is the traditional translation in this context of a Greek word of wider meaning. Aristotle holds that in a way the formal, efficient and final causes are identical. It is the essential nature of a table (formal cause) to serve certain purposes (final cause), and it was the thought of those purposes in the carpenter's mind that brought the table into being (efficient cause). It is the essential nature of a horse to perform certain characteristic functions and exercise characteristic powers, and to do this – to live the life of a mature horse – is just what horses are for; and a horse is produced by horses, that is, creatures already exercising the functions of mature horses. It should be noticed that the notion of explanation by the four causes applies to things rather than events, that it is derived from reflection on the process of production (natural and artificial), and that it implies a kind of universal teleology.

5 *Classification of the Sciences*. Aristotle divides the various branches of inquiry into theoretical, practical and productive sciences. Theoretical science studies 'what cannot be otherwise' and aims simply at truth, and it can be subdivided into three parts, distinguished by subject-matter: physics deals with things that exist separately but are liable to change, mathematics with things that are changeless but have no separate existence and 'first philosophy' (metaphysics) with what exists both separately and beyond change. The practical sciences – chiefly ethics and politics – are concerned with 'what can be otherwise' and are ultimately aimed at action. And the productive sciences are concerned with making things. As for logic, Aristotle regarded it not as a substantive part of philosophy but as ancillary to all its parts: it studies forms of reasoning and expression common to

different subject-matters, and is a necessary tool in all areas of inquiry. Hence the traditional name of Aristotle's logical works – the 'Organon' (i.e. *tool* or *instrument*).

6 *Logic.* ¯Aristotle's great contribution to formal logic is his theory of the syllogism, expounded in the *Prior Analytics*. It is a theory of great rigour but limited scope: it handles only certain kinds of statement, and the arguments it studies are all inferences from two such statements to a third. Each statement in a categorical syllogism must have one of the following forms: 'all A is B', 'no A is B', 'some A is B', or 'some A is not B'. Modal syllogisms involve such forms as 'all A *may be* B' and 'all A *must be* B'. Aristotle works out all possible combinations of premises and conclusions, determines which syllogisms are valid and investigates some of the logical relations between different syllogisms.

The *Posterior Analytics* contains Aristotle's 'logic of science'. His account of the form a completed science should take is much influenced by the model of geometry and rests on the view that nature contains 'real kinds' whose essence we can know. Aristotle rejects the notion, which he ascribes to Plato, of one grand comprehensive science; different sciences, he argues, require different premises. Any given branch of science is concerned with some limited class of objects. It starts from principles and axioms – some common to all the sciences, others peculiar to itself – and from definitions of the objects studied. It then demonstrates by means of syllogisms that certain properties necessarily belong to the objects in question. This may seem remote from what scientists do, and indeed from Aristotle's own scientific works; but it expresses an ideal for the exposition of a completed science rather than a programme for investigators.

7 *Physics.* Aristotle's *Physics* and connected works analyse such concepts as nature, change, chance, time, place, continuity, infinity and growth; they also offer proofs that movement is eternal and that there is an eternal Prime Mover, and discussions of the actual constitution and workings of the universe. The analyses of concepts are often subtle and illuminating, but much of what Aristotle says is out-of-date (and would not now be regarded as in a philosopher's province). Moreover his treatment of movement and continuity – which rejected as senseless all questions about the velocity (or direction) of a moving body at a given point – was to have unfortunate effects on the study of dynamics.

The argument for a Prime Mover starts from Aristotle's conception of change and causation. There could not be an absolutely first (or last) change. For since change implies pre-existing matter (or potentiality) and a pre-existing efficient cause to impose form on the matter (to actualize the potentiality), every supposed first change must have been preceded by something capable of being changed and something capable of causing change. But then to explain why these potentialities were actualized at a certain time, we must assume some actual change just prior to that time, that is, a change before the supposed first change. Change or movement must therefore be eternal. But can eternal change be explained? Not by the assumption of an eternal 'self-mover', for we would then have to distinguish one part of the self-mover which causes change and another which undergoes it. Hence we have to postulate an *unmoved* being which can somehow cause eternal movement. This Prime Mover – eternal, changeless and containing no element of matter or unrealized potentiality – keeps the heavenly bodies moving and maintains the eternal life of the universe.

8 *Biology*. If Aristotle's work on physics suffers from a lack of experiment and observation, the same cannot be said of his biology. He collected a vast amount of information about living creatures and, in spite of some fundamental errors, was better informed on the subject than most of his successors until comparatively recent times. He recognized that theories must wait upon facts; after giving a theory about the generation of bees he says: 'the facts have not been sufficiently ascertained', and affirms that 'more credence must be given to the direct evidence of the senses than to theories'.

Aristotle achieved valuable systematic classifications of animal life, rejecting what he regarded as an inadequate Platonic method – the method of dichotomy – and employing multiple differentiae to distinguish the main classes of creatures. He thought of the various species as eternal, but as capable of being arranged in a scale leading from the lowest and least developed to the highest and most complex. The essence of biology, he thought, was teleology, or the explanation of material structure in terms of function. Nature does nothing in vain, and the true explanation of the characteristics of a species must show how they serve some purpose in the life of the members of the species. The job of an embryo is to become a mature animal, live its proper life and reproduce itself; and its parts and characteristics are to be explained as contributing to these ends. 'For any living thing that has reached its normal development . . . the most natural act is the production of another like itself, an animal producing an animal, a plant a plant, in order that, as far as its nature allows, it may partake in the eternal and divine. That is the goal towards which all things strive, that for the sake of which they do whatsoever their nature renders possible.'

9 *Psychology*. The word '*psyche*', commonly translated 'soul', really has a wider meaning; plants as well as animals have *psyche*, because they have *life*. Living things can be ordered according to the complexity of their powers. Some (plants) have only the power of nutrition and reproduction; others have also the power of perception, desire and movement; humans have in addition the power of thought. Aristotle's main discussion of these various psychical functions is in the *De Anima*, which also contains his general account of soul and its relation to body.

A dead human body is not strictly human at all, since it lacks the powers which define humanity. A human being (like an animal or plant) is a body-with-soul; and the relation between body and soul is the relation of matter to form. Soul is the form of body, as sight is the form of the eye ('when seeing is removed the eye is no longer an eye, except in name – it is no more a real eye than the eye of a statue'). Soul, the power of life, cannot exist in any and every body (form requires appropriate matter); only a body with suitable organs can possess life. Such a body is *potentially* a living animal or plant; soul is the *actuality* of such a body. This important conclusion (closer to RYLE than to DESCARTES) enables Aristotle to dismiss the question whether soul and body form a unity: 'this is as meaningless as to ask whether the wax and the shape given to it by the stamp are one, or generally the matter of a thing and that of which it is the matter. Unity has many senses . . . but the most proper and fundamental sense . . . is the relation of an actuality to that of which it is the actuality'. On this view, psychological activity is not the activity of an immaterial substance but the actual functioning of a living body; and Aristotle's accounts of psychological concepts always bring in the relevant physical and physiological facts.

Aristotle allows one exception to the rule that soul is the form or actualization of body. The activity of *nous* (pure intuitive thought) does not depend on body and may therefore exist separately from it. His doctrine on this point is exceedingly obscure, and it is disputed whether he attributes some sort of immortality to the *nous* in the individual human soul. In general, his account of soul dissolves the question of personal immortality as effectively as that of the unity of body and soul.

10 *Metaphysics*. Aristotle expresses two views about 'first philosophy'. (The name 'metaphysics' was applied to it by an editor simply because Aristotle's treatise came after (*meta*) the *Physics* in his edition.) One view, already mentioned, is that it is the study of changeless, separable substance, which makes it equivalent to theology. The other is that it studies *being as such*, together with concepts (e.g. unity and identity) and principles (such as the law of contradiction) which are common to all particular sciences. Aristotle is not very successful in reconciling these two views. Most of the *Metaphysics* is metaphysics in the wider sense, as a brief synopsis will show.

In Book I Aristotle surveys the opinions of his predecessors on the ultimate principles of reality and confirms his view that there are just four different kinds of 'cause'. Book IV discusses the law of contradiction and the law of excluded middle, while Book V is a lexicon of important philosophical terms. Books VII and VIII discuss substance and wrestle with notions of essence, genus, universal, substrate, form, etc. The next books treat actuality and potentiality, unity, plurality and similar notions. Book XII contains Aristotle's

theology, and Books XIII and XIV discuss and reject certain views held in the Academy about immaterial substance, arguing that there are no such things as Platonic Ideas or Ideal Numbers, and that mathematical objects are not substances.

Only Book XII can be discussed here. In it Aristotle argues again (as in the *Physics*) that there must be an eternal, immaterial Prime Mover, which he now calls 'God'. God is not himself susceptible of movement, but causes movement as an object of desire and love. His life is perpetual activity – activity being perfect and complete in every moment and not, like movement, a process. The only sort of activity which can be ascribed to God is pure thought, uninterrupted intuitive knowledge of the highest object of knowledge, which is Godhead itself. 'It must be of itself that the divine thought thinks (since it is the most excellent of things), and its thinking is a thinking about thinking.'

The outer heavens and the planets are animate beings moved by a desire to imitate the eternal activity of God, and nature as a whole does something similar in that the processes of birth, growth and reproduction maintain forever the life of the various species. But of course plants and animals, unlike humans, do not imitate God *consciously*, nor is God aware of or concerned about them.

11 *Ethics*. The *Nicomachean Ethics* is one of the best books ever written on the subject: rich in analysis of moral and psychological concepts, and in ingenious arguments.

(a) 'Good' is not, Aristotle argues, the name of a single quality. Different kinds of things are called good for different reasons: an axe is good if it cuts efficiently, eyes are good if they see well. To decide what constitutes the best life for human beings one must first establish what their proper functions are (as cutting is the function of an axe); the life of those who perform those functions excellently will be the good life. Now the function of something is what it alone can do, or what it can do best. But humans are distinguished from other animals by their power of reason, so their proper functions – those whose effective performance will constitute a good life – will be those which involve reason. Reason shows itself in an ability not only to think, but also to control desires and conduct; hence human virtues are not only intellectual but also moral or ethical (i.e. virtues of character, *ethos*).

(b) Moral virtues, like skills, are acquired by practice. We become generous by being trained or habituated to doing what generous people do; and they are generous because they have acquired a settled disposition of character to do such deeds regularly, gladly and without ulterior motive. 'Gladly' is important; it helps Aristotle argue that the virtuous life is a pleasant one, in which we do as we ought because we want to: moral struggle, or a need to conquer desires, are signs of imperfection.

Moral virtue is concerned with feelings and actions, of which there can be either too much, or too little, or the right amount – 'the mean'. Virtue is a matter of striking the mean between opposite vices: for example, generosity lies between stinginess and prodigality. There are no simple rules for deciding what the mean is – it is not an arithmetical average, but always 'relative to us'. We need *phronesis* ('practical wisdom') in order to hit the mean.

The doctrine of the mean is more famous than it deserves. Aristotle admits that virtue is not just a matter of the right amount, and that it is difficult to bring *all* virtues and vices into his scheme: 'anger and pity . . . may be felt both too much and too little, and in both cases not well; but to feel them at the right *times*, with reference to the right *people*, with the right *motive*, and in the right *way*, is what is intermediate and best, and this is characteristic of virtue'. The doctrine of the mean, in fact, contains little positive moral teaching and is inadequate if considered simply as analysis of vice–virtue concepts. Supplementary discussions consider responsibility and choice. Aristotle offers acute analyses of the conditions under which responsibility can be disclaimed, and reduces them to two – duress and ignorance of material facts. Choice he finds to involve deliberation and desire: our desires and character determine our ends, and we deliberate about the *means* by which we may reach these ends.

(c) Practical wisdom is an intellectual virtue that enables us to find the right answers to practical questions of conduct. It involves skill in deliberation, but also presupposes the possession of moral virtue. Character determines ends, and to have the right aims is a matter of moral virtue. Moral goodness and practical wisdom are in fact inseparable, each involving the other in its definition. Three further points about practical wisdom may be noted. First, the means–end terminology used by Aristotle is clearly inadequate to his own account of the good life: the aim of the good person is not to achieve some future goal but to live a good life; and Aristotle came to recognize that an action can be right not as a means to a future end but as falling under some moral principle. Second, though Aristotle gives simple examples of deliberation, he does not underestimate the complexity of practical questions or suppose they can be settled easily. To appreciate all the factors in a situation and weigh their various claims one must have an experienced eye for what matters. Age and training are what count here, not mere cleverness. Third, Aristotle does not suppose that every right action is preceded by deliberation, only that practical wisdom implies being able to justify actions by reference to ends or principles. Aristotle's treatment of practical wisdom concludes with important discussions of *akrasia* (knowing what one ought to do but not doing it) and of the nature and value of pleasure.

(d) Theoretical wisdom is an intellectual virtue concerning 'what cannot be otherwise'. It involves intuitive knowledge of unprovable starting-points (concepts and truths) and demonstrative knowledge of what follows from them. Such wisdom, Aristotle argues, is the highest of human virtues: it concerns the highest objects and the divine part of the soul (for pure thought is the only activity that can be attributed to God). The happiest possible life is one devoted to theoretical philosophy, but few are capable of it (and they only intermittently); the rest of us must make do with a life of moral virtue and practical wisdom.

It is striking how Aristotle, starting from the question of human nature, concludes by identifying the highest virtue with the *imitation of God* through the exercise of pure reason.

12 Politics and Poetics. In his *Politics* Aristotle seeks to explain the nature and purpose of a state (a city-state) and discover what constitution and laws would be best. Further, since politics is a branch of *practical* inquiry, he not only expounds an ideal constitution but also makes suggestions as to how actual cities of various kinds could best be run. The main philosophical interest of the work is in its analysis of political concepts ('state',

'citizen', 'law' etc.). His *Poetics* meanwhile had an enormous – and not wholly beneficial – influence both on the writing of drama and on theories of AESTHETICS. See also CATEGORIES, METAPHOR, PHILOSOPHY OF MIND, POLITICAL PHILOSOPHY.   (J.L.A.)

Arnauld, Antoine (1612–94)   Catholic theologian, a leading defender of DESCARTES' 'new philosophy', and author (with Pierre Nicole) of *La logique, ou l'art de penser* ('Port-Royal Logic', 1662).

Atomism   Atomism arose as an explanatory scheme with the ancient Greeks, LEUCIPPUS and DEMOCRITUS, and EPICURUS, and the Roman poet LUCRETIUS. At the most fundamental level atomism is the belief that all phenomena are explicable in terms of the properties and behaviour of ultimate, elementary, localized entities (or 'fundamental particles'). Thus it prescribes a strategy for the construction of scientific theories in which the behaviour of complex bodies is to be explained in terms of their component parts. That strategy has led to many of the successes of modern physical science, though these do not prove that there actually are 'ultimate entities' of the type postulated by atomism.

The atomists made the assumption that the things which really exist are permanent and indestructible, though this is obviously not true of the everyday objects around us. Their analysis goes 'behind' the appearances to minute, unchangeable and indestructible 'atoms' separated by the emptiness of 'the void' which is said to make change and movement possible. All apparent change is simply the result of rearrangements of the atoms as a consequence of collisions between them. This seems to lead to mechanical DETERMINISM, though, in an attempt to leave room for freewill, Epicurus and Lucretius postulated that atoms might 'deviate' in their courses.

According to the atomists, colour, taste, warmth and so forth are the effects produced in our sense organs by atoms which themselves possess none of these properties: a conclusion which, as they were aware, is difficult to establish on the basis of sense experience itself. The hypothetical properties of the atoms were basically 'geometrical' (sharp-cornered, smooth, etc.), though 'solidity' was needed to distinguish them from empty space (compare LOCKE). The later atomists also regarded 'weight' as an intrinsic property of the atoms. Lucretius says that the number of atoms is infinite but the variety of shapes and sizes is finite (arguing fallaciously that otherwise there could be no limit to the size of the atoms).

However if 'what exists' is 'atoms', what of the 'void'? In different ways both ARISTOTLE and DESCARTES denied that there could be such a thing as literally 'empty space'. Physically therefore they saw the world as a *plenum*. Atomism was also associated with atheism, since as Lucretius put it, 'Nothing can ever be created out of nothing, even by divine power.' Conversely no thing can ever become nothing. Thus the atomists proposed a strict principle of conservation of matter. They strove to provide a complete picture of the world that included a materialist account of perception and the nature of mind. The mind is simply a fragile and mortal association of certain subtle atoms with those of the body; and they are disordered and dissipated in disease, insanity and death. Visual perception occurs because objects shed physical 'images' (or 'species') of themselves in thin atomic films which impinge upon our eyes. These 'images' are moving all around us, sometimes in fragments, and are responsible for dreams, phantoms and in their most

subtle form for experience of 'the gods'. This thoroughgoing materialism, and the HEDONIST ethics which Democritus and Epicurus associated with it, were responsible for the disfavour with which atomism was long regarded in European culture.

In the seventeenth century GASSENDI and BOYLE detached the atomic or corpuscular theory from its associations with atheism and MATERIALISM. Indeed they turned the tables on those, like HOBBES, who believed that the material world was a *plenum* and who denied the existence of a real 'vacuum' on the grounds that 'incorporeal substance' was impossible. In Hobbes' universe not only must the 'soul' be material and mortal, but there could be no physical empty space in which his 'corporeal' God could act. NEWTON, following the example of the Cambridge Platonist Henry MORE, justified his introduction of 'Space' as a real, infinite entity (and by implication, the existence of 'hard, massy, impenetrable, moveable particles') by claiming that Absolute Space is constituted by the Omnipresence of God.

Newton sought to make the action of Universal Gravitation across empty space believable by reference to the power of God, but as the investigation of electricity, magnetism and chemical affinity developed in the eighteenth and nineteenth centuries attempts were made to find physical explanations for 'action-at-a-distance'. In the theories of Boscovich and Faraday the dualism of Atoms and the Void is replaced by an all-pervasive 'field of force' in which there are many mathematical centres. (This vision also informs the account of gravitation in Einstein's General Theory of RELATIVITY.) Paradoxically the attraction of 'mathematical atomism' proved an obstacle to the acceptance of Dalton's atomic theory in which 'atoms' of many different sizes and weights were proposed, each associated with a different chemical element. That theory provided an explanation of the empirical regularities discovered by experimental chemists, but positivistically inclined scientists regarded atomism as a 'metaphysical encumbrance' until the early years of the twentieth century. A critical factor in convincing the doubters was Einstein's analysis of the 'Brownian' motion of microscopic particles, which dimly echoed Lucretius' discussions of the significance of dust dancing in sunbeams. Scepticism over the question of whether 'atoms' can be 'observed' raises questions about the meaning of 'observation' when sophisticated instruments are employed. A thoroughgoing POSITIVISM will continue to hold that 'atomic theories' are simply devices for talking about observable phenomena.

The ancient atomists postulated 'atoms' of many different shapes and sizes, but this variety itself stands in need of explanation. Reduction of this variety to one single type of elementary entity would be more 'satisfying', though this would not prevent one from asking why this 'ultimate entity' had its particular properties. A great simplification in the Daltonian atomic scheme was achieved when it was shown that periodic regularities in the properties of different 'atoms' could be explained in terms of inner structures constructed from just three kinds of more elementary particle (electron, proton and neutron). Subsequent collision experiments generated a profusion of other 'elementary' particles, which were eventually largely reduced to order by postulating entities which are yet more fundamental ('quarks'). It might be supposed that this process could continue forever, without any 'ultimate particles' (genuine 'atoms') ever being identified. Indeed it is difficult to see how anyone could ever prove that 'the end of the road' had been reached. However ordinary concepts of

'structure' have come under strain in these explorations, and it is by no means clear that the most elementary entities postulated at present have properties which are explicable in terms of *any* classical atomistic model.

One of the assumptions of the fundamental atomist picture is that atoms have intrinsic properties of their own and that all 'relational properties' can be analysed in terms of these properties and the *spatial* relations of the bodies. (This is another way of saying, 'There is nothing but Atoms and the Void'.) However QUANTUM MECHANICS indicates that the elementary constituents presently postulated by physical science have properties which cannot conceivably be analysed in this way.

The attempt of the ancient atomists to solve a metaphysical problem about the nature of change resulted in a brilliantly fruitful strategy for the construction of theories in the physical sciences. But there are unanswered philosophical objections to atomism and the very successes it has stimulated suggest that 'the stuff of the world' cannot ultimately be understood in terms of atomism.   [J.H.P.]

Augustine (354–430)   Saint Augustine, also known as Aurelius Augustinus and Augustine of Hippo, was born to a Christian mother and a pagan father at Thagaste in Numidia (Souk-Ahras in Algeria on the Tunisian border). He received a thorough education in rhetoric, a discipline over which the spirit of CICERO presided, and by the time he was 20 he turned his back on Christianity, intellectually repelled by the crudity, in style and content, of its Scriptures. Its canons of behaviour were also uncongenial to him, and as a very young man he was already established in Carthage with a mistress and a professorial chair of rhetoric.

His energetic and curious mind was fired with a love of philosophy by Cicero's *Hortensius*, now lost, which he read at the age of 18. This started him on an intellectual adventure that led him first to MANICHEISM, then to the thoroughgoing SCEPTICISIM of the ACADEMICS; next, about the time he was appointed to a chair of rhetoric at Milan, to NEOPLATONISM; and finally, at the age of 32, to what he called Catholic Christianity. He was baptized in Milan at Easter 387, about nine months after his conversion. In 391 he was ordained priest and in 395 he became bishop of the city of Hippo Regius (Bône, on the Algerian coast). His genius and his strenuous devotion to pastoral duties soon made him the intellectual leader of African Catholicism. After an episcopate of over thirty years, during which he won an Empire-wide reputation, he died at Hippo on 28 August, 430, as the Vandals were besieging the city.

Augustine's thought was always the expression of his personal experience – an experience of conversion to Christianity followed by a life spent in teaching it. For him, Christianity is the true philosophy, and pagan schools of philosophy were false or defective. Truth is one and divine (indeed it is what God is), and its possession is happiness, *beatitudo*. (Augustine defines beatitude as *gaudium de veritate*, enjoying Truth.) Under the pull of Truth his life had a certain splendid simplicity about it; first a quest for Truth, then the discovery of it, and after that a life spent in its exploration.

It is wisdom that gives knowledge of Truth, so the quest for Truth is a quest for wisdom. One of the first philosophical problems to engage Augustine was how one can pass from being unwise to being wise. To do so one must desire the wisdom that one lacks. But desire implies knowledge of the thing desired. Desire of wisdom therefore implies both lack of wisdom and possession of it. This conundrum was posed for Augustine by the Academics, for whom wisdom consisted in knowing that we can know nothing, and he made use of it in his *De Utilitate Credendi* against his Manichean friends, who thought they had all the answers. Dialectically he extricated himself from the impasse of scepticism by what has been called 'the Augustinian *Cogito*': *Si fallor, sum* ('if I am wrong, I exist'). But his real method was one that could be described as systematic faith. 'Unless you believe, you shall not understand' (Isaiah 7, 9) was one of his favourite texts. (The older he got, the more biblical his thought and language became.) Faith alone can provide the base from which the quest for wisdom must start, because it is both a knowing, which makes love of the thing known possible, and a not knowing, so that love is still desire, not yet enjoyment. Augustine's conversion was his discovery of wisdom by faith, and the beginning of his exploration of it by understanding.

The method is deployed most conspicuously in *De Trinitate*, a work which also displays the extent and bearing of Augustine's Platonism. His cosmos is constructed on a Platonic dialectic; there is the outer and the inner world, the lower and the higher, the sensible and the intelligible, and the carnal and the spiritual. Progress in wisdom is a movement of the mind inwards and upwards to God at the apex and the centre – an opening to the illumination of incommutable truth, which is always available for inspection, provided the mind has been purified by faith. But this progress is, so to speak, a feeling one's way backwards along the channel of influence which comes downwards and outwards, from the Creator to the creature.

The word 'Creator' indicates the limits of Augustine's Platonism. His crucial theme of the divine image in the world and in humanity depends on the wholly biblical doctrine of creation, and enabled him to regard the material world with a reverence impossible for a thorough Platonist. The goal of his vision was the resurrection of the body, not the soul's release from a bodily prison. His doctrine of EVIL as no-thing, as a privation, a lack of due order, marks his easy independence of Platonism as much as his emancipation from Manicheism.

The doctrine of Incarnation accords ill with the ultra-spiritualism and intellectualism of the Platonists, but fits smoothly into Augustine's God-imagining world. The divine image in man has been defaced by sin, which upsets the divine order, ruffles the clear surface. It is restored by a transcendent manifestation of divine order, in which the Word, the image *par excellence*, makes up for pride with humility, and disobedience by obedience, and restoring life through death, and innocence through the acceptance of guilt. The dialectical statement of the Incarnation in St Paul and St John plucks an immediate response from Augustine, the trained rhetorician. The Word incarnate is the Way back for man to the Word who is Truth, and the Way on to the risen Christ who is Life. Like creation, restoration must come from above. All the initiatives are God's. Human freedom is fully vindicated only when its derivation from divine freedom is accepted. Divine grace is displayed in divine charity – 'God so loved the world . . .' – and the human response is one of charity, which Augustine would almost say is as natural as falling off a log. *Amor meus pondus meum* ('My love is my weight'), he said. His ethics stems from grace rather than will-power, and from personal love rather than abstract principle, and is quite free from the harsh Puritanism which has often been ascribed to it. (E.H.)

Aurelius See MARCUS AURELIUS.

Austin, John Langshaw (1911–60) The Oxford Professor of Moral Philosophy J. L. Austin had a very considerable influence on the development of ANALYTIC PHILOSOPHY. His work consists mainly of close examinations of the way words are ordinarily used, without direct reference to the traditional problems of philosophy. Austin gives an admirable brief account of his reasons for this procedure in his 'A Plea for Excuses' (1956). Two of his most important sets of lectures were published posthumously. In *Sense and Sensibilia* he attempted to show that certain traditional philosophical arguments that are designed to prove that the direct object of the senses is always a SENSE-DATUM and never a physical object derive their plausibility from a systematic distortion of key terms from their normal use. In *How to Do Things with Words* he first restates his doctrine of 'performative utterances', but finds it ultimately unsatisfactory and goes on to replace the distinction between performative and statemental utterances by a distinction between the locutionary act (saying something with a certain meaning), the illocutionary act (what one does, such as promising, in saying something), and the perlocutionary act (what one brings about by saying something), all considered as abstractable components of the complete speech-act. This doctrine has greatly influenced later work on the philosophy of language.   (J.O.U.)

Averroes (1126–98) The Arabic philosopher, jurist and physician Averroes (the name is Latinized from Ibn Rushd) was born at Cordova, Spain, and died at Marrakesh. In the West, he is best known as a commentator on ARISTOTLE. On many Aristotelian writings he wrote three different kinds of Commentaries: *Summaries* in his own words, and *Middle* and *Long Commentaries* quoting portions of the text and adding explanatory and critical comments, in the light of classical commentators like Themistius, Alexander of Aphrodisias, and Al-Fārābī, AVICENNA and Avempace (Ibn Bājja). His exposition is lucid and concise, adhering more closely to Aristotle than any of the earlier *Falāsifa* (arabic religious philosophers). Not having Aristotle's *Politics*, Averroes commented on PLATO's *Republic*, which he treated as the second, practical part of the science of politics supplementing Aristotle's *Nicomachean Ethics* which was the first, theoretical part.

The significance of Averroes as a religious philosopher lies in his polemical treatises, his spirited rebuttal of attacks on the *Falāsifa*, and his Commentary on Plato. Averroes set out to prove the essential agreement between the religious law (*Sharī'a*) and philosophy (*falsafa*) by claiming that one is 'the companion and foster-sister' of the other. Truth is one and indivisible, but explicable in different ways. The theory of 'double truth' is wrongly fathered on him; it belongs rather to his Latin followers. Averroes asserts the philosopher's exclusive ability, right and duty to expound the inner meaning of the prophetically revealed Law by demonstrative argument. With Plato he distinguishes the few elect philosophers from the masses. With Aristotle he distinguishes three classes of arguments (demonstrative, dialectical and rhetorical or poetical), which he assigns to three classes of believers: philosophers, theologians and the masses. The masses must accept the stories, parables and metaphors of Scripture in their plain meaning; but they also have an inner meaning accessible only to the metaphysician. All three classes must accept certain statements in the *Qur'an* (*Koran*) in their literal meaning

as religious truth inaccessible to human reason, because they are God's revelation. On these grounds, he maintains the superiority of the *Sharī'a*, which guarantees happiness to every believer, over *Nomos* (secular law), which is only concerned with the happiness of the élite.

Averroes insisted, like Avicenna, on the superior and exceptional character of Muhammad as the divinely sent prophetic law-giver, but his vindication of the *Sharī'a* as the constitution of the ideal Muslim state is combined with a sustained critique, rooted in Plato, of the Muslim state of his time. (E.I.J.R.)

Avicenna (980–1037) Persian physician (the name is Latinized from Ibn Sīnā) and most original of the *Falāsifa* (Muslim religious philosophers). Avicenna propounded a philosophical monotheism which approaches a synthesis between the tenets of Islam and the teachings of PLATO and ARISTOTLE. Unlike Al-Fārābī, to whom he was greatly indebted, and AVERROES, whose original contribution is largely contained in his *Commentaries*, Avicenna succeeded in formulating a *Summa* of philosophy out of a critical study of Aristotle, helped by NEOPLATONIC commentators and the STOICS. His *Shifā* exerted a strong influence on Muslims, Jews and Christians. In LOGIC, Avicenna's strict adherence to Aristotle's concept of cause and effect led to a logical determinism which brought him into conflict with theological determinism, while in psychology he combined Aristotle with PLOTINUS in his widely accepted idea of the immortality of the rational soul which, as form, is also substance. More far-reaching is his contribution to METAPHYSICS. Like all *Falāsifa* he was helped by Plotinus and Porphyry, who had tried to harmonize Plato and Aristotle and, by giving Plato's thought a turn towards religious MONISM, enabled Muslims to blend traditional beliefs and convictions with Greek thought. Avicenna's view that existence and essence coincide in the being of God gained wide currency in the West, especially with the Jewish MAIMONIDES and the Christian AQUINAS. So did its corollary, that in created beings essence is separate from existence, which is only an accident. Accepting Aristotle's concept of the eternity of matter, Avicenna rejected the theological axiom of 'creation out of nothing'. Moreover, creation is a necessary consequence of God's existence as an absolute, simple unity whose knowledge, will and power are one with his essence. He is the uncaused First Cause, hence necessarily the Creator. Maimonides and Aquinas opposed this Avicennian concept, maintaining the Scriptural notion of a creation in time by God's free-will.

To close the gap between revelation and reason Avicenna escaped into a form of intellectual mysticism. The speculative mystic (*ārif*) who attained the highest degree of knowledge, gained intellectual union with God in intuitive perception. Practical philosophy is part of Avicenna's *Metaphysics* because the attainment of human happiness is only possible in society, but prophecy and *Sharī'a* (prophetically revealed Muslim Law) were indispensable for human survival and happiness. The prophetic lawgiver brings mankind a divine law guaranteeing welfare in this world and bliss hereafter. Al-Fārābī identified the prophetic lawgiver with Plato's philosopher-king; Avicenna, in contrast, grants the prophet a spontaneous, intuitive knowledge which raises him above the philosopher. The ideal Muslim state with Muhammad's law as constitution is the counterpart to Plato's concepts of Justice and Law which, for the *Falāsifa*, illustrated the political significance of the *Sharī'a* and enabled them to blend Islamic fundamentals with Greek concepts.   (E.I.J.R.)

Ayer, Sir Alfred Jules (1910–89)

Born in London and educated at Eton and Oxford, A. J. Ayer was Professor at the University of London from 1946, and in Oxford from 1959. He was also well known as a broadcaster. Ayer achieved early fame as the author of *Language, Truth and Logic* (1936), a work which did much to familiarize the English-speaking world with LOGICAL POSITIVISM. Based on first-hand acquaintance with the VIENNA CIRCLE, it ranks among the clearest and most forthright expositions of the subject in any language. In some respects, also, it represents a synthesis of British and Continental versions of EMPIRICISM. Ayer agrees with the latter in rejecting METAPHYSICS and confining philosophy to ANALYSIS. He conceives of the analytic method as the translation of problematic expressions into a logically more explicit terminology, and he typically makes use of it to resolve traditional cruxes in the theory of knowledge. Material objects, for instance, are not 'constructed' out of SENSE-DATA, but statements mentioning the former can be logically 'reduced' to statements mentioning only the latter. This linguistic 'PHENOMENALISM' is put forward as a truth already glimpsed in the writings of BERKELEY and HUME. Apart from its controversial treatment of ethical propositions (as 'emotive' rather than factual), the other main feature of Ayer's discussion is his proposal to distinguish a weaker form of the verification principle, designed to exclude metaphysics while preserving the significance of other propositions supposedly more useful to science. Difficulties of formulation proved far greater than he expected, and were reviewed in his introduction to the second edition (1946).

Ayer's later writings (especially *The Problem of Knowledge*, 1956) were largely devoted to retrenchment of his position in the light of subsequent criticism. The same epistemological problems are repeatedly tackled, with substantially the same weapons; but there is less disposition to claim finality for the results. Commonsense claims to knowledge of the external world, the past, the self and other people are now scrutinized, not in order to 'reduce' or repudiate them, but in order to elucidate the logical grounds for their acceptance. In pursuit of this inquiry, Ayer came to doubt the possibility of analysing claims about material objects into claims about the actual or possible occurrence of sense-data; and he at length forsook phenomenalism. His later position can be described as that of an analytically minded empiricist, dubious of claims made for 'ordinary language', and without commitments to any really definable school. Ayer is also the author of the article on RUSSELL in this Encyclopedia.   (P.L.H.)

B

Bachelard, Gaston (1884–1962)
French philosopher and historian of
science, more widely known to the
English-speaking world for his writings
on aesthetics and poetics, but whose
approach to the history and PHILOSOPHY OF
SCIENCE influenced a whole generation
of philosophers passing through French
universities, including such figures as
CANGUILHEM, FOUCAULT and ALTHUSSER.
Bachelard's first degree was in mathematics and he taught physics and chemistry at
his local college, in Bar-sur-Aube, whilst
working on his doctorate in philosophy.
He thus came to the history and philosophy of science from science. This is
reflected in his approach to the philosophy
of science, which is characterized by an
opposition to the imposition of philosophical ideologies (whether POSITIVIST, EXIS-
TENTIALIST, REALIST or PHENOMENALIST)
on science. He insists that any philosophy
concerned with EPISTEMOLOGY must learn
from science, and recognize the distinctive
character of twentieth-century science.
The overthrow of classical Newtonian
physics by the theories of RELATIVITY and
QUANTUM MECHANICS represented a break
with past science, which in its turn
requires epistemology to break with past
philosophies of science. (This view is
most succinctly expressed in *The New
Scientific Spirit*, 1934.) Bachelard rejects
the picture of the development of science
as a continuous, gradual accumulation of
knowledge in favour of a discontinuous,
ruptured development in which what was
once taken for knowledge undergoes
repeated re-evaluation and re-interpretation.
His concern with the development of science and with the objectivity of creative

rational thought in science is parallelled
by his concern with the subjectivity of
non-rational, artistically creative thought,
with poetic imagination and reveries. In
works such as *The Psychoanalysis of Fire*
(1938) and *Water and Dreams* (1942) he
draws on Jungian depth psychology for his
exploration of the trans-subjective power
of poetic images, images which reverber-
ate in the readers' consciousness and lead
them to create anew whilst communicating
with the poet. Such communication is
contrasted sharply with the objectivity
required of scientific discourse, which
requires that the power of images (which
present epistemological obstacles) be
broken and that the scientist learn to dream
in the austere realm of abstract mathematical structures. This duality of objective
and subjective, of concept and image, of
the scientific and the poetic, informs not
only Bachelard's philosophy, but the whole
structure of his written corpus.   [M.T.]

Bacon, Francis (1561–1626)   Francis
Bacon was born in the shadow of the
English Court, which dominated his
whole life. He was educated at Cambridge
and admitted to the Bar in 1575. In 1584,
through the help of his uncle, Lord
Burghley, he obtained a seat in the House
of Commons. He was befriended by
Essex, the favourite of Elizabeth, who
tried unsuccessfully to get him made
attorney-general in 1593. Under James I,
Bacon's fortunes improved. In 1607 he
was made solicitor-general and in 1613
attorney-general; in 1617 Lord Keeper
and in 1618 Lord Chancellor. He was also
created Baron Verulam and in 1621
Viscount St Albans. Three days after this

honour Bacon was accused of bribery, found technically guilty, and deprived of office. He had accepted presents from litigants, the usual practice of the time. To quote his own words: 'I was the justest judge that was in England these fifty years. But it was the justest censure in Parliament that was these two hundred years.' He died in 1626, in retirement, working on his scientific projects.

Bacon always claimed that his aim in seeking political advancement was to improve man's estate and to use his wealth and influence to forward the cause of a new science that might contribute to this end. But in spite of repeated attempts he obtained neither a college nor a royal foundation. He lived lavishly, and his debts prevented him spending much on the advancement of science during his lifetime; after his death they also prevented the implementation of his will, in which he provided for lectureships in natural philosophy at Oxford and Cambridge.

His actual contributions to learning and science were similarly incomplete – programmatic aspirations rather than concrete pieces of work. In 1603 he laid the foundation for his 'Great Instauration' with *Valerius Terminus* and *De Interpretatione Naturae Proemium*, followed by *Cogitata et Visa*. He announced that he had constructed a new method of scientific discovery, in which large natural histories and collections of facts were to be amassed, preferably within a college, and carefully interpreted. The same stress on natural history and a new method of interpretation runs through his *Advancement of Learning* (1605), together with a criticism of previous thinkers and passionate pleas for the use of knowledge to better man's earthly estate.

This was a preliminary to the Great Instauration itself, which was to consist of six parts, the *Advancement of Learning* forming a major section of the first part. The parts were as follows. (1) A classification and review of existing sciences which would make the gaps in them obvious. (He fulfilled this portion of his plan in *De Dignitate et Augmentis Scientiarum*, 1623). (2) A new inductive method for putting all human minds on a level in the interpretation of nature. (This was sketched in *Novum Organum*, 1620.) (3) Natural history or a collection of data and experiments arranged in accordance with the principles laid down in Part 2. (This was achieved only in extremely fragmentary form: *Parasceve ad historiam naturalem et experimentalem*, 1620; *Historia Naturalis et experimentalis ad condendam philosophiam: sive phenomena universi*, 1622; and a strange collection of facts and fables, *Sylva Sylvarum*, 1627.) (4) The Ladder of the Intellect, which was meant to consist of fully worked out examples of his method. (None of this is extant save a preface called *Scala Intellectus sive filum labyrinthi*.) (5) Generalizations reached from natural history without the use of Bacon's special method of interpretation. (Only a preface to this exists: *Prodromi sive Anticipationes Philosophiae Secundae*.) (6) The New Philosophy or Active Science, consisting of the complete science of Nature. This was to be built on the facts of Part 3, established by the methods of Part 2. (None of this is extant.)

Bacon wrote many other works which do not fit into his Great Instauration and are not easily regarded as anticipations or offshoots of it. Most famous are his *New Atlantis* (his contribution to Utopian literature), *De Sapientia Veterum* (1609) and *De Principiis atque Originibus* (1623–4), an attempt to supplant the Platonic and Aristotelian traditions with a more materialistic theory deriving from DEMOCRITUS. Also in refutation of earlier philosophers he wrote a treatise on 'the idols of the theatre',

Redargutio philosophiarum (1608). There are also several other fragments, such as *Temporis partus masculus* and *Delineatio et argumentum*, both of which were anticipations of his Great Instauration.

Bacon's main contribution to philosophy was in the sphere of scientific method. He was one of the most powerful and articulate rebels against the Aristotelian and Platonic traditions; in many respects he attempted to revive a materialism akin to that of Democritus. He claimed that Aristotelian logic was useless: it revealed nothing new and dragged experiment along like a captive. In addition, its explanations in terms of 'final causes' had wonderfully corrupted philosophy, for such explanations were only appropriate in explaining human affairs. The alternative school of thought, deriving from PLATO, was equally useless. No trust was to be placed in the abstract axioms of the geometric method. Definitions could not remedy the evil, because they themselves consisted of words: 'words are but the images of matter; and except they have life of reason and invention, to fall in love with them is to fall in love with a picture'. Rationalists were like spiders spinning ideas out of the recesses of their mind. The brute empirics, on the other hand, were no better: they were like ants, aimlessly collecting data. The secret lay in natural history, or the amassing and storing of data, and it was the bees that provided the proper model for scientific procedure.

In the endeavour to replace rash anticipations of Nature by orderly interpretations the inquirer is brought up against certain deep-seated limitations of the human mind. These Bacon called the Idols of the Tribe. We tend to generalize too readily, to find instances which suit our purposes and to believe more readily that which we prefer. Bacon therefore stressed the importance of looking for the negative instance, of seeking systematically for exceptions to generalizations. The Idols of the Tribe are due to other limitations such as the dullness of our perceptual apparatus. But there are also the Idols of the Den, which are due not so much to human nature generally as to individual differences and idiosyncrasies. Then there are the Idols of the Market Place, due to vague words and phrases that corrupt and muddle our thinking. Finally, there are the Idols of the Theatre, which arise from systems of philosophy. The remedy for these obstacles was not simply to expose the faulty reasoning of others, but to set out the new method of inquiry clearly for all to use.

This method consisted of accumulating data and dealing with them in a certain manner. Suppose the cause of heat was sought. A table of *presence* had first to be compiled containing all known instances in which heat was present, then a table of *absence* with instances corresponding to those in the table of presence. A table of *degrees* had also to be constructed with instances where heat was present in varying degrees. By examining the tables, a 'generating nature' might be found which was co-present, co-absent and co-variant with the effect or 'generated nature'. An interpretation or 'first vintage' could then be made – for example, that motion is the cause or 'form' of heat. (These tables are very similar to J. S. MILL's joint methods of agreement and difference and the method of concomitant variations.)

One of the most vexed questions of Baconian scholarship is the status of the 'forms'. He distinguished physics – which investigates efficient and material causes but 'does not stir the limits of things which are much more deeply rooted' – from METAPHYSICS, which investigates 'forms'. Forms are both 'generic' and 'generating': heat, for instance, is a limitation of the more generic nature 'motion'; and it is also in some way *produced* by motion. Such 'forms' are unlike Aristotelian formal causes because they are generators of other natures and not just correlative with matter. It is often suggested that Bacon had in mind some atomic theory akin to that of Democritus. Yet his 'forms' are observables, discovered by compiling tables, whereas Democritan atoms are not observable.

Whatever doubts there may be about the status of 'forms', there can be no doubt about Bacon's enthusiasm for the practical projects which a knowledge of the laws of the combination of forms might permit. He was one of the first to stress that knowledge gives humanity power over nature, and he has been heralded as a forerunner of both UTILITARIANISM and MARXISM in this respect. Bacon thought that the aim of his Great Instauration was 'knowledge of the causes and of the secret motion of things, and the enlarging of the bounds of human empire, to the effecting of all things possible'. He subscribed to the alchemist's ideal of transmuting substances of one kind into substances of another, but thought such an undertaking must be based on a thorough understanding of 'what is constant, eternal, and universal in nature'.

Bacon met with little concrete success either in developing his fundamental science or in inaugurating a college to house it. But he inspired many with his dream of improving the human condition by the employment of scientific method. The Royal Society, founded in 1662, was Baconian in spirit. It combined his emphasis on observation and experiment with a concern for inventions of practical use. It was founded by Puritans who

believed, like Bacon, that science could reveal the wonders of God's creation and be used to improve man's estate.

Bacon's thought influenced not only the development of science but also the typically British conception of knowledge and scientific method as developed by LOCKE, BERKELEY, HUME, J. S. MILL and RUSSELL. But his account of scientific method has been criticized by later thinkers in at least four respects. First, it is argued that he was mistaken in thinking that there is an 'inductive' method which puts all observers on a level in arriving at well-founded generalizations. There may be methods for testing generalizations once they have been made, but there are no recipes for arriving at them. Second, it is alleged that Bacon failed to distinguish between rash 'anticipations' of nature and working hypotheses. Data cannot be collected without some sort of hypothesis, nor can theory be developed. The nineteenth-century logician WHEWELL made much of this defect in Bacon's account. Third, Bacon was profoundly ignorant of mathematics and overlooked its great importance in the development of theories. He rejected the Copernican hypothesis, ridiculed Gilbert's speculations about magnetism and failed to see the importance of Harvey's work. He understood little of continental thinkers like Kepler and Galileo. Finally, Bacon ignored problems connected with the *justification* of inductive reasoning, which have troubled philosophers since Hume. But he remains important for his stress on the observational basis of science and the search for the negative instance. (R.S.P.)

Bacon, Roger (c. 1214–c. 1292) English thinker whose long career at Oxford and Paris covers the whole of the vital period in the thirteenth century when Greek and Arabic science and philosophy were assimilated into Western thought. In many respects he appears conservative and traditional, like his fellow Franciscan, BONAVENTURA, being no less observant of religion and equally convinced of the supremacy of theological knowledge. Yet he differs profoundly from him in his reaction to the new science. Where Bonaventura saw science as a possibly interesting field for human investigation, but a regrettable distraction from the contemplative activity to which all should aspire, Bacon saw a new method which could radically transform philosophy and theology by applying the new mathematical and experimental techniques to them. His most characteristic writing is to be found in his *Opus Majus* which, together with the shorter *Opus Minus* and *Opus Tertium*, elaborates his views on how to reform the teaching of Christian wisdom. These works were written at the request of Pope Clement IV and urged the political hegemony which would fall to the West as a result of the advance of science. But Clement died and Bacon remained frustrated.   (J.G.D.)

Barth, Karl (1886–1968)   Swiss theologian, see EXISTENTIALISM, RELIGION.

Barthes, Roland (1915–80)   French critic, see STRUCTURALISM.

Bataille, Georges (1897–1962) French surrealist, erotic novelist and neo-NIETZSCHEAN philosopher of religion. He was also a disciple of HEGEL in the interpretation put forward by KOJÈVE, and author of *L'expérience intérieure* (1943).

Beauty   See AESTHETICS, BURKE.

Beauvoir, Simone de (1908–86) Born in Paris, she was a key figure in French EXISTENTIALISM and a founding theorist of modern FEMINISM. Though she was profoundly influenced by the philosophy of SARTRE, with whom she maintained a life-long association, de Beauvoir's alertness to the central weakness of the doctrine of *Being and Nothingness* – its neglect of the social context of action – was itself an influence on Sartre's shift from a 'philosophy of consciousness' to the more Marxist perspective of his later work. An initial focus (see her early novels and *The Ethics of Ambiguity*, 1947) is the moral dilemma posed by the existentialist insistence on our absolute freedom: for whilst freedom from social codes and conventions may be essential to the exercise of responsible moral choice, morality itself would seem to demand that our actions be constrained by a 'conventional' concern for their impact on others. Moreover, all choices are in fact made in concrete situations which limit the possibilities of action.

The Second Sex (1949) offers a powerful and sustained exemplification of these dilemmas, exploring how the historical oppression of women can be reconciled with their possession of freedom, while at the same time exposing differences in the situation of the sexes which are obscured by philosophy's universalizing pretensions. For while women, in virtue of their humanity, have as much need for autonomy as men have, their cultural relegation to the status of 'Otherness' in relation to men has condemned them to forms of dependency and subordination irreconcilable with genuine freedom. De Beauvoir dismisses any suggestion that women are incapable by nature of transcending their situation. But her positive valuation of transcendence (which implicitly condones the Hegelian and Sartrean association of femininity with immanence) has been unacceptable to some of her readers, as has the political implication that women can only realize themselves by becoming like men. But in drawing attention to the disparities in the legal and social situation of women, *The Second Sex* helped inaugurate the practical campaigns (around such issues as abortion and equal rights for women) which led to the growth and diversification of the modern feminist movement.

De Beauvoir is exceptional among philosophers both in the range of her writings (which include novels, journalism and autobiography alongside distinctively philosophical works) and in the extent to which she uses fictional forms to convey philosophical ideas. Of note, too, is her practical adherence to the philosophy she espoused; she lived her life as a project, and not least among her achievements is the record she bequeathed in her memoirs of the existential unfolding of an individual life in its unique and unrepeatable passage from birth to grave.   [K.S.]

Behaviourism   An approach to psychology first formulated in 1913 by J. B. Watson (1878–1958), who held that a science of mind must be based on outwardly observable behaviour rather inner experience. The term was later extended, often with a hint of scorn, to philosophical treatments of mind in the tradition of WITTGENSTEIN and RYLE.

Being   See ARISTOTLE, DUALISM, EXISTENTIALISM, HEIDEGGER, IDEALISM METAPHYSICS, MONISM, REALISM.

Benjamin,   Walter   (1892–1940)
Literary critic and theorist, born in Berlin. Walter Benjamin was a close friend of Gershom Scholem, the historian of Jewish mysticism, Bertolt Brecht and THEODOR W. ADORNO, whose philosophy Benjamin's writings significantly influenced. During the 1930s Benjamin was associated with the FRANKFURT SCHOOL, in whose journal some of his best-known essays appeared.

Benjamin's philosophical thought circles around his idea of 'redemptive criticism'. This idea is revealed explicitly in the 'Epistemo-Critical Prologue' to his *Origin of German Tragic Drama* (1928), his 'Theses on the Philosophy of History', and some of his early essays; and implicitly in his historical–critical works, especially the unfinished study of nineteenth-century Paris, the *Arcades Project*. The goal of redemptive criticism was to overcome the modern split between critique, which seeks the truth content of a work of art, and commentary, which seeks to illuminate a work's subject matter. In pursuit of this goal Benjamin developed ideas on the philosophy of history and the philosophy of language, and on critical cognition. According to Benjamin the idea of history as a continuous slow progress of truth and human freedom is a vision from the perspective of the victors: 'the continuum of history is that of the oppressor'. Redemptive criticism seeks to reveal moments of discontinuity and restore that which continuous, progressive history has dominated and repressed. While Benjamin's philosophical thought is intensely idiosyncratic and problematic, especially his theologically inspired philosophy of language, it continues to command attention, in large measure because of the way it informs his uniquely powerful critical and historical writings.   [J.M.B.]

Bentham,   Jeremy   (1748–1832)
Jeremy Bentham originally expected to follow his father and grandfather as a lawyer working in the city of London, but revolted against the unnecessary technicality of current legal procedure and devoted himself instead to discovering the fundamental principles of a just, clear and rational legal system. This led him to a profound examination of the nature of thought, language, law, government and public morality. He sought to substitute

clear expressions for unclear ones, and made the fundamental innovation of substituting at the level of sentences rather than terms (the method of paraphrasis). Unclear sentences are analysed into clear ones and clarity is achieved by closeness to experience, particularly the sensations of pleasure and pain. Thus, in his account of law, Bentham analysed sentences about rights into sentences about duties, and sentences about duties into sentences about the commands of a person or group backed by the threat of sanctions (the possibility of pain). In this way he hoped to establish an account of the law as it is. Turning to the question of how the law ought to be, he appealed to the principle of utility (as previously used in various ways by HUME, Helvétius and Beccaria), declaring at the start of his first main work the 'fundamental axiom, it is the greatest happiness of the greatest number that is the measure of right and wrong'. This UTILITARIAN principle also substitutes clear goals, concerned with pleasure and pain, for unclear ones. Finally, Bentham added a self-interest psychology describing how people actually value various states so that the value varies with such factors as certainty, distance, intensity or duration. With an account of man as he is and an account of society as it ought to be, Bentham spent much time designing institutions – in particular his famous prison, the Panopticon – in which these two were united. In these institutions, be they states or prisons, men would naturally (i.e. following their own interests) do what they ought to do (i.e. promote the greatest happiness of the greatest number). From this follow the utilitarian principles of punishment in which deterrence is its only justification. As Bentham puts it, all punishment is in itself evil (i.e. it causes pain); it is only justified therefore if it causes greater good by deterring the wrong acts of others. By taking account of value, this enables the precise quantity of punishment appropriate for every offence to be measured. [R.H.]

Berdyaev, Nicholas (1874–1948)

Berdyaev lived in his native Russia until his expulsion in 1922, when he settled first in Germany and then in France. A faithful member of the Russian Orthodox Church, Berdyaev, in most of his work, should be classed as a religious thinker and as a social and political propagandist rather than a philosopher; his aim was practical – to bring about a Christian social system – rather than theoretical. But his fundamental philosophical thesis was a distinction between the material world, subject to natural law and necessity, of which man as an animal is a part, and the higher world of freedom of which man as spirit is a part, a position reminiscent of KANT'S distinction between the phenomenal and noumenal worlds.

(J.O.U.)

Bergmann, Gustav (1906–87)

Positivistic analytic philosopher, born in Austria, who emigrated in 1938 and transmitted some of the austere logical formalism he had acquired from the VIENNA CIRCLE to the United States. See also LINGUISTIC TURN.

Bergson, Henri Louis (1859–1941)

French philosopher who produced a philosophy of 'creative evolution' which made a considerable impression in literature as well as philosophy in the early years of the twentieth century (see, for example, the Preface to Bernard Shaw's *Back to Methuselah*). This was not only a romantic para-biological theory of a 'Life-Force' designed to counteract materialistic or mechanistic notions of the evolution of life in nature. It was an ingenious speculative theory of the relation of life and matter, correlated throughout with a particular theory of knowledge. Indeed, Bergson's work could either be interpreted idealistically, in which case the theory of knowledge is prior, and we have a certain kind of concept of matter because our minds work in a certain way; or it could be interpreted as an evolutionary realism in which our minds have come to think in a certain way because of the natural history of their evolution. In either case, Bergson's originality lay in the way he interpreted a theory of evolution and a theory of knowledge in terms of each other. The theory of knowledge was presented first, in *Essai sur les données immédiates de la conscience* (1889), (translated as *Time and Free-will*), and in *Matter and Memory* (1896). Here Bergson draws a sharp distinction between our intellectual knowledge of the external world and consciousness as we know it from within. The intellect proceeds by analysis and classification, interpreting the world in terms of limited kinds of discrete units, undergoing repeatable arrangements in space. Hence it thinks of static objects in spatial juxtaposition; it does not grasp fundamental changes through time, but imagines change as a succession of static states of affairs, spread out in a succession of instantaneous spaces – a limitation which was brought out by ZENO of Elea in his paradoxes about motion, and which, Bergson thought, is never transcended by mere concepts, although it may be met practically by devices such as the infinitesimal calculus, where a sequence of very small intervals is treated as though they formed a continuous movement. The intellect therefore, Bergson says, 'spatializes', and its ideal form of thinking is geometry.

Sharply contrasted is self-consciousness, where change in time is experienced from within: we are aware not of a succession of distinct states, but of our present as arising out of our past and turning into a not clearly envisaged future. The 'time' of this inner experience is not external clock time, or 'spatialized time', measured for instance by noting successive positions of the hands of a clock. It is an actual experience of change, in which stages of 'before' and 'after' interpenetrate. Bergson calls this kind of time 'duration' (*durée*), and claims that it is not merely a way of measuring a changing reality, but is the changing reality itself. The state of mind in which we are aware of the quality and flow of inner consciousness is called intuition. It is a non-conceptual kind of awareness, and Bergson says it dispenses with symbols, though what he means by 'symbol' is not clear, and indeed his own attempts to express and describe intuition are couched, perhaps inevitably, in metaphors. For a form of consciousness which uses neither concepts nor imaginative metaphors would presumably not be explicit thought at all, but *feeling*. Indeed Bergson sometimes speaks of intuition as 'sympathy', and 'integral experience'. In the *Introduction to Metaphysics* (1903), he speaks of metaphysics as 'the science which claims to dispense with symbols'. If this were the whole truth, it is hard to see how it could become articulate knowledge, since any expression must presumably use some form of symbolism. Bergson does not, however, present intuition as able to work apart from intellect, though he describes them as if they were polar opposites. Intuition is compared with the creative inner excitement which enables a writer to fuse his mass of materials into a unity, which he cannot do unless he has first gathered the materials by intellectual effort. 'Any one of us, for instance, who has attempted literary composition, knows that when the subject has been studied at length, the materials all collected, and the notes all made, something more is needed in order to set about the work of composition itself, and that it is an often very painful effort to place ourselves directly at the heart of the subject, and to seek as deeply as possible an impulse, after which we need only let ourselves go...Metaphysical intuition seems to be something of the same kind. What corresponds here to the documents and notes of literary composition is the sum of observations and experience gathered together by positive science. For we do not obtain an intuition from reality – that is, an intellectual sympathy with the most intimate part of it – unless we have won its confidence by a long fellowship with its superficial manifestations.' In neither case, however, can the 'impulse' produce a synthesis out of the materials apart from an integrating idea.

Bergson's description of intuition seems to be an account not so much of such integrating ideas as of the underlying state of mind out of which they may come. This is a form of feeling intensely concentrated on the present task, but which has behind it the resources of the person's whole past experience. Here Bergson's particular view of *memory* should be taken into account. He holds that consciousness contains implicitly the whole of one's past experience, but the function of the brain of the animal organism is to act as a 'filter', selecting for immediate awareness such memories as may be relevant in attending to the situations in which one is placed. But by reversing the habits of the intellect (always to Bergson primarily a way of thinking shaped by practical needs), it may be possible to draw on a wider range of the resources of consciousness. Bergson was impressed by the work of

Charcot on amnesia, and by experimental work on hypnotically recovered memories. He was writing before Freud's theory of the unconscious mind had been put forward, and he uses the word 'consciousness' broadly and not only for such experiences as are within the focus of attention. Indeed he imagines a rudimentary form of consciousness in all living organisms, and is prepared to interpret them by what he calls an 'inverted psychology'.

Bergson's theory of knowledge, formulated in terms of the contrast between intellect and intuition, is correlated with a view of their function within the process of evolution. Intelligence, Bergson holds, begins with the making of tools. He describes 'instinct' as an innate power of using natural instruments, either parts of the organism itself, or materials in the environment. Intelligence is first of all a power of making tools as artificial instruments: the human race at the dawn of intelligence was *homo faber*, the smith, rather than *homo sapiens*. So intelligence starts from the interest in practical construction; it always bears the stamp of this practical interest, and finds its model of intelligibility in artefacts, which are discontinuous, isolatable systems, repeatable as specified types. Instinct on the other hand is continuous with the organizing power of life, but is unreflective and unadaptive. If it becomes disinterested and self-conscious, it is intuition, and can carry forward the original impetus of life into the creation of new forms. Bergson interprets evolution as the outcome of an impulse of life (*élan vital*) manifesting itself in innumerable forms. This is not finalist teleology in the classical sense – development tied to the realization of predetermined ends, which Bergson calls 'inverted mechanism'. Nor is it vitalism as ordinarily understood, since no 'vitalist principle' is invoked over and above the physicochemical components of organisms. Rather, the whole of nature is said to be the outcome of a force which thrusts itself forward into new and unforeseen forms of organized structure. These store and utilize energy, maintaining their power of growth and adaptive novelty up to a point, before relapsing into repetitive routine, and ultimately into the degradation of energy.

The universe, Bergson says, shows two tendencies: 'a reality which is making itself within a reality which is unmaking itself'. The laws of the tendency to repetition and the dissipation of energy are the laws of 'matter'; the counter tendency is the thrust of 'life'. Here, in *Creative Evolution* (1907), 'matter' is represented as a real tendency in nature, inverse to life and representing the running down of life into uniformity. Bergson also speaks of 'matter' as the picture formed by the artificial fixing of a system of spatialized concepts by the intellect. Possibly the link is to be found in the belief that the more things display the tendency inverse to life, the more they are amenable to this kind of intellectual treatment. But the notions of pure matter, or of a purely free and creative life impulse, would be abstractions, and Bergson acknowledges that what is routine and mechanical and what is living and creative are never in fact found in complete separation from each other. But his concern to bring out the difference between them underlies his whole work; and it finds a special application in *The Two Sources of Morality and Religion* (1932), where Bergson turned from biology to moral and religious sociology. He describes the 'closed' morality and religion based on social custom as the conservative force of a limited society making for the solidarity and preservation of a social group. Groups cohering

through closed morality are always limited groups, not just by definition, but because their way of life is maintained through real or possible conflict with other groups. Humanity as a whole does not therefore form a group of this kind; and those prophets and saints who are filled with an outgoing love for humanity are drawing on a different source. The analogy of closed morality to the repetitive mechanisms studied by the intellect is apparent; 'open' morality and religion are forms of intuition, and their source lies in a direct contact with the springs of life in the *élan vital*. In this last book Bergson is prepared to call it 'love', which is 'either God or from God'. Whether he was received into the Roman Catholic Church is not known; he is reported to have held back until just before his death in order to maintain his solidarity with the Jewish people in their time of trouble.

Bergson's works are written in a non-technical, flowing and persuasive style. They show wide knowledge of the biology and psychology of his day, and an enthusiastic, sometimes visionary, power. Other philosophers have, however, remarked on his tendency to write in unexplained metaphors, and on the lack of rigorous exposition of his central concepts, notably those of *durée* and the *élan vital*, and of the case for their supposed identity.   (D.M.E.)

Berkeley, George (1685–1753)   George Berkeley was born in Ireland, in the neighbourhood of Kilkenny. His ancestors were English and Protestant, but he passed his early and later years entirely in Ireland. Although he was always of the Anglican faith, he appears to have regarded himself as decidedly an Irishman. He was excellently educated, first at Kilkenny College, and, from 1700, at Trinity College, Dublin, of which he was subsequently a Fellow for many years. He was ordained in 1707, became Dean of Derry in 1724 and Bishop of Cloyne ten years later. He married in 1728 and died in Oxford in 1753.

Berkeley's life is noteworthy, apart from his philosophical writings, chiefly for his attempt in middle life to introduce a university to Bermuda. The aim of this scheme was mainly missionary. Berkeley hoped to attract to his college not only the colonial settlers of America, but also some of the indigenous Indians, to be trained as ministers of religion and apostles of culture. Berkeley, whose energies, powers of persuasion and ingenuous charm were remarkable, succeeded in securing much public and official support for his project. He obtained a charter, a large sum of money by private subscription, and the promise from Parliament of a subvention from public funds. But his scheme was impracticable, and was in the end seen to be so. Bermuda – as he was perhaps not clearly aware – is far too distant from the American mainland to have been a suitable site for his purposes; and after he left for America in 1728, hesitations and doubts began to prevail at home. Berkeley waited abroad almost three years for his grant to be paid over, but in 1731 the Prime Minister, Walpole, let it be known that his hopes were not to be gratified. The house at Newport, Rhode Island which Berkeley built and inhabited is still preserved.

The works on which Berkeley's fame chiefly rests were written when he was a very young man. By the time he first visited England in 1713, being then 28, he had already published the *Essay towards a New Theory of Vision* (1709) and *Principles of Human Knowledge* (1710) and *Three Dialogues between Hylas and Philonous* was published that year. In his later philosophical writings he did little more than defend, explain, and at certain minor points amend, the views thus early

developed. It is clear from his correspondence that for long periods of his later life he did not occupy his thoughts with philosophy at all. In this respect he differs strikingly from LOCKE, whose main work did not appear till he was nearly 60; and in fact the young Berkeley, who was early acquainted with Locke's writings, is apt to refer to Locke's thoughts as those of a very old man – as admirable, indeed, for one so advanced in years.

There have been many philosophers who have constructed bold and sweeping, and often extraordinary, metaphysical systems. There have been some also, particularly in the English tradition, who engaged in the clarification and defence of 'common sense'. There have been thinkers, again, devoted to the defence of religious faith. It is the peculiar achievement of Berkeley that, with astonishing ingenuity and skill, he contrived to present himself in all these roles at once. This achievement exactly suited his temperament, in which a taste for ambitious metaphysical doctrine was combined with strong religious beliefs and with a solid respect for ordinary good sense; but it was of course due only to his insight and intellectual power that he was able so to frame his theories as to yield him rational satisfaction also. His synthesis of these usually incompatible roles is doubtless unstable and few readers have been able to follow him in it. At first, to his great chagrin, he was seen merely as a fantastic metaphysician; more recently, he has found occasional defenders, as an advocate of 'common sense'. But if one is to feel the full force of his theories, it is essential to see how these diverse aspects are combined.

Berkeley's position is best understood by contrast with Locke's. The picture of the world which, in his student reading, Berkeley found in Locke was roughly as follows. The universe is really a mechanical system of bodies in space. It is made, as it were, of matter; and material bodies really possess just those qualities required for their mechanical mode of operation–'solidity, figure, extension, motion or rest, and number'. These bodies operate on, among other things, the sense-organs of human beings, who possess minds – 'immaterial substances' – as well as bodies. When this occurs, the mechanical stimulation of the sense-organs and brain causes 'ideas' to arise in the mind, and these are the objects of which the observer is really aware. In some respects these ideas faithfully represent the actual character of the 'external world', but in others not; ideas of, for instance, sound, colour and smell have no real counterparts in the world, but are only modes in which an observer so constituted is affected by the appropriate mechanical stimuli.

Berkeley soon came to regard this picture of the world as at once ridiculous, dangerous and detestable. It was ridiculous because it clearly entailed a fantastic scepticism, in manifest conflict with good common sense. For how could observers who were aware of nothing but their own ideas know anything about the 'external world'? Locke himself had asserted, absurdly enough, that colour, for instance, is only an apparent, not a real, feature of that world; but how could he know that contemplation of our own ideas ever apprises us of the world's actual character? If a SCEPTIC suggests the possibility that all our ideas mislead us, Locke could in no way counter the suggestion. Locke is thus committed to the ridiculous view that, for all we know, objects in the world may be utterly unlike what we take them to be – and perhaps that, for all we know, there may be no such objects. This is surely repugnant to anyone of good sense.

But Locke's doctrine, Berkeley believed, was also exceedingly dangerous. Apart from offering a general pretext for scepticism, its tendency was towards MATERIALISM and atheism, and therefore, in Berkeley's view, towards the subversion of morals. God was brought in by Locke as the designer, creator and starter of the great machine; but how could he show that matter itself was not eternal? And if it were, would his system not make it possible, and even rational, to deny the existence of God altogether? Again, Locke himself had held that consciousness belonged to 'immaterial substances', which he would doubtless have regarded as immortal souls. But he confessed that he could not disprove the counter-suggestion that consciousness might be just one of the properties of matter, and so, presumably, wholly dependent on the maintenance of certain material, physical conditions. His theory was thus in some danger of permitting – if it did not actually encourage – denial of the existence of God and of the immortality of the soul; and with this denial, in Berkeley's opinion, religion fell, dragging morality after it.

Finally, it is clear, though less explicitly asserted, that Berkeley was utterly oppressed and repelled by the notion that the universe is really a vast machine. Those metaphors of clocks and engines, wheels and springs, in which Locke delighted, inspired in Berkeley the utmost detestation. The world, he felt, could not be really like this – particularly if, in order to maintain that it is, we have to assert that its actual appearance is delusive; that, in fact, the 'visible beauty of creation' is nothing but a 'false imaginary glare'. Why should we deny the evidence of our senses, in order to believe that the universe is so repulsive?

Now Berkeley perceived – and it struck him as a revelation – what seemed to be a bold but beautifully simple means of eliminating, at one blow, all these horrors and absurdities. It was necessary only to *deny the existence of matter*. For what would be the consequences of this? First, the actual course of our everyday experience would be quite unaffected. On Locke's own admission, we are never actually aware of anything but our own ideas; to deny the existence, then, of his 'external objects', material bodies, is not to take away anything that has ever entered into our experience, and is indeed to leave quite undisturbed the opinions of the unphilosophical masses. But it must also put an end to all sceptical questioning. Locke was obliged to concede that our ideas might mislead us as to the character of things, precisely because he regarded things as something other than our ideas. But if instead we adopt the view that things – the ordinary objects of experience – are just 'collections of ideas', it will be manifestly impossible to suggest that they are not as they appear to us, and even more so to suggest that their very existence is doubtful. If an orange is not an 'external' material body, but a collection of ideas, then I may be – as of course anyone of good sense actually is – entirely certain that it exists, and that it really has the colour, taste, texture and aroma that I find in it. Doubts on so simple a point could only arise as a result of the needless assertion that things exist, distinct from and in addition to the ideas we have.

We may next see how Berkeley counters two serious objections. First, must it not be admitted that our ideas have causes? We do not simply produce our ideas ourselves; they plainly come to us from some independent source; and what could this be, if not the 'external objects' of Locke's theory? Now Berkeley admits that our ideas are caused; but to take them

to be caused in the way supposed by Locke is, he holds, both needless and impossible. It is needless, because we can suppose that God causes them to occur in our minds as they do, with their admirable order and regularity. And it is in fact impossible, he holds, that they should be caused otherwise; for to cause is to act, and nothing is genuinely active but the will of an intelligent being.

But if matter is denied, what becomes of physics? It is plainly impossible to dismiss the discoveries of NEWTON and his fellows as mere moonshine; but matter, in the form of particles or 'corpuscles', is precisely that of which they have discovered and proved so many of the properties. What is there for the laws of physics to hold true of, if there are really no material bodies?

Berkeley's earliest reflections on this objection were rather evasive; but later, notably in the *De Motu* of 1721, he devised a strikingly ingenious reply in which, though running against the main tendency of his age, he anticipated the ideas of many twentieth-century PHILOSOPHERS OF SCIENCE. He answered, in effect, that scientific theories are not true of anything at all. If correct, they apply to the world of our experience, in that they enable us both to predict and in some degree to control its course; but their function is no more than that of predictive devices. The theory of the corpuscular structure of matter, for example, makes possible the exact mathematical expression of formulae, by the use of which we can make invaluable predictions; but there is no need to suppose that the corpuscles and particles of that theory actually exist. That there are such corpuscles is a theoretically useful supposition; so long as it proves useful it should continue to be made; but it should never be regarded as a literal truth. Thus, the practice of science need not be disturbed by Berkeley's doctrines; it is necessary only for scientists to admit that they are not investigating 'the nature of things', but rather perfecting the formulation of predictive devices.

Believing that the errors of earlier thinkers, notably Locke, had been due in part to linguistic unclarity, Berkeley devoted the Introduction to the *Principles* to an investigation of language. He rather unfairly interprets Locke's vague expressions in their most vulnerable sense, but his own insistence that the essence of language lies in its use, and on the concrete understanding of expressions in definite contexts, makes this one of his most original and stimulating contributions to philosophy.

Two of Berkeley's later works may be mentioned briefly. His *Alciphron* is a long work in dialogue form, in which the tenets of Anglican orthodoxy are defended against various current types of 'free-thinking' and DEISM. Though able enough, it has little interest now that the controversies which prompted it are dead. Berkeley's last work was *Siris*, in which a strangely rambling, ponderous and speculative statement of some of his earlier opinions leads on to an inquiry into the virtues of tar-water, a medicine which Berkeley made popular, and for the promotion of which he worked in his later years with almost eccentric zeal.

Berkeley's main work was slow to exert any influence on philosophy, though his early essay on vision became fairly well known. His criticisms of Locke were for the most part powerful and well taken; and the transition to his own remarkable doctrine of a theocentric, non-material universe, whose *esse* was *percipi* (which existed only insofar as it was perceived), and in which human beings were conceived of as conversing directly with the mind of God, was at least a triumph of ingenuity. But this doctrine was too extraordinary to be taken seriously; the fact that, so far as actual experience went, he could represent it as coinciding with the customary views of ordinary people was not enough to make it actually the same; and Berkeley was not welcomed as the defender of common sense. Even his criticism of Locke was deprived of much of its effect, since it appeared to lead straight into a position still less defensible; and his philosophy of science was much less acceptable then than it would be today. It was then generally accepted that physical theory was merely a kind of extension of ordinary observation, revealing truths of just the same kind as those of common experience. Today this has become somewhat difficult to believe; but to deny it then was probably felt to constitute an attack on the physicist's prestige. There is no doubt that this was Berkeley's intention: he had the bad luck to detest the 'scientific worldview' at a time when it was in the first flush of its ascendancy.

Today the ordinary reader of Berkeley is most likely to regard him as a pioneer of PHENOMENALISM. It is certainly part of his doctrine to maintain that material objects could be reduced to collections of ideas, or SENSE-DATA as his successors would say. This is, moreover, the classic rejoinder to theories of 'indirect' perception, such as Locke had classically expounded. But Berkeley was not engaged in cool and neutral philosophical analysis. His phenomenalism was primarily an ontological thesis; he genuinely wished to deny that there are any really material things. He was happy to believe that ordinary opinions could be so analysed as to conform with his ontology, and he believed that they ought to be understood in that way. He was, however, consciously and deliberately, as Locke had been almost inadvertently, a metaphysician, not merely an analyst.

It was remarked above that the result of Berkeley's ingenious attempt to unify metaphysics and common sense is unstable. This instability may be located in his use, adopted from Locke, of the term 'idea'. Berkeley's use of this term (like Locke's) is not so much ambiguous as insufficiently determinate. When he wishes to bring out the common-sense aspect of his doctrine, he stresses that he means by 'ideas' the *things* that we perceive; when he speaks as an ontologist, affirming that *esse* is *percipi* and that matter does not exist, he insists that ideas are 'only in the mind'. It seems likely that, if his use of this term were more closely scrutinized and made more precise, his theory would become not so much less plausible, as almost impossible to state. In so far as it rests on fluidity at this key point, it does not stand firm.   (G.J.W.)

Berlin, Isaiah (1909–97)   Isaiah Berlin was born to a wealthy family in Latvia, moved to England at the age of 11, and rose without apparent effort to become a tutor in philosophy at Oxford University in 1932. He was a follower rather than a leader in the attempts by colleagues like RYLE, AUSTIN and AYER to give a British philosophy a LINGUISTIC TURN, and his interest drifted towards high politics and Russian literature. After spending much of the Second World War on Government work in the United States, he reinvented himself as a historian of political thought, and a great talker. (It was said that the knighthood conferred on him in 1957 was 'for services to conversation'.)

The course of his intellectual career was defined by a celebrated lecture delivered in 1958 on 'Two Concepts of Liberty'. Here Berlin explored the distinction between freedom in the relaxed, liberal sense of being allowed to do whatever you like without unnecessary interference, and freedom in the romantic, demanding and totalitarian sense of realizing your better self by doing what you should. Although it was clear that Berlin favoured the first, 'negative', kind of freedom, he did not offer explicit arguments for it. Indeed he thought that conceptual diversity was an ineliminable feature of intellectual life in general, and that philosophers should do whatever they could to preserve it. He believed that the root of evil, in politics as in philosophy, lay in the assumption that there must be some 'single true solution' to all the tragic conflicts that beset us – an assumption he considered typical of all enemies of liberal or negative freedom, especially Marxists. It followed that the only justifiable attitude, in politics and philosophy, was 'relativism', or 'pluralism' as he and his disciples preferred to call it. He was perhaps unaware that his all-purpose pluralism risked becoming a 'single true solution' in its turn.

Most of Berlin's other writings are exercises in European intellectual history, designed to reinforce his passion for pluralism. The main protagonist in all of them is the 'romanticism' or 'irrationalism' of the nineteenth century, which Berlin saw, conventionally enough, as an understandable but dangerous reaction to something called 'the enlightenment'– an eighteenth-century movement supposedly founded on a monolithic belief in the ultimate harmony and intelligibility of both society and nature. Responses to Berlin's historical writings have been divided between admiration for their confident range of reference and frustration at their superficiality, vagueness and repetitiveness. In the last twenty-five years of his life Berlin seems to have been more interested in his work as a public figure and as the founding president of Wolfson College Oxford.   {J.R.}

Bioethics   See APPLIED ETHICS.

Black, Max (1909–88)   Though born in Russia, Black obtained his formal education in England, and after 1940 taught philosophy in the United States. His major interests were in the foundations of logic and mathematics, the theory of knowledge, and the philosophies of language and of science. Although his outlook was influenced by RUSSELL, MOORE and the LOGICAL POSITIVISM, he was an acute critic of various doctrines advocated by these thinkers. Moreover, while he was a prominent exponent of the linguistic method of philosophic analysis associated with WITTGENSTEIN, he was not an orthodox follower of this approach. His principal works include *The Nature of Mathematics* (1950) and *The Labyrinth of Language* (1968). See also METAPHOR.   (E.N.)

Blanshard, Brand (1892–1987)   The most prominent American exponent of a viewpoint developed from the absolute idealism which flourished in Oxford at the beginning of the twentieth century. Blanshard's most important work is *The Nature of Thought* (1939), which describes, in both psychological and logical terms, the development of human thought. Thought can, and must, be described in psychological terms, but we will not understand its development unless we see it as guided by a logical ideal. The logical ideal is a system, such as is conceived in the coherence theory of TRUTH in which all thoughts are necessarily connected with each other. We must seek necessity everywhere, and attempts to reduce it to the empirical, as in HUME's theory of causation, or to the trivial, as in conventionalist or linguistic theories of the A PRIORI, are subjected to sustained attack. (J.O.U.)

Bloch, Ernst (1885–1977)   Marxist philosopher of hope and utopia, born in Ludwigshafen. Against the reigning positivistic and reductionist philosophies of the twentieth century, as well as against Marxism's own scientific variants of the dominant culture, Bloch defended a 'process METAPHYSICS' oriented towards practice and the future, a philosophy in which 'that-which-is-not-yet' surfaces from beneath social repression to provide a focus and guide for revolutionary thought and action.

Bloch's metaphysics of the future, revolving around the concept of the 'not-yet', argues that in utopian ideas and ideals we possess anticipations of a radically different future. We are 'not-yet-conscious' of what we really desire, but a different future is adumbrated in the unrealized ideals of the past. More significantly, that different future may be really possible even if the necessary conditions for its realization are not all present, for in becoming aware of what is 'not-yet-conscious' we give the hoped-for future a practically efficacious place in the present.

There is an indecision in Bloch's thought between a heuristic, practice-oriented side, which seeks to change the present by introducing utopian ideas into it, and a systematic, metaphysical side which labours to underwrite the claims of utopian reason through the development of an expanded conception of 'real possibility'. Such indecision, however, is systematic and necessary in a theory seeking to make the imagination integral to reason and rationality. Bloch was a prolific writer. His most important work is the massive *The Principle of Hope* (1954–9). Other significant works include *Spirit of Utopia* (1918), *Thomas Münzer as Theologian of Revolution* (1921), *Subject – Object, Commentaries on Hegel* (1949) and *Natural Right and Human Dignity* (1961).   (J.M.B.)

Boethius, Anicius Manlius Severinus (c.480–c.524) Boethius was born into one of the great senatorial families in Rome, accepted public service under Theodoric, and rose to high office. Later, he was disgraced as a result of political intrigue, and wrote his most celebrated work, the *De Consolatione Philosophiae*, while in jail awaiting execution. His importance in the history of philosophy, however, rests not only upon the *Consolation*, but also on his effort to translate and transmit to the Latin West the collected wisdom of the Greeks. His declared intention was to translate and comment on all the works of PLATO and ARISTOTLE, but he achieved no more than the translation of the Aristotelian logical writings together with PORPHYRY's introductory *Isagoge*. For centuries, however, these remained the only sources of Aristotle's philosophy available to Western thought.

In his commentary on Porphyry, Boethius showed his Platonizing sympathies in a famous formulation of the problem of UNIVERSALS: 'whether *genera* and *species* actually subsist or are found in the mind and intellect alone'. This formulation proved both a starting point and a stumbling block in the controversy which played so large a part in early medieval philosophy. Boethius was also instrumental in transmitting knowledge of Greek scientific methodology by his translations and classification of the four mathematical disciplines as Arithmetic, Music, Geometry and Astronomy. This *quadrivium* of study built on the *trivium* of Grammar, Rhetoric and Dialectic and thus provided a systematic approach to education by way of the 'Seven Liberal Arts'. Elaborated later by Cassiodorus and by Isidore of Seville, this arts curriculum survived the dark ages in the monastic and court schools of the West, to become fully established in the medieval university system.

In his theological writings Boethius provided a model of theological method and the rigorous application of LOGIC to the analysis of Christian doctrine. The opening sections *De Consolatione Philosophiae* give, through the mouth of the lady Philosophy, conventional STOIC and Platonic answers to Boethius' account of his misfortunes. Thereafter his Christian convictions give a positive direction to the argument, and true goodness is found to consist in union with God. There follows a discussion of the problem of the existence of EVIL in a world governed by a benevolent providence and the difficulty of establishing a relationship between human freedom and God's foreknowledge. The *Consolation* was both a vehicle for the transmission of ancient wisdom and a model for philosophizing for the next thousand years. (J.G.D.)

Bonaventura (1221–74) John of Fidanza, known as Bonaventura, was born in Italy, joined the Franciscan order and studied in Paris, where he later held the Chair of Theology contemporaneously with his Dominican counterpart, Thomas AQUINAS. He died while taking part in the Council of Lyons and was canonized in 1482. His philosophical doctrines are found mainly in his commentary on the *Sentences* of PETER LOMBARD and in the two short treatises, the *Itinerarium Mentis in Deum* and the *De Reductione Artium ad Theologiam*.

Bonaventura's work in Paris coincided with debates occasioned by the reception of the full ARISTOTELIAN corpus of scientific writings in the West and the rise of AVERROISM in the Universities. His philosophical position can be understood as the relatively conservative reaction of a theologian who preferred to elaborate the Platonizing content of the writings of AUGUSTINE. Thus he presents explicit formulations of

Augustinian theses concerning man's knowledge of God, seminal reasons, soul as SUBSTANCE, and an illuminationist theory of knowledge. Bonaventura regarded all true speculation as a search for God, which might begin with an investigation of the physical world which bears the imprint of its Creator, *vestigia Dei*. It is only in the study of ourselves, however, and through acquaintance with our soul as an image of God, *imago Dei*, that we can begin to achieve true knowledge. Exercising our memory, understanding and will under the influence of divine illumination, we are led to the contemplation of God, not as a cause through its effects but immediately and ecstatically. Though Duns SCOTUS later became the official Doctor of the Franciscans, Bonaventura, the *Doctor Seraphicus*, is perhaps more truly characteristic of the deeply religious outlook of the Order.   (J.G.D.)

Boole, George (1815–64)   George Boole, who was born in Lincoln, England, was entirely self-educated but became a mathematician of distinction and in 1849 was appointed to the Chair of Mathematics at Queen's College, Cork. Two years earlier, he had published *The Mathematical Analysis of Logic*, which has come to be regarded as the first substantial step towards modern mathematical LOGIC. *An Investigation of the Laws of Thought*, published in 1854, though better known, is important chiefly for its application of Boole's logical algebra to the theory of probability. Earlier mathematicians had shown that algebraic methods can be used to represent relations between entities other than numbers. Boole's basic innovation was the use of methods substantially equivalent to those of ordinary algebra, to operate on variables, x, y, z,... standing for classes and the symbols 1 and 0 standing respectively for the universal class and the empty class (though the use of these terms was not introduced by Boole himself). In Boole's symbolism, if 'x' represents a class, say, the class of red things, then '$(1-x)$' stands for the complementary class of things that are not red. Operations corresponding to addition, subtraction and multiplication in ordinary algebra are introduced. If 'x' stands for the class of red things and 'y' for the class of square things, then 'xy' stands for the product of the two classes, the things that are both red and square. And '$x+y$' stands for the class of things that are either red or square but not both. (This exclusive sense of '$+$' distinguishes Boole's algebra from most later versions.)

With this notation we can represent a limited class of statements of logical importance. For example, 'All men are mortal' becomes: '$x(1-y)=0$', in other words 'the class of men who are not mortal is empty'. Moreover, we can combine these expressions and operate on them in accordance with the rules of the algebra to derive other expressions from them and solve problems involving logical relations between classes. These include the simple SYLLOGISM of classical logic as well as other much more complex problems. In an application of the algebra to hypothetical propositions, Boole came near to discovering the truth-table technique later developed by C. S. PEIRCE and modern logicians, and Boolean algebra is a recognized branch of modern mathematics.   (D.J.O'C.)

Bosanquet, Bernard (1848–1923)   Bosanquet, who was born in Alnwick, England, gave up his Oxford teaching in 1881 to devote the rest of his life to writing and social work. He was the last British philosopher to work out a complete system of philosophy covering all types of human experience. His work was influenced mainly by HEGEL and was based on a conception of individuality as the harmony of a variety of differences in the 'concrete universal', in contrast to the 'abstract universal' of scientific reason operating by general laws. This notion of individuality he found expressed in human persons, in works of art, in the State, and supremely in the Absolute as the final ideal transcending and unifying all these subordinate 'concrete universals'. Late in life he fell under the influence of F. H. BRADLEY and became more doubtful about the power of reason to grasp the unities met with in experience. The individuality of a person or picture required the conception of a type of unity in which the variety could not be so clearly distinguished nor the elements so rationally related as Hegel had supposed.   (J.D.M.)

Boyle, Robert (1627–91) Natural scientist and pioneer of 'copuscularianism', an undogmatic form of atomism which was meant to bring mathematical natural science into harmony with Christianity.

Bradley, Francis Herbert (1846–1924) English philosopher, a research Fellow of Merton College, who lived the whole of his adult life at Oxford. He suffered from poor health and was naturally retiring and reserved, devoting himself completely to philosophical thinking and writing. He wrote in a brilliant and trenchant style, with a force and vigour seldom equalled in English philosophy. He was influenced in his youth by HEGEL and the German logicians who followed him, but his philosophy was uniquely his own.

In his first book, *Ethical Studies* (1876), he criticizes utilitarian theories from a Hegelian angle and works out a theory of self-realization which is also Hegelian in its general design. The self is to be realized in self-conscious membership of the state (which is understood as an organic unity of spiritual beings) and not in isolated self-cultivation. The essay entitled 'My Station and its Duties' is the best short statement in English of the Hegelian conception of morality. But in the next essay 'Ideal Morality' Bradley passes beyond these Hegelian concepts of rational unity and of moral right as supremely embodied in Law and the State. Many fields such as science, art and philosophy itself, provide moral ends and fields of self-realization independent of national frontiers and civic allegiance; and in the last resort morality itself attains its completeness only by moving on into religion.

In *Principles of Logic* (1883) Bradley worked out a complete survey of logical forms showing how each finds its place in the hierarchy of human reason. But he emphasized at every point that these forms arise from a basic experience whose unity they all fail to express, and hence that they always involve an element of subjectivity and error. But Bradley's greatest work is *Appearance and Reality* (1893). In the first part, he offers a relentless dialectical criticism of all the general categories of human thought and experience. In arguments reminiscent of ZENO of Elea and of KANT's antinomies, he shows that quality and relation, substance and cause, space and time, self and object, are all of them, if taken as real, beset by insoluble contradictions and must therefore be dismissed as 'appearance'. Absolute reality must transcend all these categories. Relations are grounded in the nature of their terms, and no term can be understood apart from its relations. Whether relations are regarded as completely external (in a LOGICAL ATOMISM such as RUSSELL's) or as completely internal (as in the monadology of LEIBNIZ), they fail to satisfy the demands of reason. Thus the relational mode of thinking – and in the end all modes of thinking are in one way or another relational – can never attain knowledge of reality. Reality must have a unity unlike anything in our worlds of rational thought, a unity above and beyond relations, and to whose nature only the undifferentiated unity of feeling gives any clue. This absolute reality differentiates itself into finite centres of experience which however cannot be identified with human persons because of the element of time which infects all human life. In the second part of *Appearance and Reality* it is argued that each category of human experience, whose final inadequacy had been demonstrated in the first part, must somehow find a place in the real, though transmuted in it; and each of them has a degree of reality corresponding to the extent to which it is comprehensive and self-consistent.

In his later work Bradley did not go back on his fundamental metaphysical position and the suprarational and even mystical or religious view of the real to which it leads. At the time of his death he was working on a long essay on relations, and the incomplete draft published in his posthumous *Collected Essays* gives the best exposition of this central part of his philosophy. But he also developed the positive argument of the second part of *Appearance and Reality*, emphasizing the partial truth to be found in the various logical and epistemological categories which many of his readers thought he had intended totally to destroy, and by elaborating a theory of degrees of truth. Each of these categories is now justified in its own sphere and degree; what is resisted is the claim of any one of them to be (or to be the model for) the whole truth. At the same time, and no doubt for similar reasons, his work became less polemical and his style more mellow and tolerant.

Bradley's position in the history of philosophy is thus a curious one. He was probably the only first-rank philosopher

England produced in the nineteenth century; and in brilliance and acuteness his only rival is HUME. Yet his influence was slight and his followers few. This was partly because he came at the end of the idealist movement, and partly because he was a very unorthodox representative of it, so that later idealists looked back not to him but to Hegel for their inspiration. Though his main tenets have won little acceptance he can still be read with profit for three reasons: first for the vigour and effectiveness of his style; second, for his devastating criticisms of utilitarian, associationist, individualist and pragmatist theories; third because his work in philosophical psychology on such subjects as memory, imagination and introspection has permanent importance.   (J.D.M.)

Braithwaite, Richard Bevan (1900–88)

English philosopher, based in Cambridge. Though mainly a philosopher of science, he was also interested in giving an account of religious belief which would make it tenable for the thoroughgoing empiricist, and in putting moral choice on a rational basis by applying the mathematical theory of games to conflict situations. This use of the theory of games developed by statisticians is the chief innovation in his main work *Scientific Explanation* (1953), where he draws on it for 'the prudential policy' for making choices between statistical hypotheses; this provides a rejection procedure, and so guarantees that probability statements have an empirical meaning, by allowing them to be provisionally refutable by experience, the rejection being subject to revision after each new series of tests. This procedure is unnecessary for the limiting case, that of universal statements, which are of course open to conclusive refutation (by a single counterinstance). In the same book he explains the use of 'models', theoretical concepts, and mathematical reasoning in scientific theories, and discusses the status of laws of nature.   (R.HALL)

Brandom, Robert (1950–) American philosopher, student of Richard Rorty and David Lewis. In *Making it Explicit* (1994) he defended a notion of 'discursive commitment' which combined the anti-foundationalism of the American pragmatists with an uncompromising rationalism derived from KANT and HEGEL. He is also the author of *Articulating Reasons: An Introduction to Inferentialism* (2000).

Brentano, Franz (1838–1916) The German-Austrian philosopher Franz Brentano is remembered for his contributions to philosophical psychology. He became a Professor of Philosophy at the Catholic University of Würzburg, but resigned his chair and his priesthood after the declaration of Papal Infallibility in 1871. He accepted a philosophical chair at Vienna, but resigned in 1880, returning later as an instructor. His last years were spent in Florence. His two most important works are *Psychology from the Empirical Standpoint* (published 1874, second edition 1911) and *The Origin of Ethical Knowledge* (published 1889), which influenced MOORE's *Principia Ethica*. His posthumously published work is considerable and valuable.

In his *Psychology* Brentano seeks to provide a 'psychognosy', that is, a logical geography of mental concepts, which will serve as a preliminary to an empirical psychology. He assumes that the world contains two sorts of 'phenomena', the physical and the 'psychical', and seeks both to identify the distinctive features of 'psychic phenomena' and to discover the 'basic classes' into which psychic phenomena fall. Brentano holds the differentiae of psychical acts to be, first, 'INTENTIONALITY', or directedness to

objects; and second, direct and inerrant accessibility to an 'inner perception' which is identical with the act perceived. By the term 'intentionality' (derived from the scholastic *esse intentionale*) Brentano means what is revealed by the fact that most mental verbs are incomplete until they are supplemented with appropriate object-expressions, stating what the mental activity expressed by the verb is concerned with. Thus if I observe, my observation must be *of* a house or a tree, for example; if I doubt, my doubt is *about* the equality of 2+2 to 4, for example; if I am pleased, there must be something I am pleased *with*, etc. In his second edition Brentano makes the point that intentionality is not a relation between the mind and an object: it is merely *relational* or *relationlike* (*relativlich*). A relation to an object would normally entail that the object existed, whereas a mental directedness to an object usually does not. What is distinctive of Brentano's position is that he thinks this 'relationlikeness' is ultimate and needs no further analysis.

Brentano's classification of mental phenomena admits only three basic classes: (a) presentations (*Vorstellungen*), in which some object is simply present to mind; (b) judgements, in which something is *accepted* as real or factual, or rejected as the reverse; (c) phenomena of love and hate, that is cases of affective conative acceptance or rejection. In the case of (a) there is no distinction between correctness and incorrectness, but in the case of (*b*) there is, the criterion being an inward self-evidence (*Evidenz*). In regard to (c) Brentano holds that certain acts of liking, disliking or preferring have an inwardly self-justifying character which mediates the knowledge of what is absolutely good, better, or evil. Pleasure, for example, is absolutely good.   (J.N.F.)

Broad, Charlie Dunbar (1887–1971)
English philosopher, based at Cambridge,
who was strongly influenced by many
previous Cambridge philosophers, including RUSSELL and MOORE as well as
W. E. Johnson and MCTAGGART. Broad owed
little to foreign influences, and nothing at
all to WITTGENSTEIN. He claimed for himself neither the task of construction nor of
demolition, but 'at most the humbler (yet
useful) power of stating difficult things
clearly and not too superficially'. While
admitting that speculative philosophy has
value he doubted that any attempt to construct one could be profitable without there
first being a considerable advance in critical philosophy. This type of philosophy
makes progress, according to Broad, by
replacing vague and instinctive beliefs by
clear and explicit ones which have stood up
to criticism. In a series of large books, he
dissected existing theories and possible
alternatives and the arguments for and
against them, as for example in *The Mind
and its Place in Nature* (1925), where
seventeen different theories of the relation
between mind and matter are considered,
the one most favoured being a type of
'emergent materialism'. Broad took an
interest in psychical research: though not
prepared to accept the possibility of survival, he regarded alleged paranormal phenomena as due to the persistence after
death of a 'psychic factor', which had previously formed with the brain and nervous
system a compound of which mentality
was an emergent quality. Broad also wrote
on ethics, though here his interpretations of
some great philosophers are highly questionable. His greatest achievement, and the
most difficult to follow, was his monumental *Examination of McTaggart's Philosophy*
(1933–8).   (R.HALL)

Buber, Martin (1878–1965) Jewish
thinker born in Vienna who taught in
Jerusalem from 1938 and advocated
peace with the Arab world. In *I and
Thou* (1922) he argued that our relation to
others – including God – must be understood quite differently from our relation
to objects.

Burke, Edmund (1729–97) Irish-
English writer and Whig politician, whose
late work, *Reflections on the Revolution
in France* (1790), was an attack on the
revolutionaries of 1789 together with
their supposed intellectual progenitors
such as VOLTAIRE and ROUSSEAU. As
the Revolution proceeded through the
September Massacres, the execution of the
King and Queen, and the Reign of Terror,
Burke's philosophical criticism of what he
ironically called 'this enlightened age'
was widely regarded as confirmed, and
Reflections became one of the classics of
conservative political thought.

Burke argued above all for the dignity
of tradition in politics, praising English
institutions for treating political liberty
not as a claim or right but an 'inheritance' – a fragile heirloom to be cherished
'as if in the presence of canonised fore-
fathers'. The French revolutionaries, he
complained, had been undone by 'the
metaphysics of an under-graduate', in
other words 'the mechanic philosophy';
they were 'only men of theory' and lacked
'practical experience in the state'. Their
airy talk of 'rights' might be 'metaphysically true', but was 'morally and politically false'. It appeared indeed that
experience in general was 'out of fashion
in Paris'. For Burke, the best antidote to
excessive revolutionary zeal was 'a strong
impression of the ignorance and fallibility
of mankind' – a wry political scepticism
that he hoped would equip his readers
to 'admire rather than attempt to follow
in their desperate flights the aeronauts of
France'.

But Burke's traditionalist political compass did not always point in a conservative direction. Earlier in his career it led him to advocate Catholic emancipation and the removal of restrictions on Irish trade, and to support the native peoples of India and the rebels in the American colonies. And if he was hostile to the 'philosophy' behind the French Revolution, it was because it was 'false and unfeeling', not because it was philosophical. Following his education in Dublin, he always advocated a broadly empiricist method of analysing ideas by tracing them to their origins or causes in experience, and, like LOCKE, he emphasized the ways in which mere words can frame our thinking without our conscious awareness. In *A Philosophical Enquiry into the Origin of our Ideas of the Sublime and Beautiful* (1757), he proposed a new 'Logic of Taste' based on anatomizing the norms of both passion and understanding which must guide our judgements in the field of fine art. His principal conclusion was that artistic taste has two sides: as well as the familiar pleasures provided by whatever is beautiful, delicate and lovely, there were the darker joys of 'delightful horror', stemming from things that are terrible and astonishing, rugged, wild and vast – in short, 'sublime'. (KANT would seek to give a 'transcendental' spin to Burke's 'physiological' account of the sublime in the *Critique of Judgement*, 1790.) It could be said that in his later work on the French revolution, Burke simply elaborated his early interest in the combined operation of passion and understanding, extending it from the fine arts to the arts of politics.   {J.R.}

Butler, Joseph (1692–1752)   Bishop Butler holds a lastingly important place in English moral philosophy and philosophy of religion. His ethical thought is contained primarily in *Fifteen Sermons* (1726) and *Dissertation upon the Nature of Virtue*; his philosophy of religion in *Analogy of Religion* (1736), to which the *Dissertation* was an appendix. The two sides of Butler's thought are closely interconnected: conscience is not only the crucial concept of his ethics, but also provides an impressive disclosure of the being and nature of God. Virtue, to Butler, is natural to man, vice a violation of our nature, a kind of self-mutilation. Human nature is a complex structure that Butler likens to a watch with intricately cooperating parts, to a political constitution, and to a body with its component members. The full realization of this nature (and the attainment of virtue) involved the hierarchical subordination of its various elements under conscience. The promptings of hunger, thirst and other kinds of appetite form the base of the hierarchy. These 'particular passions' are disciplined and regulated by benevolence and self-love, which involve not indulging the passions, but managing them with a view to one's long-term, total well-being. Butler denied that self-love and benevolence were mutually antagonistic principles; indeed, the policies they initiate tend to coincide – for the most part in this world, and perfectly hereafter. Conscience is an essentially reflective and rational principle, which refuses to reduce all duties to one alleged supreme duty such as the production of the general happiness. Our duties are multiple, and only God, with his synoptic and omniscient view, could afford to play the UTILITARIAN. A measure of agnosticism pervades Butler's thought on account of his strong sense of human ignorance (the *Fifteenth Sermon* is devoted to this theme). Perhaps the most memorable features of his ethical thought, however, are the many shrewd analyses that make up his moral psychology – analyses of such concepts as forgiveness, resentment, self-deceit and compassion. Particularly effective are his arguments against HOBBES'S egoistic interpretation of pity.

The Analogy of Religion was conceived as an answer to DEISM. The deists held that a natural and rational religion escaped a great many intractable difficulties that beset a religion based on alleged revelation. But Butler maintained that analogous difficulties affect both spheres, though they are decisive against neither. 'The design', he wrote, 'of the following treatise will be to show, that the several parts principally objected against in this moral and Christian dispensation…are analogous to what is experienced in the constitution and course of Nature, or Providence; that the objections themselves which are alleged against the former, are no other than what may be alleged with like justice against the latter, where they are found in fact to be inconclusive.' As this suggests, Butler does not claim a priori certainty for his apologetics, but only a probability high enough for faith. (R.W.H.)

C

Cajetan, Thomas de Vio (1468–1534)
Born in Gaeta, Italy, died in Rome, he was Dominican Master-General, later Cardinal and the classical commentator on the *Summa Theologica* of Thomas AQUINAS. His criticism of SCOTISM brought him to the problem of analogy, the use of the same name for different objects in more than a purely equivocal or METAPHORICAL sense. He distinguished two proper types: analogy of attribution, based on a causal connection; and analogy of proportionality. Only this, he held, meets the requirements of metaphysical thinking. Most Thomists have agreed with him, but not Francis Sylvester of Ferrara (1474–1528), his successor as Master-General, who tried to vindicate attributional analogy.   (T.G.)

Cambridge Platonists A group of English philosophical theologians, centred on Cambridge and predominantly Puritan, who wrote and preached in the later seventeenth century. Best known among them are Ralph CUDWORTH Richard Cumberland, Henry MORE, Benjamin Whichcote, John Smith and Joseph Glanvill.

Their writings contain a mass of erudition, philosophical, mystical, ancient and 'modern', often uncritically employed and on the whole lacking logical coherence. The thought of PLATO, in particular, is seldom accurately differentiated from the speculations of NEOPLATONISTS. Nonetheless, the Cambridge Platonists made a considerable impact on EPISTEMOLOGY and ETHICS as well as theology. They attempted to disengage theological thinking from the polemics of the reformation and the earlier seventeenth

century, to restore the emphasis upon religion as above all a way of living, and to give primacy to religious – often mystical – experience. To Henry More, who was most in sympathy with mysticism, the path to knowledge of God was not learning but moral purification, a view that carries echoes of PLOTINUS. Joseph Glanvill's *Vanity of Dogmatizing* is in the main a repudiation of intellectual pretention and arrogance, whether among the over-revered Ancients, in the scholastics or in moderns infected with the same vice. Real understanding, to Glanvill, starts only from a wholesome scepticism. The Platonists had themselves, however, a humble confidence in reason. Whichcote repeatedly reminded his reader that reason is 'the candle of the Lord'. Irrationalisms were indeed as much part of their target as scholasticism; and the reconciliation of reason and revelation was the dominant aim of their work. The controversial issue to which they were most single-mindedly devoted was undoubtedly the refutation of the philosophy of HOBBES. Against his claim that matter and motion were adequate concepts for a philosophy of nature, Cudworth protested: 'as if there were not as much reality in fancy and consciousness as there is in local motion'. The activity of mind, the reality of non-corporeal spirit, were thus strenuously argued for by the Platonists against all brands of materialism. More insisted that spirit must be thought of as extended for otherwise it would lack full reality, so he regarded infinite extension as an attribute of God. Also against Hobbes, the Platonists affirmed that moral right and wrong, good

and bad are 'eternal and immutable', the products of no decrees, orders or agreements, whether human or divine.
(R.W.H.)

Canguilhem, Georges (1904–95) French philosopher based at the Sorbonne, who specialized in the history and epistemology of the life sciences. Canguilhem trained as a medical doctor, and his thesis on *The Normal and the Pathological* (1943; republished with supplementary essays, 1966) honed his interest in the origin and transformation of concepts. His ability to combine detailed historical analyses with major speculations on IDEOLOGY and rationality was an inspiration for a whole generation of students, including FOUCAULT, whose *Birth of the Clinic* (1963) is a notable development of Canguilhem's approach.

Canguilhem shared with BACHELARD (whom he succeeded as director of the Institute for the History of Science and Technology in Paris) a belief that there are radical breaks in the development of knowledge. Science, for Canguilhem, was a matter of constituting the world and determining possible ways of interacting with it, rather than uncovering the hidden structure of nature. The distinction between normal and pathological states, for example, was not a fact about the body and its organs but a way of structuring medical thought, and could be understood only by analysing its specific historical origins. Canguilhem combined detailed studies of scientific research and its controversies with wide-ranging analyses of the situations in which they occurred. Thus his most characteristic work, *The Formation of the Concept of Reflex in the 17th and 18th Centuries* (1955), is both an essay about a single organizing idea and a study of the concept of 'life', which turns out not to be a constant of human thought but, on the contrary, to have undergone sharp alterations which have redirected the entire course of medical inquiry. Further reflections on this theme are to be found in his *The Understanding of Life* (1965). See also HISTORY OF PHILOSOPHY, PHILOSOPHY OF SCIENCE.   [I.H.]

Cantor, Georg (1845–1918) German mathematician, born in St. Petersburg, one of the creators of set theory and originator of the suggestion that it is the foundation of mathematics.

Carnap, Rudolf (1891–1970) Rudolf Carnap was born in Germany and taught at the University of Vienna and later at the German University in Prague. In 1936 he left Europe for the United States, where he became Professor of Philosophy at Chicago and from 1954 at Los Angeles. He is generally acknowledged as the leading exponent of LOGICAL POSITIVISM, the internationally influential philosophical movement that originated with the VIENNA CIRCLE. This was an informal discussion group of scientifically oriented thinkers, who combined the anti-metaphysical positivism of the Viennese physicist-philosopher MACH with the logical ANALYSIS as practised by Russell and the early WITTGENSTEIN. Carnap was a member of this group for some years; and served as co-editor of *Erkenntnis*, the semi-official organ of logical positivism, until it became a casualty of the Second World War. He continued as an editor of the *International Encyclopedia of Unified Science*, an uncompleted series of monographs designed by Otto NEURATH, another member of the Vienna Circle, to exhibit the essential methodological unity of the major scientific disciplines.

Carnap was a prolific contributor to the theory of knowledge, mathematical

LOGIC, the PHILOSOPHY OF SCIENCE, and the foundations of probability and induction. His writings are a large storehouse of ingenious technical analyses and innovations, and models of formal precision and clarity. They also exhibit his readiness to revise his ideas repeatedly. One of Carnap's long-standing concerns was the construction of an adequate criterion of cognitively meaningful discourse. He first adopted and developed a stringent form of what is commonly called 'the verifiability theory of meaning'. He maintained, in effect, that the meaning of a statement consists in the sensory or introspective data which establish it directly and conclusively. However, although it can readily be shown that on this criterion metaphysical utterences whose alleged content transcends the domain of possible experience are nonsensical (and not even false), Carnap soon recognized that the criterion also rules out as meaningless most if not all scientific statements. For various technical reasons he also came to view as unpromising the task he had set himself (in *The Logical Structure of the World*, 1928) of indicating in detail how every purportedly factual statement can be translated into statements about sense-data; and he eventually came to doubt the feasibility of such translations even into the language of everyday affairs and experimental physics. He subsequently sought to develop a more liberal version of the verifiability criterion of cognitive significance, one which could be a guide in constructing symbolic systems for theoretical science but which would also help to demarcate metaphysical vagary from genuine scientific hypothesis. The general import of Carnap's proposed criterion was that a statement is meaningful if, and only if, the statement itself or some of its logical consequences can be tested by sensory observation.

Carnap's ideas on the province of philosophy underwent an analogous liberalization. In *The Logical Syntax of Language* (1934), in which he formulated some characteristic views on logic, mathematics and the philosophy of science in rich detail, he defined logical syntax as the study of how the signs in a language are related to one another in virtue of their purely structural properties. He maintained that the laws of logic and mathematics make no assertions about any subject matter, but are simply linguistic structures whose a priori necessity within the language in which they occur is derived entirely from conventional syntactical rules. Moreover, he declared that philosophical controversies are usually generated by the confusion of 'pseudo-object' statements (such as the claim that time extends infinitely in both directions, which he held to be equivalent to the syntactical statement that any positive or negative real-number expression can be used as a time-coordinate) with genuine statements about some non-linguistic subject matter. He concluded that philosophy should be identified with the logical syntax of the language of science. This recommendation apparently made illegitimate any consideration of the relations of signs to what they represented, and in particular outlawed any analysis of what is meant by factual truth. However, as was made evident by the work of Alfred TARSKI, it is possible to develop a precise theory of semantics, dealing with the relations of signs to what they signify; indeed, Carnap eventually made important contributions to this branch of logical analysis. In any event, he now enlarged his earlier conception of the scope of philosophy, and identified the latter (using the terminology of Charles MORRIS) with the semiotical analysis of the structure of cognitive discourse.

Carnap's main preoccupation during later years was with the technical development of the logic of inductive inference. On his view, statements such as 'It is highly probable on the available evidence that Smith is guilty as charged' cannot be explicated in terms of empirically ascertainable relative frequencies in some class of repeatable events, as can be done for a statement like 'The probability of obtaining heads with a fair coin is one-half' (which in effect asserts that in a long series of tosses a coin falls uppermost about half the time). In statements of the first type, Carnap believed, the word 'probable' refers to a logical relation between the evidence and the hypothesis based upon it. Since it was this logical sense of probability that Carnap thought relevant in evaluating the weight of the evidence for any conclusion in inductive inquiries, he attempted to construct an explicit symbolism for it, and also devised a variety of numerical measures for degrees of logical probability. However, although Carnap developed an imposing range of ideas and theorems on this subject, the structure was not completed, and its eventual value for scientific practice remains an open question. (E.N.)

Carneades (c.213–c.129 BC) Leading exponent of the sceptical turn at the ACADEMY, and fierce opponent of STOICISM; see SCEPTICISM, SCEPTICS.

Cartesianism See DESCARTES.

Cassirer, Ernst (1874–1945) Cassirer built up his original reputation as a historian of philosophy, especially that of the seventeenth century, and as a philosopher of science. He was a product of the neo-Kantian school of Marburg and spent most of his teaching life at Berlin and Hamburg; but on the advent to power of the Nazis he moved first to England, then to Sweden and finally to the United States, where his work came to be highly valued. He never rejected the Kantian philosophy, though he developed it. KANT had taught that human experience was conditioned by the categories, the forms of thought under which all phenomena were subsumed. Cassirer maintained (in his *Philosophy of Symbolic Forms*, 1923–9) that in addition to the Kantian categories, which inform scientific thought, there are also forms of mythical, historical and practical thinking, and that they could be brought to light by the study of forms of expression in language. Each of these kinds of thinking was valid in its own right, and though scientific thought is a later development than mythical thought the latter is not merely primitive science. Cassirer's thought is difficult and expressed at very great length; his works all contain long and learned discussions of the linguistic, anthropological and philosophical work of his predecessors. (J.O.U.)

Categorical Imperative According to KANT, the value of a morally worthy action depends neither on its happy consequences nor on any kindly sentiments it may spring from, but only on the ultimate principle or 'maxim' to which it gives expression. In the *Groundwork for the Metaphysics of Morals* (1785) he argued that morality is rooted in just one supreme principle: always to act 'in such a way *that I can also will that my maxim should become a universal law*'. (For example, I should never make a false promise, since that would imply that everyone could break their promises with impunity, which would undermine the entire practice of promising.) According to Kant, this supreme principle was absolutely binding for all free and rational beings regardless of their circumstances, and as such it was not 'hypothetical' but 'categorical'. {J.R.}

Categories   ARISTOTLE borrowed 'cate-goria' from legal parlance, where it meant 'accusation', and stretched it to mean anything that could be asserted truly or falsely of anything. If we complete 'Socrates is. . .' with any noun or adjective, or 'Socrates...' with a verb, we ascribe a predicate to Socrates. Aristotle saw that predicates are of different types. To say of what kind Socrates is, for example a man or an animal, is very different from saying merely where or how heavy he is. Aristotle distinguished several ultimate predicate-types or categories.

1 Kind, for example '...a man'.
2 Quality, for example '...pale'.
3 Quantity or size, for example '...six-foot'.
4 Relation, for example '...older than Plato'.
5 Location, for example '...in Athens'.
6 Time or date, for example '...in the fifth century BC'.
7 Action, for example '...argues'.
8 Undergoing, for example '...being prosecuted'.

Aristotle called several of his predicate-types after ordinary interrogatives, like 'what?', 'where?', 'how big?' and 'when?' Any answer to 'what is Socrates?' specifies a Kind, any answer to 'where...?' a Location and so on. All predicates of one type will answer, truly or falsely, one interrogative and will not answer any other interrogative.

To most predicates, for example '...laughs' or '...shrewd', there correspond abstract nouns, like 'laughter' or 'shrewdness'. If we ask 'what, ultimately, is laughter? or shrewdness? or slavery?' the answer names the appropriate category: 'Laughter is an Action'; 'Shrewdness is a Quality'; or 'Slavery is a Relation'. But not all abstract nouns correspond to

predicates. 'Possible' is not a predicate, for example, of Socrates, so we cannot ask to what category possibility belongs. Predicates of Kind, like '...a man' and '...gold' do not naturally yield abstract nouns. We speak of the brightness or remoteness of the planet Venus, but not of her 'heavenly bodihood'. Her brightness or remoteness might alter or cease, but Venus could not become less or more of a body. If she ceased to be a body she would cease to be at all.

Moreover, to find a particular instance of brightness we have to find a particular *bright star* or *bright torch*, etc. An instance of brightness can be found only in a member of a Kind. But we find a specimen of *star* or *torch*, just in finding a star or torch. Brightness is something that, for example, *this star* possesses. But being a star is not something extra that *this star* also possesses – else the question 'Of what Kind is it?' would arise again about the possessor of this postulated property of being a star.

What made Aristotle want to discriminate predicate-types was perhaps partly this. When a thing alters, it ceases to be what it was. So, apparently, Socrates, who is getting warm, being no longer what he was, cannot still be a man or Xanthippe's husband; which is absurd. To resolve this paradox it is helpful to be able to say that Socrates has changed from having one Quality to having another, but that this is not a change from one to another Kind, or from one to another Relation. We specify the general field of a change by specifying the category of the predicates between which the transition is. Though Socrates is never continuously the same age, he is continuously a human being. Not everything is in flux.

KANT gave to the word 'category' a different philosophical use. For him a category is a structural principle exemplifiable in scientifically ascertainable facts. Thus all facts of the form 'X's happening was due to Y's happening' come under the category of Cause and Effect. We know, before we find out the actual explanation of X, that there has to be an explanation with this structure. Today the word 'category' is used by philosophers, if at all, for any supposedly ultimate type, without any settled convention about what it is a type of. Without *ad hoc* elucidations the word is therefore nowadays a vague one. (G.R.)

Cavell, Stanley (1926–) American thinker whose philosophical development started with the teachings of AUSTIN and WITTGENSTEIN, which he took to involve not so much a cool, detached description of the operations of 'ordinary language', as an earnest effort towards self-understanding. This demanding intellectual programme subsequently led Cavell into studies of Shakespeare and of Hollywood movies, as well as to attempts to rehabilitate the work of Emerson and Thoreau (see AMERICAN PHILOSOPHY). His books include *Must we mean what say?* (1969), *The Claims of Reason* (1979) and *In Quest of the Ordinary: Lines of Scepticism and Romanticism* (1988).   {J.R.}

Chomsky, Noam (1928–) American linguist whose *Syntactic Structures* (1957) revolutionized linguistics by centring it on grammar, and turned grammar itself into a powerful formal theory. Grammar, according to Chomsky, is a device which produces all and only the grammatical sentences of a language. Although this set is infinite, the grammar must be finite. The only kind of grammar which matches actual human competences is, according to Chomsky, one which postulates a 'deep structure' together with a set of 'transformational rules' which generate 'surface structures'. Such a 'transformational grammar' can be seen as revising

SAUSSURE's distinction between *langue* and *parole*, which is fundamental to STRUCTURALISM. According to Chomsky, transformational grammars are not just scientists' theories; they are actually encoded in language-users: thus to know a language is to know, implicitly, its grammar. In *Language and Mind* (1968) Chomsky argued that his analyses of linguistic competences in terms of abstract mental structures could be generalized into 'a remarkably favourable perspective for the study of human mental processes'; and this vision partly inspired the subsequent development of 'Artificial Intelligence' at the border between computing science and psychology.

Chomsky holds that it is impossible that children should learn a language from scratch: they must, he believes, be already equipped with 'innate knowledge' of 'linguistic universals'. According to Chomsky, this theory places him in the Cartesian, 'rationalist' tradition in philosophy, as opposed to the Lockean 'empiricist' one; and moreover supports the belief in the worth of all human beings which underlies his outspoken anarchistic socialism.   [J.R.]

Chrysippus (c.280–207 BC) In 232, Chrysippus of Soli, Cilicia, succeeded Cleanthes as third head of the Stoa (see STOICISM). On coming to Athens about 260, he became a pupil in the ACADEMY of Arcesilaus, from whom he acquired an extreme virtuosity in logic and dialectic. When he converted to the Stoa, it was suffering from the divergent and unorthodox systems of Ariston and Herillus, and from a severe attack from Academic SCEPTICISM. Chrysippus, in an enormous literary output displaying great dialectical power, repelled the attacks and formulated in great detail what became the definitive system of STOICISM. He was not an original thinker, but showed great skill in refurbishing the fundamental doctrines of ZENO of Citium, the first of the stoics, an achievement which won him the title of Second Founder. 'Give me the doctrines', he said with characteristic dry humour, 'and I shall supply the proofs'. But his relentless logic led to differences of detail most noticeable in his psychology and theory of knowledge. And as his logic drove him towards extreme positions, so the paradoxes inherent in Stoicism were spotlighted. To his boast 'Without Chrysippus, there would have been no Stoa', CARNEADES, the most formidable opponent of Stoicism, could answer, 'Without Chrysippus, there would have been no Carneades'.   (I.G.K)

Church, Alonzo (1903–95)   American logician, author of *Introduction to Mathematical Logic*, 1956; see FREGE, LOGIC.

Cicero, Marcus Tullius (106–43 BC) Roman lawyer, politician and writer. Trained in philosophy from youth up, auditor and friend of the leading professors of the ACADEMY, Stoa and Epicurean School, he maintained his philosophical reading even during his busiest years in public life. At 45, personal distress and political helplessness led him to concentrate his full energies on making Greek philosophy accessible in Latin literary form. Within the next two years he produced a long series of dialogues, covering the various departments of contemporary philosophy by expounding and criticizing the doctrines of the three leading schools. By temperament and training an Academic SCEPTIC, in ethics he followed and widened the electicism introduced to the Academy by Antiochus. He admired the noble ideals of STOICISM; to EPICURUS he was unsympathetic. He thought of himself as a translator (in some cases his source books can be traced, for example, to Clitomachus, Philo,

Antiochus, Panaetius, Posidonius), but he claimed the right of independent presentation and criticism. His aim was perhaps to naturalize Greek philosophy, as his predecessors, beginning with translations, had naturalized Greek literature; he thought that his mastery of language and style could initiate the process. The creator of a Latin philosophical vocabulary which was to become dominant, his influence was immense, and he remains invaluable as a source for the history of scepticism, stoicism and epicureanism.   (I.G.K.)

Clarke, Samuel (1675–1729)   English philosopher who championed a Newtonian philosophy in opposition to the prevailing Cartesian climate of thought in the Cambridge of his day. In a famous correspondence with LEIBNIZ, he maintained that space and time were infinite homogeneous entities, against Leibniz's claim that they were ultimately relational. In *A Discourse Concerning the Being and Attributes of God* (1704–5), he contended against 'deniers of natural and revealed religion', HOBBES and SPINOZA being his most notable targets. Morality is based, according to Clarke, not on the power or command of God, nor upon 'contracts' brought into being by human communities, but on independent and self-evident relations between situations and the kind of actions they demand. A mistaken moral judgement is of the same logical order as a contradiction in mathematical reasoning. Joseph BUTLER found this rather too abstract a presentation of moral philosophy, but the most powerful criticisms came from HUTCHESON and HUME, who denied that moral judgement lay in the perception of relations, or in the activity of reason alone.   (R.W.H.)

'Cogito ergo sum'   See DESCARTES.

Cohen, Morris R. (1880–1947)   Born in Russia, he emigrated to the United States as a boy, and taught philosophy in New York. He was an outspoken NATURALIST, and a vigorous exponent of liberalism conceived as a faith in rational analysis. He subscribed in essentials to philosophical REALISM as advocated by the early RUSSELL, maintaining that philosophy, like the sciences, makes significant intellectual advances only when it grapples in piecemeal fashion with limited and clearly formulated problems. Cohen believed that the truths of LOGIC formulate the absolute invariants exhibited by all possible objects. On the other hand, he construed the laws of the positive sciences as expressions of relations which are invariant only in certain specialized domains. He therefore maintained that factual statements are inherently incapable of a purely rational demonstration. Accordingly, he recognized a fundamental polarity between what he called the rational and the empirical elements in existence; and his writings contain spirited criticisms of philosophies that ignore these as well as other polar aspects of nature. He expounded this principle of polarity in his major book, *Reason and Nature* (1931), which contains, in addition to an uncompromising critique of anti-rational currents in contemporary philosophy, a general account of scientific method, and numerous analyses of philosophical questions raised by substantive issues in MATHEMATICS, physics, biology, the social sciences and ethical theory.   (E.N.)

Coleridge, Samuel Taylor (1772–1834)

English romantic poet and philosopher whose early adherence to LOCKEAN principles was shaken when he encountered BERKELEY's idea of nature as a form of divine language. A subsequent visit to continental Europe in 1798–9 convinced him that the best philosophical work came from Germany, and he spent much of the rest of his life struggling to give form to the inspiration he drew from SCHELLING and KANT. The record of these encounters can be traced not only in his poetry, but also in *Biographia Literaria* (1817), and a series of lectures on the History of Philosophy given in London in 1818–19, first published in 1949. {J.R.}

Collingwood, Robin George (1889–1943)

English philosopher who spent all his working life at Oxford. He was a very eminent authority on the archaeology and history of Roman Britain, but his main life's work was as a very original philosopher, and his bold, fresh style makes him an unusually stimulating and exciting author even for readers who are not in agreement with him. Contrary to his own statement in his *Autobiography* (1939), his views appear to have undergone considerable change. Brought up in the Oxford REALIST school, led by Cook WILSON and PRICHARD, he early reacted to a position more nearly in sympathy with IDEALISM; in his *Essay on Philosophical Method* (1933) perhaps the best of his earlier writings, he took the view that philosophy was essentially an attempt to set forth human knowledge in systematic form. But he insisted that this was but a transmutation of knowledge already possessed in a less developed form; thus moral philosophy should simply systematize existing moral beliefs, transmuting but not challenging or adding to them. The other main contention was that philosophy works with concepts which overlap in a way not found in science and that this gives it a special character and special methods of argument. In later life, however, Collingwood became more sceptical; in *An Essay on Metaphysics* (1940), ostensibly a continuation of the *Essay on Philosophical Method*, he abandons the view that philosophy has a distinctive character and sees it rather as a part of history. Metaphysics now has the purely historical task of bringing to light the absolute presuppositions of human thought at some date in history; to any metaphysical statement in traditional form should be supplied at the beginning the 'metaphysical rubric' that 'it was an absolute presupposition of thought at such and such a time that. . .'. No assessment of the merits of these presuppositions is apparently possible. In identifying philosophy with history he was adopting a position, similar to that of DILTHEY and CROCE, which gave an appearance of unity to his historical and philosophical concerns. The attempts to trace out absolute presuppositions at the end of the *Essay on Metaphysics* and in his *Idea of Nature* are of great independent interest, as are his views on the nature of history (see his *Autobiography* and the posthumous *Idea of History*). He expresses contempt for 'scissors and paste' history, and takes seriously the view that history is the history of human thought and that the task of the historians is to relive past thoughts. He was also a major contributor to aesthetics, especially in his *Speculum Mentis* (1924) and *The Principles of Art* (1938).   (J.O.U.)

Communitarianism   See LIBERALISM AND COMMUNITARIANISM.

Comte, Isidore-Auguste-Marie-François-Xavier (1796–1857)   Auguste Comte was born in Montpellier to Catholic parents. In 1814 he became a student at the École polytechnique in Paris, and in 1816 led a student revolt which resulted in his expulsion together with the rest of the students of his year. In 1817, he became secretary to the Utopian socialist writer Saint-Simon (1760–1825), who influenced him greatly. It has been held Comte was the

principal author of much that was published in Saint-Simon's name at that period. In 1822, there appeared under Saint-Simon's auspices Comte's *Plan of the Scientific Works necessary for the Reorganization of Society*, in which most of the ideas of his subsequent philosophy are contained. In 1824, Comte quarrelled with Saint-Simon and left his service.

In 1826, Comte began a course of public lectures on 'Positive Philosophy', but had to abandon them owing to mental illness. The next year he tried to drown himself in the Seine. In 1829, he restarted his public lectures, which were published in six volumes from 1830 to 1842 as the *Course on Positive Philosophy*. This is his major work, in which he sets out his theory of knowledge and the sciences and lays the foundations for a new science, which he first called 'social physics' and then 'sociology'. The central thesis is that the attempt to discover extra-mundane causes of the natural world, whether in theological or in metaphysical terms, should be abandoned in favour of the positive method of correlating the facts of observation with one another. The positive sciences, he argued, have been developed progressively, the earlier ones forming the basis for those that came later. The sequence he sets out, in ascending order of complexity is: mathematics, astronomy, physics and chemistry, and biology (including psychology). There remains sociology, of which Comte claims to be the founder. As conceived by him, this science comprises *social statics* and *social dynamics*. As to the former, he held that the various elements are so closely bound together in a 'social consensus' that no part can be radically changed without serious effects upon the rest. As to the latter, he held that intellectual development was the prime cause of social change, and that human society therefore passes through the same theological, metaphysical and positive stages as the sciences. First, there was a theocratic and traditional stage which came to be organized around the secular power of kings and the spiritual power of priests. At the metaphysical stage there is a sort of anarchy in which both temporal and spiritual authority are attacked. This transitional stage would be succeeded by the positive era when men of science would form a new and durable spiritual power, and an ordered society would come into existence based on the cooperation that positive knowledge of social facts would bring with it.

Comte had hoped for a professorship at the École Polytechnique, but obtained only minor teaching and examining posts there. J. S. MILL and others organized financial support to enable Comte to continue his researches. In 1844, Comte made the acquaintance of Clotilde de Vaux. Comte claimed that she taught him the importance of subordinating the intellect to the heart, and after her death in 1846 his writings take on a new emphasis. It is not merely by means of the natural and social sciences and the spiritual power of scientists that society is to be regenerated, but by means of a secular religion, the Religion of Humanity, of which Comte was to be the High Priest. The details of this new religion are set out in *The General View of Positivism* (1848), *The Catechism of Positive Religion* (1852) and the four volumes of *The System of Positive Polity* which appeared between 1851 and 1854. Having made arrangements for the perpetuation of the cult, Comte died in 1857.

Comte's later writings are a strange mixture of absurdity and insight. On the one hand, there is the Religion of Humanity, with details for the worship of the Great Being (symbolized by the female form) in chapels containing the busts of the benefactors of mankind. There is the Positivist Calendar with months named after Moses, Archimedes and Frederick II, and with days for the celebration of great men (among whom Comte gratefully included friends who had vainly worked to get him a professorship at the École Polytechnique). On the other hand, Comte had pondered seriously the ritual and ideology of a society from which religious beliefs and institutions had been eliminated. He saw that in the absence of unifying sentiments a scientific society might degenerate. One of his ideas was that scientific activity itself has moral implications. Thus he held that submission to the facts of nature curbed the exorbitance of egoism, that the acceptance of a scientific argument had a certain kinship with justice, and that understanding was very close to sympathy. Yet his principle of the subordination of the intellect to the heart is an admission that there is more to morality than can be got from science. The intellect, he held, in a phrase that echoes and corrects HUME, should be not the slave but the servant of the heart. See also HUMANISM, PHILOSOPHY OF SCIENCE.   (H.B.A.)

Conceptualism   The view that the objects of thought and the meanings of general terms are concepts – mental entities which exist only in minds and are formed or constructed by them. On this view when I think about redness – when, for example, I infer from the fact that something is red the fact that it is coloured – I am scrutinizing the concept of red that I possess and discovering that it contains as a part the concept of colour. Again, when I recognize something as red, I see that it falls under or satisfies the concept. Stated in this way the theory has a somewhat uninformative appearance. It seems to repeat, in less familiar words, the state of affairs to be explained. It is more compelling in the form of imagism, where the concept is identified with mental imagery of some kind. Imagery is used as a standard of classification. To tell if a thing is red I must compare it with my standard imagery of red. For LOCKE this imagery was abstract, but BERKELEY found abstract and indeterminate images unintelligible and proposed instead a theory of representative images. But a specific representative image will have a multitude of features and so will be ambiguous. HUME's theory of a series of similar images overcomes this difficulty. Conceptualism, like other theories of UNIVERSALS, is implicitly regressive. To use a mental standard of classification I must compare the things to be classified with the standard; but this act of comparison is itself a classificatory undertaking, requiring the use of a further mental standard and so on. A difficulty peculiar to imagism – the price, perhaps, of its ready intelligibility – is that it seems psychologically false. The use of images in recognition is the exceptional case. It is often said that images are themselves symbolic in character and thus raise the same problems about meaning as words. (A.Q.)

Condillac, Étienne Bonnot de (1715–80)

Condillac was born in Grenoble and took holy orders before coming into contact with DIDEROT and other ENCYCLOPEDISTS, by whom he was greatly influenced; he was also for long a friend of ROUSSEAU. He began as a disciple of LOCKE, whose philosophy was very popular among advanced thinkers in France at that time. In his first book, *Essay on the Origin of Human Knowledge* (1746) he was content to follow Locke, but in his main work, the *Treatise on Sensations* (1754), he took EMPIRICISM

further than Locke had ever done. Not only are all our ideas derived from sensation, but all the activities of the mind are mere transformations of sensations: a memory, for example, is a mere after-effect of sensation and attention is the occupation of consciousness by one sensation to the exclusion of others. Condillac expounds this doctrine by the device of imagining a statue being gradually endowed with senses, first smell, then touch and so on; he can thus consider the contribution of each separately. It is important to his doctrine that he conceives of sensations as arousing pleasure and pain at the promptings of which our wants, instincts and habits are formed. This doctrine, which Condillac expounds with grace, simplicity and clarity had a great success in France for a time; but his views have had a more abiding influence in Britain, largely because of their influence of JAMES MILL and Herbert SPENCER. (J.O.U.)

Condorcet, Marie-Jean-Antoine-Nicolas Caritat, Marquis de (1743–94)

Condorcet was one of the ENCYCLOPEDISTS and an early supporter of the French Revolution. But he was soon proscribed and went into hiding where he wrote his most famous work, the *Sketch for a Historical Picture of the Progress of the Human Mind*; he was captured and imprisoned and immediately died, possibly from poison. He wrote biographies of Voltaire and Turgot and his *Essay on Methods of Analysing Probability in its Relation to Majority Decisions* (1785) is important in the development of the theory of probability. But it is as a philosophical theorist of progress that he is best known. He believed in a permanent human nature and invariant moral principles derived from this nature and independent of custom and religion (of which he was a fierce opponent); progress was therefore a matter of improving institutions and education. He distinguished ten epochs of human society, beginning with the hunter, then the pastoralist, then the agriculturalist; the eighth stage was that of scientific culture inaugurated in the sixteenth century, and the triumph of this culture ensured indefinite further progress. The ninth period began with the French Revolution and the tenth was yet in the future. For his idea of indefinite progress he relied on an analogy with the sciences. Though human intelligence is essentially limited, there can always be progress in mathematics and the other sciences; similarly an indefinite progress in human affairs does not presuppose perfection in human nature. These views, very influential in their time, were severely attacked in the nineteenth century.   (J.O.U.)

Continental Philosophy The rubric 'Continental Philosophy' has been used since the 1970s to designate a range of twentieth-century French and German thinkers – notably HUSSERL, HEIDEGGER, GADAMER, SARTRE, DE BEAUVOIR, FOU-CAULT, DELEUZE and DERRIDA – whose work has been condemned as 'unclear' and generally disreputable by self-appointed guardians of the purity of ANALYSIS in general and ANALYTIC PHILOS-OPHY in particular. The label is also applied to the movement within anglophone philosophy which has undertaken to translate, paraphrase and promote the works of 'continental' thinkers: indeed it has been argued that Continental Philosophy is essentially an English-language phenomenon, only indirectly related to the movements in continental Europe which it celebrates. Controversy over Continental Philosophy came to a head in 1992 with a campaign to prevent Derrida from receiving an honorary

degree at Cambridge University. A letter to the press signed by an international team of nineteen analytic philosophers, including QUINE, informed the public that 'in the eyes of philosophers, and certainly those working in leading departments of philosophy throughout the world, M. Derrida's work does not meet accepted standards of clarity and rigour'. The spectacle of a band of philosophers appealing to their own authority as professors in order to validate their status as arbiters of philosophical truth caused some amusement at the time, and Derrida was awarded the honour anyway.

Thinkers grouped under the heading 'Continental Philosophy' share a number of distinctive features. On the whole they are happy to admit the works of HEGEL, MARX, KIERKEGAARD, NIETZSCHE and FREUD into the philosophical canon; they regard ambiguities and obscurities as part of the fabric of language and existence, rather than undesirable excrescences that need to be pruned away; they take the task of reading and criticizing classic philosophical texts very seriously; and they are not particularly fussy about the supposed boundaries between philosophy on the one hand and history, art, science and politics on the other. They also share an indifference to the notion of 'Continental Philosophy'.

The pre-history of Continental Philosophy in Britain goes back at least as far as COLERIDGE with his crippling fixation on the hidden depths of German idealism. The phrase itself came into use in the first half of the nineteenth century, and gained wide circulation in a celebrated pair of essays in which J. S. MILL contrasted BENTHAM's 'short and easy method' in philosophy with the agonized elaborations of Coleridge (1838, 1840). 'By Bentham, beyond all others, men have been led to ask themselves, in regard to any ancient or received opinion, *Is it true?*' Mill wrote; 'and by Coleridge, *What is the meaning of it?*' The future of 'English philosophy', in Mill's opinion, lay with the 'Germano-Coleridgian school', or with the 'Continental philosophers' – 'for, among the truths long recognised by Continental philosophers, but which few Englishmen have yet arrived at, one is, the importance…of antagonist modes of thought: which, it will one day be felt, are as necessary to one another in speculation, as mutually checking powers are in a political constitution'.

The idea that England, or Britain, or the English language is the repository of a proud national tradition that is rooted in empiricism and suspicious of flighty foreigners can be traced back to the time of the French Revolution and BURKE's polemics against the 'men of theory' he held responsible for it; but even before that it was anticipated in the eulogies to BACON, LOCKE and NEWTON in VOLTAIRE's *Letters concerning the English Nation* (1733). The entire doctrine of philosophical national characters is highly questionable however (see 'AFRICAN PHILOSOPHY'). In any case, philosophers have always cultivated an interest in the exotic, and if there are such things as national intellectual currents, then perhaps they have an obligation to swim against them.   {J.R.}

Contract, Social   See SOCIAL CONTRACT, HOBBES, LOCKE, ROUSSEAU, HUME, POLITICAL PHILOSOPHY.

Cook Wilson   See WILSON, COOK.

Cosmogony   An account of the origin of the universe.

Cosmological Argument   See THEISM.

Cratylus   Cratylus of Athens was a sophist who lived around 410 BC. He developed an extreme form of Heracliteanism and, according to ARISTOTLE, persuaded the young PLATO that there could be no knowledge of the unstable physical world. In Plato's *Cratylus* he is shown as defending the natural correctness of names – a development of HERACLITUS' view that a thing's essence is often revealed in its name. Aristotle asserted that he also went beyond Heraclitus in saying that you could not step even once into the same river, and that he ultimately avoided speech and merely pointed. Cratylus seems to have been an extravagant and somewhat uncritical person, who must have had difficulty reconciling his exaggerations of Heraclitus' belief in the ultimate impermanence of objects with the significance of some names. It is possible that Plato's interpretation of Heraclitus as positing constant and universal physical change was derived from Cratylus. See also PRE-SOCRATICS.   (G.S.K.)

Critical Philosophy   see KANT.

Critical Theory   The interpretation of Marxism associated with the FRANKFURT SCHOOL.

Croce, Benedetto (1866–1952) Benedetto Croce was born in Naples and his first scholarly work was on the history and antiquities of that area. He turned to pure philosophy after a considerable period as a historian and art critic, and to the end of his life he continued to work in those fields. He held no academic post, but was Minister of Education in the Italian government from 1920 to 1921, and again after the Second World War. He retired from active politics on the advent of Fascism, with which he never compromised. Croce's main fame is in the field of AESTHETICS, but his aesthetic theory is essentially part of his general philosophical system, which is a form of idealism indebted to HEGEL. His general system he called the philosophy of the spirit. Spirit is for him the sole reality, and the physical world is a construction of the mind; but spirit does not transcend experience: it is the world. Though spirit is one it contains four varieties of experience: cognitive experience of the particular, where the spirit expresses itself in particular embodiments, the sphere of aesthetics; second, cognitive experience of the universal, the sphere of logic; third, practical experience in particular matters, the sphere of economic interests; fourth, practical experience concerned with the universal, the sphere of ethics. History is the description of the activity of spirit in these four grades; philosophy can be regarded as a systematic account of the task and methodology of history, and Croce often says that philosophy and history are one; hence the systematic treatise on the spirit contains a final part on the theory and history of historiography.

Croce stated his aesthetic views not only in the first volume of the *Philosophy of the Spirit* (1902) but also in a shorter *Breviary of Aesthetics* (1913) and an Encyclopedia Britannica article, *Aesthetics* (1928). Art, Croce holds, is vision or intuition; a work of art is an image produced by the artist and reproduced by the audience. The physical artefact is produced by the artist to perpetuate and aid reproduction of the image, which is the true work of art. But we cannot separate the artist's intuition from its expression: a poetic thought is nothing outside its metre, rhythm and words, and intuition and expression are one; technique is involved in mixing paints, writing down notes, or cutting stone, but the poem, the sonata and the novel are complete before the mechanical work of writing them down is undertaken. Artistic imagination must be distinguished from mere fancy: it is productive imagination expressing some feeling or emotion, though we must not separate the feeling as content from the image as its form; art is the a priori aesthetic synthesis of feeling and image.

Art then is simply the representation of feeling in an image. Though this will normally give pleasure we must not be misled into thinking that art is the utilitarian act of producing images as a means to pleasure; nor is art a moral activity; nor again must we confuse art with conceptual knowledge. Since art is an activity of spirit it is a mistake to claim that there can be beauty in nature; but nature, as much as a block of carved marble, can prompt and fix in our memories an aesthetic image: 'nature is mute if man does not make her speak'. Expression and beauty are a single concept in different words.

Such is Croce's theory of aesthetics in a narrow sense. But for Croce aesthetics is the field of the entire manifestation of spirit in which it expresses itself in particular embodiments; thus it includes all expression except pure logical thinking. This accounts for Croce's claims that his aesthetics is also a general linguistics: language is the medium of self-expression; hence, Croce says, any use of language is identical with poetry. Croce's closest follower in the English-speaking world was COLLINGWOOD. (J.O.U.)

Cudworth, Ralph (1617–88) Ralph Cudworth was the most distinguished of the CAMBRIDGE PLATONISTS. He published his chief work, *The True Intellectual System of the Universe* in 1678; his *Treatise Concerning Eternal and Immutable Morality* appeared posthumously in 1731. Cudworth took as his task the welding together of the new science of his day and a broadly Platonic tradition of metaphysics and theology. The universe, to him, is not a mechanism, fashioned and set in motion by God and thereafter self-regulating: nor is it the theatre of God's constant miraculous intervention. Rather, God works by way of a semi-autonomous 'Plastic Nature', reminiscent of the Platonic 'World-Soul'. Cudworth vigorously combated ATOMISTIC and MATERIALISTIC metaphysics, stressing in particular the active, spontaneous and creative powers of the mind.

Right and wrong, to Cudworth, cannot be established by the arbitrary fiat of ruler or deity. Both the Calvinist and Hobbesian concern with will and power as ultimates are criticized in terms of 'eternal and immutable' morality. Happiness and freedom are seen as release from self-concern, religion consisting crucially in the choice and pursuit of a way of life. Of philosophers influenced by Cudworth the most significant is Richard PRICE, whose theory of knowledge, though not his moral philosophy, might almost be called a restatement of Cudworth's. (R.W.H.)

Cynicism A philosophical movement or way of life inaugurated in the second half of the fourth century BC by DIOGENES of Sinope, from whose nickname, *Kuōn*, the Dog, it derives its name. It continued in phases of varying popularity and purity until the end of the Greco-Roman world in the sixth century AD. It comprised a succession of individuals emulating the life and practices of Diogenes, and was never an organized School with official dogmas; but a traditional core of precept and behaviour can be extracted.

The end of life is happiness, which is achieved by living a life of virtue and self-sufficiency in accordance with nature. This principle is common to Cynicism and STOICISM, but they differ in the interpretation of it. To the Cynic, happiness depends on being self-sufficient, which is a matter of mental attitude. The road to self-sufficiency was to dissociate oneself actively from any influence, external or internal, which might fetter one's individual freedom. For example, the cynic's attitude to prosperity was not untroubled indifference but uncompromising hostility. Money is the metropolis of all evil, the whip of desire. The solution lies not in moderation or temperance, but in the eradication of money and all the lower desires. Property may involve ties, so the Cynic has no property at all, and repudiates family and community, and all conventional values of birth, class, rank, honour or reputation. A life lived according to nature is restricted to the bare minimum necessary for existence. The driving force is the search for inviolability. The more one owns, the more one wants; the further one is involved, the wider one's needs; the greater one's needs, the more vulnerable one is. But if all needs apart from the absolutely basic are the result of convention, one can become free by unshackling oneself from them. This is apparent from the conduct of animals who are not bound by convention, and from the ideal of the gods who have no needs at all.

But the Cynic's asceticism did not involve leading the life of a hermit. The Cynic lived in the full glare of civilization, for two reasons. First, the cynical way of life demanded continual practice against its enemies – convention, pleasure and luxury – in order to keep both body and mind fighting trim. (To form and test one's *apatheia*, or lack of emotion, for example, it was necessary to face insults.) Second, Cynicism was a militant evangelism: as the Scout of humanity, the Cynic had to explore human conditions; as its Doctor, to cure human minds. Conventional education and the learning of the philosophical schools were both reviled. Cynicism as a purely practical ethic could be taught only by the example of the Cynic's life, (hence the deliberate public defiance of conventional decencies), and by precepts distilled from personal experience. But Cynics were characterized principally by a fearless, shameless freedom of speech, and a mordant wit and repartee which gave birth to numerous apophthegms and to a new philosophical genre, the satirical diatribe. This was misused by the less reputable members of the sect, but in the hands of the true Cynic, it was a surgeon's knife, impartially wielded to remove the cancer of illusory conventions, pretensions and sham values from human minds.

Cynicism was the most drastic of the philosophies of security which were a feature of the Hellenistic Age (see STOICISM, EPICUREANISM). Arising at a time when the old values of the Greek city-state, already weakened, were tottering under the impact of Alexander, it offered individuals, whatever their status, the prospect of freedom from fear of misfortune, by schooling them to care for nothing except what could never be taken from them. The embodiment of this self-sufficiency was Diogenes himself. Subsequent Cynics tended to stress one aspect or another of his doctrines. His pupil Crates of Thebes, who gave away his fortune to become a mendicant healer of men's souls, was well loved as a kind of consultant to the poor. In the third century BC, when Cynicism flourished, Bion of Borysthenes and Menippus developed Cynic literary satire; Cercidas of Megalopolis, prominent in politics, applied his beliefs to a doctrine of social reform; Teles was a third-rate mendicant preacher of a type later to become common. After lying dormant in the second and first centuries BC, Cynicism blazed in the Roman Empire. Apart from prominent adherents like Demetrius, Dio, Demonax, Oenomaus of Gadara, Peregrinus Proteus and Sallustius, we hear of a swarm of riff-raff

charlatans imposing on the populace under the Cynic beggar uniform of cloak, knapsack and stick. They were particularly disgusting to writers like Lucian and Julian, who nevertheless admired Cynic ideals. Perhaps the greatest philosophical importance of Cynicism lay in its influence on Stoicism, strong at the beginning in ZENO of Citium and Ariston, and later revived in the first century AD by Musonius and EPICTETUS, in one of whose *Discourses* the noblest expression of its ideals is found.   (I.G.K.)

Cyrenaics   A school of HEDONISTIC philosophers, founded by ARISTIPPUS of Cyrene, the friend of SOCRATES, or by his grandson of the same name. The school flourished at the end of the fourth and beginning of the third century BC, when Theodorus, Hegesias and Anniceris led branching sects; thereafter the school disappeared before the advance of EPICUREANISM.

ETHICS was regarded as the only useful branch of philosophy; the end was the enjoyment of the particular pleasure of the moment, which was the sole good to be desired for its own sake. This view is based partly on the observation that the prime natural instinct in all living beings is pursuit of pleasure and avoidance of pain, partly on an epistemology which denied knowledge of external objects and restricted it to the field of sensations. Pleasure and pain are motions and as such positive sensations, mere absence of pain is neither. Neither the past nor the future provokes immediate movement; philosophers will neither regret the past nor toil for the future; and since only immediate sensations constitute knowledge, they will never countenance vain opinion, envy, or superstition. Present gratification, accordingly, is the only goal, and no actions can be good except in so far as they produce this end. But the Cyrenaics also maintained that happiness lies not in slavery to pleasure, but in mastery of it. Pleasures differed in degree, and a present pleasure might be followed by a more violent pain, and hence the consequences of an act could not be ignored. Faced with choice, the philosopher's weapon is rational practical intelligence which can be taught and trained; the art of life lay in the intelligent manipulation of circumstances and prudent adaptation to them for the sake of present gratification. Thus the Cyrenaic answer to the problems of a troubled age was not the renunciation of the CYNICS, but acceptance of the vicissitudes of fortune and an attempt to control them. The master of a horse or ship, they said, is not one who declines its use, but one who knows how to guide it in the right direction.

But the school was troubled by the difficulty of reconciling sensuous ends with rational means, or external stimulus with rational control. Theodorus attempted to free himself from external dependence by redefining the end as a state of mind – joy, brought about by wisdom. Hegesias stressed that pleasure and pain depend to a large extent on our attitude to external circumstances; but he admitted that happiness was not realizable and that the philosopher could only alleviate the preponderance of pain. Anniceris softened the position in another direction, by making some allowance for the pleasures of friendship and patriotism, thus raising the problem of altruistic feelings previously denied by the egoistic hedonism of the school. Cyrenaism is mainly interesting as a curtain-raiser to the more elaborate and successful philosophy of EPICURUS. (I.G.K.)

D

Damascius See NEOPLATONISM.

Danto, Arthur C. (1924–) American philosopher and art critic based in New York. Danto is renowned for his claim that art 'came to an end' with modernism, because there was no longer any 'special way a work of art had to be'. His works include *The Transfiguration of the Commonplace* (1981), *The Philosophical Disenfranchisement of Art* (1986) and *After the End of Art* (1997).

Darwin, Charles (1809–82) Charles Darwin was one of the first naturalists to establish the theory of 'descent with modification', which implied (contrary to much theology) that the characteristics of species of plants and animals have not been fixed from the beginning of life on earth. Indeed it suggested that they could vary slightly from one generation to the next, until – given sufficiently long periods of time – whole new species could emerge, while old ones became extinct. In *The Origin of Species by Means of Natural Selection* (1859) he noted that stocks of cultivated plants and domesticated animals have been systematically improved by selective breeding, and suggested that similar mechanisms were at work within nature. His argument was that organisms with advantageous inherited characteristics would have an improved chance of surviving and having offspring, and that these descendants would pass on these advantages in their turn; over the generations, therefore, the advantaged sector of the population would grow and displace its rivals in the competition for scarce resources. In the *Descent of Man* (1871) Darwin observed that this effect, which he called 'natural selection', would be reinforced by competition for sexual partners. Although Darwin himself refrained from drawing philosophical conclusions from his account of evolution, it was evident that his doctrine endangered many traditional notions about the distinction between humans and other ANIMALS. In addition it undermined certain arguments for THEISM by suggesting that the apparent orderliness of nature came about not through the ingenuity of a divine creator but by blind chance; from now on it was possible to conceive of selection without a selector, design without a designer and indeed creation without a creator.   {J.R.}

Davidson, Donald (1917–2003) The American philosopher Davidson was born in Springfield, Massachusetts. Although he never wrote a full-length book, Davidson was amongst the most influential of analytic philosophers. In the series of articles collected in *Essays on Action and Events* (1980) and *Inquiries into Truth and Interpretation* (1984) he developed a philosophical system involving a number of interlocking themes from the PHILOSOPHY OF MIND and the philosophy of language.

In the philosophy of mind, Davidson aims to reconcile the physical basis of mental life with the fact that explanations in terms of mental events do not involve the kind of general laws that govern physical phenomena. His solution, known as 'anomalous monism', states that although each mental event is identical with a physical event, we adopt a different perspective, with different principles of organization, in considering events as mental, from the perspective of the physical sciences.

The link between mind and language, according to Davidson, is that we can only know what people think if we know what their sentences mean. To know the meaning of a sentence is a matter of knowing its truth conditions, but the identification of truth conditions hinges on what thoughts can intelligibly be attributed to a speaker. Davidson draws general philosophical conclusions from these constraints on interpretation; in particular, he concludes that there is no possibility of radical divergence in human conceptual systems. [D.P.]

de Beauvoir, Simone See BEAUVOIR, SIMONE DE.

Deconstruction See DERRIDA, POSTMODERNISM, STRUCTURALISM.

Deduction 'Deduction' is one of the technical terms of LOGIC, denoting arguments such that if their premises are true the conclusion must also, as a matter of logic, be true. A deductive argument is thus distinguished from INDUCTIVE argument where, however convincing it may be, the premises could conceivably be true and the conclusion false. In this sense the so-called 'deductions' of Sherlock Holmes should be counted as inductions. In the usage of logicians the arguments of mathematics are the most notable examples of extended deductive arguments. (J.O.U.)

Deism Deism is the belief that there is a good and wise Supreme Being who created the world but no longer intervenes in it. The God of the deists is an eighteenth century deity in every respect, to be known only by the methods of rational argument and more particularly by those arguments which lead to a First Great Cause and an Intelligent and Benevolent Designer. The importance of deism in the history of ideas is largely due to its use by VOLTAIRE and others as a weapon against Catholic orthodoxy. Its main importance in the history of philosophy is that it provoked Bishop BUTLER to write his *Analogy of Religion Natural and Revealed*. Butler tries to show that the doctrines of revealed religion and the course of nature are sufficiently alike that they probably both have the same author. In particular there are no intellectual difficulties in accepting a theology of revelation which do not arise equally for the believer in a purely natural and rational theology. But the interest of Butler's arguments concerning issues like immortality is happily independent of their connection with deism. What Butler's arguments point to is the fact that at its most vulnerable points desim is no stronger than revealed religion. While the deist aims his polemics at the Trinity and the Incarnation, he is himself undermined by sceptical attack on the very existence of God. Moreover deism is entirely a religion of the intellect. Whether God exists is for the deist a question of the same order as whether atoms exist. Deism, therefore, even if true, would have little of the type of interest which most religious doctrines possess. The classic deistic statements are John Toland's *Christianity Not Mysterious* (1696), the author of which acknowledged a debt to LOCKE, and Matthew Tindal's *Christianity as Old as the Creation, or the Gospel a Republication of the Religion of Nature* (1730). See also RELIGION, THEISM. (A.MACI)

Deleuze, Gilles (1925–95) French philosopher who started his career as a gifted but conventional historian of philosophy, with studies of HUME, KANT, BERGSON and SPINOZA. With *Nietzsche and Philosophy* (1962) and especially *Difference and Repetition* (1962) and *Logic* *of Sense* (1969) he emerged as a major philosopher of desire and difference. After 1968, he collaborated with the psychoanalyst Félix Guattari (*Anti-Oedipus*, 1972; *A Thousand Plateaus*, 1980; *What is Philosophy?*, 1991). His position is fundamentally anti-Hegelian: against the concepts of totality, origin and hierarchy, he develops a philosophy of difference and multiplicity which is etymologically anarchic. His work contains a powerful critique of the reductionisms which dominate contemporary French culture: against the Oedipal reductions of PSYCHOANALYSIS, with its interpretation of desire in terms of Law and lack, he celebrates desire as positive, productive, excessive and proliferating; against the economistic reductions of MARXISM, he gives a picture of society in terms of flows and cuts, semiotic machines rather than structures, lines of flight and bodies without organs; against STRUCTURALIST reconstructions of language, he stresses the multiplicity of semiotic levels, the struggle of minor against major dialects, the importance of pragmatic strategies and collective arrangements of utterance. This central opposition is best embodied in the metaphors of the hierarchized tree and the proliferating rhizome. The material of Deleuze's analyses often comes from literature or art, and he wrote extensively on Proust, Lewis Carroll, Kafka, Francis Bacon and the cinema.   [J.-J.L.]

Democritus Democritus lived in the fifth century BC and was a native of Abdera, Greece, which was probably also the birthplace of LEUCIPPUS, with whom he is associated as a founder of the ATOMIC theory. It is probable that Leucippus first propounded the theory and Democritus elaborated it. We have much information about his life, of which a great deal is improbable – he is said for instance to have been educated by magi

and to have blinded himself to escape from the distractions of sense. It seems that he was in fact the son of wealthy parents, and that as a young man he travelled much, including a tour of Egypt and the nearer East, thus reducing himself to poverty. On returning home he became renowned for his teachings on atomic theory, cosmology, sense-perception, biology, music and many other subjects; some of his work, such as his attempt to explain colour in terms of the atomic theory, seems to have been based on experiment. He also developed an ethical system which is essentially that adopted later by EPICURUS. The goal of life is happiness, which consists largely in tranquil freedom from fear and anxiety. The pleasures of sense are less important than mental well-being because they are fleeting and frequently lead to pain; though nothing is of value except well-being, wisdom is of importance since it allows us to know what pleasures are worth pursuing and how they can be attained. The considerable surviving fragments show a mind of great power and subtlety.   (J.O.U.)

Dennett, Daniel (1942–) American philosopher of doggedly atheistic and materialistic views, and enthusiast for the philosophical relevance of DARWIN's notion of natural selection. His campaign began with *Content and Consciousness* (1969) and continued with *Darwin's Dangerous Idea* (1995) and *Freedom Evolves* (2003).

Deontology 'Deontology' (from the Greek *deon*, meaning approximately 'obligatory') denotes the view that duty is fundamental to all moral thought. Deontologists (e.g. PRICHARD and ROSS) are usually contrasted with UTILITARIANS, who regard the obligatoriness of actions as derivative from the goodness of the results that the action will achieve.   (J.O.U)

Derrida, Jacques (1930–2004) Jacques Derrida was born in Algeria and educated at the Ecole Normale Supérieure in Paris, where he also taught for many years. His thought – often discussed under the rubric *deconstruction*, a term derived from HEIDEGGER – first had a revolutionary impact on literary criticism and 'philosophy of literature'; only subsequently was Derrida recognized as a remarkably original voice in philosophy and the history of philosophy.

His early work on HUSSERL, *Voice and Phenomenon* (1967), introduces most of his ideas concerning 'deconstruction'. These ideas centre on theories of signification, indication, ideality and sense or meaning generally; on the transcendental/empirical parallelism in metaphysics and epistemology since KANT; on theories of time and the 'spacing' of time; on the metaphysics of presence as analysed by Heidegger; on theories of intersubjectivity, alterity and *Lebensphilosophie* or 'philosophy of life'; and on the privileging of the voice and living speech in traditional philosophy, with the concomitant suppression of writing. The deconstructive strategy starts from the idea that the metaphysical, epistemological, ethical and logical systems of the past were constructed on the basis of conceptual oppositions such as transcendental/empirical, internal/external, original/derivative, good/evil, universal/particular. One of the terms in each binary set is privileged, the other suppressed or excluded. By analysing the denigrated or marginalized terms and the nature of their exclusion, deconstruction seeks to demonstrate that the preference for one term over its opposite is ultimately unjustifiable: the privileged term has meaning only in so far as it is contrasted with its ostensibly excluded opposite. In other words, the privileged term is constituted by what it suppresses, which will inevitably return to haunt it. Thus the privileged term never achieves perfect identity or conceptual purity; it is always parasitic on or contaminated by the 'marginalized' term. In *Of Grammatology* (1967) Derrida develops his understanding of the trace or *arché-writing* by deconstructing the dream of plenitude, proximity and perfect presence that dominates Western metaphysics. Important strands of his notion of trace arise from Freudian PSYCHO-ANALYSIS, LEVINAS'S 'trace of the Other', Heidegger's history of being, ROUSSEAU'S, SAUSSURE's and LÉVI-STRAUSS' condemnations of (but ultimate appeals to) writing, and NIETZSCHE's genealogy of differential force.

Derrida's deconstructionist readings of a number of important philosophers were quick to establish themselves as classics. See especially his work on PLATO ('Plato's Pharmacy', in *Dissemination*, 1972); on Kant ('Parergon', in *Truth in Painting*, 1978; '*Mochlos* – or The Conflict of the Faculties', 1980); on HEGEL ('The Pit and the Pyramid', in *Margins of Philosophy*, 1972; *Glas*, 1974); on FREUD ('Freud and the Scene of Writing', in *Writing and Difference*, 1967; *The Post Card*, 1980); on Nietzsche (*Spurs*, 1978; *Otobiographies*, 1984); on Heidegger ('The Ends of Man' and 'Ousia and Grammè', in *Margins*; 'The *Retrait* of Metaphor', 'Geschlecht I', 'Geschlecht II', in *Psyché*, 1987; *Of Spirit: Heidegger and the Question*, 1987); and on MARX (*Specters of Marx*, 1993). Interspersed with his readings of philosophers are essays and books on literary figures (e.g. Mallarmé, Joyce, Artaud, Bataille, Blanchot, Barthes, Celan, Jabès, Ponge), on political topics such as philosophical nationality and nationalism, apartheid, feminism, the Holocaust and nuclear disarmament, as well as works on law, education, art and architecture.

While it is impossible to summarize his work, one can nevertheless discern how the notion of the *trace* – which, Derrida insists, was always an affirmative idea, never a negative one – was transformed in later work on the future, on the promise of memory and on an affirmation that precedes all questioning.   [D.F.K.]

Descartes, René (1596–1650)
Descartes was born at La Haye, a small town in Touraine, France, and educated at the Jesuit college of La Flèche. He retained a lively admiration for his teachers, but was dissatisfied with the course of instruction, finding that for the most part it consisted of the transmission of the received opinions of the ancients, and that mathematics alone gave any certain knowledge. In 1618 he departed for Holland to serve as a soldier under Maurice of Nassau. The following year he was in Germany where he had dreams or visions which apparently revealed to him some fundamental part of his philosophy – most probably, the unity of mathematics and science. He did not at once set out to write works of philosophy or science, but travelled widely. In 1628 he wrote the *Rules for the Direction of the Understanding*, an unfinished work, not published in his lifetime, which sets out for the first time the rules of his 'method', which was to be a method of both science and philosophy.

In the same year he went again to Holland, where with brief interruptions he remained until 1649. In 1634 he had completed and was about to publish a treatise called *Le Monde*, when he heard of the condemnation of Galileo by the Inquisition for teaching, as did the treatise, the Copernican system, and he withdrew it from publication. In 1637, however, he published three short *Discourses* on physical and mathematical subjects, prefaced by the celebrated *Discourse on Method*. Besides being in other respects revolutionary, this was the first great philosophical work to be written in French, and created a style which became a model for the expression of abstract thought in that language. In 1640 he suffered a grievous blow from death, at the age of 5, of his illegitimate daughter Francine, for whom he cared deeply.

In 1641 he published his *Meditations on the First Philosophy*, together with six sets of Objections from various distinguished persons (including HOBBES and GASSENDI) to whom Descartes had submitted the work, and his *Replies to the Objections*; altogether these form one of the most important texts of Descartes' philosophy. He followed this in 1644 with the *Principles of Philosophy*, which contains besides other things his views on cosmology, cautiously set forth. This work was dedicated to Princess Elizabeth of Bohemia, a woman of intelligence and sensibility with whom Descartes was in correspondence.

In 1649 Descartes yielded, after much hesitation, to the requests of Queen Christina of Sweden that he should join the distinguished circle she had assembled in Stockholm, and should instruct her in philosophy; in this year he also published *The Passions of the Soul*. However, as a result of the Swedish climate and the severe régime demanded by the Queen, he caught pneumonia, and died in 1650.

Descartes' character has been the subject of much discussion and analysis: his exaggerated secrecy, which led him increasingly to disguise both his interests and his whereabouts, together with his ambiguous relations to the Church, have given rise to many hypotheses, of which perhaps the most fanciful is that he was a Rosicrucian. However, there is no real doubt that his Catholicism was sincere; he believed that his philosophy was in accordance with the faith and constituted the only way of reconciling it with the contemporary advances in natural knowledge. His principal aim was to avoid any prejudiced and hasty judgement of his views that would result in their being misguidedly suppressed. His attitude to his philosophy was self-confident, proud, almost visionary, and he did not underestimate his vocation as a solitary and privileged discoverer of the truth. However, he also enjoyed social life and had a number of distinguished and devoted friends, with whom he conducted an ample correspondence, which is happily preserved and is of the greatest interest.

1 *The Quest for Certainty.* Descartes was not only a metaphysician, or a philosopher in the modern sense; like many other 'philosophers' of the seventeenth century, he was also a natural scientist, with interests in such subjects as physics and physiology. Above all, he was a mathematician; the use of the term 'Cartesian co-ordinates' in analytical geometry commemorates his invention of such a system (even though in its present form this branch of mathematics owes more to the work, unpublished for many years, of Descartes' contemporary Fermat). Descartes' concern with mathematics, and his own contributions to its powers, above all as an instrument of science, profoundly influenced his philosophical system. In the first place, he believed that the essence of a natural science was the discovery of relationships which could be mathematically expressed; that all natural science must be capable of being unified under mathematics; and that the world, insofar as it can be scientifically explained, must be

of such a nature as to admit of mathematical treatment. Second, he thought that mathematics gave a paradigm of certain knowledge and the methods of acquiring it; hence he set himself to discover in what this certainty consisted, and to test all beliefs by the criterion of such certainty, by methods as clear and effective as those of mathematics.

The criterion of certainty which he was to apply to all received beliefs was expressed by Descartes in the rule – one of the celebrated rules of his 'method' – that we should accept only those beliefs that appear to us 'clearly and distinctly' to be true. By 'clarity and distinctness' he meant that kind of intrinsic self-evidence which he found to characterize the simplest propositions of mathematics and LOGIC – propositions which anyone could see to be true by the 'natural light' of reason. Such propositions Descartes also characterized as *indubitable*, in the sense of being not just very hard to doubt, but intrinsically incapable of being doubted; and it is as a search for the indubitable that Descartes' attempt to find certain knowledge takes its most characteristic form. He set himself to doubt anything that admitted of doubt, and to see whether anything was left over that was immune to this process. His application of this procedure of 'methodical doubt' is explained principally in the *Discourse on Method* and (in a strikingly dramatic form) in the *Meditations*.

He found that he could doubt many things generally considered very certain: for instance, the existence of physical objects around him. He reasoned that, although he felt very certain at a particular moment that he was seeing and feeling various physical objects, he had on many occasions felt just as certain of such things when later it had turned out that he had been dreaming, and all the things he had supposed to be around him had been illusions. How then could he be certain that the things apparently around him at this moment were not also illusions? He could even doubt that he himself had a body: his body was apparently one physical object among others, and it might be that this, too, was an illusion. What then could be immune to doubt? At least one thing – that he was doubting; for if he doubted this, it would still certainly be true that he was doubting. From this it followed that he could not doubt that he was thinking, for doubting was only a kind of thinking. Hence he had found at least one indubitable proposition: 'I am thinking'. From this, however, there followed another, 'I exist', for it was self-evident that nothing could think without existing. Thus Descartes could be certain of his own existence because he was thinking – a truth expressed in the famous Cartesian formula '*cogito, ergo sum*', 'I am thinking, therefore I exist'.

The expression 'I am thinking' in this formula is not, however, to be taken only in the narrow sense of 'I am doubting'. Although, principally in the *Discourse*, Descartes does approach the *cogito*, (as the formula is often called) by way of the impossibility of doubting that one is doubting, it is quite clear that more is established in the *cogito* than the one proposition 'I am doubting'. Under the term *cogitationes* (thoughts) Descartes includes a much wider range of what might be called 'private experiences', all of which he regards as indubitable and immediately evident to consciousness. For instance, although Descartes can doubt that there are objects around him and that he has a body, he cannot doubt, he holds, that at least he is having experiences as if such objects were there. The certain existence of such *cogitationes*, regarded merely as subjective experiences,

is recognized in the *cogito*; all the experiences of which he is in this way immediately aware are, Descartes reflects, in some sense *his*; and he must exist to have them.

But what is the manner of this existence? Descartes has seen that he can doubt that he has a body, but not that he exists so long as he is thinking; hence, he concludes, the 'I' that he has proved to exist is something whose essence is to think. Thus he has proved his existence as a '*res cogitans*' or 'thinking being'; or, as he also puts it with dubious justification, as a *substance* whose essential attribute is that of thought.

At this point Descartes turns naturally to the *content* of his thoughts. He finds that he has, among other ideas, the idea of a Perfect Being or God, and reflection on this idea leads him to the conclusion that there must be something outside himself corresponding to this idea – that God must exist in reality, not merely in our thoughts. Two lines of reflection lead him to this conclusion, both of them derived from scholastic or patristic sources. One is substantially the same as ANSELM's ONTOLOGICAL proof of the existence of God. The other relies on an application to the realm of ideas of the principle that the less cannot give rise to the greater. An idea of a perfect thing, Descartes argues, could not be brought into being by an imperfect agency. But he himself is imperfect, as is shown by his state of doubt, which is inferior to knowledge. Hence there must really be a Perfect Being, who is the origin of this idea. This argument is derived from AUGUSTINE; as indeed is the principle behind the *cogito*, that to doubt one's own existence is self-defeating or impossible.

Since he has established that a Perfect Being exists, Descartes has a warrant to reintroduce at least some of the beliefs which he had earlier eliminated as doubtful. For, he reasons, a Perfect Being would not allow him to be deceived to such an extent that he would naturally and systematically believe in such things as external objects if they really did not exist. Hence Descartes feels justified in accepting, though with reserve, some of the most basic beliefs of common sense. In particular, the proof of the existence of God introduces an idea of *permanence* hitherto lacking. The proof of Descartes' own existence in the *cogito* was, strictly speaking, only a proof that he existed so long as he was thinking; even though Descartes seems to have tried, illegitimately, to transcend this limitation already by speaking of himself as a thinking *substance*, that is, an enduring thing. The idea of God as a conserving principle may help to overcome this limitation. Again, Descartes sometimes says that it is only the existence of God that validates memory, and so *deduction*: a process which, unlike the instantaneous steps of *intuition*, presupposes the reliability of memory. Since, however, Descartes has already relied on deduction in his somewhat complex proofs of the existence of God, if not in the *cogito* itself (a much disputed point), there is a strong suspicion of a circular argument here.

Descartes is in further difficulties at this point. He must admit that we are sometimes deceived – this was the starting point of his whole inquiry. How is this fact to be reconciled with the existence, now proved, of a Perfect Being who would not deceive us? Descartes' answer is that the origin of our being deceived is our misuse of our will, of that freedom which also allows men to do moral evil in spite of God. This misuse of the will consists in an overhasty assent to propositions that are not really self-evident, and it

can affect even deductive reasonings – thus we make mistakes in mathematics. But if this is so, it may be objected, can we ever be sure that we have taken enough care, that our imperfect nature may not have led us into error? In particular, may not Descartes be mistaken about even the foundations of his philosophical system? Here Descartes merely asserts that God would not allow us to misuse our will to that extent; but this is hardly satisfactory, since the existence of God is itself one of the things proved in the system by reasonings to which these doubts apply. Here again, the argument seems circular. Accusations of circularity were frequently made against Descartes' system in his lifetime, and have been constantly discussed since.

2 Mind and Body. Among the physical objects which he now believes with some firmness to exist, Descartes finds one – what would normally be called his own body – which is in a peculiar relation to the mind, thinking substance, or, as he also calls it, soul, whose existence has been proved in the *cogito*. For one thing, his will can move this body immediately, unlike any other; for another, things that happen to this body affect the mind in peculiar ways; for instance, when this body is struck, pain is experienced, and when some sorts of desire are experienced, we know (as Descartes puts it, 'Nature teaches us') that the body has some need. These latter facts, in particular, mean that the soul is united to the body in a peculiarly intimate way. 'My soul is not in my body like a pilot in a ship' said Descartes, echoing Thomas AQUINAS; if it were, it would be able only to move the body, not also to feel 'through' it.

Ultimately, Descartes holds, the peculiar nature of this union cannot be explained. In this connection, he wrote to the Princess Elizabeth, there are three basic and unanalysable notions – the body, the soul and the union between them. Nevertheless, elsewhere Descartes attempts to explain at least some features of the union. In particular, he holds against much ancient and traditional opinion that the soul is not the principle of life of the body. The body is just a machine with its own internal economy and sources of energy, and 'it is not that the body dies because the soul leaves it, but that the soul leaves it because the body has died'. While the body is alive, however, a soul is joined to it in such a way that some of the movements of the body are produced by the soul, and some experiences of the soul are produced by changes in the body. In the *Passions of the Soul* Descartes suggests that there is in the body a physical place of this interaction, in the pineal gland at the base of the brain. This gland, he supposed, could be moved directly by the soul, and thus agitate the 'animal spirits' which, like many other seventeenth-century theorists, he believed to flow and to transmit movement to all parts of the body; in the opposite direction, changes in the animal spirits induced by stimuli to the body could move the gland and thus affect the soul.

This naïve causal account of the relations of soul and body was thought unsatisfactory even by many Cartesians. The OCCASIONALISM of MALEBRANCHE, and, in one of its many applications, the 'pre-established harmony' of LEIBNIZ were other seventeenth-century attempts to solve the problem. Descartes held that the problem arose only in the case of human beings. In the case of animals, he seems to have thought that all their movements were produced by purely mechanical causes in a system of stimulus and response, and that they were accordingly

merely machines, having in the proper sense no souls. However, Descartes is not always consistent on this issue, which raises important problems about his concept of consciousness. The problem of the union of soul and body is central to Descartes' metaphysics. In his view, which is the classical expression of dualism, there are in the realm of created beings only two fundamentally different sorts of substances or existing things: 'thinking' and 'extended' substances, souls and matter. This dualistic view was the heart of Descartes' attempt to reconcile the Catholic faith and the advances of seventeenth-century science. Although there was some causal interaction between souls and bodies, he thought that he had sufficiently isolated souls from the realm of extension, which alone was subject to the mechanical laws which science was developing. Natural science, he believed, could ultimately complete a deductive theory of all mechanical changes in extended nature, and so of all physical events, since every physical event must be only a change of motion in extension: these would include all movements of human bodies which were not the product of FREE-WILL, but free-will and the soul itself would remain essentially outside the reach of the scientific laws.

Apart from the difficulties already mentioned concerning the relations of soul and body, one notable problem about Descartes' dualism is the question of the number of each type of substance. It is clear that on Descartes' view there can be an infinite number of thinking substances or souls. The case is different, however, with extended substance: Descartes seems to have held, in effect, that there could be only *one* extended substance, which constituted all of mechanical nature. This substance could be more or less dense, but not discontinuous: Descartes holds that the notion of absolutely empty space is unintelligible, and that a vacuum cannot exist. Influenced by a purely geometrical concept of extension, he in fact equates extended matter and space and is faced in consequence with many difficulties, particularly in his theory of motion. These views were effectively attacked by Leibniz, as was Descartes' related belief that the quantity of motion in the universe remains always constant.

3 *Natural Science.* The only essential property of matter, on the Cartesian view, is extension. The idea of extension is, like the idea of God and the fundamental ideas of mathematics, innate; by 'innate' ideas Descartes means A PRIORI notions which the mind can find in itself alone and which it does not derive from experience. Moreover, we can form clear and distinct ideas of other qualities which can belong to physical objects, namely size, shape, motion, position, duration and number: all these are 'modes' of extension. Since we can conceive these qualities clearly and distinctly, we know a priori that it is possible that there should be in reality physical objects possessing them. However, we in fact have more than the mere innate idea of these qualities as possible attributes of physical objects; we also have what Descartes calls 'adventitious ideas' – that is, ideas formed in our minds without our willing them, and apparently caused by some outside source – of objects around us actually possessing these qualities. Since God is no deceiver, we have good reason to think that such objects actually exist.

The objects around us appear to have other qualities besides these, as we also have sensations of such things as colours, sounds, odours, tastes, degrees of hardness etc. About these qualities (often called in the seventeenth century, 'secondary' qualities, as opposed to 'primary' ones), Descartes holds that we can have little certainty. The ideas of them are confused and unclear, and while he thinks that the goodness of God makes it probable that there are in the physical objects real differences corresponding to the differences of these various sensations, he finds unintelligible the notion that these various qualities as given to sensation actually exist in the objects. Thus Descartes, although he does not commit himself firmly on the point, leans towards the view found in LOCKE and others, that primary qualities exist in objects, but secondary qualities, as we perceive them, do not. He shares with Locke the representative theory of perception that goes with such a view. He differs from Locke, however, both in the exact list he gives of primary qualities, and in holding that, although we have ideas of sensation, none of our knowledge of physical objects really comes from sensation. Sensation can give us only unclear and confused ideas, and we understand physical reality only by an act of the intellect, through the ideas of extension and its modes, which can be made clear and distinct.

Descartes' conception of a complete natural science, consonant with his other views, is of an entirely deductive system derived from self-evident a priori premises. These premises were ultimately of a philosophical or metaphysical character. Metaphysics and science are for him fundamentally one, and in his *Principles* he indeed attempts to derive the first principles of his science from reflection on the nature of God. Every physical event, including changes in the human body, was governed by the same physical laws – thus medicine, ultimately, must be part of the one physical science. All the sciences were one with physics, and physics one with philosophy, a state of affairs which Descartes pictured in his description of the Tree of Knowledge, of which the roots were metaphysics, the trunk physics, and the branches the other sciences. This science Descartes expected to be of not merely theoretical interest. In common with his older contemporary, Francis BACON, he frequently emphasizes the practical benefits to be expected from the scientific study of nature; in particular he hoped that the study of physiology might enable man to discover the causes of senescence and thus to prolong life.

Despite the entirely a priori character of the science which he imagined, Descartes admitted, from the beginning, and increasingly after discouraging experience, that experiments were necessary to the discovery of physical truths, and he himself engaged in many experiments, for example in physiology and optics. The need for these experiments and their function are not entirely clear, granted the nature of his system and its a priori claims, and his interpreters have found many problems in his various and not entirely consistent accounts of this matter.

4 *Historical Influence.* The influence of Descartes on the history of philosophy has probably been greater than that of any other thinker, with the exception of ARISTOTLE. It extended far beyond the Cartesians, such as Malebranche who adopted many of his views, or even the other RATIONALISTS, who agreed with much of his general account of the nature of philosophy and science. In particular, the British EMPIRICISTS, who rejected almost all his conclusions, were so profoundly affected by his approach that the eighteenth-century Scots philosopher REID stated not so much a paradox as the truth in writing that Malebranche,

Locke, BERKELEY and HUME shared a common 'system of the human understanding' which 'may still be called the Cartesian system'. The same influence, in various forms, has continued to the present day.

What influenced all these philosophers was the most revolutionary element in Descartes' thought, his placing at the centre of philosophy the EPISTEMOLOGICAL question 'how do I know...?' Descartes was effectively the first to try to abandon the impersonal 'God's eye view' of the world common to earlier philosophers, and to ask, not just what the world is like, but how one could know what the world is like. Descartes also transmitted to his successors the view that there could be only one valid method of answering these questions, the method of starting from the immediate data of consciousness, which alone were indubitable, and attempting to 'work out' from them to an external world. Descartes himself attempted to do this by appealing to the existence and nature of God. His arguments here represent some of the most traditional elements in his thought; when these were called in question, not just in detail but in principle, other philosophers were left with the task of constructing an external world from the immediate data of consciousness without such transcendental aids.

Thus the philosophy of Descartes, which is itself a transcendental religious metaphysics as well as a philosophy of the New Science, contained the seeds of the empiricism and subjective idealism that came later. It is perhaps only in very recent years that philosophers have determinedly called in question the fundamental Cartesian principle which underlies these systems, that there are immediate data of consciousness, more certain than anything else, from which philosophy must start in its search for knowledge.   (B.A.O.W.)

Determinism Determinism is, roughly, the thesis that any event whatsoever is an instance of some law of nature. It is usually stated in the form: 'every event has a cause', or 'nature is uniform'; a famous and very graphic formulation by Pierre Laplace (1749–1827) is that given complete knowledge of the state of the universe at some time it is in principle possible to predict all the subsequent history of the universe. The thesis cannot be proved or disproved; we cannot prove it since to do so would require a deterministic explanation of the totality of events; we cannot disprove it since any failure to find a deterministic explanation of an event can always be regarded as a temporary lacuna in scientific knowledge. The famous problem of the justification of INDUCTION can be stated in the form: science presupposes the principle of determinism, and if this principle is unprovable then science rests on unprovable presuppositions. HUME was responsible for the classic statement of this problem, to which philosophers have never found an agreed solution. It appears, however, that the deterministic hypothesis has been abandoned in some fundamental physical inquiries in which statistical laws are sought regarding events for which, taken singly, no deterministic explanation is sought. For this and other reasons it is often suggested that the principle of determinism should not be regarded as a true or false statement but as a methodological principle which may or may not be used in a scientific investigation (see QUANTUM MECHANICS).

Frequently, however, determinism is understood to involve the thesis that the will is not free, that choice is illusory and that how we act is determined. There are philosophers who accept the principle of determinism but regard it as compatible with FREEDOM OF THE WILL, but it would

he misleading to describe them as determinists. The principle of indeterminacy in physics can be thought to provide a solution to the problem of the freedom of the will only at the cost of confused thinking, for there is no way of basing human responsibility on the impossibility of simultaneously determining the position and momentum of elementary particles. (J.O.U.)

Dewey, John (1859–1952) American philosopher who was guided by the idea that philosophy is a thoroughly human undertaking which must be judged in terms of its social or cultural impact. Dewey was an uncompromising naturalist with a vigorous distrust of anything that smacked of the esoteric. Philosophizing is a mode of human behaviour arising in certain contexts rather than others; and it should be judged in terms of its capacity to meet the challenge of the very conditions which give rise to it. One can say that Dewey replaced the problem of truth with the problem of value: instead of asking 'what conclusion is true?' he tended to ask 'what conclusion, considering the conditions of the problem which gives rise to our thinking at all, is the one we *ought* to come out with?'

Dewey was strongly influenced by C. S. PEIRCE's contention that all thought is a movement from a doubtful to a settled situation of belief. Thinking (or intellection) is a form of activity engaged in by a human biological organism whenever habitual patterns of action are disrupted. Its function is described by Dewey in five stages. (1) Given the breakdown of habit, the organism nonetheless presses on to further action; when overt action is thwarted, it resorts to 'suggestions'. (2) 'Intellectualization' takes place as the problem is formulated as one to be solved. (3) The next step is the imaginative construction of 'hypotheses' which might serve as guides in the actual search for an answer. (4) 'Reasoning' consists in deducing from a hypothesis the actual differences it would make in the course of experience. (5) Experiment itself, or 'testing', is the action (overt or imaginative) of checking the differences of fact entailed by the hypothesis.

In his earlier writings Dewey, following William JAMES, described his position as a view of the meaning of truth. He tended to say that what we mean by 'true' is contained in a description of the criteria to be satisfied by any 'proper' end result of the process just described. Such a description would provide the full import of Dewey's notorious remark that 'the true is that which works'. Nonetheless, under vigorous attack (especially from Bertrand RUSSELL), Dewey's approach changed significantly. Russell argued that one must carefully distinguish the meaning of truth from the *criteria* we apply in establishing its presence. Thus, in order to establish that 'Caesar crossed the Rubicon' is true, I must no doubt engage in research to establish that, when adopted as a hypothesis, the proposition 'works'. But what I *mean* in calling it true is that it 'corresponds' with what actually took place many years ago. Dewey's concern was with the conditions under which the hypotheses we adopt are *warrantedly assertible*. It was those conditions which must guide our judgements, not esoteric notions about truth by correspondence. Russell's response was that, difficult as it is, the notion of truth by correspondence cannot be avoided, and that Dewey, while ostentatiously ushering it out of the front door, surreptitiously lets it back through the windows.

For Dewey the first task of ETHICS is to understand the nature of the biological organisms whose conjoint behaviour constitutes the social context. The second is to understand the kinds of problem-situation which give rise to our efforts to distinguish good conduct from bad. Dewey stated the main outlines of his moral theory in a book significantly entitled *Human Nature and Conduct* (1922). Human nature is analysed in terms of three key concepts: impulse, habit and intelligence. The dynamic character of the human organism is expressed in the concept of impulse; habits in turn are relatively stable patterns of activity resulting from the constant interplay of impulse from within and social pressures from without; and intelligence is the form of activity whereby an organism whose habits are frustrated or upset seeks to reinstate action. Thus, degree of intelligence will be judged in terms of the degree of permanence with which action is reinstated relative to the problem by which action was thwarted in the first place.

This conclusion is now used as a clue to the moral philosopher's search for human goodness. Dewey proposes the following definition: 'Good consists in the meaning that is experienced to belong to an activity when conflict and entanglement of various incompatible impulses and habits terminate in a unified orderly release in action.' In short, we ask the question 'what is good?' only relative to a general type of problem-situation. Societies, like individuals, are dynamic and active. Like individuals they develop habits which break down under pressures and strains. Thus the role of intelligence at the social level is comparable to the role of intelligence at the level of individual action. Societies must seek to establish patterns of activity stable enough to resist shock; and every course of action must be judged according to its degree of success in removing the conditions of breakdown. Dewey had no respect for those who approach problems 'from the top down'. It seemed to him that political philosophy had for too long sought the justification of courses of action in elaborate metaphysical doctrines. Social science should tackle concrete problems by running through the five stages of intelligent activity. It should run the risk of bold hypothesis and tackle the task of checking every hypothesis against the evidence.

Dewey's philosophy of education is an integral part of his general social philosophy. Education should be based upon the premise that all genuine thought grows out of real problem-situations. If education is to proceed 'from the bottom up' it will adjust itself to real problems felt by the child, and will educate it by training it to invent hypotheses, think out their consequences, and test them in actual practice. The emphasis is on what the child feels as a real problem in contrast to what the teacher preconceives as gospel.

Dewey attacked METAPHYSICS on two rather different grounds. The first is that metaphysical thinking really makes no difference at all to humanity's intelligent control of nature. The second is that metaphysical thinking makes a very great deal of difference – for the worse. It is said to block inquiry, to make philosophy dogmatic and stagnant, and to close our minds to possibilities inherent in natural science. Dewey attacked RELIGION on both these grounds, and they may very well be compatible. But Dewey was not an iconoclast, and he coupled his attacks on religion with a positive claim that his way alone would lead to a release of the religious energies of mankind. 'If I have said anything about religions and religion that seems harsh,' he wrote, 'I have said those things because of a firm belief that the claim on the part of religions to possess a monopoly of ideals … stands in the way of

the realisation of distinctively religious values inherent in natural experience… The opposition between religious values as I conceive them and religions is not to be bridged. Just because the release of these values is so important, their identification with the creeds and cults of religions must be dissolved.'   (J.W.S.)

Dialectic   The word 'dialectic' comes from the Greek verb meaning 'to converse', and originally meant 'the art of conversation, discussion or debate'. ARISTOTLE, in saying dialectic was invented by ZENO of Elea, was presumably referring to Zeno's paradoxes, which refuted certain hypotheses by drawing unacceptable consequences from them. But it was first applied generally by SOCRATES, who, as presented in the earlier dialogues of Plato, constantly practised two techniques, both hypothetical in form: refuting his opponents' statement by getting them to accept as an ultimate consequence of it a statement contradicting it (*elenchus*), and leading them on to a generalization by getting them to accept its truth in a series of instances (*epagoge*, translated 'induction').

PLATO himself regarded dialectic as the supreme philosophical method, 'the coping-stone of the sciences', and it was to be the final stage in the formal education of his philosopher-kings. But his references to dialectic, though always laudatory, are often vague, and his conception of it may have changed over time. Sometimes it was treated as the method of refuting hypotheses, and in his later work it included the method of 'division' of a genus into species, one of which was then divided in its turn, and so on as long as repetition was possible. Almost any form of non-specialized abstract reasoning could be described as dialectic, but it seems always to have involved the search for unchanging essences – above all, the idea of the Good.

Dialectic was put on a sound footing for the first time in Aristotle's *Topics*, a manual for finding arguments for or against given 'theses' or positions, such as the claim that 'every pleasure is good'. Such theses were probably debated in Plato's ACADEMY, and Aristotle sought to provide general methods for dealing with them. In the process he discovered many basic principles of formal LOGIC, which was developed in the *Analytics* into a theory of 'demonstration', in contrast with 'dialectic', which was restricted to reasoning from mere opinions. Amongst STOIC logicians, however, and in MEDIEVAL PHILOSOPHY, formal logic itself came to be called 'dialectic'.

One descendant of the debates in the Academy was the medieval disputation, in which the contestants continued, mainly by syllogistic reasoning, to maintain both theses and 'antitheses' (their opposites). It was by means of such disputations that candidates in medieval universities were examined for degrees. HEGEL gave a new turn to dialectic, which he regarded as a process at work not only in reasoning, but also on history, and in the universe as a whole. The Hegelian dialectic (sometimes described as a movement from thesis to antithesis, and then to a synthesis of the two) influenced MARX and was taken over by ENGELS to become part of the philosophy of DIALECTICAL MATERIALISM. (R.HALL)

Dialectical Materialism According to some authorities, Dialectical Materialism is the 'philosophical basis' of Marxism. Its origins can be traced back to 1845, when MARX and ENGELS wrote a bulky manuscript intended to reveal that the 'Young Hegelians' (especially FEUERBACH, Bauer and Stirner) were merely second-rate copies of the French IDEOLOGISTS. They were sheep in wolves' clothing: they pretended to be 'revolutionary philosophers' but 'their bleating merely imitates in a philosophic form the conceptions of the German middle class'. Marx and Engels declared that real revolutionaries must replace this 'idealist outlook' with 'materialism'; they should 'set out from real active human beings' instead of pretending to 'descend from heaven to earth'. The manuscript, entitled *The German Ideology*, was left, as Marx put it, 'to the gnawing criticism of mice': Part One was eventually published in 1926; the rest in 1932.

In the 1870s, the German reformist socialist Eugen Dühring (1833–71) brought out several books purporting to derive a policy of class cooperation within the nation-state from a materialistic philosophy of nature and history. Dühring denounced Marx for 'performing dialectical miracles for his faithful followers' and attacked 'dialectics' as a whole, by which he meant the supposedly Hegelian claim that 'contradiction is objectively present not in thought...but in things and processes themselves and can be met with in so to speak corporeal form'.

Engels responded to this attack in *Anti-Dühring* (1878), arguing that the idea that reality is 'contradiction-free' is valid only 'so long as we consider things as at rest and lifeless, each one by itself, alongside and after each other'. Drawing on a wide acquaintance with the natural sciences, Engels argued that motion and life could never be understood from this 'mechanistic' and 'metaphysical' point of view, and that dialectical contradictions really do exist in the objective natural world. He gave a lucid restatement of this position in *Ludwig Feuerbach and the End of Classical German Philosophy* (1886), where he argued that in reacting against HEGEL'S idealism, Feuerbach had simply reverted to pre-Hegelian, mechanical materialism: he had continued to regard philosophy as 'an impassable barrier, an unassailable holy thing'; hence, 'as a philosopher, he stopped half way: the lower half of him was materialist, the upper half idealist'. It was Marx alone (Engels said self-effacingly) who had seen the way forward: whilst opting for materialism back in the 1840s, he had retained Hegel's 'dialectical method'. In this way 'the revolutionary side of Hegel's philosophy was taken up again but freed from the idealist trammels which, in Hegel's hands, had prevented its consistent execution'. Unlike the Hegelians, Marx had put matter first; but unlike the 'mechanical materialists' he did not think of matter in terms of '*things*, as given, as fixed, as stable' but in terms of 'dialectical processes', driven by 'real contradictions'. This provided Marx with a philosophical outlook on nature as a whole, and also on society as a part of nature.

Engels' vivid account of the place of Marxism in the history of philosophy had a wide appeal in the international socialist movement. It corresponded to some of the ideas already being propagated by the German worker-philosopher Joseph Dietzgen (1828–88); and in 1892 the Russian revolutionary Georg Plekhanov (1856–1918), perhaps following Dietzgen, invented the name under which it was to become famous: 'dialectical materialism'. In 1909, LENIN asserted boldly, and quite falsely, that 'Marx and Engels scores of times termed their philosophical views dialectical materialism'.

The textual basis for 'dialectical materialism' was extended in 1925 with the publication of some fragments and drafts of a work on *The Dialectics of Nature* which Engels had left unfinished at his death. This codified dialectics into three 'laws' which were said to have been 'abstracted' from the 'history of nature and human society'. These were '1) the law of the transformation of quantity into quality and vice-versa; 2) the law of the interpenetration of opposites; and 3) the law of the negation of the negation'. With the help of this formula, dialectical materialism was taken up as part of the propaganda of the Third International, achieving its most forceful statement in Stalin's chapter on 'Dialectical and Historical Materialism' in the *History of the CPSU(B)* (1938). This made a sharp and influential distinction between 'dialectical materialism', which was the Marxist philosophy of nature, and 'historical materialism', which was 'the application of dialectical materialism to society and history'. In this form, and as elaborated by Mao, dialectical materialism became the best-known philosophical doctrine the world has ever seen – though perhaps not the most intelligent.

Dialectical materialism has offered a tempting target for philosophical critics of Marxism (such as POPPER) who have questioned, in particular, whether 'dialectical contradictions' (as distinct from clashes of forces) can coherently be attributed to inanimate natural processes, particularly if these are interpreted materialistically. However, its credentials as the authentic 'philosophical basis' of Marxism are themselves very questionable, and it is doubtful whether Marx's own theoretical achievements presuppose dialectical materialism in any way. Throughout the twentieth century, many of the most vital Marxist philosophers (LUKÁCS, the members of the FRANKFURT SCHOOL, GRAMSCI and SARTRE, for instance) were more or less explicitly hostile to dialectical materialism. For them, the live philosophical issues in Marxist theory were ALIENATION, IDEOLOGY and art; the nature of freedom, practice and labour; and the changing relations between society and nature, none of which has any place on the philosophical agenda of orthodox dialectical materialism. Their interpretation of Marxist philosophy often implies, moreover, that the very idea that knowledge stands in need of a 'philosophical basis' is 'idealistic'; which suggests that 'dialectical materialism' may itself be a form of 'German Ideology'. [J.R.]

Diderot, Denis (1713–84) A cutler's son, born at Langres, France, Diderot received his schooling at the Jesuit College of Louis-le-Grand in Paris. He was a natural choice as an editor of the *Encyclopédie* (see ENCYCLOPEDISTS), and became sole editor following d'Alembert's withdrawal as co-editor in 1757. From 1747 till the appearance of the seventeenth and final volume in 1765, he wrote numerous articles on philosophy, religion, political theory and literature, taking particular interest in the sections on trade and applied science, and editing the articles of the other contributors. This achievement alone would have established his reputation. The philosophy of Diderot is found in *Philosophical Thoughts* (1746); *Letter on the Blind* (1749); *Thoughts on the Interpretation of Nature* (1754); and in works of fiction such as *D'Alembert's Dream* (1769). Following LOCKE, Diderot was a convinced empiricist, accepted scientific 'facts' and rejected all metaphysical systems, especially Christian revelation, and the Church's claim to dominate the mind. (F.A.T.)

Dilthey, Wilhelm (1833–1911) The German philosopher and historian Wilhelm Dilthey is best known for his writings on the theories of history and the human sciences, though he also had a

significant influence on the development of HERMENEUTICS and PHENOMENOLOGY, literary criticism and the methodology of the social sciences. Viewing his overall philosophical task as a Critique of Historical Reason, Dilthey sought an epistemological grounding for the human sciences (*Geisteswissenschaften*, which include the humanities as well as the social sciences).

Dilthey's delimitation of the natural and human sciences is set forth in his landmark work, *Introduction to the Human Sciences* (1883), and subsequently elaborated in the 'Ideas Concerning a Descriptive and Analytic Psychology' (1894). The natural and the human sciences are both empirical, but the former deal with the outer experience of nature, while the latter are based on inner, 'lived' experience which provides a direct awareness of the human historical world. The distinction is ultimately epistemological, and the difference between their tasks is characterized as that between explanation and understanding. The natural sciences seek causal explanations of nature – connecting the discrete representations of outer experience through hypothetical generalizations and abstract laws. The human sciences aim at an understanding (*Verstehen*) that articulates the fundamental structures of life given in lived experience. Finding lived experience to be inherently connected and meaningful, Dilthey opposed traditional atomistic and associationist psychologies and developed a descriptive psychology that HUSSERL recognized as anticipating phenomenological psychology.

Although Dilthey first thought that descriptive psychology could provide a neutral foundation for the other human sciences, in his later hermeneutical writings he rejected the idea of a foundational discipline or method. In the *Formation of* the *Historical World in the Human Sciences* (1910), he claims that all the human sciences are interpretive and mutually dependent. Hermeneutically conceived, understanding is a process of interpreting the 'objectifications of life', the external expressions or manifestations of human activity and spirit. The understanding of others is attained through these common objectifications and not, as is widely thought, through empathy. Moreover, to fully understand myself I must observe the expressions of my life in the same way that I observe the expressions of others.

Whereas the natural sciences aim at ever more comprehensive generalizations, the human sciences place an equal value on the understanding of individuality and universality. Dilthey regards individuals as points of intersection of the general social and cultural systems in which they participate. Any psychological contribution to the understanding of human life and its expressions must be integrated into this more public framework. Although universal laws of history are rejected, the more systematic human sciences (e.g. economics, sociology) can establish uniformities limited to specific systems.

In his philosophy of life, Dilthey defined life as the nexus of all that is real. He focused on value, meaning and purpose as three of the principal categories of life, but maintained that there is an indeterminate number of categories available for reflection on life in general. Such reflection receives its fullest expression in a *Weltanschauung* (world-view), an overall perspective on life encompassing the way we perceive the world, evaluate and respond to it. Dilthey distinguished three recurrent types of world-view in Western philosophy, religion and art: naturalism (e.g. HUME), the idealism of

freedom (e.g. KANT) and objective idealism (e. g. HEGEL).   [R.A.M.]

Diogenes of Apollonia   See PRE-SOCRATICS.

Diogenes of Sinope   Known as 'the Cynic', Diogenes lived in Greece in the fourth century BC. A prominent citizen of Sinope, he was exiled about the middle of the century, allegedly for defacing its currency; thereafter he lived at Athens and Corinth, becoming the prototype of CYNICISM. It is likely that he was influenced by ANTISTHENES, though Antisthenes was probably dead before Diogenes reached Athens. There is thus a tenuous thread leading back to SOCRATES, and there is some point in the remark attributed to PLATO, that Diogenes was a Socrates gone mad.

Virtue, which alone produced happiness, was achieved through self-sufficiency, which was attained by freedom from all external restriction (family or public) and internal disturbance (desires, emotions or fears). By rejecting property, external goods, and conventional values, one could reduce one's needs and vulnerability to the barest natural minimum, retaining mastery of the one realm which could never be taken away – one's own soul. The aim was to live in accordance with nature; everything else was worthless convention, against which virtue must wage uncompromising warfare. In his life and teaching Diogenes sought to deface the currency of convention, as he and his father had defaced the debased currency at Sinope. This ethic required continual practice, both physical and mental: Diogenes would, for example, embrace a bronze statue in winter to train his body in hardship and combat physical desire, and he would court insults to test his mastery of his emotions. Endurance of hardship was in any case a necessary concomitant of the stark poverty of the Cynic way of life, illustrated by Diogenes' own existence as a stateless beggar in Athens, sleeping wherever he could. He despised theoretical education, convention, authority and decency: hence his nickname, the Dog, from which, in Greek, came the word 'Cynicism'. He is unreliably credited with some written works, notably *Republic* and some tragedies.   (I.G.K.)

Diogenes Laertius   At the beginning of the third century AD, Diogenes Laertius compiled a baggy collection of *Lives of the Philosophers* which, despite its flamboyant unreliablity, was for hundreds of years an unrivalled source of information about ancient Greek philosophy. He had a pronounced taste for gossip and folly, and the cumulative effect of his tales is comic rather than edifying. Take CHRISYPPUS, for example, who died of a fit of laughter brought on by one of his own feeble jokes; or Epimenides, who 'became famous throughout Greece' after taking a nap which lasted fifty seven years; or HERACLITUS, who tried to cure himself of dropsy by plastering himself with cowdung, only to be eaten alive by dogs who mistook him for a succulent meat roll. Diogenes' disrespectful frivolity has been deplored by all serious philosophers and by earnest practitioners of the HISTORY OF PHILOSOPHY; but it has endeared him to multi-faceted ironists like NIETZSCHE and KIERKEGAARD.   {J.R.}

Dogmatism   The opposite of SCEPTICISM.

Dualism   'Dualism' is the name for any system of thought which divides everything in some way into two categories or elements, or else derives everything from two principles, or else refuses to admit more or fewer than two substances or two kinds of substance. Although of course dualistic systems have to be justified by arguments, what leads some philosophers to dualism is the urge to tidy up and simplify our picture of the world, an urge which would drive them to MONISM if they were not prevented by respect for some radical and irreducible difference which their dualism expresses. The PYTHAGOREANS afford an early example of this blockage of the unifying tendency, in their case by a whole series of opposites, which they reduced in turn to two basic principles, the Limit and the Unlimited.

The term, which was coined in about 1700 to cover such theological views as MANICHEISM, has the same ambiguities as monism, and can likewise be applied to at least three distinguishable and logically independent ontological views. The most outstanding and influential example of dualism, giving precise formulation to what is probably the commonsense view, and going back at least to ANAXAGORAS, is DESCARTES' division of the world into 'extended substance' (matter) and 'thinking substances' (minds); this kind of dualism might be called *attributive*, as claiming that there are two kinds of attributes and thus that all substances are of just two ultimate kinds. This distinguishes it from *substantial* dualism, the view that there are precisely two substances, which does not *by itself* have the same psychological attractiveness: for once it is accepted that there is more than one substance, it seems arbitrary not to admit several, unless the two are of fundamentally different kinds. For the same reason, a third possibility, a *partial* dualism, claiming that regardless of the number of ultimate kinds of substance some one kind has just two substances belonging to it, is unattractive. It was in fact rejected by Descartes, who allowed only one substance in the material realm, but in the mental realm a plurality of them.

The term 'dualism' can also be applied rather more loosely to philosophical systems which have as their core some important opposition, as in PLATO between the world perceived by the senses and the world of Forms known by the mind, or in KANT the distinction between the phenomenal and noumenal world. See also MIND, PHILOSOPHY OF MIND, SUBSTANCE. (R.HALL)

Duhem, Pierre (1861–1916) French philosopher of science. Duhem was one of the outstanding French theoretical physicists of his generation on account of his austere and rigorous analysis of thermodynamics. He also established himself as a leading historian of science in a series of monumental investigations of the mechanics, astronomy and physics of medieval and renaissance precursors of 'the scientific revolution'. But it is chiefly because of his book *The Aim and Structure of Physical Theory* (1906) that he is still discussed in the PHILOSOPHY OF SCIENCE. As a young student he was at first attracted by the idea of science discovering real mechanisms hidden behind phenomena, but this ambition was severely battered by his later teachers and he began instead to pursue the Newtonian ideal of inferring laws by induction from experiment. However when Duhem came to teach he found it impossible to sustain this approach and was driven to adopt the POSITIVIST and conventionalist stance which characterizes his mature thought. This implied that no metaphysical conclusions can be derived from physics; but, as an orthodox Catholic, Duhem maintained a philosophically REALIST view of theology. He gives his name to the 'Duhem–Quine argument' according to which no scientific hypothesis can ever be conclusively refuted, since one can always adjust other hypotheses to protect it. [J.H.P.]

Dummett, Michael (1925–) English philosopher of mathematics, based in Oxford. He regards the construction of a systematic theory of meaning as the main task of philosophy, if not the sole legitimate one, and takes his inspiration from FREGE. However, he rejects Frege's central belief that mathematical and logical rationality presupposes a 'platonic' REALISM; see ANALYTIC PHILOSOPHY. Dummett's works include *Frege: Philosophy of Language*, 1973; second edition 1981, and *The Interpretation of Frege's Philosophy*, 1981, as well as the article on Frege in this Encyclopedia. [J.R.]

E

Edwards, Jonathan (1703–58)
Jonathan Edwards was born in South Windsor, Connecticut, and is now recognized as one of America's most brilliant and original philosophers. He stood midway between the Calvinist theology of the seventeenth century and the Lockean EMPIRICISM of the eighteenth century. In his own time the significance of his major writings was missed on both sides. For close to two centuries his reputation was confined to theology and distorted by a failure to appreciate his central philosophical intent.

The traditional view of Edwards was that in early life he showed great promise as a philosopher steeped in the writings and the spirit of NEWTON and LOCKE; but that when he became a minister he sought to revive the fundamental axioms of Calvinism, and must therefore be considered an 'anachronism' who smothered his latent philosophical promise with hellfire sermons and esoteric treatises which sought to justify them. A proper understanding of Edwards will recognize that his mature writings are careful and brilliant attempts to defend and reinterpret the fundamental axioms of Calvinism in terms of that a profound grasp of the spirit of Newton and Locke. However, his subtle revision of Calvinism made him unpopular among the defenders of the orthodoxy he was trying to save; while his use of the new philosophy to defend religious orthodoxy made him anathema to run-of-the-mill proponents of secularism and 'Enlightenment'. But his writings show a deeper understanding of the new philosophical insights than do the commonly adulated works of later Americans such as Franklin and Paine.

Each of his three major works was designed to reinterpret a fundamental Calvinist axiom in the light of Newton and Locke. The axiom of determinism is defended in the classic treatise on *Freedom of the Will* (1754), while the axiom of depravity is defended in the brilliant revisionary work on the *Nature of True Virtue* (1765), whose argument rests on a Lockean psychological analysis, without any appeal to theological matters such as the story of the Fall of Man. The central Calvinist axiom of God's omnipotence and inscrutability is taken up in the treatise on *Religious Affections* (1746), with its forward-looking defence of the emotive basis of religious experience. Most eighteenth-century thinkers made the mistake of proclaiming an 'argument from design' as the touchstone of empiricism in religion; Edwards however saw clearly that the only consistent way to pursue religious empiricism is to endorse mysticism. His defence of the thesis that mystical experiences are always essentially emotive is an astonishing foreshadowing of William JAMES' monumental *Varieties of Religious Experience* two centuries later.
(J.W.S.)

Eleatics   Elea was a Greek colony in southern Italy, and the home of PARMENIDES and his follower ZENO, who held that reality must be single and unchanging, and by implication that the plural sense-world is illusory. Also counted as an Eleatic, because he accepted these views, was Melissus of Samos (flourished *c.*440 BC) who amended Parmenides by arguing that Being was infinite, not finite and incorporeal. He also produced an explicit argument against sensation: we perceive plurality, yet also perceive that things change, which on Eleatic premises is logically impossible; therefore perception is false, and if there are many they must be of the same kind as the Eleatic One. This conclusion may have aided LEUCIPPUS in his conception of ATOMISM. XENOPHANES, too, was often regarded in antiquity as an Eleatic, because of the superficial resemblance of his one God to Parmenides' one Being; but in fact Parmenides' logical process of inference is radically different from Xenophanes' reversal of Homeric anthropomorphism. Parmenides and the other Eleatics had a profound effect on the development of PRE-SOCRATIC thought. The material MONISM of the Milesians and the structural monism of HERACLITUS were replaced by systems that envisaged a plurality of essentially immutable elements, and which now had to face the question of the validity of sensation.   (G.S.K.)

Emerson, Ralph Waldo (1803–82) American romantic thinker, who was inspired by German idealism to seek spirituality not in the supernatural but in what is 'common', 'low' and 'casual'. His works include *Nature* (1836) and *Essays* (1841–4) whose vision of a 'new degree of culture' that would 'revolutionise the entire system of human pursuits' enthralled the young NIETZSCHE. See also AMERICAN PHILOSOPHY.

Emotivism   Emotivism is the doctrine, associated chiefly with LOGICAL POSITIVISM, that value judgements in general, and ethical judgements in particular, express emotions rather than representing facts; see also EMPIRICISM, ETHICS.

Empedocles   Greek philosopher, physician and democrat from Acragas in Sicily, who flourished *c*.450 BC. His mystical claims (e.g. that he was a god, having previously been 'a boy, a girl, a bush and a bird and a dumb fish in the sea') gave rise to extravagant biographical inventions. To meet PARMENIDES' dilemma he claimed in his physical poem 'On Nature' that apparent coming-to-be and perishing were caused by the mixture and separation of eternally existing 'roots' or elements – fire, water, earth and air (whose corporeality he verified by observation). Attraction and repulsion of the roots were caused by specific motive agents, Love and Strife, which also possessed size and bulk. An equivalent to Parmenides' 'sphere' of Beings was reproduced when Love permeated the roots and mixed them together; then Strife gradually entered the sphere and caused plurality to assert itself. Thus the senses, if properly used, were not necessarily deceptive. Sensation was caused by physical effluences from objects entering pores in the sense-organs and meeting with corresponding roots there; thus in vision, fire activates fire in the eye. Empedocles avoided the apparent coming-to-be of traditional cosmogonies by making the entry of Strife into the sphere merely one stage out of four in a never-ending cosmic cycle: domination of Love, entry and gradual increase of Strife, domination of Strife, entry of Love. Our world belongs to the second of these. Corresponding with the transitional stages were two evolutionary stages: when Love is in the ascendant, first disunited limbs, then monsters; when Strife increases, first 'whole-natured forms', then our world. In a second poem, 'Purifications', Empedocles described a personal cycle of innocence, pollution, fall, purification and deification. Pollution is caused by bloodshed and strife, and leads to successive incarnations of the type also envisaged by PYTHAGOREANS and Orphics. See also PRE-SOCRATICS. (G.S.K.)

Empiricism   In ordinary use, the term 'empiricism' (from the Greek *empeiria*, meaning 'experience') implies the employment of methods based on practical experience as opposed to abstract theory. But in philosophy the word is used to refer to the theory that all knowledge is derived from experience. It was developed mainly by a succession of British philosophers, of whom the most important are LOCKE, BERKELEY, HUME and John Stuart MILL. (In America William JAMES developed a version he called 'Radical empiricism'.) Although such movements as ENCYCLOPEDISM in France have been inspired by empiricist ideas, empiricism has never taken hold on the Continent, whereas in Britain it has been the dominant tradition in philosophy since the seventeenth century. Moreover, Continental empiricists such as CONDILLAC have always been directly or indirectly influenced by British philosophy. The general principles of empiricism are opposed primarily to those of RATIONALISM, and it was as a reaction against the systems of DESCARTES, SPINOZA and LEIBNIZ that modern empiricism originated. There are two central questions at issue between rationalists and empiricists. The first concerns A PRIORI concepts (or 'innate ideas' as they were misleadingly called in the seventeenth century), or ideas supposedly not derived from sense-experience but independently produced by reason or intellect. Rationalists allow that some concepts are empirical (e.g. that we derive our idea of redness from our experience of seeing red objects), but they maintain that our knowledge of the world also involves a priori concepts like those of cause and substance. It is fundamental to empiricism to deny the existence of such ideas. Empiricists therefore argue either that allegedly a priori concepts can be broken down into a combination of simpler concepts derived from experience, or sometimes, and more radically, that they are not genuine concepts at all (e.g. that 'substance', as a metaphysical

term, is simply a word to which no meaning can be assigned). The second dispute between rationalists and empiricists concerns a priori propositions or statements. It is generally agreed that all necessary truths are a priori, since we can learn from experience only what has been and is likely to be the case, not what *must* be so. Empiricists, who believe that we have no means of acquiring knowledge except through observation of what actually happens, contend that necessary truths are true by definition, or ANALYTIC. Rationalists, on the other hand, hold that some a priori statements are synthetic; that is, that they tell us something about the nature of the world. The assertion 'every event must have a cause', for example, has been said to be a self-evident principle of this kind: a priori because it states a necessary connection, and synthetic because it is not simply true by definition (as 'every *effect* has a cause' is). It is characteristic of empiricism to deny that reason can assure us of the truth of a genuinely synthetic statement and therefore that any proposition can be both a priori and synthetic.

As a result of their disagreement over these matters of principle, rationalists and empiricists have very different attitudes towards natural science and towards metaphysics. Rationalists have been inclined, broadly speaking, to think of beliefs based on experience as infected with error. For them, an understanding of the world is not to be gained through sense-perception, which is confused, but through metaphysical speculation. But precisely because metaphysics claims to give knowledge of a reality transcending experience, metaphysical inquiry depends upon our having a priori concepts. The empiricist tradition has therefore been antagonistic to metaphysics, and has set a high value on science as a means of acquiring knowledge: Hume described NEWTON as 'the greatest and rarest genius that ever arose for the ornament and instruction of the species'.

The solutions that empiricists offer to particular philosophical problems are essentially applications of these general principles. Hume's account of causation is a classical example. He is well aware that the relation of cause and effect presents crucial difficulties for empiricism and that he has to show that the idea of a cause originates in experience. He maintains, like most later empiricists, that the causal connection between two events is, in fact, their regular succession, which is a matter of observation. He admits that the idea of a cause involves the idea of necessity, but this too he traces to its origin in experience. The repeated observation of B following A produces in us the habit of thinking of B when we perceive A. It is the experience of this habit which is the source of our idea of necessity. 'Necessity', Hume writes, 'is something that exists in the mind, not in objects'. He claims therefore to have refuted the rationalist account of causation as a necessary connection between objects, and to have shown that the idea of causation is a complex one that can be analysed into simpler elements (e.g. the idea of regular sequence) each of which is derived from experience.

Another typical application of empiricist principles is to the theory of mathematics. Mathematics has always been a stronghold of rationalism, since mathematical propositions are, on the face of it, a priori and synthetic: they seem to be about objects, but truths which *must* be so and which we can know in advance of any experience of them. This challenge has been met by empiricists in two ways: by denying either that mathematics is a priori or that it is synthetic. The first course is taken by J. S. Mill, who treats mathematics as a generalization from experience. '7+5 = 12' is, according to him, a law of

nature based on observation. If, however, arithmetic is only established by experience, it might possibly be falsified by experience, difficult though it may be to imagine what such an experience could be. Few empiricists have been prepared to swallow this paradox. They have usually taken the other alternative, asserting that mathematics is analytic, not synthetic. According to this view, mathematical propositions are true by definition. '7+5 = 12' is a necessary truth, but only because we define '7', '+', '5', '=' and '12' in such a way as to make it so. Mathematics therefore does not, as rationalists have thought, give us any information about the nature of the world. Though there are still considerable technical disagreements about the nature of mathematics, empiricists all agree on the essential point that its truths are necessary only because they are in this way uninformative.

Empiricism is primarily a theory of knowledge, but has also been influential in the field of ETHICS. Moral concepts (like 'rightness', 'obligation' and 'duty') must, if they are genuine concepts and if empiricism is correct, be derivable from experience like any others. But according to rationalists this derivation is impossible. We may be able to see that someone is behaving ungratefully, but we cannot similarly see that their ingratitude is wrong. Our idea of wrongdoing, it is said, is not based on experience, and we know that ingratitude is wrong only because reason intuitively grasps the a priori connection between these two ideas. The basic principles of morality are self-evident, and do not need to be justified by argument or observation, even if they could be. The empiricist reply to this intuitionist theory was that, in Hume's words, 'morality is more properly felt than judged of'. We do not, admittedly, observe the wrongness of an action, but we *feel* it, and it is this feeling that we put into words when we say that the action is wrong. This point of view – often called moral sense theory – was characteristically combined with the theory that our only duty is to produce as much happiness as possible. Although UTILITARIANISM is not an essential part of empiricist ethics, the combination is understandable: since empiricists do not believe that moral principles are self-evident, it is natural for them to hold that morality is justified by its tendency to bring about human happiness, which makes an appeal to each person's instinctive feelings of sympathy. However contemporary empiricists have come to realize that it is unsatisfactory to treat moral judgements as statements about feelings, and to regard ethics as a branch of the science of human nature, in the manner of Hume. They have therefore tended to argue that moral principles do not assert a priori truths, because they assert nothing at all, their function being solely the practical one of influencing behaviour. It has been suggested that moral judgements are really commands (e.g. that 'stealing is wrong' means 'do not steal') or that they are expressions of feelings, rather than statements about them. This 'emotive theory of ethics' rests on a naïve view of language, and has been widely criticized.

If modern empiricism is compared with that of the eighteenth and nineteenth centuries, the most significant advance is the increasingly clear separation of logical from psychological issues. The earlier empiricists were primarily interested in problems about the analysis of concepts and the logical status of propositions, rather than psychological problems about the origin of ideas. Nevertheless, they were often confused about the questions they were debating and wrote as if their intention was to give a natural history of the mind. Hume and J. S. Mill, for example, felt themselves to be committed to an atomistic psychology, which explained all mental activity in terms of the association of ideas. Modern empiricists, on the other hand, recognise that their philosophy is compatible with any psychological theory based on observation, and leave psychology to the psychologists.

The establishment of empiricism purely as a thesis about the logical structure of knowledge has been an important stimulus to the development of mathematical logic. It has also led to the conception of philosophy as the ANALYSIS of concepts and propositions, and therefore to an increased hostility to speculative philosophy and metaphysics. This hostility found its most extreme expression in the LOGICAL POSITIVISM of the VIENNA CIRCLE. The positivists held that apart from the formal or analytic statements of mathematics and logic, no statements were significant except those which could be verified by observation. Metaphysical and theological assertions were consequently rejected, not as unproved, but as 'nonsensical' or 'meaningless'. (E.B.)

Encyclopedists The first intention of the Paris printer and publisher Le Breton was to translate the English *Cyclopaedia* of Ephraim Chambers (1727), but when DIDEROT and d'Alembert became co-editors the scope was enlarged until it became the *Encyclopédie ou Dictionnaire Raisonné des Sciences, des Arts et des Métiers* (1751–65). This great work in seventeen folio volumes was a monument to the erudition of the French intellectuals or *philosophes*, intended to provide information on every branch of knowledge, with special attention to the application of science to industry, trade and the arts.

Chief among the contributors was Diderot, who, besides having the general direction of the work, wrote an immense number of articles – on religion, ancient history, political theory (his article 'Political Authority' is the most outspoken pronouncement in the whole work), philosophy, beer and the applied arts. D'Alembert contributed a celebrated 'Preliminary Discourse' which he traced the historical growth of knowledge. He was chiefly concerned with geometry, mathematics and the sciences, but also wrote an article on 'Geneva' in 1757 which provoked the ire of the local clergy and also the wrath of ROUSSEAU, who resented d'Alembert's criticism of his native city for lacking a theatre, and riposted with an indignant 'Letter to d'Alembert'. Disgusted with the outcry over this article, as well as for reasons of prudence and ambition, d'Alembert withdrew his collaboration, leaving Diderot to carry on alone. Luckily Diderot's devoted friend, the Chevalier de Jaucourt, who had studied medicine in Geneva, Leyden and Cambridge, then became the general factotum of the work, and wrote articles on the widest variety of topics – philosophy (he had previously published a study of LEIBNIZ), politics and literature, war, despotism, government and monarchy etc. Some critics claim that he was as important and as devoted to the enterprise as Diderot himself.

Rousseau contributed articles on music, and a contribution on 'Political Economy' foreshadowed some of the themes of his *Social Contract*. Later, Rousseau came to regard the *Encyclopédie* as the work of the devil, quarrelling not only with d'Alembert but with Diderot as well. The fifth volume opened with a notable tribute to MONTESQUIEU, author of *The Spirit of the Laws* (1748), whose influence on the *Encyclopédie* was pervasive. But Montesquieu kept aloof, refusing to write on 'Despotism' and 'Democracy', though he submitted an incomplete article on

'Taste', which was finished by VOLTAIRE, who otherwise contributed little – his articles, apart from one on 'History', are more important for their style than their content. Voltaire's friend Marmontel, an indifferent novelist and playwright, contributed articles on literature.

Although the editors claimed that the *Encyclopédie* had attracted the most eminent contributors, two outstanding personalities found its atmosphere too bellicose: Buffon, author of the great *Natural History* in forty-four volumes, who may have contributed one article on 'Nature'; and Duclos, a court historian, who wrote only on 'Declamation' and 'Etiquette'. The King's physician, Quesnay, contributed two outstanding articles, 'Farmers' and 'Seeds'. Turgot, who later became famous as Intendant and Minister, wrote on 'Fairs and Markets', condemning barriers to free enterprise; and on 'Foundations', showing the disadvantage of unchangeable bequests. The Baron d'Holbach wrote on mineralogy and chemistry, and there are grounds for attributing to him the entry on 'Representatives' which maintains that a state cannot prosper unless the king invites the cooperation of all elements of the population. For the rest, his general philosophy is contained in his notorious *System of Nature* (1770) where he insisted that kings must defend the liberty of their subjects. Holbach was an atheist and as such was attacked by Voltaire.

The great majority of the articles are factual and objective, written by specialists without an axe to grind. Other articles, however, were more barbed. Whereas opinions on politics were moderate, contributions connected with philosophy (deeply permeated with LOCKE'S EMPIRICISM) and religion were double-edged, despite professions of orthodoxy. For instance, under 'cowl', the absence from monasteries of 'sound philosophy' is deplored, and under 'Encyclopedia' there is a bland statement that the contribution of the Sorbonne to knowledge will be theology, sacred history, and the history of superstitions. One needs to read between the lines and follow the cross-references to detect the underlying scepticism about religion. Because of this attitude the *Encyclopédie* was suspect from the beginning, and in the course of its chequered career it came encountered opposition from Jesuits, Jansenists, the Sorbonne, the Pope, the Parliament, the devout party at Court, and private enemies. A suppression in 1752, thanks to Jesuit intrigue, was repeated in 1759, owing largely to an outcry against the materialism of *On the Mind*, a work by Helvétius, who was a friend of the project but not a contributor. But in neither case was the ban on the *Encyclopédie* enforced for long, and the work went on. In 1757 a lawyer called Moreau published a pamphlet in which the encyclopedists were called *Cacouacs*, a pejorative term which caused them intense annoyance, and in 1760 Pallissot pilloried the *philosophes*, chiefly Diderot and Rousseau, in a comedy of that name. Throughout these vicissitudes, Diderot stood firm. Thanks to his efforts the seventeenth and final volume of text appeared in 1765, and the indispensable eleven volumes of plates were complete by 1772. Diderot's avowed aim – 'to change accepted habits of thought' – was in large measure realized. (F.A.T.)

Engels, Friedrich (1820–95) German socialist, and friend, collaborator and financial supporter of MARX during his residence in Britain. It is to Engels rather than Marx that we owe the exposition of the fundamental tenets of DIALECTICAL MATERIALISM. His most important philosophical works are *Anti-Dühring* (1878) and *Ludwig Feuerbach* (1886), which treats materialism and IDEALISM, dialectical and mechanistic MATERIALISM and the materialist reorientation of Hegelian DIALECTICS; and *The Dialectics of Nature*, which contains the fullest statement of Engels' laws of development, but is incomplete and was not published in his lifetime. Engels was also co-author with Marx of the *Manifesto of the Communist Party*. (J.O.U.)

Epictetus (c.55–c.135 AD) STOIC philosopher of Hierapolis, Phrygia. A freed slave of Nero's secretary, and pupil of the stoic Musonius, Epictetus set up a school in Nicopolis when Domitian banished the philosophers from Rome in 89. His stoicism underlines freedom, providence, practicality and humanity, enjoining us to value nothing except the inviolability of our moral purpose, which alone is completely in our power and unassailable by external ills: we cannot be injured by others, but only by ourselves. The governing, indeed divine, principle is the moral will, and our sole active duty is to exercise it rightly, and by recognizing the rule of divine providence in the universe, to accept God's will. Impatient of theory, he concentrated on a practical ethic illustrated by everyday examples: SOCRATES and DIOGENES were his heroes. His message was not, like that of many stoics, addressed to an intellectual, social or governing élite, but to the community at large. The humanity and nobility of his teaching shine in his *Manual* and the four surviving books of lectures based on a pupil's notes. His later influence on both pagan and Christian thought was widespread. (I.G.K.)

Epicurus (342–270 BC) An Athenian citizen, Epicurus was brought up in Samos, returned to Athens for a short period of study as a young man, and then spent some years in Asia Minor. He finally returned to Athens in about 306 BC and set up his school in the garden where he taught until his death.

Epicurus is best known for his HEDONISM and ATOMISM; yet in neither field was he original. The only contribution he made to atomism – the suggestion that atoms originally fell in a kind of rain in parallel courses but that some of them swerved by free choice and caused collisions – is a regression rather than an improvement. And the essentials of his ethics can be found in the ethical fragments of DEMOCRITUS. But Epicurus was more interested in practice than in theory: he was a secular evangelist seeking to preach the secret of true happiness. Thus he propounded the atomic theory in order to combat the fears – of gods and demons, or of death and the torments of the underworld – that make people unhappy. The mechanistic doctrines of atomism, which denied the gods any control of nature and treated the soul as a concourse of atoms which was dissolved at death, were intended to allay these terrors. And the doctrine of the voluntary atomic swerve was an antidote to the dangers of a purely mechanistic atomism: 'it were better to follow the myths about the gods than to become a slave to the destiny of the natural philosophers'.

Epicurus' moral views have been much misunderstood and misrepresented. (The modern notion of an Epicurean as given up to voluptuous high living is based entirely on later slanders.) His theoretical starting point is that pleasure alone is good and always good. It consists in the driving out of pain, and when pain is ended pleasure can be varied but not increased. Pleasure is either bodily, perfect health being its highest form, or mental, where it consists in freedom from fear and anxiety. But though all pleasure is good in itself some pleasure brings pain as an inevitable consequence; therefore not all pleasure is desirable. Hence wisdom is of the greatest importance since without it we cannot make the best choice of pleasures.

In the letter to Menoecus Epicurus says: 'When we maintain that pleasure is an end, we do not mean the pleasures of profligates and those that consist in sensuality . . . but freedom from pain in the body and trouble in the mind. For the end is not continuous drinkings, nor the satisfaction of lusts, . . . but sober reasoning, searching out the motives for all choice and avoidance.' Pains of the mind are much more important than those of the body, which are either bearable or produce death, which is no evil. Death 'is nothing to us, since so long as we exist death is not with us, but when death comes then we no longer exist'. Moreover, though virtue is not in itself a good, only those who live virtuously can be happy, and anyway the virtuous life is pleasant as such.

Epicurus was not an atheist – he believed in gods who lived a life of infinite bliss which would be spoilt if they had to worry about human affairs – and he practised a disinterested worship of the gods. His teaching is thus paradoxical. He is a theist who regards ordinary religion as evil; a hedonist who advocates a simple life of study; a supporter of virtue and the pursuit of truth who holds them to have no value in themselves. He seems to have endeavoured to live the life he preached, gathering a simple community of disciples round him in his garden. We are told that 'he exceeded all others in the bulk of his works', of which some seventy or eighty pages survive; and on his deathbed he spoke contemptuously of his severe pains as weighing nothing against his joy of mind. The philosophical poem by LUCRETIUS, *De Rerum Natura*, well brings out both the doctrines and the practical attitude of Epicurus.   (J.O.U.)

Epistemology   There is a wide-ranging, loosely knit set of philosophical problems concerning such notions as those of knowing, perceiving, feeling sure, guessing, being mistaken, remembering, finding out, proving, inferring, establishing, corroborating, wondering, reflecting, imagining, dreaming and so on. This part of philosophy is often called the Theory of Knowledge or Epistemology – the latter word deriving from the Greek *episteme*, meaning knowledge or science.

Some of the problems revolve around the notion of a science, in the sense in which we take astronomy to be a science, but astrology not. A fairly typical problem of this kind is the problem why in pure MATHEMATICS there are conclusive proofs of theorems, when no such demonstrable certainties can be found or even looked for in, for example, history or medicine. It would be absurd for a mathematician to rest content with mere plausible conjectures or even with highly probable hypotheses. Scientists of other sorts seem not to be in a position to aspire higher than high probabilities. We incline to say that a body of truths ranks as a real science only when these are conclusively established; and then we find ourselves forced to say that, judged by this rigorous standard, even physics and chemistry are not really sciences; and this conclusion conflicts badly with our ordinary ideas.

Other problems in the Theory of Knowledge centre not upon the notion of a science, but upon the notions of our personal investigatings, inferrings, perceivings, rememberings, imaginings and so on. How can I tell for certain whether the stick half immersed in water is bent or not? How can I tell for certain whether I really recollect a past event or am merely imagining it, and whether I am now awake or dreaming? Might I not be the victim of one continuous illusion?

Whatever sorts of things we may want to find out, our attempt may fail in one of two ways. We may be simply baffled, or we may get something positively wrong. We can be stumped or we can make mistakes in calculating, in counting, in reasoning, in visual estimates of speeds and distances, in recognizing people or places, in recollecting, as well as in more executive things like spelling, aiming and treating the sick. What safeguards have we against mistakes? How, if at all, can we ever know anything? For in knowing, unlike believing, surmising and feeling confident, we cannot be wrong.

When we consider conflicting opinions about what exists and happens in the world around us, for example, about the relative heights of two church-steeples or about the migration dates of cuckoos, we think we could decide between the true and the mistaken opinion by, in the one case, simply measuring the heights of the two steeples, and in the other case by observing the arrivals and departures of cuckoos for a number of years in succession. But then we have to face the fact that there are mistakes of measurement and even mishearings of the first cuckoo. How could we decide between conflicting measurements or between conflicting reports of birdwatchers? At this point we are inclined to say that the ultimate decision, if only we could attain it, would be given by sense impressions unadulterated by any assumptions, guesses or expectations – by pure hearings, seeings or tastings in which there is not yet any place for slips or misjudgements. Here perhaps we have the absolutely firm foundation on which we might build knowledge of the world around us. The difference between having knowledge of something in the world around us and merely having a fallible opinion about it would be that the former would be at all points supported by sense-impressions, where the latter, though suggested by them, would be at best only partly supported by them. Where I am or may be mistaken, I have let my imagination jump ahead of the required impressions.

This sort of account of the difference between knowledge and fallible opinion will not be applicable inside the fields of purely abstract truths and falsehoods, like those of pure mathematics; nor yet inside some other fields, like those of ethics. Nor can my knowledge about my present wishes, fears, imaginings and broodings rest on the support of what I see with my eyes or taste with my tongue. It is for our knowledge only of what exists and happens in the world surrounding us, as well as in our own bodies, that sense-impressions, it seems, furnish the granite foundations.

In every case in this field where we would normally claim to be not merely guessing or believing something, but to have discovered or made certain of it, the fact which we claim to know goes beyond any particular momentary visual or auditory impression. If I assert that the cuckoo has arrived, I am asserting more than that at a certain moment I heard a noise of a certain sort. How then can we go beyond our present impressions and still sometimes claim to know? The natural answer to give is that we *infer* from for example the sound that we have heard to the ulterior conclusion that the cuckoo has arrived. Our knowledge of the world around us, together with our mere beliefs and conjectures about this world, are all conglomerations of interlocking conclusions inferred, sometimes legitimately, sometimes riskily and sometimes illegitimately from our impressions. Knowledge, unlike belief and conjecture, would be the product solely of legitimate and riskless inferences. But then what, if anything, can guarantee our inferences themselves against being mistaken? Even if the impressions from which we infer are exempt from slips, still the inferences that we draw from them are not so exempt.

If we knew, somehow, from the start some completely exceptionless causal laws, to the effect that whenever such and such a sequence of sense-impressions is had, then such and such other sense-impressions will always follow, then in any particular case we could, without risk of error, infer from the sense-impressions of the present moment to their successors in the next few moments. But we do not start off with any such knowledge. If we get bits of such knowledge, we get them late in the day, after a great deal of observation and experimentation. We discover the ways in which things always or sometimes happen only by finding them happening and collating our findings; and even then the laws and regularities that at any particular time we claim to have ascertained are always subject to subsequent correction. Nature is never without her surprises. The unpredicted sometimes happens and the predicted sometimes fails to happen. So it begins to look as if knowledge about the world around us, going beyond our impressions of the moment, cannot be got at all. For it would have to be knowledge by inference; but we possess, to start with, no warrant to make any such inferences. If we make jumps beyond our present impressions, we can have, to start with, no warrants for making them; and even if they happen to turn out right, this, by itself, cannot justify us in making the same jump on the next similar occasion. One lucky guess may be succeeded by another lucky guess. But we have no reason to expect it, however much we, like gamblers, are irrational enough to trust that our successes will continue.

So far we have been not expounding but rather reconstructing a line of thought that was operative in especially LOCKE, BERKELEY and HUME. We have contrasted our fallible perceptions and inferences with knowledge of what exists and happens in the world around us, with the disappointing upshot that this knowledge seems to be forever out of reach. Those very matters of everyday fact which we are inclined to adduce as obvious instances of things known and not merely guessed or opined – such as that the cuckoo has reached England, or that this church-steeple is taller than that one – seem unable to live up to their promise. The granite foundation of mistake-proof sense-impressions seems unable to carry any mistake-proof superstructure. Perhaps all that I can know from perception is that I am at this moment seeing such and such colours, smelling such and such smells, and hearing such and such noises, and these seen colours and heard noises are untrustworthy clues, if they are clues at all, to what exists or happens in the world around us – if there is such a world.

Considerations like these have led many thinkers to reverse the whole direction of the inquiry. Knowledge, as opposed to guesswork and opinion, is to be found where the sciences at their peak are to be found. What is known to some and is in principle knowable to all is any body of truths conclusively established by the rigorous methods of true science. We can get beyond guesswork and fallible opinion to knowledge by operating as geometricians and arithmeticians operate, namely by pure thought, not vitiated by the deliverance of our senses. Where we can calculate and demonstrate we can know. Where we can only observe and experiment we cannot know. No set of sense-impressions can yield knowledge. Only by exercises of pure thought can we ascertain truths. In the most exacting sense of the word 'science' there cannot be empirical sciences, but only purely ratiocinative sciences. Holders of this kind of view are called

'RATIONALISTS'. This programme leaves us discontented. We object that even granting that in pure mathematics we can discover uncontradictable truths, still these truths are bound to be completely abstract truths. Pure geometry cannot tell us the positions or dimensions of actual things in the world, but only, for example, that *if* there is something in the world possessing certain dimensions, *then* it has certain other dimensions. Geography could get nowhere without geometry, but geometry by itself cannot establish the position or even the existence of a single hill or island. Truths of reason win the prize of certainty only at the cost of being silent about what, if anything, actually exists or happens. Pure reason can arrive at uncontradictable truths, but none of these truths of reason can ever also be or yield truths of fact. We cannot learn merely from the theorems of Euclidean geometry or from the formulae of algebra whether Ptolemaic or Copernican astronomy is true, or even whether there exist any stars at all.

If these attainable certainties are, by themselves, too factually empty to yield knowledge of the actual world, and if sense-impressions, by themselves, are too anarchic to yield reliable inferences to what exists and happens in the actual world, there seems to remain just one escape route from the depressing conclusion that we cannot possibly know a single bit of what we most want to know, This escape route was the one first suggested by KANT. Knowledge of what exists and happens must have for its foundation not just the formal and therefore uncontradictable truths of pure reason, nor just the uninterpreted and therefore mistake-proof impressions of the senses, but the truths of reason as the principles organizing the sense-impressions, and the sense-impressions as the concrete material to be organized by the truths of reason. It is the application of the formal certainties of the abstract sciences to what we get by sheer seeing, hearing, etc., that enables us first to make anything at all out of our impressions, and then to sift out what really does exist and happen from what we precariously and often mistakenly suppose to exist and happen. We continue, of course, to be the frequent dupes of illusions and precipitate assumptions. But we know in principle how to check and correct them. We know the methods of making certain; and the principles of our procedures of making certain are the abstract truths of pure reason being put to work as our canons of objectivity in our experimental investigation of the world around us. Pure reason tells us no matters of fact. But it does provide, so to speak, the acid for our acid tests. When we progress beyond the infantile stage of mere sentience to the stage when we try to ascertain things, our investigations begin to be controlled not just by a Utopian ideal of mistake-proof knowledge, but by operative, though initially inarticulate procedures of testing. We begin to look, feel and listen experimentally, methodically and suspiciously. Though we make plenty of mistakes, we begin to take cautionary steps to prevent them and remedial steps to rectify them. We become alive to the contrast between 'real' and 'apparent' as we master the manifold techniques of deciding between them. We now begin to use our eyes, fingers and ears with some degree of judiciousness, and our seeings and hearings are now exercises not only of our senses but also of our wits. For our still frequent perceptual mistakes, for example for our misestimates, misrecognitions and non-discriminations, we properly confess to having been, not deaf or blind, but silly. Perception calls not only for sentience but also for rationality, though not, save in unusual circumstances, for explicit ratiocinations.

The possibility of mistakes always exists; but the possibility of detecting, correcting and forestalling mistakes also always exists. To be judicious is not indeed to be immunized against mistakes, but it is to know how to forestall and correct them. What exists and happens in the world around us is, in principle, ascertainable to creatures who possess both Sentience and Reason, that is to creatures who can examine judiciously.

It is important to be on one's guard against a tendency, deep-seated in all of us, to think of people as if they were, like large stores, divided up into departments. We tend to speak as if a person consisted, somehow, of one internal employee or agent called his 'Reason', of another called his 'Memory', of a third called his 'Imagination', of a fourth called, in the plural, his 'Senses', or in the singular, his 'Sight', his 'Hearing' and so on. Now we can indeed properly *distinguish* these and many other human capacities. My memory may be deteriorating with advancing age, while my sight and hearing remain as good as before, and my ability to calculate or argue may even be improving. The lessons, stimulations and exercises which develop the powers of the young musician are not at all like those which develop the powers of the young engineer or geometrician – or, of course, of the young swimmer or skater. The danger is that we may pass from correctly distinguishing, say, the violinist's musical taste from his manual dexterity to personifying his Taste and his Manual Dexterity as separate, internal functionaries; and so puzzle ourselves by questions like: 'Are his Taste and his Dexterity related as Master to Servant, as Partner to Partner, or even as Rival to Rival?'

Questions akin to these have often been raised in epistemology. People have asked whether our knowledge is given to us by our Intellect or by our Senses, and whether our mistakes are the faults of our Senses or of our Imaginations – as if these distinguishable capacities were themselves separate and semi-personal investigators quarrelling with one another inside our minds, and giving to us, their employers, conflicting reports about the world. But it is we ordinary people who try to ascertain things, and while we can certainly differ in eyesight, hearing, memory, judiciousness, inventiveness, and in our capacity to calculate, systematize, experiment and so on, still these distinguishable abilities are not themselves observers, experimenters, calculators, theorists – or reporters. For the sake of picturesqueness we may say that our Eyes notify us of things; that our Ears or Memories have given us false reports; that our Reason has convinced us; that our Imagination has invented things; and even that our Consciences reproach us. But in serious, theoretical discussions we need to avoid such tempting personifications.

There is another model to which we are tempted to shape our theories of knowledge, what may be called the 'Container-model'. We are tempted to suppose that because, what is true, a person who at one date had not yet learned what pineapples taste like, or what *isosceles* means, may at a later date have learned these things, therefore there must by the later date have come to exist inside him something that can be called 'the idea of the taste of a pineapple' and 'the abstract idea, notion or concept of *isosceles*'; somewhat as a bird-cage, formerly empty, may now house a canary, or as a picture-gallery may now have hanging on the wall a newly acquired picture. Using this Container-model, we are inclined to assume that in order to find out whether we have yet learned what pineapples taste like, or what 'isosceles' means, we can and must, so to speak, peer inside our own minds in order to see whether the required idea or notion is there or not. Yet when we try so to peer inside our own minds, we find the task oddly baffling. What sort of an internal thing can I be looking for when I try to peer into my own mind for the abstract idea of *isosceles*? Certainly most people, though not all, can see in their minds' eyes things like familiar faces, houses and coloured or colourless patterns. But the taste of pineapple can naturally not be visualized at all, nor, by most people, even tasted 'on the mind's tongue'; and what we visualize, if anything, when thinking of isosceles triangles, we visualize far too nebulously to meet the very precise requirements of Euclid's definition of an isosceles triangle. Yet very likely we can, without hesitation or error, discriminate the taste of pineapples from that of oranges, bananas, raspberries etc., and we can decide, without hesitation or error, whether a triangular figure of certain dimensions is or is not isosceles. We have learned and we now know the taste of pineapples and what *isosceles* means, without there existing anything 'inside our minds' to be found by inward peering.

To learn is indeed to acquire something or to come into possession of something. But what is acquired is not a thing but an ability, such as the ability to discriminate one taste from others, or the ability to classify geometrical figures, given their dimensions. When the schoolmaster wishes to find out whether a pupil has yet got the ideas of 'square number' and 'square root', he tests him on some arithmetical problems. The pupil has the ideas if he can tackle the problems; he has not got the ideas if he cannot yet tackle them. This is what it is to have the ideas.

It follows that the question 'How do we acquire our ideas?' has as many different answers as there are different kinds of acquired mental abilities. We become familiar with the taste of pineapples by tasting not only pineapples but also many other kinds of fruit, by comparing these tastes and perhaps also, what is very difficult, by trying to describe in words these different tastes. We get the ideas of 'square number' and 'square root' only when, having learned to count, add, subtract, multiply and divide, we learn to multiply numbers by themselves and to work out what number, if any, multiplied by itself produces a given number. Correspondingly different kinds of accounts would have to be given of our acquisition of the ideas of 'check-mate', 'vacuum', 'volt', 'equator', 'joke', 'weed', 'magneto', 'risk', 'virus', 'dragon', 'impossibility', 'tomorrow', 'debt' and so on. The doctrine that all our ideas come from sense-impressions, though unhelpful, is true enough if it means only that an infant born blind, deaf and without the senses of smell, taste and touch would never learn anything at all. It is false if it means that we get the idea of 'square root', say, or 'tomorrow' in just the same way as we get the idea of the 'taste of pineapples' – and even this latter idea is got not just by having a certain taste-impression two or three times, but by having this impression, noticing it, comparing it with other tastes, and perhaps trying to describe in words the differences and similarities between these tastes. To have learned something, however primitive, from one's sense-impressions, is always more than just to have had those impressions. It is to have become able to cope, in some degree, with some kinds of task or problem, however elementary.

Epistemologists are commonly divided into EMPIRICISTS, like LOCKE, BERKELEY and HUME, and RATIONALISTS, like PLATO, DESCARTES, SPINOZA and LEIBNIZ. The empiricists are said to maintain that all our ideas come from experience; the rationalists that some of our ideas come not from experience but from reason or thought. But what does this apparent tug-of-war amount to? What does 'come from' mean? What does 'experience' mean? The technical phrase 'sense-experience' is used to denote the mere having of sense-impressions. In this use, philosophers sometimes speak of a particular momentary sense-experience. In contrast with this technical idiom, we commonly use 'experience' in another way, to cover continuous or repeated practice in something or accumulating familiarisation with it. Thus a chess-player may have had much or little experience of match-playing in chess; but he would not describe himself as having had, on a particular afternoon, an experience of match-play. Experience, in this use, is what makes a person more expert than he had been. He has learned by having a certain amount of practice. He has tested and developed his abilities by exercising them. An experienced chairman is a man who has been in the chair a lot of times and in a lot of more or less difficult situations.

That all knowledge, for example, all expertness and all competence, comes from experience, in the second sense, that is, from training and practice, is an uncontentious truth – at least if safeguarded by the proviso that much of what we learn comes from instruction by others. But this is not at all the same thing as to say that whatever is known is inferred from premises provided, ultimately, by particular sense-experiences, though this is a theory maintained, with reservations, by some empiricist philosophers. The truth that we are not born already knowing anything, that is that no ideas are innate, is sometimes erroneously identified with the proposition that whatever we ascertain, when we do come to ascertain things for ourselves, we get by inference from our sense-impressions. But it is obvious that even if, what is questionable, we ascertain some facts by inference from our sense-impressions, when we have learned from training and practice to do this, still this account will not by itself cater for the enormous differences between, for example, ascertaining that the cuckoo has arrived, ascertaining that the king is checkmated, that the ship is now crossing the Equator, that there is a risk of thunder tomorrow, that a certain sentence is ungrammatical or that a certain metal object is a magneto. To ascertain things of these different kinds, we have to have acquired special abilities from special kinds of training and practice. The mere combination of good eyesight with good wits would not enable anyone to tell that the king is checkmated. He must also have studied and practised the game of chess.

Conversely, however, if an ultra-rationalist were to argue that since we cannot ascertain anything merely from having sense-impressions, therefore our only way of finding out what exists and happens is to do what Euclid did, namely to deduce theorems from axioms, without any recourse to observation or experiment, his position would also be untenable. If, which is rare, he holds that we are born knowing both these axioms and these techniques of deducing consequences, he is saying that we have masteries of things without ever having mastered them, that is, that we know without having learned, and hence are experts, though totally inexperienced. But even if, as is more common, he allows that knowledge of abstract truths and of the techniques of deriving consequences from them itself requires experience, in the sense of training and practice, he still cannot show that this special kind of training and practice can replace the other special kinds of training and practice which make us more

or less experienced observers and experimenters – or, for that matter, the other special kinds of training and practice which make us more or less experienced draughtsmen, speakers or dancers. The experience which is omitted from the theories of the empiricists is the experience which is omitted from the theories of the rationalists. Craving for something to avert the possibility of mistakes, the one finds its haven of safety in uncorrupted sense-impressions, the other in uncorrupted ratiocination. But the successful investigator is he who has made sure, not he who has remained in safety. Where mistakes are possible, the avoidance, detection and correction of them is possible. Knowledge comes not by some immunization against the chance of error, but by precautions against possible errors – and we learn what precautions to take by experience, that is training and patience. It is the expert, not the innocent, who knows.

To take a concrete example. If we ask how anyone can tell for certain whether the king is checkmated, the right answer would be that this can be ascertained by a spectator who has adequate eyesight and uses his eyes; has adequate wits and uses them, that is, is not absentminded or distracted, but is attending to the game; and lastly who has become, through training and practice in the game, expert enough to consider possibilities and to eliminate them. But if, instead, we asked whether the checkmate is ascertained by the spectator's Reason or by his Senses, and whether he was saved from being mistaken by the infallibility of his sense-impressions or by the uncontradictability of his formal principles, we should have debarred ourselves from getting a sensible answer, since these questions, unless taken as merely picturesque, are themselves not sensible questions. The spectator was not saved from making mistakes; he took good care not to make them. He was not notified by reports from his Intellect or by reports from his Senses that the king was checkmated; he found it out by visually studying the chessboard with his wits about him. He knew what to look for, since he had previously learned by training and practice how to play chess and how to follow games played by others.

Similarly, if asked whether the spectator has the abstract idea of 'checkmate', we need to construe the question as asking whether he has learned and still remembers what it is for a king to be checkmated, and whether, therefore, he can tell by suitably careful inspection, at any particular point in any particular game the king is or is not checkmated. To this question the answer is obviously 'yes'. But if we construe the question as asking whether the spectator has something special in his mind's eye, like a clear or blurred picture of a checkmate, we should answer first that there could be no picture of what is common to all checkmates; and second that it does not matter what, if anything, he visualizes when he hears or uses the word 'checkmate'. What matters is whether he has learned what it is to checkmate, to be checkmated and decide on inspection that the king is, or is not, checkmated. If he has learned and remembers these things, then he has the idea of checkmate, whether he happens to visualize things or not. If he has not learned them or has forgotten them, then he has not got the idea, whatever he may happen to see in his mind's eye on hearing the word 'checkmate'. If we forswear the personification of capacities and forswear the Container-model, we shall not suffer much from dividedness of mind between Rationalism and Empiricism. Their tug-of-war lacks a rope.   (G.R.)

Erigena, John Scotus (c.810–c.877)

Also known as Eringena ('Irish born'),

Erigena left Ireland to live and work at the court of Charles the Bald, King of the West Franks. In common with other Irish monks of the time Erigena knew Greek, and much of his work consisted in translating and commenting on Greek patristic writings. His chief philosophical work is, however, *Of the Division of Nature*, a sustained speculative treatise on the evolution of the universe in the NEOPLATONIC style of Proclus. For its comprehensiveness and speculative power it has no rival in Western thought from the time of BOETHIUS to that of ANSELM.

Erigena begins from the principle that all that exists is a divine manifestation which is to be understood by a DIALECTICAL penetration of revelation. His dialectic consists in the application to Nature of the well-known neoplatonic method of division and analysis. So elaborated, Nature is subject to four main divisions: nature which creates but is not created, nature which creates and is created, nature which does not create but is created, and nature which neither creates nor is created. So all reality consists either of God (the uncreated) or of creatures which go forth from and return to God. Being a Christian, Erigena tried to avoid the pantheistic implications of such a system by distinguishing the divine from the human as that which is not from that which is. Erigena had no immediate followers and his work exerted little historical influence. There is however, considerable systematic affinity between his speculations and later mysticism.   (J.G.D.)

Ethics   Out of the many sorts of inquiry for which the term 'ethics' has at one time or another been used, three groups of questions may be selected as the most important to distinguish from one another: (1) *Moral questions*: for example, 'Ought I to do that?'; 'Is polygamy wrong?';

'Is Jones a good man?'. In this sense 'ethical' and 'moral' mean much the same. (2) *Questions of fact about people's moral opinions*: for example, 'What did Mohammed (or what does the British Middle Class, or what do I myself) in fact think (or say) about the rightness or wrongness of polygamy?' (3) *Questions about the meanings of moral words (e.g. 'ought', 'right', 'good', 'duty'); or about the nature of the concepts or the 'things' to which these words 'refer'*: for example, 'When Mohammed said that polygamy is not wrong, what was he saying?'

These three sorts of questions being quite distinct, the use of the word 'ethics' to embrace attempts to answer all three is confusing, and is avoided by the more careful modern writers. No generally accepted terminology for making the necessary distinctions has yet emerged; but in this article we shall distinguish between (1) morals, (2) descriptive ethics and (3) ethics, corresponding to the three sorts of questions listed above. The case for confining the word 'ethics' (used without qualification) to the third sort of question is that ethics has usually been held to be a part of philosophy, and the third group of questions, which are analytical or logical inquiries, or, as older writers might say, metaphysical ones, is much more akin than the first two groups to other inquiries generally included in philosophy. Thus ethics (in the narrow sense) stands to morals in much the same relation as does the PHILOSOPHY OF SCIENCE to science. Students of ethics will nevertheless have to get used to a variety of terminologies: they will find plain 'ethics' used for what we have just called 'morals' ('normative ethics' is another term used for this); and they will find, for what we have just called 'ethics', the more guarded terms 'the logic of ethics', 'metaethics', 'theoretical ethics', 'philosophical ethics' and so on.

Works called 'ethics' usually contain questions and answers of all three kinds, and the student of ethics must be prepared to find in them ambiguous remarks in which it is not clear *what* sort of question the writer is trying to answer. It is, for example, only too easy to confuse a moral statement with a descriptive ethical one, especially when one is talking about one's own moral views; but it is nevertheless vital to distinguish the moral judgement 'It would be wrong to do that' from the descriptive ethical statement 'I, as a matter of psychological fact, think that it would be wrong to do that'. The first task, therefore, for anybody who takes up the subject, is to learn to distinguish these three types of questions from one another; and for this purpose the following rules may be found helpful. A writer is making a *moral* statement if he is thereby *committing* himself to a moral view or standpoint; if not (i.e. if he is merely writing in a detached way about moral views which are or may be held by himself or other people), it is either a *descriptive ethical* or an *ethical* statement; and this is normally indicated by the form of the statement, the moral words being 'insulated' by occurring inside a 'that'-clause or quotation-marks. Which of the two it is can be decided in the following way: if the truth of the statement depends on what moral opinions are *actually held* by people, it is a *descriptive ethical* statement; but if its truth depends only on what is *meant* by certain words, or on *what people would be saying if* they voiced certain moral opinions, it is an *ethical* statement. Thus, for example, ethics in the narrow sense is concerned directly neither with whether polygamy is wrong (a moral question) nor with whether anybody in fact thinks it is wrong (a descriptive ethical question) – though ethics may have a bearing on these two questions, as mathematics has on physics; it is concerned with the question 'Precisely what is one saying if one says that polygamy is wrong?'

1 *Relations Between these Inquiries.* Throughout the history of the subject, the chief incentive to the undertaking of all three sorts of inquiry has been the hope of establishing conclusions of the first kind (i.e. moral conclusions) by means of a philosophical inquiry. It is from this motive that inquiries of the second and especially the third kinds have mostly been undertaken. Clearly the study of the meaning of the moral words is closely related to the study of what makes arguments containing them cogent or otherwise. One of the best ways of obtaining a clear view of the subject is to consider the mutual relations between these three kinds of inquiry, and the bearing that they can have on one another.

(a) *Descriptive ethics and morals.* Some writers have proceeded directly from descriptive ethical premises to moral (normative ethical) conclusions. For example, the Greek HEDONIST Eudoxus argued that since everyone thought pleasure to be the good, it must *be* the good. In a similar way some modern writers have held that the task of the moral philosopher – the utmost he can do by way of establishing moral conclusions – is to examine carefully the opinions that are accepted by his society or by himself and reduce them to some sort of system. This is to take received opinions as data, and to regard as established a moral system that can be shown to be consistent with them. This type of argumentation will not, however, appear convincing to anyone who considers the fact that a person (e.g. in the ancient world) might have said 'Everyone thinks that it is legitimate to keep slaves, but may it not be wrong?' Universal assent to a moral principle does

not prove the principle; otherwise the moral reformer, who propounds for the first time a new moral principle, could be put out of court all too easily. Still less does it follow, from the fact that some limited set of people hold some moral opinion, that that opinion is right.

(b) *Descriptive ethics and ethics proper.* The commonest way, however, in which it has been sought to bring descriptive ethics to bear on moral questions is not directly but indirectly. It has been thought that a descriptive ethical inquiry might lead to conclusions about the *meanings* of moral terms (conclusions, that is to say, in ethics proper); and that in turn these might be used to prove moral conclusions. Those who have argued in this way have been attracted by a seductive analogy between moral terms and other predicates and adjectives. For example, it might be held possible to prove in the following way, to anyone who disputed it, that post-boxes in England are red: we should first establish by observation that everybody says that things are red when they have a certain recognizable quality, and that they are not red when they do not have this quality; we should conclude from this, that 'red' means 'having this quality'. This is the first step. We should then ask our disputant to observe that post-boxes in England have this same quality; and since we have already established that 'having this quality' is just what 'red' means, he can no longer deny that the post-boxes are red. It might be thought possible to use the same argument in ethics to prove, for example, that certain kinds of action are right. But unfortunately the analogy breaks down at both steps – at the step from descriptive ethics to ethics proper, and at the step from ethics to morals. That conclusions about what people *mean by* 'right', for example, cannot be proved by finding out what they *call* right, is evident from the case of the moral reformer just mentioned. If he said that slavery was not right, when slavery was one of things universally agreed to be right, he would, if the proposed argument were valid, be like a man who said that post-boxes were not red when everybody agreed that they were red; we should be able to accuse such a man of misusing the word 'red' – for 'red' *means* the colour which post-boxes are, so how can he deny that they are red? But the moral reformer can deny that slavery is right while still using the word 'right' in the same sense as that in which his contemporaries, who think that slavery is right, are using it. This example shows that there is an important difference between moral words and words like 'red' – a difference which invalidates the superficially plausible argument from descriptive-ethical premises to conclusions about the meanings of moral words.

(c) *Ethics and morals.* But the second step in the proposed argument is also invalid, for a very similar reason. We cannot, even if we can establish the meaning of the moral words, pass from this to conclusions of substance about moral questions. This may be shown by the following example: suppose that there are two people who know everything about a certain action (including its circumstances and consequences), and still dispute, as they may, about whether it was wrong. Since they are in dispute, they must be using the word 'wrong' with the same meaning; for if this were not so, there would be no real dispute, only a verbal confusion. But since they can continue to dispute, even though they are in agreement about the meaning of the word, it follows that knowledge of the meaning of the word cannot by itself, or even in conjunction with what they both know about the action, determine whether the action is

wrong. Some *other* difference must remain between them (a moral difference), which is neither a difference about what the action is (for this they know in the fullest detail), nor about the meaning of 'wrong' (for about this they are agreed). The plausible argument which we have just rejected is a particular application of a type of argument often used in philosophy, and known as 'the argument from the paradigm case'. Without discussing here whether the argument is cogent in other fields, we can see that it is not in ethics. The assumption that this argument has unrestricted force is linked with the assumption that to discover the use of a word is always to discover to what things it is correctly applied. This is not true of words like 'is' and 'not'; and it seems not to be true of moral words either. This assumption (to take another example) leaves us with no way of distinguishing between the uses of the two sets of words 'Shut the door' and 'You are going to shut the door'; for all the words in both sets, in so far as they 'apply' to anything, apply to the *same* things.

2 *Naturalism.* The arguments so far considered and rejected all exhibit a common feature. In them, moral conclusions are allegedly derived from premises which are not themselves moral judgements: in the one case the premise was a statement of sociological fact about what people think on a moral question; in the other it was a statement of linguistic fact about how (with what meaning) people use a certain word, together with another premise giving the description of an action whose wrongness is in dispute. This feature is common to a great many arguments which have been used by ethical thinkers; and it has been frequently stated that any argument which derives moral conclusions from non-moral premises must be invalid. A famous statement to this effect

was made by HUME (see *Treatise*, book 3, part I). Hume based his rejection of such arguments on the general logical principle that a valid argument cannot proceed from premises to some 'new affirmation' not contained, at any rate implicitly, in the premises. The correctness of Hume's view ('no *ought* from an *is*') depends, therefore, on the assumption that moral judgements contain an element in their meaning (the essentially moral element) which is not equivalent, even implicitly, to anything in the conjunction of the premises. It is this assumption which is challenged by those ethical theories known as NATURALIST. The term 'naturalist' has been used in a variety of ways, but will be used here as follows: an ethical theory is naturalistic if, and only if, it holds that moral judgements are equivalent in meaning to statements of non-moral fact.

It must be noted that, on this definition, a statement of moral opinion (that is to say a statement in the first of the three classes listed earlier) cannot be called naturalistic; for naturalism is a view about the meanings of moral terms, and nobody is committed to any form of it who merely *uses* moral terms without taking up a view about their meaning, definition or analysis. In general, no view can be naturalistic unless, in the statement of the view, the moral words occur inside quotation marks or a 'that'-clause or are *mentioned* (not used) in some other way, and remarks are made about their meaning or their equivalence to other expressions. That is to say, only statements in ethics proper, as contrasted with descriptive ethics and with morals, can be naturalistic. Thus the view that the right action (the action which ought to be done) in a given situation, is that which would produce the greatest balance of pleasure over pain, is not naturalistic, since it does not seek to *define* 'right', but only to say what actions *are*

right. To be a naturalist, a utilitarian of this sort would have to hold, in addition, that the view was true in virtue of the meaning of 'right' – that is to say, that 'right' *meant* 'producing the greatest balance of pleasure over pain'. If the naturalist refrains from trying to prove the theory in this way, 'refutations of naturalism' pass it by.

It must also be noticed that, on this definition of naturalism, to call a definition of a moral word 'naturalistic' does not imply that the properties in terms of which it is being defined are empirical, that is, perceived by the five senses. As G. E. MOORE, who coined the expression 'the naturalistic fallacy', observed, the same 'fallacy', as he thought it was, is committed if the properties are 'properties of supersensible reality', given only that they are not moral properties. Thus a philosopher who *defines* 'right' as meaning 'in accordance with the will of God' is, in this sense, a naturalist, unless the word 'God' itself is held to be implicitly a moral term. The most important argument by which Moore sought to 'refute naturalism' may be restated as follows, using the example just quoted: if 'right' meant the same as 'in accordance with the will of God', then, 'whatever is in accordance with the will of God is right' would mean the same as 'whatever is in accordance with the will of God is in accordance with the will of God'; but according to our actual use of the words it seems to mean more than this mere tautology. (Note that, as before, there is nothing in this argument which forces anybody to abandon the *moral* view that whatever is in accordance with the will of God and only what is in accordance with it is right. It is only the attempt to make this view true by definition which is naturalistic.) It has been held, though not by Moore, that what is wrong with naturalistic definitions is that they leave out the commendatory or prescriptive element in the meaning of words such as 'right' and 'good' (see below).

3 *Intuitionism.* The work of Moore convinced certain philosophers that naturalistic definitions of moral terms had to be ruled out. But Moore and his immediate followers showed a great reluctance to abandon what had been the traditional view of the way in which words have meaning. It was taken for granted that the way to explain the meaning of an adjective, for example, was to identify the property which it 'stands for' or 'is the name of'; all adjectives have the same logical function, that of 'standing for' a property, and the differences between them are not differences in logical character, but simply differences between the properties for which they 'stand'. When, therefore, it became accepted that moral adjectives did not stand for 'natural' (i.e. non-moral) properties, it was concluded that they must stand for peculiar moral properties, thought to be discerned by 'intuition'.

There are two main forms of ethical intuitionism. According to the first, we are supposed to intuit the rightness, goodness, etc. of concrete individual acts, people, etc.; general moral principles are arrived at by a process of induction, that is, by generalization from a large number of these instances. According to the second, what we intuit are the general principles themselves (e.g. 'promise-breaking is wrong'); by applying these, we ascertain the moral properties of individual acts and people. The second view has the merit of emphasizing a very important fact about the logical character of moral words, namely that the moral adjectives, etc. differ from most other adjectives in the following way: we call a thing 'red', for example, because of its redness and nothing else; it could be similar in every other way and yet not be red. But when we call

a person 'good' or an act 'right', we call them good or right *because* they have certain other characteristics – for example, an act is called wrong because it is an act of promise-breaking, or good because it is the act of helping a blind man across a road. The intuitionists sometimes express this feature of moral adjectives by saying that they are the 'names' of 'consequential' or 'supervenient' properties. Even if we reject the idea that all adjectives have meaning by being the names of properties, this remains an important discovery. It has sometimes been thought that Hume's 'no *ought* from an *is*' was a denial that we can, for example, call an act good *because* it is an act of a certain kind. This is a misunderstanding; what Hume was denying was that it *logically followed*, from an act's being of a certain kind, that it is good. The difference is crucial, but obscure. It has been one of the main problems of recent ethics to give a satisfactory account of the connection between, for example, goodness and what were called 'good-making characteristics'. The intuitionists reject the naturalist explanation that this connection is due to an equivalence in meaning between moral words and words describing the characteristics of things in virtue of which we apply moral words to them. But they give no adequate positive account of the connection, contenting themselves, for the most part, with saying that it is a 'synthetic necessary' connection discerned by 'intuition'. The explanatory force of this account is impaired by the failure to say clearly what 'intuition' is or what is meant by 'synthetic necessary connection'.

But the chief argument brought against ethical intuitionism of all sorts is the following, which is to be compared with that in the paragraph on Ethics and morals. Intuition is supposed to be a way of knowing, or determining definitively and objectively, the truth or falsity of a given moral judgement. But suppose that two people differ on a moral question, and that both, as may well happen, claim to intuit the correctness of their own views. There is then no way left of settling the question, since each can accuse the other of being defective in intuition, and there is nothing about the intuitions themselves to settle which it is. It is often objected further, that what 'moral intuitions' people have will depend on their various moral upbringings and other contingent causes. In fact, the intuitionists, who often claim to be 'objectivists', belie this claim by appealing to a faculty of intuition which is unavoidably subjective. This illustrates the extreme difficulty, to be referred to later, of stating any clear distinction between 'objective' and 'subjective' in this field. Intuitionism has waned since the early years of the twentieth century. Writers on ethics have tended, either to revert to some form of naturalism, open or disguised, or to pass on to one of the kinds of view, to be described later, which recognize that 'good', 'right' etc. have, logically, a quite different role from that of other adjectives, and that it may be misleading to call them 'the names of properties'.

4 *Relativism and subjectivism.* Great confusion has been caused in ethics by lumping together, under the title 'subjectivism', theories which are quite different from one another. Before considering subjectivism proper, we must first distinguish from it the *moral* view which is best called RELATIVISM. A typical relativist holds that we ought to do that, and that only, which we *think* we ought to do; on this theory, the mere having of a certain moral opinion by a person or a society makes that moral opinion correct for that person or society. Since this is a *moral* doctrine and not an *ethical* one (i.e. since it says what we ought to do, not what

'ought' means) it is not naturalistic (see p. 124); but it is open to the objection that it makes it impossible to say that another person's moral judgement is wrong – indeed, it has the paradoxical consequence that two people who differ about a moral question must both be right. This seems to be at variance with the common use of the moral words; we have here an illustration of a way in which ethics (the study of the uses of the moral words) can have a negative bearing on a moral question – it enables us to *rule* out a moral view as involving logical paradox, but not to *prove* one. It may also be objected to relativism that it does not do what a moral principle is expected to do, namely guide us in making our decisions on particular moral questions. For if I am wondering what to do, it is no use being told that I ought to do what I think I ought to do; for the trouble is that I do not know what to think. Relativism is mentioned, not for its own value, but because confusion of other views with it has bedevilled nearly all discussion of the views which we are about to consider. These are by contrast all ethical views (i.e. views about the meanings of the moral words). They do not commit the holder of them to the acceptance or rejection of any substantive moral opinions.

The first is a form of naturalism, which is not now often avowedly held, but dates from a time when it was thought that a moral sentence must have meaning in the same way as other indicative sentences, namely by being used to state that a certain object possesses a certain property (see earlier). It being implausible, for many reasons (some of which have been given on p. 124), to hold that the properties in question are 'objective' properties of objects, it was suggested that they are 'subjective' properties – that is, properties of being related in certain ways to states of mind of the maker of the statement in question. Thus 'he is a good man' was held to mean 'he, as a matter of psychological fact, arouses in me a certain mental state (e.g. a feeling of approval)'. This theory makes a moral judgement equivalent to a descriptive ethical statement (see introductory section on p. 120). If it is taken literally, it is open to the objection that it makes moral disagreement impossible. For if two people say, one that a man is a good man, and the other that he is not, they are, on this view, not disagreeing with each other; for one of them means that he (the speaker) is in a certain mental state, and the other means that *he* (the second speaker) is not in that state; and between these statements there is no contradiction.

Because of this objection, the view has been generally abandoned in favour of others which hold that in a moral judgement we are, not giving information about our mental state, but engaging in a use of language different from the giving of information. This development has been part of the recent realization by philosophers that it is a mistake to regard all kinds of sentences as having the same logical character and role. For at least two reasons it is best to confine the name 'subjectivism' to the view just considered, and not to extend it to those described below. First of all, the terms 'objective' and 'subjective' have a tolerably clear meaning, and draw a graspable distinction, when they are used to mark the difference between statements of 'objective' fact about objects, and statements of 'subjective' fact about the speaker (though even here there might be confusion; for in a sense it is an objective fact that the mind of the speaker is in a certain state). But the distinction gets lost when moral judgements are held not to be statements of fact, in the narrow sense, at all. This may be seen by comparing

the case of imperatives (though it is not suggested that moral judgements resemble these in all respects). An imperative expresses neither an objective statement nor a subjective statement, since it does not express a statement at all; nor does it express a 'subjective command'; for it is hard to understand what this would be. So, if it be asked whether the command 'shut the door' is about the door or about the mind of the speaker, the answer, insofar as the question is meaningful, must be 'about the door'. And in the same way the moral judgement 'he is a good man' may be held to be, in the strongest possible sense, 'about' the man in question, and not about the mind of the speaker, even by someone who holds that it is not (in the narrow sense) a *statement of fact* about the man. Thus criticisms of the theories to be described in 'outstanding problems', on the ground that they turn moral judgements into remarks about the mind of the speaker, are misdirected, and should be reserved for subjectivism as described here. The same applies to the criticism that these theories 'make what is right depend on what the speaker thinks is right'.

Second, the division between those views which hold that moral judgements are used to give some sort of information, and those which hold that they have a quite different function, is the most fundamental in ethics, and should not be concealed by using a term which straddles it. Views of the first sort (e.g. all the ethical views so far considered) are called 'descriptivist'; views of other kinds, including those considered in the rest of this explanation, are called 'non-descriptivist'.

5 *Emotivism.* Though emotivism was, historically, the first kind of non-descriptivism to be canvassed, it is a mistake to think of it as the only kind, or even as commanding general support among non-descriptivists at the present time

(1960). It is common even now for non-descriptivists of all kinds to be misleadingly called 'emotivists', even though their theories do not depend on any reference to the emotions. Emotivism proper embraces a variety of views, which may be held concurrently. According to the best known, moral judgements have it as their function to 'express' or 'evince' the moral emotions (e.g. approval) of the speaker. According to another version, their use is to arouse or evoke similar emotions in the person to whom they are addressed, and so stimulate him to actions of the kind approved. A. J. AYER when he wrote *Language, Truth and Logic* (1936), which contains the most famous exposition of emotivism, attributed both these functions to moral judgements; but he has since abandoned emotivism, though remaining a non-descriptivist. C. L. STEVENSON put forward a kindred view, with the difference that, instead of the word 'emotion', he most commonly used the word 'attitude'. An attitude was usually thought of by him as a disposition to be in certain mental states or to do certain kinds of actions. Stevenson's 'attitudes' are much closer to the 'moral principles' of the older philosophers (especially ARISTOTLE) than is usually noticed by those who use the misleading 'objectivist–subjectivist' classification. Stevenson made the important qualification to his view that, besides their 'emotive meaning', moral judgements may also have a 'descriptive meaning'. In one of his several 'patterns of analysis' the meaning of a moral judegment is analysed into two components: (1) a non-moral assertion about, for example, an act (explicable naturalistically in terms of empirical properties of the act); and (2) a specifically moral component (the emotive meaning) whose presence prevents a naturalistic account being given of the meaning of the whole

judgement. This specifically moral element in the meaning is the function which these judgements have of *expressing* attitudes and *persuading* or *influencing* people to adopt them, towards the act described. Stevenson's views did not, of course, find favour with descriptivists; and even non-descriptivists who wrote after him, while recognizing the seminal importance of his work, have for the most part rejected the implied irrationalism of the view that the only specifically moral element in the meaning of moral terms is their emotive force. This, it has been felt, makes moral judgements too like rhetoric or propaganda, and does insufficient justice to the possibility of reasoned argument about moral questions. If moral argument is possible, there must be *some* logical relations between a moral judgement and other moral judgements, even if Hume was right to hold that a moral judgement is not derivable from statements of non-moral fact. Stevenson has some important things to say about moral arguments, but his account of them has been generally held to be inadequate.

6 *Outstanding problems.* Most of the main problems which occupy ethical thinkers at the present time (1960) arise from the complexity of the meaning of moral terms, which combines two very different elements.

(a) *The evaluative or prescriptive meaning* (these more non-committal terms are now often preferred to Stevenson's 'emotive meaning'). It is not necessary, and probably false, to attribute to moral judgements, as such, any impulsive or causative force or power to *make* or *induce us to* do what they enjoin; but even descriptivists sometimes admit that moral judgements have the function of *guiding* conduct. It is indeed fairly evident that in many typical cases we ask, for example, 'what ought I to do?' because we have to decide what to do, and think that the answer to the 'ought' question has a bearing on our decision greater and more intimate than that possessed by answers to questions of non-moral fact. To take another example, it is fairly evident that there is an intimate connection between thinking *A* better than *B*, and preferring *A* to *B*, and between the latter and being disposed to choose *A* rather than *B*. This intimate connection is emphasized in the old tag (whose substance goes back to SOCRATES): 'whatever is sought, is sought under the appearance of its being good'. It would follow from this that to call a thing good is thereby to offer guidance about choices; and the same might be said of the other moral terms. Descriptivists, however, refuse to admit that this feature is part of the *meaning* of moral terms.

Their principal opponents, who may be called 'prescriptivists', hold that it is part of the meaning. Moral judgements, on this view, share with imperatives the characteristic that to utter one is to commit oneself, directly or indirectly, to some sort of precept or prescription about actual or conceivable decisions or choices. In typical cases, disagreement with a moral judgement is displayed by failure to act on it – as when someone has told me that the right thing to do is such and such, and I immediately do the opposite. Such a view does not, like the emotive theory, make moral argument impossible; for according to some prescriptivists logical relations may hold between prescriptions as well as between ordinary statements.

Prescriptivists have to face, like Socrates, the difficulty that in cases of so-called 'weakness of will' one may choose to do something which one thinks bad or wrong. The most promising line for prescriptivists to take in answer to this objection is to point out that in such cases either the chooser is *unable* to resist the temptation (as is indicated by the expression '*weakness* of will'; cf. also St Paul, Romans 7, 23); or else he thinks the thing bad or wrong only in some weaker, conventional sense, having the descriptive meaning of 'bad' or 'wrong' but lacking their prescriptive force.

(b) *The descriptive meaning.* The second main feature of moral judgements is that which distinguishes them from imperatives: whenever we make a moral judgement about, for example, an act, we must make it because of *something about* the act, and it always makes sense to ask what this something is (though it may be hard to put a reply into words). This (although it has been denied by some thinkers) follows from the 'consequential' character of moral 'properties' (see p. 125). To every particular moral judgement then, there corresponds a universal judgement to the effect that a certain feature of the thing judged is, so far as it goes, a reason for making a certain moral judgement about it. For instance, if I say that a particular act is good because it is the act of helping a blind man across a road, I seem to be adhering thereby to the universal judgement that it is good to help blind people across roads (and not merely this particular blind man across this particular road). Those who accept this argument may be called 'universalists'; and their opponents, who do not, may be called 'particularists'. A universalist is not committed to the view that, if it is a good act to help a blind man across a road on this occasion, it would be a good act on all occasions (e.g. it would not be a good act if the blind man was known to be hopelessly lost and his destination lay on this side of the road); he is committed only to the view that it would be a good act in the absence of something to make a difference between the two acts – something more than the mere numerical difference between the acts.

The universalist thesis is closely connected with the thesis that moral judgements, besides their function as prescriptions, have also a descriptive meaning (see p. 125). On this view, in calling an act, for example, good, we are commending it (the prescriptive element in the meaning), but commending it because of something about it. These two elements are well summarized by the *Oxford English Dictionary*'s first definition of 'good': 'the most general adjective of commendation, implying the existence in a high, or at least satisfactory, degree of characteristic qualities which are either admirable in themselves or useful for some purpose'. The word 'characteristic' is important; it draws attention to the fact that the word which follows 'good' makes a difference to the qualities which a thing has to have in order to be called good (e.g. a good strawberry does not have to have the same qualities as a good man). In the case of some words (e.g. 'knife'), if we know what they mean, we know some of the conditions that have to be fulfilled before we can call a thing of that kind good. Some philosophers (e.g. PLATO and Aristotle) have held that the same is true of all words – that, for example, if we could determine 'the nature of man' we should therefore be able to say what makes a man a good man. But this type of argument may be based on a false analogy between words like 'man' and words like 'knife'.

A more promising way of bringing the universalist thesis to bear on moral arguments (and thus to some extent satisfying those who insist that ethical studies should be relevant to moral questions) is that exemplified by the 'Golden Rule' and

worked out in some detail (though obscurely) by KANT and his followers. In certain cases it may be a powerful argument, if a man is contemplating some act, to ask what it is about the act which makes him call it right, and whether, if some other act possessed the same features, but his own role in it were different, he would judge it in the same way. This type of argument occurs in two famous passages of the Old and New Testament (2 Samuel 12, 7 and Matthew 18, 32). It has been held that a judgement is not a *moral* judgement unless the speaker is prepared to 'universalize his maxim'. But this raises the vexed question of the criteria for calling judgements 'moral judgements' – a question which is beyond the scope of this definition. This question, and the whole problem of the relation between the prescriptive and the descriptive elements in the meaning of moral judgements, continues to tax ethical thinkers.   (R.M.H.)

Evil   The fact that many things go badly, often through no human fault, is obviously a problem for those who believe in a benevolent, powerful and wise God. As HUME put it in his *Dialogues Concerning Natural Religion* (published posthumously in 1779): 'Is he willing to prevent evil, but not able? then he is impotent. Is he able but not willing? then is he malevolent. Is he both able and willing? Whence then is evil?' Earlier thinkers – notably LEIBNIZ in his *Theodicy* (1710) and Alexander Pope (1688–1744) in his *Essay on Man* (1733) – had sought to show that evils were no more than appearances, due to our adopting a partial and limited perspective on the world: once the universe was seen intelligently and as a whole it would become evident that in reality this was 'the best of all possible worlds', and that 'whatever is, is right'. This optimistic line of thought seems to have lost much of its appeal following the disaster that befell Lisbon on 1 November 1755: the people of the city were celebrating All Saint's Day when it was struck by an earthquake, followed by a fire and tidal wave, which together took some 60,000 human lives. Shortly afterwards, VOLTAIRE tried to make a laughing stock of Leibniz's optimism in his story *Candide* (1759). ROUSSEAU was unamused and unpersuaded, and – like KANT and HEGEL after him – thought that reason obliges us to keep our spirits up and to believe that, in the long run, everything will make sense and justice will be done. During the twentieth century, the broad old notion of evil as an attribute of the natural world was increasingly confounded with the specific idea of moral evil, in other words deliberate viciousness or sin – a development that Hannah ARENDT sought to counter in *Eichmann in Jerusalem: a Report on the Banality of Evil* (1963). See also BOETHIUS, THEISM, STOICISM. {J.R.}

Existentialism 'Existentialism' is a name for a philosophical trend or tendency whose central figure is HEIDEGGER, and of which the following marks may be noted.

1 Abstract theory is criticized for obscuring the roughnesses and untidinesses of actual life. This may take the shape, as in AUGUSTINE's *Confessions*, of a profound self-analysis, or as in PASCAL's *Pensées*, of an insistence that the mathematical methods of the exact sciences must be contested in the name of a flexible and less restricted concept of the varied and different styles of commerce with the natural and human environment. Étienne GILSON claims that AQUINAS should

be classed as existentialist, whereas the Platonic essentialist tradition should he viewed as asserting the priority of essence over existence.

2 The task of the moral philosopher is seen as continuous with that of the novelist or dramatist. (SARTRE and MARCEL achieved distinction as writers and dramatists as well as philosophers.) In this one may discern a continuity between existentialist philosophizing and PHENOMENOLOGICAL criticism of KANT's formalistic ethics. The existentialist bias in favour of the particular and the concrete conflicts with Kant's attempt to lay bare the universal principle of all moral action, though it harmonises with his doctrine of the primacy of practical over theoretical reason.

3 Existentialist thought is sometimes profoundly religious (as in KIERKEGAARD), and sometimes overtly atheistic (as in Sartre). But in existentialist atheism there is discernible an almost obsessionally religious note. Thus Albert Camus' novel *The Plague* (1947) displays a preoccupation with the problem of an atheistic sanctity which is unmistakably religious in its undertones.

4 Kierkegaard saw himself as offering a corrective to the dialectical rationalism of HEGEL, and its philosophical interpretation of the Christian religion. One might say that professional philosophers will always find in the writings of existentialist thinkers, resources to correct restricted and confined paradigms. One might mention in this connection WITTGENSTEIN's regard for Augustine's *Confessions* and the stories of Tolstoy. The enlargement of the academic imagination by recollection of the actual poignancy of human life and experience is often achieved through insights to be found in the diffuse, and sometimes unbalanced, writings of the existentialists.

The influence of existentialism in contemporary theology is better sought in the work of Paul Tillich, and of Rudolf Bultmann than of Karl Barth. The latter's early work owes much to Plato as well as to Kierkegaard and Dostoevsky; and his later work is more in debt to ANSELM than to existentialist thinkers. Indeed members of his school have been known to accuse those who pursue the method of existentialism in theology of continuing the disastrous inheritance of Augustine's self-absorption.

(D.M.M.)

F

Fallacy The term 'fallacy' is used in LOGIC to refer to an invalid argument or form of argument. Strictly, therefore, only arguments, not statements, can be said to be fallacious; an argument with true premises and conclusion may be a fallacy, while an argument with false premises and conclusion may be exempt from fallacy. If the premises of an argument are true and the conclusion false there must be a fallacy in it; in no other case can we determine whether an argument involves a fallacy simply by considering the truth or falsity of the statements it comprises.

It should be noted that the term 'fallacy' applies properly only to a deductive step in an argument (see DEDUCTION); what would be a fallacy in a deduction might well be perfectly sound in a merely probable argument. There is a fallacy known as the fallacy of affirming the consequent which is of the form 'if p then q; but q; therefore p'. An example would be 'if it has been raining the roads will be wet; but the roads are wet; therefore it has been raining'. Here the conclusion does not follow, for there may in fact have been no rain but only a burst main; but clearly wet roads are a good ground for suspecting that it has been raining.

The ways in which arguments can be bad are numberless, and many of the fallacies named in traditional logic books are of little interest. But some of them are worth knowing.

1 *Denying the antecedent.* This fallacy has the form: 'if p then q; but not p; therefore not q'; for example, 'if it has been raining the roads will be wet; but it has not been raining; therefore the roads will not be wet'.

2 *Petitio principii* ('begging the question'). This involves presupposing a premise which cannot be known to be true unless the conclusion is known to be true. Sometimes it is said that to take as a premise a proposition which cannot be true unless the conclusion is true involves begging the question; but in that case, as some have not shirked saying, every valid argument would be a case of begging the question.

3 *Simple conversion.* This means concluding from 'all A is B' to 'all B is A'; on the other hand it is of course valid to conclude from 'no A is B' to 'no B is A'.

4 *Undistributed middle.* This fallacy consists in arguing SYLLOGISTICALLY with premises in which the term occurring in both premises (the 'middle term') is not used in either premise to refer to everything to which it can refer (to its whole 'extension'). Thus in the syllogism 'all liars are rogues and all thieves are rogues, therefore some thieves are liars', the middle term 'rogues' is undistributed in both premises; in neither is anything said about the whole class of rogues.

5 *Ignoratio elenchi.* This is to produce a proof which validly proves something, but not what it was required to prove.

6 *Equivocation.* An argument in which a term is used in different senses at different stages of the argument.

7 *Post hoc ergo propter hoc.* An argument from the fact that something happened after something else to the conclusion that it must have been caused by it. Many superstitions are supported by

this argument; bad luck after walking under a ladder or breaking a mirror or spilling salt is held to be due to doing so. On the other hand, regular sequence is clearly a valid ground for an inductive argument to a causal relationship. (J.O.U.)

Fatalism   See FREEDOM OF THE WILL, DETERMINISM.

Feminism   See GENDER.

Feuerbach, Ludwig Andreas (1804–72)
Ludwig Feuerbach was born in Bavaria and deeply influenced by HEGEL'S lectures at the University of Berlin. He is best known for his *Essence of Christianity* (1841) and his philosophical manifestos, for example, *Principles of the Philosophy of the Future* (1843). Feuerbach's philosophy (or 'anti-philosophy' as he conceived it) was a HUMANISM and a naturalism: the touchstone was 'man on the basis of nature'. His position is distinguished from crude empiricism by a phenomenological approach derived from his Hegelian training. Thus his critique of RELIGION is a reinterpretation of it as an unconscious projection of truths about humanity, especially its 'species being' (*Gattungswesen*): while individuals are limited, humanity as a whole actualizes its *Gattungswesen* in its totality, which is expressed in religious imagery as God's plenitude. It is experienced most immediately when individuals recognize each other in an I-Thou relationship. This humanist reading of religion influenced modern theology. Feuerbach's critique of philosophy follows the same course: speculation hypostatizes the abstractions generated in human thought, as if they had a real existence apart from it. But truth exists there in inverted form: hence Feuerbach advised readers of Hegel to 'reverse subject and predicate'. His work encouraged MARX and ENGELS in their

turn to MATERIALISM and the theory of ALIENATION.   [C.J.A.]

Feyerabend, Paul (1924–94)   Viennese philosopher of science who worked mostly in Britain and California. His inquiries brought him to the conclusion (similar to that of KUHN, but more melodramatic) that orthodox views of scientific progress are a myth, and that there is no such thing as 'the scientific method'. His works include *Against Method* (1975) and *Science in a Free Society* (1978); his collected *Philosophical Papers* appeared in two volumes in 1981. See also PHILOSOPHY OF SCIENCE, RELATIVISM.

Fichte, Johann Gottlieb (1762–1814)
Fichte was born into a poor peasant family in Saxony, but with the aid of a local landed proprietor he studied theology, philology and philosophy at Jena and Leipzig. He met KANT in 1791 and became a close student and disciple. In 1794 he was made professor at Jena but was dismissed in 1799 on a charge of teaching atheism. An ardent patriot, he delivered his *Addresses to the German Nation* in Berlin in 1807–8 and was influential in the rebirth of Prussia after its defeats at the hands of Napoleon. He became professor at the new University of Berlin in 1810.

Fichte held that there were two possible methods in philosophy: dogmatism, which deduces the idea from the thing, and IDEALISM which deduces the thing from the idea. Which method one follows depends on one's mental make-up, but idealism is preferable since we cannot explain consciousness satisfactorily in terms of being, as dogmatism would do, but can construct experience, though not the thing-in-itself, from consciousness as a datum. Thus Fichte discarded the thing-in-itself and instead of deriving the nature of the thinking self from the manifold of experience, like Kant, he set out to deduce the manifold from the activity of the ego. The clearest statement of this not very easy doctrine is perhaps his *Introduction to the Theory of Knowledge* (1797).

Fichte's ethical views were developed in *Theory of Morals* (1798). Moral action must spring from conscience rather than obedience to authority. The basic ethical demand is that we should act according to our conception of duty, in a way we would acknowledge as ours without reservation through all time. Thus the moral life is a series of actions leading to the complete spiritual freedom of the ego. Moral evil arises from a lazy incapacity to think out our actions to the full. Certain individuals have the power to act morally in a preeminent way and their example is an inspiration to others; this is the basis of religion, and a church is really no more than an association for stimulating and strengthening moral conviction.

The State, according to Fichte, has the task of ensuring that citizens limit their freedom by regard for the freedom of others; but it cannot do this unless it also attempts to secure the same rights for all, which it can do only if it ensures property and economic self-dependence for all. In the light of this view Fichte was led to some socialistic doctrines about economic matters, including the transference of all foreign trade to the state. But, contrary to received legend, he did not share the organic view of the state typical of many German idealists. (J.O.U.)

Fodor, Jerry (1935–) American philosopher and cognitive scientist. Fodor believes that we think in a 'language of thought' that is realized in the computational structure of the brain. He is the author of *The Language of Thought* (1975), *The Modularity of Mind* (1983) and *Psychosemantics* (1987).

Foot, Philippa (1920–) In a series of concentrated articles starting in the 1950s, the English moral philosopher Philippa Foot has attacked EMOTIVISM and PRESCRIPTIVISM by arguing that moral considerations are 'necessarily related in some way to good and harm', and that there is no separate 'evaluative element' in the meaning of moral terms (see ETHICS). Like NIETZSCHE, she sees no logical reason why people ought to care about morality; but she holds that 'morality may be stronger rather than weaker if we look this fact in the face'. Her monograph *Natural Goodness* appeared in 2001, and her principal papers are collected in *Virtues and Vices* (1978) and *Moral Dilemmas* (2002). [J.R.]

Foucault, Michel (1926–84) French philosopher and historian, born in Poitiers, who worked most of his life in Paris. Foucault's work is a distinctive fusion of philosophical and historical investigations. From the HEGELIAN tradition which dominated the post-war French intellectual climate of his youth, it retains two major traits: a concern to theorize relations between general history and the history of thought, and a preoccupation with the human subject, or with how individuals are constituted as knowing, knowable and self-knowing beings. It discards, from the same tradition, the idea of history as a total process with an intelligible overall meaning and direction. It also rejects the goal of a definitive science (or sciences) of the human subject.

Each of Foucault's historical studies deals with concepts which have been used in particular periods (usually, Europe from the seventeenth century to the present; in his last books, Greek and Roman Antiquity) and thematic fields (psychiatry, medicine, linguistics, penal practice, sexual conduct) to articulate systems of thought about human beings. Foucault examines the intimate and sometimes morally disconcerting relationships between such knowledges and the social practices, techniques and power-relations through which they are developed and applied. One of his recurring lessons is that the nature and limits of the thinkable, both in theory and in practice, have changed more often, more radically, and more recently than we tend to suppose. Concepts such as those of normality or sexuality, through which we now think our selves and our identity, are contingent and potentially dispensable historical constructs. Foucault acknowledges NIETZSCHE's inspiration. His later work, notably *Discipline and Punish* (1975), contains a 'genealogy of morals' which demonstrates, for example, that punishment is a practice whose meaning can change fundamentally over time, and that familiar values may have forgotten, accidental and possibly ignoble antecedents.

Like their historical content, the ethical implications of Foucault's analyses are complex and challenging. Power and freedom are not seen as incompatible. Power, or our capacity to act on others, is not an intrinsic evil, but an ineluctable social fact. Freedom is a practice which can never be made safe by institutional guarantees. Our task is to invent modes of living which avert the risk of domination, the one-sided rigidification of power-relations. Enlightenment, the modern commitment to the pursuit of rationality, is a fortunate fact but also a source of intrinsic dangers. The search for truth, especially perhaps for the truth about ourselves, is not a sure path to freedom. In showing the historically various forms taken by the concern for truth, Foucault's intention is not to repudiate that concern as vain or culpable, but rather to assemble analytical resources enabling us to exercise it more critically and freely. His work ends in a reassertion of the practical and moral value of philosophy, which, as an effort to think the unthought, is always a thought against one's self and a readiness to 'refuse what we are'.   [C.G.]

Frankfurt School   An Institute for Social Research was founded as an autonomous section of the University of Frankfurt in 1923. Its first director, Carl Grünberg, saw it as a centre for historical and sociological inquiry inspired by Marxist theory. Within a few years, however, leading members of the Institute, including HORKHEIMER, ADORNO, BENJAMIN and MARCUSE were giving equal emphasis to purely theoretical work, incorporating elements of PSYCHOANALYSIS and EXISTENTIALISM into a new form of Marxism known as 'critical theory'. Critical theory was always centrally concerned with problems of aesthetics, culture and MODERNISM; it was Hegelian in inspiration and strongly opposed to Soviet Marxism and DIALECTICAL MATERIALISM. During the Nazi period the so-called 'Frankfurt School' dispersed and eventually regrouped in New York; it moved back to Frankfurt in 1949, where HABERMAS emerged as its leading figure.   [J.R.]

Freedom of the Will   A cluster of problems arises from an incompatibility, real or apparent, between sets of beliefs none of which we are ready to abandon. On the one hand we believe we can sometimes choose whether to act in a certain way or not; that we are responsible for so acting or refraining from action; and that we cannot be held responsible for those parts of our history which do not lie within our choice. On the other hand we believe that nature is uniform, that whatever happens results from and can be explained by a set of causes and conditions, and in particular that our actions result from our inherited character as modified by environment. But if everything that happens is determined by its context then it would seem that our actions and choices are too. In particular, if our actions arise from an inherited character as modified by our environment, it would seem that we are no more responsible for them than we are for our inherited character and environment.

Moreover a mere denial of the principle of DETERMINISM does not obviously eliminate the problem; for if our actions do not arise out of our character as modified by environment it is hard to find any other account of their genesis which will make us responsible for them; certainly we are hardly to be held responsible for what occurs purely fortuitously.

No solution to these problems has been found which commands anything approaching general consent. Those philosophers who regard determinism as incompatible with freedom and therefore deny or weaken the deterministic thesis are usually called LIBERTARIANS; they have had no conspicuous success in finding an account of human action which makes responsible choice intelligible. Those philosophers who retain the doctrine of determinism and accept that we do not in a full sense have freedom to choose are known as determinists. Many philosophers, however, are unwilling to accept either of these paradoxical positions and try instead to show that the opposition between determinism and freedom is only apparent. Thus they frequently say that the true antithesis to acting freely is acting under compulsion: the laws of nature are descriptive, not prescriptive, for example, the laws of motion describe how things move, but do not compel them to move so. Consequently they maintain that we do in fact often act freely (not under constraint) even though our actions can always in theory be subsumed under

(descriptive) natural laws. It is not however clear that in these contexts compulsion is the antithesis of freedom; and though I do not digest my food under compulsion it would be odd to say that I do it of my own free will.

It is, however, true that the determinist at least need not think of laws as prescriptive. Those who think that human actions are in some way prescribed are called fatalists or predestinationists. According to the doctrines of fatalism and predestination some powerful entity (Fate or God) has a plan according to which things happen in a prearranged fashion; the laws of nature can, but need not, be thought of as prescribed by Fate or God as a method of executing the plan. Thus the fatalist and the predestinationist accept, as the philosophical determinist does not, that human action is purposively determined or compelled; but doctrines of creation and divine foreknowledge raise notorious problems about human responsibility for the theologian.   (J.O.U.)

Frege, Gottlob (1848–1929)   German philosopher and logician. Frege's historical importance is twofold, as the founder of modern mathematical logic, and as a philosopher of LOGIC and of MATHEMATICS. He invented the notion of a *formal system* with the intention of attaining the ideal of mathe-matical rigour, and in *Concept-Script* (*Begriffsschrift*, 1879) gave what was at once the first example of a formal system and the first formulation of the sentential and predicate calculi. He drew for the first time the distinction between axioms and rules of inference and introduced the device which distinguishes modern logic from its predecessors and makes it superior to them, the use of variables and (nested) quantifiers.

Frege then turned to the application of his formal system to arithmetic. In doing so, he discovered the possibility of formalizing arithmetic without introducing any non-logical concepts or axioms, at least if the notion of a class or set is admitted as a logical one. This possibility rested on the famous definition of a cardinal number, later rediscovered by RUSSELL, as the class of all classes which can be mapped one-to-one on to a given class, together with the definition of the ancestral of a relation (i.e. the transformation of a recursive into an explicit definition) which had already been given in *Begriffsschrift*. The definition of cardinal number follows naturally from the discovery that the fundamental numerical notion is that of 'just as many as'. An unreflective person, asked what it meant to say that there were just as many things of one kind as of another, might reply that it meant that if one counted up the first set and then counted up the second, one would arrive at the same number. But Frege observes that it is possible to say that a set has just as many members as another set without being able to say how many each has; thus if a waiter checks that there is just one knife to the right of each plate, then he knows that there are just as many knives as plates on the table. He has mapped the set of plates one-to-one on to the set of knives by means of the function 'object to the immediate right of'. Moreover, counting itself is a particular case of setting up a one-to-one mapping; for what I in effect do when I count a set of objects and find that there are *n* of them is to define a function on the set whose values are the numbers from 1 to *n*. Finally, to explain 'just as many as' in terms of one-to-one mapping gives a sense to saying of some infinite set that it has just as many members as another set, whereas of course an infinite set cannot in the ordinary sense be counted.

In order to prepare the way for the symbolic work Frege wrote *The Foundations of Arithmetic* (1884), expounding his theory without symbolism. This is a classic of philosophical exposition, and contains an entirely effective annihilation of then prevalent philosophical accounts of numbers and arithmetic. It also contains some profound philosophical insights. In order to answer such a question as 'what is the number 1?', Frege says, we have to give an account of the sense of sentences in which the symbol '1' occurs. We must not make the mistake of asking for the meaning of a word in isolation: only in the context of a sentence does a word have meaning. If we ask for the meaning of a word in isolation, we shall be inclined to answer by describing the mental images which are called up in us by hearing the word. But these mental images are entirely irrelevant to the sense of the word. The same word may call up different images in the minds of different people; different words may call up the same image in the mind of one individual. In any case the image cannot determine the sense of sentences containing the word. Elsewhere, Frege distinguishes two features of the meaning of a word: the images and associations which the word calls up (which Frege calls the 'colouring' of the word), and the sense properly so called. Colouring is subjective, and can vary from person to person. The sense of the word is objective; it is that feature of the meaning which alone is relevant to the determination of the truth-value of a sentence containing the word. When we know how to determine the truth-value of sentences containing the word, then we know all there is to know about the sense of the word; nothing further can be demanded. Among the most important sentences in which a singular term can occur are those expressing judgements of identity: Frege points out that stipulating the criterion of identity for Xs is a necessary part of determining the sense of the word 'X'. It is evident that the first part of WITTGENSTEIN'S *Investigations* is deeply indebted to these ideas of Frege.

In a famous article published in 1892, Frege introduced a distinction which had not occurred in *The Foundations of Arithmetic*: that between the sense and the reference of a word. The reference of a singular term is the object about which we are speaking when we use a sentence containing it. But we must not think with J. S. MILL that the meaning even of a proper name consists just in its having the reference that it has; its sense is not uniquely determined by its reference. Thus, to use an example given by Frege elsewhere, one explorer might discover a mountain to the south and give it a name, while another explorer gave a different name to the same mountain seen to the north, and it might be many years before it was realized that it was the same mountain they had seen; the two names would then have different senses but the same reference. The sense of the whole sentence is a *thought* (somewhat analogous to the 'proposition' of Russell); the thought is what is primarily said to be true or false, and is something immaterial though objective. Hence the reference cannot be a constituent of the thought; if I am talking about Everest, the mountain itself cannot be part of the thought I express. All the same, I do succeed in talking about the mountain itself, and not some shadowy correlate of it; the reference is in general something non-linguistic, something 'in the world'.

Whether an expression is a proper name or not is for Frege a question only of its logical behaviour. Thus 'red' and '5' (used as nouns) can count as proper names since 'red is a primary colour' and '5 is a prime number' are logically of exactly the same form as 'Krushchev is a clever man'. If an expression functions like a proper name, and possesses a definite sense, then it is a proper name; and it has a definite sense if we have assigned a sense to all the sentences in which it can occur. Whether an expression has a reference or not depends upon whether we should ordinarily say that there was something answering to that designation; for example, 'the perfect number between 10 and 30' has a reference in virtue of the fact that, as we should ordinarily say, there is a number which is perfect and between 10 and 30. The idea that there is a further philosophical question as to whether there *really* exists an object for which the expression stands arises from the fallacy of 'asking after the reference of a term in isolation'. Frege calls an 'object' anything which is the reference of a singular term; for him it is as legitimate to speak of numbers (and other 'abstract entities') as objects as of men or cities as objects. Hence arithmetic is a collection of truths about objects just as much as any other science, and it is the task of the mathematician to *discover* these truths, which hold good independently of whether we discover them or not.

Frege distinguishes two fundamentally different types of expression, which he calls 'saturated' and 'unsaturated'. Singular terms are saturated, as are complete sentences. Unsaturated expressions are predicates like '...is tall', relational expressions like '...bores...' and functional expressions like 'the capital of...', in short expressions containing gaps which become saturated when the gaps are filled by saturated expressions. Unsaturated expressions are not merely sequences of words which could be written down on their own, for it is required that we can indicate where the gaps occur and which gaps must be filled with the same term and which may be filled by distinct terms (variables are a device for indicating this). Thus an unsaturated expression is a *feature* in common to several sentences rather than an isolable *part* of those sentences. An unsaturated expression has a reference as well as a saturated one; but its reference is an unsaturated kind of thing, something which can no more be thought of as standing on its own than can the expression which denotes it, and which is therefore totally unlike an object. The reference of a predicate Frege calls a 'concept' ('property' would be a happier term in English), that of relational and functional expressions 'relations' and 'functions'. The reference of an unsaturated expression is to be distinguished from its sense just as sharply as the reference of a proper name from its sense; concepts, relations and functions are just as much 'in the world' as are objects. If we say that Jupiter is larger than Mars, the relation holds between the *references* of the words 'Jupiter' and 'Mars' and not between their senses, and hence must be a feature of the world (the 'realm of reference') as are the planets themselves. It is nevertheless an entity of a quite different kind: if an expression stands for a concept or a relation, it cannot stand for an object, and indeed it cannot even make sense to try to say about a concept what it makes sense to say about an object, or conversely. We do talk about concepts, however: if I say, 'God exists', I am not ascribing a property to a particular object, but talking about a certain *kind* of thing – about a property or concept – and saying about it something that it makes sense to say only about a property, namely that there is something which has it, that there is something of that kind. Number-statements are to be understood in the same way: 'there are three trees in the garden' says something about the concept *trees in the garden*, and cannot be understood as an assertion about an object.

If we want to understand the nature of concepts and relations, we must consider functions in mathematics. The number 4 is a certain function of the number 2, namely its square, but it is not itself that function. In fact we cannot as it were isolate the function, but only particular numbers which are that function *of* certain other numbers. Indeed, Frege is able to regard concepts and relations as special cases of functions, since he holds that a sentence as a whole has a reference, namely its truth-value; concepts and relations are thus functions whose value is always truth or falsity. This doctrine cuts clean through the old controversy between NOMINALISTS and REALISTS. For Frege the colour red, for example, is a genuine object, the reference of the *noun* 'red'; but it cannot be the reference of the *adjective* 'red', and is not alluded to in the sentence 'tulips are red'. The doctrine leads in Frege's formal system to a rigorous distinction of type between predicates; classes are, however, treated as *objects* (entities of lowest type). This is an illustration of the interdependence between Frege's philosophy of logic and his formal system. A formal system is to be constructed not merely with an eye to convenience, but ought to mirror the essential features of language (this was in essence Frege's retort to PEANO's objection that his assertion sign was formally redundant). This does not mean that a formal system has to copy natural language: the use of variables and quantifiers, for instance, solves the problem of generality not by giving a coherent account of the devices used to indicate generality in natural languages, but by inventing a totally new device (the theory of quantification seems a better claimant for the title 'paradigm of philosophy' than Russell's theory of descriptions). Natural language may actually be incoherent and can be criticized as such; thus Frege regards it as a defect of natural language that in it singular terms may be formed which have a sense but no reference. The modern quest for an ideal language was initiated by Frege.

In 1893 and 1903 Frege published two volumes of his masterpiece, *The Basic Laws of Arithmetic*, which sets out his construction of arithmetic out of logic in his logical symbolism. The theory contains 'naïve set theory', that is, the assumption that for every property there exists a class having as members precisely those objects which have that property. Shortly before the publication of volume II Russell wrote to Frege explaining the contradiction he had found in naïve set theory. Frege hastily added an appendix stating how the contradiction could, as he thought, have been avoided by weakening one of his axioms. Lesniewski later proved that a further contradiction would arise, but it is doubtful if Frege discovered this. In any case many of the proofs would have broken down under the revised axiom, and Frege lost heart for rewriting and completing the book. At the end of his life he came to consider the whole theory of classes, and the project of deriving arithmetic from logic, an error. Frege produced little work of interest after 1903; and probably did not follow the work that was being done in the subject he had

founded. Nor did he receive much credit in his lifetime. The work he had done was transmitted to other logicians through the writings of Peano, Russell and WHITEHEAD; only Dedekind, Zermelo and Russell gave him the credit that was his due. He was little known among philosophers, although three of great importance were profoundly influenced by him – HUSSERL, Russell and Wittgenstein, followed later by logicians such as Church, CARNAP and QUINE. Perhaps Frege's greatest achievement in philosophy, in which he was followed by Wittgenstein though not by Russell, was to reject the Cartesian tradition that EPISTEMOLOGY is the starting-point of philosophy, and reinstate philosophical logic as the foundation of the subject.
(M.A.E.D.)

Freud, Sigmund (1856–1939) See PSYCHOANALYSIS.

Functionalism 'Functionalism' is the name for an approach to psychology – pioneered by William JAMES and revived by moderate materialists towards the end of the twentieth century – in which mental states are accounted for not in terms of their physiological basis but by their role in a larger patterns of causes and effect. See also PHILOSOPHY OF MIND.

G

Gadamer, Hans-Georg (1900–2002)
German philosopher, the main exponent
and developer of the idea that HERMENEU-
TICS is the most fundamental of all
philosophical disciplines. Much of his
work takes the form of lucid and
self-effacing essays on the figures he sees
as dominating the HISTORY OF PHILOSOPHY:
not only his friend and teacher HEIDEGGER,
but also PLATO, ARISTOTLE, HEGEL and
HUSSERL. Collectively, these essays plead
for a recognition that philosophy consists
essentially in the interpretation of philosophical tradition. With the publication of
his *Truth and Method* (1960), it became
clear that this historical approach to philosophy was based on a general theory about
the universal ontological significance of
'the phenomenon of understanding'.

Following Heidegger, Gadamer rejected
the idea that understanding or interpretation is the activity of a 'subject' confronting an independent 'object'. This
dichotomy of subject and object is itself,
he argues, a hasty interpretation with
limited validity, and so are all the other
dualisms characteristic of MODERNITY,
especially that between art and science.
For, in spite of KANT's 'subjectivisation of
aesthetics', art makes no less a 'claim to
truth' than science. Once we have discovered how truth can happen in art, according to Gadamer, we can begin to see how
understanding in general – including scientific understanding – works. We will
realize that it consists not in the pure and
timeless relation between subjective representations on the one hand and objective
phenomena on the other, but in historically situated 'events' where interpreta-
tive 'horizons' are enlarged, and eventually

'fused' with others gathered from the past.
'Understanding', he says, 'must be conceived as part of the process of the coming into being of meaning, in which the
significance of all statements – those of
art and those of everything else that has
been transmitted – is formed and made
complete'.

Gadamer's conception of understanding
as part of 'the historicity of our existence'
also led him to reject the 'prejudice against
prejudice' which he regarded as another
commonplace of modernity. Recognition
of authority, he argued, is really a condition of knowledge, rather than its enemy.
Our prejudices 'constitute our being': they
are the 'biases of our openness to the
world' and 'the initial directedness of
our whole ability to experience'. Some
left-wing critics such as HABERMAS have
seen this as involving a universal endorse-
ment of supine conservatism since, they
argue, it implies that any demand for
radical change must be irrational and a
misinterpretation of tradition. Gadamer
however sees these criticisms as mistakenly presupposing an 'unconditional
antithesis between tradition and reason',
and an 'objectivist' view of the past.
Tradition, for Gadamer, does not 'persist
by nature because of the inertia of what
once existed'; on the contrary, it is 'an
element of freedom' which perpetually
'needs to be affirmed, embraced, cultivated'. Hence even in the most fundamental revolutions, according to Gadamer, 'far
more of the old is preserved ... than
anyone knows'.   [J.R.]

Gassendi, Pierre (1592–1655)   French
scientist, whose influence on the course

of philosophical and scientific speculation was important and profound. Both
HOBBES and DESCARTES knew him well
and derived from him, not so much specific doctrines or solutions of philosophic
problems but rather certain habits of
thought. Gassendi set himself the task of
providing an explanation for the doctrines
of the current orthodoxy that would be
based upon the scientific theories of the
ancient ATOMISTS and the moral views of
EPICURUS. For example, he regarded mental activities as fully explicable in terms
of physical distortions of the material of
the brain and elaborated a complex theory
of 'traces' to account for the intelligent
behaviour of men and animals. Typically,
his solution of the problem of the interaction of imperishable soul and perishable
brain was a para-mechanical one. If brain
and soul pursued the same goals, they
would for that reason act together, a doctrine similar to, but much simpler than
LEIBNIZ's pre-established harmony.
Gassendi also exerted a marked influence
on moral and political theory, for he
reintroduced to Europe the Epicurean
doctrine that the highest moral good was
to be sought in 'tranquility of soul', a
notion which is a likely progenitor of
Hobbes' 'peace'. We act for the preservation of our soul's tranquility, which is not
always the same as pleasure.   (R.HAR.)

Gender 'Gender', as distinct from 'sex',
is whatever there is to being male or
female that cannot be attributed to innate
bodily differences. Sex, we are told, is
biologically given; gender is socially constructed. But opinion differs as to where sex
stops and gender starts. For many feminists,
gender is malleable without limit; but others
question this conception of free-floating
gender, and also challenge aspects of
the Western philosophical tradition on
which it rests.

The idea of gender as transcending
bodily sex differences is of course a modern one. But it has its roots in traditional
philosophy, with its aspirations to the
transcendence of body by mind and consciousness; or of animality by human
nature; or of the passivities of nature by
autonomous will. And the concept of
gender also has links with the traditional
philosophical concept of the person.
Gender transcends sex. But for those feminists who rest claims to sexual equality
on the supposed fundamental sameness of
men and women, it is itself transcended
by personhood. As persons, what sex we
are is not essential to us. The rational
mind is neither sexed nor gendered.

The idea of the sexless soul, which
reinforces the idea of gender as change-
able, goes back to PLATO's discussion of
the female guardians in book five of the
Republic. The sexual equality of the
guardians rests on their sameness of soul,
which co-exists with bodily difference.
Women should be given the same education as men, to fit them for the same social
roles. But in *Emile* (1762) ROUSSEAU
claimed that Plato had really excluded
femaleness from the Republic: the female
guardians did not really have female
gender. Modern feminists have often seen
this pattern repeated in women's access to
institutions and professions structured
around men. In reaction to the disappearance of female gender into a supposedly
gender-neutral norm, there was a trend in
subsequent feminism towards an affirmation of female difference. This was accompanied by a move to bring gender closer to
sex, repudiating the philosophical assumptions implicit in the picture of gender as
'free-floating', especially DESCARTES'
model of the mind–body distinction.

Some feminists also argue that social
arrangements should reflect the different
relations of the sexes to the biological

facts of reproduction. Such versions of feminism echo Rousseau's insistence that male and female are different ways of being human, and that female reproductive capacities are central to the difference. They believe in 'taking biology seriously', highlighting the connections between femaleness and nurturance, and then arguing that the philosophical dichotomy between mind and body deludes us into advocating the fundamental sameness of men and women.

Although such feminists are at pains to distance themselves from biological determinism, they continue to construe the relations between gender and sex in causal terms. The problem, however, is to see what there is to 'sex' that can provide the cause or ground of the approved forms of social arrangement. How do we know where the biological facts end and the social construction of nurturance as female begins? A merging of cultural and biological facts of reproduction is of course exactly what we should expect, if we do repudiate the sharp dichotomies inherited from the philosophical tradition. But to the extent that they do merge, the idea of sex as grounding gender becomes confused.

An alternative approach has been to see gender as the human response to the fact of sex differences, rather than their causal product – as our enactment of sex differences, our response to their significance. This view seeks to expose as illusory the KANTIAN ideal of a personhood that transcends sex difference, in favour of seeing gender as integral to personhood. But this view also has difficulty in identifying the natural facts to which gender is supposedly the truthful response.

We seem to have here a conceptual impasse. We can think of gender as floating free of sex. But then femaleness either disappears into a human norm, which coincides with socially constructed maleness; or it survives only as a complement to the essentially human. Alternatively, we can try to affirm femaleness by bringing gender closer to sex; but this may only perpetuate and rationalize existing sexual stereotypes, by naturalizing them.

A possible way out of this impasse is to see gender as neither a causal product nor a response to pre-existing difference, but an expression of power, with no existence independent of the dominance of men over women. According to this view, what is fundamental is the political fact that maleness is the standard with reference to which both sameness and difference are judged: sameness means being the same as men; difference is being different from men. Hence a feminist affirmation of what differentiates women from men is fraught with problems. For women to affirm difference is to confirm their powerlessness.

Some feminist philosophers have argued that the philosophical tradition has helped form this identification between maleness and the human norm: that philosophical ideals of reason, autonomy and personhood have privileged maleness as transcending and excluding the feminine; and that female gender has been constructed by those exclusions. But if the philosophical tradition has contributed to our present quandaries about sex and gender, it also offers resources for rethinking sexual difference; and from this perspective many of the old philosophical debates take on new dimensions.

For example, much of the contemporary dissatisfaction with our ways of thinking of sex and gender focuses, as we have seen, on Descartes' view of the mind. But on a Spinozistic view of the mind–body distinction, sex differences would reach right into the mind. The mind, for SPINOZA, is the 'idea of the body'. As ideas of differently sexed bodies, minds would have to be sexually differentiated. But does that commit us to a distinction between male and female minds? Why should the idea of a male body be male, any more than the idea of a large body is large? But the claim is not ludicrous. The idea of a large body reflects the 'powers and pleasures', in Spinoza's phrase, of such a body. And to the extent that the powers and pleasures of bodies are sexually differentiated, it will be appropriate to speak of male and female minds. A female mind will be one whose nature, and whose joys, reflect those of a female body.

Moreover, there is for Spinoza a continuity between the individual body and the socialized body. The powers of bodies are enriched by good forms of social organization, which foster the collective pursuit of reason. They are also diminished by bad forms of social organization, and by exclusion from good ones. If we take seriously the implications of Spinoza's theory of the mind, female minds will be formed by socially imposed limitations on the powers and pleasures of female bodies.

On this way of looking at sex difference, there is no sexless soul, waiting to be extricated from socially imposed sex roles. But nor is there any authentic male or female identity, existing independently of social power. With gender there are no brute facts, other than those produced through the shifting play of the powers and pleasures of socialized, embodied, sexed human beings. [G.L]

Gentile, Giovanni (1875–1944) Italian IDEALIST, and author of *The Theory of Mind as Pure Act* (1916). Gentile argued that all phenomena, however disparate they might seem, were aspects of the activity of a single spirit. Applying this theory to culture, education and the state, he became the leading philosopher of fascism and minister of education in the early years of Mussolini's fascist government.

Geulincx, Arnold (1624–1669) See OCCASIONALISM.

Gilson, Etienne Henri (1884–1978) French philosopher and pioneer of the modern understanding of MEDIEVAL PHILOSOPHY. He started by trying to understand better the philosophical antecedents of the Cartesian philosophy; they began to absorb his attention and he came to accept the position of Thomas AQUINAS on essential points. His most important historical work, *The Spirit of Medieval Philosophy*, was first published in French in 1932. He has also written independent philosophical works in the Thomistic tradition, including *God and Philosophy* (1941). (J.O.U.)

Glanvill, Joseph (1636–1680) See CAMBRIDGE PLATONISTS.

Gödel, Kurt (1906–78) Austrian mathematical logician who moved to the United States in 1940. He is best know for a theorem published in 1931 which demonstrated that no formal system of arithmetic could be complete in the sense of supplying a proof of every truth expressible within it. This put an end to attempts (by HILBERT or RUSSELL for example) to reduce mathematics to a self-contained axiomatic system.

Goodman, Nelson (1906–98) American philosopher of language who held that philosophy aims at giving precise structural descriptions of the world by formulating definitions which exhibit things as patterns of various elementary components of experience. In his first book, *The Structure of Appearance* (1951), he offered such definitions for a number of individual items in phenomenal experience (such as colour spots), using, as primitive building blocks, directly presented qualitative characteristics, such as specific shades of colour and places in the visual field. Goodman was a vigorous proponent of NOMINALISM, refusing to postulate such abstract 'Platonic' entities as classes, and although he made extensive use of modern logical techniques, he did not hesitate to reject portions of logic, mathematics and scientific theory that do not satisfy his nominalistic requirements. Like QUINE, he was highly critical of the widely employed distinction between synthetic and ANALYTIC statements.

A problem that occupied much of Goodman's thought was the analysis of contrary-to-fact conditionals, such as 'if this match had been scratched it would have ignited'. He canvassed various difficulties facing attempts at explicating precisely the sense of the connective 'if–then' in such statements, showing that this problem is intimately related to that of formulating the difference between statements expressing laws of nature (e.g. 'water expands on freezing') and those expressing merely accidental universality (e.g. 'all the coins in my pocket to-day are made of silver'). In *Fact, Fiction and Forecast* (1955), he advanced some suggestions for resolving these questions, and for clarifying the nature of inductive inference. Later works include *Languages of Art* (1968) and *Ways of Worldmaking* (1978). See also AESTHETICS, RELATIVISM.　(E.N.)

Gramsci, Antonio (1891–1937)　Italian Marxist, born in Sardinia. His activities in opposing Fascism led to his arrest in November 1926. He spent the final ten years of his life in Fascist prisons and clinics, and his major theoretical work, the *Prison Notebooks* (published 1948–51), was written during his incarceration.

Gramsci's philosophical aim was to reconstruct Marxism as a political philosophy, a philosophy of praxis, and thus to move away from the HISTORICAL MATERIALIST conception of Marxism as a scientific theory of economy and society. To this end he attempted to incorporate into Marxist thought, in radically altered form, the brand of Hegelianism and historicism he learned from the writings of the Italian philosopher Benedetto CROCE. For Gramsci 'philosophy' is a social activity; it is the universe of cultural norms and values, the world-view, shared by all as common sense. All philosophy, then, is historically concrete, belonging to a people, a time and place, even if 'philosophers' – those who produce specifically philosophical writings – are unaware of it as such. In conceiving of philosophy in this way Gramsci was attempting to refute the standard Marxist conception of the economy as the base or infrastructure which determines society's political and cultural superstructure. For Gramsci, politics, as the transformation of common sense, and the introduction of new philosophical perspectives, represented an independent element in historical change; and as such it was essential to the possibility of revolutionary change in the West.

Central to Gramsci's conception of historical change and political education was his concept of 'hegemony'. This refers either to the consensual basis of an existing political system, achieved when a ruling class imposes its world-view as common sense; or to the attainment of a new common sense by a dominated class. For Gramsci, ideological struggles are, properly speaking, struggles for hegemony, struggles for the hearts and minds of the people. In identifying philosophy, history and politics Gramsci transformed the Marxian problematic of IDEOLOGY into the question of the 'fate' of 'the political' in MODERNITY.   [J.M.B.]

Green, Thomas Hill (1836–82)   The English philosopher T. H. Green studied and taught at Oxford, and helped to spread the influence of KANT and HEGEL against the prevalent trends of empiricism and utilitarianism in England. The only book of his which appeared in his lifetime was an edition of HUME, and his influence was exercised mainly through lectures at Oxford which were published posthumously. He maintained that the world was a network of relations, and that mind was required not only to apprehend but also to constitute and sustain these relations. Any term we may seek to isolate will turn out to be itself a network of relations too; and any attempt to find in feeling or sensation the ultimate data of experience must fail. Here Green comes very close to Hegel. The distinction between appearance and reality is not a distinction between a mental world and a world independent of mind, but one between the limited, human mind and the universal, absolute mind which sustains the universe.

In ETHICS too Green goes a long way with Hegel. Desires are not, as in an animal, isolated forces. In each desire the human self seeks its own satisfaction as a whole. Only thus can one hold oneself responsible and free. Here, however, Green began to diverge from Hegel. The good is personal to the individual whose good it is, even though, being naturally social, we can achieve full satisfaction only if we confer good on others. Green firmly rejected any notion of a corporate self. The divergence dominates his political theory. He noted how ROUSSEAU'S conception of a common good led him to that of a general will. But beyond this lay Hegel's view of the State as a unity higher than that of the individual and beyond this again lay extremes of totalitarian authority and nationalistic state-worship. Green's solid English liberalism rejected all such conclusions. He maintained the importance of individual responsibility, though, unlike LOCKE or J. S. MILL, he did not allow individual rights to serve as a bulwark against social authority; indeed they depended for their existence on social recognition. See also POLITICAL PHILOSOPHY.   (J.D.M.)

Grotius, Hugo (1583–1645)   Dutch thinker, whose ideas exerted an influence out of proportion to their philosophical acuteness. Their context was political upheaval and assassination, lawlessness at sea and the Thirty Years War. His belief in toleration and rational ways of settling disputes was based on a profound respect for truth, inherited from the humanistic tradition of Erasmus. Grotius believed that piety, based on what was common to different interpretations of the Christian religion, together with reticence about doctrinal disagreements, was a sufficient basis for reconciliation between Catholics and Protestants.

His rational outlook was partly the product of his early training by the great scholar Scaliger, one of the first to stress grammatical cogency rather than doctrinal convenience in interpreting the Bible. Grotius mastered Latin and Greek by the age of 12 and became a Doctor of Law at Leyden at 16. As advocate for the Dutch East India Company he became involved in a controversy arising from the seizure of a Portuguese galleon in the Straits of Malacca, which led him to investigate the general grounds of the lawfulness of war. His *On the Law of Booty*, written in 1604 but not published till 1868, was the result; it led to an abiding interest in International

Law and formed the basis of his later masterpiece *On the Law of War and Peace* (1625). Grotius upheld the general principle that the ocean is free to all nations.

Grotius' main contribution to philosophy was his unequivocal defence of NATURAL LAW (upholding the security of property, good faith and fair dealing) as a rationally discernible set of principles binding on citizens, rulers and God alike. The validity of such a law was a commonplace of Christian thought, but the disunity of Christendom after the Reformation, together with secular challenges to the authority of the church, had made its validity difficult to defend on religious grounds. Furthermore the *Realpolitik* pursued by the rulers of the new nation-states, as popularized by MACHIAVELLI, made the content of the old law of nature look somewhat artificial. Grotius therefore sketched a foundation for natural law which would make it independent of religion.

Natural law, claimed Grotius, is 'a dictate of right reason, which points out that an act, according as it is or is not in conformity with rational nature, has in it a quality moral baseness or moral necessity; and that, in consequence, such an act is either forbidden or enjoined by the author of nature, God.' It was not obligatory because God commanded it; rather God commanded it because it was obligatory. 'Just as even God cannot cause two times two not to make four, so he cannot cause what is intrinsically evil not to be evil.' In other words Grotius assimilated moral knowledge to mathematical knowledge.

Grotius held, furthermore (with ARISTOTLE and the STOICS) that we are social by nature, and hence have a natural interest in the maintenance of social order. The rules of natural law are therefore self-evident to us as social animals endowed with reason, 'for human nature itself – which would lead us into the mutual relations of society even if we had no lack of anything – is the mother of the law of nature'. Grotius maintained that all other laws were subordinate to natural law. The civil law, for instance, depended for its validity ultimately on the natural obligation of good faith in keeping covenants. Grotius' treatment of the Law of Nations was particularly interesting and important; for he transformed what had been a system of private law establishing relations between subject and subject belonging to different nations into system of public law establishing relations between state and state.   (R.S.P.)

H

Habermas, Jürgen (1929–) Habermas is the most influential second-generation representative of CRITICAL THEORY, a tradition of Marxist social philosophy which originated in Germany in the 1930s, amongst members of what has come to be known as the FRANKFURT SCHOOL. Like earlier members of the School, including Theodor ADORNO and Herbert MARCUSE, Habermas is concerned with the predominance of 'instrumental reason' in modern industrial societies. Instrumental reason deals with the relation between means and ends, but leaves the determination of ends outside its scope. For many modern philosophers, this is the only kind of reason. Such views, Habermas argued in his early work, encourage the 'scientization' of politics: political questions are reduced to problems of technical control, and the 'public sphere' of debate and discussion concerning social goals is eroded. Habermas also believes that earlier Critical Theory failed to clarify the broader conception of reason to which it implicitly appealed.

Habermas' solution to this difficulty was to shift the philosophical emphasis from the subject–object relation to the process of intersubjective communication. Thus, in his main contribution to EPISTEMOLOGY, *Knowledge and Human Interests* (1968), he argued that the existence of society depends on two forms of action, labour (instrumental action) and social interaction (communicative action). These form the basis of distinct human interests, which in turn guide the formation of categorically different kinds of knowledge. Hermeneutic and critical modes of inquiry, directed towards understanding others and uncovering unconscious compulsions, arise from communicative action, and cannot be reduced to 'empirical-analytic' enquiry, which arises from instrumental action and aims at the prediction and control of objective processes.

Subsequently, Habermas worked on a 'universal pragmatics', an account of the normative commitments which are constitutive of linguistic communication. He wished to show, in particular, that when we attempt to reach agreement through discussion, we cannot help but assume that the conditions under which an unconstrained consensus could be reached have already been realized. Thus an 'ideal speech situation', characterized by equality and reciprocity, is an immanent goal of communication, and makes possible a critique of inequalities of social power – a critique not based simply on personal value-commitments. This account of communication was a central component of Habermas' comprehensive reformulation of social theory in *Theory of Communicative Action* (1981). Here Habermas argued that the pathologies of contemporary society could be diagnozed in terms of the invasion of the 'life-world' (the domain of social existence which is communicatively organized) by quasi-autonomous 'systems' of bureaucracy and the economy. Opposition to this invasion was no longer located only in the working class, but rather amongst all those social movements which attempt to expand solidaristic forms of social life, and to bring the dynamics of money and power under democratic control. He launched a vigorous assault on POSTMODERNISM in *The Philosophical Discourse of Modernity*

(1985); see also GADAMER, PHILOSOPHY OF SCIENCE.   [P.D.]

Hackenschmidt, George (1878–1968)
Wrestler, bodybuilder and philosopher, also known as the Russian Lion. Hackenschmidt was born in Estonia and came to prominence in 1896 when he picked up a milkman's horse and walked around with it on his shoulders. In 1898 he became world champion in Greco-Roman wrestling, and remained undefeated in more the 3,000 matches until 1911, training with a five-hundred weight sack of cement on his back. His physique was much photographed and widely admired in many remarkable poses, but he was also noted for his sweet reticence and feminine gentleness. While detained as a prisoner of war by German forces during the First World War he began to develop a system of philosophy based on the values of spirituality, vegetarianism and self-control, which he later elaborated as a trainer and teacher first in France and then in Britain, including the House of Lords. His eight books in English include *Man and Cosmic Antagonism to Mind and Spirit* (1935), and *Consciousness and Character: True Definitions of Entity, Individuality, Personality, Non-entity* (1937). 'I have never bothered as to whether I was a Champion or not', he wrote; 'the only title I have ever desired to be known by is my name – George Hackenschmidt.'   {C.R.R}

Hacking, Ian (1936–)   Canadian philosopher of science, whose belief in the relevance of history, especially the history of scientific techniques, shows the influence of both FOUCAULT and KUHN. He is the author of *The Emergence of Probability* (1975), *Representing and Intervening* (1983), *The Taming of Chance* (1990) and *Historical Ontology* (2002), as well as the article on Philosophy of Science in this Encyclopedia.

Hamilton, Sir William (1788–1856)
Scottish philosopher, who spent some time at the Bar and became Professor of history and then philosophy in Edinburgh. In philosophy his starting point was the common-sense position of REID and the Scottish school; his lectures, later published as *Lectures on Logic* and *Lectures on Metaphysics* were of great weight in the development of the Scottish philosophical tradition.

Hamilton's main work was the *Philosophy of the Unconditioned* (1829), in which he proceeds, by means of a critical examination of the views of KANT, SCHELLING and COMTE, to a theory of knowledge whose main thesis is that to think is to condition. This means that when we think of anything we inevitably determine it by its relation to something else by which it is conditioned. Hence every part is a whole of parts, and every whole a part of some greater whole; the idea of the absolute whole or part is an absurdity. Similarly we cannot think of an unconditioned beginning and can only understand a beginning as conditioned by another phenomenon; the conditioning phenomenon is thus the cause; indeed the concept of cause is treated by Hamilton merely as a special case of the general principle of conditioning. Hamilton took it that this implied that it was impossible to attain absolute truth through philosophy, and that we must be satisfied with enlightened ignorance. But though we cannot know the unconditioned, we cannot but have some faith concerning it: the unconditioned is God who, as unconditioned, is completely incomprehensible.

Hamilton is remembered as the subject of J. S. MILL's *An Examination of Sir William Hamilton's Philosophy* and as the inventor of a variant of the LOGIC of the syllogism in which the predicate as well as the subject is quantified (i.e. in which we have not simply the propositions, 'all S is

P' and 'some S is P', but rather 'all S is all P', 'all S is some P', 'some S is all P' and 'some S is some P'). (J.O.U.)

Hampshire, Stuart (1914–2004) English philosopher based at Oxford. His *Thought and Action* (1959) was an important exploration of the way in which people's knowledge of their own actions differs from the objective empirical knowledge which then preoccupied ANALYTIC PHILOSOPHY.

Hare, Richard Mervyn (1919–2002) English moral philosopher who taught at Oxford. His main position is set out in *The Language of Morals* (1952), *Freedom and Reason* (1963) and a number of papers which have been published in collected form. This position is commonly called PRESCRIPTIVISM. Hare holds that the primary task of the moral philosopher is to clarify the nature of moral terms and judgements, and that such clarification can have considerable influence on practical questions. Moral judgements, he holds, differ from descriptions of the world, not in subject matter, but by being imperatives whose primary function is to guide choice. But moral judgements are not mere commands, for they are essentially universalizable. Also notable are Hare's critical reformulation of MOORE's arguments against naturalism, or descriptivism, and his attempt to show that there can be a logic of imperatives as well as of indicatives. Hare summarizes his views in the entry on Ethics in this Encyclopedia. (J.O.U.)

Hart, Herbert L. A. (1907–92) Lawyer who taught at Oxford and, in *The Concept of Law* (1961), developed a liberal theory of law drawing on the resources of ANALYTIC PHILOSOPHY. Hart also wrote the article on Jurisprudence in this Encyclopedia.

Hartmann, Karl-Robert-Eduard von (1842–1906) Hartmann is known chiefly for his *Philosophy of the Unconscious* (1869), the most widely read of all German philosophical books of its time. Hartmann claimed to produce a synthesis of HEGEL and SCHOPENHAUER; taking from Hegel the notion of the rational Idea and from Schopenhauer that of the Will, he combined these in a new ultimate – the Unconscious. The rational Idea ought properly to guide blind Will, but the pessimistic Hartmann regarded them as at variance in sinful humanity. His reputation has much declined. (J.O.U.)

Hartmann, Nicolai (1882–1950) German philosopher, and one of the few twentieth-century practitioners of speculative metaphysics in the grand old style. He considered that European philosophy since DESCARTES had made a fundamental mistake in starting with the subject, the thinker. Knowledge, he said, was the apprehension of an independent reality, an apprehension as immediate as our apprehension of the self, according to Descartes. Properly understood, all philosophical problems are ontological: they are attempts to understand the kind of being presented to us. Metaphysical problems such as that of FREE WILL and of the relation of life to the mechanical are, according to Hartmann, essentially insoluble. According to Hartmann's ETHICS (which is indebted to HUSSERL and the PHENOMENOLOGISTS), there are two kinds of value: that of the things and situations with which agents deal, and that of agents and their actions. Specifically moral value is to be found in the disposition of the agent, and it is in this connection that Hartmann gives his famous analysis of the virtues. Agents and their actions can have value only if they are free; they must therefore be to some extent exempt from determination by natural law and even by values. In accordance with his general position on the insolubility of metaphysical problems, Hartmann admits that he cannot understand how such freedom is possible, but he is sure that it is presupposed in morality.   (J.O.U.)

Hazlitt, William (1778–1830)   English radical and essayist who was encouraged into philosophy by COLERIDGE. He published a brilliant essay on the self, the future and PERSONAL IDENTITY (*An Essay on the Principles of Human Action*, 1805) before turning to forms of literary activity that were commercially more rewarding.

Hedonism   The term 'hedonism' (from the Greek *hedone*, meaning 'pleasure') had been applied to three quite different views. First, ethical hedonism, the moral view nothing is good except pleasure. EPICURUS and BENTHAM are famous examples of moralists who have held this view. Second, psychological hedonism, which is the theory that we can desire nothing but pleasure. (Though this view has often been confused with ethical hedonism it is strictly incompatible with it, for if we can desire nothing else it is as pointless to recommend desires for pleasure as it is to recommend falling when one is released in mid-air.) This theory, frequently held by earlier British empiricists, was heavily attacked by BUTLER; but it nonetheless appears as a support for ethical hedonism in J. S. MILL's *Utilitarianism*. Third, the view that the notion of 'good' 'is to be defined in terms of 'pleasure'. Thus LOCKE in his *Essay* says that we call *good* whatever 'is apt to cause or increase pleasure, or diminish pain in us.' This view also has been confused with ethical hedonism in spite of the fact that 'pleasure alone is good' can have no moral content if it is a mere definition.   (J.O.U.)

Hegel, Georg Wilhelm Friedrich (1770–1831)   Hegel was born in Stuttgart, Germany, and was one of the most influential philosophers of all time; indeed, the entire history of philosophy since his death could be represented as a series of revolts against him and his followers. Even his opponents have absorbed much of his thought, and in order to gain some historical perspective on KIERKEGAARD and MARX, on Marxism and EXISTENTIALISM, on PRAGMATISM and ANALYTIC PHILOSOPHY, Hegel's influence must be taken into account.

Hegel himself published only four books: *Phenomenology of Spirit* (1807); *Science of Logic* (1812–16); *Encyclopedia* (1817; thoroughly rewritten edition 1827; revised edition 1830) and *Philosophy of Right* (1821). His philosophy may be divided into three phases, the first antedating the *Phenomenology*, the second represented by that book and the third by his later works, beginning with the *Logic*.

In the first phase we encounter a non-professorial Hegel, who could hardly be more different from his popular image. His earliest writings – drafts and essays from his twenties – were first published in 1907 under the misleading title *Hegel's Early Theological Writings*. In some of them, notably 'The Positivity of the Christian Religion', his style is brilliant, eloquent and picturesque, his criticism of the Christian churches, both Catholic and Protestant, and even of Jesus himself, is frequently vitriolic, and his opposition to all dogma and authoritarianism uncompromising. He does not oppose all religion but finds Christianity incompatible with reason and human dignity. In the oldest fragments, he considers the possibility of a wholly rational religion which would help us attain a harmonious personality and a high level of morality. By 1800, Hegel felt that the sort of criticism in which he had earlier engaged was all too easy, obvious and pointless. It would be a more challenging task to show how

Christianity and other beliefs held by the eminent thinkers in the past had been more than 'bare nonsense'. Perhaps one could even 'deduce this now-repudiated dogmatics out of what we now consider the needs of human nature and thus show its naturalness and its necessity'. This programme, sketched in 1800 in a preface to a never-written work, marks the transition to Hegel's second phase and to his *Phenomenology of Spirit*.

Hegel's use of the term 'necessity' in the last quotation foreshadows one of the central confusions of his subsequent philosophy. He uses it as a synonym of 'natural' and an antonym of 'arbitrary' and 'utterly capricious', and he fails to distinguish between giving reasons for a development and demonstrating its 'necessity'. In this sense he finds reason in history, but he does not claim – as many interpreters suppose – that historical events or particular entities can be 'deduced' in any ordinary sense. In the important preface to the *Phenomenology* he declares that he aims to elevate philosophy to the status of a science, but the book – and much of his later philosophy, too – is best understood in the perspective supplied by his early writings. What he wants is still a substitute for traditional Christianity – a world-view that eliminates whatever is incompatible with reason and human dignity while preserving whatever was sound in Christianity and in the thought of the great philosophers of the past. His prose, though still occasionally picturesque, has on the whole become involved and heavy, and his criticism no longer takes the form of sarcastic denunciation or outright ridicule: rather it consists in relegating all past positions, including various forms of Christianity, to the role of more or less remarkable, though plainly unsatisfactory, anticipations of the philosophical system that Hegel distils out of the cauldron of history.

Despite the scorn which Hegel's critics have lavished on his allegedly arrogant claims for his own system, the view of the HISTORY OF PHILOSOPHY on which these claims are based has been almost universally accepted; and when his claims are understood in terms of this view they prove to be much less presumptuous. Hegel does not pit his own philosophy against rival philosophies, past and present, by way of saying: 'they are wrong and I am right'. Rather he repudiates the common conception of philosophical disagreement – what one might call the battlefield view of the history of philosophy. The history of philosophy must be understood, he insists, in terms of development. It was Hegel more than anybody else who established the history of philosophy as a subject of central importance, and almost all texts on the subject show, albeit in varying degrees, his influence.

Hegel, then, does not look at his system as in any sense peculiarly his own. But he thinks he can draw on the cumulative efforts of his predecessors, showing how the excesses of one are in time pointed out by successors who, in turn, may well go to the opposite extreme. All along, there is a continual refinement, an increased articulateness, and, as it were, a progressive revelation of the truth.

This raises the question what Hegel expected from the future. Did he admit that his own system was not final? Hegel never supposed that history would stop with him. In his lectures on the philosophy of history he referred to the United States as 'the land of the future', while insisting that it must be left out of account at present, since it is the task of philosophy to comprehend 'that which is' and not to speculate about what is yet to come. The same course of lectures culminates in the pronouncement: 'to this point consciousness has come'. If he had foreseen the insights of future philosophers, he would have embodied them in his own system. Since he could not foresee them, he did not talk about them. For all that, he might have stressed, at least occasionally, that his own system was not final, instead of stressing, as he often did, that it was, if only at the time of speaking, the last word. This is surely a fault, but there are at least two extenuating circumstances. The first is that few great philosophers have not been guilty on the same score: from PLATO to WITTGENSTEIN (see preface to *Tractatus*), it is encountered in classic upon classic. Second, there was a peculiarly apocalyptic atmosphere in German philosophy in Hegel's day. We can trace it back at least to KANT's announcement, in the preface to the *Critique of Pure Reason* (1781), that he hoped philosophy would attain the truth by the end of the century. FICHTE tried to keep Kant's promise in 1794; SCHELLING, at first enthusiastic about Fichte, soon struck out on his own, publishing his *System of Transcendental Idealism* in 1800. Hegel felt he was completing what Kant, Fichte and Schelling had begun. In addition, there was a widespread feeling that an era was coming to an end, and Hegel, like the elderly Goethe, felt that the civilization he had known was drawing to a close, that he was looking back upon European history and in some sense summing it up. To cite the Preface to the *Philosophy of Right*: 'when philosophy paints its grey on grey, a form of life has grown old, and with grey on grey it cannot be rejuvenated, but only comprehended. The owl of Minerva begins its flight only at dusk'.

In the *Phenomenology* these tendencies are less prominent than in Hegel's later work. It is a work of youthful exuberance, though the Preface makes clear the author's desire to put an end to romanticism in philosophy. What is wanted is not inspiration and edification, sentiment and intuition, but careful and rigorous conceptual thinking – not the enthusiasm of a coterie but the discipline of a science. Even if one sympathizes with these programmatic declarations and with Hegel's sharp and perceptive criticism of romanticism, one may yet conclude that his own brand of rigour was misconceived from the start. The great central idea of the *Phenomenology* is that different outlooks correspond to different stages in the development of the spirit, and are not, taken as a whole, true or false, but rather more or less mature. The book is the story of the education of the spirit, and this framework allows for many penetrating observations. But it is marred by two pervasive faults: first, the above-mentioned confusion about necessity affects Hegel's attempts to show how one stage necessarily issues in the next; second, he assumes not only that some outlooks and positions are best understood in terms of a developmental sequence, but – and this assumption is surely untenable – that *all* outlooks and positions can be reasonably arranged in a single development, or even on a scale of rising maturity.

A further flaw in the *Phenomenology* is that it is never clear whose 'spirit' Hegel is discussing. Often it is clearly the human spirit, and Hegel seems to be writing about the education of humanity. But at other times, 'spirit' seems just as plainly an alias of God. Hegel clearly did not believe in a transcendent God, eternally omniscient and omnipotent; but he thought there was a force at work in the development of the material universe which eventually fashions humanity and finds expression in the human spirit, and that it may legitimately be named after its final and highest manifestation – just as we call an embryo an undeveloped human being. According to Hegel, it is only in humanity that the spirit achieves self-consciousness. Nevertheless Hegel does not repudiate traditional conceptions of the Trinity, the Incarnation, or God: he often makes use of Christian terms, praising Christianity for recognizing that God is spirit, that God becomes man, etc. This gives rise to the paradox that 'God' finds out about himself only in Hegel's system. The paradox disappears when we say that Hegel did not believe in 'God' but, like many other philosophers and theologians, did not make a point of this fact, preferring to pour new wine into old skins.

Hegel's *Logic* – the work which inaugurates his third and final phase – is marred to an even greater degree by pseudo-demonstrations and a confused notion of necessity. But again, much remains after allowance has been made for these faults: above all, perhaps the most sustained attempt since ARISTOTLE to articulate the meaning of philosophically interesting and important terms and their relation to each other. Unfortunately, many readers have never got beyond the first three terms: Being, Nothing and Becoming. Partly as a result of this, partly because it is a commonplace in the literature, they suppose, mistakenly, that all of Hegel is reducible to the three steps of Thesis, Antithesis and Synthesis. As a matter of fact, Hegel does not speak of theses, antitheses and syntheses at all, although his immediate predecessors, Fichte and Schelling, did; and neither his analyses in the *Logic* nor his dialectic in general can be reduced to any such three steps.

The point is even more obvious in Hegel's philosophy of history. He divides world history into three stages: in the first, in the ancient orient, only one is considered free (the ruler); in the second period, in Greece and Rome, some are free; in the modern world, all are considered free, at least in principle. Some English translations, however, introduce the word 'antithesis' in all kinds of places to render words that literally mean 'other' or 'opposite' and secondary sources perpetuate the legend that Hegel construed everything mechanically in terms of three concepts which he actually spurned.

The *Encyclopedia* contains his entire system in outline form. A shorter version of the *Logic*, slightly rearranged, (sometimes called the 'Lesser Logic') comprises part one; part two contains the Philosophy of Nature, subdivided into mechanics, physics and organics; and the Philosophy of Spirit forms part three. This too is divided into three parts, and each of these into three sub-parts; but these tripartite divisions cannot be reduced to theses, antitheses and syntheses. Subjective Spirit comprises sections on anthropology, the phenomenology of the spirit, and psychology. Then comes Objective Spirit which contains sections on right, morality and ethical life. Finally, the whole system culminates in a chapter on Absolute Spirit, divided into sections on art, revealed religion and – the pinnacle – philosophy.

The state belongs in the sphere of Objective Spirit – that is, spirit embodied in institutions – and is discussed in the section on ethical life (*Sittlichkeit*), after family and civil society (see also POLITICAL PHILOSOPHY). This whole realm is the basis on which art, religion and philosophy develop. 'All great men have formed themselves in solitude, but they have done so only by assimilating what has been created by the state.' Hegel's philosophy of Objective Spirit is developed in more detail in his *Philosophy of Right* and the lectures on the philosophy of history, from which the last quotation is taken. The philosophy of Absolute Spirit is elaborated in eight volumes of lectures on art, religion and the history of philosophy.

After Hegel's death, his followers quickly divided into two camps: a right wing that made the most of Hegel's theology and tried to infuse new life into Protestantism, and a left wing of so-called Young Hegelians who included brilliant atheists and revolutionaries – most notably Ludwig FEUERBACH and Karl Marx. Marx accepted Hegel's preoccupation with history and development but claimed that Hegel had stood humanity on its head, as if spirit and ideas were fundamental, while he, Marx, would set it on its feet again by pointing out that material factors are basic. Kierkegaard also protested against the Hegelian theologians. He repudiated all attempts to transcend faith, or even to comprehend Christianity (which, he insisted, is absurd but must be believed), or to use a system to hide from the problems of one's own concrete existence.

During the latter half of the nineteenth century, Hegelianism came to England and profoundly influenced T. H. GREEN, B. BOSANQUET, F. H. BRADLEY and J. M. E. MCTAGGART against whom, in turn, G. E. MOORE and Betrand RUSSELL revolted at the beginning of the twentieth century. In the United States, William JAMES rebelled against the Hegelian idealism of Josiah ROYCE and dozens of less gifted philosophers. John DEWEY was a Hegelian when young. In Italy, CROCE developed the Hegelian tradition. In France, SARTRE's *Being and Nothingness* leant heavily on Hegel. Beyond that, the historical approach to art, religion and literature, no less than philosophy, owes a great deal to Hegel. Perhaps no other thinker since Kant has had a comparable influence.   (W.K.)

Heidegger, Martin (1889–1976)

Heidegger taught at Marburg University from 1923 to 1928 and at the University of Freiburg-im-Breisgau from 1928 to 1958. His life-long preoccupation with the 'question of being' was first formulated in his unfinished magnum opus, *Being and Time* (1927), and then revised in lectures, books and essays until his death. Heidegger's *Seinsfrage* arose from a number of sources, among them ARISTOTLE's physics, metaphysics and ethics, interpreted in the light of his mentor HUSSERL's phenomenological method, KANT's *Critique of Pure Reason*, and the historical and HERMENEUTICAL investigations of Wilhelm DILTHEY. Aristotle inspired Heidegger to challenge Husserl's neo-Kantian thesis concerning 'acts of consciousness' as the sole resource of philosophy by asking: 'how does the being of *acts* relate to the being of the *objects* of those acts?' Thus the question of being was from the outset a question concerning TRUTH, understood not as the correspondence of propositions to states of affairs but as disclosure, unconcealment and what Heidegger later called the 'clearing of being', *die Lichtung des Seins*. Dilthey encouraged Heidegger to challenge Husserl's emphasis on 'evidence' as the sole philosophical recourse by asking: 'what sort of historical self-understanding lies behind philosophy's search for apodictic and adequate evidence; indeed, behind its fascination with cognition and theory of knowledge in general?'

Heidegger first elaborated the question of being as *fundamental ontology*, the 'science' of being. He set out in *Being and Time* to revise all the categories which prior philosophers had applied to the relations between human beings and their world. Fundamental ontology, as enquiry into being, was itself a possibility of human being (which Heideger called *Dasein*, 'being-there' or 'existence'). Dasein always operates within a prevailing understanding of being, or *Seinsverständnis*, even when it is not philosophizing. Traditional epistemologies and metaphysical systems appeared to have forgotten the salient features of human being as being-in-the-world: our manipulation of tools in the workaday world, a manipulation that does not depend on concepts such as 'extended substance' or 'primary and secondary qualities'; our absorption in a kind of 'public self' that defines most of the possibilities that shape our lives; and the occasional upsurge of an anxiety that exposes human being as eminently finite and mortal. None of these things pertains to 'knowledge': knowing the world is not the primary way of being in the world. Heidegger's reading of AUGUSTINE, Luther, KIERKEGAARD and NIETZSCHE had convinced him of the 'falling' character of the world and the need for human existence, as 'concern' (*Sorge*), to resist the everyday, public world. Such resistance does not take the form of an epistemological solipsism; rather, it is a matter of confronting without subterfuge one's own impending death. In this way one achieves an *appropriate* relation to one's own death. This proper relation to the finitude of Dasein Heidegger called *Eigentlichkeit*, a word that came to be translated by as 'authenticity'. Such an appropriate or 'ownmost' relation to the possibility of one's own death is said to reveal temporality and ultimately time itself as the horizon upon which the meaning of being is projected.

In essays and lecture courses of the 1930s and 1940s Heidegger expanded the scope of his question beyond human being to being as a whole, *das Seiende-im-Ganzen*. Actually, the tendency of human dispositions and moods to reveal being as a whole had long been noted by Heidegger. The expansion thus did not so much abandon the ontology of Dasein as exceed its terms of reference in the direction of 'meta-ontology'. Yet Heidegger soon let the vocabulary of ontology recede altogether: the guiding and grounding questions of METAPHYSICS now became

his principal concern. What is being? Why is there being, why not far rather nothing? How and why are beings understood as grounded in another being – for example, a Creator God? Heidegger's pursuit of the grounding question of metaphysics uncovered what he called the history or destiny of the truth of being: *Seinsgeschichte/ Seinsgeschick*. That history or destiny, viewed as a whole, unfolded essentially as oblivion of being, *Seinsvergessenheit*, the self-occultation of being. Nevertheless, the history of being consisted of more or less well-defined epochs: (1) early Greek thinking, which experienced the clearing of being without preserving that experience in texts, leaving only mere traces of being (see PRE-SOCRATICS); (2) PLATO and Aristotle, who founded metaphysics – in which 'being' is accepted uncritically as 'permanence of presence' – and who thus in some sense initiated the forgetting of the question of being, yet in whose works reminiscences of the great Greek tradition can still be found; (3) Latin and MEDIEVAL thought, which at least in its orthodox representatives obscured the Greek tradition and perpetuated an inferior version of Greek ontology; (4) modernity, which from DESCARTES and LEIBNIZ onward sought security no longer in sanctity but in certitude of cognition. The epochs of being thus culminate in an age of technology, and because technology closes off all other ways in which beings are disclosed, the age of technology completes the history in which being is forgotten. Thus it is the epoch of nihilism. Modern science is itself part of the technological framework of beings, and by no means the master of technology. Contemporary philosophy, with its compulsion to epistemological rigour, formal precision, calculability of truth, clarity and 'cashable' value of argument, exhibits both a Cartesian heritage and a technological destiny. Contemporary thinking is bound to be one-track thinking. 'The most thought-provoking thing in our thought-provoking time', wrote Heidegger in 1951, 'is that we are still not thinking'.

In writings after the Second World War, such as the famous 'Letter on "Humanism" ', Heidegger turned increasingly to the theme of language, especially the language of poetry. Language in Heidegger's view is not the vehicle of thought. Nor is it subject to manipulation – except as flattening out and vulgarizing. Nor, finally, does its 'normal' use, even in 'speech acts', allow it to serve as the arbiter of philosophical disputes. Heidegger strives to hear in language what he calls *Ereignis*, the event by which human beings, as mortals, are claimed and called upon to think. What they are called upon to think will vary from epoch to epoch, but it will invariably have to do with the 'granting' – the bestowing and preserving – of time and being, and thereby of the particular ways in which being as a whole is revealed: in our time, for example, as a stockpile of resources awaiting exploitation.

Within the CONTINENTAL tradition, Heidegger is without doubt the most powerfully original and influential philosopher of the twentieth century. PHENOMENOLOGY, EXISTENTIALISM and deconstruction (see DERRIDA) are unthinkable without him, but so are philosophy of literature and many social-critical or neo-Marxian strands of thought. His importance in the English-speaking world has also grown steadily, because no other thinker so unsettles the enterprise of ANALYTIC PHILOSOPHY. Yet the greatest single obstacle to the reception of Heidegger's work both in the Anglo-American world and on the Continent is his commitment during the 1930s to National Socialism. While his active engagement (as rector of Freiburg University in 1933–4) was brief, his antiliberal, anti-democratic sentiments endured.

For reasons that resist all explanation, he failed to speak out after the War in condemnation of Nazi atrocities. Even if his reasons for refusing had more to do with a Kierkegaardian contempt for publicity than with crass indifference, that silence more than anything else inhibits the reception of his thought. However, much research has been done on Heidegger's politics, and a more insightful and differentiated evaluation is becoming possible. Such nuanced responses are important if one of the most significant voices in modern European thought is not itself to be silenced.

Major works by Heidegger include: *Being and Time* (1927); *Kant and the Problem of Metaphysics* (1929); 'On the Essence of Truth' (1943, first delivered 1931); 'The Origin of the Work of Art' (1950, 1935); *Introduction to Metaphysics* (1953, 1935); *Nietzsche* (1961, 1936–41), 'Letter on "Humanism" ' (1947); *What is Called Thinking?* (1954); 'The Question Concerning Technology' (1954); *Identity and Difference* (1957); *On the Way to Language* (1959); *On Time and Being* (1969, 1961).   [D.F.K.]

Heraclitus   Heraclitus of Ephesus (a Greek city in Asia Minor) flourished *c*.500 BC. Of aristocratic family, he withdrew from society and, in notoriously obscure language, attacked the Ephesians, and everyone else, for their stupidity in failing to apprehend the Logos – a kind of common characteristic of all natural objects, in part identifiable with fire. Like ANAXIMANDER, he believed that things in the world were divided into opposites, and that all change was change between opposites. Despite appearances, these opposites were actually 'one and the same', being connected by the Logos in a 'joining that stretches in both directions', which ensured the ultimate balance and continuity of all changes. Thus Heraclitus located the unity of the world in its structure and behaviour rather than its matter. But the primary material was fire, which controlled the 'turnings' into each other of the three great cosmic components – fire, sea and earth. Change – or 'strife' as Heraclitus called it – was necessary for the continued unification of opposites: not perhaps continuous change in everything (as PLATO, thinking of the exaggerated Heracliteanism of CRATYLUS, maintained), but the certainty of ultimate change between opposites. Wisdom consists in understanding the Logos, how the world works; for humanity itself is part of the world and subject to the Logos, which is the active and fiery part of the human soul. This fiery part, which must be preserved from the moisture produced by sleep, stupidity and vice, makes contact with the Logos-element in external objects, and in some form can survive even death. Thus Heraclitus produced a remarkably coherent system, which gave a real motive for philosophy, and which for the first time gave some account of EPISTEMOLOGY. Its obscure presentation, and PARMENIDES' re-alignment of thought, prevented it from being as influential (until the STOICS) as it deserved to be. See also PRE-SOCRATICS.   (G.S.K.)

Hermeneutics   The theory and practice of interpretation (Greek: *hermeneia*). Originally applied to biblical criticism, the concept of hermeneutics was extended by Schleiermacher (1768–1834) and especially DILTHEY to cover the whole of human existence, and made the basis for a projected science of the human as distinct from the natural world. The concept was further developed within PHENOMENOLOGY, particularly by GADAMER and RICOEUR, and usually carries the implication that whilst some interpretations are better than others, none can ever be final. See also PSYCHOANALYSIS.   [J.R.]

Hesiod   See PRE-SOCRATICS.

Hilbert, David (1862–1943)   German mathematician and proponent of a 'formalist' interpretation of mathematics; see GÖDEL, MATHEMATICS.

Historical Materialism   The doctrine, famously articulated by MARX, that the fundamental historical discipline is the history of economic forms rather than of legal or political institutions or philosophical ideas. 'Just as one does not judge an individual by what he thinks about himself,' Marx wrote in 1859, 'so one cannot judge an epoch of transformation by its consciousness, but, on the contrary, this consciousness must be explained from the contradictions of material life.' See DIALECTICAL MATERIALISM, GRAMSCI, IDEOLOGY.

Historicism   The view that the only fully adequate way of understanding things (particularly human affairs) is by reference to their history, or the history of the contexts in which they occur or of humanity or nature as a whole is historicism. Ever since its origins in the nineteenth century, the term (alternatively *historism*) has been used polemically and mainly pejoratively – in PHENOMENOLOGY, for example, to denounce those who seek to substitute historical explanation for philosophical understanding and end up in the swamps of RELATIVISM; or by POPPER and his followers, to ridicule the belief (which they ascribe to MARX and HEGEL and associate with totalitarianism) that human affairs are governed by laws of history, just as natural processes are by laws of nature.   {J.R.}

History of Philosophy   It has commonly been agreed (too readily, perhaps) that the task of the scientist is to produce theories, and that theories are good or bad depending on how adequately they describe or explain established facts. On this view, the study of the history of science, though it can be entertaining or chastening or inspiring, is a distraction from science proper. 'A science which hesitates to forget its founders', as WHITEHEAD said, 'is lost'.

Philosophers who have aspired to model their discipline on the progress of the sciences have therefore disdained the study of the history of philosophy. KANT, for example, made a division between the authentic philosophers, 'who endeavour to draw from the fountain of reason itself', and their boring colleagues, the 'scholarly men to whom the history of philosophy is itself philosophy'. ANALYTIC PHILOSOPHERS have typically taken the same view; as QUINE put it, 'there are two kinds of people interested in philosophy, those interested in philosophy and those interested in the history of philosophy'.

In practice, however, would-be scientific philosophers have seldom succeeded in confining their attention to a supposedly ahistorical 'fountain of reason'. Whereas scientists have often discussed theories without caring about their original formulation or context, philosophers have repeatedly succumbed to historical curiosity. Many of them (RUSSELL for example) have produced both detailed studies of particular events in philosophy's past, and synoptic surveys of periods, movements or even the 'history of philosophy' taken as a whole. They have attempted to square this with their philosophical conscience by appealing to a distinction between their own approach to philosophy's past, which they take to be 'purely philosophical', and that of Kant's 'scholarly men', which they dismiss as 'merely historical'. The practical utility of this distinction is evident: it permits philosophers to insulate their histories of philosophy from historical criticism. Its theoretical justification is obscure

however; and it is hard to see why philosophers should bother with the past at all, if they are as uninterested in history as they profess to be. May it be that the entanglement of philosophy with its past is inevitable, even though unwelcome to some philosophers?

There are three main ways in which philosophy gets involved with its past. The first can be described as *connoisseurship*: just as poets or painters learn to be discriminating about their art, and hence capable of meaningful innovation, by acquainting themselves with existing masterpieces, so it is, presumably, with philosophers as well. Indeed the significance of a work of art, or poetry, or philosophy, may be wholly mysterious unless it is seen in relation to the past works to which – implicitly or explicitly, negatively or positively – it refers. This is especially true of philosophy, which is as often engaged in the exposure and diagnosis of plausible errors in the works of the illustrious dead, as with positive expositions of evident truths.

An even closer connection between philosophy and its past can be identified under the rubric of *canonicity*. The canon is, strictly speaking, the list of the books of the Bible which are accepted as genuine or inspired; by extension, it is the set of acknowledged masterpieces in which a practice acknowledges, or claims, its legitimate ancestry, and thereby forges a sense of its identity. If a discipline is uncertain or divided about its aims, objects and methods (as seems to be chronically the case with philosophy), then its canon becomes especially vital to it. The unity of the field of philosophical issues, and the cohesion of communities of philosophers, will depend on agreement about the contents of the philosophical canon. And specific theoretical projects, such as ANALYTIC PHILOSOPHY, CONTINENTAL PHILOSOPHY,

EMPIRICISM or PHENOMENOLOGY, or indeed 'Western philosophy' or 'philosophy' itself, will define themselves very largely in terms of their rival canons. Controversies as to the canonical status of works by, for example, HERACLITUS, SPINOZA, HEGEL, EMERSON, NIETZSCHE, GREEN, HEIDEGGER or DAVIDSON turn out to be debates about philosophy's nature and future, disguised as discussions of its past.

The third and most intimate link between philosophy and its past is provided by *plot*. By means of plot, the history of philosophy is divided into periods, and partitioned between various schools of thought, in such a way that it exhibits a philosophically meaningful development over time, probably leading to some present or imminent crisis. (If the addition of an idea of completeness to the objects of philosophical connoisseurship turns philosophy's past into a canon, then the addition of significant organization in time to the canon, produces philosophy's past as plot.)

These three kinds of connection between philosophy and its past can be traced back to SOCRATES, a connoisseur who defined himself against the historical background of the sophists; to PLATO, who canonized past philosophers as participants in his dialogues; and to ARISTOTLE, who conceived philosophy as a continuing cooperative enterprise whose plot should display rational progress. CICERO systematized the Aristotelian story by dividing philosophy into four Schools – EPICUREAN, STOIC, ACADEMIC (Platonic) and PERIPATETIC (Aristotelian); and SENECA drew the obvious eclectic moral; 'we must imitate the bees', he said, 'who raid whichever flowers they need for making their honey'.

The classical view of the canon and plot of philosophy's past was crystallized in DIOGENES LAERTIUS' gossipy *Lives of the Philosophers*, written in the third century AD, which defined philosophy in Europe throughout the middle ages and the renaissance. Georg Horn was the first to mount a systematic challenge to Diogenes. His *Philosophical Histories* (1655) added postclassical authors to the philosophical canon, and organized ancient (pagan) and modern (Christian) philosophy into a single 'Judaeo-Christian' plot, in which Jesus Christ played a pivotal role. But Diogenes was not definitively displaced until the appearance of Johann Jakob Brucker's *Critical History of Philosophy* (1742–4) – a monumental work which firmly established a three-part plot for the history of philosophy, with ancient philosophical wisdom at the beginning, medieval scholastic darkness in the middle and modern eclectic enlightenment at the end. This tightly articulated history had the fateful effect of presenting the whole history of philosophy as culminating exclusively in Western Europe (see AFRICAN PHILOSOPHY).

For Hegel the historicity of philosophy was a cardinal philosophical problem: true philosophy would have to go behind the apparently self-defeating quarrels of the past, and the complacent eclecticism of modern enlightenment as celebrated by Brucker, in order to reveal an underlying intellectual unity in the history of philosophy as a whole. According to Hegel, all true philosophers incorporated the principles of their predecessors, even if they thought they were rejecting or ignoring them; despite appearances, therefore, the plot of philosophy's past expressed a single unified argument, and 'the same Architect has been directing the work for thousands of years'. Whether they knew it or not, philosophers could only articulate this inherited argument for the benefit of their own age, and clarify its implications for the future. Philosophy might attempt to escape its past, but it was never going to succeed.

Of course philosophers may still try to avoid a Hegelian submission to history by imitating the progress of the sciences. But unfortunately for them, this unhistorical concept of scientific progress has been discredited by the progress (if such it is) of the PHILOSOPHY OF SCIENCE. POPPER's theory of science as a cycle of arbitrary conjectures and systematic refutations, followed by KUHN's idea of scientific revolutions as instituting new paradigms incommensurable with the old, and BACHELARD's idea of the 'breaks' which inaugurate the different sciences, have all suggested that criteria of scientific truth may themselves be contingent and perspectival. RORTY has drawn negative conclusions about the whole of 'traditional philosophy'. MACINTYRE however has attempted to get round the difficulty by arguing that whilst both science and philosophy are 'essentially historical', they are still rational, and indeed that they could not be rational unless they were embedded in particular traditions. On this view, the distinction between historical and philosophical approaches to philosophy crumbles, and many elements of Hegelian HISTORICISM are reinstated.

However, Hegel's view of the history of philosophy tends to conceal the arbitrary artifice in the smooth idea of a self-contained tradition called '(Western) philosophy' which fuses Jewish, Christian and ancient Greek elements. MARX tried to escape Hegel's emollient philosophical historicism (if not his Eurocentrism) by replacing a history of modes of philosophising by a history of modes of production. Both KIERKEGAARD and Nietzsche revolted against Hegel's homogenized conception of history by affirming the awkward and absurd irreducibility of the 'actually existing individual'.

Heidegger and DERRIDA have argued that the development of philosophy as recounted by Hegel is really an increasingly disastrous forgetting of philosophical questions, rather than a triumphantly progressive solution of them. And FOUCAULT has suggested that the whole conception of a Western philosophical tradition benignly seeking the truth is a systematic concealment of the processes in which political powers establish and legitimize themselves through a violent exclusion of those whom they define as mad or otherwise beyond the bounds of reason. Such attempts to 'invert' Hegel – whether Popperian, Marxist, Nietzschean or Foucaldian – all agree with Hegel on one point, though: detached objectivity is impossible in any history of philosophy, or for that matter in an encyclopedia.   [J.R.]

Hobbes, Thomas (1588–1679)   English philosopher educated at Oxford. In 1608 he became tutor to the young son of William Cavendish, Earl of Devonshire, and spent the rest of his long life in similar employment, mainly with the Cavendish family. He was tutor to Charles II during his exile in Paris in 1646.

Hobbes' intellectual history can be conveniently related to his three visits to the continent. His first, in 1610, inspired him with a desire to master the thought of the ancient world. His dissatisfaction with Aristotelianism was probably encouraged by his talks with Francis BACON. In 1628 he published a translation of Thucydides, partly to warn his fellow-countrymen of the dangers of democracy. In 1628, during his second journey to the continent, he developed both a passionate interest in geometry, whose method he thought he might use to present his conclusions about democracy as irrefragable demonstrations. He thought, like Bacon, that knowledge meant power, and hoped to cure the ills of a society on the verge of Civil War by sketching a rational reconstruction of society like a geometer's figure. Hobbes' third journey to the continent provided the final ingredient for his natural and civil philosophy: he visited Galileo in 1636 and conceived the imaginative idea which permeated his whole philosophy – the generalization of the science of mechanics and the geometrical deduction of the behaviour of men from the abstract principles of the new science of motion.

Hobbes claimed originality for two main parts of his work: the optics and the civil philosophy. His *Little Treatise* (1630–7) was an attack on the Aristotelian theory of sense and a sketch for a new mechanical theory. On returning to England his thoughts turned again to politics, owing to the turbulent state of the country. In 1640 he published *Elements of Law* – which demonstrated the need for undivided sovereignty – while Parliament was sitting. When Parliament impeached Strafford, Hobbes fled to the continent, priding himself in later times on being 'the first of all that fled'. In *De Cive* (1642, published in English in 1651 under the title *Philosophical Rudiments Concerning Government and Society*), he tried to demonstrate conclusively the proper purpose and extent of the civil power, and the relationship between church and state.

Hobbes' originality revealed itself not only in his views about optics and politics, but also in the links he forged between them. He thought an all-inclusive theory could be constructed starting with simple movements studied in geometry and culminating in the movements of men in political life. He envisaged a deductive trilogy comprising works on Body, Man and Citizen, but the project was constantly interrupted by events. He started on *De Corpore* soon after the publication of *De Cive*, but with the arrival of Charles II in Paris, Hobbes started work on his masterpiece, *Leviathan*, which stated in a pungent form his views on Man and Citizen. It was published in 1651 and soon afterwards Hobbes was permitted by Cromwell to return to England. For Hobbes used the SOCIAL CONTRACT theory to demonstrate the necessity of an absolute sovereign – by consent, not by Divine Right. So his doctrine could be used to justify any government, provided it governed effectively.

Soon after his return to England, Hobbes became involved in a dispute with Bishop Bramhall on the subject of FREE WILL. His *Questions Concerning Liberty, Necessity, and Chance* was the result (1656). Hobbes was then led into a most humiliating controversy; for in *De Corpore* (1655) he had inserted an attempt to square the circle. This was seized on by John Wallis and Seth Ward, both of them Puritans and foundation members of the Royal Society, who were irritated by Hobbes' criticisms of the universities and ruthlessly exposed his mathematical ineptitude. The wrangle lasted for about twenty years.

Hobbes' energy was remarkable (he played tennis up till the age of 70). In 1657 he published the second part of his trilogy, the *De Homine*. After the Restoration he was received at Court, where his wit was appreciated. But at the time of the Plague and Great Fire some reason was sought for God's displeasure, and when a bill was brought before Parliament for the suppression of atheism, a committee was set up to look into *Leviathan*. The matter was however dropped, probably through the intervention of the King, but Hobbes was forbidden to publish his opinions. He turned to history and in 1668 completed his *Behemoth* – a history of the Civil War, interpreted in the light of his opinions about man and society. (It was published posthumously in 1682.) He was also sent Bacon's *Elements of Common Law* by his friend John Aubrey and, at the age of 76, produced *Dialogues Between a Philosopher and a Student of the Common Laws of England.* (Published posthumously in 1681.) At 84 he wrote his autobiography in Latin verse and at 86 published a translation of the *Iliad* and *Odyssey.* He died at the age of 91.

His contribution to philosophy can be summarized under eight headings.

1 *Philosophical Method.* Like his contemporaries BACON and DESCARTES, Hobbes believed that natural reason was in decay for want of a proper method, and clouded over by the vaporous doctrines of the Schools. He saw philosophy as a necessary preliminary to rational government and the avoidance of Civil War – the worst of all evils, from which come 'slaughter, solitude, and the want of all things'. But he understood philosophy in a very wide sense: 'such knowledge of effects or appearances as we acquire by true ratiocination from the knowledge we have first of their causes or generation. And again, of such causes or generations as may be from knowing first their effects'. Like all his rationalist contemporaries, he believed that the reality beneath the deceptive appearances of sense was geometrical in character. He regarded the use of reason as a kind of adding and subtracting 'of the consequences of general names agreed upon for the marking and signifying of our thoughts'.

2 *The Metaphysics of Motion.* Hobbes' analysis was, as a matter of fact, usually subservient to his wider speculations. For his dream of a trilogy covering Body, Man and Citizen coloured all his work. He conceived of human actions as particular cases of bodies in motion,

explicable in terms of all-pervasive mechanical laws. This was made plausible by the introduction of the concept of 'endeavour' to postulate infinitely small motions of various sorts – especially those in the medium between man and external objects, in the sense-organs, and within the body. The phenomena of sense, imagination and dreams were regarded as appearances of minute bodies conforming to the law of inertia, and the phenomena of motivation were explained as reactions prompted by external and internal stimulation. Hobbes became famous, however, (and notorious), for his suggestion that all human motivation is a particular case of one of two basic bodily movements – appetite, or movements towards objects, and aversion, or movements away from them.

3 *Politics.* In his political writings these basic responses appeared as the desire for power and the fear of death, which were the reality beneath all the appearances of political behaviour. Hobbes thought that a multitude became a commonwealth by the device of authority in which they gave up unlimited self-assertion against each other – their 'rights of nature' – and authorized some individual or body to act on their behalf. This 'social contract', which was presupposed by sovereignty, was a consequence of the overwhelming fear of death which haunted humanity in a state of nature. Hobbes also deduced from this 'ideal experiment' that such a sovereign must be absolute, the sole reason for the institution of government being the safety of the people.

4 *Ethics.* This deductive scheme determined the general pattern of Hobbes' thinking about morals, law and religion. In moral philosophy he held that the rules of civilized behaviour ('natural law' or 'the laws of nature') were deducible from

the rules of prudence which must be accepted by any reasonable agent with a fear of death. Civilization, he contended, is based on fear, not on natural sociability. By 'good' we mean an object of desire, by 'evil' an object of aversion. He believed, too, in DETERMINISM and made important contributions to the free will controversy by maintaining that 'free' is a term properly applied to people and their actions, rather than to the will, which is but 'the last appetite in deliberating'. People are free when there is no constraint on their actions; but all actions are necessitated, in that they have causes, even though they may be free. For the opposite of 'necessitated' is not 'free' but 'contingent'. Hobbes was also singularly clear-sighted on the subject of punishment, holding that it is by its nature retributive, though its justification must be sought along UTILITARIAN lines.

5 *Law.* Hobbes is famous for his view that law is the command of the sovereign. This was, historically speaking, a very important thesis in that it attempted to make clear the procedural difference between statute law (which was then in its infancy) and Common Law, and insisted on distinguishing the questions: 'what is the law?' and 'is the law just?'

6 *Religion.* Hobbes' views on religion were, to a large extent, directed to showing that there were general grounds as well as scriptural authority for the belief that the sovereign was the best interpreter of God's will. Religion was a system of law, not a system of truth. To establish this Hobbes distinguished between knowledge and faith. He suggested that we could know nothing of the attributes of God. The adjectives used to describe him were expressions of adoration, not products of reason. He was particularly vehement in defending what he called the 'true religion' against the twin

threats of Catholicism, with its extramundane authority, and the Puritans who took seriously the priesthood of all believers. In the course of this onslaught he dealt mercilessly, from the point of view of mechanical metaphysics, with Biblical concepts such as 'spirit', 'inspiration', 'miracles' and 'the kingdom of God'. On the problem of EVIL he pointed out very acutely that the only solution was to stress God's power. Did not God reply to Job 'where wast thou when I laid the foundations of the earth?'

7 *Philosophy of Language.* Many modern philosophers hold that Hobbes' outstanding contribution to philosophy was his theory of speech. He tried to combine a mechanical view about the causes of speech with a NOMINALIST account of the meaning of general terms. He was particularly vitriolic about the scholastic doctrine of essences. Names could be either names of bodies, of properties, or of names. If one of these classes of names was used as if it belonged to another class, an absurdity would be generated. 'UNIVERSAL', for instance, was a name for a class of names, not for essences designated by names; such names are 'universal' because of their use, not because they refer to a special type of entity. Similarly redness (which is a property) is not in blood in the same way as blood (which is a body) is in a bloody cloth (which is another body). Hobbes' distinctions were crude, but he anticipated the techniques of logical analysis by supplementing the demand for concreteness and clarity of speech by a theory of how absurdities are generated by insensitivity to the logical behaviour of different classes of terms. But of much more general importance was his insistence that speech was essential to reasoning and that it was reasoning, in the sense of laying down definitions and drawing out the implications of

general names, that distinguished men from animals.

8 *Assessments of Hobbes.* Hobbes' contemporaries were alarmed at his denial of any sort of extra-human authority, at his thoroughgoing doctrine of human selfishness, and at his suggestion that we can know none of God's attributes. SPINOZA, who owed a lot to Hobbes, purged his political doctrines of their inconsistencies and converted political philosophy into a theory of power. LOCKE criticized Hobbes mainly for his doctrine of human selfishness and his willingness to substitute the terror of an arbitrary sovereign for that of a state of nature. LEIBNIZ was full of admiration for Hobbes – especially his nominalism – but aghast at his determinism and agnosticism about God's attributes. During the eighteenth century, criticism was focused on Hobbes' account of the passions – especially his attempt to show that benevolence is a special case of self-love. The UTILITARIANS regarded Hobbes as their intellectual ancestor and were impressed by his individualism, his mechanical psychology, his nominalism, and his theory of law and punishment. And MARX viewed Hobbes as a pioneer of materialism and approved of his determination to use knowledge for practical purposes rather than merely to understand. Modern philosophers have tended to criticize Hobbes for his naturalism in ethics and for his mechanical account of man. They have, however, dwelt on the startling similarity between Hobbes' account of a state of nature and international affairs. They have praised Hobbes for his interest in language, for his analytic techniques, and for his clarity in handling political concepts. And even if they disagree with most of the details of his scheme, they accord Hobbes the doubtful honour of being the father of modern psychology and one of the first systematic social scientists.   (R.S.P.)

Hocking, William Ernest (1873–1966) Hocking was born in Cleveland, Ohio, and became a disciple of Josiah ROYCE. At a time when most professional philosophers in America were abandoning philosophical IDEALISM, Hocking defended it with an eloquence which made him a significant factor in American intellectual history. His influence was especially strong in religious and theological circles. His most important books were *The Meaning of God in Human Experience* (1912) and *Human Nature and its Remaking* (1923).   (J.W.S.)

Holbach, Baron d' (1723–89) Franco-German exponent of materialistic atheism, see ENCYCLOPEDISTS, MATERIALISM.

Holism The term 'holism' (from the Greek *holos*, meaning 'whole') denotes the thesis that wholes are more than the sum of their parts. It is a rational, rather than mystical, alternative to atomism and scientific mechanism. The doctrine inhabits many disciplines: in political philosophy, for example, holism opposes individualism by collectivism; in historiography and social science, it maintains that the objects of social inquiry are wholes rather than individual actions; in psychology, it sets the focus on Gestalts, not elements; and in the philosophy of biology, it opposes both mechanism and vitalism, asserting that life consists in the dynamic system of the organism.

While predecessors like SPINOZA and HEGEL thought in a holistic way, the term 'holism' was coined by the South African statesman-scholar J. C. Smuts (1870–1950), who argued that wholes – both animate and inanimate – are real, while parts are abstract analytical distinctions, and wholes are flexible patterns that are not simply mechanical assemblages of self-sufficient elements. Like BERGSON, he rejected Darwin's theory of natural selection and argued for 'internal holistic selection', though as a natural rather than immaterial principle.

Among analytic philosophers, QUINE has opposed the atomistically formulated verifiability theory of meaning in claiming that it is not the isolated statement, but the whole ensemble of assumptions involving it, which is amenable to empirical testing. POPPER, on the other hand, though maintaining that scientific method is applicable to the study of individual aspects of social systems, has rejected holistic attempts to formulate laws holding for social wholes, regarding the latter as theoretical constructs. [M.M.]

Hook, Sidney (1902–89) American pragmatist born in New York. Hook wrote extensively on the philosophy of Karl MARX (*Towards the Understanding of Karl Marx*, 1933; *From Hegel to Marx*, 1936), defending Marxism as a version of American PRAGMATISM, rather than as DIALECTICAL MATERIALISM. But with the passage of time he decided that what he approved therein was certainly not what the usual 'Marxists' advocated (*Marx and the Marxists, the Ambiguous Legacy*, 1955). His later work expressed rancorous disillusion with Marxism. (J.W.S)

Horkheimer, Max (1895–1973) German social theorist born in Stuttgart. Along with Theodor ADORNO and Herbert MARCUSE, Horkheimer was one of the architects of the FRANKFURT SCHOOL conception of 'Critical Theory'. Horkheimer assumed the directorship of the Institute for Social Research in 1930, guiding it throughout the period of its greatest productivity; he edited the Institute's journal, *Zeitschrift für Sozialforschung* (1932–9), and oversaw the Institute's move from Frankfurt to New York in 1935 and its return to Frankfurt in 1949.

Horkheimer is best known for the numerous essays he wrote for the *Zeitschrift*, now collected in the two-volume *Kritische Theorie*; and for *Dialectic of Enlightenment*, which he wrote in 1944 with Adorno. In his writings of the 1930s, notably 'Traditional and Critical Theory' (1937), he developed an original version of the sort of philosophy of praxis inaugurated by Georg LUKÁCS. Increasingly, however, he saw the impossibility of an integration of philosophy with social science, or of critical theory with revolutionary practice. After the War, Horkheimer's critical theory became a critique of 'enlightened' reason and rationality. Reason, he argued, has been reduced to an instrumental, means-end, reason, which suppresses difference and particularity through the establishment of regimes of identity. The model for such regimes was the domination of (concrete) use values by (abstract) exchange value. The critical and paradoxical auto-critique of Reason must acknowledge suffering in the name of that which is dominated and suppressed by identity thinking. [J.M.B]

Humanism The term 'humanism' entered the philosophical vocabulary by way of the *studia humanitatis*, associated with the focus of Renaissance education on classical culture as opposed to Christian scripture. In the late nineteenth century it established itself as an umbrella term for any disposition of thought stressing the centrality of 'Man' or the human species in the order of nature. Today, in the Anglophone world, humanism is more or less synonymous with atheism or secular rationalism. In the CONTINENTAL tradition, however, it has come to designate (often pejoratively) any philosophy (FEUERBACH, the young MARX, PHENOMENOLOGY, EXISTENTIALISM, for example) premised on ontological differences between humanity and the rest of nature, and according priority to it in the explanation of society, history and culture. According to humanists, there are qualities and capacities peculiar to human beings which make their products – whether historical events, economic systems or literary works – unamenable to the objective and reductive analyses associated with standard scientific explanation.

While the epistemological reference of humanism is to the human subject as the locus of experience and source of knowledge, the political stress falls on human agency and hence control over historical process. Marxist and socialist humanists have wanted to respect the 'dialectic' between human agency and the circumstances in which it is exercised, but there has been a certain polarization in their argument: the existentialist approach has placed an emphasis on consciousness which is difficult to reconcile with the idea of 'unwilled' social forces whilst the Hegelian-Lukácsian school has emphasized the loss of humanity inflicted by generalized processes of reification and ALIENATION, though perhaps at the cost of making them appear inescapable.

In contrast to both these positions, STRUCTURALIST and 'post-structuralist' anti-humanists either insisted on the subordination of individuals to economic structures, codes and regulating forces (modes of production, kinship systems, the unconscious etc.) or attempted to 'deconstruct' the very idea of a 'human meaning' prior to the discourse and cultural systems whose qualities it is supposed to explain. Thus, Jacques DERRIDA detected a 'humanist' residue even in SAUSSURE's structural linguistics, in so far as it allows the sign to retain a reference to a 'signified'. More generally, humanist argument has been rejected by these schools of thought for its 'mythological anthropology', teleology and ethnocentricity. [K.S.]

Hume, David (1711–76) Scottish historian and philosopher, who never held any academic post, though in 1745 he stood unsuccessfully for the Chair of 'Ethics and Pneumatic Philosophy' at Edinburgh. His ruling passion, he tells us, was a love of literary fame, and this he achieved in his lifetime mainly by essays on moral, political and economic subjects, and historical works. The only important post he held was that of secretary to the British Embassy in Paris (1763–9), where he cut a considerable figure. Though not without friends in the church, he was an opponent of all established religions, and enjoyed notoriety as an 'infidel'.

Hume's first philosophical work, *A Treatise of Human Nature*, was completed by 1737, when he was 26. It was the product of ten years of unremitting intellectual effort and its aim was ambitious: to remedy the defects of previous philosophies, which seemed to 'depend more upon invention than experience', by establishing the foundations of a genuinely empirical science of human nature. The first step was to investigate the understanding and the passions, on which all human judgements and actions depend. The *Treatise* was divided into three books, 'Of the Understanding', 'Of the Passions' and 'Of Morals', and was intended to lay the foundations of the most fundamental of sciences: 'there is no question of importance', Hume wrote, 'whose decision is not comprised in the science of man'.

1 *Impressions and Ideas.* The mind, Hume said, consists of nothing but perceptions, and these are of two kinds, impressions and ideas. Roughly speaking, impressions are sensations, feelings and emotions; and ideas are thoughts. Impressions are forceful and vivacious, and ideas are faint copies of them. Impressions are of two kinds: primary

impressions of sense, which arise in the soul 'from unknown causes', and secondary impressions of reflection, which arise from our ideas. Aversion, for instance, is caused by the idea of pain, itself a copy of the primary impression of pain. Ideas too are of two kinds, simple and complex. Simple ideas are copies of simple impressions that we have actually had, while complex ideas are combinations of simple ideas and need not mirror any actual combination of impressions (if they do, and do so vividly, they are memories). That is how we are able to think of dragons and other things we have never perceived. But we cannot have a simple idea which is not derived from a corresponding impression, and all our complex ideas are constructed out of simpler ideas derived from impressions. This, Hume says, implies that we have no 'innate ideas': all our ideas are derived from experience. The objects of our thoughts are confined to such as we have experienced, or conceivably might experience, by the senses or inner feeling. All these propositions, Hume thinks, are evident from experience, known from observation of our own minds. EMPIRICISM is an empirical truth.

Though the fancy may join ideas as it pleases, it tends to join those whose corresponding impressions have been either alike, or contiguous in time or place, or related as cause and effect. Hume attached the greatest importance to these principles of association. 'Here is a kind of *attraction*, which in the mental world will be found to have as extraordinary effects as in the natural, and show itself in as many and as various forms.' 'These are the only ties of our thoughts, they are really *to us* the cement of the universe.' The meaning of a word, according to Hume, is the range of ideas associated with one another by resemblance, with which the word is associated by contiguity; in plain English, all objects sufficiently like those in whose presence we have heard the word used. Understanding a word is the activation of these associations.

Space and time, however, are evidently neither impressions nor groups of impressions, so Hume describes each of them as a 'manner' in which impressions appear to us, mirrored in the manner of appearance of the resulting ideas. Time is the 'manner' in which all perceptions occur, that is successively or simultaneously. Space is the manner in which coloured and tangible points are disposed, that is alongside one another. Since size and duration are defined in terms of the manner in which unitary perceptions are disposed, these latter cannot themselves have size or duration, and are consequently simple and indivisible. Since no ideas are infinitely divisible, we have no idea of infinite divisibility, and it is therefore inconceivable, whatever the mathematicians may say.

2 *Causal Reasoning.* Reasoning, according to Hume, consists in the discovery of relations. These may be either (a) 'relations of ideas', which yield demonstrative reasoning, showing what is conceivable or inconceivable (i.e. absurd or self-contradictory), or (b) relations in which objects as a matter of fact to stand one to another. That three is half six, and the internal angles of a triangle equal to two right angles, are relations of ideas, depending on the nature of the ideas related. That mercury is heavier than lead, that Caesar was murdered in the Forum, that the number of the planets is nine, are matters of fact, which could conceivably have been otherwise. A matter of fact cannot be demonstrated, since its opposite is conceivable without absurdity or contradiction; it can only be learned from experience. The only important field of demonstrative reasoning, Hume said, was mathematics. Consequently any books that

comprise neither mathematical demonstrations nor empirical reasoning (i.e. most works on metaphysics and theology), contain 'nothing but sophistry and illusion', and should be 'committed to the flames'.

Though matters of fact cannot be demonstrated, they can be inferred with probability, and the relation on which such inferences depend is cause and effect. There is no other relation, according to Hume, which enables us to infer the existence of an object we have not observed from the existence of one we have. This relationship is therefore of 'prodigious consequence', and Hume's account of it is the most fundamental feature of his philosophy. Hume insists that neither the proposition that everything has a cause, nor any proposition assigning a particular cause to a particular occurrence, is demonstrable. A priori, it is perfectly conceivable that some events should be fortuitous, and that anything should cause anything. Nothing but experience teaches us the orderliness of nature, or what exactly causes what.

But how do we learn that one thing is the cause of another? The effect, we all suppose, immediately succeeds the cause and is contiguous to it in space, and we can identify these features – succession and contiguity – by our impressions of sense. But there is a third feature which is more elusive. The effect *necessarily* follows the cause. It is this *necessary connexion* that enables us to infer the one from the other. And it is not a *logical* connexion, demonstrable or self-evident like the proportions of numbers. What is it then? Hume's answer is as follows. The necessary connection we seek is the foundation of inferences from cause to effect, so let us consider the foundation of the inference in common life. It is not far to seek. If, for instance, flame has always been attended by heat, and has never occurred without it, then when we see a flame we infer the presence of heat, and 'without further ceremony we call the one cause and the other effect'. The necessary connection we refer to when we say flame causes heat, consists in nothing but the fact that heat has regularly followed flame in the past, and that we cannot help expecting it to do so again. The 'must' of causal necessity expresses only our readiness to infer, which is due to experienced regularity.

Hume subsumed this account of causal inference under the general principle of association of ideas. Seeing the flame is an impression, associated by resemblance with the ideas of flames seen in the past, each of which is associated by contiguity with the idea of heat. So the impression of flame readily evokes the idea of heat. The vivacity of the impression transfers itself in part to the associated idea, and the frequent repetition of the transition from impression to associated idea gives it a customary facility, a kind of felt unavoidability. These two features, the vivacity of the idea, and the steadiness of custom, make it what we call a *belief*. Where the regularity in past cases is unbroken, and the custom consequently full and perfect, we have *certainty* and *empirical proof*. Where either the regularity or the resemblance of the present case to the past cases is imperfect, the inference is uncertain, and we speak of *probability*.

3 *Scepticism.* So far Hume has attempted to present a constructive theory of knowledge, sceptical only in so far as it undermines various pretensions – those of the metaphysicians and theologians who try to provide a priori demonstrations of matters of fact (e.g. the existence of God, or how the world began), and those of the natural scientists who try to prove exact and final truths, or provide rational explanations a posteriori. He has opened

the way for a descriptive science of man, in every way as respectable as the physical sciences. But when Hume discusses the fallibility of reason and the senses, and the nature of the mind, he reaches conclusions so sceptical that no science could possibly be founded on them.

Hume's argument against the efficacy of reason is designed to support his contention that belief is a psychological state due to instinct and habituation, not the completion of a logical exercise. If the exercise of reasoning were ever carried to its logical conclusion, it would destroy assurance about everything. Belief, therefore, since it undoubtedly occurs, must be due to something else: it must be natural, not logical. The sceptic's arguments fail to carry conviction, not because they are invalid, but because they are 'remote and strained', carrying us far beyond the experiences of common life. But now the baby of science has been thrown out with the bathwater of metaphysics, as Hume realizes: 'Shall we then establish it for a general maxim that no refined or elaborate reasoning is ever to be received? By this means you cut off all science and philosophy.'

Hume need not have despaired. His arguments for the self-destructiveness of reason are fallacious. If we make a calculation according to sure mathematical principles, we may still make a mistake. The probability of our conclusion is the probability of our not having made a mistake. But in estimating this probability we may again make a mistake, and the probability of our original conclusion sinks to that of our not having made this second mistake. And so on *ad infinitum*. This process would, according to Hume, ultimately reduce the probability to zero. But there is no reason why these probabilities should decrease. The probability of a firm's profits for the year being what the accounts show is equal to the probability of there being no error in the books. But the probability of the auditors being right in thinking that there is no error may well be greater than the original probability of the accounts being correct.

Hume's account of sense-perception is equally unsatisfactory. How can our preceptions – either impressions or ideas – give rise to knowledge of physical objects? The impressions of sense are interrupted, as well as being part of, and dependent on us, whereas physical objects are relatively permanent, and independent and distinct from us. Hence they cannot be known by sense alone; nor can they be inferred by an argument from effect to cause. For to know that a given sensation was due to a certain material thing, we would have had to be able to observe the two separately and notice the constant conjunction between them. And our ability to observe the material thing apart from the sensation is precisely the question at issue.

Since neither sense nor reason produces our belief in material things, Hume concludes that it must arise from imagination. By certain weird 'propensities', quite different from the ordinary principles of association of ideas, we are impelled to construct a picture of a relatively permanent and regular world in which the gaps in the series of impressions we call mountains and fires are filled with fictitious unperceived impressions. This 'world' provides the material for the investigations of natural science, which soon convince us that impressions and their sensible qualities, such as colour and warmth, are wholly dependent on our perception of them and cannot have an independent existence. Science consequently bids us accept an unimaginable world of atoms with no qualities at all, and sense and imagination bid us accept a world which is scientifically impossible. 'Carelessness and inattention' are the only remedies for this and other sceptical quandaries.

4 *The Human Mind.* Hume's account of the mind is similar. Nothing is discoverable but perceptions, which are distinct occurrences, like the successive pictures in a cinema display. They stand in relations of succession, similarity and causation, but there is no other real bond between them. The self is a mere figment, an imaginary string on which the beads are strung. 'I am nothing but a bundle of perceptions.' But who or what imagines the string? How is the series conscious of its own serial existence? Hume cannot answer, 'pleads the privilege of a sceptic', and says the question is too hard.

The absurdities of Hume's accounts of sensory perception and of the mind arise from the starting point of his philosophy – the doctrine of impressions and ideas. Hume supposes them to be the undeniable elements of which experience is composed, but in fact they are nothing but the fragments of a metaphysical ghost exploded by Hume himself. That ghost was the 'simple indivisible incorporeal substance', conscious only of its own ideas, and performing on them sundry ghostly acts – perception, volition, judgement, doubting etc. – which DESCARTES had foisted on philosophers as the human mind. Hume rejected ghostly substance and its ghostly acts, but retained 'ideas', or 'perceptions' as he preferred to call them, and attempted to reconstruct the world of common sense out of their spontaneous antics.

5 *Moral Philosophy.* Hume's contribution to moral philosophy is closely parallel to his contribution to the theory of knowledge. As he distinguished matters of fact from relations of ideas, so he now distinguishes ethical judgements from both of them. An ethical judgement states neither that something could not conceivably be otherwise, nor that something is

as a matter of fact the case. And just as matters of fact cannot be inferred from relations of ideas, so ethical statements cannot be inferred from either. Just as the discovery of matters of fact depends on relations of necessary connection, which seem to be objective, but are really dispositions of the mind, so ethical judgements depend on rightness and wrongness, goodness and badness, which seem to be objective qualities of persons and acts, but are really the approvals and disapprovals of the judger's mind. Just as our dispositions to expect depend on our experience of regular conjunctions, so our approvals and disapprovals depend on our past experience of pleasant and unpleasant consequences. Just as the natural scientist regulates our expectations by means of general and well-substantiated regularities, so the moralist regulates our approvals and disapprovals by means of general and well-substantiated tendencies – the tendencies of actions and character to promote human happiness. If the epistemologist describes the psychological mechanisms of belief, the moral philosopher describes psychological mechanisms of approval and disapproval. But the mechanisms Hume describes are equally fantastic in either field, and equally irrelevant to his main contentions.

The main psychological principle employed by Hume is HEDONISM. Nothing but pleasure and pain influence voluntary action. The influence may be direct, as when I let go of a hot plate because it hurts my hand, or indirect, as when fear of pain prevents me from touching a plate I believe to be hot. And this occurs because fear is a 'disagreeable' sentiment: if it were not painful, the belief that the plate is hot would not affect my actions. Reason cannot influence conduct by itself, but only 'obliquely' – by discovering either an object which arouses a 'passion', or the means to gratify it.

Hume thus has two arguments against the widely held view that reason alone distinguishes moral good and evil. The first, based on his psychological theory, is that reason alone cannot influence conduct, though moral judgements sometimes do. The second is that reason consists in the discovery of truth and falsehood, which pertain only to matters of fact or relations of ideas. Since moral judgements are based neither in matters of fact nor in relations of ideas, reason cannot decide moral questions. This second argument is sometimes regarded as Hume's major contribution to ethics: the contention that there is no logical argument from 'is' to 'ought', from description to evaluation.

The obligations of justice (e.g. keeping promises, respecting property and allegiance to the state), present difficulties to Hume, since the acts they require do not always increase the happiness of the agent, or even that of all concerned. Hume's answer is that these obligations rest on artificial conventions, without which society could not hold together, and which could not perform their function if everyone could choose whether or not to support them, depending on their particular circumstances. Our sympathetic concern for the long-term happiness of our fellows creates a *moral* obligation to be just (which is not very effective by itself), and our concern for the happiness of ourselves and our friends leads us to set up a system of laws and penalties which create a *natural* obligation to be just. But by 'obligation' Hume means only a sort of motive.

This account enables Hume to argue forcibly against the SOCIAL CONTRACT theory of political obligation, and offer a valuable suggestion about the nature of promises. Since contracts (i.e. exchanges of promises) and governments are only useful artifices, owing their obligatory power solely to their utility, it is pointless (quite apart from the fact that the social contract is a myth) to try and base one upon the other. Promising is neither uttering a verbal spell, nor performing a mental act by which a metaphysical entity called an 'obligation' is created out of the void. It is simply operating the machinery of a convention, according to which, if I make a promise and fail to keep it, I will not be trusted again. We have here the germs of the SPEECH-ACT theory of language.

It will be seen that the impartiality of genuine moral approval is for Hume founded on 'sympathy', which alone gives us a concern for the happiness of our fellows in general. Sympathy, he admits, is a pretty feeble motive, and moral principles control selfish passions mainly by means of the system of sanctions which self-interest leads us to set up. But it may be asked why virtue and vice seem important, independently of the rewards and punishments they sometimes receive. Hume's answer – interesting if not convincing – is that if we regulated our approval and disapproval according to our personal interests, we would face the inconvenience that our judgements were variable and opposed to those of others. But if we seek a common coin, as it were, for valuing human beings, we will find none so suitable as sympathy, that mild preference we have for anybody's happiness, other things being equal. So we ask of any human characteristic or institution: 'is it in general likely to promote the long-run happiness of all whom it affects?' The proper use of ethical terms is to express the feelings of approval or disapproval which we experience through sympathy in response to this question.

6 *Conclusion.* Hume can hardly be said to have succeeded in laying the foundations of an empirical science of human

nature. His contentions rest not on discoveries of new facts, but on appeals to what we all already know. We have all learned how to distinguish causal connections from coincidences, estimate likelihood, make and follow demonstrations, and make moral judgements. No one in common life looks for empirical exceptions to mathematical truths, or attempts wholly to anticipate by abstract reasoning the verdict of experience on questions of fact. It is perhaps not so clear that no one in common life approves what increases misery or disapproves what decreases it. But it can be said that many things have come to be recognized as certainly bad because of the misery they produce, and that no moral judgement has ever been justified except by appeal to some moral principle which itself either lacks justification or is controversial.

Hume's achievement is that he tries to describe clearly how we do certain things which we very well know how to do in familiar contexts, and so make it clear that in unfamiliar contexts we are sometimes not really doing these things, though we think we are. Metaphysicians who pretend to be reasoning about the origin of the universe or the immortality of the soul seem to be doing the same sort of thing as people who reason about the origin of Stonehenge or the evaporation of water. But in fact they are not: they are simply doing things we have all learned not to do in the familiar contexts. No one who has understood Hume can continue to do metaphysics in the old way. Among the more important philosophers influenced by Hume were Jeremy BENTHAM and Immanuel KANT. Bentham said that scales fell from his eyes when he read Hume. Kant claimed that Hume woke him from his dogmatic slumber. Many of Kant's important tenets, especially his accounts of space and time, causality and substance,

necessary truths, personal identity and practical reason are either explicitly or implicitly answers to problems raised by Hume. (D.G.C.MACN.)

Husserl, Edmund (1859–1938) German philosopher and founder of the movement known as PHENOMENOLOGY. The main influence on Husserl's thought was the intentional psychology of BRENTANO under whom he studied in Vienna in 1884–6. Husserl taught at Halle, and held philosophical chairs at Göttingen and Freiburg. His principal works are: *The Philosophy of Arithmetic* (1891) much criticized by FREGE; *Logical Investigations*, (1900–1, revised edition 1913–21); *Ideas for a Pure Phenomenology* (book I, General Introduction, 1913; books II and III posthumously published, 1952); *Phenomenology of Internal Time-consciousness* (1905–10, published 1928); *Formal and Transcendental Logic* (1929); *Cartesian Meditations* (1931); *Experience and Judgment* (1948); *The Crisis of European Sciences* (1954).

Husserl's phenomenology represents a vast extension and transformation of Brentano's 'psychognosy', which was an attempt to work out a logical geography of mental concepts as a necessary preliminary to empirical psychology. Husserl accepts Brentano's main thesis that states of mind are characterized by 'intentionality' or directedness-to-objects, all states of mind being *of* objects (whether real or unreal), and different states of mind being *of* their objects in varying manners. He starts by building on Brentano's classification of mental states into presentations, judgements, and affective-desiderative attitudes. But he carries the classification much further, and develops it into such a ramifying tangle of fine distinctions that it becomes an independent discipline rather than mere prolegomena to an empirical psychology. Husserl is, for example, deeply interested in the distinction between those conscious states in which something is merely 'meant' and those in which it is concretely 'present', the latter being said to 'fulfil' the former. He is also interested in the distinction, analogous to Frege's distinction between 'sense' and 'reference', between the object as such and the object as meant – the victor of Jena is in a sense different from the vanquished of Waterloo; and he is interested in the way in which successive thoughts or intuitions are 'synthesized' in the developing consciousness of the 'same' object, and in the way in which we pass from a problematic assertion to an assertion of probability; he is above all interested in the processes involved in the understanding and meaningful use of words.

Husserl also stresses, as Brentano does not, that the sort of investigation he is pursuing is conceptual or 'eidetic' rather than empirical – that he is trying to see what factors are involved in, and what possibilities flow from, the mere notions of perceiving, believing, predication etc., rather than to find out what empirically obtains when we perceive, believe or predicate. A wholly imaginary instance may therefore be as decisive in a phenomenological investigation as one that is actual. Husserl further widens the scope of Brentano's inquiry by making it include any and every object of a mental intention, not, however, in a naturalistic or realistic, but in a 'bracketed' or phenomenological form. We can, that is, discuss the ideal objects of mathematics, sense-given natural objects or sociological groups, in so far as these latter are possible *cogitata* of mental references in which, to use Husserl's terminology, they are 'constituted'. As objects 'constituted' in consciousness, both the choir of heaven and the furniture of earth enter into the subject-matter of phenomenology. The name 'phenomenology' in fact derives its significance from this 'bracketed' treatment of anything whatever: it connotes a study of things as they appear in consciousness, and from that point of view it does not matter whether what appears is ever more than an appearance. The things postulated by physics, theology or normative ethics remain phenomenologically interesting whether or not they are metaphysically real. Husserl's phenomenology in its full development is in fact not unlike the philosophy of KANT, an affinity of which Husserl himself was fully conscious. Husserl, like Kant, wished to discover a priori principles governing mind, phenomenal nature, law, society, ethics, religion etc., which should never go beyond what appears to consciousness, and which should derive their warrant from the nature of such conscious appearances.

In the actual carrying out of his phenomenological venture there are, however, some singularities. Great use is made of the terms 'intuition', 'experience', 'description' in contexts where the subject-matter is notional, and where such terms can be misleading. The notion of 'acts' is scrupulously explained, but their description reads like an account of ghostly performances. In the *Logical Investigations* there is even said to be a 'categorical intuition' of the meanings of the logical connectives 'and' and 'or', and though this use, too, is innocuously defined, it leaves a legacy of misunderstanding. After 1907 Husserl also became addicted to a quasi-Cartesian approach; the phenomenological philosopher was represented as having to 'put out of action' any sort of realistic conviction so that the 'structures' of consciousness itself might become reflectively evident. Great use was made of the notion of an *epoché* or transcendental suspension of belief: the abstraction necessary for a conceptual investigation became a mystical exercise for which the natural world dissolved, while phenomenological structures made their appearance. But Husserl, like other saints, fell a victim to his own ecstasy: he was unable to come out of this transcendental suspension. The harmless 'bracketing' of commonsense realities became the metaphysical thesis that they can have none but an 'intentional' existence in and for consciousness. Husserl does not see that we cannot suspend a belief if it is meaningless. After 1907, therefore, phenomenology passes over into a form of traditional German IDEALISM.

The works of Husserl form a slowly declining series: as the fruitful analyses diminish, the metaphysical generalities increase. *The Logical Investigations*, with its fine studies of meaning, intentionality and knowledge, is undoubtedly one of the greatest of philosophical masterpieces; in the later works there is much, but not so much, to admire. But the influence of Husserl's thought increased as its philosophical importance declined: hence the strange drop from phenomenology to EXISTENTIALISM.   (J.N.F.)

Hutcheson, Francis (1694–1747)

Hutcheson was born in the north of Ireland and ran a private academy for a time in Dublin, before moving to Glasgow where he held the Chair of Moral Philosophy from 1729 to his death. His biggest work, *A System of Moral Philosophy*, was published posthumously by his son. Hutcheson opposed any 'rationalist' and a priori account of value-judgement, such as that of CLARKE. To Hutcheson, the discernment of value was an activity not of reason but of certain 'internal senses' specially furnished by God for that purpose. The 'moral sense', for instance, inclines us by 'strong affections' to seek the greatest happiness of the greatest number. Hutcheson's doctrine looks back to LOCKE, with his distinction between the external and internal senses, and SHAFTESBURY, whose somewhat untidy 'moral sense' theory Hutcheson developed and systematized; and forward to HUME and the BENTHAMITES. For it was through Hutcheson that Hume learned that moral judgments cannot ultimately be justified by reason alone – a view he was to extend far beyond ethics into his general philosophy. And here too is the first clear statement of the UTILITARIAN 'greatest happiness' principle. Seen in the light of both Hume and the utilitarians, however, Hutcheson's philosophy – shored up by theology and proliferating in special *ad hoc* senses (sense of decency, of honour, of religion etc.) – shows up as rather unwieldy and unstable.   (R.W.H.)

Huxley, Thomas Henry (1825–95)

Self-educated Victorian scientist and exponent of an optimistic if naïve materialism. 'The mind stands related to the body as the bell of the clock to the works', he wrote, 'and consciousness answers to the sound which the bell gives out when it is struck'. He gave a polemical edge to the work of DARWIN, and coined the term 'agnostic' to describe his preferred attitude to metaphysics in general and religion in particular.   {J.R.}

I

Iamblichus See NEOPLATONISM.

Idealism In its philosophical use, the term 'idealism' is quite distinct from 'idealism' in the sense of high moral aims. While the term has sometimes been employed by philosophers to cover all views according to which the basis of the universe is ultimately spiritual, it has most commonly stood (in opposition to REALISM) for a theory according to which physical objects can have no existence apart from a mind which is conscious of them. (Thus it does not cover those who, while they believe in God, also ascribe a substantial existence to matter as quite conceivable independently of being experienced, although ultimately created by God.)

Idealism in this narrower sense originated in the eighteenth century with BERKELEY. He argued that physical objects were only 'ideas' (hence the term 'idealism'), or that their *esse* (existence) was *percipi* (to be perceived). His main argument was that we could not conceive the qualities we ascribe to them as existing in abstraction from our sense-experience. He also used the negative argument that we could not possibly know unexperienced physical objects. These two arguments in some form are common to most idealist thinkers. He then argued that ideas, being passive, cannot cause anything and that those which cannot be explained by human action must be due to the direct action of a non-human spirit, spirits being the only possible causal agents since they alone are 'active', that is possess volition. He explained the fact that physical things still seem to exist when no one is perceiving them by saying that they exist in God's mind, thus providing a new argument for God.

Berkeley made practically no converts in his lifetime, and the 'idealist' school only began to gain ground with KANT, who however approached the subject in a very different way. He contended that we can account for our a priori knowledge of things only by supposing that our mind has imposed on them a structure to which they must conform. But the human mind cannot impose on reality itself, but only on appearances, so Kant concluded that our knowledge must be limited to appearances. Appearances have to obey the conditions which our mind imposes, since they exist only as objects of actual or possible experience. This was the reason, Kant thought, why we are able to apply categories such as substance and cause to the physical world, but it also debars us from extending them beyond the realm of human experience and thus proceeding, with Berkeley, to metaphysics. This, Kant insisted, does not cast doubt on science; on the contrary it is the only way of saving it from scepticism. If we claimed that the function of science was to tell us the truth about reality, we should have to admit that it was wholly illusory; but not if it tells us only about appearances (phenomena). Kant consequently called himself both an 'empirical realist' and a 'transcendental idealist'. By this he meant approximately what some later thinkers expressed by saying that physical-object propositions have to be analysed in terms of 'SENSE-DATA'. He also argued that, if we hold that reality is in space and time, we will become involved in certain self-contradictions ('antinomies'). We will have to hold either that the world in space and time is infinite or that it is finite, and either alternative, he maintained, leads to self-contradictory conclusions; hence the only solution is to say that reality is not in space or time at all.

Unlike Berkeley, Kant did not use idealism as the basis of an argument for God; he repudiated all theoretical arguments for theism, saying we can have no knowledge of 'things-in-themselves'. He did however think that the existence of God could be established – if not with certainty, at least sufficiently to justify belief – by means of an ethical argument. He was convinced that the moral law was objective and argued that it commanded us to strive for ideals which could only be realized if we were immortal and if the world was ordered in the interests of the moral law, which implied that it must have been created and governed by an omnipotent and perfectly good being. His denial of the reality of time led to the consequence that our own real self is timeless and therefore unknowable – a paradoxical conclusion which he nevertheless welcomed, because it enabled him to reconcile freedom with universal causality by saying that the real self is free, even though the apparent or phenomenal self is completely determined by the past.

The chief idealists in the first half of the nineteenth century – FICHTE, SCHELLING and HEGEL – were all much influenced by Kant, though they completely transformed his philosophy. The first element they rejected was the concept of unknowable things-in-themselves. It was argued that there could be no ground for asserting something quite unknowable, and no meaning in doing so, and that Kant's attempts to exclude metaphysics involved inconsistencies since he himself only excluded it by making metaphysical assumptions of his own. Now, if we reject

things-in-themselves, we are left with minds and objects of experience, and we are back with what Kant called dogmatic idealism. The resultant philosophy ('absolute idealism' or 'absolutism') held that reality can be known to be ultimately spiritual, but that there must also be an objective material element since spirit would not be able to realise itself without it. Object implied subject, but subject also implied object, even if subject was ultimately prior. Reality as a whole was conceived not as dependent on a mind distinct from finite minds (God), but as itself a single all-embracing experience of which finite minds are differentiations (the Absolute). Such a view stressed the unity and rationality of the cosmos and even described it as perfect, since any evil in its parts could be seen as arising from the fact that they were only parts.

It is reasonable to class Hegel as an idealist, but it is disputable in what sense he was one. He undoubtedly thought that matter was the manifestation of spirit, but it is unclear how he saw the status of unperceived physical objects. His philosophy centred on a 'dialectic' by which he sought to show that, starting with the most abstract and empty of all concepts, mere being, we could pass by an a priori process of thought to the highest logical categories of the spiritual life. A leading characteristic of this mode of argument, which he also regarded as characteristic of reality itself, is that it proceeded in triads. An adequate concept was taken first, its inconsistencies led to its being replaced by the opposite extreme, but the latter displayed fundamentally the same defects, and the only cure was to combine the good points of the two in a third concept, solving the previous problems and taking us a stage nearer to the truth. But this concept would exhibit inconsistencies in its turn, generating a new thesis and antithesis, whose antinomy would be solved by a new synthesis, and so on till we reached the fundamental category of the 'absolute idea' and proved the whole of reality to be the expression of spirit. Hegel traced such processes not only in logic but also in ethics and politics. In politics, for example, some seek liberty at the expense of order, others order at the expense of liberty, but both can turn into the same evil, the rule of the strongest regardless of others; political development consisted of successive syntheses of the two, preserving more and more of what was of value in order and liberty. Unfortunately Hegel sometimes gave the impression that the final syntheses had been achieved in the Prussian state of his day, so that his philosophy was used to bolster stubborn conservatism, and to foster the impression that the state, as the representative of the Absolute on earth, can do no wrong. (On the other hand the 'Hegelian left' developed the almost equally one-sided doctrine of Marxism.) It may be doubted whether Hegel believed in a personal God: he regarded philosophy as superior to religion, but called himself a Christian and attached great importance to Christian dogmas, at least as symbolic representations of the spiritual nature of reality.

Idealism spread from Germany to Britain in the latter half of the nineteenth century and became dominant in Oxford and Scotland. T. H. GREEN, who exercised a great influence at Oxford, was specially concerned to bring idealism into connection with Christianity and with liberal political ideas. He used a more subtle form of Berkeley's argument to show that physical objects cannot be conceived except in relation to mind and therefore should be thought as dependent on a divine mind, but he discarded Berkeley's empiricism in theory of knowledge and insisted,

like Kant and Hegel, on the place of thought in perception. His argument for God was based mainly on the view that relations imply mind and yet are independent of human minds. F. H. BRADLEY, also of Oxford, began his leading work *Appearance and Reality* with an attempt to show that all our ordinary concepts are self-contradictory. This argument however led him not to scepticism, but to the conclusion that we must suppose the existence of a perfect thought-transcending Absolute Whole in which all these contradictions are reconciled. Bradley developed the coherence theory of truth, according to which the definition and criterion of truth lie in the coherence of a system. Truth for him was a matter of degree, all our judgements being both partly false (corrigible in the light of a wider system) and partly true (inevitably embracing some elements of the real). He did not mean to deny that in a limited system for ordinary purposes judgements could be taken as absolutely true or false. The coherence theory was also expounded by BLANSHARD in America.

J. M. E. MCTAGGART, who taught at Cambridge, developed a form of idealism according to which reality consists of a number of spirits (including human beings) united in a supersensuous harmony. By way of an elaborate a priori argument he arrived at the conclusion that matter, time and almost all the unsatisfactory features of human experience are only apparent, and that in reality nothing exists except immortal spirits loving each other. Especially in the 1920s of the twentieth century, a great influence was exercised by the Italian idealists CROCE and GENTILE.

It will be seen from the above that the idealist case against independent matter leaves room for a number of different views. It may be combined with theism, as by Berkeley, or it may take the form of absolutism, or of some kind of pluralism. It may even be maintained that physical objects are merely abstractions from human experience. Other idealists have taken the view that what we call inanimate matter is the appearance of very inferior minds (*panpsychism*). This view has been supported by the argument that the problem of the relation between the human body and mind can only be solved if we regard our body (or brain) as the appearance of our minds, which naturally led to the theory that everything physical is the appearance of something mental. It would be hard to find many philosophers who would call themselves idealists today. There are indeed many who would reject the view that physical objects should be regarded as entities existing independently of experience except in the hypothetical sense that under suitable conditions they would appear in experience; and some trends in modern science can be regarded as supporting this conclusion (see QUANTUM MECHANICS, RELATIVITY). But such views are usually referred to not as 'idealism' but as 'PHENOMENALISM'.   (A.C.E.)

Ideas The term 'idea' has a double history in philosophy in English, only distantly related to its ordinary use. It is in the first place a transliteration of the Greek word for 'form', and hence occurs commonly in translations of PLATO, and in the development of aspects of Platonism by KANT, HEGEL, SCHOPENHAUER or HUSSERL. Second, it was extensively employed by LOCKE in the late seventeenth century, and remained in philosophical use for a hundred years. The expression *idée* had already been much employed by French writers, notably DESCARTES and MALEBRANCHE, and Locke's usage no doubt derived from that source.

The word was in fact the cause of a great deal of confusion in the philosophy of the eighteenth century. An early critic, Thomas REID, went so far as to suggest that all the major errors of Locke, BERKELEY and HUME could be traced to it, and that, but for unclarity at this key point, some of their tenets could scarcely have been stated. This contention, though extreme, was by no means baseless. The root of the trouble was that the meaning of 'idea' was either made undesirably wide, or left highly indeterminate. Locke, in introducing the expression, writes of it thus: 'it being that term which, I think, serves best to stand for whatsoever is the object of the understanding when a man thinks, I have used it to express whatever is meant by *phantasm, notion, species*, or whatever it is which the mind can be employed about in thinking'. This remark is conspicuously unclear. In actual fact Locke used the word 'idea' in at least four ways. (1) He often uses it in the sense – itself not perspicuous – of the modern expression 'SENSE-DATUM', to refer to the 'immediate objects' of sense-experience. (2) He uses it also, occasionally, in the sense of an *image*, notably in his discussions of imagination and memory. (3) The term 'idea' sometimes designates the *meaning of a word* (or a *concept*): for instance to have the 'idea' of whiteness is to know what 'white' means. (4) Less clearly, Locke sometimes seems to mean by 'ideas' whatever it is that one has in mind when one *thinks* or *understands*.

The greatest danger in such a liberal use of terms is that it makes it easy to discuss very different things in identical language, obscuring how different they are. In the present case perhaps the most seriously harmful result was that, from Locke to Hume, no adequate distinctions were ever drawn between *perceiving, thinking, understanding, imagining* and even *believing*. Indeed there was a constant tendency to assimilate them all to *perceiving*. Hume sought to improve the position by distinguishing ideas from 'impressions', a term intended for separate reference to sense-data or sensations. However, since he held ideas to be *like* impressions except for a lower degree of 'force and vivacity', his subsequent analyses of belief, imagination and thinking in general retained the inappropriate underlying model of perception.

Berkeley's case is somewhat different. He proceeded, with unjustified confidence, as if the term 'idea' were already quite clear. He employed it in all of Locke's diverse senses, and exploited the unclarity of one of them, listed as (1) above. Berkeley wished to maintain the ontological thesis, that there exist only 'spirits' and 'ideas', on the basis that it was really no more than an elucidation of common-sense beliefs. If he appears to succeed, it is partly – as Reid saw – in virtue of his double, or at any rate fluid, use of the principle that we 'perceive nothing but ideas'. At times he represents this principle as a truism – ideas just are 'the things that we perceive'; but at other times he stresses that ideas 'have not any existence without a mind'; and then he can appear to have shown that the things we perceive exist only 'in a mind'. It would be unjust to the subtlety of Berkeley's argument to suggest that it rests wholly on so simple a manoeuvre. However, this concealed unclarity probably accounts for Berkeley's strange conviction that his startling doctrines were obviously correct, and scarcely needed supporting argument; and it is, perhaps, in his writings above all that the employment of the term 'idea' calls for critical scrutiny.   (G.J.W.)

Identity   See PERSONAL IDENTITY.

Ideology   'Ideology' is an indispensable but highly controversial term in Marxist theory. Before MARX it referred to a supposed 'science of ideas' devised in the 1790s by the French philosopher and political reformer Destutt de Tracy (1754–1836), and derived from LOCKE and CONDILLAC. Ideology was a branch of zoology; it analysed ideas into their sensory elements and dismissed any remainder (such as religion or metaphysics) as groundless. Its proponents believed that it would enable all citizens to decide matters of right and wrong for themselves. When Napoleon came to power in 1799, he derided the Ideologists for overestimating the reasonableness and malleability of human nature and the eliminability of religion, and the word 'ideology' acquired a derogatory connotation which has clung to it ever since.

In an early work, Marx and ENGELS wittily denounced the Young Hegelians of the 1840s as the 'German Ideologists', on the grounds that their understanding of society was based not on 'material activity' but on 'the ideological reflexes and echoes of this life-process' (see DIALECTICAL MATERIALISM). Beside Hegelianism, the chief examples of ideology were morality, religion and metaphysics; and 'in all ideology human beings and their circumstances appear upside down'.

The concept of ideology has thus acquired a double meaning. On the one hand, it refers to 'world-pictures' or bodies of ideas, as opposed to the real world which they (mis)represent. Thus in the 'Preface' to the *Contribution to the Critique of Political Economy* (1859) Marx distinguished between his own topic – 'the material transformation of the economic conditions of production' – and 'the legal, political, religious, artistic or philosophical – in short, ideological – forms in which people become conscious of this conflict and fight it out'. The Marxist doctrine that the course of history is determined by 'material conditions' rather than 'ideological forms' is known as 'HISTORICAL MATERIALISM'. But the concept of ideology also refers, on the other hand, to systems of ideas which are systematically deceptive, as opposed to scientific theories which reveal underlying truths. In this sense ideologies constantly confuse the natural with the social, the necessary with the contingent, the real with the apparent, and use-value with exchange-value; and the goal of Marxist theory is to decipher or 'demystify' the innumerable 'fetishized' forms in which capitalist societies present themselves to their participants, or in other words to provide 'critiques of ideology', perhaps allied with HERMENEUTICS.

Much controversy within Marxist theory can be understood in terms of tensions between 'historical materialists' and 'critics of ideology'. For the former, Marxism is a 'natural science' of history, but can itself be treated as an ideology – the socialist ideology of the working class, for example. For the latter, Marxism is an open-ended art of interpretation, and not itself ideological. In the formulations of Destutt de Tracy, and of Marx and Engels, the two meanings were of course not separated; despite the efforts of theorists like LENIN, LUKÁCS and ALTHUSSER, there must be some doubt as to whether they can ever be reconciled.   [J.R.]

Induction   'Induction' is a technical term in LOGIC; but unfortunately it is used in at least two ways. In one, it stands for any procedure other than DEDUCTION by which we attempt to justify some conclusion. Thus the procedures of mathematics and pure logic are deductive, but the arguments of the scientist and the detective are inductive. But the term has also been used – principally by POPPER – to stand for one particular theory about how scientists and detectives justify their conclusions. This theory, espoused by BACON and J. S. MILL, states that science proceeds by a special sort of argument in which the premises are singular statements of observation and experiment, and the conclusions, scientific laws and theories. Popper opposed this view by arguing that scientists arrive at their laws and theories by a process of testing hypotheses – though on the wider acceptation of the term this would itself be a form of induction. See also DETERMINISM.   (J.O.U.)

Intentionality   In medieval philosophy, intentionality was a status attributed to objects of thought which are in the mind but which do not, or may not, actually exist (e.g. a unicorn, tomorrow's lucky bet). The concept was revived by BRENTANO, who used it to define the psychical as distinct from the physical world, and this usage was further developed by MEINONG, HUSSERL and PHENOMENOLOGY generally.   [J.R.]

J

James, William (1842–1910) American psychologist born in New York, whose thought passed through three major stages: work in psychology, the defence of PRAGMATISM, and 'neutral monism'. James was always more interested in specific problems than in fitting his work into a consistent pattern, but each of his three periods may be looked upon as a logical outgrowth of its predecessor; and all can be read as products of a single philosophical intent.

1 *Psychology.* The key to James' work in psychology is his method, generally called 'functionalism'. Functionalism in general is the demand that things be understood exclusively in terms of the differences they make in experience, and hence our conception of mentality must be rooted in an inspection of what it *does*. At the outset of *Principles of Psychology* (1890), James stipulates that 'the pursuance of future ends and the choice of means for their attainment are the mark and criterion of the presence of mentality in a phenomenon'. James argued that mental life is always experienced as a 'flow' in which each succeeding moment grasps and 'owns' its predecessor, and came to the startling conviction that 'whenever my introspective glance succeeds in turning around quickly enough to catch one of these manifestations… all it can ever feel distinctly is some bodily process, for the most part taking place within the head'. This led to the famous 'James–Lange' theory of the emotions, which states that emotion is no more than the *feeling* of a bodily state: for instance, I do not strike a man because I am angry; my anger is simply the result of a total bodily state which includes striking him.

2 *Pragmatism.* James acknowledged the source of his pragmatism in C. S. PEIRCE, who formulated the 'pragmatic maxim' as one of several rules governing intelligent inquiry. For Peirce it was simply a rule for achieving *clarity of meaning*, requiring that the significance of any concept or hypothesis be expressed by a specification of the 'sensible difference' its being true would make. James' 'pragmatic rule' had a far more overarching status: his view was that if a concept literally *means* what you do with it, then its truth must consist in a successful doing. Ideas, like minds, were to be treated in terms of their *function*. To judge that an idea is true was simply to claim that it successfully leads one through the labyrinth of experience. Ideas were not mysteries but tools.

According to James, traditional EMPIRICISM paid too much attention to the origins of ideas and not enough to their function as pointers to future experience; moreover its concentration on the discrete elements of experience generated inattention to their equally real relatedness. For James, pragmatism was the only genuinely radical empiricism, and its essence lay in a stress upon the relatedness of ideas to future experiences, which fulfil their meaning. James repeatedly defined the mental life as a continuous 'substitution of concepts for percepts', but in the last analysis he always defined a concept as a *percept functioning in a certain way*, that is to say in a predictive manner. If James' psychology rests upon suspicion of any difference of kind between minds and bodies, his theory of knowledge rests upon suspicion of any difference of kind between percepts and concepts.

In his psychology, James always refused to distinguish mental and material 'stuff', and in his later work he defended a technical version of REALISM under the label 'Neutral Monism'. If he was to commit himself to a 'stuff' of the world, independent of human investigation, he could not label it either 'mental' or 'material', so he took the bull by the horns and called it 'neutral'. Minds were this stuff organized in one way; material objects the same stuff organized differently.

3 *Religion*. Few philosophical works are more clearly the product of personal experience than *The Will to Believe* (1897), where James describes a decision which enabled him to surmount a period of acute melancholy and depression. His argument is threefold. (a) There are 'forced options' in intellectual life – questions where one has to make up one's mind either for or against, and there is no middle course. Thus, one must either believe or not believe that one is free, or that God exists. (b) In cases where no evidence could possibly settle the matter, the only truly empirical approach is to recognize the need to transcend the evidence. One must look for evidence at second remove, examining the effects on the integrity and power of one's life which would follow choosing one option rather than the other. (c) James also makes the startling claim that in cases of this sort the act of believing tends to make what is believed more true. Thus if I seriously believe that I am free I will act as a free agent; and if not, not.

The theme was followed up in *The Varieties of Religious Experience* (1902), where James claimed that RELIGION can be 'justified' by its tendency to organize and energize men's lives. By 'religious belief' James meant a commitment to the divine or supernatural element in reality. He failed to anticipate that later pragmatists might claim that beliefs like communism and scientism could 'integrate' one's life and actions more efficiently than the religious beliefs with which he was concerned.   (J.W.S)

Jaspers, Karl (1883–1969)   Jaspers was the chief exponent of German EXISTENTIALISM next to HEIDEGGER, although he repudiated both the label and the philosophy of Heidegger. He took his doctorate in medicine, published a *General Psychopathology* in 1913 and a *Psychology of Worldviews* in 1919, and then became a professor of philosophy at Heidelberg. In 1932 he published his chief work, *Philosophy*. Under the Hitler regime he was forbidden to lecture.

His work was a sustained protest against the 'professors' philosophy' of the later nineteenth century. The two giants of the period after HEGEL are, to his mind, KIERKEGAARD and NIETZSCHE. What matters is neither Kierkegaard's 'forced Christianity' nor Nietzsche's 'forced anti-Christianity', but their shared concern with human existence and the unexampled fluidity and elusiveness of their thought: 'Out of every position one may have adopted, out of every finitude, we are expelled; we are set *whirling*.' It is only after reason has suffered 'shipwreck' in its quest for certainty that true philosophizing can begin. Extreme situations (*Grenzsituationen*) confront us with the inadequacy of all philosophies and become, to cite Jaspers' characterization of his own *Nietzsche*, 'an introduction to that shaking up of thought from which *Existenzphilosophie* must spring'. Jaspers' consistent disparagement of all content poses a problem about the contents of his own voluminous writings. They are very largely filled with highly subjective paraphrases of the alleged positions of other writers, followed again and again by an appeal to the reader (*appellieren* is one of Jaspers' key concepts) to be seriously concerned with his own existence instead of seeking refuge in finished positions.

(W.K.)

Jevons, William Stanley (1835–82)
The logician and inventor W.S. Jevons was born in Liverpool and studied chemistry at University College, London. After working for some years as a metallurgist in Australia, he went back to University College to study economics and philosophy. In 1863 he was appointed to teach in Manchester, returning to London in 1875 as professor in his old college.

Pure Logic (1864) is a study of BOOLE which introduces some notational improvements and amendments. (Jevons' later work on Boolean algebra included the construction of a calculating machine, the so-called 'logical piano'.) *Principles of Science* (1874) contains an elaborate account of inductive reasoning in which hypotheses are first framed by the informed insight of the scientist and then confirmed by evaluating evidence in accordance with a calculus of probability. The theory is developed in conscious opposition to J. S. MILL's account of induction as depending on a process of elimination, and Jevons makes an important point against Mill by insisting on the essential uncertainty of all inductive conclusions. Jevons' general view of induction keeps close to the fact of scientific practice, and received a powerful and original reformulation in the work of POPPER. (D.J.O'C.)

John of Paris (c.1269–1306) John of Paris (also known as Jean Quidort) was a Dominican friar and Paris master who bravely defended civil prerogatives against the power of the Church. His *Of Royal and Papal Power* drew on ARISTOTLE and AQUINAS to define two separate sets of divinely instituted rights, and anticipated the later doctrine of indirect control. He also defended Aquinas against the English Franciscan, William de la Mare, denying that matter can exist without form, and maintaining the real distinction between essence and existence in finite things; but he seems not to have appreciated how far Aquinas had advanced from AVICENNA. (T.G.)

Jonas, Hans (1903–93) Hans Jonas was born in Germany and studied under HEIDEGGER in Marburg in the 1920s. He believed that *Being and Time* had revitalized philosophy by orienting it to human existence in history, and like Heidegger's other Jewish students – MARCUSE, LEVINAS and ARENDT for instance – he was shocked when his brilliant teacher came out as a sullen Nazi. 'When the most profound thinker of my time fell into step with the thundering march of Hitler's brown battalions', he wrote, 'it was not merely a bitter personal disappointment for me but in my eyes a débacle for philosophy'. He left Germany in 1933, fought with the British army, and eventually moved to New York.

Jonas devoted his philosophical intelligence to questions about ethics and nature. He believed that DARWIN's account of evolution, if it had wounded human vanity, also gave a certain dignity 'to the realm of life as a whole'. In particular it demonstrated the preciousness of all those organisms that had been lucky enough to find an ecological harbour in which to shelter from extinction. In *The Imperative of Responsibility* (1979), Jonas argued that the scope of our ethical community could no longer be restricted to 'neighbours' and 'sharers of a common present'. It was necessary to fashion cautious new principles for a brash new world. Our technological reach had outgrown our moral grasp, and the future of humanity could no longer be expected to take care of itself. The kind of moral heroism that insists on justice regardless of the cost was irresponsible in view of the prospects of sublime destruction opened up by modern science. The worst of tyrannies might be preferable to nuclear holocaust and the irrevocable degradation, desolation and exhaustion of the planet. The 'principle of hope' that Ernst BLOCH had proposed as the basis for a happy human future needed to be abandoned and replaced with a 'heuristics of fear'. {J.R.}

Jurisprudence 'Jurisprudence' is the name of a loosely related group of studies concerned with certain general questions about law which knowledge of particular legal systems does not suffice to answer. Among the general questions of jurisprudence are: What is law? Can there be law without coercion? Is international law really law? How is law related to morality and justice and how does it differ from them? How do judges reason in deciding particular cases? How do social and economic conditions affect the law, and how are they affected by it? Are there any fixed principles by which laws may be appraised as good or bad? Jurisprudence is thus concerned to further the understanding and reasoned criticism of law as distinct from knowledge of its details. In pursuit of these general aims it has drawn heavily on other disciplines, especially philosophy. Distinctions are sometimes made between jurisprudence, philosophy of law and legal theory, but these mean little; it is more important to distinguish between different types of inquiry as follows.

1 *Analytical Inquiries.* The elucidation of the expression 'law' and of terms embodying fundamental legal concepts (e.g. rights and duties, legal personality, ownership, sources of law) is now regarded as an independent and important study. The systematic analysis of legal concepts was begun by BENTHAM in *The Fragment on Government* (1776), *The Principles of Morals and Legislation* (1789) and the *Limits of Jurisprudence Defined* (1782), and developed by his disciple John Austin in *The Province of Jurisprudence Determined* (1832) and *Lectures on The Philosophy of Positive Law* (1863). Modern forms of analytical study of law have been developed in the 'pure theory' of law of Hans Kelsen (1881–1973), described in *General Theory of Law and State* (1945), and by jurists influenced by linguistic philosophy. Analytical jurisprudence is usually associated with (though logically independent of) 'legal positivism', that is the doctrine that there is no necessary but only a historical connection between law and morality.

2 *Critical and Evaluative Inquiries.* The doctrines of NATURAL LAW developed by the scholastics (especially AQUINAS) from Aristotelian metaphysics and Christian theology founded a lasting tradition in the criticism of law. Its distinguishing feature is the insistence (a) that there are fixed principles for the guidance of human conduct not made by humans but discernible by reason; (b) that these principles constitute a *natural* law by which all human-made law is to be judged. Some theorists hold that failure to conform to natural law renders human law invalid; others look upon natural law not as a test of legal validity but only as a standard of criticism. Despite their objection to natural law doctrines, criticism of law (on UTILITARIAN grounds) was a major concern of Bentham and Austin. Most modern critical jurisprudence has been based on a variety of social policies and is independent of natural law theory, though its essentials have been reasserted in some quarters.

Study of the judicial process especially in America stimulated two forms of jurisprudence, one constructive, the other sceptical. Both emphasized the fact that legal rules have at best a central core of settled meaning, so that when courts apply general rules to borderline cases, their reasoning is not (despite appearances) deductive, but represents a choice between social values. One movement, led by Roscoe Pound (often termed 'functional' jurisprudence) is concerned to determine the social interests which should guide courts in the area left open by legal rules. The sceptical movement, originating with O. W. Holmes (*The Path of the Law*, 1897) and J. C. Gray (*The Nature and Sources of Law*, 1902), stressed the diversity of non-legal influences on judicial decisions latent beneath the legal forms. Later 'realist' writers challenged the conventional conception of law as consisting of rules as distinct from more or less predictable operations of the courts (see, e.g. Jerome Frank's *Law and The Modern Mind*, 1930). These developments were anticipated by the advocacy of unfettered judicial discretion by Continental jurists of the 'Free law' school (e.g. Ehrlich, *Freie Rechtsfindung*, 1903) and by Scandinavian writers such as Axel Hägeström.

3 *Sociological Inquiries.* Various general theories concerning the interplay of law with economic and social forces fall under this head. The MARXIST doctrine that law is determined by economic conditions and destined to 'wither away' was developed by Russian writers, for example E. B. Pashukanis in his *General theory of Law and Marxism* (1924). Official Soviet legal theory suppressed the anarchical side of this doctrine. Non-Marxist theories such as E. Ehrlich's *Fundamental Principles of Sociology of Law* (1913) insist that the 'formal' law to be found in statutes is a less important social influence than moral and other non-legal norms ('the living law'). Though general programmes for 'sociological jurisprudence' have often been announced, the best work consists of studies of the relation of special legal institutions to specific economic or social conditions, for example Berle's and Means' *The Modern Corporation and Private Property* (1932).

4 *Historical Inquiries.* The work of Savigny, *The Vocation of Our Age for Legislation and Jurisprudence* (1814) and Sir Henry Maine's two works, *Ancient Law* (1881) and *Early History of Institutions* (1875), are usually described as 'historical jurisprudence', but no single form of inquiry is distinguishable under this name. Savigny thought that the naturally developing law of a society should be interfered with only in accordance with its natural genius, which could best he grasped in the earliest of its legal forms. Maine wished to free the understanding of early law from modern preconceptions concerning the nature of law, and to exhibit characteristic stages of legal development followed by 'progressive' societies. (H.L.A.H.)

K

Kant, Immanuel (1724–1804)
Immanuel Kant was born in Königsberg in Eastern Prussia, the son of a saddler. He was educated at a grammar school in the city, and at its University, where he later taught first as a *Dozent* (lecturer) and then, for many years, as professor. As a student he studied mathematics and physics as well as philosophy, and, throughout life, he kept an interest in these subjects. (The so-called Kant-Laplace theory of the origin of the solar system is partly based on an early cosmological essay of his.) Externally, he lived the quiet and uneventful life of an unmarried scholar, devoted to his work and friends. He had no particular taste for music and the fine arts but was well acquainted with ancient and modern literature. His interest in the political events of his time was intense, and he sympathized with both the American and French revolutions. He was one of the greatest of all philosophers.

Two main streams of European philosophy influenced his thought: RATIONALISM, which reached him through his own teachers, in the form given it by LEIBNIZ and WOLFF; and EMPIRICISM, the impact of which he felt most strongly when he came across some of HUME's writings in German translation. His own mature philosophy begins with the *Critique of Pure Reason* (1781) and is known as the Critical Philosophy. It is a synthesis – as distinct from a mere combination – of rationalism and empiricism, each of which, in his view, give a one-sided and distorted account of the structure and content of human knowledge.

Perhaps the best approach to Kant's philosophical system is through his twofold classification of judgments. According to him every judgment is (i) either ANALYTIC or synthetic and (ii) either A PRIORI or a posteriori. A judgment is analytic if its negation results in logical absurdity. For example 'a father is male', 'a green thing is coloured' are analytic judgments, since their negations ('a father is *not* male', 'a green thing is *not* coloured') are logically absurd. Their truth is clear from a mere analysis of the terms in which they are formulated. Any judgment which is not analytic is synthetic, notably judgments about empirical matters of fact, in particular those stating empirical laws of nature, such as 'copper conducts electricity'. Such judgments, whether true or false, can always be denied without contradiction.

A judgment is a priori if it is 'independent of all experience and even of all impressions of the senses'. Thus 'man has an immortal soul', which can be neither confirmed nor falsified by experience, is – if meaningful – a priori. Again all analytic judgments are a priori. Their truth, and indeed their logical necessity, can he made evident by a mere analysis of their terms, without resort to experiment or observation.

If we combine these two classifications, and note that all analytic judgments must also be a priori, we see that there are three classes of judgments, mutually exclusive and jointly exhaustive, namely: (i) analytic a priori, (ii) synthetic a posteriori, and (iii) synthetic a priori. It is worth remarking that Leibniz considered all judgments to be analytic: according to him, even empirical judgments can in theory have their terms analysed till their connection is seen to be logically necessary; on the other hand Hume and his modern followers hold that all judgments are either analytic (and so a priori) or synthetic a posteriori; none are synthetic a priori. Kant was convinced to the contrary. He found synthetic a priori judgments both in the mathematics and science of his day and in morality. An example would be the judgment 'every event has a cause', which can be denied without logical absurdity even though, in its complete generality, it is neither confirmable nor falsifiable by sense-experience. (If no cause of a given event is known, we can always go on looking; and even if all known events had causes, there might be others which had none; the dominant interpretation of QUANTUM MECHANICS does in fact reject the principle of causality.)

For Kant, the occurrence of synthetic a priori judgments gives rise to two philosophical tasks: first, to exhibit them clearly and, if possible, completely; and second, to demonstrate that they are justified. Kant formulates this problem by asking 'How are synthetic a priori judgments possible?' It is the central question of the Critical Philosophy, and its answer required a critique of all theoretical and moral knowledge as well as an examination of METAPHYSICS and its claim to yield transcendent knowledge, that is, knowledge of what transcends every possible experience.

1 *Critique of Pure Reason.* The task of the first Critique was (i) to exhibit the synthetic a priori judgments which enter into pure mathematics and natural science, and show 'how they are possible'; and (ii) to examine the claims of metaphysics. It is important to note that Kant was convinced that the mathematics of his day, Newtonian physics, and Aristotelian logic were complete, and that, when analysed by the methods of the Critical

Philosophy, they would yield all the fundamental synthetic a priori propositions, any others being deducible from them by ordinary reasoning. Experts are divided on the question of how far the development of non-Euclidean geometry, RELATIVITY and quantum theory, and the new mathematical logic demonstrates that Kant cannot possibly have succeeded in producing a complete outline of a priori knowledge.

One of the fundamental assumptions of the Kantian philosophy is that perceiving and thinking are different. Following the psychology of his day, Kant attributes them to two distinct faculties of the mind, sense and understanding. Apart from analytical judgments – which merely elucidate the meaning of their terms – every judgment consists, or appears to consist, in applying a concept to some particular. Apprehension of particulars belongs to the faculty of sense; apprehension of concepts and the rules by which they are applied belongs to the understanding. In order to grasp the function and legitimacy of a synthetic a priori judgement it is necessary to inquire into its constituents – the type of concept and particular which make it what it is.

Concepts are of three types. First, a posteriori concepts which are abstracted from sense-perception and applicable to it (thus 'green' is abstracted from perceptual data and applied to them when we judge that something is green); second, a priori concepts which, though not abstracted from sense-perception, are nevertheless applicable to it; and third, Ideas, which are neither abstracted from sense-perception nor applicable to it. While Kant's account of a posteriori concepts contains nothing not familiar in traditional empiricism, his account of a priori concepts and Ideas is all his own, and distinctive of the Critical Philosophy. This account is essential (i) to an understanding of the nature of those synthetic a priori propositions which are contained in mathematics, natural science, metaphysics, morality, aesthetic judgement and teleological explanation; (ii) to an understanding of their claim to be true; and (iii) to the decision whether and how far they are true in each of these cases.

(a) *Kant's philosophy of mathematics.* In discussing the mathematics of his time – arithmetic, classical analysis and Euclidean geometry – Kant tries to show that the propositions embodying their axioms and theorems are synthetic a priori. Since the discovery of non-Euclidean geometries and their successful use in physics it has been fairly generally agreed that the postulates of Euclidean geometry can be denied without logical absurdity, and yet are independent of sense-perception – which corresponds to what Kant meant by saying that they are synthetic and a priori. As far as arithmetic is concerned, Kant holds that such judgments as '$7 + 5 = 12$' are synthetic because the notion of '12' is not 'contained' in the notion of adding 7 and 5. The synthetic a priori character of arithmetical propositions is, however, disputed by many experts, although some, concerning 'the totality of all integers', have been denied without contradiction and are independent of sense in that they do not describe sense-perceptions of any kind.

Assuming now that the axioms and theorems of every system of pure mathematics are synthetic a priori judgments, Kant has to ask: How are they possible? Are there, perhaps, particular objects other than sense-perceptions which the concepts of arithmetic and geometry characterize? Kant's answer is that there are.

According to Kant, space and time – as opposed to the sense-perceptions located in them – are (i) a priori and (ii) particulars rather than general notions. One of his arguments for their a priori status is the possibility of varying in imagination all the features of a perceptual object except its being in space and time. One of his arguments for the conclusion that space and time are particulars rather than general notions is that 'division' is a quite different process in the two cases: space divides into sub-spaces and time into temporal intervals, whereas a general notion divides into various species (e.g. 'animal' divides into 'vertebrate' and 'non-vertebrate'). Now if space and time are a priori particulars, then Kant can explain the legitimacy of the synthetic a priori judgments of arithmetic and geometry. Those of arithmetic describe the structure of time with its repetition of units; those of geometry describe the structure of space with its extended patterns. Mathematical synthetic a priori judgments are thus 'possible' because they involve applying a priori concepts to space and time, which are a priori particulars.

Kant characterizes this kind of explanation of the legitimacy of synthetic a priori judgments as 'transcendental'; indeed he calls his whole philosophy not only 'Critical' but also 'Transcendental', because its concern is 'not so much with objects as with the manner of our cognition of objects, in so far as it is possible *a priori*'.

(b) *Kant's philosophy of science.* Kant proceeds to show that synthetic a priori judgments are employed not only in pure mathematics but also in science and common sense factual knowledge. Here too, he urges, it is the task of the Critical or Transcendental Philosophy to recognize our synthetic a priori possessions and prove our entitlement to them. We all make judgments to the effect that a particular event caused something else to happen. Moreover, before the advent of quantum mechanics the general principle of causality – that every event has a cause – was generally accepted. The judgment expressing this principle is, according to Kant, synthetic a priori. Moreover, the concept '*x* causes *y*', which is involved in the general principle, and applied whenever we make a particular causal judgment, is an a priori concept. It is not abstracted from perceived necessary connexions, since all that we ever perceive is successions of occurrences. That we do not abstract the relation of causal necessity from perception had already been shown by Hume, whose views in this respect Kant substantially accepts. Yet we do apply this concept to perception. The name Kant adopts for concepts which are applicable to perception – but which, unlike mathematical ones, are not characteristic of space and time – is CATEGORIES. The fact that they are constituents in synthetic a priori judgments makes it necessary to list them systematically.

Kant believes there are certain clues to help us with this task. First, there is the difference between subjective perceptual judgments and judgments which are objective and empirical. Compare, for example, 'what now appears to me is green' and 'this is a green object'. The first judgment does not claim to be about a public thing or substance, independent of my perception, but the second does. Yet both have the same perceptual content. Hence, Kant argues, the concept, or more precisely the Category, 'substance' is applied in the objective empirical judgment but not in the subjective perceptual judgment. This leads to the conclusion that if we compare objective empirical judgments with subjective perceptual ones having the same perceptual content, and if we as it were subtract the latter from the former, we will be left with one or more Categories.

A second clue concerns the criterion for judging whether we have discovered all the Categories, and lies in the difference between the *matter* of objective,

empirical judgments and their *form*. The matter of such judgments is always expressed by its a posteriori concepts, the form by the fact that the judgment has a certain structure. Thus the judgment 'if the sun shines, the stone will get warmer' has the *if-then* form, or the structure of a hypothetical judgment. This, according to Kant, expresses the fact that in making the judgment we are applying the Category '*x* causes *y*'. In considering on the one hand the difference between subjective perceptual and objective empirical judgments, and on the other hand the difference between the matter and form of objective empirical ones, Kant thinks we can see that the form or structure of objective empirical judgments embodies the Categories.

It follows that if we could list every possible form of judgment – all the varieties of logical structure – we would know all the Categories. Now Kant held that traditional logic (slightly modified by himself) did contain a list of all possible logical forms of judgment. Hence it contained, implicitly, all the Categories, namely (i) Categories of quantity: Unity, Plurality and Totality; (ii) Categories of quality: Reality, Negation and Limitation; (iii) Categories of Relation: Substance-and-accident, Causality-and-dependence and Community or Interaction; and (iv) Categories of modality: Possibility-Impossibility, Existence–Non-existence and Necessity–Contingency.

Synthetic a priori judgments consist in applying the Categories to the data given to the senses in space and time, that is, to the perceptual manifold. Since the Categories are not abstracted from the manifold, their application to it is more than a mere declaration of what is found in perception. (How could we declare that we have found e.g. causal necessity in perception, when all we have perceived is regularity of sequence between events?)

Kant's account of how the Categories apply to the manifold of perception is one of the central points of his philosophy. He himself compared it with the revolutionary idea of Copernicus who 'made the observer turn round (the sun) and kept the stars still'. The applicability of the Categories transforms the subjective manifold of otherwise disconnected appearances in space and time into an objective (or inter-subjective) reality, in which we discern physical objects as SUBSTANCES capable of causal interactions and as the source of our systematically connected perceptions. To be an object – as opposed to a mere subjective impression – is thus, for Kant, to be a bearer of Categories, which are not abstracted from the manifold of perception but, as it were, imposed on it by the subject. The reality of inter-subjective objects is due to the activity of the thinking subject, the pure self which connects the manifold by means of the Categories. But Kant distinguishes sharply between the pure self which imposes the Categories, and the empirical self which apprehends its own states and does so through the application of the Categories. There can be no self-awareness of the pure self.

Once we understand that objects are constituted by the application of Categories to the perceptual manifold, we will be on the way to understanding those synthetic a priori judgments which are not mathematical. Kant conceives them as the principles according to which the Categories are applied to the manifold of perception. They express the conditions under which objective experience is possible. They are the presuppositions of the apprehension of the objects of common sense and science. The conditions for applying the Categories, expressed by non-mathematical synthetic a priori judgments, are according to Kant connected with the fact that objects and perceptions are all located in time. (i) To the Categories of quantity there corresponds the principle 'all perceptions are extensive magnitudes'; (ii) to the Categories of quality, there corresponds the principle 'in all appearances the real which is an object of sensation has intensive magnitude, that is degree'; (iii) the principle corresponding to the Categories of relation, is that 'objective experience is possible only by means of the presentation of a necessary connexion of perceptions' (more concretely expressed in three synthetic a priori propositions presupposed in Newtonian physics: the principles of conservation of substance, of causality and of interaction); and (iv) to the Categories of modality there correspond three principles which are held to explain possibility, reality and necessity as characterizing our judgments about the objective world.

Having, as he thinks, discovered all the synthetic a priori principles, Kant embarks, in the 'Transcendental Deduction of the Categories' upon their justification. His central point is that the application of the Categories to objects, in accordance with the principles, is legitimate because to be an object is nothing else than to be capable of being characterized by the Categories. Whatever one may think of his claim to have discovered the presuppositions of all objective and scientific knowledge, Kant's most important contribution to the theory of knowledge lies in the suggestion that we employ Categories in our thinking about matters of fact, and that their application constitutes objective reality.

(c) *Kant's metaphysical views.* The analysis of mathematics and theoretical knowledge results in the thesis that all theoretical knowledge consists in 'categorizing' perceptual material located in space and time. But Kant believes there must also be something apart from space, time and the Categories – a 'thing in itself', an 'intelligible' or *'noumenon'* – about which, however, we can know nothing. Kant calls this doctrine 'transcendental' idealism (as opposed to 'transcendent' idealism, which would claim that the 'things in itself' is knowable). Any attempt to apply the Categories to things in themselves, Kant says, will result in confusion and illusion.

Another source of illusion is the improper use of the Ideas of Reason. Just as Kant derived the Categories from the possible forms of judgment, so he derives the Ideas from the possible forms of logical inference. In doing so he again accepts the traditional logic as, on the whole, complete. The guiding principle is that we can always go on asking to have the premises of our inferences deduced from higher premises without limit (We can ask for the 'conditions of the conditions, of the conditions…of the truth of any statement'.). An Idea is formed when we assume that this potentially infinite series is actually given in its totality. Kant recognizes three types of deductive inference, each giving rise to a potentially infinite sequence of premises, and hence to three Ideas of Reason, namely: (i) the Idea of the absolute unity of the thinking subject; (ii) the Idea of the absolute unity of the sequence of the conditions of appearance; and (iii) the Idea of the absolute unity of the conditions of objects of thought in general. Each of these Ideas provides the spurious subject matter of a spurious metaphysical discipline; first, speculative psychology (alleged a priori knowledge of the soul); second, speculative cosmology (alleged a priori knowledge of the world); and third, speculative theology (alleged a priori knowledge of God).

Genuine metaphysical knowledge of matters of fact is, according to Kant, deducible from synthetic a priori principles. But if the Categories are taken as characterizing things in themselves, or if the Ideas are taken as characterizing something given in experience, then metaphysics becomes spurious. The mistaken employment of Categories and Ideas leads, as Kant tries to show, to obstinate fallacies, such as the alleged proofs of the existence of God – in particular the ONTOLOGICAL ARGUMENT, according to which we can deduce God's existence from the fact that we can conceive of God as a perfect being, and that as such God must exist since non-existence would be an imperfection. Kant's reply is that existence is not a predicate. Other fallacies include the so-called antinomies, of which the most important is that between freedom of the will and natural causality. Here Kant distinguishes between the Idea of moral freedom, which does not apply to phenomena, and the Category of causality, which does. Our experience of moral obligation logically implies the Idea of moral freedom. It is a notion which we must think, but cannot know, and is quite compatible with the Category of causality.

Whereas the Categories constitute phenomena as objects, the Ideas have only a 'regulative' function. They 'direct the understanding to a certain goal…which serves the purpose of giving the greatest unity and the greatest breadth at the same time'. As we have seen, they have their root in the demand that we should search for the conditions of any true judgment and in the assumption that the totality of these conditions, which form a potentially infinite sequence, is actually given. This assumption, unlike the demand, is the source of a pretended knowledge. But the demand does indeed confer greater unity on our judgments, since in following it we connect them systematically by deductive relations.

2 *Critique of Practical Reason.* The second part of the critical philosophy is concerned with the synthetic a priori principles which underlie our knowledge of what we ought to do and what ought to be the case. It aims to exhibit these principles and demonstrate their legitimacy. The moral law – which enables us to decide whether an action is obligatory or not – is discovered by analysis of our moral experience and the language in which we formulate it. The morality of an action, Kant tries to show, is not a quality of behaviour, or of a desire to bring about a certain state of affairs; it depends rather on what Kant calls the maxim on which the agent is acting, in other words the general rule which would be used to justify the action.

Kant argues that a maxim is moral if it conforms to the moral law. This law – a purely formal principle supposedly derived from the analysis of moral experience – is the famous CATEGORICAL IMPERATIVE, which states that the maxim of my action is moral if and only if I can will that it should become a universal law. (One of Kant's alternative formulations runs: 'Act in such a way that you treat humanity both in your own person and in the person of all others, never as a means only but always equally as an end.'). This formal test separates maxims into moral and non-moral, just as syllogisms are divided into valid and invalid.

Our experience of the conflict between duty and desire is supposed to commit us to the categorical imperative. But is this commitment objective, in the sense of being possible in a world which stands under the law of causality? Kant believes that it is. The Idea of freedom, which can be thought but not known, is not only demanded by our sense of duty; it is, as already noted, compatible with the rule of the principle of causality in the phenomenal world. As phenomenal beings we are causally determined, but as non-phenomenal or noumenal we are free. We know we are free, even though we are ignorant of what our freedom is. Thus the compatibility of moral freedom with the causal order of nature can be demonstrated, while the nature of moral freedom remains mysterious.

It is clear that for Kant morality 'needs neither the idea of another being above man, for man to recognize his duty, nor does it need another motive apart from the law that he should fulfil his duty.' Unavoidably, however, morality gives rise to the assumption that virtue has some connexion with happiness, that the two are adequately correlated, and it thus suggests the Idea of a power which would secure this correlation. But the connexion between religion and morality is not logical. It is based on an act of faith which explains the otherwise mysterious consistency between moral freedom and causally determined nature. To make room for this act of faith is, according to Kant, a more important task than trying to give rational proofs of the existence of God.

3 *The Critique of Judgment.* In the first two *Critiques* Kant tried to discover and justify the principles presupposed in our *objective* judgments of what is or ought to be the case. In the *Critique of Judgment*, however, he sought for the *subjective* principles at the root of (i) our search for system in our explanations of natural phenomena and (ii) our apprehension of beauty. The key notions investigated in the third Critique are 'purpose' and 'purposiveness' (the latter in the sense of a harmony we might apprehend without recognizing any specific purpose).

The notion of purpose is always presupposed by scientific explanations, which are based on the assumption that the special empirical laws which we discover are more than a heap of unrelated generalizations. We look for a certain systematic unity, treating them 'as if an understanding (though not our own) had given them to our cognitive faculties, in order to make possible a *system* of experience in accordance with the laws of nature'. This assumption is not a statement of fact, but a subjective, methodological principle. Apart from the general assumption of a harmony between our understanding and the nature which we try to understand, Kant considers particular fields of inquiry, and the teleological explanations sometimes used in them. They have their use as preparing the way for causal explanations, or as filling temporary – perhaps even permanent – causal gaps. The notion of purposes in Nature is a methodologically useful and indispensable Idea; but as an Idea it has, unlike the Categories, no objective application.

Kant argues that teleological explanations foster the assumption that 'the universe has it source in an intelligent being... existing outside the world'. But not even the most complete teleology amounts to a proof of God's existence, since teleological principles are merely subjective expressions of 'our cognitive faculties being what they are'. Kant, as we have seen, admits purposiveness without purpose. Indeed he defines beauty as 'the form of purposiveness in so far as it is perceived *apart from the presentation of a purpose*'. The unity of aesthetic experience is due to an indefinite interplay of the faculties of perception and imagination on the one hand and understanding on the other. An aesthetic experience calls for the application of concepts, but overflows every conceptual characterization. Apart from ascribing purposiveness to what is judged beautiful, aesthetic judgments also claim that the beautiful object is necessarily connected with pleasurable feeling – that *qua* beautiful is not an object

of interest, and that it pleases universally. The universality claimed for aesthetic judgments is quite different from the (objective) universality of synthetic a priori judgments. It has a merely subjective foundation in our cognitive faculties. In this respect aesthetic judgments are on the same footing as teleological explanation.

4 *Kant's Influence.* Kant's view of mathematics as a system of synthetic a priori propositions describing the structure of space and time was to a large extent adopted by mathematicians of both the formalist and the intuitionist schools. His philosophy of science has been kept alive by anti-phenomenalists, and was substantially accepted by Einstein. The Critical Philosophy also had considerable influence on the rise of German idealism – particularly the philosophy of FICHTE and his followers, who regarded the self as not only apprehending but somehow creating the world. Kant's demonstrations of the antinomies which arise when Ideas are taken to characterize objective reality is one of the sources of the Hegelian doctrine that reality is self-contradictory, and his view of the function of Ideas influenced PEIRCE and other pragmatists. His distinction between pure and practical reason has been widely accepted, and his anti-naturalism has been very influential in ethics.   (S.K.)

Kierkegaard, Søren Aabye (1813–55) Danish writer whose critique of contemporary Christianity contained a radical rejection of Hegelian philosophy, setting the stage (and providing the conceptual tools) for modern EXISTENTIALISM. He was born in Copenhagen, the youngest of seven children five of whom, along with their mother, died before he was twenty-one.

Kierkegaard's formative years were spent under the influence of his oppressively religious father. There ensued a period of extravagant socializing which, combined with a deepening personal despair, ended in an apparently rehabilitative decision to assume social responsibilities as cleric and husband. But shortly after completing his doctoral dissertation, *On the Concept of Irony* (1841), Kierkegaard gave up these plans and embarked on a writer's career which over the next ten years produced a constant flow of books and pamphlets including no fewer than twelve major philosophical essays. Beginning with *Either-Or* (1843), the focus of the early works is on the task and rewards of adopting an ethical in preference to a consciously hedonistic or 'aesthetic' way of life. From *Repetition* (1843) to *Stages on Life's Way* (1845) there emerges a need for a specifically religious orientation to support the openness required of an ethical mode of life. In *Fear and Trembling* (1843) the notion of actual conflict between ethical and divine duties is epitomized by the 'teleological suspension of the ethical' in Abraham's decision to sacrifice his son in obedience to God's command. That these are all pseudonymous works is due partly to Kierkegaard's need to distance himself from their clearly autobiographical reference to the problematic status of the social outsider, but also to the fact – as Kierkegaard later says in reference to these particular works – that they were deliberately written from an 'aesthetic' point of view to help people in its grip to find their way back to an authentic religious understanding.

In *Philosophical Fragments* (1844) and *Concluding Unscientific Postscript* (1846) Kierkegaard's principal philosophical pseudonym attacks the Hegelian notion of an objective science of human spirit for obscuring the nature and place of Christian faith, as well as for eclipsing the subjective viewpoint from which alone the questions which prompt faith can meaningfully be raised. *The Sickness unto Death* (1849) offers a systematic psychopathology of progressively deliberate renunciations of a Christian ideal of human fulfilment. Kierkegaard also published in his own name a large number of 'edifying' discourses dedicated to 'that individual', as well as extensive works on specifically Christian themes, notably *Works of Love* (1847) and *Training in Christianity* (1850). When he died at the age of forty-two Kierkegaard had become a target of ridicule and public anger, the former through a feud he had himself provoked with a satirical weekly almost ten years earlier, the latter through his savage attack, in the last two years of his life, on the State Church, its dignitaries, and the naturalized form of Christianity he referred to as 'Christendom'.

Kierkegaard is widely admired for the profundity of his psychological insight, his moral fervour, and the subtle penetration of his thought. Among his many seminal ideas are a nonsubstantialist view of the self (or 'spirit') as a 'relation which relates itself to itself', the centrality of choice and commitment in the establishment of selfhood, and the communicative role of indirect communication. Kierkegaard rejects system-philosophy, but without denying that the kinds of questions it addresses have meaning once raised from the point of view of the 'existing individual', who must still come to terms with them without recourse to rational philosophy or science. A number of modern thinkers, especially HEIDEGGER and SARTRE, owe much to Kierkegaard's writings. He is also greatly admired as an innovative literary stylist.　　　　[A.H.]

Knowledge　See A PRIORI, EMPIRICISM, EPISTEMOLOGY, RATIONALISM.

Kojève, Alexandre (1900–68) Hegelian Marxist born in Moscow, who studied in Germany under JASPERS and then taught in France. Between 1933 and 1939 he gave seminars on HEGEL's *Phenomenology of Spirit* in Paris. These were attended by, amongst others, Raymond Aron, Georges BATAILLE, Alexandre Koyré, Jacques LACAN and Maurice MERLEAU-PONTY, and they also influenced SARTRE and DE BEAUVOIR. Kojève held that 'history can never refute Hegelianism; it can only choose between conflicting interpretations of it'. His own interpretation focused on the discussion of 'lordship and bondage' in the *Phenomenology* – the so-called 'master–slave dialectic'. On this basis Kojève constructed a Hegelian reading of MARX's theory of history which bypassed DIALECTICAL MATERIALISM and connected with EXISTENTIALISM and the theory of ALIENATION. He thereby initiated a Hegel renaissance in France, and is consequently often regarded as the 'father' of French philosophy in the second half of the twentieth century. Raymond Queneau compiled an edition of the seminars, published in 1947; the English translation (*Introduction to the Reading of Hegel*, 1968) is abbreviated.   [J.R.]

Kripke, Saul (1940–) American philosopher born at Bayshore, New York State. His earliest published papers were in mathematical logic. In particular, his 'Semantical Considerations on Modal Logic' (1963) showed how different modal logics could be interpreted in terms of systems of possible worlds with different kinds of 'accessibility' relationships between the worlds.

In *Naming and Necessity* (1973) Kripke developed his thinking about modal logic into a fundamental critique of description theories of reference and epistemological theories of necessity. He argued that identities involving proper names, like 'Cicero-Tully', were metaphysically necessary, even though they could not be known to be true on the basis of the meanings of the names alone; and he accounted for this metaphysical necessity on the grounds that a proper name, like 'Cicero' or 'Tully', is a 'rigid designator', which has the same referent in all possible worlds. Allied to the notion of rigid designation was the 'causal theory of reference', according to which a proper name refers, not to the object that speakers recognize as its referent, but to the object that was the causal origin of the use of that name.

Other works by Kripke include 'Outline of a Theory of Truth' (1975), which indicates how languages can contain their own truth predicates without running into the semantic paradoxes, and *Wittgenstein on Rules and Private Languages* (1982).   [D.P.]

Kuhn, Thomas S. (1922–96) American philosopher of science, born in Cincinnatti. Kuhn trained as a physicist but turned to history of science because he was amazed by the difference between the pretty picture of scientific rationality offered by philosophers (and eagerly accepted by scientists), and its actuality. In *The Structure of Scientific Revolutions* (1962) he argued that science is not a careful construction of theories on a basis of laboriously accumulated neutral fact, but a contingent social activity. 'Normal science' is what scientists do 'almost all their time', and consists in 'puzzle-solving' within particular scientific communities. It assumes that scientists 'know what the world is like', but in reality it is based on 'world views'. Kuhn claimed that these scientific world views – or 'paradigms' as he called them – 'provide models from which spring particular coherent traditions of scientific research'. According to Kuhn, a choice of paradigm – such as Ptolemaic astronomy, Newtonian dynamics, or wave optics – is presupposed by scientific rationality, not founded upon it; it belongs to 'revolutionary' rather than normal science. Kuhn's work opened lines of communication between PHILOSOPHY OF SCIENCE and history, but many critics have been alarmed by its seeming irrationalism or RELATIVISM. See also HISTORY OF PHILOSOPHY.   [J.R.]

L

Lacan, Jacques (1901–81) The most controversial and influential French psychoanalyst of his generation; the papers collected in his *Écrits* (1966) contributed greatly to the prestige enjoyed by PSYCHO-ANALYSIS in France. The hallmarks of Lacan's work are a highly literary style, perhaps influenced by his early association with the surrealists, and a close but selective reading of Freud. Lacan concentrates on Freud's earlier texts and makes a polemical attack on post-Freudian ego-psychology, which he sees as a quintessentially American deviation. This, together with a controversy over training methods and the length of analytic sessions, led to conflict with the establishment and to Lacan's departure from the International Psychoanalytic Association. Lacan exploits the linguistics of SAUSSURE and Jakobson, and the structural anthropology of Lévi-Strauss, to argue that the unconscious is structured like a language, but the emphasis placed on the role of language in the constitution of subjectivity also recalls HEIDEGGER's dictum that language is the house of being. At the same time, Lacan draws upon HEGELIAN phenomenology, and particularly on the master–slave dialectic, for his theory of the ego and of inter-subjective relations (see also KOJÈVE). Thus, intersubjectivity is always founded in a relationship of aggression and identification, whilst the ego is not the central agency of the personality but a false self with which the subject identifies in a dialectic of ALIENATION. [D.M.]

Lakatos, Imré (1922–74) Hungarian philosopher of science who came to London in 1956, see PHILOSOPHY OF SCIENCE, RELATIVISM.

Language See ANALYTIC PHILOSOPHY, CHOMSKY, HEIDEGGER, SAUSSURE, STRUCTURALISM, WITTGENSTEIN.

Law See FREEDOM OF THE WILL, INDUCTION, JURISPRUDENCE, LOGIC, NATURAL LAW.

Leibniz, Gottfried Wilhelm (1646–1716) German philosopher, son of the Professor of Moral Philosophy at the University of Leipzig. At the age of fifteen he entered the University, graduating in 1663 with a thesis on the Principle of Individuation. This work contained many of the ideas of his later writings in embryo. From 1663 to 1666 he studied Jurisprudence at Jena and published a paper on legal education. This paper brought him to the notice of the Archbishop of Mainz who thereupon took him into his service. He entered wholeheartedly into the Archbishop's plans for preserving peace within the Empire and between Germany and her neighbours. This led him to search for a rational foundation for the Christian religion, acceptable to Protestants and Catholics alike, which would provide a sound basis for active religious toleration. Sent to Paris on a mission to Louis XIV, Leibniz stayed for four years, and made the acquaintance of MALEBRANCHE, ARNAULD, Huygens, and Tschirnhausen. He also invented a calculating machine which would be an improvement on PASCAL's in that it could extract roots, multiply and divide as well as add and subtract. In 1673 he visited London, met BOYLE and Oldenburg, and demonstrated his calculating machine to the Royal Society, which thereupon elected him to membership. In 1676, the Archbishop of Mainz died, and Leibniz became Librarian to the Duke of Brunswick at Hanover. On his way to Hanover, Leibniz spent a month at Amsterdam, where he met SPINOZA and discussed with him those parts of his writings which he had been permitted to read. This was his last personal contact with fellow philosophers. From this time till his death he was at work on a history of the House of Brunswick. In his correspondence with Clarke, he attacked the absolute space and time of the Newtonian system, opposing to it his own system of monads and relative space and time, set out in the *Discourse on Metaphysics* (1686) and the *Monadology* (1714). In his correspondence with Arnauld, he defended his view of individuality and human and divine freedom, to which Arnauld had objected on reading a summary of the *Discourse*. In his later years, Leibniz was involved in a controversy with the friends of Newton as to the authorship of the Infinitesimal Calculus. His highly original work in symbolic logic was almost entirely unknown before the twentieth century, and his discoveries had to be made over again while his work lay buried in masses of manuscripts in the royal library at Hanover. Leibniz ended his life in a similar state of neglect. The Academy of Berlin, of which Leibniz was founder and first President, ignored his death as did the Royal Society of London.

Leibniz was a first-class mathematician and scientist, sharing with Newton the honour of having discovered the infinitesimal calculus and contributing the concept of kinetic energy to mechanics. He was also an excellent philosopher whose metaphysics is peculiarly interesting in that it can also be interpreted as a system of logical doctrines. Leibniz established

his basic positions with arguments drawn from science, logic and metaphysics and believed that his 'new principle' of 'preestablished harmony' was 'proved' in all these disciplines, as well as in religious and moral theory.

Leibniz's account of SUBSTANCE as essentially active arose out of his dissatisfaction with the extended substance of the 'new philosophy' and his equal dissatisfaction with ATOMISM, and with the absolute space, time and matter of Newtonian mechanics. His objections to these concepts were both scientific and metaphysical. He showed that DESCARTES' formulation of the laws of motion was scientifically unsound, and that his view of motion as miraculously imparted to essentially inert matter was metaphysically unsatisfactory. He described 'atoms of matter' as contrary to reason, since a 'smallest particle of matter' was an absurdity: if the particle was extended, it was divisible; if not, it was not a particle of matter. Moreover, the laws of motion demanded that the elements involved should be bearers of energy. No extended being could be either active or truly unified. The only possible element must be a 'simple substance, without parts'. This simple substance Leibniz called a monad.

Since the monad has no parts, it is indestructible except by annihilation, and can come into existence only by creation. It can produce no effect on another monad, so there is no causal interaction. ('The monad has no windows.') Since it is non-extended it is not in space or time, and not material. Furthermore, since the only essential characteristic of a monad is that it is active, all monads are of the same kind. However, there is no doubt that the observed world, which is the starting point for speculation about substance, *appears* to be spatio-temporal, and to contain moving bodies in causal relations with one another, and entities of fundamentally different kinds – stones, plants, animals and humans, for instance. All these appearances are, in Leibniz's phrase, 'well-founded', in that they can be systematically connected with real properties of the system of monads.

A proper description, however, would go behind these appearances to a world comprising only monads varying in their degree of activity – an infinite series of monads ranging from the completely active to the almost inert. The proper activity of monads is perception, representation or 'mirroring', to use Leibniz's metaphor. ('Perception' as he understands it is applicable to stones and plants as well as people and animals.) Every monad perceives every other monad with some degree of clarity, and its perceptions are true in that they are in pre-established harmony with other monads. Pre-established harmony is 'proved' by the joint fact of the impossibility of interaction and the actuality of perception. The less active monads present the well-founded appearance of materiality. High- and low-grade monads mutually mirror one another, and every 'body' is a colony of monads of varying degrees of activity. A human being is such a colony and the relation between mind and body is not a Cartesian miracle but part of the natural order, a special case of the universal mirroring. The history of each monad is the unfolding of its states in accordance with its own principle, and the appearance of interaction is the result of the unfolding of each monad in pre-established harmony with others. Leibniz used the examples of two synchronized clocks and two choirs singing from the same score to explain how there could be the appearance of interaction without the reality. He described the unfolding of the states as 'appetition', a notion applicable equally to purposive human activity

and to the movement of iron towards a lodestone or a sunflower towards the sun.

Space is the well-founded appearance of the 'order of possible co-existences', and time of the 'order of possibilities which are inconsistent'. Space and time as conceived by mathematicians are abstractions. The monads form an infinite series according to their degree of activity, each term differing infinitely little from those next to it. Similarly, successive states of a monad form a continuous series, each according to its own principle. Leibniz described the *plenum* of the universe with its two ordered series of compossibles and incompatibles as the 'actual infinite'. For him, space and time were not only infinitely divisible, but infinitely divided, not into the mathematician's abstractions of atom, point and instant but into 'real beings', the monads.

In describing the series of monads, Leibniz invokes his famous principle of the Identity of Indiscernibles. If two beings have exactly the same set of properties then they are 'indiscernible', that is indistinguishable from one another. The properties of a monad are a function of its place, so no two beings could have all the same properties, since they would then be in the same place, in which case they would be one and not two. Leibniz invokes the same principle in arguing for the absurdity of absolute space and time. Space and time have meaning only as the place of material bodies; but to place a body here rather than there in absolute space, or earlier rather than later in time, would make no discernible difference, so that God, in creating the world, could not have made a rational choice between them. This objection is made in a letter to Samuel CLARKE, who replied that God needed no reason for his choice other than his will. In response, Leibniz appealed to the principle that for every matter of fact, there must be a sufficient reason why it is so and not otherwise ('the principle of Sufficient Reason'), claiming that this principle was valid not only in relation to the various parts of the world, but also in relation to the acts of God.

In the *Discourse on Metaphysics* (the elaboration of a letter to Arnauld), Leibniz tried to support the doctrine of monads by means of arguments drawn from logic. The logical counterpart of his factual arguments for simple substances was that every proposition is of the subject-predicate form and that every true proposition has its predicate contained in its subject. Just as there is no interaction between monads, there are no relational propositions; and just as every monad contains its states enfolded in it, so every true proposition contains its predicate in its subject. Leibniz's logical calculus presupposes that every true proposition has, as its subject, a name showing the analytic constitution of the subject and, as its predicate, a name for one or more of these constituents. Any true proposition is expressible in the form 'ABC is A' (or 'ABC is AB', or 'B', 'AC', ' C' or 'ABC'). This view is closely connected with Leibniz's life-long search for a 'universal characteristic', a language in which false propositions would appear as manifest absurdities ('ABC is not A' or 'not B' and so on). Calculation could then take the place of inference, and disagreement would disappear.

These logical arguments left Arnauld completely dissatisfied. If every true proposition is analytic, if the history of every monad is contained in its concept, then freedom, both human and divine, is a myth. Leibniz's reply was that every actual state of affairs has hypothetical but not absolute necessity. When God chose to create the actual Adam, he chose to create everything that goes with him too.

Moreover, in creating the actual Adam, God had regard to all the free acts that would ever be performed by his creatures, and adapted the whole state of affairs to them. Free and spontaneous activity is allowed for in the pre-established harmony. All monads choose the best and their capacity to discern the best varies with the degree of clarity with which they mirror the world. God, with perfect knowledge and goodness, freely chose to create this, the best of all possible worlds (see EVIL).

At this point Leibniz's system shows a fundamental inconsistency. He wanted to maintain the contingency of matters of fact within a system where the concept of every individual contained all that it would ever become. In the same way, he wanted to maintain a real distinction between mathematical truths, based on the principle of contradiction (their opposites being impossible), and empirical truths, based on the principle of sufficient reason (their opposites being a manifest absurdity). Our reasons for our acts, he thought, 'incline without necessitating'; yet he also maintained that the proposition 'Julius Caesar did not cross the Rubicon', properly formulated by someone with complete knowledge of Julius Caesar, would appear as a self-contradiction. God, who alone possesses complete concepts of each individual, can 'read off' any state of any monad from any other state of that or any other monad. The distinction that Leibniz certainly wished to maintain between necessary and contingent truths, was that the former are true of all possible worlds, the latter of this world only. Necessary truths depend on God's intellect but not his will; but he wills contingent truths in choosing to create this world. True statements about this world form a system such that it is not possible that some should be true and others false.

Correspondingly, while it is abstractly possible that any part of the universe should be other than it is, it could not be other than it is while the other parts remained the same. A state of affairs must be not only possible, but also compossible with all other states of affairs. Leibniz provided a formal system by which possibilities as combinations of simples might be derived. He called this the 'Combinatory Art', and it may be compared with a table of elements in chemistry. A formula for a possible combination of simples might lead us to the discovery of a hitherto unknown entity. Used with a well-chosen system of 'names', the combinatory art could provide an encyclopedia of all knowledge and a means of communication between all nations.

Leibniz's metaphysical system is completed by his proofs of the existence of God. The system of created monads is, in a sense, complete in itself, that is, it has to be as it is, granted that any part of it exists. But no one part of it contains the reason for its own existence, so the reason for its existence must lie in a being which does contain its own reason for existence – a necessary being, which we call God. This 'cosmological argument' appears in the *Monadology* but it is not peculiar to Leibniz: all RATIONALISTS took God to be the necessary creating and sustaining cause of the universe. However, Leibniz's formulation of the 'ontological argument' is peculiar to him in two ways: he couples it with a new argument, from the existence of necessary truths, and he completes it by a proof that 'God' is a possible concept. Hitherto, according to Leibniz, philosophers have succeeded in proving only that *if* God's existence is possible, then it is necessary. The argument from the existence of necessary truths presupposes that all truths are 'made true by' facts of some sort. There is no difficulty with contingent truths – they are made true by empirical

facts. But what makes the truths of logic and mathematics true? What do we know when we know them? Leibniz's answer is that we know them as they are present to the mind of God. God's intellect is the 'place' of the eternal truths. (For philosophers inclined to POSITIVISM, this whole issue is of course a pseudo-problem: necessary truths are not true *of* anything; they are either analytic or self-contradictory, and we do not need to look beyond our own concepts for their validation.)

The ontological argument is preceded by a proof that the concept of a 'perfect being' is possible. Leibniz first defines perfection: a property is a perfection, he says, if it may be possessed in a superlative degree, and if its possession does not exclude other properties. Spatial and temporal properties are not perfections, since all superlatives involving them (e.g. 'greatest size', 'last event') are self-contradictory. Properties perceptible by the senses are not perfections either, since their ascription to an object carries with it the denial of other properties: to ascribe 'red' to an object implies that it is not blue, green, etc. On the other hand, 'good', 'wise', and 'knowledgeable' are adjectives whose superlatives involve no self-contradiction, so they may be ascribed to the being who possesses all perfections in perfection. 'Perfect being' is therefore a possible concept, and since existence is itself (so Leibniz assumes) a perfection, 'perfect being' is not only a possible concept, but an actuality. (R.L.S.)

Lenin, Ulyanov V. I. (1870–1924) Lenin was a Russian revolutionary and one of the most original and ruthless political leaders and statesmen of the twentieth century. His claim to be taken seriously as a philosopher derives from three main sources: his book-length polemic against 'Machism' amongst the Bolshevik philosophers; his posthumously published philosophical notebooks; and the supposed philosophical achievements implicit in his more substantive economic and political analysis and in his approach to political practice. The ideas of the radical empiricist philosopher of science, Ernst MACH, became influential among Russian revolutionary intellectuals in the first decade of the twentieth century, and Lenin's *Materialism and Empirio-criticism* (1908) was devoted to a re-assertion of MATERIALISM as the philosophy of orthodox Marxists, against the 'IDEALISM' and 'agnosticism' of Machism. In taking their cue from the recent revolution in physical science, the followers of Mach, according to Lenin, confused specific scientific *concepts* of matter with the philosophical *category*, which refers to the mind-independent reality which is the source and object of human perception and knowledge. Their rejection of this materialist category, he argued, could only strengthen idealism, fideism and reaction.

From the outbreak of the First World War until 1916 Lenin was again preoccupied with philosophical issues. His *Philosophical Notebooks* contain extended quotation and commentary on works by HEGEL and they suggest that Lenin was developing a new and more positive valuation of dialectics. Whilst his hostility to idealism was undiminished, his denunciation of 'crude, simple, metaphysical materialism' became much sharper. It is arguable that Lenin's reading of Hegel facilitated his subsequent dismissal of the orthodox view of rigidly demarcated 'stages' in the historical process and so played some part in Lenin's change of strategic perspective in 1917. See also DIALECTICAL MATERIALISM. [T.B.]

Leucippus Probably a native of Abdera, Greece, Leucippus lived about the middle of the fifth century BC. He was the first to formulate the ATOMIC theory but he is a shadowy figure from whose work only one doubtfully authentic sentence survives. Our earliest authorities usually refer to Leucippus in conjunction with DEMOCRITUS, and it is quite impossible to determine what was the original contribution of each. It is however reasonable to believe that Leucippus is in the tradition of the PRE-SOCRATIC Milesian philosopher-scientists, but his theory was designed to take notice of the criticisms of the ELEATIC philosophers, with whom he was probably personally acquainted. In particular, the doctrine of the void was intended to answer Eleatic objections to the notion of not-being, in such a way that that which was not (the void) could be said to be (there was a void). The decisive importance of Leucippus in the history of thought was that he proposed a completely mechanistic account of the world without reference to purpose or other teleological principles, and that he singled out as fundamental those properties of matter which can be the subject of quantitative science. (J.O.U.)

Levinas, Emmanuel (1906–95) French philosopher born in Lithuania. He was indebted both to Jewish dialogical philosophy (Rosenzweig and to a lesser extent BUBER) and to PHEMOMENOLOGY (HUSSERL, of whom he was the foremost exponent in France in the 1930s, and HEIDEGGER). *Existence and Existents* (1947) and *Time and the Other* (1948) presented original descriptions of the instant, time, death, the feminine and fecundity which forced him to the limits of phenomenology and, he claimed, beyond ontology. The confrontation with previous philosophy which these analyses represented was elaborated further when in *Totality and Infinity* (1961) they were integrated into in account of the possibility of ethics. The face-to-face relation with the Other, a relation with an exteriority irreducible to thematization, exposed the neutrality of previous philosophy. In *Otherwise than Being or Beyond Essence* (1974) Levinas sought to restate this 'beyond ontology' in a language which minimized its debts to the ontological tradition. This also led him to elaborate his account of language as an address to the Other – a 'saying' as well as a 'said'. Alongside his philosophical texts, there are a number of 'confessional writings' on Jewish topics, mainly readings of the Talmud.   [R.L.B]

Lévi-Strauss, Claude (1908–)   French anthropologist, see STRUCTURALISM.

Lewis, Clarence I. (1883–1964) American philosopher, born at Stoneham, Massachusetts. He made fundamental contributions to mathematical LOGIC and the theory of knowledge. His major achievement in logic was the calculus of 'strict implication', one of the first successful symbolic systems of 'modal' logic. It is called a modal logic because it employs the modal term 'impossible' in defining '*p* implies *q*' as 'it is impossible for both *p* and not-*q* to be true'. Lewis developed his theory as an alternative to RUSSELL's system of 'material implication' because the latter yields such 'paradoxical' theorems as 'a false proposition implies every proposition', and does not capture the sense in which one proposition is commonly said to imply another. However, Lewis recognized that his and Russell's systems are but two out of a large number of distinct but self-consistent calculi, none of which is intrinsically superior to the others. He held that the sole ground of choice between them is the pragmatic one of greater convenience in organizing our intellectual experience.

Lewis generalized this claim in his pragmatic theory of the a priori. According to him, just as the map-maker provides the principles by which territory is represented on a map, so the mind supplies the categories or principles in terms of which it interprets the sensuous content of direct experience. The categories and the relations of entailment between them are thus a priori, but place no limitation upon the content of the sensuously given. On the other hand, there are alternative systems of categories, just as there are alternative logics and alternative principles of map-making. But a choice between these alternatives can be made only on the pragmatic ground that some categorical schemata may be more convenient than others.

However, Lewis also argued that every claim to knowledge of objective reality involves an interpretation of what is sensuously presented, and a prediction concerning its consequences. To claim, for example, that the round rosy thing in my visual field is an apple, is to assert among many other items that if I were to bite it I would experience a characteristic taste. But since such predictive judgements may be erroneous, Lewis concluded that empirical knowledge is only probable. He then outlined a conception of probability akin to CARNAP's notion of logical probability. Lewis also applied the main principles emerging from his general account of knowledge to some outstanding issues in ETHICS, and claimed that judgements about moral values can be as objective as judgements about matters of fact.   (E.N.)

Lewis, David (1941–2001)   American philosopher, a devoted but disobedient student of QUINE. His books include *Convention* (1969), but he is best known for his 'modal realism', in other words his doctrine that statements of necessity, possibility and impossibility imply the reality of an infinite number of 'possible worlds' (see *On the Plurality of Worlds*, 1986).

He knew his opinions were regarded as wild, but responded by saying, 'I cannot refute an incredulous stare.'

Liberalism and Communitarianism

'Liberalism' is a protean term that often means little more than giving a certain priority to individual liberty. But liberalism in this sense is consistent with very different degrees of commitment to social and economic equality. Moreover different kinds of liberals have different views of what freedom is and why it matters. Hence a great variety of political programmes and doctrines have historically qualified as 'liberal'. In the twentieth century, liberalism came to be identified with state minimalism in the political domain and free markets in the economic sphere. As such it was exposed to criticism from both right and left. Conservatives berated it for a heartless individualism that ignored the ties of community and tradition, while socialists argued for a greater role for the state in promoting social and economic equality. But by the end of the century, liberalism had made a philosophical comeback, in a form that embraces egalitarian state welfarism. John RAWLS's *A Theory of Justice* (1971) offered a systematic philosophical defence of the modern democratic welfare state on the basis of recognizably liberal principles. According to Rawls a liberal state must not only guarantee that all its citizens have an equality of fundamental liberty rights, such as voting, and freedom of speech, religion and association; it must also ensure that those who are least well off are assured as good a life as possible.

One of the fundamental marks of Rawlsian liberalism is its understanding of society as a regulated cooperative venture whose terms of cooperation must be justifiable to all. Another is its political view of citizens as entitled to live in accordance with their own freely chosen values. And the central problem it has faced had been how any set of fair principles of cooperation could be justified to all those who are subject to these principles even while they are divided by deep and enduring moral disagreements.

Rawlsian liberalism has been subject to a range of criticisms. Some accuse it of reducing political theory to a branch of applied ethics. Feminists think it mistakenly prioritises justice over other social virtues, or pays insufficient attention to injustices in the private, familial realm. Critics from the left think it too indulgent about economic inequality, while those on the right, like Robert NOZICK, think it insists too much on economic equality. Perhaps the principal opposition to Rawls's liberalism has come from so-called communitarians (such as Michael Sandel, Michael Walzer, Alasdair MACINTYRE, and Charles TAYLOR). Their criticisms are of various kinds. Some communitarians claim that liberalism overlooks the fact that people's identities are constituted in large part by their membership of communities (national, religious, ethnic, etc.). Rawls's defenders respond by pointing out that his theory was concerned with citizens in the abstract, not with concrete individuals, and by asking whether or not individuals should have the right to change and shape their lives. Certain communitarians also accuse liberalism of underestimating the importance of shared values, while Rawls's supporters reply that it would take unacceptable state coercion to keep a community united round a single moral viewpoint. Liberalism is also criticized for trying to override the particular distinctive values espoused by different societies and replace them with universal political principles. But it can be retorted that such particularism risks descending into a moral relativism which would make it impossible to criticize the values of any community. Moreover it might prove possible to ascend from divergent local understandings to agreements on principles of genuinely universal application.

Nevertheless Rawlsian liberalism may owe its critics a fuller account of the place of community in modern political life. In particular it should acknowledge that a political society united only by a commitment to abstract principles of justice might not be fragile and disorderly. On the other hand, communitarians need to give a positive account of the kind of community they favour. Must a non-liberal society be an illiberal one, or can it acknowledge individual rights? Rawls's liberalism is close to some democratic versions of socialism; but it remains to be seen whether the communitarian alternative is conservative, or socialistic or something completely different.   {D.A.}

Libertarianism   Libertarianism is the thesis which attempts to vindicate the FREEDOM OF THE WILL and responsibility for action by denying the principle of DETERMINISM at least in the case of some spheres of human activity. It is not easy to state this thesis in a positive way. If it be said that human actions are uncaused it might seem that they are attributed to pure chance, in which case it would be absurd to attribute responsibility to the agent. If we are to be held responsible for actions it would seem that in some way they must arise out of our character; indeed it is often easy to predict the actions of people whom we know well on the basis of their character, and this is not naturally taken to diminish their responsibility. But it is evident that we are not responsible for our inherited character or for the environment by which that character has been modified. Thus libertarianism is faced with a double problem: it has to justify rejection of the deterministic thesis, but it

has no obvious alternative explanation of action which would preserve responsibility. It is in fact customary for libertarians to use such language as 'a creative act of will' but it is not clear that such expressions can be used to do more than affirm choice without explaining it.   (J.O.U.)

'Linguistic Turn'   A phrase used by Gustav BERGMANN in 1964 to describe what he took to be a decisive turning point in twentieth century thought whereby philosophers (in particular analytic philosophers such as CARNAP) started to 'talk about the world by means of talking about a suitable language.'

Locke, John (1632–1704)   Locke was born in Somerset, England, the son of a lawyer of no great distinction. He went to Westminster School and, in 1652, to Christ Church, Oxford. There he was trained in the philosophical orthodoxy of the day. In 1659 he was elected to a Senior Studentship in his college – an office supposed to be tenable for life, though Locke was actually dispossessed, on political grounds, in 1684.

In the years after his election, Locke's main interests appear to have been scientific. Through his friendship with Robert BOYLE, who was in Oxford from 1654 to 1668, he was brought into close and practical contact with current work in physics and chemistry, and on his own account he had taken to the study of medicine. In fact he obtained, though with some difficulty, a medical degree from his University, and, in 1674, a licence to practise medicine. His interest in philosophy, however, was eventually re-awakened by the study of DESCARTES; and Descartes' influence is clearly discernible in the vocabulary and the pre-occupations of Locke's own philosophical work.

His connection with Lord Ashley, afterwards Earl of SHAFTESBURY, began in

1666. They first met in Oxford, but by the middle of the following year Locke had become one of Ashley's most esteemed friends and advisers, partly as his physician, but also generally on public affairs. In 1671 Locke composed two short drafts of what was to grow, over the next twenty years, into his *Essay Concerning Human Understanding*; but for the present he was deeply engaged in the private and political affairs of his patron, who became Lord Chancellor in 1672. In 1680, after many vicissitudes in the scheming Shaftesbury's fortunes, and several journeys abroad for the sake of his own health, Locke was back in Oxford. But in 1683, after his patron's death in extreme political disfavour, Locke judged it prudent to retire to Holland, in whose comparatively calm and liberal atmosphere he passed, to the great profit of his writings, the next five years. After the Whig revolution of 1688, he became a celebrated figure. The *Essay* and *Two Treatises of Government* both appeared in 1690; and until 1700, when his health became precarious, he both wrote much on current issues of controversy and held various active political appointments. In that year he brought out a fourth edition of the *Essay*.

Locke's *Essay*, by far his most important work, is a vast, untidy composition, bearing all too clearly in its wanderings and repetitions the signs of having been written piecemeal over many years. Its style is sober and usually clear; but Locke was not careful over points of detail, not always consistent with himself, and by no means rigorous in working out the full consequences of his position.

1 *The Way of Ideas.* Locke's official concern is with EPISTEMOLOGY, the theory of knowledge; his purpose is, as he puts it, 'to inquire into the origin, certainty, and extent of human knowledge, together with the grounds and degrees of Belief, Opinion, and Assent'. However, underlying this 'analytic', clarificatory programme, and greatly influencing its course, is an unsystematic and indeed almost unconscious metaphysical doctrine. Locke believed that philosophers ought to take account of the impact of scientific discoveries upon their own beliefs, and on 'common sense'. But, half unwittingly, he went much further: he evidently believed that the world is really what the physicist says it is. He even adapts to this conviction a fragment of the medieval apparatus which he had acquired in his student days: the 'nominal essence' of a substance, he says, consists in those observable qualities which determine the ordinary application of its name; its 'real essence', on the other hand, consists in the physical structure of its 'insensible parts'. In this and in many other passages, Locke in effect erects the current physicists' atomic, or 'corpuscular', theory of matter into an ultimate metaphysical truth. It was, incidentally, this aspect of Locke's position which was regarded by BERKELEY as most odious, dangerous and mistaken.

The general picture of the world which Locke thus took for granted may be summarized as follows: the physical universe really consists of indefinitely many material bodies, which are composed of corpuscles, or 'insensible particles', which are themselves very small bodies. This whole system operates mechanically; indeed Locke sometimes refers to ordinary objects as 'machines', and says that impact, or 'impulse', is 'the only way which we can conceive bodies operate in'. Now besides this system of mechanically interacting material bodies there exist also, Locke believes, immaterial substances, some at least of which are associated, in a manner not clearly understood, with particular material things, namely human bodies. These bodies have certain physical features known as sense-organs; and it is a fact, perhaps not further explicable, that when these sense-organs are stimulated – mechanically of course – the resultant motion 'produces in us those different sensations which we have', or 'produces in our minds...particular *ideas*'. In addition to such 'ideas of sensation', we acquire further 'ideas of reflection' from 'the perception of the operations of our minds within us, as it is employed about the ideas it has got'. These IDEAS together, Locke holds, supply the whole of the material of consciousness, experience, perception and thought; all are derived 'from experience' (the vague but fundamental tenet of EMPIRICISM); and 'we can have knowledge no farther than we have ideas'.

Thus the mind, Locke says, 'in all its thoughts and reasonings, hath no other immediate object but its own ideas, which it alone does or can contemplate'. This conviction leads to serious difficulties about perception and knowledge. As to perception, it is of course possible, on Locke's principles, to ask whether the 'ideas' of which we are aware faithfully represent the character of the 'external' material things which cause them. Locke's own answer is that, in part, they do: our ideas of 'primary qualities' – 'solidity, extension, figure, motion or rest, and number' – represent qualities that bodies do really possess. Ideas of 'secondary' qualities, on the other hand – 'as colours, sounds, tastes, etc.' – are merely modes in which bodies happen to appear to organisms constituted as we are; they are 'in truth nothing in the objects themselves, but powers to produce various sensations in us by their primary qualities, that is, by the bulk, figure, texture, and motion of their insensible parts'. In making this distinction Locke gives

striking expression to his conviction that the world is nothing but a physical mechanism; the qualities he asserts to be really 'in' bodies are precisely those relevant to their mechanical behaviour. However, he seems not to notice the difficulty that, if we can 'contemplate' only our own ideas, it is not apparent how we could ever decide what relations hold between these and 'external' bodies: how could we tell that our ideas are faithful representatives in any respect, if we can never contemplate that which they represent to us? It was indeed urged by Berkeley that, on Locke's view, we should have no solid ground even for the conviction that any 'external' bodies exist; still less, then, is Locke in a position to assert so confidently that those bodies really do have certain qualities, but only appear to have others.

Locke's difficulties as to knowledge are somewhat similar. Defining knowledge as 'the perception of the connexion and agreement, or disagreement and repugnancy, of any of our ideas', he is first obliged to add the inconsistent rider that our ideas must be perceived also to 'agree with the reality of things', and then to evade the resulting question as to how, on his principles, this latter perception can occur. He sometimes appears to hold that knowledge, strictly speaking, extends only to the relations between ideas; but even if so, it is not clear how he could consistently admit that even so much as a well-grounded opinion could be achieved as to the relation between ideas and 'the reality of things'.

It will be observed that these major difficulties in Locke's position derive from his basic principle, that we can be actually – 'immediately' – aware only of the contents of our own minds. It is in this way that ideas, in his system, become what has been described as an 'iron curtain' between the observer and the world. And it is important to notice that this principle was not, as Locke seems to have supposed, forced on him by his adherence to scientific theory. For the scientific account of perception addresses itself to the question, how perception occurs – the orthodox answer being, in Locke's day, that it occurs by means of the mechanical operation of 'insensible particles' upon the sense-organs. Now this is not an answer to the question, what it is that is really perceived. It may be that some occurrence 'in the mind' is the last item in the causal trans-action between the observer and the environment; but it does not follow that what occurs in the mind is all that is really observed.

2 *Political theory.* Locke's political writings were for the most part directed towards supplying a theoretical justification for the views of those who wished to overthrow the arbitrary government of the Stuarts, and replace it by a monarchy of strictly limited powers. Of his *Two Treatises of Government*, the first is a successful refutation of a view that scarcely deserved such extended notice. Locke's target here is the absolutist theory, not, unfortunately, of the powerful HOBBES, but of the zealous Royalist Robert Filmer, who had argued that the authority of a king is identical with that of a father over his children, and is derived directly from God's grant of such authority to Adam. Locke gravely points out, first, that a father's authority over his children is not absolute, at least when they become adult; second, that the relation between a king and his subjects is not genuinely analogous with that between a father and his children; and third, that it would in any case be a matter of some difficulty to trace the direct descent of patriarchal authority from Adam to Charles II. It is in the second *Treatise* that Locke states his own case.

In the exposition of his political principles Locke adopted the pseudo-historical convention of the period. He describes, purporting to trace an actual process, societies as emerging from a pristine 'state of nature', as a result of a 'contract' by which individuals jointly agree to submit themselves, for the sake of certain advantages, to a ruler or rulers. Now Hobbes had argued that, in such a case, the designated ruler could only be absolute; if any members of society were to be effectively restrained, the ruler must have absolute power over all. Locke argues against this, first, that the ruler's rights are limited, as are those of everyone, by the 'law of nature'; and second, that in any case they are assigned as a trust for the good of the members of society, and hence can properly be taken away if that trust is broken. Though thus opposed to authoritarianism, Locke was of course in no sense a democrat. He had no uncritical faith in elected assemblies, still less in the populace at large, and he did not envisage universal suffrage. He believed that monarchy was the best political arrangement, provided some assembly could hold the monarch to account, and itself be in some degree answerable to the people. Unlike Hobbes, he did not think it essential that any person or persons in society should be a centre of final sovereignty, and able in the last resort to settle all disputes. No doubt this was because, unlike Hobbes, he believed in the rational basis of the principles of conduct, and also believed that human beings were rational enough to be trusted, with certain safeguards, to follow those principles. This made it possible for him to rely upon some measure of enlightened cooperation in political affairs.

It may be said, in summary, that Locke's real achievement was to bring together most of the threads of the 'advanced' thinking of his time. In his philosophy he seemed to have escaped from the mazes of minute and insignificant subtlety into which the scholastic tradition had degenerated; to have taken account of the new stirrings of Cartesianism; and above all to have brought philosophy firmly into line with the latest and best in scientific theory. The general picture of the world, against the background of which Locke pursued his epistemological inquiries, was, as has been said, exactly that of the seventeenth and eighteenth century physicist; and there is little doubt that Locke's views owed much of their prestige to their declared alliance with the flourishing physical sciences. The fact that those views embodied serious misunderstandings was soon observed by philosophical critics, notably Berkeley and LEIBNIZ; however, they expressed so exactly the spirit of the age, that they easily survived such criticism. Moreover, there is merit enough in Locke's many discussions of particular problems to ensure that he will continue to be read with close attention, as being at least in the historical mainstream of modern philosophy in the English language.

In his political theory also – unadventurous as it may seem, and artificially presented as it undoubtedly is – Locke was giving clear expression to the enlightened opinion of his day. It is true that he presented his theory as stating the conditions to be satisfied by any good society at any time; but in fact – not surprisingly – its real contribution was to the political thought of his own society and age. The seventeenth century in English politics was a period in which the character and role of kingship, or more generally the relations of ruler and subject, were topics of incessant uncertainty, conflict and debate; that age was, more than most, an age of transition. It can hardly be said that Locke contributed directly to the comparatively enduring settlement of 1688, but he did express the thought of those who worked for it. In this also he was the embodiment of his age, and in his good sense, sobriety and devotion to reason, he remains a justly admired representative of it.   (G.J.W.)

Logic Logic may be defined as the theory of the conditions of valid inference or, more shortly, as the theory of proof. Inference is a process by which we pass from a belief in one or more statements (the *premises*) to a belief in a further statement (the *conclusion*) whose truth, if the inference is a good one, is either guaranteed or at least made probable by the truth of the premises. Inference is therefore a mental process and it might be thought that this means that logic is connected in some way with psychology. But in fact logical study of the *conditions* of valid inference does not involve studying processes of thought, but only the formal or structural properties of arguments.

1 *The Scope of Logic.* In its simpler forms, logic may be considered as a natural history of arguments. Just as the biologist studies the structure and working of plants and animals and tries to see how different species are related to each other, so the logician studies the structure and working of different types of argument and tries to relate them together systematically. But the logician is interested only in those features of arguments in virtue of which they are admitted to be *valid*. It is clear that we all rely on inference to provide much of our knowledge and that our inferences may be more or less reliable. At a common sense level, we all distinguish between good inferences and bad ones, though we may not find it easy to explain the rules by which we tell the difference. It is one of the tasks of logic to provide an explicit and systematic way of making these distinctions.

However logic has other tasks too. In ancient and medieval times, logicians were interested mainly in the classification and working of arguments, and modern symbolic logicians have sought to give a detailed and complete account of the various kinds of valid arguments and their connexions. An equally important task, at least since FREGE, has been the critical examination of mathematical concepts and methods. The study of mathematical proofs falls under the general heading of the theory of proof; it is an important aspect of logic, but technical and difficult. No further reference will be made to it here, but we should remember that modern developments in logic are almost entirely due to the work of mathematicians.

Two main types of inference have interested logicians, _deductive_ and _inductive_. Well-known examples of deductive inference are the geometry of Euclid or SYLLOGISMS such as:

(1) If all mammals are warm blooded, and all mammals suckle their young, then some warm blooded creatures suckle their young.

To say that a deductive argument is valid means that the conclusion follows rigorously from the premises, or in other words that the conclusion cannot be false if the premises are true. It is part of the task of logic (and a matter of some difficulty) to give a complete and satisfactory account of the conditions under which a statement can be said to be inferable from, deducible from, or entailed by others.

The process of inductive inference has received a good deal of attention from logicians, though some would argue that the concepts of proof and valid inference should be restricted to cases that conform to the rules of deductive logic. A brief account of some of its problems will be given in Section 6; Sections 2 to 5 relate to deductive or formal logic.

2 _Logical form._ It has been a common practice of logicians since ARISTOTLE to use symbolic devices for the expression and study of arguments. This is because logicians are interested not in the subject matter of particular arguments or the linguistic expressions in which they are formulated, but only in the _general rules_ governing their validity. The formal study of argument-structures can reduce the enormous diversity of reasonings on all sorts of topics and in different languages to a few standard patterns which can be systematically related together. That the validity of a deductive argument depends upon its structure (or _logical form_) and not its subject matter can be seen in the following examples.

(2) If no metals are soluble in water, and some crystalline substances are metals, then some crystalline substances are not soluble in water.

(3) If no Christians are pantheists, and some mystics are Christians, then some mystics are not pantheists.

The logical form common to (2) and (3) can be represented thus:

(4) If no A are B, and some C are A, then some C are not B.

Here the terms expressing the subject matter of the deduction have been replaced by _variables_. The use of variables may be familiar from the use of 'x', 'y' and so on in algebra. Variables can be defined as symbols which do not themselves refer to anything, but, like pronouns, stand for (and can be replaced by) words or phrases that do refer. Variables can be regarded as convenient devices for marking blank spaces. We could (rather less conveniently) write (4) as:

(5) If no ••• are ---, and some ∗∗∗ are •••, then some ∗∗∗ are not ---.

Aristotle introduced the use of variables into logic, and modern logicians have added symbols other than variables, some of which will be explained later. Meanwhile, it is worth noting that the use of symbols has important advantages besides the exhibition of logical form and the formulation of general rules. They bring a clarity and conciseness to logic without which little progress could be made. Consider how inconvenient it would be to paraphrase in ordinary language even a simple algebraic expression like '$(x+y)^2 = x^2 + 2xy + y^2$'. The development of logic, like that of mathematics, depends on concise and apt symbolism.

3 *Propositional calculus.* The simplest branch of logic is the logic of propositions or, as it is often called, the propositional calculus. It was not the first part of logic to be developed: Aristotle paid little attention to it, and though the Stoics and some medieval logicians investigated it, its systematic development was the work of FREGE, PEIRCE and other modern logicians. The propositional calculus treats arguments whose basic constituents are propositions. (The defining property of a proposition for this purpose is that it must be either true or false and cannot be both; propositions correspond to indicative sentences, as opposed for example to questions or commands.) A typical example of a simple propositional argument is:

(6) If smoking is not a cause of cancer, then statistical correlations are not a reliable sign of causal connexion; but statistical correlations are a reliable sign of causal connexion; therefore, smoking is a cause of cancer.

The logical form of this argument may be shown by replacing the proposition 'smoking is a cause of cancer' by 'p' and 'statistical correlations are a reliable sign of causal connexion' by 'q' and rewriting it

as follows:

(7) If, if not-p then not-q; and q; then p.

(7) exhibits the logical form of (6); it is an *argument-form* which becomes a concrete argument if the variables 'p' and 'q' are replaced by particular propositions. And since this form is a valid one, whatever propositions we substitute for 'p' and 'q' will yield a valid argument.

All propositional arguments can be conveniently symbolized by replacing their constituent propositions with variables ('p', 'q', 'r' etc.), and finding further symbols for the words and phrases ('if...then...', 'and' and 'not' for example) that are used to bind one proposition to another. These words and phrases are known as *propositional connectives* or *logical constants*, and their symbolic equivalents in the notation of RUSSELL and WHITEHEAD's *Principia Mathematica* are as follows:

not: ~
and: . (alternatively, &)
if...then.... : ⊃ (alternatively, →)

A further commonly occurring constant is:

or: ν

('Or' is taken here in its *inclusive* sense: '$p \, \nu \, q$' means 'either p or q or both'). After further translation, (7) thus becomes:

(8) $[(\sim p \supset \sim q) \cdot q] \supset p$

(Brackets are used to show the *scope* of the logical constants; without them a formula like (8) would be ambiguous.)

4 *Validity in propositional arguments.* Once we have a method of formalizing propositional arguments, we can confront the question how to distinguish valid argument forms from invalid. At this level of logic, the so-called *decision problem* can be solved easily enough. One simple decision procedure is provided by 'truth-tables'. By this method, we first list all the

possible combinations of truth and falsity ('T' and 'F') for the constituent propositions of the argument-form in question. For an argument comprising n propositions, there will be 2^n such combinations. Argument (8) comprises 2 propositions, p and q, so there are 2^2 or 4 possibilities: p and q both true, p true and q false, p false and q true, and p and q both false. We will therefore need to work out what the truth-value ('T' or 'F') of the whole formula will be in each of these four cases. As a preliminary, we define the four logical connectives ('~', '.', '⊃', 'ν'), in terms of truth-values, which is done in tabular form as follows:

p	q	$\sim p$	$\sim q$	$p \cdot q$	$p \vee q$	$p \supset q$
T	T	F	F	T	T	T
T	F	F	T	F	T	F
F	T	T	F	F	T	T
F	F	T	T	F	F	T

(Thus, to take the bottom row, when p is false and q is false, then $\sim p$ is true, $\sim q$ is true, $p \cdot q$ is false, and $p \supset q$ is true.)

Applying these rules, we can now complete a truth-table for (8) in four stages. First, we set out the truth-values of the four negated and unnegated variables ($\sim p$, $\sim q$, p, q) in columns:

$\sim p$	$\supset$	$\sim q$	$\cdot$	q	$\supset$	p
F		F		T		T
F		T		F		T
T		F		T		F
T		T		F		F
1		2		3		4

Second, observing the truth-values in columns 1 and 2 and the rules for '⊃', we complete a column under the logical constant of narrowest scope:

$\sim p$	$\supset$	$\sim q$	$\cdot$	q	$\supset$	p
F	T	F		T		T
F	T	T		F		T
T	F	F		T		F
T	T	T		F		F
1	5	2		3		4

Third, observing the truth-values in columns 5 and 3 and the rules for '.', we complete the column under the logical constant of next widest scope:

$\sim p$	$\supset$	$\sim q$	$\cdot$	q	$\supset$	p
F	T	F	T	T		T
F	T	T	F	F		T
T	F	F	F	T		F
T	T	T	F	F		F
1	5	2	6	3		4

Lastly, observing the truth values in columns 4 and 6 and the rules for '⊃', we complete the remaining column under the logical constant of widest scope:

$\sim p$	$\supset$	$\sim q$	$\cdot$	q	$\supset$	p
F	T	F	T	T	T	T
F	T	T	F	F	T	T
T	F	F	F	T	T	F
T	T	T	F	F	T	F
1	5	2	6	3	7	4

It will be seen (from column 7) that the argument form comes out true for all the truth-possibilities of its component propositions. This shows that it is a valid formula, since an invalid one would reduce to F for at least one assignment of truth values to its component propositions.

But a decision procedure like this merely tells us whether or not a given argument-form is valid. It provides no means of systematizing valid forms or generating new ones. For this purpose, a standard method is to construct a system in which all the valid formulas of the calculus can be deduced from a small number of formulas (the *axioms*) taken as a starting point. (An imperfect but well-known example of an axiom system is the geometry of Euclid.) Deduction consists in operating on the axioms and on the formulas derived from them in accordance with the rules of the system. These rules must specify what symbols may be used and how they may be combined (Rules of Formation) and what manipulation of the axioms and derived formulas is permitted (Rules of Transformation). Axioms may be chosen in any convenient way provided that the set we select is consistent, that is to say, yields only valid formulas. It should also, if possible, be 'complete', or capable of yielding *all* valid formulas of the system. Proofs must be found that these conditions of consistency and completeness are satisfied – which can be done without much difficulty in the case of the propositional calculus.

5 *Predicate Calculus.* Propositional calculus is only the first level of logic, and there are many arguments which cannot be expressed in its symbolism or tested by its method. One example is:

(9) If A is larger than B, and B is larger than C, A is larger than C.

Another example is provided by arguments (2) and (3) or their formalization in (4): they are clearly valid – but not in virtue of their propositional form. (In the symbolism

of propositional calculus they can be formalized as

(10) $(p \cdot q) \supset r$

which is clearly not a valid form.) The argument is valid not because of the relations between its constituent propositions but because of their *internal structure*. More particularly, it is valid because of the way in which the words 'all', 'some' and 'not', and the descriptive phrases (or *predicates*) – 'metals', 'soluble in water' and 'crystalline substances' – link the premises with each other and with the conclusion. To formalize such arguments we need, in addition to the symbols of propositional logic, three further sets of signs:

(i)   *Variables* – 'x', 'y', 'z' etc. – standing for particular things, or *individuals*;

(ii) Signs for *predicates* – 'F', 'G', 'H' etc. – standing either for *monadic* predicates, like 'blue' or 'square'; or for *dyadic* predicates (predicates needing two individuals to complete them) like 'larger than' or 'loves'; or *triadic* predicates, like 'between' or 'lends'.

(iii) The two *quantifiers*: the *universal* quantifier, '(x)', meaning 'for all xs'; and the *existential* quantifier, '(Ex)', meaning 'there is an x such that…'.

With the help of this apparatus, (2) can now be formalized as follows:

(11) $[(x)(Fx \supset {\sim}Gx) \cdot (Ex)(Hx \cdot Fx)] \supset (Ex)(Hx \cdot {\sim}Gx)$

And (9) can be formalized thus:

(12) $(x)(y)(z)(Fxy \cdot Fyz) \supset (Fxz)$

Having established this *predicate calculus*, we face the same two problems as in the propositional calculus: finding a decision procedure and constructing a satisfactory axiom system. There are axiom systems for the predicate calculus for which proofs of consistency and completeness can be given; but it has been proved (by Alonzo CHURCH) that no general decision procedure is possible for this part of logic although decision methods can be devised for important fragments of it.

Propositional and predicate calculus are comparatively elementary levels of logic and it is easy to find sentences which cannot be formalized using their apparatus. (For example: 'There is only one god' or '$2 + 2 = 4$'.) These must be taken care of by further developments of logical technique which cannot be explored here.

6 *Inductive Arguments.* Broadly speaking, a proof by inductive methods is one which seeks to establish a general statement by considering a sample of particular cases. For example, we may conclude, on the basis of observations made on a limited number of specimens of a limited number of species, that all green plants form starch in the presence of light. Since we have gone beyond our evidence, our conclusion may turn out to be false, and in general it appears that such conclusions never follow rigorously from their premises. Whereas a deductive argument is either valid or invalid, an inductive argument will give more or less support for its conclusion but cannot guarantee it completely.

The mere fact that we tend to make generalizations on the basis of our past experience does not of itself present a problem for logicians. All animals capable of learning show in their behaviour an expectation that future events will resemble past ones, and that unobserved instances will resemble those which have been observed. Our tendency to generalize is merely a fact of biology. But some of our expectations about the future course of nature are justified by events and some are not. It is clearly a matter of great importance to have procedures for distinguishing generalizations that are

well-founded from ones that are not. The main task of inductive logic is therefore the study of the critical checks which are necessary to discipline our proneness to generalize.

Natural science provides us with a large body of well-established generalizations and so offers us a model of inductive reasoning. The influence of this model has been such that the phrase 'inductive logic' has come to be synonymous with 'the logic of science'. And it is interesting to note that the earliest important study of inductive reasoning was made by Francis BACON at a time when the experimental study of nature was beginning to play a significant role in intellectual life. The example of natural science also shows that inductive reasoning aims to produce not only generalizations but *explanations* as well. Indeed regularities or uniformities in nature have often been established in the course of the search for explanation of some apparently exceptional observed event. It was in this way, for example, that attempts to explain Galvani's observation of a mysterious contraction in the muscle of a dead frog led to the formulation of laws about the behaviour of electric currents.

The logic of induction has had two main lines of development: the study of devices for eliminating irrelevancies and the study of methods for confirming hypotheses. MILL's 'methods of experimental inquiry', variously criticized and improved by later writers, consist essentially in a technique for eliminating irrelevant factors in phenomena under observation. They are embodied in a practical way in various experimental techniques used in natural science. Indeed, this part of inductive logic may be said to consist in the logical analysis of experimental procedures. In the same way, the logic of confirmation has had to take account of advances in statistical techniques. It has sometimes been said that there are no precise rules for assessing inductive evidence, but mathematical statistics at least allows the extent of their inexactness to be be measured.

7 *The limits of logic.* Having considered both deductive and inductive methods of inference, the question arises whether there are any other kinds of arguments. In the ordinary sense of 'argument', there clearly are. There are many fields of dispute – such as literary criticism, theology, political theory, much of traditional philosophy and many parts of law – where issues cannot be decided by formalized deductive methods nor rendered more or less probable by inductive procedures. And it is clear that many of these arguments, though indecisive, are intended to be rational, so it would seem that logic ought to concern itself with them. It would certainly be unwise to try to prescribe in advance what the science of logic can achieve. Logicians at the end of the eighteenth century thought that logic was a completed science and would no doubt be astounded by its subsequent development. Whether future developments will extend the province of logic to include the 'arguments' of the literary critic, the theologian or the metaphysician, no one can say. But it is clear in the light of the history of logic that the prospects for making such arguments respectable are not promising.
(D.J.O'C.)

Logical Atomism   A doctrine first developed by Bertrand RUSSELL in the course of conversations with WITTGENSTEIN, and published in 1918. Russell wanted above all to avoid IDEALISM and HOLISM: he disliked 'the monistic logic of the people who more or less follow HEGEL' and wished instead to endorse 'the common-sense belief that there are many separate things'. Just as physical analysis reaches its bedrock in physical atoms, or the ultimate constituents of matter, so (Russell argued) logical analysis must terminate in 'logical atoms' – on the one hand universals ('predicates or relations and so on'), and on the other particulars ('such things as little patches of colour or sounds, momentary things'). Wittgenstein developed a far more subtle version of the doctrine (based on 'facts' rather than 'things') in the *Tractatus*. The doctrine has not prospered.   {J.R.}

Logical Positivism   'Logical Positivism' is a name given (by Blumberg and Feigl, 1931) to the philosophical movement emanating from the VIENNA CIRCLE. Often applied, in a vaguely opprobrious sense, to ANALYTIC PHILOSOPHY in general, it is best confined to its original purpose, in which usage it is largely synonymous with so-called 'logical', 'scientific' or 'consistent' empiricism.

The Vienna Circle originated in the early 1920s as an informal discussion group at the University of Vienna, presided over by Moritz SCHLICK. The more prominent members included Rudolf CARNAP, Otto NEURATH, Friedrich WAISMANN, Philipp Frank, Hans Hahn, Herbert Feigl, Victor Kraft, Felix Kaufmann and Kurt GÖDEL. Other associates, more or less remote in distance, time or opinion, were Hans Reichenbach, Carl Hempel, Karl Menger, Richard von MISES, Karl POPPER, Joergen Joergensen, C. W. MORRIS and A. J. AYER. A fair number of the original circle were not philosophers by training, but mathematicians, physicists or social scientists, sharing a common interest in the philosophy of science and a common distaste for the academic metaphysics then prevailing in Germany and Central Europe. Historically, their logic was that of FREGE and RUSSELL, while their 'positivism' owed less to COMTE than to the 'neo-positivism' of MACH and Poincaré, Einstein's general RELATIVITY, and by way of these, to Karl PEARSON, J. S. MILL, the writers of the Enlightenment and the earlier British empiricists (most notably HUME). The strongest immediate influence, however, was that of WITTGENSTEIN, who though not a member of the circle was acquainted with some of its members, and whose *Tractatus Logico-Philosophicus* (1921) supplied the background to many of its discussions, as also did Schlick's *Allgemeine Erkenntnislehre* (1918–25), and Carnap's *Logical Structure of the World* (1928).

After some years of comparatively private and unselfconscious existence, the group was formally constituted in 1929 as the Vienna Circle, the name – due to Neurath – being chosen for its agreeable associations with woods, waltzes and other local amenities. A manifesto-cum-bibliography (*Wissenschaftliche Weltauffassung: Der Wiener Kreis*) was issued under the auspices of a cognate body, the 'Verein Ernst Mach'; a conference was held at Prague; and the journal *Annalen der Philosophie*, purchased in 1930, retitled *Erkenntnis*, and edited by Carnap and Reichenbach, enabled the circle to establish and maintain contact with an increasing body of sympathizers in Britain, the United States and Northern Europe. Further conferences, in the name of the 'unity of science', were held at Königsberg (1930), Prague (1934), Paris (1935 and 1937), Copenhagen (1936), Cambridge, England (1938) and Cambridge, Mass. (1939). Other enterprises included the publication of several series of books and monographs, the most ambitious of these being Neurath's uncompleted project for an 'International Encyclopedia of Unified Science'.

This enlargement of activities was accompanied by some loss of identity, and

by the mid-thirties logical positivism was already diffusing into the wider and vaguer movement of logical empiricism. The meetings of the Vienna Circle proper were abruptly terminated, in 1936, by the murder of Schlick; and its dissolution was soon completed under the pressure of events in Europe, which drove the majority of its members into exile in Britain or the United States. The residual influence of the movement was probably strongest in the United States; elsewhere its explicit contentions soon ceased to excite much controversy, though many of its ideals are still operative within analytic philosophy.

The logical positivists preached a quasi-scientific agreement among philosophers, and at first were surprisingly close to practising it, at least among themselves. Some technical differences apart, it is therefore possible, if hazardous, to credit them with a collective point of view. Its main features are: a thoroughgoing empiricism, backed by the resources of modern logic and tempered only by a possibly exaggerated respect for the achievements and capabilities of modern science; an equally thoroughgoing rejection of metaphysics, on logical grounds, as not merely false or futile, but meaningless; a restriction of philosophy, therefore, to the task of eliminating its own problems, by clarifying the language employed in framing them; and the more constructive aim of analysing and unifying the terminology of the sciences, by reduction to a common denominator in the language of physics.

EMPIRICISM is the doctrine that all knowledge is ultimately derived from experience. As stated by Hume, it involves the psychological claim that all ideas are direct or indirect copies of sense-impressions, from which the conclusion is drawn that knowledge is either of internal relations between ideas (as in mathematics), or else has reference, in the last resort, to the content of sense-impressions ('matter of fact and existence'); all else being committed to the flames as 'sophistry and illusion'. Following Wittgenstein, logical positivism began by adopting a more logically orientated version of the same view. Experience (it was held) can be resolved into its ultimate constituents, namely the immediate and incorrigible sensory observations of which the observer's world consists. The structure so presented is reflected in language; more precisely, it can be shown by logical analysis that the propositions in which knowledge is expressed are similarly reducible to elementary propositions, corresponding one-to-one with actual or possible items of sense-experience. The relation between complex and elementary propositions is 'truth-functional', inasmuch as the truth of a complex proposition depends solely on the truth or falsity of its simple components. Complex propositions do not add anything to simple ones, except a greater degree of logical complexity. Nothing is added, because the propositions of logic and mathematics are concerned only to regulate the formal relationships between symbols. In themselves, they say nothing about the world, and have no content; their function is to state equivalences and relations of derivation between other propositions, and although, if true at all, they are necessarily true, this is only because they are 'tautological', true by definition, or, in an older terminology, 'analytic'. From this it follows directly, as Hume saw, that there can be no hope of a deductive metaphysics; for if logic is empty, the manipulation of empirical data cannot be expected to lead beyond experience. It remains to be shown that the propositions of metaphysics are literally without meaning.

Truth, on the view mentioned earlier, is either formal or factual, and in the latter case it consists either in direct correspondence between elementary proposition and sensory datum, or else, at a more complex level, in an (implicit) correspondence of structure, plus the occurrence of appropriate sense-experiences. A proposition has meaning only if it can, in principle, be true or false. Hence the class of meaningful propositions is exhaustively divisible into those whose truth-or-falsity can be established on formal grounds (i.e. logic and mathematics), and those in which it is, or could be, factually confirmed by verification (or falsification) through sense-experience. The principle involved is known as the *verification principle*; it is crudely stated in the slogan that 'the meaning of a proposition is the method of its verification'. A more judicious, if less incisive, formulation would be that a proposition *has* meaning if sense-experience would be sufficient to decide its truth. The 'propositions' of metaphysics and theology are plainly not formal, since they claim to report on matters transcending ordinary experience. Yet metaphysicians have no dispute with ordinary facts, and from this it appears that no empirical evidence could serve to confirm or discredit their conclusions. Since their statements cannot be tested by experience, they are no more factual than formal, and must therefore be reckoned (in this somewhat technical sense) 'nonsensical' or 'meaningless'. Strictly speaking, indeed, they are not propositions at all. The same applies to the 'pseudo-propositions' of EPISTEMOLOGY and ETHICS, so far, that is, as they refer to 'things-in-themselves' or 'subsistent values', and are not reducible, on the one hand, to factual statements about the psychology, etc., of perceptual or moral judgment, or, on the other, to logical analysis of the language in which these judgments are formulated. One result of such analysis has been the claim that ethical judgments do not state ethical facts, but express the emotions of the speaker, and perhaps incite others to share them. Metaphysical utterances may also be said to do this, and so to convey poetical emotion, or a possible 'attitude to life'. The objection to them is that they do so under a misleading appearance of imparting information about supersensible fact. If all formal propositions belong to logic, and all factual propositions, in a broad sense, to the empirical sciences, it is not easy to find a haven for the propositions of philosophy, including, of course, the verification principle itself. Wittgenstein, faced with this difficulty, had been ready to denounce even his own arguments to this end as 'nonsense', albeit of an important and elucidatory character. Unwilling to accept such a paradox, logical positivism was prepared to grant the legitimacy of analysis, which thus becomes the whole duty of philosophers. Philosophy is not a theory, but an activity – the logical clarification of the concepts, propositions and theories proper to empirical science. The verification principle was similarly interpreted as a definition, recipe or criterion of meaning, rather than an assertion which could be either true or false.

The simple identification of meaning and method of verification has many curious and improbable consequences. The literature of logical positivism is much preoccupied with them, and they have been largely responsible for later divergencies within the school. Briefly, the difficulties are that the principle appears to distort or deny the meaning of many propositions acceptable in science and everyday life; and that its conception of meaning is in any case private, incommunicable and variable from one observer to another. Historical propositions, for example, are not directly verifiable in terms of events, and have to be interpreted as predictions about what *would* be found

on a future inspection of records, etc. The content of such propositions is thus identified with the indirect evidence for their truth. Nor is there any means of distinguishing a future statement of observation from a present one, since their method of verification is the same. General propositions, such as natural laws, etc., are also in principle unverifiable, since no finite series of observations would be sufficient to guarantee their truth. Similar difficulties attach to statements about material objects, whose verification in terms of immediate sensory observations would likewise require an infinite series of such experiences to complete it. Rather than discard them as meaningless, it was declared that propositions of this type were not really propositions at all, but directions for making observations. Alternatively, they were hypotheses, capable of confirmation (or, as some said, falsification) by experience, and to that extent legitimate for the purpose of science. (Generalizations can, of course, be conclusively *falsified* by a single observation, and by that test would rank as genuine propositions; but the refutation of a particular claim that at least *one* X was Y, would then require an exhaustive enumeration, as before.)

In order to avoid these complications, some writers (notably Ayer) sought to distinguish 'strong' and 'weak' forms of the verification principle. The weak version does not require a proposition to be conclusively verifiable, allowing that its meaningfulness may be sufficiently warranted if there are sensory observations which are 'relevant' to its truth or falsity. The intention of this formula was to deny meaning to metaphysical propositions, while conceding it to empirical assertions of the kind mentioned earlier. It was soon recognized, however, that it is altogether too lenient in this respect, since metaphysicians need not scruple to declare that sense-observations are in some degree relevant to their speculations. Later formulations of the principle have sought to remedy this defect, only to run into other and more technical difficulties; with increasing complexity it has increasingly taken on the appearance of an *ad hoc* device for the exclusion of an already proscribed class of statements, rather than being in itself a reason for excluding them.

Further problems arise from the all-important role allotted to sense-experience in the process of verification. Since such experience is necessarily private to the observer, it would appear that propositions can only have meaning for him if they can be rendered in terms of what would, in principle, be accessible to immediate experience. Carnap's *Logical Structure of the World* is an elaborate attempt to perform this reconstruction of scientific and empirical discourse from within the confines of an 'egocentric' terminology. The SOLIPSISM involved is 'methodological' only, since the aim is to effect a theoretical reduction of concepts and propositions merely, and not of facts. But doubts remain as to how, on these assumptions, communication is possible, or how the data of the sciences are inter-subjectively verifiable. Logical positivism was much divided on this question. The more orthodox opinion, expounded chiefly by Schlick, was that the 'structure' of individual experience *could* be communicated and compared with that of others, though its 'content' must remain ineffable, even to the observer himself. The more radical party, headed by Neurath and Carnap, would have none of this lapse into 'metaphysics', and preferred to secure the objectivity of science even at the cost of abandoning its supposed sensory basis. Scientific hypotheses, they argued, are tested not by private sensations in the

observer, but by publicly observable facts. The mental life of the observer is of no interest to science, and allusions thereto are, indeed, strictly without meaning. The observer's reports, bodily states and general behaviour are another matter, however, since they can be publicly checked and recorded; and it is these, or rather the records thereof, that form the 'protocols' or elementary data of scientific theory. This thesis, of 'physicalism', has a close resemblance to BEHAVIOURISM, but differs in that it does not explicitly deny the facts of mental life or reduce them to facts of bodily behaviour. Its contention, rather, is that statements in the language of introspective psychology are formally replaceable by statements in the language of physics; and that it is only in the latter format that they are of any use to science. As such, the thesis is certainly questionable, but it is not refuted by the traditional arguments for dualism.

A more far-reaching claim of this sort, chiefly associated with Neurath, is that all the sciences depend ultimately on protocols couched in terms of physical objects and processes, and hence that all empirical statements can be expressed in the language of physics. Particular sciences may well have laws of their own – that is an empirical question; but the concepts employed can all be defined in physical terms, which thereby form a *lingua franca* of science. This was the theoretical foundation of Neurath's energetic campaigning for the 'unity of science'.

The physicalist retreat from empiricism was carried still further, for a time, by Carnap and Neurath, in proposing to dispense with the correspondence theory of TRUTH. The parallel between language and fact is an essential, yet suspiciously metaphysical feature of Wittgenstein's theory of meaning, since, on his own showing, the extra-linguistic relationship involved is inexpressible within the resources of language. Schlick's pursuit of 'incorrigible', immediately verifiable protocols equally ends in the unutterable. Yet the problem was easily disposed of: statements, it was insisted, are comparable only with other statements, not with external facts; and knowledge must accordingly be depicted as a system of mutually supporting statements, to which newcomers are admitted as true if found to be consistent with those already accepted. The belief in a set of 'basic' propositions underlying knowledge thereby becomes otiose; the 'protocols' required are simply a relevant selection of propositions drawn from the established system; and coherence becomes the test of truth. The difficulty, of course, is to know which system is the right one; for many are possible, and some, at least, must be false, since their internal consistency does not prevent them from being inconsistent one with another. Carnap's declaration of trust in the system underwritten by the protocols of accredited scientists was understandably viewed as an anticlimax, if not a confession of defeat – an impression soon confirmed by his abandonment of this theory and return to a qualified admission that sentences could be 'confronted' with facts.

These changes of front are less radical than they seem, particularly when account is taken of Carnap's other views. Much of his energy as a logician was devoted to 'formalizing' the internal structure (or 'syntax') of language, very much as Hilbert and his followers formalized mathematics by treating its propositions as meaningless marks on paper and discussing the rules for their combination (in a 'metalanguage'). Carnap's 'logical syntax' embraces the grammatical (or 'formation') rules of language, by which sentences are formed from its vocabulary, and the logical (or 'transformation') rules, by which

sentences are formally derived from one another. Much importance is attached to a threefold classification of these sentences: syntactical sentences, which make reference to words or other sentences, are said to be in the 'formal mode of speech'; empirical or object-sentences are those dealing with things and states of affairs; but there is also a third class, of 'pseudo-object sentences', which *seem* to be about things (as when a table is said to *be* a thing), when in fact they really are, or can be translated into, statements about words (namely, that 'table' is a thing-word). These are said to be in the 'material mode of speech'. The main point of these distinctions, in the present context, is to enable it to be argued that most, if not all, of the not hopelessly metaphysical propositions of philosophy, which appear to be alluding, for example, to the existence or status of abstract entities, such as universals, are actually syntactical assertions about words, misleadingly cast in the material mode of speech. Philosophy is thereby identified with logical syntax, the higher-level discussion of language, and long-standing philosophical controversies – such as that between IDEALISM and MATERIALISM – turn out, when translated into the formal mode, to be disputes between alternative 'languages', rather than issues of transcendental importance.

Hence the ready and even nonchalant passage of logical positivism from the phraseology of a quasi-idealist sensationalism to that of a quasi-materialist physicalism; the decision between them being a matter of methodological convenience, not a substantial change of belief. Hence also the urge to eliminate the 'semantic' element – the reference to external fact – from notions of truth and meaning, and to bring the whole compass of language under one syntactical roof. The collapse of this position led Carnap to turn his attention to the semantic field itself, but his contributions to that subject scarcely belong to the literature of logical positivism.

If logical positivism soon became unfashionable, the reason is largely that its approach to language came to seem unnecessarily rigid and doctrinaire. Its assumptions have turned out too simple, and its methods too elaborate, to deal successfully with the informality of 'natural' languages, and restriction to the analysis of artificial model-languages has also limited the interest of the results (see TRANSLATION). Apart from some notable contributions in the relatively technical fields of INDUCTION, PROBABILITY and the methodology of science, the main legacy of the school has been to concentrate attention on the problem of meaning, and to establish standards of logical rigour and clear, unrhetorical expression, that were widely emulated. The attack on metaphysics, if not wholly conclusive, may be said to have damped the ardour, chastened the style and improved the understanding of its remaining devotees. Nor is the influence of the controversy by any means exhausted; ethics and epistemology have both had something to learn from it; and its repercussions are still plainly audible in philosophical theology. See also A PRIORI, LOGICAL ATOMISM, PHILOSOPHY OF SCIENCE.   (P.L.H.)

Lucretius, Titus Lucretius Carus (98–55 BC) The only personal information we have about the Roman poet Lucretius is that he was driven insane by a love potion, wrote some books (which are presumably the six books of the philosophical poem *De Rerum Natura*) in sane intervals, and committed suicide at the age of forty-four. There is no reason to doubt that this is true. The poem is a complete account of the Epicurean theory of the soul, sense-perception, astronomy, heredity, thunder, earthquakes, magnetism

and indeed all that was most likely to seem to the credulous to be supernaturally caused and therefore a source of religious terror. There is not a systematic treatment of the Epicurean ethical theory, but orthodox Epicurean views – that pleasure is the sole good, that the most worthwhile form of pleasure is freedom from fear, and that the main reason studying nature is that we will thereby liberate ourselves from superstitious fears of the gods and life in the underworld – are presupposed throughout. There may not be anything original in Lucretius (he himself made no such claim) but his poem is an accurate and passionate statement of the Epicurean position. It is also one of the greatest masterpieces of Latin literature.   (J.O.U.)

Lukács, Georg (1885–1971) Hungarian Marxist born in Budapest. Lukács was a student of Georg Simmel, and his friends included Ernst BLOCH, Karl Mannheim, Max Weber and Bertolt Brecht. He joined the Communist Party in December 1918, and was active thereafter, as conditions permitted, in Party and national affairs.

From his pre-Marxist *Theory of the Novel* (1916), which re-worked HEGEL's critique of KANT in the context of the novel, to his last work, *The Ontology of Social Being* (1971), which includes chapters on Hegel and MARX, and treats labour as a model for social practice, Lukács' theoretical work focused on problems of dialectic. Throughout, dialectic is conceived of as a mode of historical and categorical thinking which transcends the dualisms constitutive of modern philosophy: subject and object, freedom and necessity, theory and practice, history (time) and eternity. Dialectic, so conceived, is clearly of Hegelian inspiration.

Lukács' most important philosophical work is *History and Class Consciousness*

(1923), which introduces the idea of REIFICATION as a cultural generalization of Marx's concept of commodity fetishism, and thereby seeks to transform Marxism from a reified theory of the economy into a philosophy of praxis. For Lukács the problems of modern philosophy are historical and social problems because the categories of philosophy are, in truth, historical and social categories. Hence the overcoming of categorial dualisms becomes possible in thought through their placement within the social totality, and in reality through the practical transformation of the categorial structures of modern society. Revolutionary praxis becomes, in Lukács, an ontological experiment. *History and Class cconsciousness* is the seminal work of 'Western (Hegelian) Marxism' and is largely responsible for bringing the problems of Marxism into a philosophical purview. Lukács spent the war years in Moscow. During this time he studied Marx's *Economic and Philosophical Manuscripts* of 1844. The impact of that reading is evident in *The Young Hegel: On the Relation between Dialectic and Economics* (1948). His cultural conception of Marxism led him, throughout his long career, to write numerous works on literature and the philosophy of art. Prominent amongst these are: *The Historical Novel* (1938); *Goethe and his Age* (1946); *The Meaning of Contemporary Realism* (1957); and *The Specificity of the Aesthetic* (1963).　　　　　[J.M.B.]

Lyotard, Jean-François (1924–98)
See POSTMODERNISM.

M

McDowell, John (1942–) Anglo-American philosopher whose attempts, in the tradition of DAVIDSON, WITTGENSTEIN and SELLARS, to overcome the legacy of dualism have led him (see *Mind and World*, 1994) into dialogue with such exotic partners as HEGEL and GADAMER.

Mach, Ernst (1838–1916) Austrian methodologist of science who served as Professor of Physics at Prague and then at Vienna. His general philosophical position was extreme POSITIVISM; he held that KANT's *Critique of Pure Reason* 'banished into the realm of shadows the sham ideas of the old metaphysics', but that metaphysical notions were still prevalent in the philosophy of science and even within science itself. His main aim was therefore to give an account of the nature of science which would free it from all metaphysical and non-empirical elements and to reconstruct the basic science of mechanics in accordance with these philosophical requirements. 'We know', he said, 'only one source which directly reveals scientific facts – our senses'; therefore science must be reconstructed so as to be manifestly an account of sense-given facts. But the objects of our senses are colours, warmths, smells, sounds and the like, not bodies and still less atoms, absolute space, absolute time, absolute motion and other conceptions of Newtonian mechanics; therefore science must in the final analysis be an account of sensations. No other statements can have any scientific significance. Experience, claimed Mach, provides us only with a manifold of constantly changing and unrelated sensations; we cannot claim to find objectively in the world any basis for our concepts of bodies in motion in space or of laws of nature. 'According to our conception, natural laws are a product of our psychological need to feel at home with nature; all concepts transcending sensation are to be justified as helping us to understand, control and predict our environment, and different conceptual systems may be used to this end in different cultures and at different times with equal propriety.'

But Mach does not consider that there is nothing to choose between any two conceptual schemes. A conceptual system is better if it is simple, comprehensive and free from internal contradictions; such a system is more useful to us and more fruitful. But we must not be misled into saying that nature itself is simple, economical and the like; the difference between economical and cumbersome conceptual systems is one of utility, not truth. We must not however go to the other extreme and regard our choice of scientific laws as purely conventional; the system of concepts must be suited to the facts which it is used to describe and laws of nature are descriptions of the world, even if schematic, and so must be judged true and false by reference to experience. Critics have frequently noted the difficulty of reconciling Mach's empiricism with the more a priori elements in his view. In accordance with the view of the nature of science described earlier, Mach claimed that it was misleading to talk of proof in science. If scientific laws are conceptual tools they cannot be inductively proved from the facts, and the deduction of laws from other laws is of no ultimate significance and may give a misleading appearance of rigour. The only justification that can or should be given for accepting a scientific law is, according to Mach, that it survives testing in use.

Mach was not satisfied with giving this general picture of the nature of science; he considered that contemporary science was to some extent vitiated by not conforming to this picture. In particular he held that science constantly hypostatized the elements in its conceptual system, ascribing to them counterparts in nature for which experience could give no warrant and which were therefore metaphysical. In *The Science of Mechanics* (1883) Mach therefore applied his general position to a criticism of the form given to mechanics by NEWTON and his successors and attempted to show how the scientific content of mechanics could be retained without appeal to absolute space and time, force and other non-empirical notions.

Mach's influence on the development of EMPIRICISM on the continent of Europe was very great; the VIENNA CIRCLE of logical positivists acknowledged him as their basic guide. His pure sensationalism was abandoned quite early in favour of 'physicalism', but most of the leading ideas of LOGICAL POSITIVISM can be traced to him. On the other hand, LENIN attacked Mach as an enemy of materialism.   (J.O.U.)

Machiavelli, Niccolò (1469–1527) Florentine historian whose advice book *The Prince* (published posthumously in 1532) discarded the traditional assumption that political and moral virtues coincide. A prince who clings to morality will come to grief, Machiavelli argued, and thus do damage not only to his own interests but to the public good as well. This is a hard doctrine, and was vociferously condemned,

not least by those whose political practice implicitly endorsed it.   {J.R.}

MacIntyre, Alasdair (1929–) Scots-Irish philosopher who has worked both in England and America. MacIntyre's abiding interests circle round the two poles of his first book, *Marxism and Christianity* (1954), which argued that MARX had 'humanised certain central Christian beliefs' and that Christians ought to learn 'from both the achievements and the failures of Marxism'. Since then he has explored a wide range of topics in the HISTORY OF PHILOSOPHY (especially ethics) and the philosophy of social science, with an unusual sensitivity to their social, historical and political dimensions. But all his work is focused on a single object: the need for moral philosophy to ground itself in history so as to provide positive guidance amidst the dilemmas of MODERNITY. *A Short History of Ethics* (1965) was an attack on the unhistorical approach of writers like HARE (author of the article on ETHICS in this Encyclopedia). The strident polemic in *Marcuse* (1970) discovered élitism, intolerance and irrationalism in a thinker whose interpretation of Marxism is actually quite close to MacIntyre's own. *After Virtue* (1981) is a mournful analysis of the ways in which moral thought and practice have been wrecked by the liberal individualism of the Enlightenment, and *Whose Justice? Which Rationality?* (1988) reinforces the argument by showing how 'standards of rational justification themselves emerge from and are part of a history'. He is the author of articles on Deism, Pantheism and Theism in this Encyclopedia.   [J.R.]

Mackie, John L. (1917–81) Australian philosopher with positivistic sympathies who taught at Oxford and propounded the view (known as 'error theory') that moral discourse ascribes objective moral qualities to the world, and that in doing so it makes a mistake (see *Ethics: Inventing Right and Wrong*, 1977).

McTaggart, John Ellis (1866–1925)

The Cambridge philosopher John Ellis McTaggart was an IDEALIST, a systematic metaphysician, and an admirer of HEGEL. In his great work *The Nature of Existence* (1921, 1927) he set out, with the aid of two empirical premises to the effect that something exists, to show by rigorous a priori argument the general nature of the universe as a whole and of its constituent parts. The conclusion that the universe is a society of minds in close relation to each other is arrived at by a process of argument of great ingenuity and clarity; in the course of this argument occurs the celebrated proof of the unreality of time. In the second part McTaggart attempts to draw by less rigorous methods various conclusions from the results of the first part. The formal simplicity, rigour, lack of rhetoric and candour of this work, combined with unusual audacity of thought and ingenuity, make it of value even to those who are out of sympathy with idealistic metaphysics in general. Among his many uncommon views was his combination of atheism with a belief in the immortality of the soul.   (J.O.U.)

Maimonides (1135–1204)

Moses ben Maimon was born in Spain, and – under the Latinized version of his name – became the most eminent of the medieval Jewish thinkers who attempted to synthesize Greek philosophy and Jewish monotheistic religion. His writings greatly influenced not only his orthodox co-religionists but such unorthodox philosophers as SPINOZA and such orthodox Christian philosophers as AQUINAS. His most celebrated work is *The Guide of the Perplexed* in which he attempts to reconcile Aristotelian philosophy and the Greek sciences with the literal truth of the Old Testament; in this task he relies greatly on the Arab philosophers AVICENNA, to whom he is much indebted for his doctrine of immortality, and AVERROES, from whom he took the notion of the identity of essence and existence in God. Philosophy and revealed theology were treated by Maimonides as quite different in nature but as complementary. It is the task of philosophy to confirm rationally the truths of religion and to disprove doctrines which seem to contradict revelation.   (J.O.U.)

Malebranche, Nicolas (1638–1715)

The heterodoxy of DESCARTES divided the philosophers of his time into bitterly opposed factions. Those who followed Descartes found their authority in AUGUSTINE and those who opposed him took AQUINAS as their master. The French philosopher Nicolas Malebranche was the most celebrated of the Augustinians. He believed individual things to be limitations of the one material substance and individual minds limitations of an immaterial substance, against which was contrasted the perfect freedom of God. Malebranche provided an OCCASIONALISTIC solution of the problem of the causal interaction of the two substances, for he held that there was no capacity for action whatever in finite things, whether minds or bodies – a doctrine which he claimed to be the mark of a Christian philosophy. These considerations, coupled with the problem of how an immaterial mind-substance could perceive material bodies, led him to a kind of neoplatonic metaphysics. We perceive nothing directly, but God implants in our minds the idea of a corporeal world. This world does in fact exist and corresponds to our ideas of it because the ideas of God which are the source of our perceptions are also the archetypes of the world of material things.   (R.HALL.)

Manicheism Manicheism is the doctrine of an early sect of Christians who held that Satan was as real as God, or more generally that EVIL is as real as goodness.

Marcel, Gabriel (1889–1973) French philosopher and playwright. Marcel's philosophical work was communicated to the world principally through his diaries, which appeared in three parts: *Metaphysical Journal*, 1927; *Being and Having*, 1935; and *Presence and Immortality*, 1959. The Gifford Lectures on *The Mystery of Being* (1950) represent the nearest he came to a sustained exposition of his views. While his use of the diary-form makes him an impossible writer to summarize, it gives his philosophical work a suggestive and exploratory quality which is peculiarly valuable to those patient enough to read it.

Marcel is often characterized as a 'Christian Existentialist', and as such contrasted with SARTRE; but this is a serious misdescription. He wrote doctoral thesis on COLERIDGE's relation to SCHELLING, and was initially a student of the English-speaking idealists, BRADLEY and ROYCE, and of BERGSON. With Royce he shared a profound sense of the depth of people's attachment to the community to which they belong. The reader will perhaps learn more from Marcel's diaries than from any other source, of the precise sense of COLLINGWOOD's distinction between 'proposition' and 'presupposition'. Marcel's diaries also reveal his preoccupation with the Cartesian problem of the relation of mind and matter. In his later years he gave serious attention to the implications of para-psychological phenomena, especially telepathy, interpreted as a mode of human communion. Marcel was received into the Catholic Church in 1929, but remained aloof from the neo-Thomist enthusiasms of MARITAIN. For all its looseness of texture and diffuseness of exposition, Marcel's thought has a critical and analytical quality, evidenced, for example, in his discussion of the notion of an *argument* for the existence of God, in his laying bare of the precise content of the hope of immortality, in his contribution to the pervasive debate concerning the nature and possibility of metaphysics, and through his distinction between 'problem' and 'mystery'. For all his stress on the dimension of subjectivity, he remains profoundly hostile to any sort of radical individualism, which he would judge false to the subtle actualities of the human situation.   (D.M.M.)

Marcus Aurelius Antoninus (121–180) Roman Emperor, who in his latter years wrote the *Meditations* as a personal refreshment amid the burdens of his lonely office. His STOICISM is rooted in EPICTETUS, but he felt the natural communion of humanity in the organic unity of the universe with a deeper religious fervour than other Stoics. An all-beneficent providence has placed within us a divine control, reason; hence it is in our power to make ourselves one with the rational purpose of the universe. This is our active duty to ourselves as citizens of God's State. As Emperor of Rome, however, he saw equally important duties to his fellow humans, his natural kin. Yet his love of humanity did not blind him to depravity; and, convinced of the transitory nature of temporal affairs, he found no incentive in his Stoic principles to fashion an ideal state, only a sense of urgency to do what he could in the post assigned to him by God. The philosopher-king remained a moral not a political ideal; Marcus is fundamentally concerned with his own moral character functioning in relation to others; his thoughts turn readily from Rome to the City of God.   (I.G.K.)

Marcuse, Herbert (1898–1979)
German-American philosopher who developed his own version of 'critical Marxism' in an attempt to update Marxian theory in response to changing historical conditions from the 1920s through the 1970s. Marcuse gained notoriety in the 1960s when he was perceived as both an influence on and defender of the so-called 'New Left' in the United States and Europe. His first published article, which appeared in Weimar Germany in 1928, attempted a synthesis of PHENOMENOLOGY, EXISTENTIALISM, and Marxism of a kind, which was to be carried out again decades later by various 'existential' and 'phenomenological' Marxists. Marcuse's study of *Hegel's Ontology and Theory of Historicity* (1932) contributed to the HEGEL renaissance that was taking place in Europe. In 1933, he anticipated the tendency to revise interpretations of Marxism from the standpoint of the works of the early MARX, publishing the first major review of Marx's *Economic and Philosophical Manuscripts* of 1844.

In 1934, Marcuse fled from Nazism and emigrated to the United States where he lived for the rest of his life. His first major work in English, *Reason and Revolution* (1941), traced the genesis of the ideas of Hegel, Marx and modern social theory. After service for the US government from 1941 to 1950, which Marcuse always claimed was motivated by a desire to struggle against fascism, he returned to intellectual work and published *Eros and Civilization* (1955), which attempted an audacious synthesis of Marx and Freud and sketched the outlines of a non-repressive society. In 1958 Marcuse published *Soviet Marxism*, a critical study of the Soviet Union, and in 1964 *One-Dimensional Man*, a wide-ranging critique of both advanced capitalist and communist societies. This book theorized the decline of revolutionary potential in capitalist societies and the development of new forms of social control. The book was severely criticized by orthodox Marxists and theorists of various political and theoretical commitments. Despite its pessimism, it influenced many in the New Left as it articulated their dissatisfaction with both capitalist societies and Soviet communist societies. *One-Dimensional Man* was followed by a series of books and articles on politics and capitalist societies, including 'Repressive Tolerance' (1965), *An Essay on Liberation* (1969), and *Counterrevolution and Revolt* (1972).

Marcuse also dedicated much of his energy to aesthetics and his final book, *The Aesthetic Dimension* (1979), is a defence of the emancipatory potential of aesthetic form in so-called 'high culture'. His work in philosophy and social theory generated fierce controversy and polemics, and many studies of his work are highly tendentious and frequently sectarian. Although much of the controversy involved his critiques of contemporary capitalist societies and defence of radical social change, in retrospect, Marcuse left behind a complex and many-sided body of work comparable to the legacies of BLOCH, LUKÁCS, ADORNO, and BENJAMIN. See also ALIENATION, DIALECTICAL MATERIALISM, FRANKFURT SCHOOL.   [D.M.K.]

Maritain, Jacques (1882–1973)
French Catholic philosopher. Originally a follower of BERGSON, Maritain later became one of the best-known modern exponents of THOMISM; his *Introduction to Philosophy* (1920) is orthodox scholasticism in traditional scholastic terms. His best-known philosophical work is *The Degrees of Knowledge* (1932), in which he distinguished natural scientific knowledge, metaphysical knowledge and mystical

knowledge, all of which he regarded as valid forms of knowledge, complementary to each other. (J.O.U.)

Marx, Karl Heinrich (1818–83) Karl Marx was born at Trier in Rhineland Prussia. At the University of Berlin he came under the influence of the radical Young Hegelian movement. Because of these associations a University career was closed to him, so in 1842 he assumed the editorship of the *Rheinische Zeitung*, a new liberal paper at Cologne. The paper was suppressed in 1843, and Marx went to Paris where he made contact with German workers and French socialists and became a communist. There he also met Friedrich ENGELS who became his life-long associate. Expelled from Paris at the end of 1844 he stayed in Brussels for three years and participated in the foundation of the Communist League. When the 1848 revolutions broke out he returned to Cologne to found the *Neue Rheinische Zeitung*. After its suppression in 1849, he took refuge in London where he remained for the rest of his life, often in considerable poverty. In spite of all difficulties, he embarked on a massive research programme, using the facilities of the British Museum reading room. At the same time he was the moving spirit in the International Working Men's Association (1864–72), achieving more notoriety as a revolutionary than as a scholar in his lifetime.

Marx characterized his theoretical work as materialist, dialectical and scientific, and as expressing the standpoint of 'the class that holds the future in its hands' – the proletariat. He was the founder of what Engels called 'scientific socialism'. At the time of his death he was known mainly for *Capital* (Vol. 1, 1867) and the *Communist Manifesto* (1848). Also available were works of contemporary history such as *The Eighteenth Brumaire of Louis Bonaparte* (1852) and *The Civil War in France* (1871). The specifically philosophical elements of his work were known only through his critique of Proudhon, *The Poverty of Philosophy* (1847), and a two-page summary of historical materialism in the Preface to the *Contribution to a Critique of Political Economy* (1859).

It fell to Engels to articulate the philosophical views which, after later elaboration, became known in vulgarized form as DIALECTICAL MATERIALISM. But since then the gradual appearance of unpublished works and drafts by Marx has administered a series of shocks to this doctrine, and promoted a stream of reinterpretations of 'what Marx really thought'. Important manuscripts that became available were: *Theses on Feuerbach* (1845) – put out in edited form by Engels in 1888; *The German Ideology* (1845–6) – not available in full until the 1930s; *Economic and Philosophical Manuscripts of 1844* – published in 1932; and finally the *Grundrisse* (1857–8) – of which there was no accessible edition until 1953. These posthumous publications clarify Marx's relation to German philosophy, and especially the work of HEGEL and FEUERBACH.

The greatest shock was the publication of the *1844 Manuscripts*, which led to considerable debate about the writings of the so-called 'young Marx' and their continuity with the later, supposedly less philosophical, work. However, in the *1844 Manuscripts* Marx already saw productive activity as ontologically constitutive of human being, and the critique of POLITICAL ECONOMY as the key task. In these manuscripts Marx argued that in the private property system, labour is estranged from its object; that this state of estrangement is the result of the ALIENATION of labour from itself; and that private property must be seen as the *product* of alienated labour. From this,

Marx held, there flows an all-pervasive experience of alienation in modern social institutions and culture. The end of alienation requires 'the positive supersession of private property', that is, the re-appropriation of the human essence presently estranged in it. Marx acknowledged that his account of the way in which labour grasps its other (private property) as its estranged self, and negates this negation, has obvious parallels with Hegel's *Phenomenology of Spirit*; but he criticized Hegel for taking activity as essentially spiritual labour, and equating objectivity with estrangement.

Although the young Marx's theory of alienation is not (as ALTHUSSER alleges) simply a materialist inversion of Hegel's, it follows Hegel in treating the history of humanity as a development through self-estrangement to recovery of itself. HISTORICAL MATERIALISM, with its clear periodization of history in terms of successive modes of production, did not emerge till one or two years later. This theory is documented in the first part of the *German Ideology*, and the Preface to the 1859 *Critique*.

Marx distanced his materialism from that of Feuerbach through the key role he gave to practice, especially to productive activity. Because we are natural beings, we have to interact with nature to secure our material existence. Labour converts the raw material provided by nature into goods for human use. This has to be done before anything else and hence fundamentally conditions everything else. Production, moreover, is always social production; and it is the guiding thread to history, Marx believed. History can be divided into distinct periods, in each of which a different mode of production prevails; but each system has its own laws of motion and considerable empirical work is required to discover them.

Marx begins by identifying the *relations* of production, which are seen as corresponding to stages in the development of the productive *forces*. 'The hand-mill gives you society with the feudal lord; the steam-mill, society with the industrial capitalist', as he wrote in 1847. And in 1859: 'The sum total of these relations of production constitutes the economic structure of society, the real foundation, on which rises a legal and political superstructure and to which correspond definite forms of social consciousness. The mode of production of material life conditions the social, political and intellectual life process in general. It is not the consciousness of human beings that determines their being, but, on the contrary, their social being that determines their consciousness.' Social revolution arises out of class struggle rooted in changes in the economic foundation. Of course, the protagonists themselves are not typically aware of such changes. The French Revolution, for example, was fought under the slogan 'Liberty, Equality, Fraternity'. But the development of a market economy and the rise of the bourgeois class was the real content of the event, and its outcome cleared the path for the capitalist mode of production.

It is unfortunate that Marx's architectural metaphor of foundation and superstructure suggests that social consciousness is merely epiphenomenal. In truth, Marx did not deny the reality of ideas, nor their effectivity in moving masses of people to act. He held only that reference to such ideas is not a 'rock bottom' explanation. Definite material and social preconditions must be fulfilled if revolution is to be on the historical agenda. Human liberation depends more on such premises than on any philosophy of freedom. Thus socialism is based on tendencies immanent in history, not on an ideal preached to people in abstraction from their present needs and interests. The historically created conditions for communist revolution include the development of productive forces adequate to sustain a society free from want, and also the emergence of a class that can solve its problems only by overthrowing the existing order.

Marx held that if history continually generates new structures of social being, and thus of individuality, then the socialist project cannot simply be dismissed as 'against human nature'. He had no quarrel with the visionary aims of Utopians like Charles Fourier (1772–1837) and Robert Owen (1771–1858); he shared them (as the doctrine of 'the withering away of the state' shows). But he differed from the Utopians in his conception of political practice. Where they looked with disdain on the existing class struggle, Marx held that the practical reality of communism lay in this very struggle, and that his science laid bare its motor of development and revolutionary potential. This was why Marx devoted most of his life to the study of the workings of capitalist society.

In *Capital* Marx acknowledged his debt to Hegel's *Logic*, but unfortunately gave no details. One could mention such features as: the articulation of the whole as a hierarchy of determinations and its presentation at successively more concrete levels of mediation; the representation of premises as results; the demonstration of capital's tendency to assimilate, and reproduce, its conditions of existence; the dialectic of essence and appearance; and the deployment of such categories as 'contradiction' and 'negation of the negation'. It is also noteworthy that there are distinct parallels between Marx's criticism of the 'mystified form' of Hegelian dialectic and his critique of the 'fetishistic' forms of value – commodity, money, capital.

For Marx, philosophy is part of the 'ideological superstructure'. He sometimes spoke as if it had been superseded by his new science of history: 'When reality is depicted, philosophy as an independent branch of knowledge loses its medium of existence' (1846). But more significant is his famous verdict: 'The philosophers have only *interpreted* the world, in various ways; the point is to *change* it' (1845). Thus philosophy is to lose its independence not so much in subjection to positive science, but through changing its conditions of existence, overcoming in reality the dualities of subject and object, real and ideal, duty and inclination, that bedevil it. Scientific socialism conceives itself as the theoretical expression of a revolutionary process which will put an end to philosophy in so far as it abolishes the alienating material relations which require such compensatory speculation. Marx's project of displacing philosophy from its throne in favour of a unified science of humanity, nature and history thus itself speculatively prefigures such a non-alienated society. But philosophy has effective social reality still. And, as long as the revolutionary project of transforming society in its totality lacks immediate historical actuality, Marxism is condemned to remain engaged with philosophy as such. See also IDEOLOGY.   [C.J.A.]

Material mode   The 'material mode' of utterance, as distinct from the 'formal mode', concerns objects as opposed to words. See LOGICAL POSITIVISM.

Materialism   Philosophical materialism is the view that all that exists is material or is wholly dependent upon matter for its existence. This view comprises: (a) the general metaphysical thesis that there is only one fundamental kind of reality and that this is material, and (b) the more specific thesis that human beings and other living creatures are not dual beings composed of a material body and an immaterial soul, but are fundamentally bodily in nature.

The best-known form of materialism is the speculative ATOMISM of DEMOCRITUS and EPICURUS. This view arises as an attempt to give an account of change in terms of the ultimate elements of the world. According to this theory, the ultimate elements are indivisible and indestructible particles moving about in empty space. The things, animals and people of the natural world are formed by the coalescence of these particles. On this view, thought is a form of sensation and sensation can be explained in physical terms. When the body decays or is destroyed, sensation is no longer possible and the soul itself disintegrates into its ultimate atoms. Thus the distinction between soul and body is not a distinction between the immaterial and the material, but between different sorts of material wholes. Materialistic atomism was revived in the seventeenth century and became the creed of such eighteenth-century atheists as the Baron d'Holbach, who defines feeling in physical terms as a way of being moved and of receiving impulses through the body.

With the growth of the physical sciences speculative atomism was adopted as an explanatory principle of physics and chemistry and thus gave rise to scientific materialism. This outlook gained support from the evidences of geology and the theory of organic evolution, from which is appeared that life and mind had developed from inanimate matter. Advances in physiology reinforced this view, since it was claimed that the existence and scope of mental life depended upon the size and configuration of the brain. The German physiologist Karl Vogt (1817–95) became notorious for his statement that thought was related to the brain much as bile is related to the liver and urine to the kidneys. (In fact Vogt's utterance was an echo of some phrases from Cabanis' *Relations of the Physical and the Moral in Man* (1802) where it is suggested that the brain may be regarded as digesting impressions or secreting thoughts.) But neither Vogt nor his better known contemporary Ludwig Büchner (1824–99) provided any clear account of the nature of mind. Thus, although Büchner recognized that thought is not something that could be 'secreted', he has little positive to say about it except that it is 'caused' by physical processes.

In the twentieth century there have been two main forms of materialism, DIALECTICAL MATERIALISM and PHYSICALISM. Dialectical materialists describe Vogt and Büchner as 'vulgar materialists', but their own view, while it is clear as regards the dependence of mind upon matter, is vague as regards the nature of mind itself. Physicalism was formulated by some members of the LOGICAL POSITIVIST movement. It rests upon the view that whatever can be meaningfully said must be verifiable. The Physicalists argue, however, that there can be no genuine verification of a statement about an individual's private experiences. One may say that one feels a pain, but others cannot test the statement: they can only hear utterances or see movements. Nothing can be verified publicly by more than one observer except physical occurrences. The Physicalists concluded that meaningful statements about minds must refer to bodily behaviour of some sort, and that psychology was, in a broad sense, a part of physics. Whereas some psychologists had advocated BEHAVIOURISM as a policy of only admitting those data that could be observed by more than one observer, the Physicalists advocated it on the ground that any other policy would have no meaning.

It is important to note that materialists do not deny the existence of mind or consciousness; they merely deny that mind or consciousness are characteristics of immaterial souls. The strength of the case of materialism is a reflection of obscurities in the notion of a wholly incorporeal existence. This is held to be non-spatial and hence incapable of movement. But then its mode of operation on and with material bodies seems inexplicable. On the other hand, to describe sensation in terms of physical movements or chemical changes is obviously to omit what is most characteristic of it. The most acceptable form of materialism appears to be the view that mind is not a thing, whether material or immaterial, but the powers, capacities and functioning of certain sorts of bodies. Yet the critic of materialism is on strong ground in insisting on the gulf between experience on the one hand and physical processes on the other. (H.B.A.)

Mathematics Mathematics has always been a subject of great interest to philosophers not only in its own right but also as of crucial importance for the problem of the nature and extent of the knowledge that the human mind can gain through pure reasoning and without recourse to observation or experiment. No doubt we come to grasp such truths as '2 + 2 = 4' only in the course of experience, but it is not an experimental truth comparable to the fact that if two drops of water are put with two drops of water one small puddle results. Mathematical knowledge may be occasioned by experience, but it is not based on it; we do not need to send expeditions overseas to see if '2 + 2 = 4' holds there also. Thus mathematical knowledge seems to be a case of pure rational knowledge, gained by thinking alone and independent of empirical verification; it is what is

technically called A PRIORI knowledge. Consequently mathematics appears to be a refutation of the EMPIRICIST thesis that all knowledge is based on sense-experience, a counter-example so indisputable that among empiricists only J. S. MILL has been so bold as to try to deny it by claiming that mathematical truths are really no more than well-established empirical generalizations.

But mathematics is a challenge to philosophy in yet another way, for it is hard to discover what mathematics is about; what is the number two, and what is it to add two to two? Two is surely not a physical thing, and 'adding' is not 'putting with' as two eggs can be put with two eggs? The problem arises also with regard to geometry, for if the theorem that the internal angles of a triangle are equal to two right angles is understood to refer to triangles drawn on paper it is almost certainly false; what then are the triangles, rectangles, lines and points of which the geometer speaks?

When we consider these difficulties it is not surprising that PLATO, the first great philosopher of mathematics, regarded mathematics as the supreme example of knowledge of a supra-sensible world of intelligible entities accessible to the reason alone and that RUSSELL, at the beginning of his career, accepted an essentially similar position. Yet such a view is not one which can appeal to a robust common sense; the empiricist must find an alternative to it. The most famous attempt prior to the end of the nineteenth century is that of KANT, for whom the problem of mathematics was central.

Then FREGE in Germany and, independently, Russell in England developed the logistic theory. Briefly, their view was that mathematical, terms – number, addition and the like – could be defined in purely logical terms and that mathematical theorems could be deduced from purely logical axioms; mathematics was therefore an extension of LOGIC. This theory will now be briefly sketched.

In the late nineteenth century the Italian mathematician Peano had succeeded in showing that the arithmetic of finite cardinal numbers could be derived from five primitive propositions or axioms and three undefined terms – *zero, number* and *successor of*. Now it is clear that mathematics cannot be regarded as continuous with logic unless all the terms of mathematics can be defined in terms of logic; this meant that Russell and Frege, basing their work on that of Peano, had to define *zero, number* and *successor of* in logical terms. This task they claimed to have successfully performed, Frege in *The Foundations of Arithmetic* (1884), a masterpiece of philosophical writing that is neither very long nor very difficult, and Russell in *The Principles of Mathematics* (1903). The key terms Russell used in his definition are *class, belonging to a class* and *similarity*; thus he defined number in general as 'the class of classes similar to a given class'. Definitions of the basic terms of mathematics were given so that any mathematical proposition could be rewritten so that every reference to numbers was replaced by reference to classes, membership of classes and relations between classes.

But if mathematics is to be identified with logic we must not merely be able to reduce the vocabulary of mathematics to that of logic; we must also be able to deduce the five axioms of Peano, or whatever else we take as a set of axioms for mathematics, from purely logical axioms. This gigantic task was undertaken by Frege in *The Basic Laws of Arithmetic* and by WHITEHEAD and Russell in *Principia Mathematica*. Many philosophers would claim that Whitehead and Russell essentially succeeded in this project, and regard the logistical theory of mathematics as established. The whole of mathematics, it is claimed, has been shown to be but an elaboration of a set of trivial logical axioms.

Opponents of the logistic thesis urge that not all the axioms required are so trivial. Russell's definition of number implies that to speak of the number three is to speak of the class comprising all classes having three members and to speak of the number nine is to speak of the class of classes with nine members and so on; but if there were only eight objects in the universe then the class of classes with nine members would be empty – it would be a null class – and similarly for all numbers greater than eight; so that all numbers greater than eight would be equal to each other and equal also to zero, which is absurd. To avoid ever getting to a stage in the sequence of finite integers when they would all become equal to zero Russell and Whitehead introduced the 'axiom of infinity', which in effect says that there are an infinite number of objects in the universe; but this is not obviously true and if true is not obviously a logical truth. Whether such difficulties can be surmounted without abandoning the logistic thesis is still an open question.

Of alternative theories, the best known is formalism; as stated by its best-known exponent, HILBERT, this is the view that mathematics is to be regarded as an abstract calculus of which the terms, numbers, are given no interpretation beyond being things which satisfy the axioms; the essential characteristic of mathematics is self-consistency, which is a purely formal property. Critics of this view claim that mathematical terms must be given more than this purely formal meaning if mathematics is to be applied – as it obviously can be; even within mathematics we need to say such things as that four has two square roots, and here 'two' must be given more than a formal meaning.

There is no agreed answer to the central problems of the nature of mathematics; but in spite of disagreement it is still probable that an account of mathematics can be given which, while admitting its a priori character, will not require us to accept a Platonic view of it as involving some rational insight into a world of eternal essences.   (J.O.U.)

Medieval Philosophy   The Middle Ages are significant in the history of thought as the period in which living religious traditions came into full contact with Greek philosophy. This experience was common to Muslims, Jews and Christians, and in each case the chief philosophical factor was the text of ARISTOTLE, accompanied by a vague current of NEOPLATONISM which affected the interpretation of Aristotle and occasionally showed itself independently. All three religions were faced with a choice between the primacy of theology, the primacy of philosophy, and the possibility of a harmonious synthesis of both. The efforts at synthesis provided the most interesting thinking of the period.

The Muslims came into contact with Greek philosophy as they extended their conquests over Asia Minor towards the gates of Constantinople. AVICENNA succeeded to his own satisfaction in harmonizing the Koran with a neoplatonic doctrine of the emanation of all things from God, worked out in Aristotelian terms. AVERROES was regarded throughout the Middle Ages as the Commentator of Aristotle *par excellence*, but his adherence to the theory of the eternity of matter and his denial of personal immortality were incompatible with orthodox Islam. After his death a theological reaction, already

anticipated by the notable mystical thinker Al Gazali (1058–1111), put an end to the creative period of Arabic philosophy.

Jewish thinkers living in Muslim countries, especially Spain, underwent similar philosophical influences. Avencebrol (Solomon ibn Gabirol, 1021–58), the author of *The Source of Life*, was thoroughly neoplatonic in spirit. MAIMONIDES wrote *The Guide of the Perplexed*, which is the most remarkable development of Aristotelian philosophy in harmony with Jewish monotheism and had considerable influence on AQUINAS. But, as in Islam, a theological reaction stifled medieval Jewish philosophical speculation.

The earliest period of Christian philosophy in the Middle Ages, from the end of the eighth to the end of the eleventh century, saw a gradual but by no means uninterrupted recovery from the barbarism of the Dark Ages. Philosophy had no independent existence, but philosophical notions persisted through the study of the Fathers, especially AUGUSTINE, and through the reading of BOETHIUS. The more elementary parts of Aristotelian logic were taught under the name of dialectic among the seven liberal arts, and the remarks of Porphyry in his *Isagoge* directed attention to the question of the relation of universal concepts to fact. The neoplatonic system of ERIGENA in the ninth century was an isolated product.

The twelfth century was the period of the recovery of the text of Aristotle, but already the need of more material for study was evident in the new speculative urge of ANSELM, the originator of the ONTOLOGICAL ARGUMENT. The brilliant speculative mind of ABELARD was partly stultified by the lack of material for reflection and criticism. In the course of this century however, and in the earlier part of the next, the writings of Aristotle were made available in Latin translation and came to be understood. It should be borne in mind that for the Middle Ages Aristotle was the leading source of what we should now call science as well as what we should now distinguish as philosophy. The rise of universities, as at Paris and Oxford, was also a stimulus to systematic study.

The thirteenth century was the most important in medieval philosophy because it was the period of the critical assimilation of Aristotle. The more conservative theologians (such as BONAVENTURA), sometimes described as Augustinian, made use of the new Aristotelian knowledge and method while keeping them in strict subordination to Christian theology. ALBERT THE GREAT gave himself wholeheartedly to the new learning, and his disciple AQUINAS provided the classical medieval synthesis of Aristotelian philosophy and Christian theology. His pacific manner sometimes obscures the fact that he was ready to suggest modifications on either side whenever he thought them desirable. The nearest comparable synthesis is that of SCOTUS in the next generation. Meanwhile the more radical Aristotelians, sometimes called Averroists, arrived at philosophical conclusions which they could not square with theology. SIGER of Brabant seems to have honestly expounded his difficulties, but others come under theological suspicion of substituting philosophical conclusions for doctrines of faith.

While Aquinas remains important as having tried to erect a metaphysical philosophy on an empirical basis, that basis needed further analysis. In the fourteenth century the criticism of WILLIAM OF OCKHAM brought philosophy to a more completely empirical starring point. This might have been an invitation to a more critical metaphysic, but there was no great mind to take up the challenge. Medieval

philosophy tended to decline into that sterile logic-chopping which a later age was to consider characteristic of scholasticism. The neoplatonic system of Nicholas of Cusa (1401–64) was again an individual achievement.

The revival of scholastic philosophy after the Renaissance, associated above all with Francisco Suarez (1548–1617), failed to last because it did not come to terms with the rise of modern science (see also NEO-THOMISM). The spirit of medieval philosophy is sometimes summed up in the phrase which speaks of philosophy as the handmaid of theology, but this was coined by a conservative theologian, Peter Damian (1007–72), who was anxious to curb the pretensions of rational speculation. It is better summarized by Anselm when he speaks of faith seeking understanding. The great medieval philosophers, while presupposing the truth of Christianity, sought with candour and persistence for whatever new light could be thrown on their view of the world by what they could recover of Greek philosophy.   (D.J.B.H.)

Meinong, Alexius (1853–1920)
Austrian philosopher who developed BRENTANO's intentional psychology. His REALISM greatly influenced RUSSELL, MOORE and other British and American Realists. Meinong spent most of his life as a professor at the University of Graz. His principal works are: *Hume Studies* (1877, 1882); *Psychological-ethical Investigations towards Value-theory* (1894); *On Assumptions* (1902); *On Possibility and Probability* (1915); *On Emotional Presentation* (1917); *Groundwork of the General Theory of Value* (1923).

Meinong's psychology is rooted in that of Brentano: he assumes that directedness-to-objects is the distinguishing property of the mental. The analysis of mental states is, however, complicated by distinguishing two 'elements' in them: (a) an 'act-element' which represents the manner in which a state of mind is directed to its object, and (b) a 'content-element' which is defined as that which gives a state of mind its direction to one object rather than another. The difference between thinking of dragons and believing in dragons is a difference in 'act', whereas the difference between believing in dragons and believing in ghosts is a difference in content. By the 'content-element' Meinong does not mean a mental image or representation, much less the object itself: rather he refers to the fact that being *of* a certain object is intrinsic to a state of mind. Meinong builds on Brentano's threefold classification of states of mind into Presentations, Judgments and Affective-Desiderative attitudes. But he divides Presentations into those involving Passive Perception and those involving Active Production, for example, ideas of relations. He also places beside judgments certain judgment-like attitudes which lack conviction, that is, *Assumptions* (*Annahmen*), and shows how important these are in art, play, pretence, fantasy, hypothesis etc. And he separates the affective and desiderative attitudes which Brentano confounded.

The main interest of Meinong's doctrine does not, however, lie in his psychology but in his object-theory. According to Meinong, if we ask ourselves exactly what our various mental states bring to mind, we shall see that different types of mental state correspond to typically different objects. Thus our various 'productive presentations' introduce us to various 'objects of higher order' which are founded on the objects of passive perception. For example, a

particular grouping or pattern is 'objective' and yet is not something that we passively see. Such founded objects are said by Meinong to *subsist* (*bestehen*) or have subsistence (*Bestand*), and not to exist – a usage taken over by Moore and Russell. Meinong further held that *what* we judge or assume is a peculiar complex object called an 'objective', which involves other objects as its material, and which cannot be said to exist, and which may or may not be a fact (*tatsächlich*). 'Objectives' are what Russell and Moore called 'propositions'. They are expressed by a complete sentence or 'that' clause, for example 'that Caesar conquered Gaul', but their status as objectives does not depend on their being expressed or thought.

The most famous (or notorious) of Meinong's doctrines is concerned with objects which do not exist or with objectives which are not facts. According to Meinong such objects or objectives are *genuine* objects or objectives, with a make-up which is independent of thought or expression. Their very non-existence or not-being-the-case entails this objective status, for the non-existence of a golden mountain is quite different from the non-existence of a round square, and the not-being-the-case of the former differs from the not-being-the-case of the latter. But Meinong did not hold, as Russell for a time did, that non-existent objects subsist, or have any sort of being (*Sein*); he maintained only that they have a describable nature or *Sosein*, which is unaffected by their existence or non-existence. We may say, for example, that a round square is round and square, but not that there is a round square. For Meinong, therefore, 'something is F' is not equivalent to 'there is an F', as it is for Russell. Meinong holds further that objects which cannot be said to exist play an extremely important role in knowledge. Objects which are incompletely determined, or violate the law of excluded middle, are none the less the means through which the mind refers to objects which exist and are completely determinate. In his theory of knowledge Meinong makes use of Brentano's concept of self-evidence (*Evidenz*), but he adds to absolute self-evidence the important notion of a surmise-evidence (*Vermutungsevidenz*), with which he justifies sense-perception, memory and induction.

In his theory of value, Meinong holds that feelings may fuse either with the act or content element of our presentations or judgments, yielding four types of-feeling: (a) presentation-act-feelings in which we sensually like or dislike something, without caring about its reality or its character; (b) presentation-content-feelings (aesthetic feelings), in which we do not care about the reality of something but do care about its character; (c) judgement-act-feelings, in which we do care about the reality of something but not about its character (scientific feelings), and (d) judgement-content-feelings, or valuations proper, in which we care about both the reality and character of something. In Meinong's earlier work no absolute or impersonal values are admitted: so-called absolute values are merely values for an impartial spectator. But in his later work he argues that feelings and desires may be the mental index or 'content' corresponding to peculiar objective determinations. Feelings introduce our minds to 'dignitatives' (beauty and goodness for example), while desires introduce them to 'desideratives', that is to various objective 'oughts' – that a picture ought to be re-hung for instance. The objects thus introduced sometimes really subsist and there can be considerable surmise-evidence that they do so.   (J.N.F.)

Merleau-Ponty, Maurice (1907–61)
French phenomenologist and leading proponent of EXISTENTIALISM. Merleau-Ponty also taught for many years at the Collège de France and, with SARTRE and DE BEAUVOIR, co-edited the influential journal *Les temps modernes*. The publication of his monumental *Phenomenology of Perception* in 1945 established his reputation as one of the foremost academic philosophers of post-war France. The principal originality of this work was to apply HUSSERL's phenomenology of intentional consciousness to the *corporeal* dimensions of human existence: hence the concept of the 'body-subject' which is always 'situated' in a concrete lived experience. The fact that we are bodies, pre-reflectively immersed in the 'flesh of the world' is in no way incompatible with our status as free and creative subjects intentionally related to history. Merleau-Ponty rejects the positivistic view of the body as a mere object amongst objects. It is to be understood rather as an expressive subject which reveals itself through our everyday perceptions, gestures and symbols.

Merleau-Ponty criticized his existentialist colleague, Sartre, for putting excessive emphasis on the autonomy of human consciousness, arguing that all subjectivity is inter-subjectivity – that the freedom of consciousness is inextricably bound by with preconscious structures of collective meaning. On this point, he came close to Lévi-Strauss and STRUCTURALISM. His analysis of the body-subject as both a producer and product of historical meaning gave rise to a philosophy of ambiguity, which expresses itself in the following basic phenomena: (1) Physically, the human hand can both touch and be touched. (2) Linguistically, we create new meanings on the basis of a language already acquired. (3) Politically, we are both agents who transform society and recipients of the 'sedimentations' of our social institutions and traditions. (This political ambivalence was evident in Merleau-Ponty's controversial exchanges with Sartre on the nature of revolutionary Marxism – which they both supported in different ways – in *Les Temps Modernes* and in his collection of political essays, *Adventures of the Dialectic*, 1955). (4) Ontologically, human existence is expressed in the intertwining of the visible and invisible dimensions of being. This last phenomenon was a central preoccupation of Merleau-Ponty's two final works, *Eye and Mind* and the unfinished *The Visible and the Invisible*, both published posthumously in 1964. It also recapitulates his life-long interest in the 'indirect languages' of art and literature as evidenced in earlier works such as *Sense and Non-Sense* (1948) and *Signs* (1960).

Merleau-Ponty's preference for interpreting existence aesthetically (in terms of style and signification) rather than scientifically (in terms of objects and statistics) epitomizes his conviction that truth is an ongoing project rather than a fixed possession, a task of living experience rather than a *fait accompli*. See also MIND. [R.K.]

Metaphilosophy Metaphilosophy is theory about the nature of philosophy.

Metaphor ARISTOTLE spoke of the use of metaphor as a 'sign of genius'. His own definition, in the *Poetics*, is a useful starting point: 'the application to one thing of a name belonging to another'. Although it blurs the finer rhetorical discriminations (metonymy, synecdoche and catachresis), this definition nevertheless highlights the central philosophical question about metaphor, namely: how is it possible to apply terms 'figuratively', beyond their normal range of application,

without lapsing into nonsense? What theory of meaning, communication, or thought, is required to explain this possibility? A second, related, philosophical concern is with the truth-bearing potential of metaphor. Do metaphors afford a special kind of cognition?

Philosophical attitudes have been mixed. HOBBES and LOCKE dismissed figurative usage as a superfluous distraction in intellectual discourse, a sign of sloppiness or deceit. Other philosophers have argued that metaphor is pervasive and inescapable; NIETZSCHE and DERRIDA draw the sceptical conclusion that the pervasiveness of metaphor undermines any search for fixed, timeless truths. A third attitude, hinted at by Shelley but refined by recent analytic philosophers associates metaphor with unique truth-bearing, even truth-creating possibilities.

In contemporary philosophy of language, the debate is initially focused on meaning. Two general approaches are discernible here, loosely labelled 'semantic' and 'pragmatic'. Semantic theories locate metaphorical meaning in *langue*, the language system, seeing it as a complex semantic property of phrases or sentences. If metaphor has cognitive potential then, according to this view, it resides in the embodiment of a novel thought or proposition within this special semantic content. Pragmatic theories, in contrast, locate metaphorical meaning in *parole*, as a property of specific, contextualized utterances. What cognitive potential there might be is thought to lie not in the linguistic representation of a thought but in the evocation of a particular response, imaginative or intellectual.

The simplest, most traditional, semantic theory identifies the semantic content of a metaphor with the literal meaning of a corresponding simile. Thus 'time is a tyrant' is taken to mean the same as 'time is like a tyrant'. However plausible for certain examples, this account is now widely regarded as inadequate. In a complex metaphor, like WITTGENSTEIN's famous aphorism 'a cloud of philosophy condensed into a drop of grammar', it may not be possible to construct an exactly equivalent simile. In any case, the standard criticism remains that something integral to metaphor is lost in literal translations of this kind.

A further objection to reducing metaphors to similes is that a metaphor and a corresponding simile ought to have different truth-conditions. John SEARLE illustrates this with the example 'John is a gorilla', which would normally be taken to imply, metaphorically, that John is fierce, nasty, prone to violence, and so forth. However, gorillas, as we now know, are shy and sensitive creatures, so quite different implications are carried by the literal comparison 'John is like a gorilla'.

Responding to the weaknesses of the simile account, other semantic theorists have tried to capture the features that make metaphor distinctive. Max BLACK, in a landmark paper of 1955, argued that the terms in a metaphor interact by invoking and 'filtering' systems of associations. This interaction, elsewhere described as 'interanimation' (I. A. Richards) or 'tension' (Monroe Beardsley), generates a novel semantic content, going beyond the literal meanings of the metaphor's constituent elements. An important aspect of Black's theory is the idea that the creation of metaphorical meaning depends not only on the meanings of words but on the beliefs of those involved.

The introduction of non-semantic factors, in the form of beliefs, might seem to weaken the claim that metaphor is a purely semantic phenomenon. Some theorists, notably L. J. Cohen, have argued for a more uncompromising semantic position, whereby metaphorical meanings are deemed to be already present in literal meanings and reachable by a process of selection and elimination. Such austere semantic accounts, however, face the problem of explaining the spontaneity and novelty of certain metaphors.

Interaction theories like Black's confront other difficulties of detail. First, there is the problem of how semantic interaction could discriminate relevant from irrelevant 'associations'. What semantic rule selects the connotation of fierceness for the interaction of 'John' and 'gorilla', but not the connotation of, say, living in Africa or being popular in zoos? Second, it is hard to see how the relevant associations in some metaphors, for example 'time is a tyrant', could be transferred in any non-metaphorical sense from one constituent to another. Few, if any, properties of tyrants could be attributed literally to time. But then the semantic content yielded by the interaction is just a further series of metaphors.

A problem for all semantic theories lies in the initial identification of a phrase or sentence as metaphorical. Although some metaphors, like 'time is a tyrant', contain semantic clues to their metaphorical nature, in the form of anomalies, mixed categories or patent falsehoods, other metaphors, like 'The rats went down with the ship', display no semantic irregularities and rely entirely on the context of utterance to prompt a metaphorical reading.

Pragmatic theorists take relativity to context and the dynamics of metaphorical interpretation as their starting point. Their paradigm is that a speaker issues a metaphorical utterance on a particular occasion and intends thereby to invoke a certain kind of response in the hearer. Different accounts have been offered of such metaphorical communication. One view, widely held, and expounded in detail by Searle, is that metaphor is an instance of 'speaker's meaning' rather than 'sentence meaning', that is, a speaker says one thing but means something else. Recognizing that the speaker's words cannot, given the context of utterance, be understood in their usual, literal, meaning, the hearer invokes principles of (metaphorical) interpretation to recover the meaning intended. This account allows that the search for a metaphorical reading might be prompted not only by semantic anomalies in the sentence, but by features of its context too. One major criticism of this view is that it demands too determinate a meaning for metaphorical utterances, failing to acknowledge their 'open-endedness'. Another is that it gives undue authority to a speaker's intentions.

A different pragmatic approach is to postulate a distinctive speech act associated with metaphor. One suggestion is that a metaphorical utterance is an 'invitation' or 'instruction' to a hearer to think of one thing in terms of another. Here the speaker might have no special authority over how the instruction might be carried out. Speech act accounts, however, face the complication that metaphors themselves can occur in different speech acts and in indirect speech. Does the metaphorical speech act override, or get subsumed by, the wider speech act?

A far more radical theory, introduced by Donald DAVIDSON in a seminal paper of 1978, proposes that there is no such thing as metaphorical meaning, either semantic or pragmatic: 'Metaphors mean what the words, in their most literal interpretation, mean and nothing more.' The power and interest of metaphorical utterance, according to this theory, lies in its ability to jolt us into new ways of thinking. A metaphor does not convey a propositional content, other than that of its literal sense,

so there is no question of 'metaphorical truth'. This 'no-meaning' view of metaphor emphasizes the causal and psychological features of language use. But psychological responses can be unpredictable and arise under a variety of conditions. To retain any distinctive concept of metaphor the no-meaning view needs to offer some constraints on the relevant responses and also on the modes of utterance that are their causes. It also needs to account for the prominent role of metaphor in cognitive discourse, including science and philosophy, where rational argument, rather than causal efficacy, is paramount. Finally, whereas this view presupposes a secure concept of literal meaning, the boundaries between literal and metaphorical language or even between 'dead' and 'live' metaphors are in fact blurred. This encourages the thought that metaphors are more pervasive and more intractable than neat theories of meaning are prepared, or able, to acknowledge. [P.L.]

Metaphysics Metaphysics is that part of philosophy which has the greatest pretensions and is exposed to the greatest suspicions. Having the avowed aim of arriving at profound truths about everything, it is sometimes held to result only in obscure nonsense about nothing. This equivocal status is not the least of those features of metaphysics which require explanation.

1 *Descriptions of Metaphysics.* It will be well, first, to set out a number of descriptions of the subject given by some who are themselves metaphysicians or critics of metaphysics or both. From these descriptions we may gather a list of characteristics each of which we may expect to find in some examples of metaphysics and some of which we may find in all. The task will then be to explain how these

characteristics are related; to decide, if possible, which of them are central; and perhaps to distinguish different kinds of metaphysics.

The name of the subject is the name given by scholars to a treatise of ARISTOTLE. Aristotle described the subject of his treatise in a number of different ways which he regarded as equivalent. He called it the study of the first principles of things. He said it was the science of existence in general, or of 'being as such', contrasting it in this respect with the various special sciences which each studied only one part or aspect of being. He described it also as the study of 'SUBSTANCE', a term which occupies a central position in the work of most of the great metaphysicians who came after him. Substance he declared to be what primarily existed, and was prior to all other things in respect not only of existence, but of explanation and of knowledge as well; that is to say, the explanation of anything else involved the idea of substance; knowledge of anything else involved knowledge of substance; and the existence of everything else depended on the existence of substance. Metaphysics, then, is regarded by Aristotle as a single, comprehensive study of what is fundamental to all existence, all knowledge and all explanation. It will at once be evident that different identifications of substance, that is, of what has this fundamental character, will yield different systems of metaphysics.

If we set beside Aristotle's account of his subject the words of the English metaphysician BRADLEY, we notice a different element in the definition. Bradley says: 'we may agree, perhaps, to understand by metaphysics an attempt to know reality as against mere appearance, or the study of first principles or ultimate truths, or again the effort to comprehend the universe, not simply piecemeal or by fragments, but somehow as a whole'. The mention of first principles, and the contrast with 'piecemeal' studies, are Aristotelian. But the emphasis on knowledge of reality as *against mere appearance* is an additional element.

There is a more striking shift of emphasis when we turn to the great critical metaphysicians, HUME and KANT. Kant emphasized above all the non-empirical character both of the subject-matter and of the method of traditional metaphysics. Its method was A PRIORI, the employment of pure reason alone; its subject matter was transcendent. Neither its results nor its methods could be checked by experience. For it argued to conclusions about things which transcended experience, in accordance with principles which experience did not establish. The resulting controversies were endless; and 'the battlefield of these endless controversies is called metaphysics'. Kant concluded that we should turn the light of reason on reason itself, that we should undertake the critical examination of pure reason in order to determine what it is, and is not, capable of. The first, and perhaps the only, task of metaphysics is to determine its own limits. Kant here echoes, in a more specific form, the suggestion of Hume that we should 'inquire seriously into the nature of human understanding and show, from an exact analysis of its powers and capacity, that it is by no means fitted for such remote and abstruse subjects'. This inquiry Hume describes as 'cultivating true metaphysics with some care in order to destroy the false and adulterate'.

There is a certain modern account of metaphysics which does not seem at all obviously related to what has gone before. John WISDOM describes a metaphysical proposition as, characteristically, a sort of illuminating falsehood, a pointed paradox which uses language in a novel way in order to make us aware of differences and similarities which are concealed by our ordinary ways of talking. And WITTGENSTEIN compares a metaphysical suggestion to the invention of a new kind of song. The thought common to both is, perhaps, that it is characteristic of the metaphysician to propose for use, or to offer for contemplation, a shift in our ideas, a revision of our concepts, a new way of looking at the world.

2 *Characteristics of Metaphysics.* The composite picture which these descriptions yield is not a very clear one. (a) Metaphysics is a comprehensive study of what is fundamental in the order of knowledge, explanation and existence; (b) it is the study of reality as opposed to mere appearance; (c) its subject is, or has been, what transcends experience; (d) it is, or ought to be, a study of the intellectual equipment and limitations of human beings; (e) its method is, or has been, a priori rather than empirical; (f) it proposes a revision of the set of ideas in terms of which we think about the world, a change in our conceptual scheme, a new way of talking.

This list of characteristics is heterogeneous, and may seem scarcely coherent. Before we relate the list to actual examples of metaphysics, perhaps we can trace some general connections between some of its items. For instance, while it might be possible to interpret a metaphysical system as (f), a proposal for conceptual revision, an invitation to look at the world in a new way, the system will not generally be presented by the metaphysician as such a proposal, but rather as (b), a picture of things as they really are instead of as they delusively seem, a description of reality as opposed to appearance. Again, starting with a concern with

(a), what is fundamental to existence, the metaphysician may reach the same antithesis, (b), for he may express his sense of the importance of what he regards as fundamental by saying that it alone really exists and all else is appearance. If this revised picture of reality is a radical enough revision, the distinction between appearance and reality may have to be drawn between what falls within and what lies outside experience, (c); and evidently, if the concern is with what transcends experience, the method must be non-empirical (e). It is obviously less easy to connect (d), the recommendations of Hume and Kant, with many of these characteristics; but at least there is an easy connection between the examination of the intellectual equipment of human beings and part of (a), *viz.* the determination of what is fundamental in the order of knowledge and explanation.

3 *The History of Metaphysics.* Now to compare this list of characteristics with actual systems of metaphysics. It is certainly true that most of the great metaphysicians have proposed radically revised pictures of the world, bold, comprehensive and often startling; and that most of them have accorded a central place in the picture to some few key concepts, or to some specially favoured type of entities given the title of 'substance'. It is also true that the choice of key concepts and entities, and the resultant picture of the world, have varied greatly from one metaphysician to another. Sometimes even 'substance' has been dethroned, for example, in favour of 'process'; and among candidates for the role of substance the choice has been wide. Besides God, the divine substance, who has a place in most systems, DESCARTES recognized two types of substance, matter and minds; BERKELEY one only, minds or spirits; LEIBNIZ a class of entities (monads)

each of which, though non-spatial and non-temporal, was somehow a model of the entire universe. SPINOZA recognized only one comprehensive substance, God or Nature, infinite and eternal, of which mind and matter were merely two aspects. Kant regarded substance as belonging to the world of our ordinary experience, yet set Reality itself, as totally unknowable, outside that world. Hume, though inclined to deride the whole notion of substance, thought that if anything deserved the title, as being capable of independent existence and fundamental in the order of knowledge, it was particular sense-impressions and the imagination's copies of these. It is inevitable that we should inquire into the reasons for this diversity; and it is impossible not to decide that it reflects in part historical changes in the general intellectual situation as human thought advances or develops in different particular spheres, and in part individual variations in the interests, attitudes and preferences of different metaphysicians. These interests and preferences, those advances and developments, are dramatized into cosmic *tableaux*, expressed in the form of highly abstract myth, uncontrolled, as Hume and Kant remarked, by a critical examination of the kind of reasoning employed. The point may be illustrated from the case of Descartes. His main interest was in the development of science, and he had very clear ideas about the proper direction for this development. Mathematics, and in particular geometry, seemed to him to provide the model for scientific procedure. He thought that the fundamental method in science was the deductive method of geometry, which he conceived of as rigorous reasoning from self-evident axioms; and he thought that the subject-matter of all the physical sciences must be fundamentally the same as the subject-matter of geometry, and hence that, from the point of view of science in general, the only important characteristics of things in the physical world were the spatial characteristics which geometry studies. It is not the holding of these beliefs which makes Descartes a metaphysician. It is rather the dramatic expression they receive in his doctrines about the essential nature of knowledge and existence. He offers a picture of a world in which the only realities, apart from God, are purely material substance with none but spatial characteristics, and pure thinking substances whose being essentially consists in the ability to grasp self-evident axioms and their deductive consequences. Knowledge is nothing but the results of exercising this ability. Whatever else ordinarily passes for reality or knowledge is downgraded, given an inferior status. Such a drastic revision of our ordinary scheme of things naturally creates problems, and calls for further explanations and adjustments. Thus Descartes teaches, on the one hand, that it is only through confidence in God's veracity that we can have reason to believe in the existence of material things; and on the other that it is only through our wilfulness that we ever believe what is false.

Again and again in the history of the subject such a preoccupation with some advance, achieved or hoped for, in a particular branch of thought, has found expression in some similarly bold new vision of the nature of the world. Not only mathematics and the physical sciences, but history, biology and formal logic as well, have all inspired metaphysics. Developments in the study of history underlay the Hegelian system; and the metaphysics of LOGICAL ATOMISM can be seen, in part, as the expression of a profound satisfaction with advances in formal logic at the end of the nineteenth and the beginning of the twentieth century.

Nor is it only a concern with theoretical disciplines that supplies the drive to metaphysical revision. Religions and moralities too may seek and find metaphysical support. Elements of diverse kinds may be fused in a single system, such as that of Spinoza, which expresses an attitude at once thoroughly scientific and profoundly moral.

4 *Critical Metaphysics.* The critical metaphysicians, Hume and Kant, demand separate and special attention. Kant pointed our that the metaphysician necessarily employed concepts which have an application in our ordinary experience or at least are derived from concepts so employed; but that the metaphysician's own use of these concepts characteristically ignored or went beyond the empirical conditions of their employment. Any such extension of the use of these concepts, so far from extending our knowledge beyond the limits of experience, was quite illegitimate, and the results were empty or senseless. Kant maintained that the positive task of metaphysics was to show how the most general and fundamental concepts we employed were interrelated to form an organizing framework of ideas and principles, a framework which supplied the necessary conditions of the kinds of knowledge and experience which we in fact possessed. The negative task was to show both how inevitable was the metaphysical temptation to use these general concepts in ways which disregarded the empirical conditions of their employment, and how inevitably empty were the results of succumbing to this temptation. At this point we find in Kant a residue of that very kind of metaphysics which he declared to be impossible. For the framework of ideas which it was the positive task of metaphysics to elucidate was thought of by Kant as the framework of things only as they appeared to beings

with our cognitive constitution, not of things as they were in themselves. What was ultimately real was in principle unknowable; and this unknowable reality acquired a more positive role when Kant was concerned to secure metaphysical foundations for morality: it appeared as the authoritative source of morality's commands. Hume, Kant's predecessor in time, shared with Kant the conviction that significant discourse was limited by the conditions of actual experience, and that much traditional metaphysics trespassed beyond those limits. But Hume inherited from LOCKE and Berkeley a curiously limited conception of what experience actually supplied us with. The real elements of experience, he held, were separate and fleeting impressions of sense and feeling. Our ordinary picture of a world of continuously existing and interacting material things and persons could not be rationally justified on this basis; but it could be explained, as the product of the associative mechanism of the imagination set in motion by the ultimate elements of feeling and sense.

It will be obvious that both Hume and Kant, while criticizing in principle the revisionary schemes of other metaphysicians, were to some extent metaphysically revisionary themselves. Kant's doctrine that only what is unknowable is ultimately real, and Hume's doctrine that it is imagination which makes us believe in the existence of material bodies, are alike in doing violence to the concepts of imagination, reality and knowledge which we actually employ. Nevertheless, in virtue both of the positive and of the critical aspects of their work, these two great philosophers exercised an influence on metaphysics which may well appear decisive. This is particularly true of Kant. Both philosophers concerned themselves with the general structure of our thought about the world. Both wrote, much of the time, in an idiom more suggestive of empirical psychology than of an investigation into concepts and the conditions of their use. But behind the psychological idiom of Kant we can find the outline of a far more coherent account of the general structure of our conceptual scheme than we can find either in Hume or in those later empiricists who wrote in the spirit of Hume while discarding much of his psychology. The criticisms made by both Hume and Kant of the metaphysical employment of concepts without regard to the conditions of their empirical use still stand. But on the critical as on the positive side Kant's contribution is ultimately more effective than Hume's. For though these criticisms were later expressed most vociferously and in their most extreme form by the school of Logical Positivists who were heirs of Hume rather than of Kant, the effectiveness of this expression suffered from the weaknesses and limitations of the associated empiricist metaphysics.

5 *Repudiations of Metaphysics.* Over much of the philosophical world in the twentieth century the doctrine of the impossibility of metaphysics became almost an orthodoxy, and the adjective 'metaphysical' a pejorative word. Some of the reasons for this devaluation should now be clear. The conceptual distortions and final incoherence of systems, the abstract myths parading as Reality, the grandiose claims and the conflicting results – these seemed to many the essence of the metaphysical enterprise and sufficient reason for condemning it; and the extravagances of metaphysics were by some of them contrasted with the sobrieties of a method of philosophical ANALYSIS which aims to make clear the actual functioning of our concepts in use. But though the repudiation of metaphysics was natural, it does not follow that it was justified. Metaphysical excess might be no more essential to metaphysics than tyranny to government. To show that the repudiation was not justified calls for some reordering of the facts which we already have before us.

When Aristotle described the subject of his treatise, he distinguished it sharply from the special or departmental disciplines. But the distinction was not drawn in a wholly clear way. It was implied that the 'science of being as such' was more general and comprehensive than the special sciences. Clearly this most general science was not to be merely a *compendium* of the others; yet when the special sciences are put on one side, what subject for study is left? It is difficult to avoid the impression that the projected science of being, if such a study exists at all, must have some curiously elusive yet very fundamental subject-matter of its own, somehow lying behind those aspects of reality which are studied in departmental disciplines. Behind these aspects of reality is Reality itself, 'being as such', the subject-matter of metaphysics. Already the tendency of metaphysics towards the transcendent becomes intelligible. In default of a further clarification of the nature of the enterprise, it will inevitably appear as the gropings of pure reason in a mysterious realm to which ordinary access is impossible. Another consequence may appear equally inevitable. For in order to describe this realm, the only materials that we have, or can make, available must be taken, or fashioned, from the conceptual equipment which we use for the less rarefied purposes of daily discourse or departmental studies. If we are to put such concepts to work to describe the transcendental realm, we must cut them off from the conditions of their ordinary employment and deprive them of their ordinary force; yet they must seem to retain something of their ordinary force, or we shall not even seem to be saying anything significant. So transcendental metaphysics proceeds by way of conceptual distortion to a termination in uncashable METAPHOR.

This is a kind of caricature of the rake's progress of metaphysics. Its purpose is to enable us to see more clearly the significance of the Kantian revolution. When Kant denied that knowledge of reality was possible, he was in effect denying that metaphysics had, or could have, any such peculiar subject-matter of its own. But he did not thereby deprive the metaphysician of employment. The positive task of the metaphysician was not to think about a special world, but to think about the structure of our thinking about the ordinary world; not to acquire knowledge of objects beyond our experience, but to clarify the nature and conditions of knowledge of objects within our experience. So metaphysics is indeed a more general and comprehensive study than any special science; for it aims to make clear the fundamental general structure of all our ordinary and scientific thinking. Its method is indeed non-empirical; for it inquires into the conceptual structure which is presupposed by all our empirical inquiries.

This conception of metaphysics may appear to differ from the Aristotelian conception. There is no mention of 'being as such', of what is prior in the order of existence. But this difference is apparent only. If we investigate the fundamental categories of human thought, the connexions between them, and the dependencies of one on another, we are thereby committed to inquiring into the relations between the various types of entity, or being, which we admit into our conceptual scheme. The idea of ontological priority is not

discarded, but simply given a clearer meaning. It is the idea of a transcendent reality as a possible subject of inquiry which is abandoned. The Aristotelian conception is not rejected, but rescued from perversion.

It might be said that the aims of metaphysics, so understood, are no different from those of philosophical analysis in general, which also proposes to investigate the actual functioning of our concepts; or that, at most, the difference will simply be one of scope and generality. But this is an important difference, which entails another: a difference in method. When the analytic philosopher proposes to investigate some particular concept – say that of memory, or cause, or truth – he finds the surest method of procedure to lie in a careful examination of the actual use of the verbs, adjectives and nouns by means of which we introduce this concept into our discourse. Such an examination has great power to reveal the complexities of the concept, the multifariousness of the phenomena which it covers, and, up to a point, its connexions with other concepts. The results arrived at in this way may be perfectly adequate for the purposes of a regional analysis, which legitimately takes much for granted; and they provide an indispensable corrective to the conceptual distortions to which metaphysics is prone. But this method of illuminating the workings of a particular part of our conceptual apparatus is apt to assume, rather than to reveal, the fundamental structure of the apparatus as a whole; and it is precisely this general structure which the metaphysician wishes to understand. The connexions and dependencies which the metaphysician has to make explicit lie below the surface of the linguistic phenomena. They do not lie so far below the surface that they cannot be detected and recognized. But their detection and recognition require a wider-ranging vision than is compatible with attention to the surface phenomena alone.

We have seen that many traditional metaphysicians have not been content to describe the actual structure of our thought about the world in its most general and fundamental aspects. Rather they have wished to substitute a revised structure, which somehow symbolized their own intellectual preoccupations and attitudes. It is almost as if, in order to record their sense of the importance of a certain change of direction in thought, they had to exaggerate the extent and implications of the change; as if our *whole* view of the world had to be at least temporarily altered, in order to accommodate a new vision of one of its aspects. Perhaps indeed there was a certain historical necessity about this; and it is not surprising that to some historically minded critics this side of metaphysics has seemed to be the only side. We have seen reason to think that this is a mistake. The most fundamental concepts and categories of human thinking are not those which undergo drastic changes with advances in the sciences or alterations in social living; and the investigation of this central core of thought provides metaphysics with a constant subject-matter. But it would be a mistake on the opposite side to suppose that the central tasks of metaphysics can be performed once for all, and the subject regarded as closed. For even though its central subject-matter does not significantly change, the idiom, the needs, and the emphases of metaphysical elucidation vary from age to age and even from one philosopher to another. Old truths have to be restated in a new idiom; different parts of the picture call, from time to time, for more or less emphatic illumination. Metaphysical elucidation can reach no final and complete form. But that does not mean it is impossible. Some projections of the picture involve less distortion than others; and even those projections which involve the grossest distortions of the picture as a whole may nevertheless represent a part of it with a peculiar clarity.   (P.F.S.)

Mill, James (1773–1836)   James Mill was born in Aberdeenshire, Scotland, and studied for the ministry at Edinburgh. But religious doubts led him to give up this career and at twenty-nine he went to London, where he met BENTHAM and became his chief lieutenant. In 1819 he entered the East India Company and eventually became its chief administrator. A remarkable account of his character and opinions is given in the *Autobiography* of his eldest son, John Stuart MILL.

In his *Analysis of the Phenomena of the Human Mind* (1829) Mill tries to show that all knowledge is reducible to feelings (sensations, ideas, pleasures, pains) occurring in certain orders – some successive, some simultaneous – and the patterns into which they become associated if they regularly occur together. The doctrine of association did not fulfil the author's intention, which was to make the human mind as plain as the road from Charing Cross to St Paul's.

Mill's doctrine led him to think that almost anything could be accomplished by education, and that human beings (who necessarily seek only their own happiness) could be so educated as to find their own happiness in devotion to the common good. The test of right actions lay in their consequences, and the right was that which promotes general happiness, rather than the happiness of the agent. Moral praise and blame, reward and punishment were social devices for encouraging actions useful to society and discouraging harmful ones.

Mill rejected the idea of 'natural rights' and made perhaps the first attempt to defend representative institutions on purely utilitarian lines. People need government in order to defend their interests from other people; but any government is made up of people who will have an interest in plundering and enslaving their subjects. A power is therefore needed to act as a check on the 'sinister interests' of government. The only effective way of setting up such a power was through representatives, and the only way to ensure an identity of interest between community and representatives was by frequent elections. (This is not so much representative government as representative anti-government.) Mill excluded women and the young from the electorate on the ground that they had a natural identity of interest with their husbands and fathers, and confined votes to the middle class as the real leaders of society. He had unbounded confidence in representative institutions and complete freedom of discussion. (K.B.)

Mill, John Stuart (1806–73) John Stuart Mill was born in London and educated at home by his father James MILL. At eighteen he entered the East India Company, where his father was also employed, remaining with the Company until its extinction in 1858, by which time he had become its chief London administrator. At the age of twenty, he suffered a 'mental crisis' followed by a long period of depression and disillusion, during which he found consolation in Wordsworth's poetry. On his recovery he reacted for a time against the opinions of his father, and came under the influence of COLERIDGE, Carlyle and John Sterling. In 1831 he met Harriet Taylor and the two formed an attachment which gradually came to be tolerated by her husband but not by most of their friends.

Mill's first original writings were on economic questions (written 1830–4, published 1844). At about the same time he began work on the philosophy of logic and devoted to it the 'spare time' of his most fruitful years. *A System of Logic, Ratiocinative and Inductive* was published in 1843 and made Mill famous. *Political Economy* appeared only two years later. In 1851 Harriet Taylor's husband died, and the two friends married and began work together on a number of essays and on the *Autobiography*. They both worked in the shadow of death, and were attempting to complete a compendium of their views to serve as 'a sort of mental pemmican, which thinkers, when there are any after us, may nourish themselves with, and then dilute for other people'. The partnership came to an end in 1858, when Harriet died in Avignon. *On Liberty* (a 'joint work') was published the following year. Mill now retired, and living in Blackheath and Avignon, became a well-known public figure, a champion of women's rights, of the working classes and of electoral reform. In 1865 he became M.P. for Westminster and was able to propose votes for women as an amendment to Disraeli's Franchise Bill. He died in Avignon at the age of sixty-seven, the outstanding English radical of his day and a main link between liberal thought in England and the rest of the world.

1 *Ethics.* At the age of fifteen, Mill gave enthusiastic assent to the ethical system of Bentham, with its total rejection of intuitive modes of reasoning in morals. In his subsequent logical inquiries, and reflections on justice and liberty, he attempted to show that the ultimate ethical test must be an experimental and UTILITARIAN one. He also agreed with Bentham in holding that all our conduct is determined, our deliberate acts being

motivated by the belief that they will lead to our own greatest good. But decisions rest upon character and belief as well as situation, and Mill held that we can correct our beliefs and improve our characters, provided we want to: this, Mill says, embodies what is really inspiriting and ennobling in the (incorrect) doctrine of free will. The function of moral discussion is to help people decide what sort of person they would like to be.

The fundamental principles of Mill's ethics are: (a) that pleasure alone is good or desirable in itself; and (b) that actions are right in proportion as they tend to promote the happiness of all concerned, where happiness means pleasure and the absence of pain.

(a) Mill was neither the first nor the last to hold that there must be some intimate connexion between goodness and desire. He claimed that to desire a thing is to think of it as pleasant – to hold that it brings or would bring pleasure. But Mill was not prepared to treat all objects of desire alike: some desires were primitive, others the result of experience, training, or self-discipline. He also postulated different *kinds* of pleasure, suggesting that we ought always to prefer the 'higher' pleasures, including the social and generous pleasures and those of the cultivated feelings and intellect.

(b) For Mill, the rightness of actions depends on their tendency to promote happiness – not that of the agent, but that of all affected. In effect he argues that we ought to choose the action which (at the time of decision) *looks most likely* to produce most happiness, since in practice we can never be completely sure. But we cannot usually stop to calculate the results of our actions, and Mill accepts that we should for the most part let ourselves be guided by traditional general rules: 'the beliefs that have come down are the rules

of morality for the multitude, and for the philosopher, until he has succeeded in finding better'. The importance Mill attached to rules of morality marks a departure from Bentham: only where there was a clash of duties (where one and the same action is required by one rule and forbidden by another) should one choose simply by reference to the probable consequence of the action individually considered.

Mill recognized that there were many good, noble and generous deeds which went beyond the requirements of duty, and this left a wide front on which individuals could do or become whatever they wish. In *On Liberty*, he argued that this freedom is endangered by public opinion: society had a right to make laws governing such conduct as might damage the interests of others, but there was 'no room for entertaining any such question where a person's conduct affects the interests of no person besides himself, or need not affect them unless they like'. But when Mill argues, for example, that censorship could not be expedient in any civilized society, utilitarian language hardly suffices to state his case, that 'it is the privilege and proper condition of a human being, arrived at the maturity of his faculties, to use and interpret experience in his own way.'

Mill also worked to bring about a government based on the working classes and committed to socialism; but he believed the workers should first be educated, and he insisted on constitutional safeguards of the rights of minorities. The State was to pay for education but not provide it, and social ownership, for him, did not imply ownership by an omni-competent State.

2 *Politics.* In Book VI of the *Logic*, Mill distinguishes two types of sociological inquiry, one special, the other general. The first handles particular hypothetical

issues, such as 'what would be the effect of repealing the corn laws in the present state of society in England?' We suppose that 'the state of society' remains constant, and make use of the deductive method to arrive at an answer which will hold good in the present state of society. The second notes that societies pass through different general states, and makes the assumption that the causes of any such state lie in its immediate predecessor. Mill believed (with COMTE) that economic, social, and cultural conditions mutually affect each other, the state of knowledge being the most important factor. History, when judiciously examined, will yield empirical laws of society, stating for example that an age of Faith will lead to an age of Reason, and an age of Reason to a scientific or 'positive' age. This general science of society tries to explain a given type of transition by reference to the laws of certain special sciences (geology, botany, economics, psychology, genetics), in accordance with Comte's 'inverse deductive method'. (Mill's notion of a 'law' of the successive total states of society was vehemently rejected by POPPER.)

3 *Logic.* In logic as in politics, Mill fought a battle on two fronts: against a priori and intuitive philosophy, and against simple empiricism. He described his logic as 'a logic of experience' but went on to show that science must be systematic, analytic and (at some points) deductive. In the *Logic*, he attempted to show: (a) that 'necessary propositions' are merely verbal; (b) that traditional immediate inferences are 'merely apparent' and not real inferences; (c) that the SYLLOGISM, considered as an argument from premises to conclusions, is also 'merely apparent' inference; (d) that the syllogism is important on account of the assertion of the major or universal

premise; (e) that the assertion of a universal proposition on the basis of particular evidence is a genuine inference; (f) that the principles of mathematics are inductive and rest upon observation; (g) that in some cases we can properly claim to know universal propositions based on induction.

Mill's account of mathematical knowledge has satisfied nobody. He never properly distinguished between pure and applied mathematics, and confused errors of counting and measurement with those of calculation. But his logical doctrines have proved fruitful. His approach rests on the notion that not all words are simply names for things. He recognized several types of names. There were 'singular names' like 'John' and 'Mary' and – a many-worded name – 'the King who succeeded William I'. There were also 'general names' (e.g. predicates like 'man', 'old', 'white'), which were 'capable of being truly affirmed, in the same sense, of an indefinite number of things'. But there were also 'proper names', which merely 'denote' things or places, unlike descriptive names which say something which may be true or false. 'The King who succeeded William I' denotes Rufus for anyone who understands what the phrase means, and sees its truth. Mill calls this kind of meaning 'connotation' as opposed to 'denotation'. The word 'man' connotes certain properties, and as Mill says 'it denotes whatever individuals have those properties'. But Mill was mistaken: general terms are not names. A definite description may denote an individual (Rufus) but a predicate term does not: if I state that John is not a great scientist, for example, I am not referring to any great scientist. But Mill at least recognizes that general terms have a dimension of meaning which does not involve naming, and he also realized that words like 'and', 'of', 'in', and 'truly', have 'no title what-soever to be considered as names'. Naming, then, is not the only kind of meaning – a truth not fully assimilated by philosophers for several generations.

A proposition which does no more than assert part of what its subject-term connotes is, according to Mill, tautological or 'merely verbal'. Moreover the immediate inferences of traditional logic are also tautological, depending for their truth on the *meaning* of the logical words employed. (Thus the validity of 'if all men are mortal then some men are mortal' depends on the meaning of 'all', 'some', and 'if…then…'.) As for syllogisms, it is notorious that their conclusions must be 'contained in' their premises if they are to be valid. All the same I can know that all men are mortal without knowing that the Duke of Wellington is so: I might never have heard of him. Mill sees that the 'novelty' of the conclusion of a syllogism arises from the fact that we can know a universal proposition without knowing all its particular instances: when we discover a new instance we make a new *application* of the proposition. But Mill was also concerned with the question of how we can have knowledge of factual universal propositions, which, he insisted, was by inference from a set of instances – by induction.

4 *Induction.* In Book III of the *Logic* Mill argues that induction depends on the 'assumption' that the course of nature is uniform – that what has happened once in certain circumstances, will happen again if the circumstances recur – and that we know from experience that 'the assumption is warranted'. Simple inductions proceed by enumerating similar instances: thus 'the swans we have seen are all white – therefore all swans are white'. And it is by the same method that we learn that nature is uniform. Mill distinguishes two kinds

of uniformities – uniformities of co-existence, such as the 'togetherness' of the properties of natural kinds, and of spatial and numerical properties, and uniformities of sequence, which may be loosely characterized as *causal*.

By 'cause' Mill means a factor which, added to the ordinary course of events, is sufficient to produce a given effect. We know (according to Mill) a most important truth about causes: that every event has one. We know it by simple observation, but having learned it we can use it to discover and prove particular causal laws. For the cause of any effect must lie in its immediately antecedent events and circumstances. Hence if we find that X is preceded by the circumstances A, B, C etc., we know that one or other of these, or some combination of them, must have caused X. But that is insufficient: we need, first, to eliminate those circumstances that do not always precede X, and second, we need to seek out cases where other factors are present amongst the antecedents of X. Mill proposes four 'Methods of Induction' – Agreement, Difference, Agreement and Difference, and Concomitant Variation – for this purpose, but he claimed too much when he described them as 'a scientific test'. In the first place, the initial identification of likely factors must depend on a knowledge of the field gained without the help of these Methods; and second, this 'knowledge' is itself subject to revision. (A factor initially considered irrelevant might turn out to be vital.) Methods of elimination cannot lead to a decisive verdict in favour of the candidates that remain, unless the set of possible candidates is decisively circumscribed, which it can never be in such inquiries. And repeated experiment, while it increases *probabilities*, falls short of being a decisive test.

The Methods of Induction are supposed to apply across the most basic level of experimental inquiry; at higher levels, Mill argues in Book VI of the *Logic*, different observational sciences employ strategies of their own. Mill distinguishes four of these Methods: the Geometrical, which applies where different laws do not modify each other's action; the Chemical, where direct experiment is needed in order to separate causes which are combined in a way that has defied analysis; the Physical, which is used when the laws of different causal factors are already fairly well known; and finally the Historical, which is required where phenomena are complicated and beyond the scope of experiment, as in the social sciences.

Mill referred to his own position as 'the experience philosophy', and his approach is near to Hume's in that he tries to account for bodies in terms of our perceptions of them. He distinguishes clearly between the uniform causal order which governs bodies and the order which connects different ideas or impressions in our minds and leads us to conclude that they all apply to the same individual thing. The first kind of order is a uniformity, the second not: uniformities hold between bodies rather than sensations. Mill attempts an analysis of this order and goes on to define a body as a 'permanent possibility of sensation', meaning that to talk of a table is to talk of an order of this type in actual or possible sensations. Mill makes no attempt to found this possibility upon an actual external substance, or upon God, but he recognizes that there are 'other successions of feeling besides those of which I am conscious'. But when it comes to describing the order of experiences which constitutes an individual mind, Mill comes upon 'a final inexplicability' – the fact that a mind which is a series of feelings should be aware of itself as past and future.

Mill appeared to many to be atheistic, but in his essays on natural theology he defends the theoretical possibility of a mind existing without a body, hence the possibility of immortality. He also finds that the argument from design carries some weight: it suggests that there is a God who desires the good of his creatures, though he evidently has many other tasks in hand. At this point Mill switches from the question of belief to that of hope. We do not need to believe in order to contemplate the notion of divine perfection, meditate upon the gospels, and hope for immortality; and such agnostic hope has practical value.   (K.B.)

Mind The expression 'PHILOSOPHY OF MIND' designates a certain group of problems commonly recognized by English-speaking philosophers, but the expression is hard to translate into other languages. This is only partly due to the impossibility of finding exact equivalents for the English word 'mind'. It is also a reflection of the fact that the classification in which this label figures is itself based on certain profound philosophical assumptions, often unexpressed.

The crucial assumption can perhaps be tersely described as the view that a whole host of rather different things belong together, and can usefully be treated as members of one class. The items which are gathered together under 'mind', or under the associated adjective 'mental', include such disparate things as tickles and pains, feelings of nausea and discomfort, emotional experiences like love or anger, perceptions of the world around us, and thoughts of the most abstract and exalted character. The idea of treating all these together is perhaps first clearly propounded by DESCARTES, and contrasts strikingly with the preceding dominant view, descended from ARISTOTLE, which offered a highly differentiated picture of our experiences and capacities and located sensations and thoughts, for example, in distinct parts or faculties.

What all the items on the long, diverse list of the 'mental' have in common, for Descartes, is that they are all essentially present to first-person experience. That is, there cannot be any such a thing as a thought, a perception, or a tickle, without a thinker who can experience it as his or her own; whereas this is manifestly not true of a rock or a tree or a house. Descartes' crucial move was to deem all such things as consisting exclusively in what they present to experience, and hence to see them as distinct from 'outer' realities, even though causally related to them. This way of sorting things into 'inner' and 'outer' is what gives rise to the philosophical category of the 'mental', and what licences the grouping together of all sorts of problems under the heading 'philosophy of mind'.

Descartes' inner/outer sorting was motivated by a number of things, of which two are perhaps crucial: the essential place in his method of a kind of self-scrutiny which circumscribes inner experience the better to focus on it; and his uncompromisingly mechanistic notion of body, which forces one to the complementary category of the mental as what is excluded from the physical and cannot be perceived in outer reality. The continuing force of both these leading ideas in modern philosophy, particularly in the Anglo-Saxon world, is what ensures the continued currency of the term 'philosophy of mind'. By the same token, the dominance in French and German philosophy of views which are highly critical both of these notions of method and of mechanistic reduction helps explain the relative untranslatability of the expression.

It is also understandable in the light of this background that the major problem of the philosophy of mind is the 'mind-body problem' itself. This is the term for a congeries of difficulties which beset any attempt to make 'mind' and 'body' into a coherent whole once they have been distinguished by the inner/outer sorting. Descartes' own approach was a metaphysical DUALISM: mind and body are seen as different substances, causally related in virtue of being brought together in a substantial union by God. But this solution has very little support any more. Some neurophysiologists espoused it (notably Sir John Eccles, 1903–97); but generally it has seemed incredible for a number of reasons. One is the difficulty of conceiving causal relations between mind and body once separated in this way. This is what led MALEBRANCHE and BERKELEY to even more extravagant views, respectively OCCASIONALISM and a denial of matter altogether. But beyond that, dualism has seemed to many incompatible with the obvious dependence of mental function on the physical substrate. And in addition, one important stream of European philosophy has rebelled against Descartes' downgrading, as irremediably obscure and confused, of our experience of ourselves as embodied and social agents. HEIDEGGER and MERLEAU-PONTY are among the most influential philosophers in the twentieth century to have articulated this reaction.

The obvious recourse for those who hold to mechanism is a kind of materialist MONISM which treats mind as just a reflection of underlying material process. Thoughts reflect the firing of neurones in the brain, emotions our endocrinological state, and so on. A number of theories of this kind have been propounded, some of them taking computer technology as a source of models, and proposing to see mental functions as the inner reflection of highly complex programmes of computation.

But monism has its own problems. Quite apart from possible objections to reductive mechanistic explanations of our thought, action, language and social life, there is the difficulty of placing inner 'reflections' themselves in a monistic world-view. The analogous situation is well-understood, where a solar system in which the earth 'really' spins on its axis and orbits the sun 'looks' to us as though the sun were circling an immobile earth. The appearances here are external to the phenomena explained (the solar system) and can be disregarded when explaining them. But when we come to consider 'inner' experience as the reflection of neural process, it cannot be so easily sidelined. In this case, it is part of our brief to account for there being such a thing as an inner reflection at all. Why is it that ordinary computers made of transistors don't have such an inner life and we do? Or perhaps they do after all? Or at least their more sophisticated descendants will? The discussion goes off into bizarre science fantasy at this point – a sign of deep malaise.

The difficulty is that here the 'appearances' themselves are part of what needs to be explained, and it is hard to conceive how they can be accommodated in a monistic materialist world. Either they are left unexplained; or various heroic attempts are made to subsume them under physical reality, though they always fall short of explaining why the problem should have arisen in the first place.

It would appear that there is a better hope of making coherent sense of ourselves if we start from a perspective which (as Merleau-Ponty does) makes embodied agency central. But that entails abandoning the inner/outer sorting altogether, and hence the portmanteau categories of 'mind' and 'mental'. These approaches take us outside the classification in which 'philosophy of mind' figures as a term.

The actual situation in English-speaking philosophy is a mixed one. The traditional Cartesian sorting is still sufficiently acknowledged, so that the classification 'philosophy of mind' is a recognized one, and lots of people still worry over 'the mind-body problem'. At the same time, Cartesian assumptions are often challenged in some of the particular fields which are included in the broad category. These include the philosophy of action, analyses of feeling and emotion, issues about the FREEDOM OF THE WILL, and questions about the self and PERSONAL IDENTITY. The philosophy of mind also overlaps with EPISTOMOLOGY, because any theory of knowledge must make some assumptions about philosophical psychology in the very choice of its key terms. Thus the classical Cartesian and empiricist epistemologies relied on the notion of an 'idea', impression', or 'SENSE-DATUM', as the immediate object of consciousness.

Cartesian, dualist assumptions have been strongly challenged in the field of philosophy of action, partly under the influence of the later WITTGENSTEIN. Most philosophers now reject a construal of action as an external movement caused by an inner act of will, and search for an account which does not artificially separate mind and body. Some attempts in this field also draw on European developments, like the notion of INTENTIONALITY, as defined in the work of BRENTANO and HUSSERL. At the same time, the philosophical psychology of classical epistemology is widely considered outdated if not absurd. Very few thinkers defend sense-data, and many have become sensitive to the role of language, which in turn has led them to recast the problem entirely. Since language is a social institution, the question arises whether we can offer a coherent view of the origin and bases of knowledge confined to the individual mind, as classical epistemology tries to do.

But alongside this, other questions, such as the issues about freedom and determinism, continue to be treated very much on the old assumptions. The conception of determinism, in relation to which freedom and responsibility seem to be problematical, is itself largely inspired by a mechanistic view of the human subject. And the most widely-discussed issue in this field is that about 'compatibilism', that is, whether there is, after all, any conflict between a deterministic account of human action and the kind of freedom that seems to be inseparable from moral responsibility. The thesis that there is no such conflict goes back to HOBBES and HUME at the period of origin of the inner/outer sorting. The self and personal identity are also often discussed in traditional terms, as though the main issue were that of the unity of an object through time. The idea that the self may have another kind of unity has barely begun to impinge on this debate.

The whole field of the philosophy of mind offers a strange and contradictory prospect, in that it is held together by certain fundamental ideas which are nevertheless frequently challenged in the discussion of some of the particular issues which fall within it.   [C.T.]

Miracles Miracles can be defined as exceptions to the laws of nature; if they occur, they must either be uncaused, or have causes beyond the natural world; see THEISM.

Mises, Richard von (1883–1953) Richard von Mises was a leading associate of the LOGICAL POSITIVISTS of the VIENNA CIRCLE until he sought refuge from Nazism in the United States. He wrote a general account of positivism in 1939, but is best known as a theorist of probability. In *Probability, Statistics and Truth* (1928), he defined probability as the limiting value of the frequency of an event within a collective, where a collective is an indefinitely large class whose members occur in random order. Thus to say that the probability of heads is one half is to say that the limiting value of the fraction given by dividing the number of heads by the number of tosses is one half. Von Mises was able to show that the axioms of mathematical probability followed tautologically from this definition, which has however been attacked, especially for its use of the notion of limiting frequency outside pure mathematics; others have objected that it gives no account of probability statements which are not of the form 'The probability of event e within the collective K is P'.   (J.O.U.)

Modernism According to a widely accepted but not unquestionable theory, the last few years of the nineteenth century witnessed an international upheaval in the arts which was to continue for at least 30 years. It was called modernism and it overthrew 'traditional' forms which, it is argued, had unthinkingly presupposed an incontrovertible 'real world' which art was expected to 'express' or 'represent'. Thus modernist writers replaced narrative and dialogue with 'stream of consciousness', modernist composers moved to 'atonalism', and modernist painters discovered 'abstraction'; in general the medium, or 'language', was treated as an object in its own tight, rather than a stand-in for an ulterior reality. PHENOMENOLOGY and LOGICAL POSITIVISM, RELATIVITY and QUANTUM MECHANICS are sometimes seen as further manifestations of modernism. In original intention, modernism appears as a rejection of the domineering epistemological optimism of MODERNITY; but in a wider perspective it can be seen as a continuation of it by sophisticatedly self-conscious means: see POSTMODERNISM.   [J.R.]

Modernity The idea of modernity – which is common to sociology, economics and historiography, both in their professional and in their popular or 'folk' forms – is an attempt to grasp the peculiarity of the present by contrasting it with a preceding age. Various criteria of modernity have been proposed: science, commerce, capitalism, police, print, surveillance, cheap travel, atheism, bureaucratic rationality, urbanism, consumerism, or democracy, and above all, ALIENATION. But the underlying contrast is always epistemological: the modern world is enlightened, scientific and disappointed, whereas its predecessor was superstitious, gullible and magical. Hence philosophical debates about the scope and limits of reason or science touch the crux of the concept of modernity.

Within philosophy, 'modernity' has been used to designate various moments of abundant epistemological optimism. In the fourteenth century, NOMINALISM was the *via moderna* in contrast with the discredited *via antiqua* of realism; in the eighteenth, DESCARTES was hailed as the 'father of modern philosophy' thanks to his confidence in mathematics and natural science.

ROUSSEAU initiated a reaction in which reason was seen as an ailment rather than an adornment of humanity; and HEGEL consolidated this argument by invoking a superior form of knowledge – dialectical or speculative reason which was supposed to transcend the rationalistic one-sidedness of the eighteenth century 'enlightenment'. Thus it became a commonplace to blame 'the Enlightenment' for the calamities of modernity, and particularly for the excesses of the French Revolution, The same theme was carried forward by MARX's theory of IDEOLOGY; and in NIETZSCHE (followed by HEIDEGGER and DERRIDA) it was inflated into a blanket condemnation of the whole of Western philosophy since SOCRATES.

The old ambitions of modernity were occasionally reactivated in twentieth-century philosophy, notably by LOGICAL POSITIVISM and DIALECTICAL MATERIALISM; but the barrage of criticism has been maintained by philosophers like HORKHEIMER and ADORNO (see their *Dialectic of Enlightenment*, 1944), MARCUSE, HABERMAS and MACINTYRE. The philosophers of POSTMODERNISM, however, have attempted to trump these criticisms of modernity by accusing them of a secret complicity with what they criticize, in that they cling to the 'enlightenment' idea of a final truth toward which, in spite of everything, we may at least hope to draw nearer. See also HISTORY OF PHILOSOPHY.   [J.R.]

Monads Monads are the ulitimate spiritual constituents of the world according to LEIBNIZ.

Monism Monism is the doctrine that there is only one substance, or one 'world', or that reality is in some sense *one*, that is, unchanging or indivisible or undifferentiated. For instance, the alternative claims that 'everything is mental' or 'everything is material' are crudely expressed forms of monism, each opposed to the common sense DUALISM of mind and matter. The term was invented by Christian WOLFF, who used it only of these two theories, which have the best right to the labels 'IDEALISM' and 'MATERIALISM' respectively. It later came to be used also of the theory of absolute identity held by SCHELLING and HEGEL, namely, that mind and matter are not reducible one to the other, but both to one common substance of which they are phenomenal modifications. (Compare the later 'neutral monism' of William JAMES and, at one time, RUSSELL.) Subsequently the term was applied to any theory attempting to explain phenomena by some single principle; it was opposed not merely to dualism but also to pluralism, for example to Russell's Logical Atomism, which he also called 'absolute pluralism'. As a result of these extended uses, the term is systematically ambiguous. (a) *Substantial* monism is the view that the apparent plurality of substances is due to different states or appearances of a single substance – 'God-or-Nature' to SPINOZA, for example, or 'the Absolute' to BRADLEY. (b) *Attributive* monism, on the other hand, is the view that whatever the number of substances, they are of a single ultimate kind, that is, there is only one realm of being. One could also distinguish from these absolute views (c) *partial* monism, which states that within any given realm of being (however many there may be) there is only one substance. These varieties of monism need not all stand or fall together; and have, for reasons requiring lengthy argument, been held selectively: for example, Spinoza held (a) and hence trivially (c), but rejected (b) in favour of an infinity of ultimate kinds, whereas DESCARTES rejected (a) and (b), but accepted (c) within the material realm, and LEIBNIZ rejected (a) and (c), but accepted (b), all monads being souls; thus each of these thinkers accepted monism in at least one sense but not in all. But in each of its forms it is the supreme expression of a will to metaphysical tidiness. See also MIND, PHILOSOPHY OF MIND.   (R.HALL.)

Montaigne, Michel de (1533–92) French author, remembered by historians of philosophy for reviving the ancient SCEPTICISM of Sextus Empiricus, but equally important for inventing a new form of philosophical writing. The inconclusive but humorous literary experiments that proliferate through the three editions of his *Essais* (1580, 1588, 1595) seek to make a virtue of systematic inconstancy, even inconsistency: 'The uncertainty of my judgement is so evenly balanced', he wrote, 'that I would happily submit to the decision of chance and of the dice'.   {J.R.}

Montesquieu, Charles-Louis de Secondat (1689–1755) French politician and author who made a name for himself with *Persian Letters* (1721), purportedly a translation of a correspondence in which some Persian visitors to France express their astonishment at the weird and exotic habits of the French. His *Spirit of Laws* (1748), with its systematic investigation of monarchy, despotism and republicanism, is credited with launching modern political theory. See also ENCYCLOPEDISTS.

Moore, George Edward (1873–1958) The English philosopher and Cambridge professor G. E. Moore had an immense personal influence on British philosophers of his time. The three main topics dealt with in Moore's writings are philosophical method, ethics and perception.

1 *Method.* Moore wrote little about his method because he preferred to practise it, but it appears clearly in an early article on 'Necessity' (1900), in the programmatic 'A Defence of Common Sense' (1925) and in the autobiographical remarks in *The Philosophy of G.E. Moore* (1942). As regards the things we say in ordinary life, he was concerned neither with their meaning nor their truth (he thought they had well-known meanings, and were on the whole certainly true), but with what he called an ANALYSIS of their meaning. As regards philosophical views – which were often analyses whose results denied the commonly accepted meaning and truth of what they analysed – he was anxious to discover what they could mean and whether they were true.

In these analytic investigations Moore makes two independent appeals (often confused by critics): one to the truth of what we hold in common sense, the other to the propriety of what we say in ordinary language. His attitude to common sense, like that of Thomas REID, is that while many of its beliefs are not provable, there are far better reasons for accepting them than for accepting any philosophical doctrines which contradict them. Unlike any philosophical belief, we cannot help holding them, and various kinds of inconsistency issue from our attempts to deny them. Since the expressions whose meaning Moore analyses – like 'good', 'know', 'see', or 'real' – are in common everyday use, he felt he could assume that we understand them very well, and that it was legitimate to use ordinary language to interpret the strange things that philosophers say, and to accuse any philosopher who goes against it of 'an abuse of language'.

In common with many philosophers since PLATO, Moore holds that the meaning of an expression is a kind of entity – often called a concept, notion or proposition – which the expression stands for, and which is called up before the mind of anyone who understands it. Analysis of a concept involves inspecting it and trying to describe it; in particular it involves either saying how it can be divided into a set of constituent concepts and how these constituents are interrelated or saying how it is to be distinguished, by way of similarity and difference, from other concepts which are brought before the mind by the given expression and by other related expressions. The division method, with its dependence on the concept theory of meaning, has a very ancient history and predominates in the work of RUSSELL and the early WITTGENSTEIN, while the distinction method, in a form uncommitted to the concept theory, is favoured by Wittgenstein's later work and that of his followers. Moore often thought, in addition, that in order to give an analysis of a concept one must find a concept or set of concepts identical with it and, therefore,

an expression synonymous with the expression used to express it.

2 *Ethics*. Taking 'what is good?' as the central question of ethics, Moore distinguished the analysis of the notion of *good* from the inquiry into what things are good or what kinds of things are good. In *Principia Ethica* (1903), he attempted a brief answer to the question 'What kinds of things are good?', claiming that there was an 'immense variety' of such kinds of things, including 'the pleasures of human intercourse and the enjoyment of beautiful objects'. But most of his work here and elsewhere was devoted to analysing the notion of good. In accordance with his method of inspection, he advises the analyst of *good* to 'attentively consider what is actually before his mind' in the hope that 'if he will try this experiment with each suggested definition (i.e. analysis) in succession, he may become expert enough to recognize that in every case he has before his mind a unique object'. And in conformity with his method of division, he assumes that a definition 'states what are the parts which invariably compose a certain whole', concluding that 'in this sense the notion "good" has no definition because it is simple and has no parts'. The simple concept for which the expression 'good' stood was, he thought, a 'non-natural' quality, and he called any attempt to identify it with another concept the 'naturalistic fallacy'. When, however, he used the 'distinction' method of analysis, he counted it as an analysis of *good* if he could 'distinguish this from other' concepts. In his later writings he held that the word 'good' is not after all the 'name of a characteristic' but that it may be used to express an approval. Like the UTILITARIANS, Moore made the notion of *right* dependent on the notion of *good*, arguing that it stands only for the causes of things which are good in themselves.

3 *Perception.* In discussing the notion of perception, Moore assumes that there is no doubt about the meaning of such expressions as 'I see a book' and 'this, which I see, is a book', and usually no doubt about the truth of what they say. He then argues that whenever we see an opaque material object, such as a book, we *ipso facto* see, in a second sense, a particular part of it, such as the surface turned towards us, and also see, in a third sense, what he calls a SENSE-DATUM, such as a particular patch of colour. His task then is to distinguish and relate the three concepts expressed by the one word 'see' and the three concepts expressed by their respective grammatical objects, namely 'material object', 'part of the surface of a material object' and 'sense-datum'. To the question how these various concepts are related to each other, he provided many answers, none of which satisfied him or other philosophers. This failure is, it seems, mainly due to two assumptions – that 'sense-datum' is the name of a peculiar kind of entity, present in every perceptual experience, and that when I say 'this, which I see, is a book', I must be trying to *identify* the sense-datum *with* something.   (A.R.W.)

More, Henry (1614–87)   Henry More was an early British enthusiast for DESCARTES, whom he regarded as the greatest teacher since Jesus; he also appealed to PLATO in support of Christian spirituality, and is regarded as a leading figure amongst the CAMBRIDGE PLATONISTS.

More, Thomas (1477–1535)   English politician, humanist, martyr, and saint, and author – under the inspiration of PLATO's *Republic* – of *Utopia* (1516).

Morris, Charles (1901–79)   American philosopher whose main contributions were to the philosophy of language. He sought to fuse the behaviouristic pragmatism of his teacher, George H. Mead, with the logical empiricism of the VIENNA CIRCLE, and to develop systematically the fertile but sketchily worked out ideas of C. S. PEIRCE on signs. However, Morris went far beyond Peirce in taking into account non-linguistic as well as linguistic signs (see *Foundations of the Theory of Signs*, 1938). His division of semiotics (or the general theory of signs) into three major branches, has been widely adopted. The first is syntactics, which studies the relations signs have to one another in virtue of their purely formal or structural properties. The second is semantics, which analyses the relations of signs to what they designate. The third, of which he may be regarded as the founder, is pragmatics, which examines 'the relations of signs to their interpreters'.   (E.N.)

N

Nagel, Ernest (1901–85) Ernest Nagel was born in Czechoslovakia and emigrated to the United States in 1911. He is best known for his work on probability and the philosophy of science (*The Structure of Science*, 1961, is acknowledged to be a classic in this field). In METAPHYSICS Nagel counts himself as a NATURALIST, holding that the world must be understood in terms of efficient causation and as involving no ultimate ingredients beyond matter. He is also the author of articles on Carnap, Cohen, Goodman, Lewis, Morris and Popper in this Encyclopedia. (J.O.U.)

Nagel, Thomas (1937–) American philosopher with anti-positivist views and a special interest in subjectivity. His writings include *The View from Nowhere* (1986) and 'What is it like to be a bat?' (1974); see PHILOSOPHY OF MIND.

Natural Law Natural law comprises a set of supposedly universal principles of justice that are more or less implicitly recognized in all societies. It is usually taken to be rooted in divine wisdom, and open to discovery by reasoning about human nature. See also AQUINAS, GROTIUS, HOBBES, POLITICAL PHILOSOPHY, JURISPRUDENCE.

Naturalism Like most of the words ending in 'ism' that are used to name a type of philosophical position, 'naturalism' has only a vague and imprecise sense. More widely, a naturalist considers that the totality of things which we call 'nature' and which are studied in the natural sciences is the totality of all things whatever, and denies the need of any explanations of the natural in terms of the super-natural; such a philosopher will normally hold that any reference to a deity, or to a realm of values, or to mind as something more than a natural phenomenon is illegitimate. With such nineteenth century thinkers as T. H. HUXLEY, naturalism connoted especially a belief that life and thought could be completely explained, in principle, as arising by evolution from matter. In ETHICS naturalism is the view that statements about the rightness, wrongness, goodness and badness of things are statements about the natural world and not about special values beyond the ken of science; thus a naturalist might maintain that to say that something is good is to say that it is likely to satisfy desire, which is a scientifically testable statement. But in *Principia Ethica* G. E. MOORE widened the notion of naturalism for his special purposes so that everyone was guilty of the 'naturalistic fallacy' who attempted to define ethical concepts in terms of concepts which were not specifically ethical; thus even those who defined 'good' as meaning 'willed by God', a view clearly utterly opposed to naturalism as ordinarily understood, were said by Moore to have committed the naturalistic fallacy. Unfortunately this usage of Moore's has become so widely known that the term 'naturalism' may have lost whatever utility it ever had. On the other hand, see also ANALYTIC PHILOSOPHY. (J.O.U.)

Negative Theology See NEOPLATONISM.

Neoplatonism 'Neoplatonism' is a modern term designating the last creative effort of pagan antiquity (*c*.250–550 AD) to produce a comprehensive philosophical system which could satisfy all our spiritual aspirations. Its exponents, who – rightly or wrongly – regarded themselves simply as Platonists, sought to present an inclusive, logically coherent image of the universe and our place in it, and to explain how we can achieve salvation through being restored to our original condition. Neoplatonism synthesized Platonism with other schools of philosophical thought (particularly those of ARISTOTLE, the STOICS, and the PYTHAGOREANS; only EPICUREANISM was excluded). But it also assimilated many myths, rites, and cults of Greek and of Oriental polytheism, including alchemy and magic (often based on affinities between planets and metals etc.) and found a place for the traditional deities and semi-deities of popular religions.

Neoplatonism teaches belief in a deity (or supreme principle) as the source from which all things flow without ever becoming separated from it, so that it is also immanent in everything. This 'flow' is not a temporal process, but a permanent, involuntary effulgence or emanation whose source remains forever unconsumed and undiminished. It is, so to speak, a timeless history, above being, and no predicates can really be applied to it. The best we can do is call it 'One', to express the fact that it is undifferentiated and therefore without quality. If we think of it as the source of all being, we can also refer to it as 'goodness' in the sense that it is the ultimate 'why' of everything.

The timeless process of effulgence is best described as a gradual 'dispersion' of the original unity. The process begins with supra-sensible reality (first: mind, or thought thinking itself, or spirit; next: the soul); then comes sensible reality (in time and space); and at the end there is annihilation (rather as light, receding from its source, gradually fades into darkness). Neoplatonism sees this annihilation as the effect of matter, which is both

sheer nothingness, and 'evil' – the 'why' of nothingness. The successive steps or 'hypostases' of effulgence follow each other with some kind of necessity, and it follows that everything in the universe is just as it ought to be. But Neoplatonism is keenly aware of the imperfection which stems from the human soul's remoteness from the deity, an imperfection which engenders a longing to undo 'progress' (which may also be interpreted as some kind of flaw or fall) and 'revert' to an original position. Humanity shares this longing with other beings, the path to its satisfaction being taught in ETHICS. Thus, whereas Neoplatonism is MONISTIC in theory, its practical implications are dualistic.

The concept of a deity inaccessible to reflective thought demands as its correlate a kind of knowledge that transcends rational thinking. To achieve this higher knowledge we must suppress determinateness and recall ourselves from our 'dispersion'. Having finally become one, we are able in rare moments to face the One, either in rapt contemplation or in unity with it. This condition of ecstasy is the main purpose of moral life. As we progress, our steadfastness, self-control, fairness and prudence will appear successively as civic, purificatory and exemplary virtues. In the moment of ecstasy all our intellectual and moral aspirations will be satisfied.

One of the most striking aspects of Neoplatonism is its derivation of all sensible reality from a supra-sensible one, which represents a type of causation radically different from causality in space and time. The Neoplatonist would think of modern scientific explanations as shallow; the scientist, on the other hand, is likely to consider Neoplatonism utterly fantastic.

It is customary to see PLOTINUS as the founder of Neoplatonism (though Platonism from the time of CICERO on – so-called Middle Platonism – can be seen as the soil from which it developed). It is also customary to consider the year 529, in which the Emperor Justinian ordered the closure of Plato's ACADEMY in Athens, as marking the end of pagan philosophy in general and Neoplatonism in particular.

Two outstanding representatives of the early phase of the school of Plotinus are Porphyry (234–c.305) and Iamblichus (died c.330). The former edited Plotinus, and showed great acumen and erudition in *Against the Christians*, whose arguments over chronology and the authorship of parts of the Scriptures have not been superseded. His *On the Cave of the Nymphs* is a good example of the allegorizing interpretation of poetry (in this case Homer) practised by many Neoplatonists. His aphoristic *Starting Points* make an excellent introduction to the main doctrines, and his consolatory *Letter to Marcella*, his wife, is very readable. His *Introduction to Aristotle's Categories*, a commentary on five fundamental concepts (genus, species, difference, property and accident) was particularly influential. A passage in which he posed (but did not answer) the question whether UNIVERSALS have an existence independent of both minds and particular things gave impetus to the medieval controversy between NOMINALISM, REALISM and CONCEPTUALISM. Porphyry gave much more stress than Plotinus to will as the factor responsible for the 'fall' of the soul. Meanwhile Iamblichus expounded what he considered Pythagorean doctrines in a series of treatises (*Exhortation to Philosophy, Life of Pythagoras, General Mathematics* etc.), while his *Egyptian Mysteries* is a philosophico-allegorical interpretation of Egypt's rites and religious doctrines. He tended to subdivide the entities of the supra-sensible realm (e.g. he has two Ones,

two Minds) and later Neoplatonists carried such subdivisions still further. It is possible that he was the institutor of the neoplatonic mysteries, a blend of Greek and Oriental mystery religions.

The school of Pergamum, founded by Iamblichus' disciple Aidesios, was particularly interested in the practice of magic. Its best-known representative is the Emperor Julian the Apostate (born 332) who, in his attempts to stem the growth of Christianity, used Neoplatonism to provide polytheism with allegorico-philosophical interpretations, thus making it attractive to the educated, while permitting the rest to practise it according to tradition.

The main representatives of the later phase of the school of Plotinus were Proclus (410–85) and Damascius. The former, sometimes called Neoplatonism's schoolman, gave a particularly comprehensive and systematic presentation of Neoplatonism in two works, *Elements of Theology* and *The Theology of Plato*. In his writings some tensions inherent in Neoplatonism come to light. Though he derives everything from the One, he also acknowledges two principles (ultimately Pythagorean and Platonic), namely, the Limit and the Unlimited, both of which he considered to be some way present in the One. In addition, he assumes the existence of a plurality of Ones, identifying them with gods. And he explicitly derives matter from the One. He attached great importance to the 'triadic' principle according to which everything remains, in one aspect, in that from which it emanated, in another is turned away from it, and in a third turns back to it. His hymns are remarkable documents of neoplatonic religiosity. An unknown author pretending to be St Paul's disciple Dionysius the Areopagite (and therefore enjoying great authority), compiled a series of writings – for example, *Divine Names* and *Mystical Theology* – combining Proclus with Christianity. They are particularly well known as representing 'negative theology'. As for Damascius, he was head of the Academy when it was closed, and presents the consummation of a latent tendency of Neoplatonism by declaring all rational knowledge to be merely parabolic so that no aspect of reality is accessible to it.

The Neoplatonism of the school of Alexandria is comparatively simple – in some respects closer to Middle Platonism than to Plotinus – and a number of its members accepted Christianity, whereas the school of Athens remained to the very last one of the strongholds of polytheism. Hypatia (murdered by Christian fanatics) and her pupil Bishop Synesius are among its representatives.

Despite the anti-Christian attitude of many Neoplatonists, Neoplatonism always had a great attraction for Christian philosophers and – after the Arabs discovered and assimilated Greek philosophy – for thinkers within the orbit of Islam and Judaism. This is natural, considering Neoplatonism's sympathy for religion in general, the loftiness of its concept of the divine, its assumption that the supra-sensible is more real than the sensible, and its asceticism. But it is also paradoxical: Christianity is a strictly historical religion (as are Judaism and Islam): the Incarnation is an event in time, and wholly contingent, whereas Neoplatonism, true to its Hellenic heritage, is a rational system, presenting the universe as a giant SYLLOGISM with one event following from another in a timeless manner. In spite of this fundamental difference, Christian thinkers – perhaps unwilling to accept the contingent, historical character of Christianity – have time and again tried to express Christian doctrines in terms of Neoplatonism. See also AUGUSTINE, CAMBRIDGE PLATONISTS, CUDWORTH, ERIGENA.   (P.M.)

Neo-Thomism   The scholastic philosophy which had its origin in the Middle Ages gradually faded out in the course of the seventeenth and eighteenth centuries on account of its failure to maintain contact with the development of the experimental sciences and the new approach to the theory of knowledge. Since the later scholastics had failed, it was assumed that their medieval predecessors were equally unworthy of attention. But the incapacity of modern philosophy to evolve a realistic metaphysic eventually aroused the suspicion that it might be useful to re-examine the thinkers of the creative period of medieval philosophy, especially AQUINAS.

The pioneer of this Thomistic revival was an obscure seminary lecturer at Piacenza, Vincento Buzetti (1777–1824). Among his students were the brothers Domenico and Serafino Sordi (1790–1880, 1793–1865). Both became Jesuits and tried, at first with little success, to influence members of their order in the direction of Aquinas. In the end, however, they won over a few thinkers of some prominence in Italy, Luigi Taparelli d'Azeglio (1793–1862), Matteo Liberatore (1810–92) and Giovanni Maria Cornoldi (1822–92), together with the German Joseph Kleutgen (1811–83). These, along with Gaetano Sanseverino (1811–65) at Naples and the Dominican Tommaso Zigliara (1833–93), made the movement known. Another supporter was Giusepppe Pecci (1807–90), whose brother Giocchino became Pope Leo XIII and lent official support to the revival of Thomism.

What was required to make the revival effective was both an intensive study of medieval thought and a practical demonstration that it was relevant to contemporary philosophical problems. In Italy and Spain Neo-Thomism tended to remain a clerical preserve, but the Institut Supérieur de Philosophie at Louvain, founded in 1889 under Désiré Mercier (1851–1926), became the most powerful centre of a progressive Thomism, followed by scholars like Martin Grabmann in Germany and MARITAIN and GILSON in France.

Neo-Thomists claim that the central tradition of Greek thought had its legitimate development in the theism of the medieval Aristotelians, and that this tradition has not been made obsolete by modern philosophy. They have therefore sought to produce a theory of knowledge which will answer questions which have arisen from DESCARTES onwards, and to show that Aristotelian and Thomistic metaphysics harmonizes with modern science. Amongst the most notable efforts to fulfil these requirements are Gilson's *Being and Some Philosophers* and *The Unity of Philosophical Experience*; but it is evident that Neo-Thomism has not yet attained the results for which its originators hoped.

(D.J.B.H.)

Neurath, Otto (1882–1945) Otto Neurath was a positivist philosopher, a Marxist sociologist, and an inventor. After studies in Vienna and Berlin, he became a member of the short-lived socialist administration in Bavaria, before escaping to Vienna where he directed a museum. He believed that the struggle for a unified, materialist science would promote social as well as theoretical progress, and became an active member of the VIENNA CIRCLE. But he dissented from the reductive phenomenalism of most of his colleagues (notably CARNAP), insisting in 1931 that scientific verification appeals to 'the totality of existing statements' rather than to particular

facts of experience. 'There is no way of making pure perceptual statements the starting point of the sciences', he wrote in the positivist periodical *Erkenntnis* in 1932–3; and 'there is no *tabula rasa*'. In a comment later adopted as a motto by QUINE, he added: 'we are like sailors who have to repair their boat on the open sea, without any chance of taking it into dock to dismantle it and build it again from scratch'. During the 1930s Neurath began to devise a system of visual communication known as Isotype, and the international system of road and hotel signs established in the second half of the twentieth century is only one of his lasting legacies.   {J.R.}

Newton, Isaac (1642–1727) Isaac Newton was still a student at Cambridge when his prodigious mathematical talent was noted. He became Professor of Mathematics there in 1667, and was elected to the Royal Society four years later on the strength of his small but powerful reflecting telescope. He became dreamy and sociophobic, but in 1684 he was persuaded to commit his main ideas to paper for the benefit of posterity. Within 18 months he had completed the *Philosophiae Naturalis Principia Mathematica* (1687), which quickly won recognition far beyond the small circle of readers who could understand its mathematics and its Latin. Its most splendid achievement was the postulation of a universal force of 'attraction' which explained, with mathematical exactness, both the heaviness of earthly bodies and the movements of the planets. Philosophers of a sceptical inclination were quick to note, however, that attraction itself remained an occult mystery for Newton: he himself concluded the *Principia* by noting that its causes were unknown, adding enigmatically 'I frame no hypotheses', and insisting that the order and variety of nature pointed to the inscrutable 'counsel and dominion of an intelligent and powerful Being'. In the second half of his life, Newton led the life of a prosperous and fashionable London gentleman, becoming President of the Royal Society in 1703 and ruling it tyrannically until his death. Apart from a popular work on *Opticks* (1704) he devoted the remainder of his intellectual energies to Biblical chronology and alchemy. {J.R.}

Nietzsche, Friedrich (1844–1900)

Friedrich Nietzsche was born in Röcken, Prussia. Amateur psychologists have often tried to 'explain' his ideas, but Sigmund Freud is said to have remarked that 'he had a more penetrating knowledge of himself than any other man who ever lived or was ever likely to live'. Freud also remarked that Nietzsche's 'premonitions and insights often agree in the most amazing manner with the laborious results of PSYCHOANALYSIS'.

Nietzsche was the son of a Protestant minister and the grandson of two. He studied classical philology and was appointed to a professorship at Basel, Switzerland, before he had completed a doctoral dissertation. The degree, a prerequisite for such a position, was conferred hurriedly, and Nietzsche went to Basel in 1869 and applied to become a Swiss subject. In the Franco–Prussian War of 1870–1 he served briefly as a medical orderly on the Prussian side before returning to Basel with shattered health. He formed a friendship with Richard Wagner (born like Nietzsche's father in 1813) but the composer treated Nietzsche mainly as a brilliant apostle and errand boy. When Nietzsche showed an independent mind, Wagner showed no interest. The inevitable break came when Wagner made his peace with the young German Empire, which Nietzsche loathed, and settled in Bayreuth where his anti-Semitism became as influential as his

music. Nietzsche had no sympathy for the idealization of 'the pure fool' in Wagner's *Parsifal*, which he considered an insincere obeisance to Christianity, and Wagner, a Francophobe, was so displeased by Nietzsche's enlightened, anti-romantic *Human, All-too-Human*, also published in 1878, with a dedication to Voltaire, that he refused to read it.

The following year, Nietzsche retired from his professorship for reasons of health, and for the next ten years he devoted himself entirely to writing. He lived modestly and in solitude in Switzerland and Italy, and every book represented a hard-won triumph over half-blind eyes, intense migraine headaches, and manifold physical agonies. His writings were ignored until Georg Brandes began to lecture on them in Copenhagen in 1888. In the following decade Nietzsche attained world-wide fame, without knowing it. For he suffered a mental and physical breakdown in January 1889, and remained insane until his death.

His first book, *The Birth of Tragedy* (1872) was ill-received by German scholars; but by 1912 F. M. Cornford hailed it as 'a work of profound imaginative insight which left the scholarship of a generation toiling in the rear' – an estimate shared by most later classicists. The book broke with the 'sweetness and light' conception of Greek culture and called attention to the 'Dionysian' element and the tragic outlook. Nietzsche published four equally unacademic essays, collected as 'Untimely Meditations' (the title alludes to DESCARTES), before he changed his style to write books of aphorisms, studded with psychological observations: *Human, All-too-Human* (1878, with two sequels, 1879 and 1880); *Dawn* (1881); and *The Gay Science* (1882; second edition with substantial additions, 1887). Nietzsche thought that his aphorisms, though lacking the gravity of the German academic style, were closer to the true scientific spirit and to the experimental method. He was struck by the apparent psychological importance of the striving for power and of fear, and in *Dawn* he tried to see how human behaviour could be explained in terms of these two concepts.

Eventually he came to the conclusion that Greek culture had been based on an unsentimentally competitive spirit and that 'the will to power' is the most basic human drive. What every human being – and, according to Nietzsche's next book, *Thus Spoke Zarathustra*, every living being – wants above everything else is a higher, more powerful state of being in which the manifold frustrations of our present state are overcome. It is only when we fail in our endeavour to perfect and recreate ourselves that we settle for crude physical power over others. Nietzsche's conception of 'will to power' cannot be understood apart from 'sublimation' – a word which he was the first to use in its modern sense. His anti-Christian polemics, which became more and more central in his later works, depend in part on his claim that Christianity 'demands not the control but the extirpation of the passions', and that it therefore 'made something unclean out of sexuality'. Still, Christianity too was an expression of the will to power – but only that of the weak and frustrated. Their resentment gave rise, he argues, to a pervasive antagonism to physical and intellectual excellence, a hatred of body and intellect, and a levelling predisposition in favour of everything low, and of a fictitious other world. In one of his last works, *The Antichrist*, in which his style has become shrill, and no attempt is made to offer judicious qualifications, he cites I Corinthians I to illustrate his claims: 'God has chosen the weak things of the world to ruin what is strong, and base things of the world…and what is nothing, to bring to naught what is something.' Here he finds an

outlook 'born of resentment and impotent vengefulness'. And he also cites Chapter 6, 'the saints shall judge the world' and 'we shall judge angels'. Here he finds a will to power that has run amuck.

His critics may feel that it is Nietzsche who ran amuck; but they have generally misunderstood him because they overlooked the fact that he did not find in Christianity what they find in it. He associated Christianity with resentment and the hope for boundless power in another world from which, according to some of the greatest Christians, the blessed will behold the torments of those who got the best things in this world.

Nietzsche was not only a moralist but also a moral philosopher. His view of traditional ethics might be summed up in the words which F. H. BRADLEY used to characterize metaphysics: 'the finding of bad reasons for what we believe on instinct'. But Nietzsche did not believe that moral idiosyncrasies were literally instinctive. On the contrary, he was struck by the great variety of moral views in different times and places; and derided the philosophers' conceit 'that they have long known what is good and evil for man'. His views on this subject are best cited from *Beyond Good and Evil* (1886), especially sections 186 and 260: 'With a stiff seriousness that inspires laughter, all our philosophers… wanted to supply a *rational foundation* for morals; and every philosopher so far has believed that he had provided such a foundation. Morality itself, however, was accepted as "given".' Moral philosophers had always been parochial and myopic: 'poorly informed, and not even very curious about different peoples, ages, and the past, they never laid eyes on the real problems of morality; for these emerge only when we compare *many* moralities'.

Nietzsche divides moralities into 'two basic types' – master morality and slave morality – arguing that every moral code originated 'either among a ruling group whose consciousness of their difference from the ruled group was accompanied by delight, or among the ruled group, the slaves'. The first type of morality is rooted in self-affirmation: the noble people call themselves 'good' and the rest 'bad', but they also 'help the unfortunate, though not…out of pity, but more from an urge begotten by the excess of power'. Nietzsche's 'masters' resemble ARISTOTLE's 'great-souled man', feeling, in Aristotle's words, that 'it is vulgar to lord it over humble people'. Indeed it was Aristotle's ethics that helped convince Nietzsche that modern bourgeois morality is not the whole of morality, and also that Christianity represented the 'revaluation of all the values of antiquity'. Our prevalent morality, though different philosophers have sought to supply it with 'rational foundations', is one of many mixed types, and profoundly inconsistent.

The first of the three essays that comprise Nietzsche's next book, *Toward a Genealogy of Morals* (1887), bears the title: 'Good and Evil versus Good and Bad'. It deals at length with slave morality, which, according to Nietzsche, is rooted in the contrast between good and evil, and in resentment – 'the resentment of those who are denied the real reaction of the deed, and who compensate with imaginary revenge'. The slave's preoccupation is not self-affirmation but the evil of others – an evil 'from which he then derives, as an after-image and counter-instance, a "good one" – himself'. Only the strong and noble can rise above resentment and really love their enemies: 'how much respect has a noble person for his enemies! – And such respect is already a bridge to love'. The move 'beyond good and evil' does not take us beyond good and bad; it simply means, in the

words of *Zarathustra*, being '*delivered from revenge*'. In one of his last works, *Twilight of the Idols*, Nietzsche leaves no doubt that he does not by any means accept master morality as whole, and in the final analysis he finds both types of morality 'entirely worthy of each other'.

As to morality as a whole, Nietzsche makes two points. The first is that 'every morality is…a bit of tyranny against 'nature', and against 'reason'; but this in itself is no objection'. Some discipline and constraint is the prerequisite of all those achievements that make 'life on earth is worthwhile: for example, virtue, art, music, dance, reason, spirituality'. The second is that a morality is a prescription for living with one's passions. Nietzsche tries to show this in the cases of STOICISM, SPINOZA, Aristotle, and Goethe, and claims that moralities are 'baroque and unreasonable in form – because they are addressed to "all" and generalize where generalizations are impermissible'. It would be folly for St Francis to try to live like Goethe, or vice versa. Nietzsche finds the greatest power in those who can sublimate and control their passions, employing them creatively. The libertine, who lacks self-control, has less power; and the ascetic, who cannot master his passions short of extirpating them, strikes Nietzsche as weaker than figures like Socrates or Goethe.

Although religion and ethics were Nietzsche's primary interests, he also ventured into epistemology, making many fruitful suggestions without ever working out any theory. He also has a twofold importance for metaphysics. First, he argued that this world is the only one, offering a psychological analysis of belief in another world and, especially in *Twilight of the Idols*, criticizing metaphysical conceptions of mind, consciousness, ego and will. Second, he offered a metaphysic of his own by suggesting, especially in *Zarathustra*, that 'the will to power' is the ultimate reality. His psychological explanations can probably be reconciled with his critique of metaphysical conceptions, but his reification and cosmic projection of the will to power seems clearly inconsistent with his own central intentions. It appears as a misguided attempt to outdo SCHOPENHAUER, whom the young Nietzsche had admired. Nietzsche's doctrine of the eternal recurrence of the same events at gigantic intervals, finally, has struck practically everyone as merely bizarre. But it was not intended as a metaphysical theory: Nietzsche was under the mistaken impression that modern science entails such a view. He thought that for most of us, nothing could be more depressing than the prospect of eternal return, whereas the 'overman' (*Übermensch*) – the one who has become a creator rather than a creature – would welcome it and say, unlike Goethe's Faust: 'abide, moment – and if you cannot abide, at least return'.

(W.K.)

Nominalism Nominalism is the theory that the objects of thought are simply words and that there is no more to the meaning of a general term than the set of things to which it applies. At its most modest, nominalism holds that there is no independently accessible thing, UNIVERSAL or concept, which constitutes the meaning of a word. The only way to find out the meaning of a word is to see what things it is applied to. To say that the meaning is this class of things, the word's extension, is to go further and seems to entail that we never really know the meaning of any general word since many words with the same extension differ in meaning (e.g. *man* and *featherless biped*). A more traditional version of nominalism contends that there is nothing more in common to the things a general term applies to than

the fact that it applies to them. But to say this, it is argued, makes classification arbitrary and cannot explain why it is that people have made the classifications they have or how it is that they all make the same classifications. In practice, therefore, most nominalists follow HOBBES in holding that the things a general term applies to are related by resemblance. But this similarity theory, it is often claimed, is only a disguised form of REALISM, since resemblance is itself universal. Nominalism was one of the possibilities envisaged in the work which posed the problem of universals for medieval philosophy: PORPHYRY's celebrated commentary on ARISTOTLE's *Categories*. Roscellinus believed that only individual sensible things were real, and took the doctrine of the Trinity to be an assertion of the existence of three gods, while Berengar of Tours, on similar grounds, rejected transubstantiation. Many analytic philosophers followed Hobbes in upholding the similarity theory, but RUSSELL remained faithful to realism; see also GOODMAN.

(A.Q.)

Nozick, Robert (1938–2002) American philosopher born in New York, and author of *Anarchy, State and Utopia* (1974) – a work of POLITICAL PHILOSOPHY which argues (against RAWLS in particular) for an 'entitlement theory' of justice based on the primacy of individual rights. Acknowledging that this 'libertarian' conclusion is 'apparently callous toward the needs and suffering of others', Nozick nevertheless holds that anything more than a 'minimal state' is morally wrong. 'The state', he says, 'may not use its coercive apparatus for the purpose of getting some citizens to aid others, or in order to prohibit activities to people for their own good or protection'. This minimal state – 'the only morally justifiable one'– is also,

Nozick claims, 'the one that best realizes the utopian aspirations of untold dreamers and visionaries'. Nozick had a horror of repeating himself, and instead of getting drawn into the controversy provoked by his first book, he took up a range of different issues in a series of works displaying great brilliance and an extraordinary, lunar detachment, even in the face of the fatal illness that dogged the last years of his life: see in particular *Philosophical Explanations* (1981); *The Examined Life* (1989). *The Nature of Rationality* (1995); *Socratic Puzzles* (1997); and *Invariances: The Structure of the Objective World* (2001). See also LIBERALISM AND COMMUNITARIANISM.

[J.R.]

O

Occasionalism For DESCARTES a human being was the point of union of material substance and immaterial substance, and he proposed a curious mechanism by which these two disparate sub-stances could act on each other in the pineal gland at the base of the brain. Even his most devoted followers found this suggestion unacceptable, and it was in order to provide a better explanation of this interaction that the theory of Occasionalism was developed, particularly by Arnold Geulincz (1624–69). The chains of cause and effect were supposed to be complete and independent in both mind and body, since it was clear that modifications of an immaterial substance could be neither the causes nor the effects of modifications of material substance. The correlation between the run of events in the one substance and the run of events in the other was attributed to the intervention of God. Since doing something involves knowing how to do it, material bodies, knowing nothing, cannot act at all; their apparent action upon each other is the act of God. Hence there was no problem of psycho-physical causation, since the occurrence of an event in the mind merely provided the Occasion for a Divine Act in the body, and vice versa.   (R.HAR.)

Ockham   See WILLIAM OF OCKHAM.

Ontological Argument   The argument that, since God is conceivable as a necessary existent, God exists. See ANSELM, DESCARTES, LEIBNIZ, KANT, THEISM.

Ontology   Ontology is theory as to what exists, or inquiry into the nature of being.

P

Pantheism Pantheism, or the doctrine that everything is divine, and that God and Nature are identical, is more often an instrument of poetic expression than a conclusion of philosophical argument. The great exception here is SPINOZA. Spinoza's initial definition of substance inexorably leads to the conclusion that there can only be one substance, truly so-called, and that it must be infinite. For there could be nothing other than itself to limit it and so constitute it finite. Spinoza's definition of God, which follows the traditional definitions, makes God the possessor of infinite attributes. But the only being of infinite attributes is the one substance, which is Nature. Hence God and Nature must be identical. The history of Spinoza's reputation illustrates the knife-edge along which the pantheist walks. From the standpoint of the theist, a pantheist appears to reduce God to Nature, and is thus essentially an atheist. From the standpoint of the Sceptic, the pantheist takes an unwarrantedly religious view of Nature, and appears as a covert theist. All metaphysical doctrines, such as IDEALISM, which assert that the Universe is a Unity tend towards pantheism. For the Universe is then something more than any of its finite parts; and there can be no deity distinct from it. It may be surmised that the collapse of such metaphysical doctrines deprives intellectual pantheism of its only support.   (A.MACI.)

Parmenides Greek philosopher from Elea in Southern Italy, born about 515 BC. He wrote a philosophical poem consisting of a prologue and two parts, of which considerable fragments have survived. The prologue describes Parmenides' meeting with a goddess who reveals the truth outlined in the first part of the poem; of the two possible paths of inquiry, *It is* and *It is not*, only the first is tenable – 'for you could not know what *is not* (for this is impossible), nor could you give expression to it'. Thus Parmenides recognized the existential 'is not' as an artificial concept, but was then misled – by his inability to distinguish the existential and predicative 'is' – into denying that negative predication was possible. This seemed to entail that there could be no differentiation in the real world (since if A can be distinguished from B then A *is not* B, which was, by Parmenides' logic, impossible). Thus reality, 'that which is', had to be single, homogeneous, indivisible, everlasting and motionless. Being itself was spatially finite, 'like the mass of a well-rounded sphere'. Some of Parmenides' arguments against not-being were perhaps directed against PYTHAGOREAN dualism. But he himself, in the fragmentary second part of his poem, which professedly gave 'the opinions of mortals' and was 'deceitful', outlined a cosmology in which the world was composed of two opposed substances or 'forms', fire and night. What was evidently quite an elaborate account included explanations of thought and knowledge (produced by the excess of one opposite, the hot or the cold, in the limbs), and astronomy, which had points in common with ANAXIMANDER. The purpose of this 'Way of Seeming' is obscure. Perhaps Parmenides felt that his conception of Being was too austere for practical life and ordinary people, and wished to show that the apparent world could be accounted for on the basis of a single pair of sensible opposites, without introducing so-called reality-principles like the 'Limit' and 'Unlimited' of the Pythagoreans. (G.S.K.)

Pascal, Blaise (1623–62) French mathematician, scientist and theologian, and one of the earliest great French prose writers. His earlier years were devoted to mathematics and the physical sciences; his experiments with the barometer are famous, the ascent of the Puy de Dôme by his brother at his direction being a decisive confirmation of the new theory of air pressure. In 1654 Pascal underwent a profound experience of religious conversion; he became a strong adherent of the Jansenists and much of his energy was henceforth devoted to theological and religious propaganda and controversy. He continued however to work occasionally at mathematics, doing work on the theory of the cycloid preparatory to the theory of the calculus, and laying the basis of the mathematical theory of PROBABILITY. Pascal's posthumously published *Pensées* cover a range of philosophical issues; most notably he argues for the reasonableness of faith on the ground that there are no rational grounds either for belief or disbelief and so belief is not less reasonable than disbelief; but this being so it is wiser to gamble on the truth of religion since this policy involves success if religion is true and no significant loss if it is false. The section on geometry also has some wise and clear remarks on definition and the nature of deductive systems. (J.O.U.)

Peano, Giuseppe (1858–1932) Italian mathematician who pioneered the project of reducing MATHEMATICS to LOGIC.

Pearson, Karl (1857–36) English scientist, supporter of an austere positivism and authoritarian socialism, and author of *The Grammar of Science* (1892).

Peirce, Charles Sanders (1839–1914) C. S. Peirce was born in Cambridge, Massachusetts, son of America's leading mathematician Benjamin Peirce. Much of his early formation was scientific; he came to philosophy through reading Friedrich SCHILLER and was later enthralled by KANT. He associated with most of the leading American thinkers of his day – including JAMES, Wright and Holmes – but obtained little academic recognition and was never appointed to a permanent university post. He spent most of the latter part of his life almost as a recluse and died in comparative poverty in 1914. He published a number of articles but no book on philosophy. Much of his best work remained unpublished until the appearance of the *Collected Papers of C.S. Peirce* (8 vols, 1931–58).

1 *Epistemology.* The central problem in modern EPISTEMOLOGY has been to reconcile the subjective nature of thought with our claim to know things distinct from thought. This had not been a problem for ARISTOTLE, who considered that the mind simply discovered an order in reality. But Kant inverted Aristotle's position and claimed that the order in our knowledge came from the mind. Peirce accepted the modern problem and offered his own solution.

He began by maintaining that we are conscious that we have direct experience of the real – that is, of things that exist whether we think about them or not. Moreover, if we are to avoid unpleasant surprises, we must endeavour to adapt our conduct to these things. So far he agrees with Aristotle. But it is clear that we deal with things according to our ideas of them – on selective constructions which are based on partial experience coloured by our history, circumstances and purposes. The selective nature of knowledge led Peirce to agree with Kant that the order in knowledge is to some extent constructed by the mind. He next set about showing that if we examine what an idea or concept is we should be able to reconcile what is true in Aristotle and Kant.

In reply to the question, 'what is a concept?', Peirce formulated in 1878 his famous PRAGMATIC maxim: 'Consider what effects, which might conceivably have practical bearings, we conceive the object of our conception to have. Then, our conception of these effects is the whole of our conception of the object.' He illustrates the maxim by saying that our idea of 'wine' means nothing 'but what has certain effects, direct or indirect, upon our senses'. So too, if we call a thing 'hard', we mean that 'it will not be scratched by many other substances'. He summed up: 'Our idea of anything is our idea of its sensible effects.' Peirce offers his maxim as an instrument for distinguishing true knowledge from false. True knowledge – a correct idea of an object – enables us to predict what will happen when we come to deal with that object. In fact for Peirce all our ideas are analogous to scientific hypotheses.

Peirce's 1878 formulation of the maxim contained in germ his later views. But it was formulated for explaining our ideas of material things, and seemed to leave no place for regulative ideas such as moral goodness. Furthermore, William James and the popular pragmatists took the maxim in a phenomenalist sense. In later years Peirce insisted that pragmatism (or 'pragmaticism' as he called his doctrine, to distinguish it from that of James and others) teaches that an idea has meaning through any possible practical

conduct that it can lead to or regulate. It does not have to lead to immediate sensory verification; it need only give meaning to our conduct in some way – like the notion of truth as an ideal – limit, which has no direct sensory content, but inspires us to keep adding to our knowledge. Peirce completed his theory by saying that each idea gives rise to a possibility of regular conduct in regard to what it expresses. Hence each idea is finally interpreted in a 'habit', and these habits – the interpretants of our ideas – are 'guides to action'. Our ideas find living and consistent expression in our habitual modes of conduct.

But any inquirer's knowledge of a given object or situation will always be inadequate, so it is not enough for a single individual to apply the maxim. A research community gathers more knowledge than any single individual and works to overcome mistakes in individual verification. Knowledge is pooled and correction is a cooperative affair. But the community may itself be wrong, and every inquirer has to envisage their research within the indefinitely continuing, constantly growing company of inquirers. Searchers after truth are always on their way towards a state of perfect knowledge; but they will never reach it.

The need for honesty in scrutinizing one's data, integrity in cooperating with others, and a genuine love of truth, led Peirce to believe that the struggle for truth is not only intellectual, but moral. The work of forming concepts, drawing consequences, and verifying them must be carried out in a self-disciplined and cooperative way within the community of seekers and against the background of the social ideal-limit of truth.

2 Categories. Like Aristotle, Peirce wanted to classify the main aspects of reality through a doctrine of CATEGORIES.

But where Aristotle's categories had been objectivist, Peirce believed that categories should express aspects of the world in terms of our direct perceptive experience. He formulated three such categories: Firstness, Secondness, and Thirdness. (a) Firstness is the spontaneous aspect of things, exemplified especially in the free surge of the mind in the formation of hypotheses: it indicates life, growth and variety in the universe. Any instance of Firstness, such as an act of immediate consciousness before it is reflected on, is an undifferentiated unity; but otherness and the struggle it leads to are also inescapable facts of experience – hence the next category. (b) Secondness points to the element of resistance and duality in experience – to 'existence', or 'that mode of being which lies in opposition to another'. For Peirce, 'a thing without oppositions *ipso facto* does not exist', and existence is not a predicate but something that is experienced when our willing and perceiving come up against the 'brute' aspect of the world and the sheer individuality of things. But spontaneity and opposition do not exhaust our experience of reality–there is also continuity or regularity, or Thirdness. (c) Thirdness, according to Peirce, is 'Law'. We can reflect on an idea like 'wine' or 'hard' and see that it applies to many things; this shows that there is regularity in the real, and this is the foundation of law. 'Law' or 'general principles' are 'active' in things, and the uniformities we discover in the real order have meaning for us only insofar as we can act regularly in their regard; hence we can conceive the laws of the universe as analogous to our own habits of action.

3 *God, self and immortality.* Peirce accepted as a philosophical hypothesis the idea of a personal and omnipotent God, and outlined several arguments for the reality of such a Being. (a) The living variety of the universe and the spontaneity that finds its highest expression in human personality enables us to perceive an infinite Spontaneity or Firstness at the source of all instances of Firstness. (b) It is clear that an order of dynamic finality exists in the world – exemplified in the manner in which the human mind is adapted to interpreting and predicting the course of nature through the hypotheses of science. The only explanation of this mutual adaptation of parts of the world is that an absolute Mind has presided over their creation and development. (c) When we reflect on the hypothesis of God as the creative source of the universe, we are gradually impelled to accept it: an instinctive belief in God fits every movement of our nature. Peirce concluded that God is unlimited in knowledge and power, and if we are forced to conceive him to some extent in the human image, such anthropomorphism is not so much false as figurative.

Peirce laid such stress on the connexions that each ego has with others and the rest of the universe that some passages suggest that he rejected the Cartesian unitary self. He also insisted that we have to interpret our own thoughts: they are as much signs to us as are the words of other people and the things of the universe. But where other pragmatists sought to reduce human personality to a 'bundle of habits', he argued that 'unity must be given as a centre for habits'. About immortality, Peirce never made up his mind. Early in his career he argued that the inability of MATERIALISM to explain much of the universe counted in its favour, while the dependence of the mind on the body counted against. As the years went on he laid more stress on the spiritual aspects of the universe as evidence for personal immortality, but stopped short of saying that such evidence was conclusive.

Peirce exercised little real influence during his life. William James popularized a form of pragmatism derived largely from a misunderstanding of Peirce's pragmatic principle and his insistence on moral effort in the search for truth. ROYCE's theory of the social infinite owes a lot to Peirce's teaching on the community of inquirers but Peirce dismissed Royce's logic. DEWEY took over some of the empirical emphases in Peirce's methodology. But by and large Peirce's general philosophy made no impact until the publication of the *Collected Papers*. See also AMERICAN PHILOSOPHY.   (J.O'C.)

Peripatetic 'Peripatetic' is an ancient nickname for ARISTOTLE and his followers, based on the tradition that when they discussed philosophy they walked as they talked.

Personal   Identity   In   PLATO's *Symposium*, the wise Diotima raises the question how any of us can be said to continue in existence from infancy to old age, when both body and soul are bound to change out of all recognition. If the successive episodes in a life are like beads, what is the thread that strings them all together? Her answer is that such continuity is guaranteed only for the Gods, and that the rest of us can only approximate to it, partly by working to sustain our physical and intellectual fitness, and partly by having lots of children. Socrates is more puzzled than satisfied with Diotima's solution, but the question was left in suspense in the high philosophical tradition for nearly two millennia; it seems to have been generally assumed that the basic subject of experience was a SUBSTANCE – either spiritual or material or some kind of combination of the two, perhaps the 'substantial form' of the Aristotelians (see AQUINAS). In the seventeenth century, however, the concept of substance began

to come under pressure. In the *Essay concerning human understanding* (1689), Locke insisted that complex IDEAS could only be understood if they were broken down into simple elements drawn directly from experience, and ideas of substances began to appear far more fragile, problematic and artificial than they had ever seemed before. But Locke had an implicit belief in immortality, and in a God who would issue eternal rewards and punishments adjusted to how we have conducted ourselves in this life. He realized that this belief would be quite empty if our afterlife were not in some sense a continuation of our earthly existence: otherwise we might just as well be annihilated on our death and replaced with someone completely different. Locke's proposal was that the continuity that mattered for moral and theological purposes depended not on substances but on relations, specifically relations of 'sameness' (or 'identity', to use the scholastic word). Moreover the subject of these relations was essentially a moral agent (or 'person', to use another scholastic word). That was how, in Section I of Book II of the *Essay*, the notion of 'personal identity' first saw the light of day. Locke argued that the relations that underlay it were not a matter of substantial permanence, but a combination of 'consciousness', or an intimate interior knowledge of one's own past experience, and 'concernment', or an intimate involvement with one's future prospects: 'for if we take wholly away all Consciousness of our Actions and Sensations, especially of Pleasure and Pain, and the concernment that accompanies it, it will be hard to know wherein to place personal Identity.'

This doctrine, barely sketched in the first edition of the *Essay*, was elaborated in the second (1694), where Locke asserted boldly that the boundaries of a 'personal self' coincide with those of consciousness. Moral responsibility for past deeds extends 'as far as that consciousness reaches, and no farther; as everyone who reflects will perceive'. The 'self' in short was a product of consciousness as much as its object; and it was only through consciousness that it could 'appropriate' past deeds and make them its own. The doctrine that our memories define who we are is a hard one, and perhaps irredeemably paradoxical: how after all can we identify our memories as ours unless we are already able to identify ourselves as ourselves? In the *Treatise of Human Nature* (1739–40) David HUME revelled in the difficulties, suggesting that personal identity is an illusion or a 'fiction', and citing the absurdities it gives rise to as a further incentive to general philosophical SCEPTICISM. During the nineteenth century, however, the dissemination of Locke's argument led to a change in the meaning of 'personal identity', and eventually of 'identity' itself: the words no longer referred to a supposed principle of permanence behind the jumbled confusion of experience, but to people's subjective memories and their conscious sense of who they were, or indeed of which group they belonged to. This shift in meaning gave rise to 'identity politics', and obscured the historical and conceptual origins of the problem of personal identity.   {J.R.}

Peter Lombard (c.1095–c.1160) Author of a compilation of theological wisdom known as the *Sentences*, which became one of the most popular textbooks for philosophical instruction in medieval Universities; see also BONAVENTURA, SCOTUS.

Peter of Spain Petrus Hispanus, also known as Peter of Spain, lived in the thirteenth century, and is now generally identified with Petrus Juliani who was born *c.*1210 in Lisbon, studied at Paris, and was elected to the Papacy as John XXI in 1276, dying in 1277 owing to the collapse of a study which he had had built. His *Summulae Logicales*, with its new method of describing the SYLLOGISM, remained a fundamental logical text till the seventeenth century.   (I.T.)

Phenomenalism Phenomenalism is the doctrine that human knowledge is confined to the appearances (phenomena) presented to the senses or, less restrictively, that appearances are the ultimate foundation of all our knowledge. It takes two main forms: first a general theory of knowledge and second a theory of perception.

(1) As a general theory of knowledge, phenomenalism states that we can know nothing that is not given to us in sense-experience; hence it denies, with more or less thoroughness, the validity of inferences made from things that fall within our sense-experience to things lying outside it. One version, sometimes called gnosticism, asserts that, although we cannot infer the character of what lies outside our sense-experience, we can at least infer that there is something outside it. KANT's Thing-in-itself, HAMILTON's Unconditioned and SPENCER's Unknowable are outcomes of this line of thought. Some philosophers, understandably reluctant to suppose that we can know that there is something that lies beyond the bounds of possible knowledge, maintain that nothing at all exists beyond the appearances presented to our senses. This view, sometimes called sensationalism, is roughly exemplified by the doctrines of HUME, J. S. MILL and RUSSELL, although both Hume and Mill were dissatisfied with their attempts to explain the observing mind that is the subject of sense-experience in terms of the appearances presented to it. To describe phenomenalism, as

is often done, as the view that we do not know things as they really are but only as they appear to us, is misleading. By implying that there are things over and above the appearances presented to us, it begs the question in favour of agnosticism.

(2) In its usual modern form, as a theory of perception, phenomenalism was first clearly expounded by J. S. Mill in 1865 and his compact formula – that a material thing is a permanent possibility of sensation – is as good as any. Much the same point is conveyed by Russell's remark that the thing is the class of its appearances. Later phenomenalists preferred to state their doctrine in a linguistic, instead of an ontological, idiom. Material-object statements, they said, are reducible to or translatable into statements about SENSE-DATA, and the entire content of our beliefs about material things can be expressed in terms of what is immediately given in sense-experience. The usual argument for this conclusion starts from the straightforward consideration that everything we know by perception must be either inferred or uninferred. Now unless some of it is uninferred we are landed with an infinite regress. This inescapably uninferred perceptual knowledge, it is widely agreed, is knowledge of appearances, that is of sense-data. So much is common ground to many theories of perception. The characteristic phenomenalist contention at this point is that there can be no valid inference from appearances to the existence of transcendental things – to things, in other words, that do not appear to us and of which we therefore have no direct knowledge. What reason could we have for believing that there now exists something unobserved that stands in a certain relation, that of being its cause for example, to what we are now observing? Only that we have in the past actually observed such things

regularly standing in that relation to sense-data like our present ones. It is, of course, logically impossible that we should have such evidence for things transcending sense-experience since these are unobservable by definition.

Phenomenalists are not, however, solipsists. They do not believe that there is nothing we can know to exist apart from our own sense-experiences. But, while not rejecting all inference from sense-data, they will only countenance inference to things that could in principle be experienced. The permitted variety of inference is simple extrapolation to what are variously called 'possible sensations' (Mill), 'sensibilia' (Russell) and 'hypothetical sense-data'. Our actual experience displays enough regularity for us to establish laws of correlation between experiences of different kinds. When some part of one of these regular patterns is presented to us we can reasonably understand that the rest of the pattern is available if we modify the conditions of observation appropriately (e.g. by stretching out our hands or opening our eyes). Our experience, though fragmentary, is orderly enough to enable us to construct from it a material world that is, in Hume's phrase, 'continuous and distinct'. There is some disagreement about the way in which this conclusion should be expressed. Russell speaks of 'sensibilia', actual entities just like sense-data except that no observer is aware of them. Others, feeling that there is still a faint whiff of the transcendent, even of the self-contradictory, about this, prefer to say that what we infer is the truth of hypothetical propositions.

There are three main lines of objection to this theory. First, it is argued that the phenomenalist translation could never, even in principle, be carried out, either because we lack the verbal means to effect it or because the appearances associated with a given material object are infinitely numerous and complex. Second, it is said that the translation is spurious since the antecedent clauses of the hypothetical statements making up the translation must themselves mention material objects, for example, the bodies and especially the sense-organs of observers, and the physical conditions of observation. Third, a lot of discomfort has been felt, even by philosophers well disposed to phenomenalism such as H. H. PRICE, about the fact that unobserved material things, which are only clusters of possibilities according to the theory, exert a causal influence. How can the collection of possible sense-data, which is all the water at the bottom of a well consists of, manage to emit an actual noise when an unobserved, and so equally hypothetical, stone strikes it? A more fundamental line of objection starts further back by attacking the presumption shared by phenomenalists with many other theorists of knowledge, that the only immediate objects of perception are sense-data.

Phenomenalism has close affinities with the theory of perception put forward by BERKELEY, who at one point, indeed, explicitly propounds phenomenalism but fails to follow it up. What we infer, in his view, is not possible experiences of our own but actual, and pretty transcendent-looking, experiences of God's. Mill could be said to have derived his phenomenalism from Hume's account of perception by making one crucial change: what Hume regarded as an imaginative fiction Mill saw as a legitimate intellectual construction. With his theory of sensibilia, Russell was never a complete phenomenalist, and Price was led by the argument about the causal efficacy of clusters of mere possibilities to augment his families of sense-data with ghostly relics of

Lockean substance called Physical Occupants. A far more thorough and unwavering phenomenalist was AYER.

Phenomenalist theories of mind (which see the mind as simply a related cluster of actual experiences) have been advanced with more or less conviction and enthusiasm by Hume, Mill, Russell and Ayer. MACH and PEARSON expounded a phenomenalist philosophy of science which gives an attractively hard-headed account of the theoretical entities of natural science (electrons, viruses etc.). In CARNAP's *Logical Structure of the World* a completely generalized phenomenalism is worked out in impressive formal detail in which our entire conceptual apparatus is decomposed into its ultimate phenomenal constituents.   (A.Q.)

Phenomenology   In its broadest meaning, 'Phenomenology' signifies a descriptive philosophy of experience. The name of HUSSERL is most closely associated with this term in twentieth century thought. (C. S. PEIRCE defined a discipline of 'phaneroscopy' or 'phenomenology', but without reference to Husserl.) In his later years, Husserl evolved a 'philosophy of spirit', but he was hostile to speculative philosophy in his formative period, and his version of phenomenology is unrelated historically to Hegel's 'phenomenology of spirit'. The indebtedness of Husserl's phenomenology is nevertheless many-sided. The influence of BRENTANO, JAMES, the British empiricists, DESCARTES, LEIBNIZ and KANT is to be noted particularly.

Husserl developed his version of phenomenology slowly and painstakingly, hoping to extend the scope of the a priori to the entire field of experience. At first he defined phenomenology as 'descriptive psychology', but he clarified that definition by elaborating a 'TRANSCENDENTAL' phenomenology. From the beginning, phenomenology was committed to the ideal of the greatest possible freedom from presuppositions, which ruled out speculative constructions and all talk of a 'TRANSCENDENT' realm beyond possible experience. His slogan 'Back to the things themselves!' expresses this principle very well.

Kant indicated the general nature of the 'transcendental' when he explained it in terms of attending to the experiencing of an object, rather than to the object itself. The aim of phenomenology is to make this reflection as 'radical' as possible, proceeding to the sources of certainty or 'evidence' in immediate experience, and 'questioning' everything with regard to its evidence. To that end, a procedure of 'reduction' is instituted, requiring the suspension of all beliefs, and of scientific knowledge as well. Descartes' method of doubt serves as a convenient means of introducing the method of phenomenology. One could be mistaken in one's judgments about anything 'transcending' experience, but 'immanent' experiences concerning the world, or concerning any alleged or imagined objects, could not be doubted.

The aim of phenomenology, then, is to delimit the entire, endless realm of experiences, in all their diverse types – perception, phantasy, etc. All beliefs are suspended, and we are left with the experiences themselves, and with the objectivities meant by them. These two aspects – the meaning and the meant – are called the *noetic* and *noematic* sides of experience, and this 'correlative' or 'intentional' mode of viewing experience is essential to the procedure of phenomenology. With all beliefs placed in abeyance as a matter of method, one is left with 'pure subjectivity', or 'pure experience'. The world is not 'discarded' or denied, however: the 'thesis' of existence is simply 'put out of play' and the 'world' is regarded not as independently real but as the correlate of meaningful experience – it becomes a 'bracketed' world.

The 'reduction' to the stream of inner experiences means that one must begin with 'transcendental egology' – one's own individual experiences; but solipsism is avoided when other minds are 'exhibited' by means of 'empathy', 'appresentation', and 'apperception by analogy', based upon the resemblance of other bodies to one's own. The phenomenologist can then speak of 'transcendental intersubjectivity', and of the 'constitution' of the objective world.

The term 'constitution' is used to name the *constructive* programme of descriptive analysis which commences once 'purification' by 'reduction' is completed. The 'constitution' of the world within the frame of pure consciousness does not mean that it is made out of consciousness; but when all things are viewed as objects for experience, it is appropriate to speak of the synthetic and 'idealising' processes by which complex structures and meanings are 'constituted' out of the stream of experiences. Both meaning-giving (noetic) experiences and meant (noematic) objects fall within the scope of phenomenology.

Historically, phenomenology was created as a means of outflanking NATURALISM. In this respect it was in harmony with the dominant academic philosophies of its time, concerned as they were with circumscribing the methods of the sciences, and defending the traditional preserve of a spiritual philosophy of values. But the abiding justification of phenomenology lies in its descriptive findings. Its studies of time-consciousness, its 'origin-analyses' of the basic concepts of LOGIC, and analyses of perception and other modes of experience have greatly extended the range of our descriptive vision.

The subjective method of phenomenology should not be presumed to displace the objective empirical methods of the sciences. Like many other innovators, Husserl did not know when to stop, in his relentless drive towards a universal philosophy. At times, he revealed awareness of the limits of his achievements, as when he mused that he would never set foot on the 'promised land'. But phenomenology can still render an indispensable service by 'clarifying' the basic concepts of the sciences in terms of immediate experience, and making clear the contributions of the knower to experience.

The impact of phenomenological findings on psychology was impeded by misunderstandings on the part of some psychologists, and righteous indignation on the part of Husserl. His critique of psychology was intended to show the need for a 'rational psychology' which would do for naturalistic psychology what geometry did for physical science. The influence of phenomenology has been extensive, and to some extent it has borne fruit of a type quite uncongenial to Husserl. The broader phenomenological movement includes a prominent religious wing, and the 'intuition of essences' has been extended to include the non-rational, and has sometimes deteriorated to the level of banal descriptions of familiar objects of experience. Attempts have been made, with varying degrees of success, to develop phenomenological approaches to social science, history, art, mathematics, psychology, PSYCHOANALYSIS, and Marxism (see FRANKFURT SCHOOL), as well as logic and the philosophy of values. Husserl denounced the 'EXISTENTIALIST' movement (see BEAUVOIR, HEIDEGGER, MERLEAU-PONTY, SARTRE), despite its debts to phenomenology.

It is possible to formulate a strictly methodological version of phenomenology, with no ulterior commitments to idealism or any other dogma. The phenomenological procedure is then regarded as one method of inquiry alongside all the 'objective' methods – inductive, causal and explanatory. Although its findings may well be valuable for all other disciplines, it could have no subject-matter without the factual 'mother-ground' represented by the natural and cultural sciences. A strict phenomenology, freed from all pretence to metaphysics, and from excessive claims to 'absoluteness', would, however, be as defensible in its way as symbolic logic has always been in its own.   (M.F.)

Philosophy of Mind   In virtue of having minds we are able to think, to experience the world, and act upon it: three unique capacities which are difficult to reconcile with one another. In order to explain our capacity for conscious thought, DESCARTES postulated a special kind of substance. He argued that minds are essentially conscious, thinking, immaterial, non-spatial things, distinct from but related to the essentially spatial, mechanical, matter of which our bodies are composed. This explanation was unsatisfactory. In 1643 Princess Elizabeth of Bohemia asked Descartes to explain 'how man's soul, being only a thinking substance, can determine animal spirits so as to cause voluntary actions'; a question, Descartes admitted, 'that can be most reasonably asked', but to which he had no satisfactory answer. For Descartes, the problem was to explain how the mind – something non-material, non-spatial and non-mechanical – could affect the material world. If the answer is, as it seems it must be, that it could not, then Cartesian dualism leads to 'epiphenomenalism' – the view that our mental life can exert no causal influence on the material world. If our mind exerts no causal influence on the material world, then nobody ever acts upon it. The philosophy of mind still confronts a version of this problem, and much work has centred on the attempt to explain how minds can be both conscious and affect the material world.

The physical world is a causally self-contained system, and any changes that occur in it can be explained by appeal to purely physical causes. When we act we move our bodies and so change the physical world; hence our actions must be completely explicable in physical terms. But in that case our minds are causally irrelevant. When I withdraw my hand from something hot, I would have done so whether or not I was conscious of feeling pain.

One way to avoid this epiphenomenalist conclusion is to suppose that the mind itself is physical, that every mental state is identical with a physical state. On this view – a version of physicalism known as the 'type identity theory' – pain is just a physical state of the brain, and the experience of pain can thus affect the physical world because it is itself physical. Our actions have complete physical causes, some of which are mental too. Although it successfully avoids epiphenomenalism, this view is no longer popular. The problem is that mental states seem to be 'multiply realisable' by physical states. There could be creatures physically quite unlike us – silicon-based Martians, say – who nonetheless experienced pain, and in that case pain cannot be identical with the physical states that occur in us when we feel pain.

Even if mental states are not identical with physical states in us, they may still depend on them in such a way that our physical states are sufficient to determine them. This relation (known as the 'supervenience' of the mental on the physical) concedes that the mind is composed of physical matter, and so avoids the ontological extravagance of Cartesian dualism, but it still faces the problem of mental causation. If when a mental state causes a physical state that physical state must be explicable in physical terms, then the physical properties of the mental state must be the cause of the physical state, and its mental properties become irrelevant again.

We might be able to solve this problem if we had a better understanding of the relation between mental and physical properties. Assuming that the mind is, in some sense, physical, then what is it that makes it conscious? This was not a problem for Descartes, for whom the mind was a non-physical and essentially conscious thing. A number of philosophers (e.g. Thomas NAGEL and Frank Jackson) have argued that it is impossible to explain why anything physical is conscious, and some of them (notably David Chalmers) have concluded that consciousness cannot be physical. Their arguments, though they differ in detail, have a common structure. First they argue that there is an 'explanatory gap' between the kinds of explanations available to science and those that are necessary for explaining consciousness; and second, they argue that this gap reflects a deep metaphysical difference between physical matter and consciousness.

The arguments for the existence of an explanatory gap are concerned with the kind of consciousness associated with perceptual experiences and sensations. If you look at a vase of red flowers there is *something that it is like* for you to see the flowers, a particular way your experience is for you. Had you looked at yellow flowers rather than red ones, your experience – and so what it is like for you – would have been different. (*What it is like* is not used here in a comparative sense, but to pick out *how* things are for you in virtue of having an experience.) Similarly (to use Nagel's example), assuming that bats are conscious, we can never know what it is like for the bat. We could have an excellent understanding of both the physiology and psychology of a bat, but without any insight into the bat's consciousness. To gain such knowledge we should have to have the bat's (subjective) point of view on the world, and no amount of (objective) scientific knowledge could provide us with that.

Again, imagine that Mary is a scientist who has grown up colour blind: she experiences the world in black and white. She has nevertheless come to know all the physical facts about the operation of the visual system and the physics of light and colour. Then, one day, her condition is cured and she sees colours for the first time. She looks at a ripe tomato and finds out *what it is like* to see something red. Since she already knows *all* the *physical* facts, what she has learnt cannot be such a fact. In the same way, we can conceive of the existence of zombies – creatures physically just like us, but lacking consciousness. There could then be a zombie that was physically just like you, except that, since it lacks consciousness, there is nothing that it is like to be it. But if it is physically just like you, then the fact that you are conscious but it is not cannot be explained by reference to physical facts.

The existence of an explanatory gap does not entail a metaphysical gap, and some philosophers (e.g. Colin McGinn) have argued that it simply reflects the limitation of our understanding. According to them, consciousness is a physical or natural phenomenon, but one whose nature will always elude us. Others conclude that the reason we are unable to explain consciousness in physical terms is that consciousness is not physical; they are forced to adopt a kind of dualism. Thus although no one wants to revive Cartesian dualism, the problems that led Descartes to it have not gone away.

Empirical studies of the mind have revealed a great deal that is surprising about how the mind functions. These studies suggest, for example, that we may not notice significant changes in our perceptual experiences; that we act before we are conscious of deciding to act; and that we can see without being conscious of what we see. This has led some philosophers to draw a more radical conclusion: that many of our everyday ways of thinking about, for example, self-knowledge, intentional action, and perception, are false. If that is so, then many of the traditional problems of the philosophy of mind may be illusory; and therefore, rather than supposing that consciousness is elusive or adopting metaphysical dualism, we should change the whole way we think about the mind. Here science would have a direct impact on philosophy. In reply, it might be questioned whether our everyday understanding of the mind is subject to empirical revision. What exactly the relation is between the kind of understanding of our minds we employ in everyday life and the understanding provided by science, and whether we should revise our everyday understanding in the light of empirical studies, is perhaps the most pressing question for philosophy of mind today.   {M.N.}

Philosophy of Science The questions that arise in this field fall roughly into three divisions: those about science in general, those bearing on groups of sciences, or relations between them, and conceptual problems in individual sciences.

As far as science in general is concerned, the problems fall under three heads. (a) EPISTEMOLOGY, and, in particular, questions about reasonable grounds for knowledge: Is scientific method the only rational route to knowledge and understanding? Is it rational at all, and if so, why? Are there best methodologies? What might support a theory that cannot be directly checked by observations? To what extent can we assume that the future will resemble the past, or that past generalizations will hold up in the future? (The problem of induction.) Can one measure the degree to which a hypothesis is supported by or made credible by evidence? (Probability) And is scientific knowledge founded upon observation independent of theory, or are all observations 'theory-laden'? (b) METAPHYSICS, and, in particular, questions about reality: Is a scientific theory a representation of the world? Is a theory a set of statements trying to describe, in literal terms, how things are? Or is it just an instrument for organizing experience and experimental results, and for making better predictions and revealing interrelations between phenomena? As for causes, are they constant regularities in experience, or necessary connexions in nature? And what is an explanation? When theories postulate entities that cannot be observed – for example, electrons, the superego, or the money supply – do these literally exist, or are they merely intellectual constructs? (c) ETHICS: What are the responsibilities of a scientist in choosing fields of research, and in communicating or using discoveries that may be harmful? What are the parallel responsibilities of society, and of public or private patrons of science? Issues range from debates about weapons research through the use of scarce resources (including mental resources) to questions about whether it is immoral even to investigate certain areas, for example, correlations between race and physical and intellectual abilities, or

brainwashing, or the discovery of ever more potent modes of destruction.

Many questions about groups of sciences bear on the 'unity of science'. Should the human or social sciences use a methodology which is fundamentally different from that of the natural sciences? Or is there a single scientific method, appropriate to all fields of inquiry? There are related questions about nature itself. Are all phenomena ultimately the consequence of the same basic laws of nature? On one simplistic picture, sociology is reducible to psychology, which is reducible to biology and biochemistry, and those in turn to chemistry, which reduces to physics, with an ultimate goal of a 'Grand Unified Theory' in physics. There are logical issues here (what is meant by 'reduction?'), factual ones (has unification been proceeding apace, or are we witnessing increasing diversification?), and methodological ones (does the drive towards unifying theories always tend to produce greater or deeper knowledge?).

As regards individual sciences, there are at least as many questions as there are sciences. How are we to understand space and time after RELATIVITY theory? Or causality and determinism after QUANTUM MECHANICS? What, in evolutionary biology, is a species? What is the relation between artificial intelligence and human thought? Some writers hold that the only function for philosophy of science is participation in conceptual debates within the special sciences.

1 *Origins of the philosophy of science.* ARISTOTLE, DESCARTES and LEIBNIZ made contributions of the first rank to both science and philosophy (as we now understand them), and Francis BACON is widely regarded as the first philosopher of the scientific revolution of the seventeenth century, when EMPIRICIST and RATIONALIST

traditions divided on questions of methodology. There were important REALIST-anti-realist controversies about, for example, the 'reality' of gravitational force, or whether it is literally true that the earth rotates about the sun. And HUME is commonly considered the originator of a well-defined problem about induction, and author of the definitive 'constant conjunction' analysis of causality. But it is not till the nineteenth century, with the emergence and 'professionalisation' of distinct sciences such as what we now call biology or physics, that 'philosophy of science' arose as a distinct family of inquiries. Important figures in the first generation are Auguste COMTE, William WHEWELL and J. S. MILL. The first two represent opposed attitudes to the sciences that persist to this day.

Comte invented the label POSITIVISM for his philosophy. Positivism includes the following ideas: the only significant propositions of science are those that can be verified or falsified in experience; there is no power of necessity in nature; causality is no more than the regularities and uniformities that we observe; theoretical entities are intellectual constructs, invented to enable us to organize phenomena and make successful predictions. Many positivists have said outright that they were opposed to metaphysics. Hume is often cited as a forerunner. Whewell's *Philosophy of the Inductive Sciences* (1840) was in contrast strongly influenced by KANT. It was committed to the existence and possible discovery of fundamental but unobservable entities, and to explanations that reveal the necessary causes of events. The progress of science was, in Whewell's opinion, a matter of comprehending the reality that underlies phenomena.

Many discussions among today's philosophers of science can be seen as continuations of the disagreement between Comte and Whewell. However, science has changed a lot since the end of the nineteenth century. At that time Alexander Bain was able to describe atoms, electrons and the like as mere 'representative fictions': nothing could be done to them or with them, and if one believed in them it was only because of their utility in organizing one's understanding of experimental results. But this is no longer the case: nuclear fission and genetic engineering are dramatic examples of our now common ability to manipulate and use what were earlier regarded as mere postulates.

2 *Logical Positivism.* The most influential twentieth century school of philosophers of science originated with groups in Vienna and Berlin, meeting in the 1920s. Impressed by positivist doctrines, and by the results of symbolic logic, many gladly called themselves LOGICAL POSITIVISTS, later preferring the term 'logical empiricist'. Major figures were Moritz SCHLICK, Hans Reichenbach (1891–1953), Rudolf CARNAP and Karl POPPER. All were deeply moved by the triumphs of relativity and quantum mechanics, and wished to produce criteria that would distinguish that kind of science from what they regarded as pseudo-science, for example, Marxist history or Freudian PSYCHOANALYSIS. Most of them insisted that scientific propositions should be verifiable, but Popper – who distanced himself from the others, and rejected the 'positivist' label – insisted that verification and confirmation were not decisive; instead scientific assertions should be testable and open to refutation. He strongly urged that all scientific pronouncements are fallible. Carnap spent many years attempting a theory of probability, to be called inductive logic, which would explain how generalizations are

supported by positive instances. In contrast Popper, like Hume, argued that all such induction is invalid. Instead we learn from experience by a process of conjecture, testing and refutation.

All surviving members of this group emigrated in the 1930s and became influential in the English-speaking world. In Germany their work has encountered considerable opposition, as shown, for example, by a debate in 1961 between ADORNO and HABERMAS on the one hand, and Popper on the other, later published as *The Positivist Dispute in German Sociology*. The main issue was whether the natural and human sciences involve distinct methodologies and types of knowledge.

3 *The historical dimension.* Criticism of a different sort arose in America. Popper and the positivists were committed to a strong contrast between what Reichenbach called the context of justification and the context of discovery. There might be an economic, historical, sociological or psychological explanation of why a particular discovery (or error) was made, but such 'external' circumstances had nothing to do with its correctness or acceptability. A number of writers, notably T. S. KUHN, fundamentally challenged this confident rationalist picture of science. His *Structure of Scientific Revolutions* (1962) describes scientific development dialectically, in terms of periods of 'normal' science being followed by 'crisis', then 'revolution' and then new normal science. Kuhn is not speaking of science as a whole, or even one of the sciences such as chemistry, but rather of small fragments of a field in which there may be fewer than a hundred significant workers. Normal science conducted by these research workers is a matter of solving puzzles or problems according to an established pattern, or 'paradigm'.

Crisis arises when central problems become intractable – for example, when there is no way to explain anomalous results inconsistent with a theory. New concepts are evolved which displace old ones, so that there may be no way of systematically comparing the successes and failures of abandoned theories and their successors. Thus the very notion of 'the facts' is called in question, and doubt is cast on the most fundamental of positivist tenets, that theory-neutral observations suffice to decide between competing theories. It is suggested instead that all observations are tinctured by theory.

Kuhn's work forced a rather radical reassessment of the ideas that had been inculcated in anglophone philosophy of science by its German and Austrian teachers. Some wanted to preserve their rationalist ideology. For example, one of the more iconoclastic and polemical retorts to Kuhn came from Imré LAKATOS, a Hungarian refugee who settled in London. His *Methodology of Scientific Research Programmes* (1970, 1978) is a revision of Popper's philosophy, aiming at criteria of rationality couched in terms of the track record of an entire programme of investigation. It is notable, however, that for all his criticism of Kuhn's work, on one point he is in complete agreement. Where the logical empiricists had thought of the logic of scientific method as being essentially timeless, Lakatos' philosophy of science is entirely historicized.

Most philosophers investigating the questions about science in general mentioned earlier will pay attention to this historical dimension; but the approach is not strictly new, but rather a return. Whewell's *Philosophy of the Inductive Sciences* was preceded by a three volume *History of the Inductive Sciences*, and Comte's monumental *Course on Positive Philosophy* is first of all an overview of the history of science. In consequence of this return to an historical vision of scientific activity, some Anglo-American philosophers have found that their concerns were already partially addressed by French historian-philosophers of science such as Gaston BACHELARD and Georges CANGUILHEM.

A more critical attitude towards science itself has also blossomed. It is epitomized by Paul FEYERABEND's question in *Against Method* (1975): 'What's so great about science?' Many of Kuhn's core ideas had been put forward simultaneously and independently by Feyerabend, who described himself as an 'anarchist' about science and argued, most specifically against Lakatos, that there is no peculiarly 'scientific' method and that fixed canons of procedure lead to stultification. Feyerabend on occasion urged that the modern scientific establishment is as effective in closing minds as was the religious orthodoxy challenged at the time of Galileo.

A related critique was advanced a little later as the 'strong programme in the sociology of science'. We are accustomed to providing sociological explanations for the acceptance of patently false theories, for example, the preference for Lysenkoism over Western genetics under Stalinism, and the strong programme is committed to providing similar explanations for the discovery of truths: the truth of a proposition, the compelling character of evidence, or the rationality of a method, it is maintained, can never explain their acceptance. Moreover the notion of a 'discovery' is held to be disingenuous: it suggests an analogy to discovering a continent or an island, which we think of as being there in the ocean whether people get to it or not. One should think not of discovering scientific facts, but of constructing them in the

course of an ongoing process of social interaction among research workers. Thus the strong programme and its variants tend to be anti-rationalist in epistemology, and anti-realist in metaphysics.

4 *Pluralism.* Most philosophers of science hold such views to be extreme and wrong-headed. The strong programme does, however, indicate a substantial shift in philosophical interests in the sciences since the days of the logical positivists. These days were perhaps too much dominated by a certain image of science furnished by the twin successes of relativity theory and quantum mechanics. Since then, people have become more aware of the enormous diversity of scientific activities. Where the logical empiricists and Popper wrote extensively about theory and said virtually nothing about experiment, there has recently been a good deal of work on experimental science in its own right. Sometimes this has been combined with the attitudes of the strong programme, with philosophically minded participant-observers describing what goes on in a laboratory in the course of making a 'discovery'.

These tendencies towards pluralism on the part of philosophers have also affected the tenor of discussions about the relationship between the natural and social sciences. Anti-positivist philosophers once argued that the social sciences had to have their own methodology, which was autonomous and independent of the methods of the natural sciences. But as scientific methodology has increasingly come to seem very piecemeal and fragmented, this debate has appeared less pressing.

This summary has concerned only the most general of the philosophical issues mentioned at the outset. These are undoubtedly the ones that have attracted the attention of philosophers with little interest in science for its own sake, and also of the reading public at large. But there is increasing interest in the sorts of question that have arisen within individual sciences. [I.H.]

Physicalism Physicalism is a version of reductive materialism about the mind favoured by LOGICAL POSITIVISM.

Plato (c.427–347 BC) Plato was born in Athens and lived there for most of his eighty years. Though at first marked out for politics, both by his lineage and by his interests, he devoted himself almost wholly to study, theory and teaching. One cause of this was the disgust he came to feel at the low level of politics in his time; he found that bad faith and injustice and cynical selfishness were widespread, and that ingenuous good faith could not stand against them. The only hope for politics, it seemed to him, was to found a school and create therein a new kind of political character.

The main cause of his renouncing political practice was probably SOCRATES. He fell deeply under the spell of Socrates' magnetic and searching thought, and was profoundly shocked when, at the age of about 27, he saw Socrates condemned to death on the absurd charge of corrupting the young and not believing in the city's gods. He has left us unhistorical but magnificent pictures of Socrates' defence, imprisonment, and execution, in his *Apology*, *Crito* and *Phaedo*.

After this disaster, most of Socrates' friends left Athens for a time. Plato visited the Greek cities of Sicily and southern Italy, and made political and scholarly friends there. By about 385 at the latest, he was back in Athens, and was founding, near the grove of the hero Academus, what has come to be called the 'Academy', which may loosely be called

the first university. He gathered about him a number of pupils and fellow students, who united themselves in a 'museum', or society dedicating itself to the patrons of letters and music, the Muses. The members might stay there for twenty years or even for life, taking part in common studies, religious exercises and meals. The ultimate practical purpose of the society was the restoration of decent government to the Greek cities. Some of the members left after a time and went into practical politics. Some, including Plato himself, wrote political advice to their friends elsewhere. But the studies were far from wholly practical. Plato held the restoration of decent government to require a complete foundation of theoretical knowledge; and he sought to lay such a foundation, as deep and as firm as possible. The studies which he encouraged hence came to appear to the general public as obscure, fine-drawn, and impractical; and there is a story that, when he advertised a lecture on 'The Good', people came hoping to learn how to be happy, but heard only what seemed to them to be higher mathematics. Mathematics certainly became, after philosophy, the study most pursued by the society.

Plato devoted himself to his school for most of the remaining forty years of his long life. He had, however, two very important relations with the outside world; his interventions in the politics of Syracuse and his published writings.

During his travels Plato had made a friend of Dion at the court of Syracuse. In 367 Dion urged Plato to come to Syracuse and instruct the new ruler, Dionysius II, who being young and well-intentioned might be made into the new kind of statesman desired by Plato. Plato went; but he had little hope of realizing his ideal in Dionysius, and by this time had probably lost most of his original eagerness for political practice. The matter turned out very badly. This was not because the royal pupil had no relish for Plato or philosophy. On the contrary, he became very attached to his teacher and to the subject. But Plato had not been at Syracuse six months before Dionysius expelled Dion on the ground that he was plotting against him. Loyalty compelled Plato to support Dion and demand his recall, while jealousy and suspicion drove Dionysius to try to separate Plato from Dion. Dionysius never let Dion return, and for some time he did not let Plato leave.

Six years later, in 361, Dionysius sent for Plato again, and ensured Plato's compliance by making it a condition of the restoration of Dion. Once he had Plato, however, he did not recall Dion but on the contrary confiscated Dion's property in Syracuse. Plato had to use the influence of a neighbouring ruler in order to be allowed to return to Athens.

Jealousy begins with false beliefs, but by acting on them makes them true. Dion now became the irreconcilable enemy of Dionysius. He invaded Syracuse and drove Dionysius from it in 357, ruled it himself for four years, and was then assassinated. The assassin had apparently had relations with Plato and was considered a member of the Academy. This was a terrible blow to Plato.

Plato's publications are all preserved, and make five large modern volumes. They constitute not merely the greatest philosophical work there is, but also one of the greatest pieces of literature in the world. If anyone asks what philosophy is, the best answer is: 'read Plato'. For it was Plato who brought the word 'philosophy' into use; and it was he who mainly invented and first practised the sort of study for which 'philosophy' is the name. To say that there is little philosophy in a

major work by Plato is self-contradictory; or it expresses an arbitrary change in the meaning of the word. The so-called PRE-SOCRATIC philosophers, and even Socrates, were not philosophers in the full sense of the word, though they were certainly Plato's inspirers.

1 *The Early Dialogues.* Plato's works can for the most part be confidently assigned to one of three periods: early, middle and late. The early works constitute an extremely striking presentation of the figure of Socrates.

All but one of these works are dialogues; and this is part of Plato's conception of philosophy as well as of his literary originality. Philosophy is essentially a kind of *logos*; and Plato's notion of *logos* may be analysed in modern terms as 'the reasonable use of words in thinking'. The reasonable use of words involves submitting them to criticism by others and testing their implications; and this involves dialogue. The typical early Platonic dialogue draws out the implications of a statement, in order to test it for consistency with itself and other statements. The question whether to adopt a statement must not be answered until we have discovered its implications and connexions. Since more implications may become visible to us in the future, it is usually better to adopt a view provisionally and until someone persuades us otherwise with a better argument.

2 *The Middle Dialogues.* In the middle dialogues Plato shows some dissatisfaction with the hypothetical and negative procedure of the Socrates of his early dialogues, and some hope of finding an unhypothetical starting-point on which to base intuitive certainty and good politics. He thinks that such a starting-point can be found, if at all, only in the region suggested by the following statements.

Through all the multiplicity and variety of just and unjust acts, persons, and situations in this world, there evidently is in some way only *one* Justice and *one* Injustice. And so with every other collection of things to which we apply the same name, as 'beautiful' or 'couch'. Various and divergent as beautiful things are, there is only *one* Beauty. We can distinguish from each and all of the many beautiful things the *one* Beauty itself, what Beauty itself *is*, which must be there because otherwise there would be no sense in calling anything beautiful. The one Beauty itself is not merely distinct from each and all of the beautiful things. It is also separate from them. For it must be completely beautiful, purely beautiful, unchangingly beautiful; and no beautiful thing is such. This comes out very clearly when we consider the one Equality itself; for probably no two sticks in this world ever are exactly equal; and if they were our measurements would never be able to tell us that they were. Thus we arrive at an astounding and thrilling conclusion: there is a second world, other than our world of visible things, consisting of the Ones Themselves, each of which is perfectly, purely and eternally what it is, visible only to the mind itself, or rather not visible but intelligible, grasped only by the pure intellect using bare words.

Can this be right? Let us go back and approach by a slightly different way. Socrates has made us familiar with the enterprise of asking what a thing *is*. He has asked what courage is, what virtue is, what knowledge is. And he has rejected such answers as: 'look at Laches if you want to know what courage is; he is a courageous man'. Socrates has replied that he seeks, not this or that courageous person or act, but courage itself. And surely he was right. The question 'What is courage?' expresses a possible enterprise which is not that of collecting examples. The Socratic search for 'Definitions' was in fact the search for one or other of these elusive but necessary Ones in Themselves. They must be there, to make sense of our world and our speech; but their forms are to be discerned only by the eye of the mind. There is an intelligible world of 'Forms' or 'Ideas'.

To Plato the word 'idea' meant first visible form and then form in general. Thus it meant something objective. It never carried the subjective meaning it has today. In any case it is hardly more than a label to him, a label for 'that one thing itself which (something) in itself is, complete, pure, and eternal'; and this phrase in turn is Plato's distillation from the fact of common names and from Socrates' search for definitions.

These Forms, then – so unexpectedly but so simply discovered – are the required starting-point, both for good practice and for good theory and indeed for religion of a kind (Plato called them divine). To believe in them and pursue them is to be a philosopher; that is the deeper definition of what philosophy or the pursuit of wisdom is. To be ignorant of them, or disbelieve in them when they are pointed out (which unfortunately is the usual human state), is to be essentially not a philosopher. Knowledge of them is the first possible kind of knowledge. Indeed strictly speaking it is the only kind of knowledge; for strictly speaking only the unchangeable can be known, and only the Forms are unchangeable. If you say that the moon is full, and the moon then wanes, you cannot, strictly speaking, have known that the moon was full. Only what completely is can be completely known. There is a difference of kind between knowledge which has the Forms for its object, and opinion, which has for its object this transitory and confused world.

The Forms are, however, the explanation of the visible world, so far as it has one. This cosmos is the mixed result of Mind and Necessity, and hence our account of it cannot be better than a likely story. But whatever reality there is in visible things comes to them from the Forms after which they are called. A visible couch shares in, or perhaps imitates, couch itself, and derives its half-reality therefrom. We may also suppose that, beside the Forms and the visibles, there is a Third Thing, a receptacle of all becoming, which like gold takes any shape, and is to the Forms as mother is to father, a sort of room or seat of becoming, to be grasped imperceptibly by a kind of bastard reasoning.

3 *Politics and Philosophy.* All opinion is defective; but it is not all equally defective. On the contrary, those who know the Forms will have far better opinions about this world than those who do not. And that is the key fact for good politics, since it implies that kings should be philosophers. The only good government is by those who know, and this means those who know the Forms. The ideal city would be a philosophocracy.

Whether such a city could ever come into existence is very doubtful; but how it would maintain itself if it did come into existence is clear. The ruling philosophers would see to it that their rule was absolute and not limited by unchangeable laws or by popular votes, that they handed it over only to other equally adept and right-minded philosophers, and that the supply of suitable successors was assured by appropriate education of the best persons. Education would be in fact by far the most important part of practice. Those chosen to receive it would be primarily the children of the rulers; but impartial selection would reject some of these as inferior, and add some superior children

from the common people. The same kind of impartial search for the best, overriding all useless customs however dear, would give us women as well as men rulers, would make these women exercise naked as well as the men, and would abolish family life among the rulers in favour of a conventional system of common parents and common children, which, together with communion of property, would fuse the whole ruling class into a united and selfless whole whose ascendancy would never be in doubt.

The primary education of these rulers would not be very different from what Plato had himself received. It would, however, be publicly organized and intense; and the physical or gymnastic part would be more military in character. The two greatest differences would be, first, an ever present risk of failure in the next examination and consequent relegation to the masses, and, second, the complete absence from their music and poetry of all corrupting or degrading suggestions, such as frenzied music and Homer's assertion that the gods could not restrain their laughter on a certain occasion. For whatever is read in literature in early years goes deep into the soul, especially any suggestion of self-abandonment.

Those who passed all tests up to the age of twenty would be guaranteed some sort of place in the ruling class for life; but whether this was to be higher than that of a private in the army would depend on their success in their studies and exercises and examinations in the following fifteen years. Here Plato is strange indeed; for what he proposes as a suitable training for the higher ranks of the army and for administrators and rulers, is advanced MATHEMATICS followed by abstract study of the Forms and finally of the Form of the Good. Nothing is said about history or politics or economics. His reason is that those who are to keep a city as good as possible must above all know what pure and absolute Goodness Itself is. To this end they must previously know about the other pure and absolute Forms Themselves, to which end in turn they must first know mathematics. Mathematics provides a bridge from the sensible to the intelligible world. For in mathematics we draw sensible squares and triangles, and yet are interested in intelligible triangles and squares. We use the visible as a suggestion of the intelligible, and are thus gradually brought to the desire and power to study the intelligible itself, by mere words without accompanying visible images, as the adept philosopher does.

Only those who can and will persevere the whole way up this path will be governors of our ideal city. They will by then be at least fifty years old. One curious consequence of this education will be that the rulers will dislike ruling. They will have a passion for the Forms and wish to be left alone with them. But this is no disadvantage. On the contrary, the love of power makes bad rulers; and our reluctant rulers will nevertheless rule willingly enough, because they are just and they recognize the justice of recompensing the city for the supreme education it has given them. Besides, they will have plenty of leisure to devote to abstract philosophizing.

This ideal city of Callipolis, the first surviving Utopia and by far the most interesting one, is constructed in Plato's splendid dialogue *Republic*, which is one of the ten best books there are. It is a work of his maturity, and the high point of his powers. Later in life he published two more dialogues on politics, and they show a change of interest. Here he still affirms that knowledge is the only right basis for government, that it may and should dispense with laws, and that communal

living is best. But he seems to think now that knowledge and communal living are hardly ever practical possibilities, and therefore we had better spend our efforts in finding what is best to do in their absence. He has no doubt that in their absence we should have recourse to the reign of law. Law, while much inferior to the man who knows the Good, is much the best ruler for us ignorant and ill-tempered persons; and should be sacred among us. So when in his old age he plans another ideal city, which he calls Magnesia, his account consists mainly in a mass of legal details, and the dialogue is named *Laws* (see POLITICAL PHILOSOPHY).

4 The Later Dialogues. Philosophy in the narrow sense is the analysis of conceptions; and this is mainly the invention of Plato's later dialogues. However, Plato himself continued to think of his theoretical philosophy as a study of the world rather than humanity, as metaphysics rather than logic and epistemology. And his results were often not of great value; there are weary wastes of logical and metaphysical oddities, tiresome enough in Plato himself, intolerable when expounded by devoted interpreters. Yet it is never to be forgotten that these late dialogues, or rather that activity in the Academy of which these dialogues are an expression, formed the best analytical thinker there has yet been, ARISTOTLE.

The best of the late dialogues are the first two, *Parmenides* and *Theaetetus*. The conflict of opposed views natural to a good dialogue is at its greatest in the *Parmenides*, which consists of two parts. The first appears to destroy Plato's own theory of Forms with well-founded and unanswerable arguments. The second appears to be a formidably long and boring kind of metaphysical nonsense; it is described by the main speaker as 'a laborious game', and ends with the following words: 'Let this be said, then; and also that, as it seems, whether one is or not, both itself and the others, both to themselves and to each other, all in every way both are and are not and appear and do not appear. – Very true.' Whatever this be – a joke, or ultimate truth, or something between – it is a remarkable achievement and has a queer value of its own. The discussion of the Ideas in the first part does in fact amount to a pretty clear revelation of the reasons that make the theory impossible, and is therefore a fine example of candid self-criticism. It is very strange that the *Parmenides* thus contains both an extreme example of frankness and an extreme example of mystification.

The *Theaetetus* is Plato's most successful work in purely analytical philosophy. The conceptions analysed are perception, knowledge, subjectivity, truth, change, error, *logos*, simplicity and (by implication) definition. Plato introduces there the classical comparisons of the mind to a wax tablet and to a dovecote, and the classical comparison of Socrates' conversation to midwifery. The conclusions are mostly negative and valueless by themselves: 'Knowledge is not perception: it is not true opinion; it is not even true opinion with *logos*. Error is not thinking one thing instead of another, or misrelating what I see to what I know, or misusing the knowledge that I have; it is hard to see how it can occur at all.' Nevertheless, anyone who studies and absorbs this dialogue will be greatly enlightened.

After the *Theaetetus* and the *Parmenides*, the *Sophist* is the greatest of Plato's late works. In outline it is a series of attempts to define the sophist by successive divisions of a genus, as when we define the angler by dividing the genus craft, to which he belongs, into acquisitive and constructive craft, and place the

angler in acquisitive craft. We can then subdivide acquisitive craft into acquisition by consent and acquisition by subjugation, and again place the angler in the half to which he belongs. If we continue long enough, we should come to a class that is co-extensive with the angler and constitutes a definition of him. This process of definition by division is prominent in the late dialogues. Plato appears to have hoped that it would supply a sure way of constructing definitions, as opposed to merely destroying definitions as Socrates' technique had done. Aristotle, however, showed that there is nothing sure about the procedure; every step in it is merely an unsupported assertion. And its prominence in the late dialogues is a large cause of their relative unfruitfulness.

The *Sophist* fortunately contains, besides six long divisions, a long passage of much more value. Here Plato resumes some puzzles about not-being, error, and falsehood from the *Theaetetus*. He then discovers as many puzzles in the notion of being, finding difficulties both in the notion of being as many and in the notion of it as one only. He finds that in the battle of giants between materialists and idealists neither side can defend itself. If we say that the real is what we can grasp with our hands, we deny the obvious facts of justice and wisdom and soul. On the other side, if we say that only the Ideas are real, we deny that the real can live or move or think.

Plato believes that he now has a solution to these difficulties. It consists in analysing the way in which we apply many names to the same thing (whereas the theory of Ideas was reached by considering that we apply one name to many things). From the fact that we may call the same man both white and squat and short and brave he develops the doctrine that some pairs of things communicate with each other and others do not, and that some things communicate with everything but most do not. Among the things that communicate with everything are Same and Other; for everything is the same as itself and other than everything else. But to be other than another thing is *not to be* that other thing. Thus otherness is a kind of not-being; and this kind of not-being is omnipresent, since everything is other than every other thing. Now this is a perfectly respectable kind of not-being, unlike the not-being that has puzzled us; for there is nothing queer about being other than something else. This kind of not-being is not opposite to being but merely other than it. Not-being therefore firmly exists and has its own nature, even though PARMENIDES forbade us to say so.

Not merely does not-being exist; it is also shared in by thought and statement, which therefore admit of being false. That appears as follows. A simple statement consists of a name followed by a verb, such as 'man learns'; it cannot consist of anything less complicated. It necessarily has a subject and is either true or false – false if what it says about its subject is *other* than what is true about it. As it really can say, about a really existing subject, something that is really not so as if it were so, it really can be false. False statement is possible. But then false thought is possible; for thought is the same as silent internal statement.

In his old age Plato returned to the ethical topics of Socrates and made Socrates his main speaker again. This was in the *Philebus*, an ugly and disappointing but acute and still useful dialogue. It begins with a last statement of the method of division – the most puzzling and least rewarding of them all. It then devotes itself to what appears to be a solution of the problem left open in the *Republic*, namely, what is the Good? The Good must be perfect, adequate, and desired by all who know it. The main contenders for the place are pleasure and knowledge. No one would choose either alone if he could have both; but which is the better? Socrates develops a strange classification of things into the definite, the indefinite, the mixture of these two, and the cause of their mixture; and decides that pleasure falls into the indefinite class but mind falls into that of cause. He then goes into a long and close analysis of pleasure. It is caused by the restoration of living substance. But there are also mental pleasures of expectation. Pleasures are often accompanied by false opinions, and can themselves be false. There is a neutral state of neither pain nor pleasure; and pleasure itself is not the mere absence of pain. The greatest pleasures and pains occur in bad states of the body or soul. States of pleasure mixed with pain can occur in several ways. But there are also true and absolute pleasures. Pleasure cannot be the Good, because it is a genesis, and therefore exists for the sake of something other than itself. In the course of this long psychological analysis of pleasure, Plato has some useful remarks on perception, memory, desire, imagination, envy, comedy and laughter.

He then gives a much shorter analysis of knowledge, observing that some arts are more exact and mathematical than others, distinguishing between popular and philosophical arithmetic, and praising dialectic as the most accurate of all the arts, though perhaps not the most useful. Finally the dialogue returns to the Good. The Good cannot be either knowledge or pleasure alone, for neither of them is perfect. It must be a mixture of the best of each of them, including all the sciences, and those pleasures that are pure and necessary. In this mixture the most valuable part is beauty and symmetry and truth, and that is the cause of its goodness. Each of these three is more akin to knowledge than to pleasure. Knowledge therefore stands nearer than pleasure to the Good. And we may finally announce the following order of value: measure, beauty, mind, science, pure pleasure.

Another dialogue of Plato's old age, the *Timaeus*, is devoted to the physical world, and offers an elaborate cosmogony, cosmology, physics, chemistry, and human physiology, pathology, and medicine, while at the same time declaring in the manner of the middle dialogues that there can be no science of such matters. For a long time the western world read only this dialogue of Plato's, thus obtaining a very inaccurate impression of him. At all times, however, most of Plato's readers have tended to take his second-best and leave two-thirds of his best. They have tended to take his authoritarian politics and his mystical religion of the Ideas with its inclination to unreason. But of his best they have taken only his literary beauty. They have ignored his great lead in the analysis of conceptions, that is, his invention of philosophy in the narrow sense; and they have ignored his magnificent ideal of reasonable thinking and acting. This ideal is presented to us in the person of Socrates; but it is presented only by the writings of Plato.   (R.R.)

Plotinus (205–70) Plotinus stands at the origin of the philosophy known in modern times as NEOPLATONISM. The not very reliable fourth century writer, Eunapius, says he came from Upper Egypt, but his education and cultural background were completely Greek. In 232 he came to Alexandria to study philosophy. He could find no teacher to satisfy him until he encountered Ammonius Saccas, with whom he remained for

eleven years. Ammonius was a self-taught, non-writing philosopher and we know next to nothing of his teaching, but his influence on Plotinus and his other pupils – probably including the Christian theologian Origen (185–254) – was very considerable. In 243 Plotinus set off with Emperor Gordian's expedition to the East, in the hope of learning some Persian and Indian philosophy; but Gordian was murdered in Mesopotamia in 244 and Plotinus escaped with some difficulty to Antioch, and went from there to Rome. There is no evidence that at this or any other period in his life he acquired any knowledge of Indian thought.

Plotinus spent the rest of his life in Rome teaching philosophy, and after ten years began to write the treatises which were gathered by his disciple and editor, Porphyry, into the collection we know as the *Enneads* (composed of six sets of nine treatises). Porphyry also wrote a life of his master, which is our main source of information about him, giving a vivid and detailed picture of his life and work in Rome. His method of teaching was informal, based on reading of PLATO and ARISTOTLE and their commentators, and including a great deal of free and vigorous discussion of difficulties raised by members of his audience; traces of these discussions are to be found in the published treatises.

The philosophy of Plotinus – though professing to be an exposition of the real thought of Plato and owing a great deal to close and critical study of Aristotle and of the Platonists, Pythagoreans and Aristotelians of the century or so before his own time – is in many ways thoroughly original. The primary purpose of his teaching was to lead people – those few who were capable of it – back to the source from which they and all things came, the One or Good, which in giving them being also gave them an impulse to return. This journey required perfect moral purity and the utmost intellectual effort.

The One or Good himself (Plotinus uses the masculine pronoun in speaking of his First Principle) is held to be beyond all determination or limitation and so beyond description or definition. Language can point towards him but never reach him. Even the names 'One' and 'Good' are inadequate. But though he is beyond the reach of language he is by no means mere negation or abstraction. It is because he is more, not less, than any conception we can form of him that he is beyond thought and language. He is present to all according to their capacity to receive him.

Reality proceeds from the One or Good in a series of stages of steadily increasing multiplicity, limitation and separation. Its generation from the One is both free, in the sense of being perfectly spontaneous and unconstrained, and necessary, in the sense that it is inconceivable that it should not happen. Like the radiant sun, the Good cannot but be self-diffusive or self-communicative. The process of generation is timeless, and all the stages of reality are eternal. Even the last and lowest, the physical universe, is eternal as a whole, though individual parts of the sublunary world are continually perishing and being replaced by others. But in the timeless process of generation, at each stage, two elements can be distinguished in thought, one in which the product proceeds from the producer as an unformed potentiality, the other in which it returns upon its source in contemplation, is formed and actualized by it, and gains in its turn (except at the last and lowest stage) the power to produce. This double rhythm of outgoing and return runs through the whole of Plotinus' universe.

The One is beyond being, and the source of being. In the Platonic language of Plotinus, 'being' denotes the totality of beings, and there is no such thing as indeterminate or unlimited being. True being for Plotinus is the first level of reality proceeding from the One – from the Divine Intellect in which thought and its content are one, and whose Ideas are themselves living intelligences, each of which thinks and so is the whole. Intellect is also the highest level of our consciousness, and its Forms are, as in Plato, the archetypes of the world of the senses. They are finite in number, though infinite in productive power. Plotinus, in the writings where he considers the question most carefully, makes an important departure from Plato in admitting individual as well as universal Forms – a Form of Socrates as well as a Form of Man – an admission which he reconciles with the traditional doctrine that the Forms are finite in number by adopting the Stoic idea of cyclic world periods, repeating themselves endlessly in every detail.

From Intellect proceeds Soul, the active principle which forms and orders the visible universe. Its characteristic intellectual activity is discursive thought, and time is the life of the soul in this discursive motion. But Soul in Plotinus has a very wide range: at its highest it is fully illuminated and formed by Intellect, but it also has a lower phase ('Nature') which is the immanent animating principle of the entire material universe. From Nature come the forms of bodies, the lowest and weakest of realities, incapable of further production. All levels of soul from the lowest to the highest are permanently present in us and we have to choose whether we will remain on the level of the lower soul, immersed in the concerns of body, or whether we wake to the higher realities present in us.

For Plotinus the material universe is a living organic whole, bound together by a force of universal sympathy. Plotinus himself believed in the reality of magic, but since it could not affect the higher life of the soul, it was of no importance to him. Matter itself, though like all else it proceeds from the Good, is the principle of EVIL because it is the utter deficiency of being and marks the end of the descent from the Good. But Plotinus' attitude to the material universe – unlike that of the Gnostics, whom he detested – was by no means merely negative or pessimistic: though affected by the evil of its materiality, it was also good and beautiful as a living structure of forms and the best possible work of soul.

Plotinus had a considerable influence on early Christian theologians and on the philosophy of Islam, and the publication of Ficino's Latin translation of the *Enneads* in 1492, and of the Greek text in 1580, made Plotinian Neoplatonism an important current in Renaissance thought; but the last group of philosophers deeply influenced by his thought were the CAMBRIDGE PLATONISTS. (A.H.A.)

Political Economy   Political Economy is a school of social theory created in the eighteenth century by James Steuart and Adam SMITH. It describes how the mechanisms of a modern commercial society ought to ensure that the uncoordinated activities of individuals pursuing their private interests will automatically maximize the wealth of a nation, without any need for political intervention. Ruskin and other romantic anti-capitalists denounced political economy as 'a lie'; but MARX respected it enough to devote his theoretical energies to providing a 'critique' of it.   [J.R.]

Political Philosophy   The words 'political philosophy' can cover almost any abstract thought about law, politics, and society, particularly if it addresses normative questions about the way in which political power should be used or the way citizens should behave. Thus, democratic theory, jurisprudence, political morality, APPLIED ETHICS, social theory, and POLITICAL ECONOMY have all been thought of as parts of political philosophy. A political philosopher might study subjects as diverse as punishment, representation, feminism, private property, judicial review, economic inequality, civil disobedience, rational choice and the morality of abortion. In these and similar areas, people who think of themselves primarily as philosophers have become immersed in recent times in the study of what we may call 'public affairs', and they have contributed to a large body of literature in which the issues and controversies of public life are debated and discussed.

Behind this concern with public issues, however, there is a deeper and more abstract agenda which defines political philosophy as a branch of philosophy proper. That agenda consists in the traditional questions that have dominated the subject since PLATO's time. What is the state? What is society? What is the human individual? How are they related to one another? Is a society greater than the sum of its individual parts? Is the state just a social construction or a construction of individuals, or does it have an irreducible reality of its own? Unless these questions are addressed, the study of 'public affairs' is bound to remain superficial. Apart from anything else, we need to be able to answer these questions before we can say with any confidence what makes an issue 'public' or 'political', what it is for something to be an issue or a concern for a whole society as opposed to an issue or concern for some of the individuals who make it up.

Philosophical questions about the relation between society and the individual spring from a deep paradox in our thinking. On the one hand, it is beyond question that each of us is the product of a particular society: I do not make myself; I owe everything I have, including my sense of self, to the community and culture in which I live. On the other hand, as soon as I start thinking or reflecting on society and the way it has constituted me, I appear to be doing so *as an individual*, and my own thoughts, preferences and purposes seem more real to me than the community in which they were fashioned. Society may have made me, but what it has made is something that can regard society as separate from itself.

The two sides of this paradox mark a fundamental division in political thought (see LIBERALISM AND COMMUNITARIAN-ISM). If we take society as our point of reference and regard the individual as derivative, then our values and ideals will be defined in terms of forms of communal life. We will not, of course, be unconcerned with individual men and women, but we will value their aspirations and fulfilments strictly as part of an overall communal ideal. However, if we take the individual as our fundamental point of reference, then community will appear valuable only as a means to the goals and ideals that individuals have adopted as their own. We may still think it desirable that one person's behaviour should be constrained by respect for others. But it will be respect for the interests of the other *individuals*, rather than a respect for social life as such.

Individualists differ about the nature and importance of individuality. For HOBBES, individuals are voracious consumers of utilities, driven inevitably into deadly competition with their fellows. For others, in the tradition of KANT, we are better conceived as moral beings, autonomously pursuing goodness as we happen to conceive it. Such beings still have needs which must be fulfilled and ideals which may be better pursued depending on the resources at their disposal. But they aim to *make* something of their lives, not simply engage in accumulation and consumption for their own sake. It is arguable that principles of individual *liberty* and *rights* are much easier to defend from this second perspective than from the first, for there seems nothing intrinsically important about the unimpeded motion of a utility-seeker. Still, philosophers in the individualist tradition have been wary of tying the value of freedom too closely to the idea of striving after goodness. That may lead to the illiberal conclusion – sometimes described as 'positive liberty' – that freedom to do wrong is not worth having or not worth fighting for. And it would move them uncomfortably close to the communitarian version of that idea – that true freedom involves submerging oneself in the life of a well-ordered society.

It is perhaps easier to maintain that we are essentially social animals than that we are *political* animals, for law, politics, and the state seem to be artificial constructions in a way that basic human sociability is not. When we talk about *politics*, we seem to be talking about the way people come together deliberately to express their sense of how society should be run and to articulate their differences; and we are talking about the relatively formal practices and institutions of debate and conflict that make this expression possible. Because it has this formal and artificial character, both individualists and communitarians may view the realm of politics as something derivative, to be judged in terms of more fundamental values and ideas that are not themselves political.

One way of approaching the matter is to think of the social and political structure of a society as something which people design, as an architect designs a building, and hence as answerable to the 'specifications' that such a designer might have in mind. The earliest example of this type of thinking is found in Books II and Ill of Plato's *Republic*, where justice is thought of as the idea of order and harmony that would guide the founding of a new colony or the institution of a new society.

In Plato's approach, both the social designer and the specifications he is guided by are thought of as external to the society he is constructing. That approach can be contrasted with the more individualistic view of politics as artifice expressed in the theory of the SOCIAL CONTRACT propounded by thinkers like Hobbes and LOCKE. Here political society is taken to be designed by the very people who are to live in it, and the specifications for the design are not derived from any transcendent ideal but are simply their individual needs and purposes. The state is thought of as the product of an agreement among individuals to remedy certain problems that arise for them when large numbers, each with their own interests and concerns, try to make lives for themselves in circumstances of moderate scarcity. On this account, government and law do not come naturally to us, but we agree to set them up so that each of us can realize gains from cooperation and mutual forbearance that would otherwise be unobtainable. This agreement then provides an artificial basis for political authority: it legitimizes institutions like legislatures and courts, obligates each contracting party to respect the decisions of those institutions, and places limits on what can be done with state power.

There are, however, a couple of well-known difficulties with the social contract view. First, though everyone gains from cooperation, an individual may do even better for himself if he defects from a cooperative arrangement while others do not. The contractarian, like every other political philosopher, has to find some response to the question posed by Plato in the *Republic*: 'What advantage is there in being just?' Second, even if it can be shown to be rational to keep one's agreements, it is implausible to claim that any of us has ever actually agreed to abide by the principles of the state. In fact, most of us were never given the opportunity; the social contract seems to be an elaborate fantasy. And if it is just a fantasy, it is hard to see how it can provide any actual basis for political obligation.

These worries have led people to try and express the individualist approach in other ways. If we take individual values as the basis of political evaluation, surely we can simply ask how well a given set of institutions serves those values now. We don't have to assume that it was set up for that purpose; the question is whether we should alter or abolish it. Of course, that is not a straightforward question, for a given set of institutions may serve some individuals better than others. UTILITARIANISM is the theory that we should maximize the existence of whatever we take to be valuable: if individual satisfaction is valuable, we should seek to promote a set of social arrangements that satisfy as many individual preferences as possible. Other theories take *equality* as their basic value, or stress that certain interests – in liberty or basic well-being – should have priority as matters of right over ordinary utility.

For much of the century, it seemed that this more direct approach to social and political evaluation was preferred to the social contract approach. The publication in 1971 of John RAWLS's book,

A Theory of Justice, however, heralded a revival of interest in contractarianism. Rawls argued that one could use the image of the social contract as a theoretical or intellectual device for expressing the force of certain individualist values, particularly non-utilitarian ones. As much as any critic of the contract idea, he conceded that society was not actually a voluntary arrangement. Nevertheless, he thought that by asking, 'What basis for institution-building *would* people have agreed to, if (contrary to fact) they had come together to settle terms for cooperation instead of having institutions thrust upon them?', we could come up with answers that were, in some sense, impartial *between* individuals, while retaining the image of the consent of each and every individual as our fundamental point of orientation. Rawls' answer to this question – his principles of liberty and economic equality – have not been universally accepted, but his book has had an enormous influence in setting the modern agenda for political philosophy in the English-speaking world. It has initiated an intense discussion of the basis of social justice, liberty, equality, rights and – most recently – community, which has dominated the subject ever since.

Among those who regard the state as an artificial construction, not all view it in individualist terms. MARX, for example, maintained that though man is naturally social there is nothing natural about political life. Rather, politics is the institutional expression of class struggle, the state serving to maintain the conditions for the economic dominance of one class and the orderly exploitation of others. Many Marxists maintain that, with the overcoming of class struggle, the need for a specially organized apparatus of power, superimposed on the forms of society, will gradually 'wither away'.

Other philosophers have taken an even more jaundiced view of the state. In the anarchist tradition, the institutions of state and law have always been thought disruptive of social and moral life. Either the state is seen as a coercive order superimposed on what would otherwise be a well-functioning social organism. Or it is seen as an order which, in the force it uses and in the obsessive sense of obligation it evokes, precludes and interferes with the exercise of autonomous moral judgment by the individual. Either way, it is seen as a structure of force, representing an attempt by some faction in society or some gang of individuals to gain the upper hand over others.

So far we have discussed those approaches which seek to explain the state in terms of something else – as the embodiment of some ideal, as an instrument for the fulfilment of individual interests, as a crystallization of class conflict, or as an excrescence of power. On the other side are those philosophies which accord the state and politics reality and moral significance in their own right, and which use this as their point of reference for thinking about justice and political obligation.

In modern times, the most striking theory of this kind has been that of HEGEL and the English idealists who followed him like GREEN. According to Hegel, the institutions of the state embody the reality of human consciousness. In the life of an individual, consciousness is something incomplete, but in the life of the state it attains 'final unity' and 'universality', as Hegel put it. 'Since the state is mind objectified, it is only as one of its members that the individual himself has objectivity, genuine individuality, and an ethical life.' From this perspective, patriotism, legality, and the performance of social duty take on aspects quite different from what they have in an instrumental, individualist tradition.

Between the individualism of the social contract and the collectivism of Hegel are theories like those of ARISTOTLE and ROUSSEAU which see in political life a possibility of transforming man from an animal dominated by its natural desires into a genuinely moral being. Rousseau, like the anarchists, was profoundly sceptical about existing political forms. But he held open the prospect that active participation in the democratic life of a small-scale polity might still 'enlarge' and 'ennoble' the human spirit.

Aristotle's theory was expressed slightly differently. 'Man is by nature a political animal', he said: 'it is his nature to live in a state'. He argued that man was naturally fitted for political life by his ability to engage in discourse about the good, to reach conclusions in ethics that would be impossible for individuals to reach on their own, and to live in a society with others on the basis of a shared and articulate view of right and wrong, just and unjust.

This Aristotelian view of society as essentially a *moral* community has always been worrying to liberal individualists, who stress the diversity of moral conceptions and argue for political structures which are, as far as possible, *neutral* between rival accounts of what makes life worth living. Liberalism is in part the product of an attempt to disengage the state from the enforcement of virtue (not to mention religious belief). It should be clear, nevertheless, that liberal arguments, however well-founded, are not themselves 'neutral' between different views of political morality. We have seen that political philosophy is still largely a debate about the basis on which judgments and evaluations are to be made in the political realm. Respect for the moral autonomy of the individual is one

possible basis, but it has to be one that can defend itself against the rival claims of Aristotelian, communitarian, and collectivist approaches to politics.   [J.J.W.]

Popper, Karl R. (1902–94)   Born and educated in Vienna, Popper taught in New Zealand 1937–45 and then at the London School of Economics. His major contributions have been to the PHILOSOPHY OF SCIENCE. Although he never subscribed to the early PHENOMENALIST tendencies of the VIENNA CIRCLE or to the instrumentalist interpretation of scientific theory professed by some adherents of logical empiricism, the general orientation of his thought is similar to that associated with this philosophical movement.

In his first book, *The Logic of Scientific Discovery* (1935), Popper defined scientific statements as ones which deny that something logically conceivable is actually realized. Accordingly, for a statement to be counted as scientific it was not sufficient that there should be confirmatory observational evidence for it; it was essential that such a statement should be capable of being disproved by some conceivable spatio-temporally located event exemplifying a possibility which the statement excludes. It is this feature of its statements that Popper thinks demarcates science from non-science. He therefore proposes an amended version of the relative frequency notion of PROBABILITY, in order to make such probability statements refutable and so scientific; but he also outlines a conception of logical probability which, unlike the frequency notion, he believes to be relevant to assessing evidence for a hypothesis (see CARNAP). In addition, the book contains a vigorous critique of BACON'S view of scientific procedure (which he calls 'inductionism'), and argues that it is the 'hypothetico-deductive method' which is distinctive of modern science. These themes are developed further in the essays comprising *Conjectures and Refutations* (1963).

Popper is perhaps better known as the author of *The Open Society and Its Enemies* (1945). Although it contains many reflections on the logic of science, the book is primarily a thorough-going criticism of social philosophies (in particular, those of PLATO, HEGEL and MARX) which minimize the efficacy of individual human effort and subscribe to a belief in laws of inevitable historical development. In opposition to such philosophies, Popper advocates piecemeal social engineering as the sound scientific approach to social problems. Popper pursued this argument further in *The Poverty of Historicism* (1957). See also PHILOSOPHY OF SCIENCE, RELATIVISM. (E.N.)

Porphyry (c.232–c.305) Greek NEO-PLATONIST, editor of PLOTINUS, and author of the *Isagoge*, an introduction to ARISTO-TLE's logic that which was to be a standard text for a millennium.

Positivism The name 'positivism' is given (a) to the doctrine and movement founded by the nineteenth century French philosopher Auguste COMTE; and (b) to a general philosophical view of which Comte's is only one instance. Positivism in the broader sense (referred to here with a small p) is the view that since all genuine knowledge is based on sense experience and can only be advanced by means of observation and experiment, metaphysical or speculative attempts to gain knowledge by reason unchecked by experience should be abandoned in favour of the special sciences. All positivists hold that the task of philosophy is to understand the methods by which the sciences are advanced but not to seek for any independent knowledge of the world.

They often argue that as soon as means have been found for advancing knowledge of a subject, it ceases to belong to philosophy and becomes a separate science, or a part of one.

Francis BACON, who considered himself the 'trumpeter' of the new sciences which were becoming detached from philosophy in the sixteenth and seventeenth centuries, may be regarded as the source both of positivism and of the name that was given to it in the nineteenth century. In his *On Principles and Origins* (1621–4) he refers to an ancient legend according to which Cupid was the oldest of the gods and existed at the beginning of things alone with Chaos. Cupid, according to this myth, had no parents, and Chaos no beginning. Bacon interprets the absence of parents to mean the absence of any cause, and surmised that 'Chaos' meant the ultimate matter from which all material things are formed. This ultimate matter, he writes, 'is a thing positive and inexplicable and must be taken absolutely as it is found, and not to be judged by any previous conception'. It is improper, he says, 'to require or imagine a cause when we come to the ultimate force and positive law of nature…for nothing has corrupted philosophy so much as this seeking after the parents of Cupid; that is, that philosophers have not taken the principles of things as they are found in nature, and accepted them as a positive doctrine resting on the faith of experiences; but they have rather deduced them from the laws of disputation, the petty conclusions of logic and mathematics, common notions, and such wanderings of the mind beyond the limits of nature'.

Bacon here gives expression to a number of important items of the positivist doctrine. He rejects the idea of 'deducing' the ultimate facts of nature. He believes that philosophers should not attempt to wander beyond 'the limits of nature'. He thinks that there are ultimate facts that should be approached without any 'previous conception'. He warns against a too enthusiastic search for causes. He says that there are ultimate facts that should be accepted 'on the faith of experience'. When he applies the adjective 'positive' to these 'inexplicable' facts and to the doctrines based on them, he is not using the word in the sense in which it is opposed to 'negative', but in the sense in which positive religion (consisting of revealed doctrines, accepted by faith, and not provable by reason) is opposed to natural religion (the doctrines of which are established by rational proof), or in which positive law (laid down by specific authorities for particular populations) is opposed to natural law (held to be rationally apprehended and independent of the will of legislators). Probably as a result of Bacon's usage – Bacon was much admired by the eighteenth century empiricist philosophers both in England and in France – the adjective 'positive' came to be applied to the methods of the natural sciences in respect of their reliance on observation and use of experiment. Saint-Simon, whom Comte later served as secretary, in his *Essay on the Sciences of Man* (1813) applies the word 'positive' to the sciences which are based on 'facts which have been observed and analysed'. The sciences which are not so based Saint-Simon calls 'conjectural'. Comte himself uses the word in this sense in an article entitled *Plan of the Scientific Works necessary for the Reorganisation of Society* which was published under Saint-Simon's auspices in 1822. He later brought it to full prominence in the title of his major work, *Course on the Positive Philosophy* (1830–42), where he explains that he used the word 'positive'

to emphasize that the function of theories is to co-ordinate observed facts rather than explain them in terms of causes. It is Comte's 'Positive Philosophy' which later came to be called 'Positivism', a name which Comte welcomed but did not himself invent.

Comte's Positivism can best be understood in terms of his famous Law of the Three Stages, according to which the human mind advances from a theological stage through a metaphysical stage to the final positive stage. At the theological stage the attempt is made to penetrate to the inner nature of things and explain their behaviour in terms of supernatural beings. At the metaphysical stage, which is really only a sophisticated modification of the earlier one, explanations are given in terms of abstractions, essences or forces, which, on Comte's view, are nothing but depersonalized deities. As examples of this mode of thought Comte cites the physical doctrine of the ether, the chemical doctrine of affinities, and the biological doctrine of vital spirits. At the final, positive stage the attempt to penetrate to the inner nature of things and to discover the origin and destination of the universe is abandoned. Instead, the positive thinker tries to establish, by means of reasonings based on observations, the invariable co-existences and sequences of phenomena. It was Comte's view that all the sciences pass through these stages, as for example, astronomy in its development from sun-worship and astrology, and chemistry in its development from alchemy. Like Bacon, Comte emphasized the enhanced power over nature that the advance of science brings with it.

Comte's Positivism, however, was much more than a philosophy of science and an account of intellectual history. Comte held that the time will come when human society itself is studied by positive methods. He called this positive science 'sociology' and sought to lay its foundations in the *Course on Positive Philosophy* and later writings. It was his view that to each of the three stages of intellectual development there corresponded forms of society and social outlook. The theological social outlook displays respect for tradition and authority upheld by priestly learning; metaphysical criticisms of the traditional doctrines bring with them an era of social criticism – in Europe, the Reformation and the French Revolution – based on such unverifiable doctrines as belief in natural rights and the sovereignty of the people; but with the advance of positive social science, the negative and sterile disputations of the revolutionary era would be replaced by a stable society based on incontrovertible social knowledge. A new form of authority would then reside in a new spiritual power consisting of scientists whose knowledge would enable humanity to achieve a peaceful unity of thought and action. In his later years Comte elaborated this part of his doctrine into a Religion of Humanity. Some of the most eminent of his early supporters such as Littré in France and George Eliot and J. S. MILL in England refused to follow him in this. Nevertheless, Positivist Societies were established in various parts of the world on the model of that which Comte himself founded in 1848. In these, Humanity was the object of ceremonial worship, and sociology was taken as the warrant for sociolatry. The movement was particularly strong in Latin America, but flourished for many years in England, mainly in London and Liverpool. Leaders of the movement here were Richard Congreve, who resigned his fellowship at Oxford in order to devote himself to its promotion, and Frederick Harrison. *The Positivist Review*, later called *Humanity*, was published from 1893 until 1925.

Both the theoretical side of Comte's Positivism and positivism in the more general sense are natural developments in an age of scientific advance. Bacon may be regarded not only as the first positivist, but also as the forerunner of Comte's ceremonial Positivism, since in *The New Atlantis* he writes in some detail of a cult of great men. And positivism has always formed a part of the empiricist tradition in philosophy: HUME argued that all genuine human knowledge is concerned either with matters of fact or with 'relations of ideas', especially logic and mathematics. The latter kind of knowledge is certain – it has that character which philosophers call 'necessity'. But no mathematical or logical reasoning, can, on its own, tell us anything about the nature of the world. Its conclusions are as Bacon said, 'petty'. Knowledge of matters of fact, on the other hand, is knowledge about the world: it is not 'petty', but can never have the certainty and necessity of logic and mathematics. We can always conceive of the facts of the world as different from what they actually are, and there is no way of proving that the world must be as it is. But this is just what metaphysical philosophers have tried to prove. They have claimed to provide knowledge of the world which has all the necessity of mathematics. But this is confusion. Knowledge is either of matters of fact in the world, or it is logical and mathematical, and hence not about the world at all. Any book which falls into neither of these categories must be filled with 'sophistry and illusion'.

This view was very widely held in the nineteenth century, but was not strongly represented in the universities, where various forms of Idealist metaphysics prevailed. In the 1920s, however, Hume's positivist arguments were revived and strengthened. It was now argued that a form of words that expressed neither a verifiable matter of fact nor a truth of logic or mathematics was meaningless. The field of what is meaningful contains only what is in principle verifiable or what is a mere matter of logic. This criterion excludes most of the things said in books on metaphysics which are therefore not false but without sense. This view is known as LOGICAL POSITIVISM.

Positivism gets much of its strength from the contrast between the continuous and agreed progress which has been achieved in the natural sciences since the time of Galileo, and the situation of deadlock and disagreement that has at all times obtained in metaphysical philosophy. This seems to suggest that in the special sciences a fruitful method has been employed, whereas metaphysical philosophers have got lost in an intellectual impasse. Comte and the earlier positivists argued that metaphysical problems are beyond human powers, whereas the logical positivists argued that when verifiability is taken as a criterion of meaning, the problems of metaphysics are revealed as mere pseudo-problems, which remain unsolved not because they are difficult but because they have no sense. The weakness of all types of positivism is the assumption that there are facts, each distinct from every other, which observation and experiment can reveal and correlate. When they attempt to explain what these facts are, however, positivists cannot agree, and Bacon's 'simple natures', Hume's 'impressions', and the 'atomic facts' of twentieth century positivists raise theoretical problems which are as elusive as those of self-confessed metaphysicians. (H.B.A.)

Postmodernism The word 'postmodern' gained currency in architectural criticism in the 1950s and 1960s, where it designated a movement away from the shiny machine-like austerity of the 'International Style'; soon it was extended to apply to reactions against MODERNISM in other branches of art as well.

In the 1970s the term was adopted within philosophy as a rough synonym for deconstruction (see DERRIDA) and post-structuralism (see STRUCTURALISM). Philosophical postmodernism has two aspects: it is a reaction against both MODERNISM and MODERNITY. According to its most prominent advocate, Jean-François Lyotard, the essence of post modernism is a carefree scepticism about every possible attempt to make sense of history. It anarchically rejects all the 'meta-narratives' of progress – whether Marxist or liberal – by reference to which modernity and modernism have identified themselves (see *The Post-modern Condition*, 1979).

However, the fact that modernism is itself acutely critical of modernity threatens the coherence of the whole project of philosophical postmodernism. Moreover, the postmodernist desire to escape the superstitions of a preceding epoch is not so much a break with traditional modernity, as a repetition of its oldest refrain. Postmodernism encountered formidable criticism in HABERMAS' *Philosophical Discourse of Modernity* (1985). [J.R.]

Post-structuralism See STRUCTURALISM.

Pragmatism The term 'pragmatism' was introduced into philosophy by the American philosopher C. S. PEIRCE in 1878 to describe the theory that the meaning of a word 'lies exclusively in its conceivable bearing upon the conduct of life; so that, since obviously nothing that might not result from experiment can have any direct bearing upon conduct, if one can define accurately all the conceivable experimental phenomena which the affirmation or denial of a concept could imply, one will have therein a complete definition of the concept, and there is absolutely nothing more in it'. This doctrine undoubtedly has, as Peirce intended, important consequences, such as that 'almost every proposition of ontological metaphysics is either meaningless gibberish...or else downright absurd'. But Peirce took 'pragmatism' as a name for a method of getting clear about the meanings of words rather than a complete philosophical position; being a confirmed coiner of technical terms he would have been quite as willing to subscribe to 'synechism' and 'fallibilism' as to 'pragmatism'. And he certainly did not regard his pragmatic maxim as being in a theory of truth as opposed to meaning; to him it seemed evident that truth consisted in correspondence between statement and fact.

But very early the word 'pragmatism' was borrowed by other philosophers who gave it new and vaguer meanings, and Peirce responded by writing that 'to serve the precise purpose of expressing the original definition, he begs to announce the birth of the word "pragmaticism", which is ugly enough to be safe from kidnappers'. The earliest philosophers thus to borrow the concept of pragmatism were William JAMES, F. C. S. SCHILLER and John DEWEY; what they have in common is first and foremost a theory about truth which has since been regarded as the essence of pragmatism. In his *Pragmatism*, James said that 'ideas become true just so far as they help us to get into satisfactory relations with other parts of our experience' and that 'the true is the name of whatever proves itself to be good in the way of belief'. The connexion with Peirce's views perhaps comes out when James says that the question of the truth of an idea or belief comes down to the question 'what concrete difference will its being true make in one's actual life? How will the truth be realized? What experiences will be different from those which would obtain if the belief were false? What, in short, is the truth's cash-value in experiential terms?' But the similarity to Peirce is superficial: his doctrine that the meaning of an hypothesis can be determined by considering its experimental consequences is conflated with the doctrine that the true is the good in the way of belief to yield the conclusion that the true is what has good experimental consequences.

The notion of pragmatism became connected with this doctrine about truth, partly owing to the controversies between James, Dewey and Schiller on the one side and RUSSELL on the other. The gravamen of Russell's attack (see 'Pragmatism', 1909, and 'James' Conception of Truth', 1908) is that the pragmatists have confused the meaning of 'true' with the criteria we use for deciding whether a belief is true, thereby surrendering to an irrationalist position. Largely as a result of Russell's attacks Dewey simply abandoned the use of the word 'true' and claimed that it could be adequately replaced by a notion of 'warranted assertibility'.

Lying behind this view about truth is the conviction of James and Schiller that everything, including thought, must be understood in the light of human purpose: thoughts are but tools for achieving certain ends, and they must be judged as such. Hence 'pragmatism' has come to be a name for any position which lays emphasis on results as a test of satisfactoriness. The sense which Peirce, its inventor, gave to the word is now obsolete. See also AMERICAN PHILOSOPHY. (J.O.U.)

Predestination See FREEDOM OF THE WILL, DETERMINISM.

Prescriptivism   Prescriptivism is the doctrine, derived from KANT and revived by HARE, that ethical judgments are essentially commands or imperatives, rather than representations of facts. See ETHICS.

Pre-Socratics   The term 'Pre-Socratics' denotes a dozen or so of the earliest Greek thinkers, down to the time of SOCRATES, who attempted to define the constitution of the world and the nature of reality. They range from THALES, active in the early sixth century BC, to DEMOCRITUS in the latter part of the fifth. The earliest Pre-Socratics came from Ionia, the Greek colonization area in the centre of the west coast of Asia Minor. City states like Miletus were materially prosperous in the first half of the sixth century and had close trading contacts with the foreign cultures of Egypt and Lydia (and so with Babylonia) as well as with the Greek colonies of the Black Sea and the west. In addition, Ionia was itself heir to an old literary culture going back beyond Homer. These conditions encouraged the surge of speculative thought in Miletus, Ephesus, Colophon and Samos. The interest in philosophy soon spread overseas: PYTHAGORAS migrated from Samos to one of the Greek colonies of Southern Italy, while XENOPHANES wandered all over the Greek world. PARMENIDES and ZENO were natives of Elea in south-west Italy and EMPEDOCLES came from Acragas in Sicily. Thus most of the Pre-Socratics belonged either in the east or the west of the Greek world, and Athens became involved only when ANAXAGORAS moved there from Ionia in the seventies of the fifth century.

In spite of their differences from each other, the Pre-Socratics form a logical, not merely a chronological, category. Socrates turned Greek speculative thought in a totally new direction by rejecting physics and concentrating on ethical questions. Except for the SOPHISTS, in whose tradition Socrates in this respect belonged, earlier *philosophoi* or 'lovers of wisdom' had subordinated human problems to the assessment of external physical reality. Thus those whom we term Pre-Socratics were called by ARISTOTLE 'investigators of nature', *physiologoi*, because they studied the *physis* – the nature or constitution of things as a whole. Many of them had more specialized physical interests too; indeed some of the earlier ones, like the Milesians Thales and ANAXIMANDER, were many-sided thinkers who won fame with their contemporaries not for their theoretical accounts of reality – which in some cases may have been of only incidental importance even to their authors – but for their ability to solve practical problems like measuring the distance of a ship at sea, transporting an army over a river, or accurately delimiting the seasons. All the Pre-Socratics tried to describe the nature of the heavenly bodies; some – Thales and Pythagoras most conspicuously – had special mathematical interests apart from astronomy; Empedocles, Anaxagoras and Diogenes of Apollonia were concerned with medicine and embryology; and most of them seem to have attacked notorious natural problems like the causes of earthquakes, rainbows, magnetism or the flooding of the Nile. It is important not to overlook this strong practical interest, combined as it surprisingly was with a quite unempirical dogmatism when it came to dealing with larger problems of the nature of the world. What gave these thinkers the right to be considered as philosophers, unlike the other astronomers, geographers and doctors who were active especially in the latter half of the period, was their assumption that the world possessed some kind of integral unity and determinability which could be understood and explained in rational terms. The first part of this assumption can be found in earlier quasi-mythological cosmogonies and theogonies, but it was the treatment of these problems in straightforward descriptive terms and the rejection of personification that gave Thales and his successors, for later Greeks as for us, the title of 'philosopher'.

Although they abandoned much of the mythological language, the Pre-Socratics continued to be affected at certain points by pre-philosophical assumptions. When Thales declared that all things came from water, he was probably giving rationalistic expression to a partly mythic Egyptian idea, paralleled in Babylonia, that the world arose from Nun, the goddess of primeval waters, which was itself a reflexion of the annual re-appearance of the earth as the Nile recedes. A more important debt to myth appears in the central presupposition that the world is coherent, intelligible and unified in spite of the diversity of its appearance. This presupposition formulated itself in the anthropomorphic *genetical* tendencies of traditional mythology. Thus in the Hesiodic *Theogony*, a poem probably compiled in the early seventh century, the family of gods is traced back to the very beginning of the world, when Gaia, mother earth, together with the different parts of the underworld, appears as the first distinct cosmological entity out of an originative gulf called *chaos* (which means, not confusion, but simply 'gap'). Eros or sexual love – the anthropomorphic motive for further differentiation – comes on the scene at the same time. Gaia gives birth to the male sky-god, Ouranos, and to mountains and the inner seas; then sky-god and earth-goddess mate to produce Okeanos, the encircling river that connects them. Further generation takes place from these same parents; according

to other accounts rain is the seed of sky which fertilizes earth so as to produce plants and crops. This quasi-mythological cosmogony is complicated by the synthesis in the *Theogony* of several different versions. A cruder and more completely mythopoeic story which occurs later in the poem, according to which Ouranos lies continuously with Gaia and refuses to allow her to bring forth offspring until he is mutilated by Kronos, probably represents a more primitive version by which the original *chaos* was produced by the initial separation of earth and sky. At all events the mythological idea that different components of the world are connected with deities who have a traceable ancestry, as human beings have, led on to the view that the world as a whole can be derived from a single ancestor or pair of ancestors – for example, earth, or earth and sky. This assumption deeply affected the earlier Pre-Socratics, who replaced the Gaia or *Chaos* of Hesiod with a single originative material like the water of Thales or the air or mist of ANAXIMENES. Even where cosmogony was rejected – as, for example, by HERACLITUS, who declared that the world-order was made by neither gods nor men, but had existed always – the assumption of an essential unity and determinability in the world was retained. This important general presupposition, the reasons for which were not discussed by the Greeks themselves, was presumably also due in part to the observation of natural regularities, of the sun, the seasons and so on, which encouraged the comfortable belief that the world worked in accordance with laws not completely unlike those which ordered human societies. The narrower view of the main natural constituents as divine people with a single remote ancestor was a more specialized manifestation of this anthropomorphic approach.

The survival of anthropomorphism can also be seen in the devices used by some Pre-Socratics to account for the ultimate source of physical change. The Eros or sexual love of Hesiod found its counterpart in the idea of legal retribution in Anaximander, of war or strife in Heraclitus, or of love and strife in Empedocles. Indeed, less primitive thinkers have had to fall back on metaphor here; for example, Aristotle used Eros to explain how the Prime Mover can move without being moved. Two other points at which the Pre-Socratics were influenced by inherited pre-philosophical assumptions were in their conceptions of divinity and of the soul. To a large extent they abandoned the traditional Olympian pantheon, but they all retained the idea that what was all-powerful and indestructible was divine (thus the Milesians seem to have applied this description to their primary kinds of matter). As for soul, its constitution was largely ignored by the earliest Pre-Socratics; but the Pythagoreans, Heraclitus and Empedocles saw it as a physical link between humanity and the outside world. These thinkers were reinterpreting the popular idea that the soul is related to *aither*, the material of the pure upper air and of the stars. At the same time confusion was caused in Pre-Socratic psychology by failure to distinguish perception from intelligence or mind; here the effects are evident of the influential but inconsistent treatment of soul in Homer, where psyche meant sometimes life-stuff, sometimes consciousness-stuff, and sometimes intelligence.

1 *Sources.* We do not possess anything like the intact works of any Pre-Socratic thinker. What we have takes the form of isolated fragments, varying in length from a word to a few sentences, which have survived through being quoted by later authors of antiquity. Of the Milesians there is almost nothing – a phrase or a sentence of each; of Pythagoras, nothing at all; of Heraclitus, just over a hundred genuine sayings, mostly very short (the longest consists of fifty-five words). There are about one hundred and fifty hexameter lines of Parmenides, about three hundred and forty of Empedocles; but this may have formed something over a third of the original works, which were probably quite brief. Of Anaxagoras we possess about a score of fragments amounting to approximately a thousand words in all; these form probably not less than an eighth and not more than a half of his original book. Of Democritus, known to have been an extremely prolific writer, between two and three hundred fragments survive, nearly all of an ethical character and largely irrelevant to his more unusual physical theories. Extracts from original works are, of course, only one source of information about the ideas of a dead thinker, and we rely heavily for our knowledge of the Pre-Socratics upon summaries and commentaries made by historians of thought in ancient times. Thus PLATO himself made brief incidental judgments, many of them of a humorous or ironical kind, on some of his predecessors – Heraclitus, Parmenides and Anaxagoras in particular. Plato seems to have taken Pythagoreanism seriously, but used most of the other Pre-Socratics as symbols for various kinds of wrong-headedness. Aristotle, on the other hand, attempted systematic assessments of his predecessors. The Pre-Socratic physicists were of special interest to him because, in spite of grave misunderstandings about causation, they seemed to have been making what he called 'lisping' attempts to express the truths which he revealed. The

value of Aristotle's detailed opinions on his early predecessors is disputed, and it has been demonstrated that he was capable on occasion of seriously distorting their views. At the same time Aristotle's information and judgments are always valuable and often indubitably correct; and they can only be safely rejected in those cases where we possess reliable contrary evidence, which for the most part can be provided only by relevant original fragments, and where in addition his motives for distortion can be detected.

The correct evaluation of Aristotle's judgments is particularly important because virtually all subsequent ancient accounts of the Pre-Socratics were strongly influenced by him. The chief source of information for later writers was The *Opinions of the Physicists*, a history compiled by Aristotle's colleague THEOPHRASTUS as part of the great Peripatetic encyclopedia of knowledge. But Theophrastus himself, though on many points he seems to have checked original sources, was also heavily influenced by Aristotle's opinions, which are sometimes reproduced in words borrowed from Aristotle's *Physics* and *Metaphysics*. In many cases he seems to have been unable to ascertain disputed points, no doubt partly because not all the Pre-Socratics were still readily available in their own words. Indeed, although the Greeks themselves assumed that each Pre-Socratic (though not Pythagoras) wrote at least one book, to which they usually assigned the stock title 'On Nature', it is doubtful whether some of the earlier ones produced written works that achieved wide currency even in their own time. They may have relied more on oral propagation, and the extracts from Heraclitus, notably, are primarily framed as oral apophthegms. Even when Pre-Socratic books were available their often

metaphorical and poetical language did not always meet with sympathetic interpretation from the scientist Theophrastus. Thus his history, even if it had survived entire, would itself require much interpretation and modification, and even then would often not take us back beyond Aristotle; but except for a section on sensation it too exists only in fragments. Fortunately an unknown Stoic in the second century BC made a summary of it; this was recopied and expanded by one Aetius three or four hundred years later, and his work has been reconstructed from extracts in two slightly later extant writers. One more source must be mentioned: the Neoplatonist Simplicius is of great importance because, although he lived a thousand years after the Pre-Socratics, he found it desirable for the purposes of his commentaries on two treatises of Aristotle to set out the views of some of Aristotle's predecessors in their own words; for by his time many of the Pre-Socratic writings, and even the later summaries of them, had become extremely rare. To him, then, we owe in particular a great proportion of what we possess of the original words of Parmenides, Empedocles, Anaxagoras and Diogenes of Apollonia.

Of the chronology and biography of the Pre-Socratics we are also imperfectly informed. For a crucial hundred years between the rise of the Sophistic movement and the foundation of the Lyceum they did not greatly interest most Greeks. Aristotle was interested in their ideas but not their personal lives; so it was left to the mendacious Alexandrian biographers from the third to the first century BC to produce such dubious stories as that Heraclitus buried himself in dung or that Empedocles cast himself into Mount Etna. A few plainer facts have survived, which depend upon more reputable sources. Most of the chronological information, too, goes back to a more respectable but still largely speculative side of Alexandrian learning. Sotion classified the Pre-Socratics into eastern and western schools and, following Theophrastus, related them to each other as master and pupil. Then the chronographer Apollodorus left a standard account, in verse, of the dates and opinions of philosophers and others; he assumed that each thinker's period of greatest activity came at the age of forty, which he made to coincide with the nearest of a series of epochs or dated historical events. Further, a pupil was regularly made forty years younger than his putative master. Fortunately we know a few objective dates by which to check Apollodorus: for example, the eclipse predicted by Thales must have been that of 585 BC, and Melissus, the follower of Parmenides, was Samian admiral against Athens in 441. In general the Apollodoran dating, though over-schematic, seems to be roughly reliable.

The ancient distinction between East-Greek and West-Greek schools is useful up to a point. The westerns were less materialistic in their search for unity, indeed the Eleatics rejected the sense-world altogether. In Pythagoras and Empedocles there was a mystical or religious trend that would not have been tolerated in the more matter-of-fact, if no less dogmatic, atmosphere of eastern, Ionian thought. But there are many exceptions: Pythagoras was an Ionian by upbringing, though he moved to southern Italy; the Ionian Heraclitus discovered unity in structure rather than material; Melissus, though a follower of Parmenides, was an Ionian from Samos. Apart from the Sicilian Empedocles, the post-Eleatic pluralists came mostly from the eastern end of the Greek world (e.g. Anaxagoras,

and the atomists Leucippus and Democritus) and tended to revert to traditional Ionian explanations of detailed cosmological phenomena.

2 *The Milesians.* Thales and his two successors, Anaximander and Anaximenes, are sometimes grouped together as 'Milesians'. They considered that the unity of the world was to be found in the material from which it had originated, which Thales thought to be water. Aristotle claimed, rather vaguely, that Thales 'took his supposition from seeing the nurture of all things to be moist'. Now Thales may have been affected by observations like this, but the primary stimulus for his choice of water was probably the near-eastern story that the world arose from a great surrounding flood. He was undoubtedly interested in Egypt and also had opportunities, through Sardis, for contact with the Babylonian records on which his most famous exploit – the prediction of an eclipse – must have depended. Unfortunately it is hard to tell how far Thales carried these theories. Was the unity of the world founded, in the old genetical manner, on a distant origin from a single parent, namely water? Or was the world still somehow made of water? Aristotle naturally assumes the latter, since it fits his own idea of a persistent material substrate. But Thales probably did not distinguish the alternatives very clearly, or specify precisely how the world achieved its present diversity. According to Aristotle he declared that all things are full of gods, and that magnetic stone, since it can move iron, must possess soul. But if apparently inanimate things possess soul and therefore life, then the world as a whole might be penetrated with soul or life, which – because of its immense power and scope – must be divine and so could cause the development of the present plurality.

Anaximander was somewhat younger than Thales, whom he must have known. He seems to have felt that if the originative stuff were identical with a present world-component like Thales' water, then the other components – for example fire, which is in many ways opposed to water – could not have asserted their identity. Anaximander accepted the idea of a single originative material, divine and all-encircling, but called it 'the Indefinite' – implying that it was both boundless in extent and different from any nameable constituent of our world. Cosmogony took place when a nucleus that produced fire and dark mist became separated from the Indefinite; the mist at its centre solidified into earth, and was surrounded by a ball of fire which burst to form the heavenly bodies. These were wheels of flame encased in mist, each shining out through a single aperture. The earth, according to Anaximander, was a broad flat-topped cylinder which stays in its place because it is equidistant from everything else – a brilliant advance on Thales or Anaximenes who held that the earth floats on water or air. Within the world, things are divided into mutually opposed substances like heat and cold, winter and summer, day and night, whose interactions are motivated and regulated by a sociological metaphor: first they encroach on each other and then they 'pay penalty and retribution for their injustice according to the assessment of Time'. (The use of traditional poetical language and the absence of an abstract vocabulary was a constant brake on philosophical development in this period.) The cosmological regularity was derived from the divine Indefinite substance itself, which thus transmitted its unity to the developed world.

In the next generation Anaximenes reverted to the concept of a specific cosmogonical substance: air/mist (*aer* in Greek) or breath. Anaximander's probable objection was circumvented by the hypothesis that the originative stuff can take on other forms, and become the other materials of our world, as a result of condensation and rarefaction – variation of its amount in any one place. This explanation of physical change – wrongly thought to be confirmed by the observation that the temperature of exhaled breath varies with the compression of the mouth – succeeded in making material monism logically feasible for the first time. The consequent cosmogony and cosmology were not too implausible, since mist does seem to permeate many changes in Nature: rarefied, it turns into fire (for lightning bursts out of cloud), condensed, it becomes earth by way of water, which seems to turn into earth, for example, when the sea recedes. But Anaximenes' choice of basic substance was not entirely scientific; he likened the cosmic material (also called 'breath') to the human soul, which is often associated with breath; in this way the motive of change was still largely anthropomorphic.

3 *Pythagoreanism.* In Anaximenes' maturity (around 535 BC) Pythagoras migrated from Samos to Italy and established an exclusive semi-religious, semi-philosophical society. He wrote nothing himself, so assessments are particularly precarious. He taught that the soul migrates from one body and species to another; consequently all living things are akin, and abstinence from meat, as well as other taboos, had to be observed. In common with those known as Orphics he believed that the soul must be kept pure. An important means of purification was music. Here the mystical and scientific trends link up, for Pythagoras discovered by the experiment of stopping a single string that the major harmonic intervals

can be expressed in ratios of whole numbers. If music, which is related to soul, is numerical, then the whole world must somehow be numerical too. Pythagoras' followers, developing this typically overbold induction, seem to have assigned concrete bulk (which they took to be the mark of existence) to the points which, as units, made up numbers and delimited lines, planes and volumes. Hence physical objects, composed as they were of determinable geometrical shapes, could be resolved into sums of concrete unit-points. Further, the world could be analysed into ten pairs of opposites, of which the archetype was limit and the unlimited. These were the elements of number, too: odd numbers were limited, even numbers unlimited. The world came into being when the unit as limit drew in the unlimited and subjected it to various determinations. Most of these ideas were probably later than Pythagoras; but the master himself had ascribed special importance to the decade, and there is no reason to remove from him the famous theorem associated with his name. It may have been a follower, though, who drew the full damaging implication from the consequent irrationality of the diagonal: that some natural lengths, all of which should be composed of unit-points, could not be expressed in terms of whole numbers at all.

Pythagoras' longer-lived coeval Xenophanes, likewise an emigrant from Ionia, devoted much of his poetry to attacking the traditional Homeric description of the gods – both their immortality and the very basis of their anthropomorphism: it seemed absurd that each species should envisage gods in their own shape. Xenophanes replaced them with a single, motionless god who 'shakes all things by the thought of his mind'. This idea of a divine, intellectual source of change may have affected Empedocles and Anaxagoras; his destructive rationalism was probably more generally influential. Apart from attacking anthropomorphism, he appears to have parodied the exaggeration and dogmatism of Ionian physical theories by such suggestions as that the sun continues each day in a straight line. Although not primarily interested in physics, and a professed sceptic over the acquisition of certain knowledge, Xenophanes is not without scientific importance. He used the testimony of marine fossils found inland to show that the earth must once have been mud – a rare use at this period of rational inference from a well-testified and correctly assessed observation.

Further modifications of the Milesian approach were made by Heraclitus, active in Ephesus probably around 510–480. Philosophically as well as socially an extreme individualist, he abandoned traditional cosmogony and insisted that the unity of things was to be found in their essential structure or arrangement rather than their material. This common structure or *logos*, which was not superficially apparent, was chiefly embodied in a single kinetic material, fire. It was responsible both for the regularity of natural changes and for the essential connexion of opposites (Heraclitus accepted this traditional analysis of differentiation) through balanced interaction. The regularity underlying change was for Heraclitus the significant thing, but like the Greek poets he also emphasized the ubiquity of change (and was consequently subjected to exaggerated interpretation, for example by Cratylus). He likened change to strife or war; for without reaction between opposites and world-masses the *logos* and the unified cosmos would cease to exist. Philosophy was not a game: knowledge of physics was ethically essential, for humanity is part of its environment, and the soul, which in its unadulterated state is a kind of fire, is connected through sensation and breathing with the fiery *logos*-constituents of the outside world. This enabled understanding to be distinguished from mere perception.

4 *The Eleatics.* The development of these fruitful ideas was interrupted by a philosophical explosion on the other side of the Greek world. Parmenides wrote a poem claiming that we can only meaningfully say of anything that 'it is'. The predicate 'is not' was literally nonsense: not-being was impossible, inexpressible, and inconceivable; and since not-being was equated at this time with empty space, it followed that there could be no movement. But Parmenides rejected change on metaphysical rather than physical grounds, since any change involved its subject in *not-being* what it was before. (This argument involved a confusion between the existential and the predicative 'is' which was not cleared up until Plato.) From the single premise 'it is' Parmenides proceeded to the conclusion that reality or 'being' is homogeneous, motionless, solid and indivisible: 'since there is a furthest limit, it [Being] is bounded from every side, like the mass of a well-rounded sphere'. Parmenides was still obliged to use materialistic language, and would no doubt, if pressed, have said that this reality was concrete. From now on, however, a more abstract language was developed, and it became possible to attribute to the new kinds of reality a status different from that of phenomena. Parmenides, ignoring Heraclitus here, seems to have started from the old problem of how an initial unity can turn into a plural world. His emphasis on 'limit' suggests that he was deliberately rejecting the 'unlimited' component of Pythagorean DUALISM. His follower ZENO of Elea, too,

is thought by many to have directed his paradoxes (which show that space is continuous, not composed of discrete points) against the Pythagorean view of matter. A curious and professedly 'deceitful' appendix, in which Parmenides outlines a cosmology based not on one but on two substances probably reflects, as well as some reaction against Pythagoreanism, his doubts over rejecting the world of manifest experience. Certainly it gives a hint that pluralism is a possible escape from his dilemma.

To meet this dilemma Empedocles posited no less than four 'roots' or permanent kinds of matter: fire, water, earth (Heraclitus' world-masses), together with air, the concrete existence of which he confirmed by observation. To these were added two kinetic agents, Love and Strife – motives of attraction and repulsion which, anthropomorphic as they obviously are, were described concretely as 'equal in length and breadth' to the four roots. The different substances in Nature, apart from unmixed earth, water, and so on, were compounds of roots welded together by the admixture of Love. Empedocles felt obliged to propose a uniform stage of existence – not a true cosmogonical origin, which might imply illegitimate 'becoming', but a recurrent period in a cycle – in which all things are mixed by Love in a homogeneous mass equivalent to Parmenides' 'sphere' of Being. Only Strife, by coming somewhat obscurely to 'the lowest depths of the vortex', is excluded. Then, by the gradual intrusion of Strife, the roots begin to separate into different combinations, until eventually Love is excluded in turn and Strife has separated the roots into isolated masses. A world could only be formed in one of the two intermediate stages between the total domination of Love or Strife: our world belongs to the stage when Strife is increasing. Each intermediate cosmological stage produces different stages of animal evolution, generating monsters and bisexual creatures as well as the more efficient species of our present world. Sensation can be valid, since it is caused by material effluences from objects entering pores in the sense-organs: earth is perceived by earthy components in the body, fire by fire, as in vision, and so on. Empedocles also wrote a more mystical poem called 'Purifications', in which the soul, originally divine, is polluted by Strife and cast into the world of opposites; after successive incarnations it may purify itself and regain the realms of Love.

Anaxagoras, like Empedocles active around the middle of the fifth century, also maintained that physical change, being merely the aggregation and dispersion of different kinds of permanently existing matter, did not imply that 'what is' must turn into the vicious 'what is not'. But for him these kinds of matter were not four or six, but as many as there were different natural substances. Originally these were all mixed together in a sort of Parmenidean One; then the motive substance, now described as Mind, and 'subtlest of all objects and purest', started a rotation and so, by separation and re-aggregation, a cosmogony. Objects in the world were compounded of lumps or particles called 'seeds'. There is 'a portion of everything in everything' – a portion, probably, of every natural substance (except Mind, which only exists in some things) in every seed. Each seed has the apparent character of the portion that predominates. Thus the original unity is preserved in the developed world, while evident alterations can be explained by the ratio of the portions of different seeds. Anaxagoras argued, against both the Pythagoreans and the Eleatic Zeno, that matter is infinitely divisible, evidently failing to notice that this was incompatible with the principle of 'a portion of everything in everything'. At all events his theory, though complicated and in places self-refuting, preserved appearances without contradicting the Eleatic premise; it further avoided the difficulties of Empedocles' cyclical scheme, and the objection that the formation of natural substances out of Empedoclean 'roots' seemed to involve coming-to-be of a kind.

5 *The Sophists*. It was at about this time that the Sophists, professional teachers of wisdom, made themselves felt. They believed that the current physical theories and the Eleatic rejection of the phenomenal world were either over-complicated or absurd or both, and were in any case irrelevant to practical life. PROTAGORAS and Gorgias, the most important of them, taught that the constitution of the world lay outside human knowledge, and that we should assess things on the basis of our own individual experience. Yet there now appeared a much simpler physical explanation of the world and its changes. ATOMISM was probably invented around 440–30 by LEUCIPPUS, of whom we know very little, and elaborated by Democritus, before being adopted by EPICURUS and expounded by LUCRETIUS. The atomists began by denying the Eleatic contention that empty space, or the void, cannot exist. There is not-being, in this sense; in addition there is homogeneous, solid matter, which is not continuous (as was Parmenides' Being) but contained in an infinite number of indivisible, invisible, atoms. Reality consists, then, in atoms and the void. The atoms are constantly in motion, colliding and rebounding; no metaphorical cause of motion was needed. Atoms differ only in position and shape, but sometimes they

get caught up with each other to form complexes, and a world arises when the collisions and rebounds of an isolated group of atoms happen to start a vortex, where heavy complexes of atoms are driven to the centre, light ones to the circumference. Human beings are themselves mere complexes of atoms, their souls being made of mobile spherical ones. Leucippus adapted the Empedoclean theory of sensation: objects emit effluences, 'membranes' of atoms which, sometimes distorted in passage, make physical contact with the atoms of the sense-organ and then of the soul. It follows that there are no real qualities: appearances are secondary (but not therefore negligible; Democritus had a developed ethic, aimed at moral well-being), and in reality there are only atoms and void. Thus atomism simultaneously fulfilled the conditions of Eleatic logic and the aims of Milesian material monism. An entirely a priori construction, it has little in common with modern atomic theory, though this itself grew out of GASSENDI's revival of Democritean atomism.

Various other theories of an eclectic nature were propounded from the mid fifth century onwards; by Hippon, for example, and Archelaus. Cratylus exaggerated Heracliteanism by holding that everything is in flux all the time, while Diogenes of Apollonia produced an unusually coherent old-style monistic system in which air is basic substance, with warm air as divine and intelligent, directing all things for the best. This was the kind of teleology that Socrates wanted; but Socrates rejected physics and concentrated on ethics and the soul – soul or mind being the obvious teleological agent in his still anthropomorphic view. In many ways the Socratic reaction, aided by the Sophists and by current anthropological, medical and social ideas,

brought physical speculation to a depressingly sudden halt; but by his interest in definitions Socrates initiated a deeper study of logic, without which philosophy could not have made further progress.

The Pre-Socratics, who for the most part made little appeal to their lay contemporaries, plainly had great influence on their philosophical successors; negatively, in the main, on Plato, but positively on Aristotle in his revival of physics. Atomism, furthermore, survived for centuries through Epicurus, while Stoicism was deeply indebted to Heraclitus. But it may legitimately be asked whether their fragmentary science and philosophy have any value other than as a necessary primitive stage on the way to serious speculation. The inevitable deficiencies of these lively thinkers are striking but instructive: their love of inference unconfirmed, for the most part, by observation, let alone experiment; their retention of mythical and metaphorical explanations of change; their inadequate linguistic resources, which delayed or distorted the formation of abstract concepts; their reluctance to examine what was implied by knowledge, and their rudimentary logic. Yet they also had great virtues; and apart from the admirable quality of the rapid and systematic intellectual progress from Thales to Democritus, or the comprehensiveness of systems like that of Heraclitus, the Pre-Socratics illustrate in a particularly clear form certain problems of materialistic philosophy and the limitations of some of their classical solutions: problems, for example, of presupposed unity and observed plurality; of unseen or structural types of unity; of the physical source of change; of the evaluation of sense-perception, and the interrelation of ethics and physics. In this respect Pre-Socratic thought may perhaps be said to have philosophical as well as historical value. (G.S.K.)

Price, Henry Habberley (1899–1984)
English philosopher, who worked at
Oxford and wrote mainly on perception
and PHILOSOPHY OF MIND, and also on psychical research. In his first book,
Perception (1932), he rejected previous
theories about the relation between
SENSE-DATA and material objects, especially the theory that the latter *cause* the
former and so are known solely by their
effects. In his view, sense-data not only
belong to the physical object, but are
related intimately among themselves,
forming a 'family', or a set of series
each converging on a standard member;
these standard members compose the
Standard Solid, which has the shape
ordinarily called 'the real shape of the
thing'. For Price a 'thing' is a family of
sense-data *together* with the coincident
physical object, but he could say so little
about the object that he ran close to
PHENOMENALISM. His later *Thinking
and Experience* (1953) rejected theories
which make thinking consist entirely
of the use of symbols or of images or
of concepts treated as subsistent objects,
contending that recognition is basic
and that concepts are 'recognitional
capacities'.   (R.HALL.)

Price, Richard (1723–91) English
theologian and Minister at Newington
Green, London. His *Review of the
Principal Questions in Morals* (1758) is
the earliest clear and cogently developed
DEONTOLOGICAL theory – that is, an
account of morality based on the concepts
of 'right' and 'obligation'. At loggerheads
with the school of HUTCHESON and HUME,
Price saw these as indefinable, a priori
and objective. He attacked not simply
their arguments for an ethic of 'sentiment', but the basis of their EMPIRICISM
itself. Universal notions and concepts
such as substance, duration, and infinity

cannot, he thought, be explained from a
radical empiricist standpoint; nor could
the basic notions of morals. Price followed BUTLER in his rejection of psychological HEDONISM, but did not share
Butler's confidence that duty and interest
for the most part coincide in this life. He
argued that a hereafter must be postulated
in order to make sense of our moral experience; but he saw that an *infinitely* long
after-life cannot be demonstrated in this
way. Particularly valuable throughout
Price's moral philosophy are his serious
acknowledgement of the facts of moral
conflict and his tough-minded refusal to
accept over-simplifying 'supreme principles', such as those of the egoists and
utilitarians of his day.   (R.W.H.)

Prichard, Harold Arthur (1871–1947)
The English philosopher H. A. Prichard
was probably the outstanding member of
the realist movement at Oxford of which
Cook WILSON was the acknowledged
leader. His only large-scale publication on
the theory of knowledge was *Kant's Theory
of Knowledge* (1909), a polemical work in
which he opposes his realism to KANT. In
later years he modified these views, holding that we perceive only coloured
patches and not bodies, of which we
could have only inferential knowledge. In
moral philosophy his paper 'Does Moral
Philosophy Rest on a Mistake?' (1912)
was influential in the revival of intuitionist ethics: Prichard claimed that we could
know, simply by attending to the matter,
that certain acts are duties, while any
attempt at a general theory of why such
acts are duties was a mistake. In ethics,
however, as in epistemology, he grew
sceptical in later years; in *Duty and
Ignorance of Fact* (1932) he admitted a
considerable element of subjectivity into
the assessment of our duties.   (J.O.U.)

Probability Probability has given rise to several conflicting philosophical theories. If we concentrate on such statements as 'the probability of heads when a penny is tossed is one half', then the *frequency theory* may well seem most plausible. The statement will be taken to mean, roughly, that in the long run the frequency with which a tossed coin will fall heads upwards will be one in two. Special attractions of this theory are that, in a well-known version of it, it follows from the definition of probability that the axioms of the mathematical theory must be applicable and that it manifestly ties up probability very closely with statistical data. On the other hand it is very difficult indeed to give a satisfactory version of this theory when, as is necessary, more accurate expressions are substituted for 'in the long run' to indicate what frequency is relevant. The frequency theory was first stated in detail by VENN in his *Logic of Chance* (1866); other well-known exponents are von MISES and Reichenbach.

If we turn our attention to such statements as 'there is probably life on Mars' the frequency theory becomes specially unplausible; when dealing with the probability of theories, hypotheses and special events it is hard to see how we could be referring to any sequence of events or any frequency within such a series, though some philosophers have attempted to sustain such a view. When dealing with such examples it is much more plausible to regard the word 'probable' as indicating that the statement 'there is life on Mars' should be accepted with some reserve; that it is made in a condition of *evidential satisfactoriness* midway between those we might indicate by saying 'we know there is life on Mars' and 'there is no ground for supposing life on Mars'.

CARNAP, BRAITHWAITE, RUSSELL and many other philosophers agreed that the notion of probability is used in both the frequency way and in the evidence-assessing way and that we must understand it according to context. When a numerical statement is in principle possible, some explanation of a frequency type is given; but where a statement takes the form 'it is probably the case that so and so', where no numerical valuation seems plausible, the word 'probably' is taken to be indicative of caution. It should be added that the great classical French mathematical writers (see PASCAL) defined the probability of an event as the ratio of favourable to total possibilities; this is quite inadequate for philosophical purposes, since the 'possibilities' referred to are hardly distinguishable from probabilities and it is hard to see how to add up favourable possibilities without falling into severe logical difficulties.   (J.O.U.)

Proclus See NEOPLATONISM.

Protagoras The Greek sophist Protagoras of Abdera, who flourished *c*.450–40 BC, is credited with several books on logic, cultural origins, and human behaviour, and was famous as a teacher of *areté*, practical excellence or political and rhetorical skill, working in several cities and taking fees for his teaching. He attacked the dogmatism of contemporary religion and philosophy, saying 'I am unable to know about the gods either that they exist or that they do not, or what form they have; for there are many things that prevent knowledge – both the obscurity of the subject and the shortness of human life.' It was possible to make contradictory statements on any subject, and each could be true according to circumstances; and we could never discover any single absolute truth, since our own nature is intimately involved in any judgment. This is probably the reference of Protagoras' famous dictum 'Man is the measure of all things, of the existence of the things that are and the non-existence of the things that are not', and seems to be directed particularly against the extreme ELEATIC ontology, which was also subjected to critical examination by Protagoras' contemporary, Gorgias. See also PRE-SOCRATICS.   (G.S.K.)

Psychoanalysis Psychoanalysis, or 'depth psychology', was invented in Vienna in the 1890s by Sigmund Freud (1856–1939), who described it as 'a procedure for the medical treatment of the nervously ill'. But it is a very unusual kind of medicine: it consists in frequent and regular private consultations between a patient and an analyst, sometimes spread over many years; and as Freud said, 'nothing takes place between them except that they talk to each other'. The patient's side of the conversation comprises reminiscences, self-descriptions, reports of dreams, and verbal free associations. The analyst's contributions are carefully-considered 'interpretations' of what the patient has said. The aim of psychoanalysis is to discover experiences which haunt the patient's memory, but which are so painful that they have been 'repressed' into 'the Unconscious'. It is these repressed memories, according to Freud, rather than physiological abnormalities, which cause most nervous illness; they are also the nucleus of non-neurotic personalities. Freud's enormous experience as an analyst persuaded him that the crucial memories in everyone's life refer to early childhood, and that they are all essentially concerned with the child's experience of itself as either a boy or a girl and its sexual feelings about its mother-figure, its father-figure, and itself (the 'Oedipus Complex').

Freud made two basic claims about psychoanalysis: that it affords unrivalled insight into individual personalities; and that skilful 'interventions' by analysts can cure nervous disorders, and so replace 'misery' with 'common unhappiness'. Logically these claims are independent, of course: psychoanalytic treatment might be successful even if the interpretations on which it was based were untrue; and profound insight into neuroses need not necessarily help to cure them.

Freud conceived of psychoanalysis as part of the inexorable progress of dispassionate scientific materialism, the third and final blow to humanity's inflated view of its uniqueness and importance. Copernicanism, he said, had demonstrated that the earth is not the centre of the universe; Darwinism, that *homo sapiens* is not the lord of the animal kingdom; and now psychoanalysis proved that the conscious self 'is not master in its own house'. Philosophy, according to Freud, was incorrigibly prejudiced in favour of consciousness, and hence inseparable from pre-scientific superstition.

In fact, however, many philosophers have welcomed psychoanalysis. Freud's apparent faith in the healing powers of self-knowledge could be assimilated to the traditional Socratic imperative: 'Know thyself'; and followers of WITTGENSTEIN could see the philosopher and the analyst as engaged in essentially the same enterprise – offering painstaking and intricate therapy so as to relieve people of conceptual and psychic disorders, respectively. Their main reservation about psychoanalysis concerned Freud's tendency (as they saw it) to treat concepts like 'repression' as literal descriptions of quasi-hydraulic processes inside a pseudo-material machine called 'the mind', rather than as METAPHORS.

Some philosophers have been totally hostile to psychoanalysis. Ironically, these critics align themselves with the very same current of scientific materialism as Freud. To the LOGICAL POSITIVISTS, for example, or to POPPER, psychoanalysis is a perfect example of a pseudo-science: the analyst's 'findings' are protected from open scientific scrutiny by the confidentiality of the psychoanalytic session; and the idea of the inexhaustible interpretability of the Unconscious prevents analysts from venturing specific predictions which could be definitively tested.

The third and most prolific philosophical response to psychoanalysis regards it as a significant event within philosophy itself. According to GADAMER, for example, Freud taught philosophy to 'get behind the surface of what is meant' and to 'go behind the subjectivity of the act of meaning'; for him, as for HABERMAS and RICOEUR, Freud was a key innovator in the development of philosophy as HERMENEUTICS. To socialist philosophers like MARCUSE, psychoanalytic ideas of repression and the Unconscious are in part descriptions of the misery and ALIENATION peculiar to modern capitalistic bureaucracies. Moreover, as ALTHUSSER noted, the idea that people's consciousness is systematically at odds with their real situation corresponds closely to the Marxist theory of IDEOLOGY. SARTRE, though critical of Freud's 'materialism', thought of his own version of phenomenology as 'existential psychoanalysis'. According to Sartre, Freud's leading achievement (especially in the later writings, where the conceptions of 'consciousness' and 'the Unconscious' were overlaid by the more developmental ideas of 'Ego', 'Id', and 'Superego') was that, like HEGEL, he devised a way of thinking of the mind, and particularly the 'I' or the 'Ego', as constructed in a historical, social world, rather than as the expression of some pre-established interiority. For many feminists, Freud's achievement was to uncover one of the repressed themes of philosophical thought, namely GENDER.

The philosophical adoption of psychoanalysis was taken still further by LACAN, and by neo-Nietzscheans like DELEUZE and neo-Heideggerians like DERRIDA: for them, Freud has unmasked the self-deceptions not just of consciousness and the ego, but also of the very ideas of 'Reason' and 'the Real', which they take to be the unquestioned presuppositions of the entirety of Western philosophy. Like FOUCAULT, they criticize Freud for failing to pursue his ideas to their true conclusion, namely that the whole idea of pursuing the truth is dangerous and deluded. Freud, of course, would hardly recognize these philosophical views as developments of his own work; but, given his doctrine of the Unconscious, he could not consistently claim the authority to disown them. See also MIND, PHILOSOPHY OF MIND.

[J.R.]

Putnam, Hilary (1926–) American mathematician and philosopher who was trained in logical positivism and has been trying to escape from it ever since, with special help from QUINE and WITTGENSTEIN. He holds that modern philosophy has been impaled on a dilemma – 'either ahistorical unchanging canons of rationality *or* cultural relativism' – which is fundamentally misconceived (see *Reason, Truth and History*, 1981). His other books include: *Mind, Language and Reality* (1975); *Realism with a Human Face* (1990); *Renewing Philosophy* (1992); *Pragmatism* (1995), and *The Collapse of the Fact/Value Dichotomy* (2002).

Pyrrho of Elis (*c*.360–*c*.270 BC) Pyrrho is by tradition the earliest of the SCEPTICS. His name is associated with an extreme variety of SCEPTICISM (sometimes called 'Pyrrhonism'), as opposed to the moderate variety espoused by the Middle and New ACADEMY.

Pythagoras The Greek philosopher Pythagoras of Samos flourished *c*.530 BC. He left Samos to escape the tyranny of Polycrates and settled in Croton in South Italy, where for a time he had great political influence. He established there a community of disciples, partly religious and partly scientific. The master himself wrote nothing and since his followers, out of piety, attributed their own works to him it is especially hard to assess his ideas. Some lines of Xenophanes prove that Pythagoras believed in the transmigration of the soul, even between different species, since all living things were akin. He was also renowned for his scientific and mathematical knowledge, and there is no reason to disconnect him from the theorem that bears his name. He also probably made the important discovery that the musical scale has a numerical basis, that is, that its main harmonic intervals can be expressed in ratios of the first four integers. These integers together formed the Decad, to which sacred significance was attached in his community; but whether Pythagoras himself maintained that not only music, but the whole world, was somehow numerical, and made up out of 'limit' and 'the unlimited', is uncertain. See also PRE-SOCRATICS, PYTHAGOREANS. (G.S.K.)

Pythagoreans PYTHAGORAS founded a community of disciples in Croton in Southern Italy, which split into a mathematical and a religious group. The latter lived according to taboos based on Pythagoras' idea of the kinship of living things and the necessity for purification of body and soul. The 'mathematicians',

while probably not rejecting these ideas, associated them with developments of Pythagoras' discovery that the musical scale is numerical. Since music was held to have special power over soul, which permeated the cosmos, the whole world must be somehow numerical. The elements of number, and thus of the world, were the even, representing the unlimited, and the odd, representing limit. A table of ten pairs of basic opposites within the world was drawn up, in which odd, male, straight, good, at rest, etc., came under 'limit', their contraries under 'unlimited'. Unfortunately there is little evidence here apart from ARISTOTLE's rather vague account, which did not distinguish early from later Pythagoreanism. Most of these ideas were probably formed by the time of PARMENIDES, who seems to attack Pythagorean DUALISM. By this time, too, the units which formed number were probably conceived as possessing spatial magnitude, so that lines, surfaces and solids could be expressed as sums of units, and objects were literally made out of number. According to the Pythagorean cosmogony, which may have developed a little later, an initial unit 'drew in' the unlimited, in the form of the void, and somehow divided into other units separated by the unlimited. These unit-point-atoms then grew into lines, planes and solids. At the centre of the universe lies fire; the stars, of which the earth is one, each produce a sound according to the speed of their revolution, and these make up a 'harmony of spheres' inaudible by human beings. See also PRE-SOCRATICS, ZENO. (G.S.K.)

Q

Qualities   Primary and Secondary, see ATOMISM, DESCARTES, LOCKE.

Quantum Mechanics   Max Planck, Albert Einstein and Nils Bohr originally developed Quantum Theory in the early 1900s, to explain the interactions between atoms and radiation. 'Energy' was found to be packaged in finite 'quanta', so that the energy in a tight 'wave' behaved like a stream of 'particles'. In the 1920s de Broglie extended this 'duality' by showing that material 'particles' could behave like waves and a radically new mechanics was created by Schrödinger, Heisenberg, Dirac and von Neumann. As a formal calculus for predicting experimental results it is astonishingly successful, but its interpretation is racked with controversy. Quantum Mechanics is philosophically interesting because of its implications for DETERMINISM and REALISM, and some argue that it also has implications for LOGIC. A remarkable body of 'meta-theory' has developed on the question of whether its revolutionary features could be reversed by future science.

Quantum Mechanics represents a system by a complex mathematical function which ascribes ranges of *potential* properties to the component entities in a coordinated fashion. Which properties are realized when a measurement is performed is a matter of PROBABILITY. Furthermore, certain properties are 'paired' so that, according to Heisenberg's Uncertainty Principle, closer definition of one implies more 'uncertainty' in the other. Since this appears to make precise prediction impossible in principle, quantum mechanics is often taken to have refuted determinism.

Bohr's Complementary Interpretation sets its face against theoretical realism by treating the micro-system and the measuring apparatus as an indivisible whole. Thus properties whose measurement requires mutually exclusive experimental arrangements cannot be simultaneously real. In Quantum Mechanics the HOLISTIC coordination of a system remains even when its components are apparently separate, so a measurement on one 'entity' fixes the state of another. Alternatives to quantum mechanics, such as that of David Bohm, which treat properties as real, can model this only if they permit instantaneous action-at-a-distance.

But can it be measurement which makes properties actual? If Bohr's way of looking at the situation is applied to an enlarged system which incorporates the observer, then his argument seems to imply that the new system will be undefined until observed by someone else! And so on *ad infinitum*. To block this regress Wigner argued that consciousness makes measurement definite, thus committing physics to IDEALISM. Conversely, Everett and Wheeler's Many-Worlds Interpretation rescued realism, but only at the cost of claiming that interactions continually split the world into more and more parallel universes. The theory's technical triumphs only deepen our metaphysical perplexity.   [J.H.P.]

Quine, Willard V. O. (1908–2000)   The logician and philosopher Willard van Orman Quine was born in Ohio and studied under WHITEHEAD at Harvard, where he was to spend the rest of his life. In the early 1930s he was converted to LOGICAL

POSITIVISM and went to Warsaw to study with CARNAP, whom he regarded as his 'greatest teacher'. Carnap migrated to America in 1936 and Quine recalls how he, GOODMAN and other young American philosophers 'moved with Carnap as henchmen through the metaphysicians' camp'.

Quine never broke with Carnap's orientation towards the natural sciences and his belief that the heart of philosophy is mathematical logic. But his numerous writings, all cast in a bright laconic style recalling Chandler and Runyon, have apparently left Carnap's vision of scientific philosophy in ruins, since in Quine's system natural science is presented as a (superior) form of metaphysics, not a radical alternative to it.

Carnap and other logical positivists had divided knowledge into two components: empirical propositions, which were supposed to correspond one-by-one to sensory experiences; and logical propositions, which were no more than explications of structural properties of signs. Quine came to believe, however, that this view of knowledge depends upon an indefensible 'myth of meaning': it proceeds 'as if there were a gallery of ideas, and each idea were tagged with the expression that means it'. So, according to Quine, the stark anti-metaphysical programme of logical positivism was secretly in league with an extravagant metaphysic. The 'linguistic theory of logical truths', so dear to Carnap and other logical positivists, had 'less to it than meets the eye'.

Quine's 'adverse treatment', as he put it, of the idea of meaning, led him to discard two cardinal doctrines of logical positivism. The first was the 'belief in some fundamental cleavage between truths which are ANALYTIC, or grounded in meanings independent of matters of fact, and truths which are synthetic or grounded in fact'. The second was the 'reductionist' doctrine that 'each meaningful statement is equivalent to some logical construct upon terms which refer to immediate experience'. The effect of abandoning these 'two dogmas of empiricism' was, as Quine intended, 'a blurring of the supposed boundary between speculative metaphysics and natural science', and 'a shift towards PRAGMATISM'. Observations, experiments, and common sense formed, together with logic and the sciences, parts of a seamless 'web of knowledge'. The laws of logic were not rigid necessary truths, but simply statements which, for various practical reasons, we are particularly unwilling to revise; there was no clear boundary separating them from empirical facts, that is to say experiential opinions which we can freely revise, even though no experience could definitely require us to do so. LOCKE and HUME had espoused 'term-by-term empiricism'; FREGE had attended to 'statements' rather than 'terms'; but, for Quine, 'the unit of empirical significance is the whole of science'. Quine drew the conclusion that 'our statements about the external world face the tribunal of experience not individually but as a corporate body' – a doctrine which he credited to DUHEM, and which has come to be known as the 'Duhem-Quine thesis'.

These arguments are all contained in 'Two Dogmas of Empiricism' (1951), which was anthologized in *From a Logical Point of View* (1953), a collection which also contains 'On What There Is' (1948), which argues that every theory involves an ontology. Of course, many of the objects apparently named in a theory may not actually be required by it: their apparent names can be eliminated by means of RUSSELL's theory of descriptions. According to Quine's doctrine of 'ontological relativity', existence can then be defined as follows: 'to be is to be the value of a variable'. On pragmatic grounds (he acknowledges no others), Quine then implores scientists to reduce their ontological commitments to a minimum, so as to escape, if they can, from 'Plato's beard' – a 'tangled doctrine' which, with its luxuriant population of shadowy entities, 'has proved tough, frequently dulling the edge of OCKHAM'S razor'.

For Quine, the objects of the physical sciences and of ordinary common sense are 'cultural posits', just like Homer's Gods: 'in point of epistemological footing the physical objects and the gods differ only in degree and not in kind.' Or, as he argued in *Methods of Logic* (1952), 'statements, apart from an occasional collectors' item for epistemologists, are connected only deviously with experience', so that 'there is many a slip twixt objective cup and subjective lip'.

Quine gave a systematic portrayal of his position in *Word and Object* (1960), which proposed an austere 'canonical notation', purged of singular terms, as the likeliest framework for scientific progress. In this notation it was manifestly absurd to yearn for a solid foundation for empirical knowledge – 'a fancifully fanciless medium of unvarnished news'. Quine's scepticism about the very idea of meaning was dramatized in his doctrine of 'the indeterminacy of TRANSLATION'. This went far beyond 'the platitude that uniqueness of translation is absurd', to the astonishing thesis that there could be different ways of translating one language into another, which would offer incompatible translations of the same sentences but which would still fit all the observed facts. This thesis does not assert, of course, that there are shades of meaning which no translation can capture; on the contrary, it implies that the very idea of uncaptured shades of meaning is pointless. Critics have wondered, nevertheless, whether the indeterminacy thesis, and the idea of rival translations, can have any sense at all within Quine's system. Quine's other books include: *The Ways of Paradox* (1966); *Philosophy of Logic* (1970); *Ontological Relativity* (1969); and *Quiddities: an Intermittently Philosophical Dictionary* (1987). See also AMERICAN PHILOSOPHY, PHILOSOPHY OF SCIENCE, RELATIVISM. [J.R.]

Quinton, Anthony (1925–) British philosopher with sceptically materialistic opinions and broad but conservative sympathies. He is the author of *The Nature of Things* (1973) and of articles on Conceptualism, Nominalism, Phenomenalism, Scepticism, Sense-Data and Universals in this Encyclopedia.

R

Ramsey, Frank P. (1903–30) Mathematical logician who made significant contributions to theories of TRUTH and PROBABILITY, and whose early death was deeply mourned by many, including WITTGENSTEIN.

Rationalism In the usage of philosophers, the word 'rationalism' refers to the kinds of philosophical theory which claim that we can arrive at substantial knowledge about the nature of the world by pure reasoning, without appeal to any empirical premises. It is in that sense that DESCARTES, LEIBNIZ and SPINOZA are traditionally quoted as classical examples of rationalism. Rationalism is opposed to EMPIRICISM – the doctrine that experience is a necessary basis to all our knowledge – but neither term has a precise meaning. Thus we might expect that a pure empiricist would claim that all knowledge requires empirical premises, and J. S. MILL did at times make this claim; for him even mathematical truths are empirical generalizations. But most empiricists have admitted that mathematical truths are a priori; they are still considered to be empiricists if they claim that mathematical truths are analytic, formal truths which give no information about the nature of the world. Thus there is a tendency to consider that a rationalist is one who claims to have synthetic a priori knowledge, and who claims to know, wholly or in part, what the world is like by pure reason. But Leibniz is usually considered to be the most extreme of the rationalists because he claimed that in principle all truths could be known by pure reasoning, experience being but an inferior substitute for reason; yet Leibniz held that all truths of reason were guaranteed by the principle of contradiction and therefore, in modern terminology, analytic. However, Leibniz's claim that the contradictory of every true proposition is self-contradictory is very paradoxical, and we may say that the rationalist is one who claims knowledge which is not based on sense-experience and which cannot be regarded as purely formal. But this is still inadequate: KANT recognized synthetic a priori knowledge, only about phenomena as opposed to things themselves; he thought that it was one of the main virtues of his critical system that it avoided both rationalism and empiricism. (J.O.U.)

Rawls, John (1921–2002) American political philosopher, born in Baltimore, who transformed Anglo-American POLITICAL PHILOSOPHY with a series of articles published in the 1950s and 1960s culminating in *A Theory of Justice* (1971). In opposition to UTILITARIANISM, with its exclusive concern with aggregate happiness, Rawls argues that the fundamental political value is individual rights, or 'justice as fairness'. Rawls proceeds by reviving and generalizing the hypothesis of the SOCIAL CONTRACT as found in LOCKE, ROUSSEAU and KANT. The best political principles, he argues, are those which rational citizens would agree upon if they were to choose the 'basic structure of society' whilst a 'veil of ignorance' prevented them from knowing their own eventual position within it. According to Rawls they would recognize a general presumption in favour of equality, and hold that 'all social values – liberty and opportunity, income and wealth, and the bases of self-respect – are to he distributed equally unless an unequal distribution of any, or all, of these values is to everyone's advantage'.

On this basis, Rawls attempted to justify two principles of justice. The first and over-riding one states: 'each person is to have an equal right to the most extensive basic liberty compatible with a similar liberty for others'. The second specifies conditions under which inequalities may nevertheless be justified: 'Social and economic inequalities are to be arranged so that they are both (a) to the greatest benefit of the least advantaged and (b) attached to offices and positions open to all under conditions of fair equality of opportunity.'

Debate about Rawls' system has concentrated on part (a) of the second principle, which is known as 'the difference principle'. It implies that inequalities cannot be justified unless they are to the advantage even of the least privileged. Left-wing critics have feared that this opens the way for attempts to justify unacceptable inequalities. Right-wing critics (such as NOZICK) have argued that, provided the better-off gain their advantages rightfully, they are under no obligation to bother about the disadvantaged. Either way it seems that 'self-respect', which Rawls regards as 'perhaps the most important primary good', may not be safe in Rawls' system.

Rawls consolidated his positions in *Political Liberalism* (1993); *The Law of Peoples* and *Collected Papers* (1999); and *Lectures on the History of Moral Philosophy* (2000). See also LIBERALISM AND COMMUNITARIANISM.   [J.R.]

Realism   Realism is sometimes said to be the view that some things exist essentially independently of any mind. For example, realism about UNIVERSALS holds that they exist independently of any mind;

and NOMINALISM denies it. Mathematical realism claims that numbers exist independently of mind, which discovers rather than creates them. Realism about the external world asserts that physical objects exist essentially independently of the mind of any perceiver. PHENOME-NALISTS (sometimes called 'subjective idealists') deny realism about external physical objects; John Stuart MILL, for instance, held that physical objects are nothing more than sets of actual and possible sensory data, which themselves have existence only as the contents of a mind. Realists about social phenomena deny that social wholes can be accounted for entirely in terms of the psychological states of individuals (cf. HOLISM).

Some realists formulate their claims in terms of essential independence from human activity, since acting, in its proper sense, presupposes that the actor has intentions and purposes, and hence a mind. Contemporary thinkers normally restrict 'mind' to human minds; but traditionally, anti-realists such as BERKELEY and HEGEL allowed objects to be essentially independent of all human minds, but dependent on infinite mind, or the Deity.

The word 'essentially' is important here. It would not refute a realist about the external world if every bit of reality had depended in some causal or contingent way upon mind, and one can be a realist about objects (for instance, to use MARX's example, a cultivated cherry tree), which would not have existed without human activity. If such dependence is inessential to the thing, in the sense that the object logically could have existed independently of mind or activity, it poses no problem for a realist. But this characterization of realism has the unfortunate consequence of rendering realism about the mind impossible by definition, since obviously no mind can exist essentially independently of itself. One could avoid this difficulty by defining realism as the view that a thing could exist independently, not of mind in general, but more specifically of any beliefs or thoughts we might have about it. We are realists about mental contents like pain if we hold that one can be in pain even if one does not believe it. We are realists about morality if we think that actions can be right, or things can be good, whether or not anyone believes that they are. In this sense, realism is connected with the epistemological idea that what is real can always serve as an objective 'other' against which our beliefs can be tested. The important point for realism, recharacterized in this way, is that it is always possible either that our beliefs are wrong, or that we are wrong about which beliefs we have. Error and mistake are always possible. In epistemology, the correspondence theory of TRUTH is naturally associated with the metaphysical doctrine of realism.

Scientific realism can be characterized using this second definition. It is the view that scientific theories about unobservable entities should be construed at face value, as attempts to describe an independent even if unobservable reality. Instrumentalists (like PEIRCE) and phenomenalists (like MACH) argue for an antirealist view, that scientific theories do not refer to an independent reality, but are either heuristic tools for the prediction of empirical data, or shorthand summaries, equivalent to the set of empirical statements which follow from them. Of course, scientific realists need not deny the factual or causal dependence of some part of reality upon theory, for example, in the case of self-fulfilling predictions which bring about the facts that make them true. But for the scientific realist, any factual ties between reality and scientific theory are always logically or conceptually inessential.

Sometimes anti-realism is described more weakly as the view that our knowledge of reality is theory-dependent, or that it necessarily depends on language. It then might seem an easy step to conclude that reality itself is dependent on language or theory. But this characterization would be a mistake: a clear distinction must be drawn between the mind-dependence of language or theory and the alleged mind-dependence of the world itself. A scientific realist can accept that all descriptions of the world are theory-dependent (POPPER is a clear example of this). Suppose we have to use theory T in order to describe reality. Our descriptions of the world will be T-dependent, and T is certainly something we have created. But it does not follow that without theory T the world could not have been the way it is; all that follows is that without the theory we would not be able to describe the world that way.

The great problem that faces realism is that, since it places a gap between mind on the one hand and reality on the other, it has to say that real objects transcend the contents of our experience. Realists believe that material objects and theoretical entities are more than the experiential content of our minds; that social phenomena are more than the individuals who participate in them; and that universals are irreducible to the particulars of which those universals are true. But if real objects transcend experience, how is knowledge of reality possible? See also RELIGION. [D.-H.R.]

Reductio ad absurdum A technique of refutation in which a proposition is shown to entail a contradiction.

Reid, Thomas (1710–96) Thomas Reid was the originator of the Scottish philosophy of common sense. He was educated at Aberdeen and worked as a professor first at Aberdeen and then at Glasgow, where he succeeded Adam SMITH. Like KANT, he was prompted to his original philosophical position by reading HUME. Reid noted that all the modern philosophers – DESCARTES, LOCKE and BERKELEY, for example – assumed that the immediate objects of the human mind in thought and perception are peculiar mental entities called IDEAS, and that Hume had recognized that if we have access only to discrete and unconnected ideas we cannot have connected knowledge transcending ideas. But Hume's conclusions were too extreme in their skepticism to be tenable. Therefore his basic premise – the theory of ideas – must be abandoned. In the *Inquiry into the Human Mind* (1764) Reid therefore attacked the theory of ideas as neither intuitively evident nor helpful in explaining what it was introduced to explain.

In the *Essays on the Intellectual Powers of Man* (1785), Reid set out a realist account of perception, memory and conception, to replace the way of ideas. Common sense, he says, is 'that degree of judgment which is common to men with whom we can converse and transact business'. But, Reid held, 'all knowledge and all science must be built upon principles that are self-evident, and of such principles every man who has common sense is a competent judge when he conceives them distinctly'. First principles may be necessary, as in mathematics, or contingent. Reid gives a list of principles of common sense in the contingent sphere which is very similar to the one MOORE gave in his 'Defence of Common Sense'. It includes: (a) 'the existence of everything of which I am conscious'; (b) 'that the thoughts of which I am conscious are the thoughts of a being which I call myself, my mind, my person'; (c) 'that

those things did really happen which I distinctly remember'; (d) 'our own personal identity and continued existence'; and (e) 'that those things do really exist which we distinctly perceive by our senses, and are what we perceive them to be'. Anyone who doubts these principles will be incapable of rational intercourse and those philosophers, such as Hume, who profess to doubt them cannot do so sincerely and consistently. Reid's critical work is at all times clear and acute, though his own positive views do not emerge so clearly from his writings as do the inconsistencies and unplausibilities of Locke and Berkeley. (J.O.U.)

Reification Reification is the mistake of treating an abstraction, or relation, or convention, or artificial construct, as if it were a natural *thing* (Latin *res*). See ALIENATION.

Relativism Relativism can be characterized as the view (which PLATO reports PROTAGORAS as expressing) that 'man is the measure of all things'. Plato's discussion of the saying shows that it was construed as asserting that any person's views are as good as any one else's. Relativism, then, is a doctrine about differences between individuals (individualistic relativism) or between societies (social relativism). It may focus on differences in factual beliefs (scientific relativism); in morals (ethical relativism); in concepts (conceptual relativism); or in logic. Relativism asserts that in some sense what is true in one situation may not be true in another; that what is right or good in one situation may not be right or good in another; that the concepts used in one situation might be unintelligible in another; or that what is rational in one situation may not be rational in another.

Relativism does not simply assert that different things are believed or said or done in different times and places. Such differences may be only derivative and therefore compatible with there being some fundamental higher-order principles or rules or concepts, valid always and everywhere, which explain, in combination with different local facts about the circumstances in which the two things occur, such variations. There might, for example, be a single rule of scientific support which licenses inquirers with different information to believe incompatible theories. Or there might be a single ethical principle which entitles or requires persons in different circumstances to perform different actions. The mere fact that some languages use several concepts where other languages use only one (e.g. English and Eskimo concepts of snow) does not show that there are no fundamental concepts common to all languages. Nor does the fact that a sentence such as 'it is raining' can be true in one situation but not in another prove that truth is relative. Relativism should be defined as the assertion that some of these differences are (or at least may he) fundamental rather than derivative.

The idea that what is true in one situation might not be true in another may seem more plausible than it is. This may arise from two confusions: the belief that 'true in one situation but not in another' means nothing more than 'believed to be true in one situation but not in another'; and the failure to specify statements fully. The truth of 'it is raining' appears to be 'relative' because the sentence is incomplete; but the truth of 'it is raining at place p at time t' does not even appear to be relative.

Is there some scientific methodology, valid universally, for judging when one scientific theory or set of empirical beliefs is better than another? POPPER and LAKATOS believe there is; KUHN and FEYERABEND deny it. Popper, for example, requires that the theory withstand attempts to falsify it. Kuhn, on the other hand, argues that scientific change from one theory to another is essentially non-rational. On his view, transitions between scientific paradigms can be explained but never justified in terms of methodological considerations.

Some writers have held that different societies or individuals could employ fundamentally different logics (either deductive or inductive). GOODMAN's 'new riddle of induction' poses the possibility of an inductive logic fundamentally different from our own. There is also a great deal of controversy concerning the possibility of non-standard deductive logics, and the possibility of a logic which rejects the law of excluded middle, and thereby modifies the classical conception of TRUTH, certainly seems coherent. On the other hand, the idea of a society whose logic rejected the law of non-contradiction does seem deeply incoherent.

Conceptual and ethical relativism are more plausible. It is unlikely that we will find genuine empirical evidence of societies that differ fundamentally from us in concepts or in morality, but we can ask whether it is logically possible for two societies to differ in the most fundamental concepts they employ? QUINE, with his doctrine of the indeterminacy of translation, thinks it is: that there could be a society which used concepts of object stages or undetached object parts, for instance, rather than our concept of an object as enduring through space and time. If one society used a fundamental concept that another society had neither as a fundamental nor as a derived concept, the languages of the two societies would be, to that extent, mutually unintelligible.

Could what was fundamentally right or good in one society differ from what was fundamentally right or good in another? The answer to this depends on whether one regards values as being as much a part of the universe as facts are. If they are, then there is no more reason for good or right to differ fundamentally between societies than there is for truth to differ. But if, as for example HARE and SARTRE say, values are something we create, then there is a logical possibility, if not a real one, that different societies or individuals could create fundamentally different moralities. [D.-H.R.]

Relativity The theory of Relativity derives its name from the so-called Principle of Relativity, according to which the same laws of physics obtain whatever frame of reference is adopted. It is primarily due to Albert Einstein (1879–1955), and its philosophical interest lies in the overthrow of what were previously regarded as *necessary* truths about space and time.

Einstein's Special Relativity Theory (1905) removed a deep conflict between classical mechanics and electromagnetic theory by making the astonishing 'Light Postulate', which states that the velocity of light is *invariant*, that is, the same in every frame of reference. Einstein explains this postulate by showing that any measurement of velocity requires the synchronization of spatially separated clocks. His method is based (with benign circularity) on the Light Postulate, which implies that distances and time-intervals are relative to frame of reference. Thus 'relativity' undermines the idea that there is a unique, universal 'flow' of time. Special Relativity Theory was devised in opposition to 'Aether Theories' which attempted to interpret phenomena in terms of picturable mechanisms. Einstein's idea of 'invariance' generated more elegant and more fruitful strategies for theory construction. Contrary to popular belief, the theory does not abolish

'absolute' (i.e. invariant) quantities but creates new, 'four-dimensional', ones (Minkowski 1908).

In General Relativity Theory (1916) Einstein attempted to show that the structure of space is determined by matter, thus eliminating 'Absolute Space' from physics. By taking the paths of light rays in a vacuum to define 'straightest lines', Einstein was able to treat 'gravitation' as the curvature of space-time, and show that the world has a non-Euclidean geometry. The theory explained known anomalies and predicts novel effects (most dramatically the Expansion of the Universe).

Relativity's success in displacing the entrenched assumptions of Newtonian theory shows how hazardous it is to claim a priori status for concepts in physics, and how easy it is to mistake a long-lived theory for the final truth. Nevertheless some argue that the general outline of Relativity Theory can be deduced a priori, and it seems certain that future developments will not reverse the changes wrought by Relativity. [J.H.P.]

Religion The human race seems small and weak compared with the vastness of nature, and each of us occupies the stage of history but briefly. Are our lives really significant? If so how? In all cultures over recorded human history religions have offered answers to such questions through ideas rooted in experiences which seem to transcend the mundane routines of ordinary life. Typically a religion traces the value of human life to a 'TRANSCENDENT realm' beyond nature and human society. Rituals, prayer, and meditation are justified by sacred stories about transactions between the two realms.

Philosophers who interpret the religious idea of a transcendent realm in a REALIST fashion face a dilemma: either this realm has effects on the world of everyday experience or it does not. If it does not, then it is difficult to see how it can have any relevance for human life. But if it does, then it seems that the progress of science threatens its 'transcendent' status. Since the scientific revolution of the seventeenth century, one tendency, running from DESCARTES to WHITEHEAD, has endeavoured to construct metaphysical systems which encompass both sides of this dilemma. But another tendency, from BERKELEY to DUHEM, has counter-attacked with anti-realist interpretations of science, intended to leave room for realist accounts of Religion.

Following KANT, most philosophers have accepted that knowledge of a transcendent reality is unattainable, and religious thinkers such as Karl BARTH, have welcomed this conclusion, believing that it leaves room for 'faith'. Indeed Barth embraced the LOGICAL POSITIVISTS' conclusion that the tenets of faith are literally meaningless, arguing that this underscores our utter dependence on Divine Grace. Religious language provides a means for talking about experiences of 'numinous' awe, or 'mystical' ecstasy or tranquility. It is clear that religious symbolism can express or evoke such experiences, and that those who have them feel that they are of immense significance – it matters a great deal to them that their 'nirvana' is attained through a moral and meditative discipline and not by injecting a chemical which disrupts normal brain function. However it is hard to seehow the occurrence of such experiences can provide a basis for religious conviction. NIETZSCHE and the EXISTENTIALISTS took the collapse of theistic realism to signal the need for a fundamental reappraisal of human values, and many followers of WITTGENSTEIN have come to the conclusion that statements like 'God is love' can only be understood as expressions of belief in the importance of human love. Such analyses accord with Matthew Arnold's comment that religion is 'morality touched by emotion'.

Anthropological studies have vastly extended out understanding of different forms of religious life, showing how religious doctrines can fulfil such social functions as legitimizing the distribution of power by reference to a 'transcendent' source of authority supposedly beyond renegotiation. This complements philosophical scepticism about realist accounts of religion.

Some thinkers (such as HEGEL) have argued that the philosophical quest and the religious quest have the same goal, and indeed that the questions with which religions are concerned can be answered only by philosophy. Much philosophical analysis is destructive of the metaphysical pretensions of traditional religious doctrine and of the idea that religious commitment can yield knowledge which cannot be attained by other means. At the very least the philosophical enterprise calls for detachment from one's preconceptions and a refusal to adopt beliefs which cannot be rationally justified. That such a commitment can be as total as any religious commitment is symbolized in the story of how SOCRATES met his death. Although philosophy no longer seems able to offer metaphysical consolations of the sort which sustained him, the quest for significance remains at its roots.

[J.H.P.]

Ricoeur, Paul (1913–) The French phenomenologist Paul Ricoeur has been hailed as one of the few twentieth century thinkers to surmount the division between European and Anglo-American philosophy (see CONTINENTAL PHILOSOPHY). Ricoeur is principally renowned for his original development of the HERMENEUTIC method in philosophy, which consists in interpreting the meaning contained within pre-rational signs or symbols. Ricoeur's famous phrase 'the symbol gives rise to thought' expresses the basic premise of hermeneutics: that the symbols of myth, religion, art and ideology all carry messages which may be uncovered by philosophical interpretation. Hermeneutics is defined accordingly as a method for deciphering indirect meaning, a reflective practice of unmasking hidden meanings beneath apparent ones. While this method was originally used by theologians to investigate the inner meanings of sacred texts, it was radically redeployed by thinkers like DILTHEY, HEIDEGGER, GADAMER and Ricoeur to explore the linguistic dimension of human being-in-the-world.

While a prisoner of war in Germany during the Second World War, Ricoeur became acquainted with the writings of German phenomenologists and existentialists. Afterwards he launched his philosophical career with major works on JASPERS and MARCEL and an extensive commentary on and translation of HUSSSERL's *Ideas* (1950). In contrast to SARTRE and MERLEAU-PONTY, who developed French phenomenology in a polemical existentialist direction, Ricoeur turned it into a hermeneutic project. Concerned throughout his career with the ultimate ontological question – the meaning of Being – Ricoeur rejects what he sees as the 'short cuts' of Hegel and Heidegger. He proclaims the inevitability of a 'truncated ontology' which, instead of presuming direct access to truth, accepts the obligation of always approaching it sideways, through the mediation of symbols, images, stories and ideologies. This indirect questioning of meaning, necessitated by the finite nature

of human understanding, is what Ricoeur calls the 'hermeneutic detour'. It has led him through such inquiries as *The Symbolism of Evil* (1960), which analysed the symbols of myth and religion, and *Freud and Philosophy* (1965), concerned with the interpretation of dreams and unconscious desires, to an impressive variety of studies of the signifying activity of language, ideology and fiction – *The Conflict of Interpretations* (1969); *The Rule of Metaphor* (1975); *Hermeneutics and the Human Sciences* (1981); and *Time and Narrative* (1984–5).

Unlike the existentialists, who held that the human subject is the ultimate origin of all meaning, Ricoeur insisted that meaning is always mediated through cultural, linguistic and social signs. But unlike the STRUCTURALISTS, he never abandoned the basic phenomenological notions of world, self and history. An astute synthesizer of rival theories, Ricoeur sought to chart a course beyond both the traditional ontology of absolute truth and the *avant-garde* ideology of the absolute text. Relentlessly faithful to an open-ended 'conflict of interpretations', Ricoeur would seem to have placed his own philosophical bet on the possible existence of some TRANSCENDENT meaning, even though, on his own principles, such a meaning could never be known directly.   [R.K.]

Rights   See ETHICS, POLITICAL PHILOSOPHY, LIBERALISM AND COMMUNITARIANISM, LOCKE, NOZICK, RAWLS.

Rorty, Richard (1931–)   Richard Rorty is an American philosopher and critic whose central interest is in METAPHILOSOPHY. Starting from the work of QUINE and others he has developed a comprehensive criticism of ANALYTIC PHILOSOPHY. In the editorial introduction to his anthology, *The Linguistic Turn* (1967), Rorty argued that 'the entire philosophical tradition' had been put 'on the defensive' in the twentieth century. 'What makes most philosophers in the English-speaking world linguistic philosophers', he wrote, 'is the same thing that makes most philosophers in continental Europe phenomenologists – namely, a sense of despair resulting from the inability of traditional philosophers to make clear what could count as evidence for or against the truth of their views'. This raised the question whether modern culture was moving into a 'post-philosophical' phase, in which 'philosophers will have worked themselves out of a job', and also posed problems for 'talking about the HISTORY OF PHILOSOPHY'. The way forward, Rorty suggested, might lie in overthrowing the 'spectatorial account of knowledge' which had dominated philosophy 'since Plato and Aristotle'. Rorty detected 'the beginning of a thoroughgoing rethinking' in the works of DEWEY, HAMPSHIRE, SARTRE, HEIDEGGER and WITTGENSTEIN.

Rorty sought to execute this programme in *Philosophy and the Mirror of Nature* (1980), which argued that 'traditional philosophy' in general is a desperate 'attempt to escape from history'. Ever since Descartes' 'invention of the mind', philosophers had dreamed of providing timeless 'foundations' for knowledge, morality, language, or society; but they had never been able to establish that they were doing anything more then 'eternalize' contingent prejudices. To replace the pretensions of 'systematic philosophy', Rorty recommended the 'edifying philosophy' which he claimed to find in Wittgenstein, Heidegger and Dewey – philosophers who aimed 'to help their readers, or society as a whole, break free from outworn vocabularies and attitudes, rather than to provide "grounding" for the intuitions and customs of the present'.

Philosophy as Rorty conceives it is 'a voice in a conversation', rather than 'a subject' or 'a field of professional inquiry'. He elaborated this conception in *Consequences of Pragmatism* (1982) and drew some political conclusions in *Contingency, Irony, Solidarity* (1989), which argued for social solidarity not as 'a fact to be recognized' but 'a goal to be achieved'. These themes were made more explicit in *Achieving our Country* (1998), a controversial defence of American leftist traditions; while Rorty's continuing engagement with mainstream philosophy is demonstrated by three volumes of *Collected Papers* (1991–8). See also AMERICAN PHILOSOPHY.   [J.R.]

Ross, W. David (1877–1971)   W. D. Ross was a Scots philosopher who taught at Oxford. His editions of the *Metaphysics, Physics* and *Analytics*, with elaborate commentary and textual apparatus, are amongst the most important twentieth century work on Aristotle. But he was also responsible (*The Right and the Good*, 1930) for an influential formulation of intuitionism in ETHICS: the doctrine that we apprehend our various duties directly and do not derive them from any ulterior principle such as that of utility. Ross's statement of the position is a model of precision, clarity and moderation. (J.O.U.)

Rousseau, Jean-Jacques (1712–78) The Swiss writer Jean-Jacques Rousseau spent his life wandering from country to country, from faith to faith, from job to job, often in bad health and always the victim of his oversensitive and emotional temperament. His early essays portray the natural man as a creature of good instincts and simple tastes who has been corrupted and deprived of happiness by civilization, and particularly by urban life, class distinctions, and governmental tyranny. His novel *La Nouvelle Héloïse* (1761) glorified sentiment and emotion against the contemporary claims of reason and self-restraint. Its popularity and influence were immediate and immense. His next book, *Emile* (1762), the greatest of all writings on education, had an even wider and more lasting effect. It held that education should not curb or discipline the natural tendencies of the child but encourage them to grow and blossom. Teaching should come not from books and verbal instruction, but by example and direct experience of people and things. The family, not the school, is its proper field; and love and sympathy, not rules and punishments, the tools for the task. Religion should not be an affair of creeds and dogmas, of texts and formalities, but the infusion of the heart with feelings of awe and worship, feelings revelatory of a God who is beyond our reason. In his posthumously published *Confessions* Rousseau claimed to be giving the world the first completely uninhibited picture, in all its colours bright and dark alike, of a human soul.

Rousseau's work was of great historical importance as the first attack of the romantic movement on the eighteenth century stronghold of classical rationalism. But the works noted earlier are not in the narrow sense philosophical, and his claims as a philosopher rest on his theories of government. These are found chiefly in the *Discourse on the Origins of Inequality* (1755) and the *Social Contract* (1762). Rousseau was not a systematic nor even a coherent and orderly thinker. His writing is passionate and rhetorical; he saw society as Carlyle saw history – by flashes of lightning.

In the *Social Contract* Rousseau urges that government is justified only if sovereignty remains with the people. Every law must be passed by the direct votes of all the citizens. Representative democracy is rejected, along with any

limitation on the majority and any notion of individual rights, and absolute power is given to the majority. He realized that such a system would work only in very small states (and was influenced by the examples of the Greek city state and the Swiss canton). To remedy the weakness of such states he looked to federation, though he never elaborated this solution.

The application of laws to particular cases was assigned to a body which Rousseau called 'the Government' whose constitution would vary according to the size of the state and other local conditions. All associations within the state should be eliminated so that the individual should feel no rival loyalties to those of citizenship. But Rousseau was well aware of the objections to direct democracy. It is incapable of continuous legislative activity, and the people may be ill-informed, short-sighted and irrational. The remedy here is a 'Legislator' a semi-divine individual who should draft legislation and persuade the assembly to enact it.

In formulating these problems Rousseau was led to his key conception of the 'General Will' and the 'Will of All'. The former is the will of a body of citizens directed to their own common interests, the latter a mere aggregate of private individual selfish wills. This conception had two separate aspects each of which had a more subtle and long-term influence than the obvious revolutionary implications of the theory of direct popular sovereignty. First there is the suggestion that a state is a person with a will of its own, which arguably leads to a mystic nationalism with unlimited claims on individual loyalty. Second there is the suggestion that the General Will is infallible, in that we cannot call any law an expression of it unless it is genuinely in the public interest. Thus the General Will becomes an ideal to which actual laws can only approximate.

Direct democracy is justified by the argument that if the people themselves make the laws under which they live they lose no freedom. But obedience to the General Will is justified by the argument that it is directed to a common good which is bound to be my good too, or at least the good at which I am morally obliged to aim. Law is not an external command with the sanction of force, but the voice of my own moral or higher or true self. Hence political obligation can be (like the service of God) 'perfect freedom'.

But now it was not obvious what democracy was for. As SPINOZA said, 'if the laws are good, it does not matter who makes them'. In this respect Rousseau foreshadowed the theories of KANT and HEGEL which identified duty with freedom, the State with the moral ideal, and laws with right and justice. This led to the glorification of the State as the supreme expression of morality. Rousseau never reconciled these different strands, and his work is more important as a source of ideas than a system of arguments. See also POLITICAL PHILOSOPHY.   (J.D.M.)

Royce, Josiah (1855–1916) American philosopher, born in California, and leading exponent of IDEALISM. The first of the two main elements of his philosophy was what may be called the principle of self-applicability, which requires that every philosophy should be able to account consistently for the fact of it being expressed. Royce used this principle to discredit evolutionism and PRAGMATISM, believing that only his idealism could conform to it. The second principle is that of idealism itself. Royce insisted that everything has both a 'that' and a 'what' and that no philosophy is satisfactory if it asserts 'that' when it cannot specify 'what'. The 'what' of anything is simply its 'meaning', and it follows for Royce that the core of sound philosophy is a clear account of meaning. There are, he maintains, two types of meaning – external and internal. The external meaning of a thing consists in its relations to all other things; its internal meaning is its peculiar 'embodiment of purpose'. Royce then argues that 'embodiment of purpose' is the mark of 'mentality', and that, therefore, the internal essence of anything is mental. This is his version of idealism.

But if everything (including the false and the fictitious) embodies purpose, what is the criterion of truth or reality? Royce's answer is that the test of reality is conformity with the 'ideal community' of purposes of humanity as a whole – past, present and future. Thus Royce's 'Absolute' is the ideal community of all human purposes. Aware that absolutism in Germany had led to anti-individualism, Royce devoted much labour to a defence of American democratic individualism, based on proofs of the reality of Time, Evil and Freedom. His efforts to interpret Christianity in terms of natural science also had considerable influence upon theology. See also AMERICAN PHILOSOPHY.
(J.W.S.)

Russell, Bertrand Arthur William (1872–1970) Bertrand Russell's father, Viscount Amberley, was the eldest son of Lord John Russell, the Liberal statesman, who became the first Earl Russell, and his godfather was John Stuart MILL. Both his parents died before he was four years old and he was brought up by his grandmother, Lady Russell. After being privately educated, he won a mathematical scholarship to Trinity College, Cambridge, in 1890. In 1893 he turned from mathematics to philosophy, obtaining first class honours in 1894. Two years later, he published a work on German Social Democracy, the first of his many books. He was a Fellow of Trinity from 1895 to

1901 and a Lecturer in Philosophy from 1910 to 1916. During this period he was mainly occupied with mathematical logic, but retained an interest in politics, unsuccessfully fighting a parliamentary by-election on behalf of the National Union of Women's Suffrage Societies in 1907. He was a militant pacifist in the First World War and was dismissed by Trinity after being prosecuted and fined for writing a leaflet about the case of a conscientious objector. In 1918 he was prosecuted again, for an article in which he was held to have libeled the British Government and the American Army and he was sent to prison for six months. While in prison, he wrote his *Introduction to Mathematical Philosophy* (1919) and began work on the *Analysis of Mind* (1921).

In the years following the war Russell paid visits to Russia and China. He was disillusioned by the results of the Russian revolution, of which he had at first approved, but very favourably impressed by the old civilization of China. Though reinstated by Trinity in 1919, he never took up his duties there. He stood unsuccessfully as a Labour Candidate in the General Elections of 1922 and 1923 and in 1924 went on the first of many lecture tours to the United States. In 1927, in collaboration with his second wife, he founded a progressive school at Beacon Hill near Petersfield and tried to put some of his theories into practice. In the following decade he engaged extensively in political and social journalism. He continued to uphold pacifism but renounced it on the outbreak of the Second World War, the greater part of which he spent in the United States. In 1940, after holding professorships at the Universities of Chicago and California, he was judicially pronounced unworthy to be a professor at the College of the City of New York. He was then employed to lecture at the Barnes Foundation in Philadelphia, from which he was ejected in 1943, in circumstances which led him to bring a successful legal action for wrongful dismissal. In 1944 he returned to England having been re-elected to a fellowship at Trinity. After the war he continued to write, lecture and broadcast on a variety of subjects, his numerous books including two volumes of short stories. For a time he was in favour of the atomic bomb as a deterrent to the Russians, but he was later a protagonist in the Campaign for Nuclear Disarmament. Russell succeeded his elder brother in the earldom in 1931.

1 *Logic and Mathematics.* Russell stated that he was induced to take an interest in philosophy by his desire to find some reason for believing in the truth of mathematics. Under the influence of the works of F. H. BRADLEY he became a convert to HEGELIAN Idealism, but was soon re-converted by G. E. MOORE to an extreme form of REALISM. Among other things, he was impressed by the argument that the fundamental idealist doctrine, that what is known is conditioned by the knowing of it, denies to the propositions of mathematics any objective validity. Further, it seemed to him clear that mathematical propositions are irreducibly relational, and this led him to reject both the idealist thesis that relational judgments are vicious abstractions and the view – ascribed to ARISTOTLE and LEIBNIZ – that all propositions are of the subject-predicate form. In an early book on Leibniz, Russell argued that it was Leibniz's acceptance of this view that provided the key to his metaphysics. On the other hand, while admiring Mill, Russell was not satisfied with his theory that the propositions of pure mathematics are empirical generalizations, for this did not seem to him to afford a sufficient guarantee of their truth.

His own solution was to reduce mathematics to logic. This involved, first, an analysis of the fundamental terms of mathematics into purely logical concepts, and second the elaboration of a system of logic which was adequate to furnish the premises from which the propositions of mathematics could be deduced. The first part of the undertaking was carried out in the *Principles of Mathematics* (1903) and the second in *Principia Mathematica* (co-authored with WHITEHEAD, 1910–13). His definition of number, in which he was anticipated by the German mathematician FREGE, made use of the concept of a one-one relation; that is, a relation such that if x is so related to y, no other term is so related to y, and x has the relation to no other term. Two classes are said to be similar if their members can be correlated by a one-one relation. Then the number of a class is defined as the class of all those classes that are similar to it, and a cardinal number is defined as anything which is the number of some class. At that time Russell believed in the existence of classes. Later, he came to think that they were logical fictions, and thereby put the status of numbers again in question. This was a difficulty which he never resolved.

Principia Mathematica occupies an architectonic position in the development of symbolic logic. The breach with Aristotelian logic consisted not so much in the use of a special notation as in the greater generality of Russell and Whitehead's system, and above all in their attempt to make it rigorously formal. How far they succeeded in this, or in their programme of deriving mathematics from logic, is a technical question about which there is still some dispute. Other systems of logic have since been developed which can lay claim to a greater rigour, but to a large extent they are constructed on the basis of Russell and Whitehead's work.

Perhaps Russell's most original contribution to this field was his theory of types. This arose out of his discovery of a contradiction which made Frege say, when the news was communicated to him, that the whole foundation of mathematics had been undermined. It can be fairly easily set out. Most classes appear not to be members of themselves: for example, the class of men is not itself a man. But some classes do appear to be members of themselves: for instance, the class of all the things that can be counted would itself appear capable of being counted. Now consider the class of all classes which are not members of themselves. Is it or is it not a member of itself? If it is, it is not, and if it is not, it is. Similar contradictions can be found in other fields. A notorious example is the paradox of Epimenides the Cretan who said that all Cretans were liars. Another starts from the point that some words are predicable of themselves and others not. Thus the word 'short' is short but the word 'long' is not long. Let us call those that are so predicable 'autological' and those that are not 'heterological'. Is the word 'heterological' predicable of itself? If it is, it is not, and if it is not, it is.

Russell's solution to these paradoxes was to arrange objects into a hierarchy of types, so that what can be true or false of objects of one type cannot significantly be said about those of another. In particular, if a given class is the extension of a given predicate, it is nonsensical to apply that predicate to that class. Thus it is not false but nonsensical to say that the class of men is human, and the question whether the word 'heterological' is itself autological or heterological is meaningless. Even when a predicate does appear to characterize objects of different types, it does not have the same meaning in each case. Thus a predicate like 'being countable' becomes, as Russell put it, systematically ambiguous.

The theory of types, of which only the outline has been given here, has a certain *ad hoc* air about it. Not all forms of self-reference are logically vicious, and we seem to have no adequate rules for picking out the cases in which it is to be prohibited. But the theory has had a strong historical influence. By calling attention to the fact that a sentence might be grammatically well-formed and yet succeed in saying nothing, it prepared the way for the LOGICAL POSITIVISTS' declaration that metaphysical statements are not even false but literally meaningless.

2 *Theory of Knowledge.* Russell always tried to integrate his logic with his theory of knowledge, and accordingly identified the statements that formed the basis of his semantic hierarchy with those that were epistemologically primitive. In *The Problems of Philosophy* (1912) he drew a distinction between what he called knowledge by description and knowledge by acquaintance and took as his basic propositions – those which supply the foundation for all our empirical knowledge – propositions which refer only to things with which one is directly acquainted. The meaning which he here gave to 'acquaintance' was such that if one was acquainted with an object it followed that the object really existed and really had the properties that it was apprehended as having. On the other hand he regarded the existence and properties of things known only by description as problematic.

At that time Russell held that the things with which one could be acquainted were one's own private SENSE-DATA, images, thoughts and feelings (both present and past since he allowed memory to be a form of direct knowledge), one's own self, and UNIVERSALS. Subsequently

he dropped the self from the list, for he came to hold that selves did not exist as entities distinct from the experiences attributed to them; but he continued to hold that we are acquainted both with our own sense-data and with universals. Contemporary criticisms of the notion of sense-data did not disturb him, but there is reason to think that he would have liked to dispense with universals. The recognition of such abstract entities runs counter to the 'robust feeling for reality' which he always claimed for his philosophizing. He did not, however, think it possible to dispense with them. He allowed, perhaps wrongly, that one can successfully take the NOMINALIST step of reducing them all to the single relation of resemblance, that one can, for example, substitute for the quality 'whiteness' the relation of 'resemblance in being white'; but he did not think that much is to be gained by this as resemblance, in his view, is itself a universal.

When he wrote *The Problems of Philosophy* Russell believed that physical objects were known only by description, being postulated as the causes of sense-data. But following a principle which he called the supreme maxim in scientific philosophy – 'wherever possible substitute constructions out of known entities for inferences to unknown entities' – he abandoned this view in favour of the theory that physical objects are logical constructions out of actual and possible sense-data. This amounts to claiming that statements about physical objects can be faithfully translated into statements about sense-data. This theory was developed in *Our Knowledge of the External World* (1914) and in two of the essays reprinted in *Mysticism and Logic* (1918). Roughly speaking, his view was that at any given moment each observer perceives a private three-dimensional world with its own private space (or spaces: he distinguishes the space of sight from the space of touch). He called such private worlds 'perspectives'. In addition to these perceived perspectives, there is also an infinite number of unperceived perspectives, namely all those that would be perceived if an observer were in the appropriate state and position. These contain not sense-data but what Russell called 'sensibilia', entities which are generically similar to sense-data but are not actually sensed. He did not fully work out this theory, which encounters obvious difficulties even if one is willing to assume that sensibilia and unperceived perspectives literally exist.

In later years, Russell reverted to a causal theory of perception. He came to think that it alone can do justice to the evidence which is furnished by science. A curious feature of his causal theory was that he located sense-data in the percipient's brain. He did not mean that when we think we are perceiving the world around us we are really observing only our own brains. His argument was rather that an event's position in space-time is determined by its causal relations and that 'the causal and temporal connections of percepts with events in afferent and efferent nerves gives percepts a position in the brain of the observer'. It might be thought that if percepts are to be admitted as entities one would do better to maintain that they are not the sort of things that can be located in physical space at all.

Russell's reductionism was carried to its furthest point in *The Analysis of Mind* (1921), where he adopted a theory akin to the neutral monism of William JAMES. He held that both mind and matter are logical constructions out of elements – primarily sense-data – which are themselves neither mental nor physical. They are distinguished by the fact that certain elements, such as images and feelings, enter only

into the constitution of minds, and by the operation of different causal laws. Thus the sense-data which help to constitute minds when correlated according to the laws of psychology, constitute physical objects when correlated according to the laws of physics. In their mental aspect they engage, among other things, in what Russell called *mnemic causation*, a kind of action at a distance by which experiences produce subsequent memory images. Though Russell gave up the reductionist view of the nature of physical objects, he retained it with respect to minds, in the sense that he rejected the notion of consciousness or the self as a substantial entity. On the other hand, while he dallied with BEHAVIOURISM, he never denied the existence of states of consciousness which are not definable in physical terms.

3 *Names and descriptions.* Russell's predilection for WILLIAM OF OCKHAM's razor was not due merely to a love of intellectual economy for its own sake, though this may have played its part. His main reason was epistemological: the belief that the more entities you allow yourself to postulate, the greater the risk of your being wrong. There are also semantic considerations which are displayed in his famous theory of definite descriptions, a theory which he himself regarded as one of his most important contributions to philosophy. It was first sketched in 'On Denoting' (1905), more rigorously formulated in the first volume of *Principia Mathematica*, and further explained in the *Introduction to Mathematical Philosophy*. The philosophical problem which gave rise to it was that of showing how it was possible to speak meaningfully of non-existent objects, such as the present King of France, or even of objects which could not possibly exist such as the round

square, as in the statement 'the round square is a contradiction'. His solution was to show that expressions of the form 'the so and so', at least in this usage, never function as names. It does not follow from the fact that they are meaningful that there is any object which they mean. He showed this by giving a rule for translating the sentence in which the definite descriptive phrase occurs, in such a way that the phrase no longer looks as if it were a name. Thus, to take his own example, the statement 'The author of *Waverley* was Scott' becomes in his translation a conjunction of the three statements 'At least one person wrote *Waverley*'; 'At most one person wrote *Waverley*'; and 'It is not the case that anyone both wrote *Waverley* and was not identical with Scott'. To put it symbolically, as Russell would have preferred, he held that to say that the thing which has ϕ has ψ, when ϕ is the property concealed in the definite description and ψ the property attributed to what it describes, is to say that there is an x, such that x has ϕ, and, for all y, if y has ϕ, then y is identical with x, and x has ψ. Thus, any description of the subject goes into the predicate, and what Russell called a 'bare particular' is left to be the value of the variable x.

This theory, which has been called 'a paradigm of philosophy', later came in for criticism on the ground that it makes definite descriptive statements false when they fail in their reference, whereas it would be more in accordance with ordinary usage to say in that case that they were neither true or false. A more serious objection, which does not directly impugn the truth of the theory but does diminish its importance, is that Russell throughout assumed a defective view of meaning, in that he identified the meaning of substantives with their denotation. The main reason why definite descriptions – and even

ordinary proper names, like 'Homer' and 'Napoleon' – are turned by him into predicates is that they do not guarantee the success of their reference. It is always logically possible that they should denote nothing. But if the statements in which they occur are to be meaningful Russell thought that their analysis must terminate in statements containing substantival words whose denotation was guaranteed. The ultimate values of his existential variables are denoted by what he called logically proper names.

This is the basis of the doctrine of 'LOGICAL ATOMISM' which Russell, under the influence of his pupil WITTGENSTEIN, put forward in the years following the First World War. The view is that, in the last analysis, the world consists of atomic facts and that these facts correspond directly – as it were photographically – to elementary propositions. The elementary propositions are those which are expressed by conjoining a lowest level predicate with one or more logically proper names. Once more tying up his logic with his theory of knowledge, Russell tended to assume that these logically proper names stood for sense-data: for it is plausible to argue that only demonstrative expressions which stand for sense-data are bound to succeed in their reference. It may be thought, however, that the whole enterprise was misconceived, since there seems no good reason to suppose that for a referential statement to be meaningful it is necessary that its reference should be logically guaranteed.

In the *Inquiry into Meaning and Truth* (1940), Russell gave this theory a new aspect by identifying particulars with qualities. His motive was to eliminate what he regarded as the metaphysical notion of substance. He therefore followed BERKELEY in treating the things of common sense as collections of qualities, united by what he called the relation of compresence. This view is retained in

Russell's last important philosophical work, *Human Knowledge: Its Scope and Limits* (1948), which is otherwise of interest chiefly for its attempt to deal with the problem of INDUCTION. He took the view that inductive reasoning stands in need of justification and elaborated a set of principles which he thought would be sufficient for the purpose. He did not, however, claim that any of these principles can be known to be true.

From the purely philosophical point of view, Russell's work in the field of ethics and of social and political philosophy was not of comparable interest with his work on logic and the theory of knowledge. He had been persuaded that ethical statements have no objective validity, a conclusion which he confessed to disliking on emotional grounds; and was therefore inclined to hold that the main issues in ethics are psychological and social: questions of what people desire and how they may attain it. In the sphere of education and politics he was above all an advocate of liberty. Though he was more keenly aware of the irrational features in human conduct, his political position was in many ways strongly reminiscent of that of John Stuart Mill.

Russell often changed his philosophical views, but his approach to philosophy was highly consistent. His aim was always to find reasons for accepted beliefs, whether in the field of mathematics, natural science, or common sense. He was a consistent sceptic, not in the sense that he denied our claims to knowledge, but that he questioned them. He adhered also to a single method: the method of starting with propositions which are the least susceptible to doubt, and trying to reconstruct the edifice of knowledge on this basis, with as few assumptions as possible. The result was that his justifications usually took the form of analyses: even so

he was not interested in analysis for its own sake, but only as a method of proof. In this way, as in the power and elegance of his literary style, he remained in the high tradition of British Empiricism, the tradition of Hobbes, Locke, Berkeley, Hume and Mill. He was its outstanding representative in the twentieth century.
(A.J.A.)

Ryle, Gilbert (1900–76) Gilbert Ryle, who was born in Brighton and spent his life teaching at Oxford, was probably the most influential British philosopher of his generation. He was at one time much impressed by the earlier writings of HUSSERL, but already in the early 1930s he was adumbrating one of the characteristic doctrines of modern linguistic ANALYSIS when he suggested that the task of philosophy was 'the detection of the sources in linguistic idioms of recurrent misconceptions and absurd theories'. In *Dilemmas* (1954) he suggested that philosophical problems arise from apparent conflicts between general truths none of which we could sincerely abandon; the task of philosophy was therefore to resolve these apparent conflicts by an elucidation of the concepts which were used in stating these truths; philosophy was then essentially the dissolution of dilemmas arising from our imperfect understanding of our own conceptual apparatus. This position is akin to, but not identical with, that of the later WITTGENSTEIN.

Ryle's best-known work, *The Concept of Mind* (1949) exemplifies this theory of the nature of philosophy. Ryle considers that problems about the nature of mind and the relation of the mind to the body arise from a misunderstanding of the concept of mind and of concepts of such mental 'states' and 'activities' as willing, thinking or imagining. We are inclined to construe the mind as an extra object situated in the body and controlling it by a set of unwitnessable activities; this is what he calls the dogma of the ghost (the mind) in the machine (the body). Ryle regarded this picture as totally misleading and, in a series of brilliant studies, he attempts to disabuse us of it by showing that mental concepts refer not to ghostly acts but to dispositions to behave in certain ways in appropriate circumstances, to the style of actual witnessable performances, and similar unproblematic matters. He protested vigorously that he was not putting forward a doctrine of BEHAVIOURISM, or in any way denying the reality of the mental life, but only attempting to clarify the nature of the mental. But the work has often been attacked as behaviouristic and it has been suggested that Ryle at this stage had not wholly freed himself of the 'reductive' tendencies of RUSSELL.

In his treatment of mind and elsewhere Ryle made much use of the notion of a 'category mistake'; we make a category mistake when we misunderstand what kind of concept we are using or considering, as if we were to think that the University of Oxford were something that we could visit in addition to the Colleges. To think of the mind as a hidden substance is to make such a category mistake. Apart from his studies in the nature of philosophy and the concept of mind Ryle's main work was on the nature of meaning and the philosophy of logic; he also contributed to Platonic scholarship. Ryle also wrote the articles on Categories, Epistemology, and Solipsism in this Encyclopedia.   (J.O.U.)

S

Saint-Simon, Claude-Henri de Rouvroy, Comte de (1760–1825) French socialist and philosopher of history, see COMTE, POSITIVISM.

Santayana, George (1863–1952) As a SCEPTIC, the American philosopher George Santayana denied that the existence of anything can ever be proved, and insisted that all beliefs as to existence are based upon 'animal faith'. As a Platonic REALIST, however, he insisted that we have indubitable knowledge of UNIVERSALS or 'essences'. The proposed bridge between these two sides of his thought is the claim that essences (which both are and are not real) do not *exist*.

The above paragraph uses the word 'real' in PLATO's sense, but Santayana does not generally so use it. 'To be real' for him means to exist in space and time; and he insists that all reality in this sense is material. In his metaphysical scheme the 'Realm of Matter' is the basic reality. Essences, according to this way of talking, are ideal only. Thus, in an unorthodox way, Santayana seeks to combine REALISM and IDEALISM. Another strange union in his philosophy is between hard-boiled naturalism and aesthetic romanticism. He could combine the harshest naturalistic description of what exists in space and time (the stone of sculpture, the canvas of painting, the sound waves of music) with the most sensitive appreciation of the ideal content of the work of art. His metaphysical distinction between the 'reality' of matter and the 'ideality' of essence assists him in this. He was himself a poet of considerable talent; and the literary quality of his prose is generally very high.

In RELIGION Santayana repeatedly proclaimed his NATURALISM and materialism, insisting that the essence of religion is myth and poetry. Emotionally, however, he was unquestionably Roman Catholic. He never concealed his utter disdain for Protestantism, and his later works show that his Catholicism was more than skin deep. The last years of his life were spent in a Catholic retreat in Rome.   (J.W.S.)

Sartre, Jean-Paul (1905–80) The French writer Jean-Paul Sartre worked with great originality in a vast range of philosophical, critical, literary and dramatic forms. He was the epitome of the 'committed' intellectual, and his name became almost synonymous with EXISTENTIALISM throughout the world. Instead of opting for the life of a professional philosopher in an academic institution, he communicated his ideas to a wider audience by adopting a popular style in several of his theoretical works and by composing a series of plays and novels which earned him international acclaim as a writer. He was offered the Nobel Prize for literature in 1964, but refused it.

Having taught for a brief spell at a Lycée in Le Havre, Sartre travelled to Germany in 1933 to study PHENOMENOLOGY at first hand. HUSSERL and HEIDEGGER were his main influences, though HEGEL, KIERKEGAARD and KANT also figured strongly in his existentialist writings. What most fascinated him about the phenomenological movement was its determination to describe human consciousness as it exploded into the world, intentionally relating to the everyday things around it and dynamically projecting new meanings for its future (see INTENTIONALITY). Human existence was thus revealed as first and foremost a being-in-the-world (*être-au-monde*). And this meant in turn that even the most ordinary objects of our environment could be treated as matters of immediate philosophical concern. Sartre has described the enthusiasm with which he and other French thinkers like MERLEAU-PONTY and Simone de BEAUVOIR greeted the phenomenological invitation to 'philosophize about everything – even the essence of a gas street lamp'. Nothing appeared more important to these French existentialists than the 'promotion of street lamps to the dignity of philosophical objects'. Philosophy had abandoned its academic haven and was now to be found in the streets.

All of Sartre's works share a commitment to a philosophy of freedom. His famous claim that existence precedes essence exemplifies this. There is no such thing as a given 'human nature', determining how we act and behave. On the contrary, it is our everyday acts and choices that make up our identity. Man first of all exists, Sartre argues, and defines himself afterwards.

Sartre did not deny that we are always 'situated' in a concrete world. His claim was that it is precisely our way of responding to such situations which constitutes our freedom. We can choose either to abandon ourselves to the prevailing state of affairs, passively conforming to the *status quo* and reducing ourselves to the level of a mere object among objects. Or we can choose to transcend what is given by projecting ourselves authentically towards a new horizon of possibility. Either way, we are always choosing what we are, and never able not to choose. We are what we make of ourselves, as Sartre proclaims in his polemical essay *Existentialism and Humanism*

(1947). It follows from this that 'man is condemned to be free'. Even such factors as the unconscious or social class could not, for Sartre, deprive us of our ultimate responsibility and freedom. While we do not of course decide what class, sex, language or world we are born with, we do decide what is to be made of them. In other words, we are at all times free to create and recreate the meaning of our world in terms of a project of possibilities reaching into the future.

Not surprisingly, Sartre's first two philosophical works – *Imagination* (1936) and *The Psychology of Imagination* (1940) – were devoted to an analysis and assessment of imagination. His basic argument in these works is that consciousness negates the world as it is and invents a possible one in its stead. Here we find the seeds of Sartre's decisive ontological conviction that human being is free and for-itself precisely because it has this capacity for negation – the power not to be what it is and to be what it is not. This conviction was developed in Sartre's subsequent writings – and most notably his monumental work *Being and Nothingness* (1943). Here Sartre explored the central existential dilemma – how can human consciousness relate positively to other people and things in the world if its very freedom as a being-for-itself is defined *against* what is other than itself? Existence is described accordingly as an absurd conflict between freedoms, each one trying to 'nihilate' the other in order to preserve its own sovereign autonomy.

But how is moral action or political commitment possible? This question was relentlessly pursued in Sartre's novels (*Nausea* and the *Roads to Freedom* trilogy) and plays (*No Exit, The Condemned of Altona, The Flies, The Respectful Prostitute* and *The Devil and the Good Lord*). It also figured centrally in most of his post-war philosophical works and accounts for his growing interest in Marxism – an interest which began as early as *What is Literature?* (1947), where Sartre first raised the controversial notion of 'committed writing'. The attempt to reconcile the existentialist claim for individual freedom and the Marxist claim for collective revolution became most explicit in *The Critique of Dialectical Reason*, the first volume of which was published in 1960. (Volume Two appeared posthumously in 1985.) Indeed the debate between existentialism and Marxism dominated much of French intellectual life in the post-war period and featured centrally in the columns of *Les Temps Modernes*, the left-wing journal founded and co-edited by Sartre, Merleau-Ponty and de Beauvoir.

In his later writings, Sartre seems to have rediscovered his early fascination with the powers of imagination. He devoted several full-length works to the study of the existential crisis of creativity experienced by writers such as Genet, Mallarmé and Flaubert (the last of which extended to three massive volumes published in 1971–2). He even wrote an autobiographical account of his own imaginative journey through childhood (*Words*, 1964). But Sartre's return to the theme of imagination was not a retreat from the political fray. He retained his combative stance up to his death in 1980, frequently crossing swords with structuralists, psychoanalysts, doctrinaire Marxists, and of course the right-wing French bourgeoisie whom he took great delight in denouncing as *salauds*. Perhaps the most abiding feature of Sartre's work was his unswerving attachment to the freedom of a critical intellect that always refuses the compromise of certainty. [R.K.]

Saussure, Ferdinand de (1857–1913)
The Swiss philologist Ferdinand de Saussure founded modern structural linguistics with his *Course in General Linguistics* (1916). The book was created after his death, out of various sets of students' notes, by two of his disciples. To this apocryphal but seminal text we owe above all a theory of the sign, conceived as the union of a signifier (a form) and a signified (an idea). The relationship between these is not natural, but arbitrary; nor is it autonomous: it depends on the network of relationships within language as a whole – a sign has a 'value' before it has signification. Thus, language is conceived as a system: the *Course* distinguishes *langue*, the code common to all the speakers of a language, from *parole*, the individual speech-act which externalizes the system. Finally, the object of linguistics is defined as synchronic rather than diachronic: the linguist studies the system in a particular state, without reference to its evolution in time. There is another, darker side to Saussure: the never-published notebooks in which he develops the theory that Latin poets concealed anagrams in their texts. This dubious theory nevertheless anticipates contemporary conceptions of the free play of the signifier.   [J.-J.L.]

Scepticism   Scepticism is a doctrine which holds the possibilities of knowledge to be limited. In one form it contends that there are things which cannot, in principle, be known at all; in another that knowledge of some things can be attained only with difficulty and given certain precautions. In this second form it supports a methodological policy of reserve and circumspection in the formation of beliefs. Its opposite is dogmatism. Different species of scepticism are distinguished in two principal ways: by reference either to the methods of inquiry whose reliability is questioned or to the kind of objects whose knowability is doubted. Doubt about methods may be general, based on the ground that there is no infallible way of getting knowledge and that all methods have failed at some time or other. But more usually scepticism about methods is partial and depreciates the trustworthiness of one recognized source of knowledge in the interests of another. Reason and sense-experience have been set against one another and again jointly defended against the pretensions of authority, revelation and intuition. On the other hand, defenders of faith like PASCAL, have expressed a radical scepticism about the ability of reason to arrive at religious truth. Thus AVERROISM, which distinguishes the natural truth accessible to reason from the supernatural truth that is beyond its reach, is ambiguous. It may be a sincere belief that the unaided human intelligence cannot acquire religious knowledge, but it may also be ironical and imply that since reason is unable to acquire such knowledge it cannot be acquired at all.

It is more usual for particular and limited varieties of scepticism to be defined by means of the objects held to be unknowable. Sceptical arguments have been used to deny that we can get knowledge of any matters of empirical fact, of the external world of material objects, of the minds of others, of the past, of the future, of nature as a whole, of values and of any objects of religious or metaphysical speculation which lie beyond sense-experience. Scepticism about objects has three levels or degrees. The sceptic may admit that the objects in question exist but deny that we can ever know more than this about them. KANT's position on things-in-themselves is sceptical in this sense, as is that of the inductive sceptic about laws of nature. Second, the sceptic may assert that the objects in question do not in fact exist: this is the standpoint of the ordinary religious sceptic about God,

of the ethical sceptic about an order of values, and of many philosophers about a substantive and immortal soul. Finally, the sceptic may assert that the objects in question could not possibly exist and therefore that knowledge of the sort he is doubting is logically ruled out. BERKELEY's attitude to material substance and HUME's to real or intrinsic connexions between events are instances of this type.

General or total scepticism has always been rare, most sceptics being partisans of one method or one type of object. There are good reasons for taking general scepticism to be a kind of dialectical extravagance. To start with there is an obvious air of paradox about it. It seems self-refuting to say that nothing at all can be known, for to assert it is to claim at least one piece of knowledge – the sceptical principle itself. This was clear to Pyrrho of Elis (c.300 BC), the first sceptical philosopher, who concluded that the principle could only be held tentatively – a rather enfeebling manoeuvre. According to RUSSELL's theory of types, general scepticism, since it refers to itself, is not capable of significant formulation. In general, it can be argued, if one is to have any reasonable ground for skepticism, there must be something of which one is not sceptical. The usual reason for sceptical doubt is the experience or possibility of failure in claims to knowledge. Failure reveals itself through inconsistency and to recognize this we must be aware that contradictory statements have been made and that the law of contradiction is true. Furthermore, past experience of failure in a given type of thinking is only relevant to one's future confidence in it if the rationality of inductive argument is assumed. One could conceivably exhibit complete scepticism by refusing to claim any knowledge at all; what one could not do is offer a rational defence for this procedure.

Scepticism began with Pyrrho in the same way as it has from time to time recurred – as an expression of discontent with the intellectual chaos produced by the conflict of dogmatic systems. For Pyrrho philosophy was a practical art whose aim was detachment and peace of mind (*ataraxia*). This goal could not be attained unless the inevitably frustrating search for truth were abandoned. Most of the conceivable arguments for scepticism are to be found in the thought of the Greek SCEPTICS as reported by Sextus Empiricus. Aenesidemus put forward ten 'tropes' which set out in detail the reasons for doubting the reliability of perception. Agrippa's five 'tropes' are more compact and more far-reaching. As well as the relative or subjective nature of perception, he lists the infinite regress of proof propounded by Carneades, the conflict of opinions between men, the inevitably hypothetical character of all ultimate premises and the logical circularity of the syllogism, later emphasised by J. S. MILL. Some Sceptics – Arcesilaus for example – concluded that since certainty was not to be had we must make do with probability, and Carneades suggested that coherence of beliefs was a measure of reliability, that the more systematic one's body of beliefs the more reason there was for confidence in it. Since the period of the Greek sceptics (of the fourth to second centuries BC) scepticism has reappeared from time to time in the history of thought. ABELARD's *Sic et Non* ('Yes and No') – a collection of contradictory opinions by the Fathers on points of doctrine – introduced a sceptical technique that was used by KANT in setting out the antinomies with which he sought to prove the impossibility of constructive metaphysics. The anti-Aristotelian and anti-Scholastic logicians of the Renaissance prepared the way for the more thorough-going sceptics of

the sixteenth century whose most distinguished representative was MONTAIGNE. HUME is the most penetrating and comprehensive of modern sceptics. He argued that our belief in bodies, minds and causes rested not on reason or the senses but on the workings of the imagination which was naturally constituted so as to make a coherent structure out of the disorderly flux of sense-impressions that was all we really knew. Hume's intentions are ambiguous and insecure enough for it to have been plausibly argued that he was not really a sceptic at all but rather a defender of 'natural belief' against irrelevantly rigorous criteria of knowledge.

This interpretation is in sympathy with a doctrine deriving from G. E. MOORE, and ultimately from REID, which argues that common sense beliefs are more deserving of our confidence than the arguments of sceptical philosophers and that philosophical scepticism is insincere, or, at best, 'methodological' – a technique for bringing to light principles and criteria of knowledge ordinarily taken for granted. To the followers of WITTGENSTEIN, philosophical scepticism is a symptom of conceptual confusion and disorder, an indication that language is being misunderstood and put to improper use. It is argued that we can only learn what 'knowledge' and 'certainty' mean by hearing them used in connection with material objects, past events, other people's feelings and so on, and that it is senseless to inquire whether these paradigm cases are genuine instances of knowledge and certainty. WISDOM and AYER suggested that problems in the theory of knowledge have a characteristic pattern and commonly arise in a sceptical form. In each case there is an apparent conflict between (a) our evidence, what is given or known directly (sense-impressions, present events, other people's

words and deeds, particular occurrences); and (b) what we claim to know (material things, past events, other people's feelings, laws of nature); and (c) the fact that what we claim to know goes logically beyond the evidence for it. Sceptical theories say that we must abandon the claims to knowledge (b), but there are less catastrophic ways out of the difficulty. Causal and analogical theories resolve the inconsistency by appealing to principles that validate inference from the evidence to logically distinct conclusions. Reductive theories like PHENOMENALISM deny (c); intuitionist theories like naïve REALISM deny that we are confined to the evidence specified in (a). To many philosophers scepticism is of no serious importance as a philosophical theory. Its point is to make us aware of what is involved in our claims to knowledge and perhaps, by doing so, to render them more secure.
(A.Q.)

Sceptics The name 'sceptics' is given to certain groups of philosophers in the Hellenistic-Roman period who, doubting the capacity of senses and reason to furnish knowledge of the nature of things, advocated suspension of judgment. Their common ground was an epistemological attack on all philosophies which were dogmatic, that is which claimed to have discovered truth. There seems no way, they said, of penetrating beyond 'appearances' to knowledge of external objects. Sense perception gives contradictory reports and there is no criterion in sensation itself to distinguish true from false impressions. Nor is there any criterion of correct judgment, and an attempt to find one must lead to infinite regress. Thus we must withhold our judgment. Classical skepticism went through three phases.

1 *Pyrrhonism* (late fourth and third century BC). Pyrrhonism was inaugurated by Pyrrho of Elis (*c*.360–*c*.270) and expounded by his pupil Timon. For Pyrrho, as for many in his troubled age, the state of imperturbability was the ethical mainspring of philosophy, and his originality lay in the method by which he sought to attain it. With no means of arriving at knowledge, nothing could be said to be in itself any more this than that, and no argument could be judged more certain than its opposite. The external stimulus of belief, desire, and emotion was thus severed, and this produced indifference, followed by tranquility, and one was left with no guide for action other than custom.

2 *Middle and New Academy* (third to first century BC). Pyrrhonism faded out before the dialectical scepticism of the Middle and New ACADEMY – a logical attack directed principally against the STOIC theory of knowledge, which held that special sense-perceptions caused by real objects irresistibly demanded the assent of the wise. Arcesilaus of Pitane (315–*c*.241) argued that there is no discernible difference between true and false perceptions, and that the latter may be as irresistible as the former. In teaching he adopted the basic sceptical practice of arguing impartially on both sides of any question. His scepticism may have had roots in SOCRATES as well as Pyrrho. Carneades of Cytene (*c*.214–*c*.129), the most formidable of the Sceptics, systematized the attack on dogmatism. With a wealth of brilliant argument against the possibility that true and false sense-impressions are distinguishable in themselves, and against the capacity of any rational process to do more than test formal validity, he swept the EPISTEMOLOGY of the Stoa from the field. He severely damaged their anthropocentric theology and their theories of divination, providence and fatalism. In a systematic review

of all ethical ends he demonstrated logical difficulties in the Stoic moral goal, and on a famous embassy to Rome in 166–5 he argued the relativity of moral terms. In practical life he proposed a theory of probability as a guide for action: there were three grades of probability – the probable; the probable and undisputed; and the probable, undisputed and tested; and the latter was the highest state of belief, attained when a whole system of logically connected ideas is formed. Carneades left no writings, but was fully reported by his voluminous successor, Clitomachus of Carthage. Philo of Larissa was still maintaining scepticism in the first century BC but his successor, Antiochus of Ascalon, turned the Academy towards an eclecticism which incorporated Stoic views.

3 *The new Pyrrhonism* (from the first century BC). It was outside the Academy that the sceptical movement flowed strongly for the next two or three centuries. The new sect professed to go back to Pyrrhonism, arguing that the Academic sceptics had no right to deny the possibility of knowledge: they should have withheld their assent even from this. On the other hand there seemed no basis even for opinion; one could only take things as one found them and live by custom, convention, tradition. But the new Pyrrhonists gladly accepted the Academic tradition of dialectical argument, and combining with this the EMPIRICISM of the Empiric Medical School, made a complete systematization of sceptical arguments. Aenesidemus of Cnossus, probably an earlier contemporary of CICERO, dealt with the relative nature of sense-perception in his Ten Tropes (or Modes) of Withholding Assent, arguing that every perception is relative to percipient, object and concomitant external and internal circumstances, so that the object itself was inapprehensible. Agrippa, in his Five

Modes of Attack, followed Aenesidemus in his use of relativity and found four types of fallacies in dogmatic arguments: discrepancy of theories, infinite regress, hypothetical assumption and circular reasoning. We finally hear of two ultimate Modes: nothing is apprehended intuitively, as is shown by the disagreements of philosophers; nor can anything be apprehended through something else, as this would involve circular reasoning or infinite regress. The sceptical attack on causation is likewise classified by Aenesidemus in Eight Modes, directed against the inadmissibility of a dogmatic jump to the non-apparent, unconfirmed by any evidence from appearances. There is no certain connexion between reality and phenomena; a reason is arbitrarily chosen to suit the theory of the moment. There is also an interesting argument on the relativity of cause and effect: if cause is productive of effect it must exist before it (which will lead to an infinite regress); but since cause is relative to effect it cannot be prior in existence (and their relativity makes any argument concerning them circular). The whole edifice of scepticism may be explored in the works of Sextus Empiricus (late second century AD) which are all the more valuable for their lack of originality.

Scepticism was of immense importance in an age dominated by the dogmatic philosophies of Stoicism and Epicureanism; indeed a persistent movement of doubt and inquiry which insists on keeping open for examination any assertion seems fundamental for all philosophy. In addition, stoic examinations of sense-perception, causality and probability are of great interest for much recent philosophy. (I.G.K)

Schelling, Friedrich W. J. (1775–1854)

The *Wunderkind* of German IDEALISM and 'the Proteus of philosophy' to his contemporaries, Schelling must be recognized as a magnificent failure. However, the failure is that of METAPHYSICS and moral philosophy themselves. The fact that failures are often more instructive than successes may explain why after long being buried under a flourishing HEGEL renaissance Schelling has returned to haunt contemporary philosophy. Interest has concentrated less on his last, highly religious works – *Philosophy of Mythology* and *Philosophy of Revelation* (1821–43) – than on the major works of his early and middle periods, for example, *Ideas for a Philosophy of Nature* (1797); *On the World-Soul: A Hypothesis of Advanced Physics toward an Explanation of the Universal Organism* (1798); *System of Transcendental Idealism* (1800); and *On the Essence of Human Freedom* (1809), along with a series of sketches, *The Ages of the World* (1810–14). As the titles indicate, the two principal themes in Schelling's philosophy are NATURE and FREEDOM. Yet why 'failure'? And why 'magnificent'?

The problems of nature and freedom in modern philosophy arise from the notorious Cartesian split between extended substance and thinking substance. Schelling regards all philosophy after DESCARTES as sterile and even mutilated, inasmuch as its 'subjective idealism' has cut it off from nature. He traces the Cartesian split back to the MANICHEAN-Augustinian tradition in theology. As long as DUALISM vitiates philosophy, with its oppositions of mind/matter, subject/object, good/evil, etc., the genuine problems remain insoluble. Schelling tries to confront those problems head-on by developing an 'objective' or 'real' idealism and a philosophy of absolute 'identity'. Yet as he tries to absorb the negative sides of each duality back into the positive sides – matter back into spirit, evil back into the good, etc. – in

order to account for their ultimate unity, the entire Judaeo-Christian tradition of ONTOLOGY and ETHICS is made to tremble. Whereas Hegelian dialectic often seems to be a machine that bulldozes its path of progress, Schelling's meditation never forgets the damage done: however nostalgic for 'eternal joy', it stresses the 'source of sadness' in moral philosophy, 'the veil of melancholy draped over all nature, the profound and indestructible melancholy of all life'.

Major influences on him were PLATO, NEOPLATONISM, Bruno, Jakob Böhme, KANT, FICHTE, Hegel and Hölderlin. Schelling, in turn, should be studied by philosophers interested in SCHOPENHAUER, NIETZSCHE, HEIDEGGER, WHITEHEAD, MERLEAU-PONTY, contemporary philosophy of biology, ecology or ANIMAL rights, and also by anyone interested in the fate of Kantian 'moral freedom'.   [D.F.K]

Schiller, Ferdinand Canning Scott (1864–1937)

The British philosopher F. C. S. Schiller worked in Oxford and, in later life, in Southern California. He was a personal friend of William JAMES, with whose pragmatic philosophy he was in close sympathy, though he claimed to have arrived at the basic principles of PRAGMATISM independently. Unlike James he was a polemical writer; he was convinced that the fashions in philosophy prevalent at his time in Oxford were obscurantist and quite without worth. As a result most of his writings are attacks, particularly on F. H. BRADLEY and those whom he called the 'formal logicians', often couched in an *ad hominem* form which at a later date is somewhat tedious. But he had a powerful and original mind and his now little-read works contain much that is worth reading. Schiller's basic thesis was that all human activities are moulded by human purposes and only intelligible by reference to them. This, he held, was true of thinking as well as action; the conceptual frameworks we employ, the modes of reasoning that we adopt and the beliefs we hold have their only justification in their utility for human aims. To call a statement true is to evaluate it favourably, just as to call an action good is to evaluate it favourably. Much of Schiller's effort was devoted to the application of his 'HUMANIST' thesis to this logic. In his *Formal Logic* (1912) and his *Logic for Use – An Introduction to the Voluntarist Theory of Knowledge* (1929), Schiller maintained that the view of reasoning exhibited in the logic books was wholly mistaken; his principal charges were that formal logic operated with illegitimate abstractions in speaking of propositions since meaning and truth were dependent on the time, place and circumstances of communication, and second that validity as a criterion of success in reasoning was useless since no concrete argument could be formally valid, and unquestionably good arguments in all fields made no attempt even to approximate to such an ideal. In place of formal logic he offered an account of reasoning which in its stress on verification, hypothesis and approximation anticipated later accounts of scientific thought.   (J.O.U)

Schiller, Friedrich (1759–1805)   The German poet and playwright Friedrich Schiller reacted against the subjectivism of the theory of aesthetic taste expounded in KANT's *Critique of Judgement*. In his *Letters on the Aesthetic Education of Man* (1794–5) he postulated an 'aesthetic' or 'play' impulse that was supposed to unify the Kantian opposites of form and matter. His contention that judgements in aesthetics are as objective as in any other field was developed further in *On Naïve and Sentimental Poetry* (1795), which argues

for the essential diversity of poetic style, and *On the Sublime* (1801), which postulates that the mysteries of nature will always triumph over our attempts to comprehend them.   {J.R}

Schleiermacher, Friedrich (1768–1834)   German romantic and protestant theologian, who extended the scope of HERMENEUTICS to cover the art of textual interpretation in general; see THEISM.

Schlick, Friedrich Albert Moritz (1882–1936)   Moritz Schlick was educated in Berlin, originally as a physicist. In 1922 he took over MACH's chair in the Philosophy of the Inductive Sciences in Vienna, where he later founded the VIENNA CIRCLE (see also LOGICAL POSITIVISM). Fourteen years later he was assassinated by a demented student, and his death hastened the break-up of the Circle.

Despite his scientific training, Schlick's early writings are largely on moral and aesthetic questions, and display a poetic sensibility not conspicuous in his later work. He then gained notice as an expositor of RELATIVITY-theory (1917), and as author of a treatise on EPISTEMOLOGY (1918) which argues, in opposition to KANT, and from an EMPIRICIST standpoint, that the propositions of LOGIC and MATHEMATICS are not synthetic A PRIORI but ANALYTIC, or true by definition, and hence empty of content. Scientific theories, on the other hand, were a posteriori systems of concepts, whose truth depended on correspondence, inasmuch as their consequences must be capable of verification by observed facts. Nor are these facts sensations merely, as they were for Mach; anything answering to a scientific concept may legitimately be taken as real. Schlick also tackles the mind-body problem, which he regards as spurious, in that the supposed dualism involved is merely a duality in our ways of describing the phenomena.

Schlick's later opinions reflect the influence of WITTGENSTEIN and CARNAP, and consist, in effect, of an extension of his views to all the traditional problems of philosophy. Such problems arise 'only from an inadequate description of the world by means of a faulty language', and the task of philosophy is not to solve them, but merely to clarify the question in dispute. It will then appear that the answer is either ascertainable, in principle, by scientific methods, or else void from the start, the question itself being so framed that there could be no evidence relevant to its decision. The metaphysical assertions of IDEALISM, MATERIALISM, REALISM, etc. are all meaningless in that no possible combination of sense-experiences could either verify or falsify their claims.

In basing verification (and meaning) on immediate sense-experience, the later Schlick, like other empiricists, was seeking an incorrigible foundation for knowledge. But the attempt leads to many paradoxes, and even imperils the foundations of communication, since meaning defined in terms of private experience is plainly inaccessible to anyone else. Schlick's explanation, that the 'structure' of experience is communicable, but its 'content' beyond description, did not give general satisfaction, and the problem of formulating the 'basic' or incorrigible propositions required by this theory was a source of much subsequent dissension in the Vienna Circle. (P.L.H)

Scholasticism See MEDIEVAL PHILOSOPHY.

Schopenhauer, Arthur (1788–1860)
After his father's death, the German metaphysician Arthur Schopenhauer devoted himself entirely to philosophy, being able to live comfortably on his inheritance. His ridiculously vehement essay *On Women*, which has probably been read more widely than anything else he wrote, airs a deeply personal resentment. His diatribe 'On University Philosophy' also has a personal background. He applied to become a lecturer at the University of Berlin, was found acceptable by a committee including HEGEL and decided to offer his lectures at the same hours as Hegel. But he failed to attract any students, so his university career ended in failure. After that, he outdid himself in vituperating Hegel, SCHELLING and FICHTE, calling them windbags and charlatans, though he heard Fichte as a student, and owed a great deal to his conception of the will.

The two philosophers he most admired were KANT and PLATO. He considered himself the rightful heir of Kant, while Fichte, Schelling and Hegel were usurpers. Like Fichte, he found Kant's doctrine of the unknowable thing-in-itself unacceptable, and thought he had discovered the ultimate reality: will. In his best-known work, *The World as Will and Idea* (1818), he argued that will is blind striving: it had no purpose or aim and was neither reasonable nor rational.

The details of Schopenhauer's METAPHYSICS and ETHICS have had little influence. His historical importance can be summed up in three points. First, he was the first major European philosopher to make a point of atheism. Second, he was the first to call attention to the Upanishads and Buddhism. He is often described as a pessimist, and insisted on the universality of suffering. He claimed that we can find salvation only by overcoming the blind cosmic will, but outright suicide was unacceptable because it was itself an assertion of will. There are three aids to salvation: philosophical knowledge, contemplation of works of art, and sympathy for others, based on the recognition that in reality we are all one. This ethic of sympathy contrasts very sharply with

Schopenhauer's life, for few philosophers have been more unsympathetic to others. Third, he inaugurated an increased emphasis on will and the irrational in modern philosophy. Although KIERKEGAARD, NIETZSCHE, VAIHINGER, JAMES, BERGSON and Freud clearly did not agree with him, their ideas show that Schopenhauer marks an important point of departure in the history of thought. His conception of the intellect as an instrument of the will is especially noteworthy in this connexion.

Initially, *The World as Will and Idea* attracted no attention at all, even after Schopenhauer added a second volume (1844) by way of elaborating his metaphysic. Of two essays on ethics which he submitted for prizes, one won a prize, the other not; so he published them together, specifying on the title page 'crowned by...' and '*not* crowned by...' – confident that he would thus immortalize in infamy the academy that had passed him by. Late in life, he witnessed and relished his growing fame. It may be that the widespread disillusionment after the unsuccessful revolutions of 1848 helped to make his pessimism popular. Certainly, his clearly written essays, published as *Parerga and Paralipomena* (1851), helped to find him an audience. Among his declared and devoted admirers were Richard Wagner, whose *Tristan and Isolde* tries to realize in music Schopenhauer's blind will, and the young Nietzsche, who later outgrew his infatuation.   (W.K)

Scotus, John Duns (c.1266–1308) Born in Scotland, Scotus joined the Franciscan order in 1281 and later studied and taught both at Oxford and at Paris. His main works are two commentaries on the *Sentences* of Peter Lombard, which combine acceptance of the typically Aristotelian theory of knowledge directed to the nature of physical objects with a typically

Franciscan view of the soul as a substance in its own right, whose intellectual powers are not confined to sensible reality. The subtle mingling of these two divergent tendencies earned him his title of *Doctor Subtilis*.

Scotus argues that the proper object of philosophical speculation is reality or being, without any of the determinations which restrict it to one mode (e.g. infinite being or God) rather than another (e.g. sensible being). But the human mind is hampered by having to draw its knowledge from the sensible. So METAPHYSICS is an abstract science of essences bearing upon a single field which is differentiated in terms of purely formal distinctions. These forms fall short of actual differences but are not merely the product of the mind's activity; physical existence is accounted for by a form of 'thisness' or *haecceitas*. Scotus was a profound thinker but, in the hands of less able followers, his work degenerated into an endless verbosity which contributed greatly to the collapse of scholastic thinking.   (J.G.D)

Searle, John (1932–) The American philosopher John Searle was trained in Oxford, and is the author of *Speech Acts* (1969), *Intentionality* (1983) and *The Construction of Social Reality* (1995); see METAPHOR.

Sellars, Wilfrid (1912–89) Wilfrid Sellars is regarded by some as the greatest American philosopher of the twentieth century. His education in France and Britain inspired him with respect for the natural sciences, accompanied by doubts about LOGICAL POSITIVISM and indeed ANALYTIC PHILOSOPHY as a whole. These reservations took shape very slowly, eventually finding expression in the attack on 'the Myth of the Given' in his very celebrated essay on 'Empiricism and the Philosophy of Mind' (1956). Sellars thought that the vaunted 'clarity' of authors like AYER or

MOORE was achieved at the expense of 'adequacy', remarking towards the end of his life that in philosophy it was important to 'give one's muddiest intuitions the fullest benefit of the doubt'.   {J.R.}

Semiology   See STRUCTURALISM.

Seneca, Lucius Annaeus (c.5 BC–AD 65)
The Roman dramatist, poet, and STOIC philosopher Lucius Annaeus Seneca was born in Cordoba, Spain. He switch-backed from a dangerous philosophical and rhetorical eminence under Caligula, to banishment under Claudius; soared as millionaire tutor and confidant of Nero, before sinking into prudent retirement and death by enforced suicide. He was a follower of CHRYSIPPUS, but his works have a Latin flavour both in thought and presentation; Cato was his hero, Roman rhetoric his medium. He changed the doctrine of the Stoics by grafting the Roman concept of will onto their intellectualism, and altered its direction by applying their individualistic philosophy to the government of the Roman Empire. His shortcomings as philosopher and politician are due to contradictory leanings towards worldliness on the one hand and stoic IDEALISM on the other; the resulting discrepancy of actions and professions may perhaps be excused by his honest belief that he was compelled politically to justify means by ends, and that his philosophical teaching was the result of examination of his own moral struggles. But the weakness of his character formed his stoicism, rather than his philosophy his character; thus the question of the capacity of the Stoa as an educative force in politics remained unanswered.   (I.G.K)

Sense-data   'Sense-data' (singular: 'sense-datum') is a comparatively new word for an idea that is almost as old as philosophy, namely the immediate object of sense-perception. In the past, philosophers have spoken of 'sensible species', 'ideas', 'impressions', 'representations', 'sensations' and 'the given', but preference has been given to 'sense-datum' on the grounds of its comparative neutrality. As a technical term it presupposes as little as possible about the nature and origins of perception's immediate objects. But it is as hard to find a neutral definition for sense-datum as it is to find a neutral term for the idea it expresses. From the time of HERACLITUS, PROTAGORAS and DEMOCRITUS many philosophers have been persuaded that independent, external, material things are not the direct or immediate objects of perception. In any perceptual situation we can always doubt that what we perceive is a real material thing. It might be a hallucination or we might be dreaming. But there is something we cannot doubt, for whatever, if anything, may be going on outside us, we may be sure that our senses are affected in a certain way and this indubitable residue is our current sense-datum. Though we may be in doubt as to how things are, we cannot be in doubt as to how things now appear to us to be. So to say how things appear to us now, with no implication that this is how they really are or how they would appear to anyone else, is to describe our current sense-data. Most of our ordinary perceptual beliefs involve a good deal of inference. In taking what I now see to be a chair, I ascribe to it a back, a texture and a weight, but none of these are at the moment present to my senses. The inferred elements of our perceptual beliefs are the dubitable ones. The sense-datum is what remains when they are suppressed.

It is clear that sense-data are private. My sense-data may resemble yours but this likeness can only be established by a complex and precarious inference and is always a contingent matter. The fact of hallucination shows that it is possible to have a sense-datum to which nobody else's sense-data correspond at all. The privacy of sense-data follows from their being defined in terms of what appears to *me*. There is no very clear or uniform convention about the extent or complexity of sense-data. Are we to call all dreams, hallucinations, memories and images sense-data even when we are not in the least tempted to suppose that we are perceiving some real material thing? Is my current sense-datum the whole of what I am sensibly aware of at this instant or is it what I am aware of by means of any one sense, my current visual field, for example; or is it any one discriminable part of a current sense-field? Philosophical usage tends to favour the last of these. A more substantial problem arises about the duration of sense-data. Can I be aware of the same sense-datum twice or do sense-data endure only for one specious present? Some philosophers have held that sense-data can have properties which they do not appear to have (cf. H. H. PRICE). Against them AYER has argued that sense-data are by definition precisely and entirely what they appear to be.

There are two main arguments to prove that sense-data are necessarily distinct from material objects. First, the argument from illusion. My sense-datum, what I immediately perceive, may be just the same in a case where I am really perceiving a friend as it is in a case where I am undergoing the hallucination of seeing him. Since what I immediately perceive is precisely the same in both cases and cannot be a material object in one of them it cannot be a material object in either. Second, the causal or time-lag argument. The perception of very remote events, such as the explosion of stars, brings out dramatically that perception is always of something that is temporally earlier, even if only minutely, than the event of perceiving it. But, it is argued, we can only perceive what is present, since to say that something is present is simply to say that it is contemporary with my current perception.

If sense-data are distinct from material objects, the fundamental and traditional problem of perception presents itself: what is the relation of sense-data to material objects, and how can we have any knowledge about material objects if all we immediately perceive is sense-data? Some philosophers, HUME for instance, have been sceptical of the validity of any inference from sense-data to material things. More commonly it has been held either, with LOCKE, that we can reasonably infer material objects as the causes of our sense-data, or, with BERKELEY and PHENOMENALISM, that material objects are entirely composed of sense-data, actual or possible or both. In opposition to the sense-datum theory two main tendencies can be discerned. One view, that of RYLE, is that there are no such things. Another, less radical, view is that though there are sense-data they are not the only things that we immediately perceive: they are the causes rather than the grounds our perceptual beliefs and for the most part their existence and character is a matter of inference.　　　　　　　　　　(A.Q.)

Sextus Empiricus　　See SCEPTICS.

Shaftesbury, Earl of (1671–1713)
Anthony Ashley Cooper, third Earl of Shaftesbury, argued in his *Characteristics* (1711) that we have innate senses of beauty and morality independent of religion.

Sidgwick, Henry (1828–1900)　The English philosopher and Cambridge professor Henry Sidgwick wrote on economics as well as philosophy and was a founder member of the Society for Psychical Research and its first President.

The work for which Sidgwick is remembered is *The Methods of Ethics*, published in 1874 but modified and expanded in subsequent editions. He adopted a hedonistic UTILITARIAN position, but with an unusually clear recognition of the many-sidedness of moral problems. Having denied that moral terms can be defined in non-moral terms Sidgwick goes on to contend that morality is founded on the A PRIORI moral intuition that 'we ought to aim at pleasure'. Any other basic moral knowledge is concerned with the way pleasure should be distributed; thus we know that similar cases ought to be treated similarly and that 'the good of any one individual is of no more importance, from the point of view of the universe, than the like good of any other'. From these basic positions Sidgwick deduces the principle of benevolence: 'each one is morally bound to regard the good of any other individual as much as his own'. Sidgwick acknowledges that in practice people are swayed morally by rules of conduct and not by general principles of universalistic hedonism; he himself is willing to accept these rules of conduct on the ground that they are a means to the utilitarian end. This position is however complicated by the fact that Sidgwick finds himself compelled to acknowledge as self-evident the principle of rational ethical egoism, that 'it is irrational for me to sacrifice my happiness to any other end'. Sidgwick is well aware of the apparent incompatibility of this principle with the universalistic hedonism which is his other main contention; he regards this incompatibility as the basic problem of ethics, but simply finds himself unable honestly to deny either the principle of egoism or the principle of benevolence. His solution is to suggest that the universe is so arranged that egoism and universal benevolence never come into conflict and that we

can follow the principle of benevolence with the assurance that we shall not thereby violate the rational principle of egoism. Thus Sidgwick, in his anxiety to do justice to all the facets of morality, attempts to harmonize a number of positions which are usually regarded as essentially opposed; he is utilitarian and DEONTOLOGIST, egoist and universalist. (J.O.U)

Siger of Brabant (c.1235–81) The French philosopher Siger of Brabant was a leader, with Boethius of Dacia and Bernier of Nivelles, of the so-called Latin AVERROISTS, who claimed to be pure philosophers of the school of ARISTOTLE, rather than theologians. They accepted the Averroist distinction between truths of reason and truths of faith, and ruthlessly worked out a philosophy which was an Aristotelianism coloured by Averroes and AVICENNA. Some of their doctrines, such as that of the eternity of the world, the unity of intellect in all human beings and the determination of human affairs by astral influences, went straight against Christian dogmas of creation, the individual soul and divine providence; these doctrines were condemned in 1270 and 1277, but the authors insisted that their philosophical tenets did not conflict with their faith in revelation. (J.O.U)

Singer, Peter (1946–) The Australian philosopher Peter Singer reacted against the domination of ETHICS by meta-ethical inquiries (such as those of HARE) when studying at Oxford. His works on *Animal Liberation* (1975) and *Practical Ethics* (1979) helped turn the discipline towards practical applications usually informed by UTILITARIANISM; he is also the author of the article on Applied Ethics in this Encyclopedia.

Smith, Adam (1723–90) Adam Smith was one of the greatest of that line of eighteenth century Scottish philosophers who shifted the study of human nature from its traditional concerns with theology and the pursuit of happiness in the life hereafter, to one which was based on philosophy, history and the pursuit of happiness in the world of common life. In doing so he helped to challenge the claims of the theologians to provide an adequate guide to the problems of living in the increasingly complex world of commerce.

Like his close friend David HUME, Smith was interested in the principles of social interaction and the processes by which we acquire the metaphysical, moral, political and religious skills which are necessary to ordinary living – matters which he discussed in his first book, *The Theory of Moral Sentiments* (1759). But he was also interested in the role of labour and property in shaping social behaviour and social institutions and in transforming society from its barbarous to its civilized state – matters discussed in his greatest work, *The Wealth of Nations* (1776). All of this required him to elaborate a fine-meshed account of the way in which any society disposes of its land, labour and capital resources and develops the political, cultural and religious institutions it needs in order to maintain its stability. In so doing, he developed the first fully-fledged 'materialist' model of society and its history, on which all subsequent models have been based. See also POLITICAL ECONOMY.   [N.P.]

Social Contract   Social contract theories are attempts to explain the duty of obedience to the laws and civil authority by reference to a contract or compact or promise to obey made for the sake of the benefits gained from the civil society thereby instituted. There are many different versions of the contract theory; one, not accepted by PLATO, is given in

Republic Book II; famous modern versions are those of HOBBES in *Leviathan*, LOCKE in his *Second Treatise of Civil Government* and ROUSSEAU in *The Social Contract*. These versions differ from each other as regards both the parties to the contract and its terms; they also differ in the degree to which the historicity of the contract is affirmed, since some authors content themselves with a tacit or implied contract. The theory was destructively criticized in HUME's 'Of the original contract' and HEGEL's *Philosophy of Right*. See also POLITICAL PHILOSOPHY, RAWLS.   (J.O.U)

Socrates (469–399 BC)   Socrates of Athens was perhaps the greatest of the Greek philosophers, but he left no writings of his own, and probably never produced any. Our information about him comes from four sources: Aristophanes, Xenophon and PLATO, whose lives overlapped his, and ARISTOTLE, who was probably born some thirteen years after the year in which, according to Plato, Socrates was tried and sentenced to death for 'corrupting the young men and not believing in the gods of the city'. The only statement common to all four of these writers is that there was a philosopher called Socrates. Beyond that, the picture of Socrates in Aristophanes' farce *The Clouds* should be entirely disbelieved: it contains nothing agreeing with the other three, and nothing individual or unusual, but only the popular idea of a sophist dubbed 'Socrates' and given a mask with the features of the real Socrates.

Xenophon's *Memories of Socrates*, a work of some 180 pages, consists mainly of amusing little dialogues between Socrates and various other persons, at some of which Xenophon says he was present. He also wrote an *Apology of Socrates*, a short report of the trial, which, however, Xenophon does not claim to have attended; an *Oeconomicus*, in which Socrates discusses household management; and a *Symposium*, depicting a party at which Socrates is present. Though Xenophon was a serious historian, his Socratic writings are clearly fictions exploiting the storyteller's device of saying 'I was there'. They should be believed only so far as they agree with Plato or Aristotle.

In the *Metaphysics* Aristotle gives us the most likely account we have of Socrates' thought. 'Socrates occupied himself with the excellences of character, and in connexion with them became the first to raise the problem of universal definition. ...It was natural that Socrates should be seeking the essence, for he was seeking to syllogize, and "what a thing is" is the starting-point of syllogisms. ...Two things may be fairly ascribed to Socrates, inductive arguments and universal definition, both of which are concerned with the starting-point of science; but Socrates did not make the universal or the definitions exist apart.' All these points except the last are well supported by Plato and not contradicted by Xenophon, and should therefore be accepted.

Plato's portrait of Socrates is by far the most copious and impressive. Socrates is the main speaker in all Plato's early and middle dialogues. His conversation there concerns the nature of virtue and of particular virtues, and tends to the view that virtue is knowledge, and vice ignorance. He takes a particular virtue and tries to find its essence by giving a general definition of it. He produces SYLLOGISTIC arguments (where two premises when put together necessitate a new proposition, the conclusion), and often recommends one of the premises by an inductive argument from similar cases. In these respects Plato agrees excellently with Aristotle.

But Aristotle does not prepare us for the strange fact that the Platonic Socrates uses his inductions and syllogisms not for but against proposed definitions of the virtues. His conversation takes the form of putting questions to a single respondent. The first question, being a request for a definition, does not admit the answers yes and no and is a matter of doubt, but the subsequent questions demand the answer yes or no. Having obtained a number of apparently disconnected answers in this way, Socrates 'syllogizes' them, as Aristotle says, and shows that they refute the respondent's answer to the first question. He then asks the respondent to find another answer to the first question, and treats that in the same way. The effect is to show that the respondent is contradicting himself, and does not know what he thought he knew. Socrates does not, however, claim to understand the matter himself. On the contrary, he denies all knowledge of it, and claims that he never intended to convict his respondent of ignorance: 'I was never a teacher of anybody'. He claims – though it is hard to believe – that his questions might, for all he knew beforehand, have led to the confirmation rather than the refutation of the answer given. Hence his victims tended to call him 'sly', for pretending to know less than they do when actually he knows more. The Greek for slyness is 'irony'; and this is the origin of the conception of irony as the conveyance of a statement by words which literally convey its contradictory.

There is something repellent about this pattern of talk, and Plato says it incurred some condemnation. He represents Socrates as having some other questionable traits, but still he makes us feel that his character was wonderful and uniquely valuable. In the *Symposium* he shows Socrates first as the deep thinker who has got stuck in contemplation outside the host's door, then as the lover easily obtaining the seats next the most attractive young men, then as a benign cross-examiner of his host, then as the philosophical sublimator of earthly love into a religion of Beauty, and then as the subject of a daring encomium by Alcibiades. Alcibiades likens him to a statue of the ugly Silenus that opens to show hidden beauties within, and confesses to having persistently tempted Socrates and thus experienced his unbreakable self-control. He also praises Socrates' formidable calmness and endurance on campaign, and affirms his wonderful unlikeness to any other human being alive or dead. All this is to be believed.

Like Xenophon, Plato offers us an *Apology of Socrates*. It professes to comprise the three speeches made by Socrates at his trial, but they are certainly not transcripts, bearing at best a remote resemblance to what was actually said. Some think that Socrates offered no defence at all. But it is probably true that the indictment was that 'Socrates corrupts the young men, and does not believe in the city's gods and believes in new divinities', and that if thirty more jurors had voted the other way he would have been acquitted. It is also probable that Socrates proposed as a penalty that he should be fed at public expense, and that he changed this to a fine at the request of Plato and others. And, if we believe that he was intransigent in his choice of a 'penalty' after conviction, we should believe that Plato's work is probably true to life in the magnificently proud and unbending tone it makes Socrates take with the court.

It is very probable that Socrates was, as Plato makes him claim, a courageous opponent of the injustices both of tyrants and of the people. It is also probable that

he claimed to enjoy a mysterious 'divine sign', a sort of inner voice which frequently forbade him to do what he was thinking of doing, and whose advice he believed to be always good. It is doubtful, however, whether Socrates really thought that he had been 'ordered by the god, both by oracles and by dreams and by every means by which a divine destiny was ever imposed on a man', to convict men of their ignorance by refuting their opinions in cross-examination.

It would have been easy to escape from the Athenian prison; and those who voted for his death may well have assumed that Socrates would do so. In his exquisite little dialogue, *Crito*, Plato shows Socrates' old friend Crito pleading with him to escape, and Socrates refusing. The reason he gives is that, by choosing to pursue his life in Athens, he has promised – in deed, though not in word – to obey the laws of Athens, and that he must keep his promise. Finally, in the magnificent *Phaedo*, 'Plato depicts Socrates' last conversation and death, while letting us know that he himself was not there. We may believe Plato when he tells us that Socrates' wife and children visited him on his last day but were not present at his death; that his friends wept loudly when he drank the poison and were rebuked for it by the unmoved Socrates; that his last words were 'Crito, we owe a cock to Asclepius; pay it and do not neglect it'; that Crito answered 'it shall be done; think if there is anything else'; and that no answer came. The last pages of the *Phaedo* are of extraordinary beauty and grandeur.

We had better not believe, however, that Socrates really defended the doctrines which Plato represents him as defending on his last day. In the *Phaedo* Plato shows Socrates convinced that there is a life after death; but in the *Apology* he is probably more accurate, making

Socrates treat it as an open question. In the *Phaedo* Plato has Socrates say that in his youth he took an interest in physical questions, but the passage is probably only a dramatic way of setting certain points of view in opposition to each other. In the *Phaedo* Plato also makes Socrates expound and assume the theory of Ideas, thus coming into conflict with Aristotle's statement that 'Socrates did not make the universals or the definitions exist apart.' It is very probable that Aristotle is right, as tradition holds, in saying that the theory of Ideas was the invention of Plato. It was a natural step forward from Socratic definition, but probably not one that Socrates himself took. Plato introduced it into the *Phaedo* as a way of dedicating to Socrates the fruits of his teaching, rather than as a record of that teaching itself.

The greatest value of Plato's Socrates is his superb championship of the ideal of reason, and his high and clear conception of what reason demands. He impresses us, more than any other figure in literature, with the supreme importance of thinking as well as possible and making our actions conform to our thoughts. To this end he preaches knowledge of one's own starting-points, hypothetical entertainment of opinions, exploration of their consequences and connexions, willingness to follow arguments wherever they lead, public confession of one's thoughts, invitation to others to criticize, readiness to reconsider, and at the same time firm action in accordance with one's present beliefs. Plato's *Apology* made Socrates the chief martyr of reason as the gospels made Jesus the chief martyr of faith. (R.R.)

Solipsism Sometimes we idly fancy that the whole world is merely our dream. Solipsism is a theory, rather like this fancy, but based on argument. If asked why I believe in the existence of stars, trees and people, I have to reply 'My sight, hearing, touch, in short, my perceptions tell me so. Certainly my perceptions are sorted and supplemented by memory, inference and conjecture, but without perceptions such thinking has nothing to work on. Now perceiving is having sensations. But you cannot have, for example, my visual or tactual sensations, any more than you can have my toothaches. So you cannot perceive anything that I perceive. The world that my senses acquaint me with is private to me. Even the you that I see and hear could no more exist without my existing than my toothaches could. I hanker to believe that independently existing, unperceived things tally with the perceived contents of my private world, but I ought to believe that I alone (*solus ipse*) exist in my own right, all else depending on me as my toothaches do.' No important philosophers accept this repellent conclusion. But many, accepting the argument for it, have to postulate non-perceptual reasons for believing in independently existing things and people. We should, instead, reject the step in the argument 'perceiving is having sensations'. (G.R.)

Sophists In ancient Greece traditional education consisted of music (poetry, drama and in general the subjects presided over by the nine muses) and gymnastic. In the more sophisticated social conditions of the fifth century BC the need for a further education became apparent, and the sophists came forward to supply it. They were itinerant professors, wandering from city to city giving courses of lectures, mainly on rhetoric and the art of getting on, in return for fees from their audiences. Thus the term 'sophist' originally meant something like 'professor'; and with some exceptions, such as PROTAGORAS, the sophists were not specially concerned with philosophy, and it is quite mistaken to think of them as forming some philosophical school. The establishment of such permanent centres of higher education as the schools of PLATO and ARISTOTLE (who were of course sophists to the general public) led to the disappearance of the sophists in the middle of the fourth century BC.

The opprobrium which now attaches to the word 'sophist' is due to skilful propaganda against their rivals by Plato and Aristotle. The basic charge was that what the sophists taught was not knowledge but an art of getting on which neglected the highest values. The best known of the sophists are Protagoras, Gorgias, Prodicus, Hippias, Antiphon, Thrasymachus, Lycaphron and Isocrates.   (J.O.U.)

Speech Acts   See AUSTIN, SEARLE.

Spencer, Herbert (1820–1903) Herbert Spencer achieved an enormous popular reputation in England towards the end of the nineteenth century by projecting a 'System of Synthetic Philosophy' which would unify the biological and social sciences by means of a generalized philosophical notion of evolution. In *First Principles* (1862) Spencer maintained that we could have knowledge only of phenomena, but that we could nevertheless infer to an Unknowable, an Incomprehensible Power which is the source of phenomena, the most important of which is the Law of Evolution which he obscurely phrased as follows: 'an integration of matter and concomitant dissipation of motion, during which the matter passes from an indefinite incoherent homogeneity to a definite coherent heterogeneity'. He also defined progress as a change from homogeneity; thus he identified evolution and progress and could claim that 'progress is not an accident, not a thing within human control, but a beneficent necessity'. This general conception of evolution is based on the work of German biologists and antedates the publication of DARWIN's work.

Spencer defined life as a continuous adjustment of the internal to the external environment; to live is to be the sort of thing which continually adapts its own nature to be able to deal better with its environment. This is the fundamental viewpoint of the *Principles of Biology* (1864–7) and *Principles of Psychology* (1870–2). He claimed in the *Principles of Ethics* (1879–93) that ETHICS has 'a natural basis' because moral conclusions follow the general law of evolution. Human beings were capable of indefinite adaptation to circumstances, in particular to the change from wild to settled, civilized life; in this adaptation humanity represses old selfish traits and develops new ones by virtue of a principle of sympathy. Moral principles are rules which aid the harmonious, readjusted life of civilization. A hedonistic element can be legitimately recognized since 'pleasure promotes function' and the law of evolution ensures that those actions we find pleasant will be such as tend to have survival value. Spencer's attempt to draw ethical conclusions from evolutionary principles still has imitators today.   (J.O.U)

Speusippus The Athenian philosopher Speusippus was born towards the end of the fifth century BC. He was PLATO's nephew and a member of the ACADEMY, which he headed from Plato's death in 347 until his own in 339. Only fragments of his many works survive, but four points are clear. First, Speusippus maintained – against Eudoxus – that pleasure is not good but that pleasure and pain are opposite evils. (Plato's *Philebus* is partly concerned with this controversy in the Academy.) Second, he wrote a number of works of 'Classifications', and seems to have held that nothing can be satisfactorily defined unless all other things are also; to understand a concept was to know how it is related by similarities and differences to all others. Third, he held that the account of the making of the world in Plato's *Timaeus* was simply an expository device. Lastly, it is clear from Aristotle's *Metaphysics* that Speusippus abandoned Plato's theory of Ideas and also recognized more kinds of entity than Plato, assigning different principles to each kind. (J.L.A)

Spinoza, Benedict de (1632–77) Born in Amsterdam of Jewish parents, Spinoza was brought up to speak Spanish, Portuguese and Hebrew, but he had a less sure command of Dutch. He attended a Jewish High School in Amsterdam where one of his teachers was Rabbi Manasseh Ben Israel, who negotiated with Cromwell the re-entry of the Jews into England. At the age of eighteen, Spinoza went to a Dutch teacher, Van den Ende, to learn Latin and the 'new science', studying the works of Copernicus, Galileo, Kepler, Harvey, Huygens and DESCARTES.

Spinoza wished to lead a quiet life, attending the Synagogue and pursuing his studies. He became critical of orthodox interpretations of the Bible, but had no wish to disturb the beliefs of others. When his orthodoxy was called in question, the leaders of the Synagogue offered him a pension if he would leave Van den Ende and conform. He refused and was excommunicated, thereupon moving to a suburb of Amsterdam. In conformity with Jewish custom which required all men to learn a trade he had mastered the art of grinding and polishing lenses, and now proceeded to earn his living by this means. His *Short Treatise on God, Man and his Well-being* was composed at this period. In 1661 he moved to a lodging in a small house at Rhijnsburg – now the Spinoza Museum – where he wrote his *Tractatus de Intellectus Emendatione*.

About this time, Spinoza became acquainted with Henry Oldenburg, one of the Secretaries of the Royal Society, and began a correspondence which lasted for fifteen years. In 1663, he moved to Voorburg, near the Hague and published his *Renati des Cartes Principia Philosophiae*, together with *Cogitata Metaphysica* (1663). A Dutch translation appeared immediately, and his room became a meeting place for the intellectual leaders of the day, among them Huygens and Jan de Witt. In the *Tractatus Theologico-Politicus* (1670) Spinoza tried to show that the Bible gave no ground for violence and intolerance, but the work was immediately condemned by the theologians. In 1673, Spinoza was offered the Chair of Philosophy at Heidelberg, but declined, saying he preferred to pursue his investigations 'in accordance with his own mind'.

Spinoza now moved into Amsterdam, completed his *Ethics*, and made plans to publish it. Information was laid against him to the authorities and Spinoza withdrew the book. He worked on a Hebrew grammar and a translation of the Old Testament into Dutch, with the object of enabling his fellow citizens to become directly acquainted with the Bible. These plans were brought to a sudden end by his death, at the age of forty-five. The *Ethics* was published immediately afterwards.

In the *Tractatus de Intellectus Emendatione* Spinoza declared the object of his work to be the discovery of 'the life of blessedness for man'. This entailed a search for that 'by whose discovery and acquisition I might be put in possession of a joy continuous and supreme to all eternity'. It involved a clear understanding of human nature, the universe, and the rejoicing which is essential to human beings, and Spinoza called it 'the intellectual love of God'. For Spinoza, knowledge is to be pursued by freeing the understanding from the vague and confused ideas of sense-perception and imagination, and from inappropriate attachment to objects. It is for these reasons that Spinoza's main work, a largely metaphysical treatise, is called the *Ethics*. In it we are shown finding our freedom and blessedness in the realization that we are part of a system which is determined throughout. We rejoice in this state, and in Spinoza's sense of the word, this is to love God.

When the intellect is working well it is in possession of true ideas and of certainty. ('He who has a true idea knows at the same time that he has a true idea.') True ideas are expressed in definitions which may then be deductively developed, the connexion between each proposition and the next being self-evident. We thus reach a system of true propositions. Those who proceed in this way enjoy knowledge of the second grade, *ratio*; knowledge of the highest or third grade, *scientia intuitiva*, belongs to God alone. The lowest grade, *imaginatio*, is knowledge by sense perception and imagination, by vague signs and hearsay. These sources are not erroneous in themselves, but they lead to error unless they are recognized as states of the body rather than parts of a system of ideas. Error is a privation of knowledge, an unacknowledged confusion of ideas. Vague signs are ones like 'man' and 'horse', which stand confusedly for any number of particulars, in contrast to 'Peter', which stands unequivocally for one body-mind in a determinate place in the spatio-temporal system. 'Man' has no place in a system of ideas, but 'Peter' may be understood as a body-mind in a system of interacting bodies or body-minds (see GENDER).

The *Ethics* consists of a system of definitions, axioms and theorems. The definitions in Part I are not derivable from any more fundamental concepts. Taken together, they form a basis for rational theology and the sciences. Substance is defined as 'that which is in itself and is conceived through itself', attribute as 'that which the intellect perceives of substance as if constituting its essence'. Definition VI equates 'God' with 'substance consisting of infinite attributes' and leads to a concept of God as One, infinite, necessarily existing, containing all being and the sole cause of every existing thing. This inference depends on an axiom stating that 'the knowledge of an effect depends upon and involves the knowledge of the cause'. That is to say, the causal relation for Spinoza is the relation of ground and consequent. Substance, since it is conceived through itself, is its own ground, that is, it is self-caused and so necessarily existing. There could not be two such beings, for if there were, then either one would have to be understood in terms of the other, or both would have to be understood in terms of a third thing which would then itself be substance. Everything except substance is 'in something else, through which also it is conceived', so that there is nothing outside substance.

Substance is also manifested in infinite attributes, each infinitely modified into 'modes' which are 'conceived through' substance under one or other of its attributes. Of the infinite number of attributes, we know only two – extension and thought – which are perceived *as if* constituting the essence of substance. Philosophers had mistakenly supposed that thought and extension are substances, so creating the problem of connecting things 'which have nothing in common with one another, and so cannot be conceived through one another'. Extension and thought are two attributes of the one substance, not interacting, but each infinitely diversified into modes which occur together. The most interesting case of this 'occurring together' is in human beings, where mental events are paralleled by physical events. The mind is 'the idea of the body'.

The system of extension is *facies totius universi* (the aspect of the entire universe), and is studied at different levels in different sciences: in geometry, through the concepts of point, line and plane; in mechanics, through those of smallest bodies, motion and rest; while in biology, the concept of *conatus* – 'the endeavour with which each body perseveres in its own existence' – is fundamental. These three sciences were all founded in the concept of substance under the attribute of extension; there had been no comparable development under the attribute of thought, but this is what Spinoza hoped to provide: 'I shall consider human actions as if I were considering lines, planes or bodies.' Just as a human body is to be described in terms of 'smallest bodies' moving in ways determined by earlier motions, so a human mind is to be described in terms of action, passion and adequate ideas, and mental events in terms of earlier events. The essence of an individual is its *conatus*, and the cohesion of physical parts is patterned by the mind's awareness of its own unity and its union with the body.

Differences between simple bodies are expressible in terms of degrees of motion, those between complex bodies in terms of their own motion and that of their parts. The differences among minds are expressible in terms of the degrees of clearness and adequacy of their ideas. People whose ideas are clear are said to be free and active in the sense that the causes of their actions lie, as far as is compatible with their finitude, within their own nature. The causes of action of a finite being cannot lie completely in its own nature; the body is a part of a system of interacting bodies. Free persons have an adequate idea of their own state as such an effect; and even though it may be painful, the appropriate emotion is joy, in that the pain is known to be occurring in its proper place. If the pain has arisen as the result of the action of other human beings, the free person will neither blame nor hate them. Love is 'joy accompanied by the idea of an object', and 'hatred is sorrow accompanied by the idea of an object'. The free person, who sees all human beings as parts of a determined system, can only rejoice in this knowledge, and cannot hate anyone.

The important concept in explaining human actions, as in explaining any other event, is not purpose but cause. Spinoza's favourite example of error is the belief in free will: people are aware of their 'actions' but ignorant of their causes, and when they say have they acted freely, this only shows the obscurity in which the causes of our 'actions' are for the most part hidden. Indeed the so-called 'actions' of those whose ideas are confused and inadequate are in fact passions, and their explanations are to be sought in our circumstances, not our nature. There are three primary emotions: desire, which is *conatus*; joy, which is the organism's passage to a higher state of perfection; and sorrow, which is its passage to a lower state. All other emotions are compounded of these three, together with ideas of objects appropriately or inappropriately conjoined. To pass to a higher or lower state of perfection is not to become better or worse in the moral sense, but to become more or less active. People with inadequate ideas are passive in that what they do depends on what happens to them, not on what they are.

Spinoza's moral theory is relativistic and naturalistic. ('We call that good which we certainly know to be useful to us.') Nothing is good in itself, but persons with adequate ideas will attach the term to whatever increases their power of action, whilst those who are passive will apply it to whatever they see as ministering to their purposes. They attach emotion to objects instead of assigning it to its proper place in the causally connected phases of their mental life. Praise and blame are equally inapplicable to human action, though they may be used as causes in affecting the actions of those for whose conduct we feel responsibility. Nothing can be more useful to the free than the society of other free people, so that Spinoza's 'good man' will in fact be good in the normal sense. He will naturally try to bring it about that others are free and wise, understanding that hatred and resentment are as inappropriate towards human beings as towards rocks and stones. He knows that the only object worth pursuing, knowledge, is better attained in companionship than alone, but he also knows that everyone has their own *conatus*, and no matter how mistaken they may be about how best to 'persevere in their own being', they have the same right as the wise so to persevere. The wise will be tolerant of others, interfering with the harmless beliefs of nobody, whether in politics or religion. They will choose the religion which promotes a good life, and the social system which gives security to its citizens and strengthens their 'natural right to exist and work without injury to themselves or others'. Since there are people of all grades of perfection, some must be led by authority. For this reason, it is of immense importance that theologians and civic leaders should understand the conditions of the good life.

If resentment of other people is inappropriate, it is a thousand times more inappropriate towards God. God is above good and EVIL, and though he is equally the cause of perfect and imperfect beings, his power is equally manifest in both. A physical or mental cripple is such because of his place in the system: God has not tried to produce perfection and failed. ('To him material was not wanting for the creation of everything, from the highest down to the very lowest grade of perfection; or to speak more properly, because the laws of his nature were so ample that they sufficed for the production of everything which can be conceived by an infinite intellect.') Such a God can be loved and worshipped by the wise, but they will not expect him to love them in return, or to allot rewards and punishments. Those who love God do not look to a future life: this life may be one of blessedness; and in thinking adequately, we think God's thoughts, and share in his rejoicing self-knowledge, that is to say in 'the love with which God loves Himself'. To this extent, we may be eternal. (R.L.S.)

Stevenson, Charles Leslie (1908–79)

The American philosopher C. L. Stevenson is best known for *Ethics and Language* (1944), which gives an elaborate statement of the emotivist theory of the significance of ethical terms. Stevenson's principal contention is that to say that something is good is to state that one approves of it and to seek to evoke the same attitude in one's hearers. He also maintains that the concept of valid argument is not applicable to moral discourse. These ideas had been hinted at by HUME and summarily stated by the LOGICAL POSITIVISTS, but never so carefully treated: the book is undoubtedly the classical statement of emotivism.   (J.O.U.)

Stewart, Dugald (1753–1828)

The Scottish philosopher Dugald Stewart built on the work of Thomas REID to create the so-called 'Scottish school' of 'common sense' which was widely admired, especially in France and America, in the nineteenth century.

Stoicism Stoicism was one of the dominant philosophies of the Hellenistic-Roman period. It was founded by ZENO of Citium at the end of the fourth century BC, receiving its name from the painted Stoa (colonnade) where he taught in Athens. All the fundamental doctrines of stoicism are attributed to him, but they were formulated as a definitive system in a series of works by CHRYSIPPUS in the following century. Panaetius and Posidonius made some changes of emphasis and detail in the second and first centuries BC. In the Roman Empire it was modified still further by SENECA, EPICTETUS and MARCUS AURELIUS, but it always remained in essence the unified comprehensive system of Zeno and Chrysippus. It faded out after the end of the third century AD.

The Stoics divided philosophy into LOGIC (dialectic and rhetoric), ETHICS and physics (which included theology); these were intertwined and interdependent, but not of equal importance. The Stoic interest in logic was mainly confined to perfecting arguments in defence of their system; it was the wall protecting the garden, the shell safeguarding the egg. Physics, on the other hand, was both the starring point and culmination of their ethics: Chrysippus said there could be no other basis for justice, and their definition of happiness was 'to live in harmony with nature'.

Stoic ethics was a response to the needs of the time. At the close of the fourth century, the break up of the Greek city state produced not only physical, economic and political insecurity but also a moral vacuum. The response of the philosophical schools reflects this: the ACADEMY allowed ethics to slip into the background and turned SCEPTIC; the PERIPATETICS engaged in scientific research, and acknowledged many different human goods; and the EPICUREANS offered HEDONISM. Zeno's reaction was to devise a philosophy of security for individuals without divorcing them from the circumstances in which they found themselves. His starting point was that of the CYNICS – that insecurity and unhappiness were the result of pursuing what was not wholly under our control. No physical or external 'goods' can be ultimate goods: health can deteriorate, fortunes be lost, or reputation vanish through external causes. The only thing completely in our power is the correct moral attitude of mind, which is virtue. Further, this attitude is based on knowledge (courage was the *knowledge* of what was and was not to be feared). For the Stoic, happiness arose from knowing the right thing to do at any given moment, and knowing that the actual attainment of the object was irrelevant since happiness depended solely on the moral functioning of human reason. It was argued that the wise want only what they can achieve, and thus can always achieve what they want.

The Stoics imparted a special flavour to the Cynic ingredients through their conception of the universe. All reality was material, mind as well as matter; for, they argued, only matter can move or be moved. But there was an important distinction between active force and passive matter; the active force was *logos*, divine reason, the governor of the universe. Indissolubly diffused through passive matter, it fashioned the universe into a rational purposeful living whole of which humanity was an integral part. It was this *logos*, identified with creative fire (or warm air) among the elements, which was the substance of the human soul. Reason is all-important in us just as it is in the rest of the universe, and our happiness must depend on it alone; and since human reason is the same as the universal reason, our knowledge of ourselves and our duties cannot be complete until it comprises the universe and our place in it. It is by understanding the working of reason in the universe that we can identify with its purpose. We thus have the power to accommodate our own nature to universal Nature, or in the Stoic phrase, to live in harmony with nature.

Physics afforded a justification for the supremacy of moral intelligence rather than an account of its field of exercise; for that the Stoics turned to psychology. They observed certain natural impulses and aversions which point to certain ends; the attainment or avoidance of these appear natural for a human being and involve appropriate actions. For example, the principle of all life, the securing of one's own existence, led to physical and external satisfaction, health, comfort, adequate wealth, etc. The instinct to perpetuate the race was the basis of family life and thus of friendship and society in general, and the responsibilities they entail. The impulse of the intellect fostered reflection, curiosity, and the fine arts. It accords with our nature to pursue all these and avoid their opposites, and is therefore appropriate; but as they are based on the conception of human nature alone, and not on human nature as part of the universe, their importance is subordinate to that of the rational. They form a class of intermediate objects having relative value, but not absolute (i.e. moral) value. Their relative value, determined by a study of human psychology, makes possible the formation of general rules for their attainment or avoidance which is the subject of 'appropriate' duties. But the attainment of 'intermediates' cannot be good, nor can 'appropriate' duties be perfect acts, because the general rule is sometimes wrong; such actions may be done by good people or bad or for a wrong or insufficient reason; and it is never completely in

our power to fulfill all or any of them. The 'intermediates' are nevertheless the material (though not the end) of perfect duties, and the field in which virtue functions. But virtue alone is good. The 'intermediates' accord with human nature, but only the right exercise of moral choice among them can bring us into harmony with universal nature. Thus the Stoics retained the self-sufficiency of the Cynics, while refusing, like the Peripatetics, to divorce morals from human nature.

It is just this distinctive relationship between virtue and 'intermediates' which formed the core of Stoicism and roused most criticism and misunderstanding. This was fostered by certain shifts of emphasis in different Stoics, and not least by their love of paradox. They were fond of stressing the absolute importance of moral intelligence by insisting that there were no half measures. If one perfected it, all one's acts would be right; if not, none. Everyone was either perfectly good and wise, or a fool and a knave; all mistakes or vices were equal. Although all Stoics accepted this position, some emphasized it more than others, notably Ariston (a pupil of Zeno), whose complete indifference to the 'intermediates' largely eliminated the practical side of Stoicism. Chrysippus showed that the paradox 'all sins are equal' meant that all moral mistakes were equally mistakes in comparison with perfect virtue, but regarded solely by themselves one could be worse than another. The objects of our natural impulses and the 'appropriate' duties involved were not always valueless; some had a *prima facie* 'worth' and were to be 'preferred', others 'unworth' and to be 'relegated'; others were completely indifferent. Thus health is to be preferred as a general rule, and pain avoided; but neither health nor pain is good or evil in itself, and circumstances may arise where it is right to reject the preferred or vice versa: 'appropriate' duties receive absolute value only from the decision of moral intelligence. The position finds clear expression in the educative methods of the Stoa, for if those who are not wise are fools, fools could nevertheless be introduced to the material of ethics by the rules of 'appropriate' duties, and thus make progress towards virtue. But Stoicism concentrated on concrete acts, and the rules always required interpretation; hence fools remained fallible and vulnerable until they grasped that the infallible directing principle of morality came from within. In every instance they must know what they should choose and why; for this they must comprehend the *logos*. Each individual alone can be the captain of his own soul. Yet it was apparent that most if not all men were still in the progressive stage; consequently Panaetius (*c.*185–110 BC) and Posidonius (*c.*135–50 BC), when faced with a Roman audience demanding a more practical approach than Greek theory, concentrated on the topic of 'appropriate' duties, with its emphasis on human beings and their relations to others. Thus Panaetius derived from the virtues a series of moral and political rules for action. This did not mean that he abandoned the higher study of man in the universe; but it led in the first century BC to the criticism that the Stoics were saying nothing different from the Peripatetics.

It was this essential framework of the end and scope of morality which gave unity to the diverse ramifications of Stoicism. In *ethics*, since the condition for right action was the soundness of moral reason, the greatest danger came from irrational movements of the mind, or passions. Stoics classified the passions under the *genera* of pleasure, pain, desire and fear, and regarded them as springing from impulses externally roused and overriding correct judgment. Chrysippus, who regarded all mental forms as modes of reason, went so far as to call them evil reason arising from mistaken judgments; but this view was criticized by Posidonius, who once more posited an irrational faculty in the mind to explain moral predicaments. But all the Stoics thought that passions depended on an assent which could only be granted if reason was weak, and that they should therefore be eradicated. Stoic moral education was intended as a prophylactic cure for this mental sickness. But the Stoics never banished emotion; the wise would feel correct emotions derived from their sound state, but their reason would never be clouded by emotions from other sources. And despite the influence of Panaetius, who held that the wise had a duty to enter politics since they had duties to their fellow human beings, Stoicism remained fundamentally an ethic for the individual. Since the only goal was virtue, or the soundness of moral reason, the wise were at liberty to commit suicide: they would merely be following the summons of divine purpose. Life and death were alike indifferent, and the door was always open. Although Stoics had no belief in an afterlife, there were periods when suicide became almost a Stoic obsession.

Despite their interest in *physics*, the Stoics did not engage in scientific research. Even to Posidonius, physical phenomena had interest purely as displaying the rational, purposive nature of the universe, which was to be regarded not with scientific curiosity, but with religious awe. They argued that the universe is completely material, without void; that everything is a mode of the original single being, combining passive unqualified matter with force; and that this force is reason and God. Just as a drop of wine could suffuse a whole ocean, so divine reason penetrates the entire universe, making it an organic whole. There was nothing without a tincture of the divine, and nothing not subject to rational law. This position involved, first, a rigid fatalism: all events were part of an unbroken chain of cause and effect, and 'chance' was a name bestowed by human, while possibility means only that a future event is not excluded by a known law of nature (cf. SPINOZA). Second, since God is good, providence rules for the good of the whole: the *logos* varied in purity and 'tension', with lower forms contributing to the good of higher (e.g. animals which do not possess active reason are created for the benefit of humans who do).

This physical doctrine may have buttressed Stoic ethics, but critics lost no time in pointing out two consequent difficulties. In the first place, the problem of EVIL became acute. While Stoics maintained that most things regarded as evil are morally indifferent, only vice being evil, they did recognize its existence, and the variety and contradictory nature of their answers show that they did not quite know how to meet the problem. There were three main lines of argument. The first was that God could not create evil for its own sake, so it must be the result of the material with which he has to work, or a secondary result of his provisions for the world. The second was that evil is not the fault of God, but a result of human misuse of his bounty, which has granted us control of our virtue. The third was that evil is necessary: (a) for there to be good, since opposites only acquire meaning from each other (cf. Plato, *Theaetetus*); (b) as a punishment or test; (c) by some arrangement beyond human comprehension, for the good of the whole.

The second difficulty was that while their physics involved fatalism, their ethics required FREEDOM OF WILL.

Chrysippus replied by distinguishing between the external cause which immediately precedes an action, and the all-important internal cause furnished by the nature of the thing. External causes bind us with the fatalistic chain, but our own nature gives us the power of decision over our own virtue and vice. Yet even so, we can do no more than run willingly between the shafts along the road appointed by fate; otherwise we will be dragged willy-nilly in the same direction. Our nature is subject to Nature's direction, but it is in our power to work hand in glove with Nature itself. Our happiness is under our control, but not our part in the functioning of the universe. The Stoics' view of humanity as part of a single divine organism gave them an affinity for divination and astrology, and a deep religious feeling, especially marked in Cleanthes (pupil of Zeno), Posidonius, Epictetus and Marcus Aurelius.

One of the principal tasks of Stoic *logic* was to provide a theory of the knowledge on which virtue depended. Since all reality was material, knowledge depended on sense-perception, tested by reason. Material images of objects were reproduced directly in the mind. Some images corresponded so exactly to the real object as to demand assent from sound reason; such assent became 'comprehension' (or 'grasping', as one grasps an object in the hand), and thus unshakeable certainty. However the Sceptics pointed out that there is no mark to distinguish true from false perceptions, that the latter may be as irresistible as the former, and that there is no criterion of judgement. This remained the weakest link in Stoicism. In their desire to perfect their arguments, the Stoics made considerable contributions to the study of the syllogism. Believing that speech is thought in sound, and that words arise from the nature of things, they engaged in etymology, and also in the study of grammar, to which they made significant contributions.

Most of the components of Stoicism were not original, but the attempt to unify them into a comprehensive system produced something new, including a magnificent crop of paradoxes. Not least paradoxical was the combination of an emphasis on everyone's capacity to achieve happiness with a recognition of human depravity. Over time, the idea of wisdom became more and more of an ideal, but it always remained a practical one: no one was born perfect, but anyone could become so. This combination of practicality and noble ideals gave the Stoa dominance for some five or six hundred years; it survived both the savage attack of the New Academy, and the acquisitive eclecticism of later Academics and Peripatetics. Although its natural basis and intellectual framework was Greek, and completely alien to Christianity, there were many points of contact between the two in ethics; Seneca was later represented as a secret Christian in correspondence with St Paul; and Epictetus appeared in the Christian curriculum. The influence of Stoicism on later philosophy is not easy to trace, but there are some remarkable echoes in the philosophy of Spinoza. (I.G.K.)

Strawson, Peter Frederick (1919–)

P. F. Strawson was for many years a professor at Oxford. In his *Introduction to Logical Theory* (1952) he examined the general nature of formal LOGIC, demonstrating that the gulf between formal and informal discourse is wider than orthodox accounts suggest. He criticized the semantic and correspondence theories of TRUTH and put forward the view that the phrase 'is true' has no assertive or descriptive function but is used to perform the act of confirming or endorsing a statement. In 'On Referring' (1950) he criticized RUSSELL's theory of descriptions. His most important work is *Individuals: An Essay in Descriptive Metaphysics* (1959), in which he studies the ways in which we actually distinguish individual things of all kinds, concluding that the space-time location of bodies is fundamental to all our ways of locating all kinds of things, including ourselves. This study he calls descriptive METAPHYSICS in contrast with speculative metaphysics which, in Strawson's opinion, is largely concerned to set up new conceptual systems. Later works include: *The Bounds of Sense, An Essay on Kant's Critique of Pure Reason* (1966); *Freedom and Resentment, and other Essays* (1974); and *Scepticism and Naturalism: Some Varieties* (1985). Strawson is also the author of the article on Metaphysics in this Encyclopedia. (J.O.U.)

Structuralism

The method of structural linguistics was first developed by the Swiss theorist Ferdinand de SAUSSURE at the beginning of the twentieth century, but it was not until the 1960s that a structuralist philosophical movement took shape and began to occupy a commanding role in European thought, vying with EXISTENTIALISM, PHENOMENOLOGY and humanist Marxism for the centre stage. The proliferation of a number of controversial works by French thinkers like Roland Barthes, Louis ALTHUSSER, Michel FOUCAULT, Jacques LACAN and Claude Lévi-Strauss, put structuralism on the intellectual map. These thinkers developed Saussure's rather abstract model of linguistic structures into a fully-fledged 'semiology' – that is, a science of signs which goes beneath the surface events of language (*parole*) to investigate a variety of concealed signifying systems (*langue*).

Although few of these thinkers adopted the label 'structuralist', the term did have some general basis in its reference to a number of diverse applications of Saussure's method. Most structuralists also shared a predilection for the psychoanalytic model of the unconscious and the Marxist model of determining social structures. For the French structuralists, Saussure, Freud and MARX represented a new intellectual trinity which radically challenged the prevailing existentialist gospel of the autonomous human subject. In contrast with existentialism, structuralism was deeply anti-HUMANIST. In response to Sartre's maxim that we are what we make of ourselves, the structuralists declared that we are as we are because of structures which lie beyond conscious will or individual control. It is not we that speak language, they argued, but language that speaks us.

While Saussure was the first to adumbrate a science of structural linguistics, or semiology, it soon became evident that such a project could be extended to embrace a considerable range of 'translinguistic' signifying systems. These could include mass media communications, anthropology, literature, social science or information theory. As Roland Barthes argued, semiology can account for any system of signs, regardless of content or limit – 'images, gestures, musical sounds, objects, and the complex association of these, which form the content of ritual, convention or public entertainment: these constitute, if not *language*, at least systems of signification' (*Elements of Semiology*, 1964). Barthes' own most spectacular contribution to the structuralist debate was probably his analysis of the signs of popular media culture in *Mythologies* (1957). This was followed by Foucault's interrogation of the underlying assumptions guiding Western notions of reason and madness, sexuality, sickness and crime; Lacan's exploration of the unconscious structures of desire in speech and language; and Lévi-Strauss' painstaking disclosure of a hidden 'wild thought' (*pensée sauvage*) which operates as a timeless mythological logic beneath the veneers of cultural and historical progress. Rigorously analysing the systems of binary opposition governing the patterning of mythic narratives and rites, Lévi-Strauss concluded: 'myths are machines for the suppression of time'. They attempt to resolve the fundamental contradictions of human existence – for example, the conflict between the one and the many, eternity and transience, permanence and change – by translating the disorder of empirical experience into the order of systematic structures. What cannot be solved at the everyday level of fact can be resolved at the structural level of fiction.

The polemical public disputes which raged between structuralists and humanists in the 1950s and 1960s were by no means confined to Paris. Structuralism exerted an enormous influence on intellectual life throughout Europe and the English-speaking world, particularly in the fields of literature, linguistics, humanities, history, politics, social science and media studies. In the 1970s, structuralism began to be challenged and in many cases superseded by a movement called post-structuralism. The basic structuralist claim to uncover hidden unconscious structures behind surface meanings was now being questioned by DERRIDA and the deconstructionists. The post-structuralists rejected the binary oppositions between surface and depth, event and structure, inner and outer, conscious and unconscious as revived forms of metaphysical dualism. Renouncing the structuralist quest for a science of signs, they celebrated instead the irreducible excesses of language as a multiple play of meaning.   [R.K.]

Subjectivism Like most terms ending in 'ism', the word 'subjectivism' is used very vaguely and loosely in philosophy; roughly a view is said to be subjectivist if it maintains that the truth of some class of statements depends on the mental state or reactions of the person making them. Thus in ETHICS and AESTHETICS a subjectivist will hold that to describe something as good or beautiful is to say something about one's reaction to it (that it gives one a special feeling of pleasure, perhaps), rather than about its 'objective' characteristics. It is necessary to distinguish such a subjectivist view from the expressive theory (found for example in Ayer's *Language Truth and Logic*) which holds that when we say something is good we do not make a statement about our reactions to the thing but rather are thereby reacting to the thing in words in a way analogous logically to cheering or throwing one's hat in the air. The view that what is perceived exists only because it is perceived (BERKELEY's *'esse est percipi'*) is also termed subjectivism or subjective IDEALISM; subjectivistm in this sense asserts – usually on the basis of the fact of perceptual illusion – that colours, sounds, smells, etc. exist only 'in the mind' and not in the natural world.   (J.O.U.)

Substance The word 'substance' has a distinct meaning in philosophical contexts, roughly equivalent to 'thing' or 'individual' (as opposed to properties or relations), or reality (as opposed to appearance). The word originates in the Latin *substantia*, which is standardly used to translate ARISTOTLE's notion of *ousia* ('nature', 'essence', or 'being'). In *Categories*, Aristotle defines a substance as something that exists on its own, or 'that which is neither predicated of a subject nor in a subject, such as a particular man or a particular horse'. This notion was transformed in the seventeenth century, when DESCARTES suggested that the material world comprises not many different substances but just one, which could be identified with space. LOCKE also broke with tradition by treating ideas of substances not as basic and natural but as complex and artificial. See also DUALISM, LEIBNIZ, MONISM, PERSONAL IDENTITY, SPINOZA, UNIVERSALS.   {J.R.}

Syllogism Syllogism is a form of argument comprising three steps, each of which is a proposition containing two terms. If the first step (or major premiss) links A to B, the second (or minor premiss) will link B to a further term (C), and the third (the conclusion) will link A to C. (For instance: 'All A are B, C is A, therefore C is B', or 'All humans are mortal, Socrates is human, therefore Socrates is mortal.') It will be noted that the two premises share one term (A or 'human'), which does not figure in the conclusion; it is known as the 'middle term' and is sometimes said to 'mediate' between the other two terms, which are known as 'extremes'. The theory of the syllogism – especially the classification of syllogisms into various 'figures' and 'moods' – was the bootcamp of classical LOGIC from ARISTOTLE to FREGE. See also PETER OF SPAIN.   {J.R.}

Synthetic The opposite of ANALYTIC. For 'synthetic a priori', see A PRIORI.

T

Tarski, Alfred (1902–83) Polish-American logician, author of the celebrated paper 'The Concept of Truth in Formalized Languages' (1935); see TRUTH.

Taylor, Alfred Edward (1869–1945) The British philosopher A. E. Taylor began his philosophical career as an idealist and follower of BRADLEY. But in *The Faith of a Moralist* (1930) he argued that our moral knowledge necessarily presupposes the existence of a God who controls the universe with a moral purpose, and the immortality of the human soul.   (J.O.U.)

Taylor, Charles (1931–) In his first book (*The Explanation of Behaviour*, 1964), the Canadian philosopher Charles Taylor argued that there was little chance that scientific psychology would ever be able to dispense with the apparently unscientific concept of human purpose. In his later work – including a study of *Hegel* (1975) and an inquiry into modernity (*Sources of the Self*, 1989) – he has strengthened and elaborated his view that human beings cannot be understood except in terms of their histories, their cultures and their self-understandings (see LIBERALISM AND COMMUNITARIANISM). He is also the author of the article on Mind in this Encyclopedia.

Teleological Argument An attempt to derive the existence of God from the appearance of purpose or design in the world; see THEISM, DEISM.

Thales of Miletus Thales, who lived in the sixth century BC, is by tradition the first philosopher, and predicted an eclipse which occurred in 585–4. He was a *sophos* or sage with many interests: among other things he organized the diversion of a river, and urged federation on the Ionians. His mathematical and astronomical discoveries, later somewhat exaggerated, included methods of mensuration, for example, of the height of pyramids, and the compilation of a star-catalogue for nautical use. He probably visited Egypt, and for his estimation of the eclipse must also have had access to Babylonian celestial records. We do not know how prominent and how precisely formulated his more theoretical cosmology was. He certainly believed that the flat earth floated on water, from which it had originated. Here he was probably adapting a common motif of Near-Eastern, and especially Egyptian, mythology. He may also have thought, as ARISTOTLE asserts, that the world and its parts were still essentially watery. He seems to have said: 'all things are full of gods', meaning that they are permeated by soul. Even the magnet-stone, apparently inanimate, causes motion and is therefore alive. It was by abandoning personification and attempting to explain the whole world rationally that Thales earned his traditional title of the originator of Greek philosophy. See also PRE-SOCRATICS.   (G.S.K.)

Theism Theism is the belief that there is a God and that God is omnipotent, omniscient and benevolent, distinct from the universe which he has created and in which he intervenes. To be a theist is not in itself to hold a philosophical theory, but it is to be committed on philosophical issues, both of truth and of meaning. At the same time, a belief shared by AQUINAS, DESCARTES and BERKELEY obviously has a certain chameleon-like quality. The grounds on which the existence of the God of theism has been asserted are very various. There is first the Cartesian view that 'God exists' is a necessary truth: 'recurring to the examination of the idea of a Perfect Being, I found that the existence of the Being was comprised in the idea of it, in the same way that the equality of its three angles to two right angles is comprised in the idea of a triangle...and that consequently it is at least as certain that God, who is this Perfect Being, is, or exists, as any demonstration of geometry can be'. Descartes made a mistake – one which Aquinas had identified four centuries earlier – in thinking that any assertion of existence could be a necessary truth; but this mistake is not committed by those who have accepted either the cosmological or teleological arguments.

Both these arguments attempt to derive the conclusion that God exists from premises about the world. The cosmological argument takes as its premise the assertion that something exists, the teleological assertion that the universe manifests traces of intelligent design. The cosmological argument then proceeds by way of the assertion that the existence of anything at all can only be explained by supposing that there exists an uncaused First Cause. The teleological argument passes from the assertion of design in nature to the assertion of a supernatural designer. Both arguments have been, perhaps over-frequently, pulverized by the charge that they attempt a causal inference from the universe to its maker; and HUME showed that it only makes sense to speak of causal relations as holding between observable states of affairs, and, whatever God is, he is certainly not an observable state of affairs.

These arguments – the Cartesian (or 'ontological'), the cosmological and the teleological – became a standard triad in eighteenth-century apologetics. The habit of reading the arguments of medieval theism as earlier versions of them is however a questionable one. Clearly the chief difficulty in advancing a proof of the existence of God lies in the elementary logical point that in a valid proof nothing can appear in the conclusion which was not already contained in the premises. A valid proof of God's existence could therefore be nothing other than the making explicit of a belief which was implicit in the premises. Those who are prepared to deny not only those premises which state, but also those which imply, divine existence must necessarily be left untouched by the theistic arguments. The concept of theistic proof as proceeding by unquestionable inferences from undeniable premises is ruled out not by any special difficulty in theism but by the prerequisites of proof in general. Aquinas, at least, was well aware of the central issues here. All that you can do, on a matter of first principles such as theistic belief, is to show that your opponent's position fails.

The failure of the eighteenth-century triad, however, led not to a re-examination of the notion of proof but to an appeal to inner religious experience. This appeal became characteristic of Protestant philosophy of religion and led to the quest for an experience at once plainly identifiable as *the* religious experience by those who enjoyed it and as plainly witnessing to the existence of God. The 'feelings of absolute dependence' of Friedrich Schleiermacher (1768–1834) and the 'numinous' of Rudolf Otto (1869–1937) are the most notorious candidates in this field. This whole movement had fruitful consequences for the phenomenological study of religious experience. But as an attempt to provide grounds for theistic belief it fails, for it becomes either another version of the familiar invalid causal inference, passing in this case from an alleged introspectible state of affairs to an unobserved author of this state of affairs, or a simple irrationalist affirmation that because I feel that it is so, it is so.

The latter alternative must be distinguished from another Protestant position, which rests belief neither on argument nor on experience. For some Protestants the whole ground for belief is faith in a divine revelation; the belief that there is a God is from the standpoint of rational argument simply groundless. This is not to say that theistic belief lacks grounds which it might possess, but that theistic belief necessarily lacks grounds. Such a belief is not however invulnerable to rational argument even on its own assumptions. For, if God has revealed himself, it must be at some time and place to some specific person and the allegation that there was such a person is a purely historical affirmation which can be challenged on historical grounds. So the revealed belief of Islamic theism depends upon historical assertions about Mahomet and that of Christian theism depends on assertions about Jesus.

How in any case can the assertion that a given event is revelatory of the divine be warranted? A necessary condition presumably is that the event in question should either be a miraculous occurrence or be accompanied by such occurrences. In this way the problem of miracles arises for the theist, and since the assertion that God intervenes miraculously is essential to theism, as contrasted with DEISM, an a priori proof of the impossibility of miracles would be a disproof of theism. That Hume provides such a proof has often been asserted. Hume accepts the theological definition of a miracle as a breach of a law of nature, and argues that when we speak of a law of nature we mean that a certain course of events has been

uniformly experienced to occur. Now where such a sequence of events has been uniformly experienced by the whole of mankind it is to the highest degree improbable that such a sequence should be interrupted. And when someone testifies that such a sequence has been interrupted, as the apostles testified that Jesus walked on the water, it is always more probable that the testimony is erroneous than that the hitherto observed regularity of nature should have been contravened. But this is an argument against accepting reports of the miraculous rather than against believing in the possibility of miracles; and it ignores one essential feature of claims about the miraculous. What distinguishes a miraculous event is not just its apparent inexplicability; but also the fact that it appears as an answer to a human command or need. The concept which demands scrutiny is not that of a 'miraculous event' but rather that of 'performing a miracle'.

This relationship between divine intervention and human life is characteristic of the religious content of theism, so it is not surprising that it should affect the conceptual problems which theism raises. It emerges notably in the difficulty posed for theistic belief by physical and moral EVIL. If God is all-powerful, then he must be able to prevent evil. If God is all-good, then he must wish to prevent evil. But evil occurs. So that God cannot be both all-powerful and all-good. And to assert that he is both these things and to allow that evils occur is to admit that theism involves the starkest contradiction. The theistic answer to this charge is usually that God's willing some good end such as human freedom and the possibility of human moral achievement made it logically necessary that God should create a world with possible or actual evils in it. Among the difficulties which this answer encounters is the fact that so much animal suffering, for example, must have taken place before man ever appeared and must therefore be considered irrelevant to any divine purpose for human freedom. Theists however are normally disposed to admit that the facts of evil constitute at least a *prima facie* objection to theism. That they admit this perhaps assists them in meeting another type of problem.

Critics of the theistic proofs argue that there are no good reasons for believing that God exists; exponents of the problem of evil are apt to claim that there are good reasons for believing that God does not exist; neither scepticism cuts as deep as that which claims that it is equally meaningless to assert or to deny the existence of God. This may be asserted on the general positivist ground that the meaning of a statement is the method of its verification, and that there is no method of verifying theistic statements. But the same charge can also be made in a way that brings out the nature of theistic belief more strikingly. For to make an assertion is always to allow that one may be wrong – that there is some conceivable state of affairs incompatible with one's assertion which, if it occurs, shows that one's assertion is false. If one does not rule out anything by making what appears to be an assertion, then one simply has not succeeded in asserting anything. But the theist does not seem to allow that anything conceivable could falsify the assertion that there is a good and all-powerful God. Whatever disasters happen the theist claims that their occurrence is not incompatible with the care of an all-loving, all-powerful God. This seems to evacuate words like 'loving' and 'powerful' of all meaning. To this the theist will reply that his assertions would be falsified by the occurrence of pointless and irredeemable evil, but that no actual evils can be shown to be pointless and irredeemable, especially in the light of the

possibilities of an after-life. Thus the theistic claim comes into logical connexion with the claim that human beings are not mortal, a connexion which is already made in most of the great religions on theological grounds.

There is no one problem or group of problems which can be labelled 'the theistic question'. Proof, introspection, laws of nature, free-will, falsifiability – almost all the topics of philosophy – can arise in theistic contexts. The conceptual problems of the theistic philosopher are thus for the most part the ordinary conceptual problems of philosophy, raised from a particular point of view. See also RELIGION.

(A.MACI.)

Theophrastus (c.370–c.286 BC) Born in Lesbos, a Greek island in the Aegean, Theophrastus was ARISTOTLE's most famous pupil, and took over as head of the Lyceum when Aristotle left Athens in 323. Of his surviving works, the *De Plantis* introduced important botanical concepts while the *Metaphysics* raised problems about some of Aristotle's doctrines, especially concerning the Prime Mover. Most of his many writings are lost, but it seems that he remained fundamentally an Aristotelian, while criticizing Aristotle on particular points and making useful additions to Aristotle's logic, and paving the way for STOICISM and EPICUREANISM. Theophrastus compiled a large work summarizing the views of previous Greek philosophers on nature, God etc., which became the source for numerous later historians of Greek philosophy (cf. PRE-SOCRATICS). Historians of Pre-Socratic philosophy were dominated by the influence of Theophrastus until comparatively recent times; this was unfortunate because he saw all earlier philosophers as precursors of Aristotle and forced their ideas into an Aristotelian framework. (J.L.A.)

Thomism   See AQUINAS, NEO-THOMISM.

Thomas of Sutton   Thomas was one of the Oxford Dominicans who rallied to the support of Thomas AQUINAS; his early writings, dating from about 1286, centre on the soul as single substantial form of the body; in his later writings, to about 1315, he confronted a new attack, from the developed Aristotelianism of SCOTUS, becoming a resolute defender of the distinction between essence and existence in finite beings.   (T.G.)

Toulmin, Stephen Edelston (1922–)
The English philosopher Stephen Toulmin worked mainly in the United States. His *Place of Reason in Ethics* (1950) was the earliest book on ETHICS from the viewpoint of linguistic ANALYSIS. *Philosophy of Science: An Introduction* (1953) gives an account of scientific theorizing as being more like the making of maps to enable one to find one's way about than the process of generalization which is described in the classical theories of induction. His *The Uses of Argument* (1958) is an attempt to redescribe the nature and function of arguments in terms more revealing than those traditionally used in logic textbooks. He also wrote widely on the history of science, and produced a systematic treatise on *Human Understanding* (1972).   (J.O.U.)

Transcendent   The word 'transcendent' means *going beyond*, or *exceeding*. In this sense, individual things or SUBSTANCES can be said to transcend our experience of them, and God to transcend the world, or vice-versa. It is more or less systematically opposed to *transcendental* which, in the Aristotelian tradition, refers to notions (like *one*, *good* and *true*) which can be applied across all categories of being, while in KANT it signifies the A PRIORI conditions that make knowledge possible.   {J.R.}

Transcendental Arguments   Transcendental Arguments move from the premise that a certain kind of knowledge is possible (say, arithmetic), to the conclusion that certain A PRIORI 'conditions of its possibility' must be fulfilled. The view that such arguments are crucial to philosophy is due to KANT's proposal for a 'transcendental' philosophy, 'concerned not so much with objects as with the mode of our knowledge of objects'. HUSSERL's project of PHENOMENOLOGY can be seen as an extended Transcendental Argument, as can WITTGENSTEIN's case against the possibility of a private language. Indeed the term can be applied to any argument purporting to establish a proposition by showing that if it were false, it would not even be possible to discuss it: for example, ARISTOTLE's argument that the law of contradiction must be assumed even by those who would argue against it.   [J.R.]

Translation   The philosophical interest of translation is common ground between various factions in modern philosophy, from QUINE and DAVIDSON on the one hand (mainly concerned with the translation of simple experiential statements) to HEIDEGGER and DERRIDA on the other (more interested in the translation of history-laden words like 'being' or highly wrought works of literary art). Indeed, if philosophy is (as often said) mostly about meanings, then it is inevitable that its preoccupations should coincide in large part with those of the practice and theory of translation. Both philosophy and translation could be defined as arts which take ready-formulated meanings and seek new ways of expressing them, and perennial philosophical doubts about the existence or accessibility of such invariant meanings can be said to correspond to (or even to translate) problems about the nature and feasibility of true translations.

But philosophy is entangled with translation in less abstract ways as well. It is perhaps the most systematically multilingual of all literary traditions, and many of the books on any philosopher's bookshelf will be either translations, or works in foreign languages, or both. Philosophy is also the only secular discipline that can lay claim to an unbroken literary tradition of more than two thousand years, and its continuity could not have been sustained without the labours, often unacknowledged, of philosophical translators. Even the ancient Greeks, who are usually credited with creating philosophy out of nothing, had an uneasy sense that their wisdom had been acquired, through THALES and other PRE-SOCRATICS, from the cultures and languages of Egypt and the East. The Romans in turn regarded philosophy as essentially Greek, preferring to transliterate many of its key concepts (such as *dialectic*, *logic* and indeed *philosophy* itself) rather than devising Latin equivalents for them (see CICERO, SENECA, etc.). The same applies to the Islamic philosophers (AVERROES, AVICENNA, *et al.*) who sought to convey the lessons of philosophy (or *falsafa*) in Arabic, and saved many of its classic Greek texts from complete extinction.

For both the Arabic philosophers and the Romans, philosophy's mother tongue was a foreign language, and their own philosophising had to take place in an ambiguous territory where their native forms of speech were in some measure overshadowed or intimidated by the prestige of ancient Greek. The old anxieties of philosophical multilingualism were exacerbated in the intellectual culture of Western Christendom (see MEDIEVAL PHILOSOPHY). Philosophers like AQUINAS were conscious of having no direct access to the Greek that unmistakably haunted their learned Latin, and Latin itself was at best a second language even for those who were completely at ease in it. (The resulting linguistic alienation was perhaps the most important barrier excluding women from philosophy and making it the most male-dominated of cultural domains.) While DESCARTES is often praised for turning a modern vernacular into a medium for serious philosophy by using French in his *Discours de la Méthode* of 1637, it is worth remembering that he returned to Latin for the *Meditationes* five years later. Later philosophers who are famous for forcing their own languages into the service of philosophy (from HOBBES and LOCKE to KANT and HEGEL) were also conscious of sacrificing a wealth of philosophical resonances, and were relieved when they could return to the Latin or Greek languages where philosophy seemed more at home.

The linguistic plurality that philosophy is heir to has sometimes been regarded as an unnecessary encumbrance that ought to be cast aside in the name of scientific progress. From LEIBNIZ to the LOGICAL POSITIVISTS, philosophers have dreamt of an intellectually perfect language that would transcend the often baffling and sometimes irrational complexities of ordinary natural languages. Such an immaculate language would perhaps be symbolic or graphic rather than linguistic and verbal, and it would no doubt be able to provide rigorous equivalents for certain existing concepts with a modicum of technical or practical stability – say *three*, *triangle*, *syllogism*, *quantification*, *transcendence*, or *water*. But if it had to exclude everyday words like *spirit*, *love*, *goodness*, *being*, *nature*, *death* or *end* – exactly the kinds of terms that have traditionally been at the centre of philosophical discussion – it might well be felt that the luxury of conceptual clarity was being purchased at an exorbitant price. A rigorously transparent language, purged of METAPHOR, irony, allusiveness and ambiguity could have all the proverbial horror of a wish come true, its perfection leading not to an invigoration of philosophical thinking but to death through linguistic asphyxiation. For whilst philosophy can be seen as a prolonged quest for a perfect conceptual system, it has also typically undertaken the more humdrum task of elucidating local problems of knowledge or practice as they crop up in everyday existence; and its principal method has always been one of piecemeal, pragmatic and experimental paraphrase, either between languages or within them. It is striking that modern philosophical cultures which attempt to operate within the confines of a single language (mainly those in the English-speaking world since the middle of the twentieth century) typically pay much attention to the more or less formal vocabularies of LOGIC, which enable them to replicate the salutary experiences of inter-linguistic translation without having to learn a real foreign language. It would perhaps be possible to envisage a future HISTORY OF PHILOSOPHY that would be a history not of would-be systematic thinking but of humble and fastidious translating.   {J.R.}

Truth Philosophers have been concerned principally with two questions about truth, the first concerned with the meaning of 'true', the second with the criterion or criteria by which we can decide on the truth or falsity of statements. Most commonly philosophers have failed to distinguish these two questions and have offered as an answer to one of the questions what might be regarded as a possible answer to the other. But it is easy to see that there is such a distinction if we consider the views of a philosopher who does see and make the distinction; thus F. C. S. SCHILLER maintained that 'true' was an evaluative term, meaning something like 'good to believe', but as a PRAGMATIST he maintained that the criterion of truth was utility.

The two most famous theories of truth, the correspondence theory and the coherence theory, have usually been represented as theories about the meaning of 'true'. So interpreted the correspondence theory asserts that 'true' means 'corresponds to the facts' and the coherence theory asserts that 'true' means 'coheres with the body of accepted statements'. The most obvious criticism of the coherence theory is that while it has considerable plausibility as a statement of one criterion of truth it hardly gives the meaning of 'true'; we do treat the coherence of a statement with what we already believe as one reason, though not a sufficient reason, for accepting it as true; but if coherence is a test of truth it cannot be the same thing as truth. Criticism of the correspondence theory is more difficult and complex; from one point of view it seems that to say that truth is correspondence with fact is a mere platitude, but we get into difficulties when we try to give clear meaning to 'correspondence' and 'fact'. No doubt it is true that there are no centaurs, and we may say that the statement that there are no centaurs corresponds with the facts; but it is hard to see what sort of status the 'fact' of there being no centaurs has and what sort of relation, called 'correspondence', it can enter into with a statement. Thus the correspondence theory is liable to resolve itself into a mere metaphor.

Another much-noticed difficulty is that the phrase 'it is true that' seems to add nothing to the meaning of sentences in which it occurs; it is hard to see what extra value is added if, instead of saying 'the cat is on the mat', we say 'it is true that the cat is on the mat'. The real use of the word 'true' appears to lie in such expressions as 'that is true', where it enables us to confirm a statement without repeating it. These points have led some philosophers, notably STRAWSON, to hold that the word 'true' is rather a signal of assent, or concession, or admission, functioning more like the word 'yes', than like a word signifying a quality or relation. Schiller's view, mentioned earlier, that 'true' is a term of evaluation is closely related to this view.

Incautious pragmatists have sometimes spoken as though they identified the meaning of 'true' with 'useful to believe', though cautious pragmatists like Schiller avoided this trap. In putting forward utility as a criterion of truth, the pragmatists were not wishing to say that if it would be pleasant if something were true, we should count it as true; they rather wished to emphasize that systems of human beliefs and the concepts employed in them are interpretations of the world designed to help us cope with it. If we thus think of statements as interpretations, we cannot divorce the question of their satisfactoriness from the question whether they do the job that they are intended to do. TARSKI, in a celebrated paper, defines 'truth' in a way that gives it a function in a calculus analogous to the function of 'true' in ordinary language. It is quite certain that this definition cannot be applied directly to our ordinary notion of truth; whether it has any relevance to the philosophical problem of truth is a highly technical and disputable question. Such views as Tarski's are called semantical theories of truth. See also DAVIDSON.

(J.O.U.)

Turing, Alan (1912–54) The English logician and mathematician Alan Turing was an early theorist of computing, famous for suggesting that if a machine could respond to questions with replies that were indistinguishable from those supplied by a human being, then the machine could be said to think.

U

Universals Universals are, in the first instance, abstract objects such as qualities, relations and numbers – things which cannot be straightforwardly located in space and time. They are contrasted with particulars and are sometimes defined as the objects of thought, while particulars are the objects of perception or sensation. Particulars are sometimes identified with concrete objects in space and time, sometimes with that element of a concrete object which individuates it, that is, distinguishes it from everything else however similar in character. It is perhaps preferable to retain the term 'particular' for the latter idea and to call concrete objects 'individuals', as being made up of both a particular and universals. On this view a particular would be an uncharacterized spatio-temporal position, the bare possibility of an object. Some such idea is one of the roots of the traditional concept of SUBSTANCE.

Two main sorts of universals can be distinguished: predicative universals, the properties and relations that are the meaning of general terms or predicates, and formal universals, the abstract entities of MATHEMATICS. The difference is that while predicative universals can and usually do have instances, formal universals are rather ideal limits to which actual things more or less closely approximate. The existence of predicative universals (redness, justice, betweenness etc.) is argued for as a necessary condition of the predicative use of general terms. We cannot think or speak without general terms: every statement contains at least one such term as 'red' or 'earlier than', and we are never aware of anything except as having

some property or standing in some relation. In other words, individual things fall into kinds, and the world exhibits recurrences and similarities. Clearly there are general terms and they have meanings. But does it follow that there actually exist things which are the meanings of general terms? Could one not say that there is one set of things, namely concrete objects, to which singular terms are related in one way (each standing for one concrete thing) and general terms related in another (each applying to many)? The difficulty with this view (a form of NOMINALISM) is that we can use general terms correctly without having been told in advance all the things to which they apply. There are, that is to say, sets of things in which a few members of the set are representative of the rest. Positive theories of universals are attempts to explain this peculiar and important fact. A predicative universal is what the members of a natural set of this kind have in common.

The existence of formal universals is argued for on two related grounds: abstract reference and necessary truth. Some true statements ('$2 \times 2 = 4$' and 'tuberculosis is decreasing') refer not to concrete things but to entities that are neither in space nor time. But what a true statement refers to must exist. Again, there are some truths which we know for certain simply by the use of reason and without any observation of the spatio-temporal world (such as '$axb = bxa$' and 'Red is a colour'). Universals, then, may be thought of as the subject-matter of necessary or A PRIORI knowledge; to use one's reason is to examine and elicit their invariable qualities and relations. In recent times the argument from predication has been employed more than the argument from abstract reference and necessary knowledge. For it is widely held that all abstract reference is apparent rather than real and that the principle of reference does not apply to necessary truths. Contingent propositions with abstract subjects must refer to existing things if true. But what they refer to, and so presuppose the existence of, is ordinary concrete things. 'Tuberculosis is decreasing' really refers to tuberculosis sufferers, not to the disease itself. It is an idiomatic, and potentially misleading way of saying 'fewer people suffer from tuberculosis nowadays'. Necessary propositions refer to nothing, for they depend for their truth, not on the existence of anything, but on the meaning of the words used to express them. 'Mary's husband is married to Mary' is a necessary truth whether Mary is married or single.

The most famous account of our ability to apply predicative general terms to things we have not come across before is REALISM, or, less confusingly, conceptual realism. On this view we can apply one general term to many things because we are aware of the common property they possess. This common property cannot be in space and time since, if it were, it would exhibit the logically insufferable characteristic of being in many different places at one and the same time. Furthermore there would be many such properties in many places at the same time. This theory suggests that universals are directly accessible to the mind in a way that is not easy to accept. It also has a formal defect common to all theories of universals in seeming to generate an infinite regress. I can tell that this particular thing is hard because I am aware of the abstract universal Hardness and of the fact that the universal inheres in the thing.

But to discern this fact of inherence I must be aware of the abstract universal Inherence and so on. This defect of Platonism, first formulated in PLATO's *Parmenides*, led ARISTOTLE to say that universals were not abstract and 'separated' from the things they inhere in, but to be found in the common world of space and time along with particular objects. What this presumably means is that Hardness is a vast fragmentary object, cropping up here and there all over the place. If so it would be little suited to its theoretical task, for people who know the meaning of the word *hard* perfectly well are acquainted with only a minute portion of this total object. They could only find out what the rest of it was composed of if they already knew the meaning of the word. Furthermore universals with no instances such as *Ghost* and *Female Pope* would be one and the same universal, and the two terms would have one and the same meaning, which they plainly do not.

The two traditional alternatives to realism are CONCEPTUALISM, which asserts that we apply general terms to new things through the use of some mental standard, a concept or image, and nominalism, the view that the things to which a general term applies have no more in common than the fact that men apply that general term to them. In practice neither of these theories is often held in its full rigour. Without some basis in the nature of the things in question, the general correspondence between different people's concepts and linguistic practices would be an unintelligible miracle. Thus conceptualists like ABELARD and LOCKE say that concepts are based on the similarities of things; and nominalists like HOBBES and many contemporary philosophers explain the application of general terms by the similarity of the things they apply to either to one another or to some standard thing or group of things. Realists argue that since similarity is itself a universal these modifications are no more than realism in disguise.

Apart from absolutely pure nominalism all theories of universals are exposed to the regress argument. But this does not mean that what they say is false. It is rather that what is really a repetition in other words of the puzzling fact of the reapplicability of general terms has been misinterpreted as an explanation of it. To say that we can recognize hard things as hard because they all have the common property of being hard, or fall under the concept of hardness, is uninformative. To be aware of the common property or to possess the concept is simply to know how to use the general term, above all in the recognition and classification of things. (A.Q.)

Urmson, James O. (1915–) The English philosopher J. O. Urmson is a compiler of posthumous editions of works by AUSTIN, a sympathetic but critical historian of ANALYTIC PHILOSOPHY (*Philosophical Analysis*, 1956; *The Emotive Theory of Ethics*, 1968), the original editor of this Encyclopedia, and author of many articles in it and also of *Berkeley* (1982). Although many of his writings focus on theories about the nature of philosophy, he holds that 'on the whole the best philosophy is little affected by theory; the philosopher sees what needs doing and does it'. [J.R.]

Utilitarianism Utilitarianism is a theory of ethics based on a principle formulated in BENTHAM's *Principles of Morals and Legislation* (1789): 'By the principle of utility is meant that principle which approves or disapproves of every action whatsoever, according to the tendency which it appears to have to augment or diminish the happiness of the party whose interest is in question...if that party be the community in general, then the happiness of the community.' Thus actions are to be judged only by the contribution they make to increasing human happiness or decreasing human misery. The moral validity of a law or rule, or the value of an institution, depends on the same considerations. If the tendency of an action to increase the happiness of the community is greater than any tendency to diminish it, then it is 'conformable to the principle of utility'. Revelation, authority, tradition, conscience, contract and history are all irrelevant: an action may pass such tests and still be wrong; the only pertinent consideration is its contribution to happiness. Moreover happiness itself is simply a matter of pleasure and freedom from pain.

Utilitarianism had its origins in Greek thought, but in modern times it arose from certain views of HOBBES and LOCKE, and was formulated by HUTCHESON in 1726. A version of it was elaborated by HUME as a purely descriptive account of how moral judgments are made; directly moralistic versions were given by Joseph Priestley and William Paley; and practical applications in JURISPRUDENCE were worked out by Helvétius in France and Beccaria in Italy. Jeremy Bentham drew upon all these sources to create a comprehensive theory with which he launched his assault on the constitutional, economic, legal and social problems of his day. James MILL's version is simpler and more egotistical. J. S. MILL's *Utilitarianism* (1863) is much more complicated, and re-introduces many factors which Bentham had painstakingly eliminated. Henry SIDGWICK and Herbert SPENCER stand in the same tradition, but G. E. MOORE (*Principia Ethica*, 1903) made a fundamental modification: he accepted the view that the rightness of an action depends on the good or bad consequences that follow it, but held that many sorts of things apart from pleasures and pains are good or bad in themselves. Rejecting the original utilitarian view that nothing matters except happiness or pleasure, he argued that the key question was what is good, which he held could be known by intuition.

1 *'Pleasure and pleasure alone is good in itself'*. According to Bentham we should call an object 'good' because of the pleasure it brings and 'bad' because of the pain; it is only for the sake of such pleasure that we should eat, or rest, or fight, and we should undertake to labour or suffer pain only for the sake of future pleasures. He insists moreover that the only way one pleasure can be better than another is if it is bigger. This ethical doctrine is often associated, though not to its advantage, with psychological HEDONISM. Thus Mill appeals to the psychological doctrine in the hope of establishing that even a person who aims at knowledge or virtue for its own sake is in reality still pursuing 'pleasure'. They are (he says) objectives which were once pursued as a means to pleasure, but which (by association and habit) continue to be pursued without reference to the original end. Saving money is one of Mill's examples; abiding by the rules of virtue at all costs, is another. But this is a muddled argument; it treats as 'pleasures' things that are pursued by mere habit and without desire, or desired only by a confusion of thought.

Mill goes on to introduce a distinction between 'lower' and 'higher' pleasures, claiming that whilst the higher pleasures may not be 'greater pleasures' in Bentham's quantitative sense, they are nevertheless to be preferred. On this view it is a trivial point that only pleasure can be desired for its own sake; what really matters is that we should choose higher

rather than lower pleasures. 'Pleasure and pleasure alone is good in itself' has some value as a war-cry, but it is bound to end up by expanding the meaning of 'pleasure' to cover every object of desire. The moral justification for the distinction can hardly be that all pleasures are good; it is rather that persons should choose for themselves – a doctrine which (however congenial to Bentham as to Mill) lacks the 'scientific' quality which the calculation of pains and pleasures was supposed to introduce into ethics.

2 *'Actions are right in proportion as they tend to produce happiness, wrong as they tend to produce the reverse of happiness.'* In his account of utilitarianism, G. E. Moore maintained that an action is right if its consequences would in fact be better than those of any alternative action. Since we can never be sure what all the consequences of an action will be, it follows that we can never know what action is right. The earlier utilitarians, on the other hand, took the more reasonable view that 'right' and 'wrong' should be decided by reference to probable consequences as they appear at the time of decision.

Moore also held (as did Bentham) that when deciding whether a given action would be right, we should take account of the consequences of that individual action considered on its own. This view offends against common sense, however, which thinks rather in terms of kinds of action: some kinds (cheating or lying for instance) must never be performed; others whenever opportunity arises; while with other kinds we must choose on the basis of particular circumstances. Utilitarians may reply by saying that actions like cheating and lying have got a bad name because they usually have bad consequences, so that the moral rule against them should be regarded as a rule of thumb stating that such actions are to be avoided in the main. They will also say that social life would be impossible if certain conventions – truth-telling for example – were not generally followed. On a given occasion the immediate consequence of lying may be good; but there is a more distant consequence to be considered: any breach of the convention is likely to lower public confidence in it and hence weaken it, which might do grave damage to 'general happiness' in the long run. For this reason lying may be generally wrong even when its immediate consequences are good. But in a case where the consequences of telling a lie are not so bad as the consequences of not doing so, the utilitarian would favour telling the lie.

It has been argued that the utilitarianism of Mill's essays is not the same as that of Bentham, Sidgwick and Moore. Mill's utilitarianism is said to be 'restricted' in that it recognizes that the test of the rightness or wrongness of individual actions does not normally lie in their specific consequences, but in the application of a moral rule, or what Mill calls a secondary principle. Morality consists of 'rules and precepts for human conduct', and an act of theft, for example, is wrong because there is a rule against stealing. But these rules are themselves subject to a utilitarian test: they are valid only if their observance will have better consequences than their non-adoption. According to this interpretation, Mill would consider it proper to follow the moral rule unless there was a conflict of rules, or unless the validity of the rule could be questioned on utilitarian grounds. In the latter case Mill clearly says that the proper procedure is to appeal directly to 'first principles' – that is, to test the consequences of doing or not doing the action in question.

Mill attached great importance to following moral rules even at great cost to oneself. But can a utilitarian consistently recommend following a rule for its own sake? The situation is complicated in the case of what Hume called the 'artificial virtues' – justice, keeping promises, telling the truth etc. – which, as he showed, are possible only where certain rules of conduct are generally followed. One could not keep or break a promise unless there was an institution of promising; and one could not defraud a residuary legatee in a society which had no practice of testation. Hence it would be impossible to cultivate the artificial virtues if one were guided simply by the principle of doing whatever will have the best consequences. Irregular conduct would undermine the artificial virtues, since the only reason for observing them would be the expectation that everyone else will do the same. (This does not apply to Hume's 'natural virtues', such as kindness, generosity, or saving lives.) The argument may succeed in explaining, on utilitarian principles, why rules about justice and promise-keeping should not lightly be ignored, but it cannot of course show that they must never be broken.   (K.B.)

V

Vaihinger, Hans (1852–1933) The German philosopher Hans Vaihinger was one of the founders of modern KANT-scholarship. His interpretation of Kant placed special emphasis on the regulative function of Ideas, a doctrine which he bolstered with the help of such unlikely comrades as BENTHAM and NIETZSCHE to produce a general doctrine of 'Fictions', according to which we can only have access to truth if we are prepared to make certain assumptions which we know to be untrue. His masterpiece was *The Philosophy of As-If* (1911), which had a wide influence on literature in English thanks to a translation made by C. K. Ogden in 1924.   {J.R.}

Vegetarianism See ANIMALS.

Venn, John (1834–1923) The English logician John Venn taught philosophy at Cambridge, and is the author of three influential books on LOGIC. *The Logic of Chance* (1866) gives the first statement of the 'frequency' theory of PROBABILITY, which has been extensively developed and criticized since. *Symbolic Logic* (1881) is a thorough survey of previous work in the field, notable for drawing attention to FREGE'S *Begriffsschrift*, then very recently published. *Principles of Empirical or Inductive Logic* (1889) relies largely though not uncritically on the work of J. S. MILL, and makes curiously little use of Venn's own ideas about probability   (D.J.O'C.)

Verification Principle The verification principle is the thesis, central to LOGICAL POSITIVISM, that the meaning of a proposition is the method of discovering whether it is true.

Vienna Circle The group of LOGICAL POSITIVISTS (or logical EMPIRICISTS) who belonged to the University of Vienna in the 1920s and 1930s. In 1895 a Chair of Philosophy of the Inductive Sciences had been founded in Vienna for Ernst MACH. Moritz SCHLICK was elected to this chair in 1922 and very soon an informal circle of colleagues and senior pupils formed about him; they were united by a common interest in the sciences and mathematics, a general acceptance of the positivistic outlook of Mach, and a recognition of the importance of the developing science of mathematical logic. Among the more important of these are Friedrich Waismann, Rudolf CARNAP, Otto NEURATH, Herbert Feigl, Felix Kaufmann, Victor Kraft, Hans Hahn and Kurt Gödel. They were deeply influenced by WITTGENSTEIN's *Tractatus Logico-Philosophicus*, but though he was living in Austria at the time, and a personal friend of some members of the group, he never joined it himself. In 1929 the Circle was given a more formal status and a pamphlet was issued setting out its basic tenets and aims. In 1930 the magazine *Erkenntnis* was founded as the organ of the group, and the Circle began to arouse great interest both in Europe and in America. The group itself, however, soon collapsed, because of the assassination of Schlick in 1936, the hostility of the Nazis, and finally the War in 1939. Many members of the group emigrated and it had its greatest influence outside the German-speaking countries where it originated.   (J.O.U.)

Vitoria, Francisco de (c.1490–1546) Born in Old Castile, Spain, Vitoria became a Dominican Master at Paris, Valladolid, and Salamanca, and brought a new dignity and warmth to the teaching of scholastic philosophy. The founder of the great school of Spanish Thomists, he took a leading part in the university movement for promoting justice for the natives of Spanish America which earned him the admiration of Dr Johnson. In his *Reflectiones* he criticized the NOMINALISM then prevalent in philosophy, but he is most famous as the creator of International Law. He developed the jurisprudence of Thomas AQUINAS, extending the *Jus Gentium* (law of nations) of the Roman legal texts into an organic instrument of concord for the whole *Respublica Humana* (community of mankind) which allows for pacts between States but also appeals to a higher sovereignty.   (T.G.)

Virtue Ethics   In the ancient world ethical theory was more or less co-extensive with the doctrine of virtue, that is to say of qualities of individual character. With the rise of complex social and political institutions and complex theories to match (see MACHIAVELLI), it became clear that people who cultivated personal virtuousness did not necessarily promote the happiness or welfare of others. The extension of capitalist relations of production underlined the point: as Bernard de Mandeville (1670–1733) put it in *The Fable of the Bees* (1714), private vices could (by stimulating productivity) prove to be public virtues. The notion was further developed in POLITICAL ECONOMY and UTILITARIANISM and the rule-based moral theory of KANT. Towards the end of the twentieth century, thanks to initiatives originating in the work of ANSCOMBE, FOOT and many others, there was a large and influential movement to go back to ARISTOTLE and CICERO and revive an ethics of virtue.   {J.R.}

Voltaire, François-Marie Arouet de (1694–1778)   French dramatist and philosophical writer, see ENCYCLOPEDISTS.

W

Ward, James (1843–1925) The
English philosopher James Ward studied
at Berlin and Göttingen and taught at
Cambridge. He was once a Congregational
Minister, and his interests ranged from
biology to METAPHYSICS. His *Naturalism
and Agnosticism* (1899) recommends history as a model of reality and is critical of
SPENCER and 'physics treated as metaphysics'. *The Realm of Ends* (1911) follows LEIBNIZ in developing a pluralistic
system of minds (matter being composed
of interacting mindlike monads), which is
intended to 'leave room for' a unifying
THEISM. His work as a philosophical psychologist was of great historical importance. His *Encyclopaedia Britannica*
article on 'Psychology' (1886) was a blow
to the old associationist psychology,
which had attempted to reduce mental life
to a system of experiences, or 'presentations', mechanically interrelated by laws
like those which relate bodies in physics.
Ward maintained that there must always
be a *subject* to which these presentations
occur – a 'Pure Ego' which is not only
aware of presentations, but feels pleased
and pained in consequence, and has the
power of variously distributing attention
to the presentations, which form a continuum at any one moment (a 'field of consciousness') and from one moment to
another. The argument was elaborated in
Psychological Principles (1918), but the
blending of philosophy with empirical
psychology was attacked as confusion by
BRADLEY.   (R.HALL.)

Weil, Simone (1909–43) The French
philosopher Simone Weil is best known
for the Christian and mystical doctrine of
her later works. She established her reputation in France as a radical and iconoclastic teacher of philosophy and
revolutionary trade-union activist. She
was schooled in the 'activist'
Cartesianism developed by Jules Lagneau
and her own teacher, Alain, and her philosophy is marked throughout by a belief
in the importance of the individual quest
for knowledge and self-enlightenment. Its
particular character, however, derives
from its synthesis of Marxist, Pre-
Socratic, Platonist, pacifist and religious
arguments.

One of her major concerns, made more
acute by her own experience as a factory
worker, was the servitude and humiliation
of the industrial proletariat. Her positive
philosophy of human dignity and humility
was developed through a conception of
'decreation', which means a systematic
release of the self from the 'personal',
modelled on God's abdication of interference in the universe. Weil's most important
work of social philosophy, *The Need for
Roots*, published posthumously in 1949,
was written in an occupied and defeated
France. It is an extended indictment of the
politics which substitutes the pursuit of
power and national glory for the realization
of the more fundamental spiritual needs of
the collectivity. Other principal writings
translated into English include: *Gravity
and Grace* (1947); *Waiting on God*
(1950); and *The Notebooks of Simone
Weil* (1953, 1956).   [K.S.]

Whewell, William (1794–1866) The
British philosopher William Whewell
taught at Cambridge and pioneered the
study of scientific method, stressing the

importance of INDUCTION. In line with Kantian philosophy he regarded the 'mysterious step' from the observation of particular facts to the discovery of general principles as dependent on IDEAS formed by the understanding. That is to say, for the production of a scientific theory the mere collection of facts is inadequate; what is necessary is 'a true *colligation* of facts by means of an exact and appropriate conception'. His main contribution to philosophy lies in his emphasis on the value of hypothesis in science – in effect, the 'hypothetico-deductive' method, or what he called 'framing several tentative hypotheses and selecting the right one'. This led directly to controversy with J. S. MILL. Whewell maintained that induction was no more than the formation of an explanatory hypothesis, and that since the facts explained could then be deduced from the hypothesis, Mill was mistaken in regarding induction and deduction as different kinds of reasoning: 'deduction justified by calculation what induction has happily guessed'. The dispute was unreal, for Whewell was concerned with the method of discovery in science, whereas Mill was interested in the logic of induction as a method of proof, or 'process of analysis', proceeding from particular premises and usually terminating in a general conclusion.

Whewell's views on induction and scientific method were expounded in *Philosophy of the Inductive Sciences* (1840). They rested on the immense store of information in his earlier *History of the Inductive Sciences* (1837), without which Mill, by his own confession, would have been unable to write the parts of his *Logic* dealing with induction and attacking the later book. Whewell also defended intuitionism in mathematical and moral philosophy, incurring Mill's accusation that he was turning philosophy into a support for 'any opinions which happened to be established'. Whewell was indeed the champion of the established order in every field. Whewell was probably the most learned man of the early Victorian age, when he was famous; as a philosopher of science he deserves more attention than Mill. See also PHILOSOPHY OF SCIENCE.   (R.HALL.)

Whitehead, Alfred North (1861–1947)

The English philosopher A. N Whitehead was born in East Kent, where his father was a vicar. His boyhood gave him a strong sense of the continuity of the life of a society over the generations, and of RELIGION as intimately bound up with it. He went to Cambridge in 1880, and was subsequently elected to a fellowship in MATHEMATICS. Here he wrote a *Treatise on Universal Algebra* (1903), and *Mathematical Concepts of the Material World* (1905), and began the collaboration with RUSSELL which led to the three volumes of *Principia Mathematica* (1910–13). Whitehead held the chair of Applied Mathematics at Imperial College, London from 1910 until 1924, when he moved to Harvard University, remaining in Cambridge, Massachusetts, until his death.

Whitehead's philosophy was an attempt to combine (a) a logico-mathematical interest in abstract relational systems, with (b) 'cosmology', in the sense of an interpretation of the world suggested by general notions underlying physical science; and (c) a moral, religious and aesthetic interest in human relationships within societies. In his early logical work he pursued the suggestion, originating from FREGE, that mathematics is derivable from certain formal logical relationships. These make possible the development of deductive systems which supply, as it were, blank cheques of possible forms of relations, some of which may be filled in by 'values' in empirical applications. In his interest in the general ideas underlying the physical science of his time, he was impressed chiefly by field theories in physics, and the notion of energy as he learnt it from J. J. Thompson, who regarded it as a vector magnitude, a measurable flux passing from one natural event to another. This notion, he thought, implied that the physical ultimates should be thought of as lines of force with a direction, not as particles of matter occupying points of space at instants of time. This led him, as early as 'Mathematical Concepts of the Material World' (1905), to an attack on classical Newtonian concepts. The notion of lines of force overlapping one another in 'fields' was seen as analogous to the logico-topological device of 'Extensive Abstraction', a method he had devised by which geometrical elements such as points and lines are defined not as real or ideal entities, but relationally in terms of ways in which volumes of different kinds, such as circles rectangles or ellipses, may systematically extend over or overlap one another. The logical and epistemological notions connected with this way of regarding the physical world were developed in the three books of Whitehead's 'middle' period: *The Principles of Natural Knowledge* (1919); *The Concept of Nature* (1920); and *The Principle of Relativity* (1922). Here he was concerned on the one hand with framing deductive systems of precise concepts, and on the other hand with interpreting them in terms of the data of experience. 'Experience', he believed, comes to us in the first instance in the form of vaguely interconnected *continua* of feelings, rather than clear-cut SENSE-DATA. Thus he considered that his basic logical notions of the relations of 'Whole and Part', systematic overlapping, and 'Extensive Connexion' were

more congenial than atomistic notions to the analysis of our basic experience; we should start, he believed, not from clear cut items, but from the sense of *something going on*, with a spatio-temporal spread. Whitehead at times claimed that his logical schemes could be reached by a process of idealizing and abstracting from the crude data of experience. This seems to underestimate the extent to which a notion such as the Method of Extensive Abstraction is a topological device for defining points and straight lines, and very unlike anything that can be derived from sense experience. But in seeing the need to devise logical and topological notions to deal with structures within an indeterminate continuum, he was fastening on a genuine problem, even if his own formulation of it was not sufficiently clear to hold the interest of his contemporaries or immediate followers, most of whom continued to work with logical notions related to the atomistic form of analysis.

In the books of his last period – *Science and the Modern World* (1926); *Process and Reality* (1929); and *Adventures of Ideas* (1933) – Whitehead turned to the construction of a comprehensive metaphysical system, based on his earlier notions of 'relatedness of nature' and 'Extensive Connexion', but centering in a speculative account of what it is to be an 'actual entity' in process of development within nature. Here he presents a perspectival view of structures within the continuum of natural events, each unified from its own centre, this centre being looked on as the locus of an active subject of experience, forming itself from its interrelations with the whole of its environment; in Whitehead's own terminology, it is a 'concrescence of prehension'. The nearest analogy among traditional metaphysical views would be LEIBNIZ's monads;

Whitehead's 'actual entities' are, however, not 'windowless', but in active interaction with each other throughout nature. Whitehead looked on this as a generalized notion of organic interconnexion; indeed he described his later work as a 'philosophy of organism'. Its treatment in his later books is complicated by the use of terminology drawn not only from biology but from introspective psychology (e.g. the notion of 'feelings' is used in a highly general sense). It is also complicated by his attempt to combine logical, mathematical, physical, biological, psychological, and indeed aesthetic and religious notions within the same scheme, looking on these as all in various ways descriptive of elements in real processes within nature, and also (he hoped) all finally to be seen as particular exemplifications of certain very general 'metaphysical' principles. He acknowledged that the attempt to reach these completely general principles was unlikely to be successful, though he hoped metaphysical schemes might be produced which should approximate to them. His belief in the importance of aiming at a comprehensive system led him to try and produce such a scheme by generalizing principles derived from varied sources. These, however, may belong to different levels of abstraction or to different logical types, so that as Whitehead presents them they do not readily cohere in a single system. In the earlier work he had been concerned with logical devices by which orderly schemes of exact concepts could be connected with sensory experience, which is vague and fragmentary and also (he believed) qualitative, emotionally toned and teleologically directed. In this later work there is a gigantic attempt to bridge this gap by representing the scheme of general notions itself as derived by 'descriptive generalization' from the kind of structure he believed we find in our actual experience. In this way he hoped to overcome the 'bifurcation' between human beings and nature, and also the gap between general theory and actual experience. But in so doing he may have underestimated the artificiality of general theories, and his phenomenology of actual experience may at times be over-influenced by his theoretical schemes.

Whitehead's work is many-sided, and has the faults as well as the virtues of a vast attempt to construct a comprehensive system which will 'get everything in'. Except for the great influence of his work with Russell in *Principia Mathematica*, it has remained on the whole a self-contained form of thought with little direct effect on contemporary philosophy. But some features of his view of organic interconnexion, thought of in terms of overlapping fields of relationships, have been drawn on in sociological theory. And certain of his books, notably *Science and the Modern World, The Aims of Education* and *Adventures of Ideas* are likely to be read not only for their theoretical notions, but for their wealth of humane, and sometimes witty and penetrating, observations on the history of ideas, society and human life.   (D.M.E.)

William of Ockham (c.1285–1347)

The English Friar and scholastic philosopher William of Ockham began to lecture at Oxford as a Bachelor about 1318 and since he never proceeded Master became known to his followers as *Venerabilis Inceptor*. In 1324 he was summoned to a Papal commission at Avignon to reply to criticisms of his teaching. After four years he threw in his fortunes with the Emperor Lewis of Bavaria who had just declared Pope John XXII deposed, and from that time on his pen was at the service of the Empire. He died in Munich while negotiations for his reconciliation with the Holy See were still in progress.

The influence of Ockham and his 'terminist' school was immense and lasting. In EPISTEMOLOGY he discarded all theories of abstraction or illumination and propounded an intuitive knowledge of material singulars which he held to act directly, naturally and infallibly on the mind so as to produce a total impression of themselves. Ockham's formal LOGIC exhibits a tendency to regard propositional logic as more basic than syllogistic. As for ONTOLOGY, Ockham regarded the object of intuition as irreducibly singular, though often composite. No common or universal nature was to be discovered in it, no distinction of essence and existence, no principles of change on the Aristotelian pattern, above all no relations. He admitted matter and form, but conceived of them as no less absolute and singular than the singulars composed of them. 'I say then...that no natural reason can be found to prove that there is anything imaginable which is not absolute, and hence that no one thing depends on another or postulates another, and conversely that the fact that some things coexist does not prevent each being absolute.'

'Plurality is never to be posited without need' is one form of the principle which – because he applied it frequently and thoroughly – came to be known as 'Ockham's razor'. Change was a mere reshuffling of the singulars, and (contrary to AQUINAS) the causality of the first cause remains wholly exterior to them. This atomistic theory of knowledge and being is faithfully reflected in the moral order. The obligatory law of right reason was not rooted in the nature of God or the world, but imposed by an inexplicable divine command. With regard to it every human will has the fullest autonomy, as indeed has God himself. For Ockham the will is a power not of choosing between goods with which it has a natural affinity, but of self-determination in the face of isolated beings towards which it has been given some arbitrary rights and duties.   (I.T.)

Williams, Bernard A. O. (1929–2003) Witty but waspish English philosopher who taught at Oxford, Cambridge, London and Berkeley; his first book was *Morality* (1972), followed by *Problems of the Self* (1973), *Descartes* (1978), *Moral Luck* (1981), *Ethics and the Limits of Philosophy* (1985), and *Truth and Truthfulness* (2002). He also wrote the article on Descartes in this Encyclopedia.

Wilson, John Cook (1849–1915)   The British philosopher and Oxford professor John Cook Wilson published little in his lifetime; his one book, *Statement and Inference* (1926), was compiled from the lecture notes of his pupils after his death. But his personal influence was immense; though brought up in the idealistic tradition of the late nineteenth century he was regarded as the leader of the Oxford realists, of whom PRICHARD and ROSS are other notable examples, in their opposition to the hitherto supreme idealistic movement represented by F. H. BRADLEY. In particular he insisted that knowledge was a simple indefinable apprehension of the real in opposition to the idealistic contention that the given was inevitably affected by thought. He was also a notable Aristotelian scholar, and deeply interested in the philosophy of mathematics, where he bitterly opposed the logistical theory of RUSSELL.   (J.O.U.)

Wisdom, (Arthur) John Terence Dibben (1904–93)   The work of the British philosopher and Cambridge professor John Wisdom touched on an enormous variety of topics but was remarkably consistent in method: he would follow up almost any philosophical assertion by saying just the opposite, in order to see what might come to light. One of his main theses was that philosophical statements are mere verbal recommendations, but he was quite prepared to say the contradictory since in this way both likenesses and differences would be brought out. He was heavily indebted to WITTGENSTEIN, not least in rejecting traditional METAPHYSICS; but he still found traditional philosophy valuable because it expresses dissatisfaction with linguistic usages where they contain conflicting conventions or none at all. He compared these conflicts with the obsessional doubts of the neurotic, which also have a point; indeed, philosophy has a therapeutic value in ridding us of perplexity, and is in some ways comparable to PSYCHOANALYSIS. (R.HALL.)

Wittgenstein, Ludwig Josef Johann (1889–1951) Ludwig Wittgenstein was by birth an Austrian of Jewish descent. He studied engineering at Berlin and then, from 1908, at Manchester where he became especially interested in aeroplane engines and propellers. The mathematical aspects of this work led Wittgenstein to develop an interest in pure MATHEMATICS and the philosophy of mathematics and he thus became aware of the work of RUSSELL and FREGE on mathematical logic. Consequently he moved to Cambridge where he spent the greater part of 1912–13 working with Russell, first as a pupil but soon as a partner. Wittgenstein served in the Austrian army in the First World War, being captured in Italy at the end. By this time he had completed his *Tractatus Logico-Philosophicus* which was published in Germany in 1921 and London in 1922. At this time Wittgenstein believed that this work was a definitive solution to the problems of phi-

losophy; he had also undergone a deep mystical experience while on the Eastern front during the war, apparently as a result of reading Tolstoy. On his release after the war he consequently gave away the considerable fortune which he had inherited and went to work as an elementary schoolmaster in Austria; at this time also he began to lead the very simple life which he never abandoned. However, during the 1920s he began to re-establish contact with philosophy; under the auspices of J. M. Keynes he revisited Cambridge in 1925 and about the same time he established personal contact with SCHLICK and Waismann, two of the leaders of the positivist movement in Vienna. In 1929 he returned permanently to Cambridge, and eventually became a British subject. During these years he was gradually led, largely through self-criticism, to a new position in philosophy which was extremely influential on Anglo-Saxon thought in the 1950s and 1960s. It was first stated in the *Blue and Brown Books*, which are notes of lectures dictated to pupils in 1933–5, widely circulated at the time but not printed in his lifetime. He became Professor of Philosophy at Cambridge in succession to G. E. MOORE in 1939; but on the outbreak of war he went to work as a porter in a hospital. In 1947 he resigned his chair in order to devote himself entirely to research; but his health soon deteriorated and he died of cancer in 1951.

He was an unusual man; even as a professor he invariably wore an open-neck shirt; his room in Trinity College, Cambridge, was furnished by little more than a few deck-chairs; he never dined at the High Table; his candour was so extreme that it could easily be regarded as rudeness; to the philosophical world in general he often gave the impression of being the high priest of a secret cult rather than a fellow-worker.

Wittgenstein's work as a philosopher divides clearly into two periods. The definitive account of his earlier views is contained in the *Tractatus Logico-Philosophicus*, written in 1914–18; he himself published no account of his later views, but we have an earlier version of them in the *Blue and Brown Books* and a later version in the *Philosophical Investigations* (published 1953) which contain his thoughts, constantly revised, from the mid-1930s until his death. *Remarks on the Foundations of Mathematics* (1956), contains his most mature views on the philosophy of mathematics. Many other posthumous publications have followed.

The *Tractatus Logico-Philosophicus* is without doubt a modern classic of philosophy; but it is a very difficult work, written in aphoristic style. It presents a position in many ways similar to Russell's LOGICAL ATOMISM; but it has been perhaps too frequently interpreted in Russellian terms, for Wittgenstein differed from Russell on important points and adopted a much more extreme and consistent EMPIRICISM. Wittgenstein first states a metaphysic according to which the world consists entirely of simple facts, none of which is in any way dependent on any other, these facts being the ultimate subject-matter of empirical science. Wittgenstein, unlike Russell, gives no examples of what he regarded as simple or elementary facts; he was convinced there must be such, but was not prepared to claim that he had identified any. However, he would presumably have regarded John's shouting at Johann as being more nearly a simple fact than Britain's being at war with Germany, and would have regarded most of what are usually called facts as being in truth mere assemblages of elementary facts. Language, he held in the *Tractatus*, has as

its purpose the stating of facts, which it does by picturing them. By saying that language pictures facts Wittgenstein especially wanted to claim that language must have a structural similarity to what it describes; an informative statement will be a picture of some possible state of affairs in the same way as a sketch-map can picture a battle or the arrangement of furniture in a room. This is true even though ordinary idiomatic language is so full of special conventions and *ad hoc* rules as to be hardly recognizable as a picture – just as a map of Australia might have such a queer projection that we would not recognize it intuitively as such. But a perfect language is imaginable and in principle constructible – a language in which, for example, the spatial relationship of objects will be pictured quite clearly by the spatial relationship of their names. The only fully significant use of language is thus to picture facts; beyond this there is a derivative but legitimate use of language for stating tautologies, of which a simple example would be 'It is raining or it is not raining', but which Wittgenstein held to include the whole of logic and mathematics, which are vacuously true and tell us nothing. Picturing facts and expressing empty tautologies were the only legitimate uses of language; any attempts to use it otherwise would be nonsensical: in particular all ethical or metaphysical utterances would be pseudo-propositions, nonsensical violations of the proper use of language. (Here we have a glimpse of what the LOGICAL POSITIVISTS were later to call the verification principle as a criterion of significance.) By a famous but unavoidable paradox, Wittgenstein denounced his own metaphysics and theory of language in the *Tractatus* as meaningless nonsense: to say, for example, that language pictures facts is to try to give a picture of the pictorial relation which holds between statement and fact, which is absurd; this pictorial relation shows itself and what shows itself cannot be said. Wittgenstein regarded his metaphysics as useful or important nonsense because it could help us to recognize it itself and all other nonsense for what it was. Our tendency to talk nonsense, particularly in philosophy, was caused by the complications of ordinary language, and Wittgenstein devoted a great deal of attention to the technical problem of constructing an ideal language which would not tempt anyone to talk nonsense. But those who had understood the *Tractatus* would not wish to concern themselves with philosophy any more, since it was neither empirical like science nor tautological like mathematics; they would abandon it, as Wittgenstein himself did in 1918.

Wittgenstein's later philosophy received its most simple, general and intelligible statement in the *Blue Book* of 1933. It is largely directed, though not explicitly, to showing why the whole way of thinking adopted in the *Tractatus* is mistaken, though it tends also to destroy all traditional approaches to philosophy. The basis of the new approach is a new view of language; the old view in the *Tractatus* that there is in principle the one perfect scientific language with the sole task of describing the world is abandoned and language is seen as an indefinite set of social activities, each serving a different kind of purpose. Each of these distinct ways of using language is called by Wittgenstein a language game. No doubt there is a use of language for describing the world, and there may be one way of doing so which may reasonably be called 'picturing' as in the *Tractatus*; but there is a host of other uses of language – giving orders, asking, thanking, cursing, greeting, praying. Wittgenstein gives a considerable list of such different language games in paragraph 23 of *Philosophical Investigations* and ends with the remark: 'It is interesting to compare the multiplicity of tools in language and of the ways they are used, the multiplicity of kinds of word and sentence, with what logicians have said about the structure of language (including the author of the *Tractatus Logico-Philosophicus*).'

Though, in Wittgenstein's opinion, we learn to play our language games by practice rather than by theoretical instruction, we are liable to become overimpressed with one or two of the possible ways of using language, giving ourselves an oversimplified account even of these (as his own account of the language of science had been oversimplified). Thus we think of a word as being always the name of something, to be learnt by ostensive definition or pointing ('that is a cat'), and of sentences as typified by 'the cat is on the mat' or 'Tom is fat' – accounts of the way the world goes. It thus comes about that when we reflect on uses of language which are in fact quite different, and of which we are masters when we employ language unreflectingly in its proper context, we try to force them all into one pattern. We may, for example, reflect on the language game of wishing or hoping and try to force it into the pattern by taking is as 'a description of my present mental state'; we may then introspectively attempt to isolate the special mental event of hoping or wishing. Wittgenstein sees here the main root of philosophical perplexity and metaphysical paradox; philosophical puzzlement arises when we utterly misunderstand the functioning of some of our conceptual tools. We may talk as though our problem is of precisely defining a hope or wish, as though we knew well enough roughly for ordinary purposes but in philosophy needed greater accuracy; whereas, Wittgenstein held, what we need philosophically is to see that we are utterly misconstruing the concept of hoping if we take 'hoping' as the name of some psychic process. Therefore to have a philosophical problem is like being unable to find your way about a town through not understanding its plan, or like being a fly in a bottle, buzzing against the side instead of flying out of the top; it is a bewitchment of the intelligence. What is needed in such a predicament is not a revelation, a theory or an explanation, for these do not cure radical misunderstanding. The concepts which perplex us are ones over which, out of our studies, we have complete mastery (in railway travel the notion of time does not perplex us). What we need, therefore, are simple reminders of the purposes for which we make use of these concepts, judiciously assembled so that we cease to be blind to what 'already lies open to the view'. A well-arranged selection of such reminders will make us see how we employ the concepts in question, and thus remove the causes of our philosophical puzzlement.

Apart from our tendency to interpret all uses of language in terms of one over-simplified model, Wittgenstein found another important source of philosophical perplexity in the search for the feature common to all things called by the same name. Thus we may try to find, and even invent, some feature common to all games, in virtue of which they are called games. But Wittgenstein held that there need be no such feature; if we call tennis a game it is easy to find similarities between it and bridge and between bridge and patience, and this is enough to explain the common name 'game' without our looking for some feature common to both football and patience and possessed by each and every game. In such a situation as this Wittgenstein spoke of a family resemblance. Thus we may tend to look for some psychic occurrence common to all cases of hoping or intending not only because we think that the verbs 'hope' and 'intend' must name some process but because we think there must be a common feature to all cases of each; Wittgenstein will then suggest that there may be only a family resemblance between them.

The bulk of Wittgenstein's later work consists of the application of this method of philosophy to a wide variety of problems and tracing their interconnexion. He will take a set of concepts, from mathematics or from ordinary conversation, set out the paradoxical things which we are inclined to say about them under the influence of philosophical puzzlement, and then attempt to banish the puzzlement by reminding us of the normal use of these concepts, by inventing new language games which will be both revealingly similar and revealingly different, always by description of actual and possible uses of language in various contexts.

Given this view of philosophy as a fall into conceptual puzzlement from which one is rescued, or rescues oneself, by reminders of the use of these concepts in their natural context, Wittgenstein could find no place for any philosophical theories, doctrines or opinions. He conceived his task to be to remind us of what lay on the surface, not to express any opinions or offer deep explanations. In his own words (*Investigations*, 126 and 129): 'Philosophy simply puts everything before us, and neither explains nor deduces anything…Since everything lies open to view there is nothing to explain…The aspects of things that are most important for us are hidden because of their simplicity and familiarity.' This makes the actual content of Wittgenstein's later work quite impossible to summarize; there is no doctrine and no single method: one must simply describe things in such a way as to end the intellectual bewitchment of the perplexed.

The influence of Wittgenstein on philosophy, particularly in the English-speaking countries, was very great. His *Tractatus Logico-Philosophicus* was also of importance for the growth of logical positivism in Continental countries, particularly Austria. Very few analytic philosophers would accept Wittgenstein's view that the whole object of philosophy is to banish puzzlement, but few would dispute that among analytic philosophers – between whom there is but a family resemblance – Wittgenstein stands out as a great and original philosophical genius. See also MIND, PHILOSOPHY OF MIND.   (J.O.U.)

Wolff, Christian (1679–1750) German protestant philosopher who adapted Leibnizian philosophy to the needs of university education, laying the foundations for professional academic philosophy in the German language.

X

Xenophanes The Greek poet and thinker Xenophanes lived at Colophon, 570–*c*.475 BC. Leaving Ionia when young, he travelled round the Greek world, particularly Sicily and the west, reciting his poems, which ranged from banqueting-songs to speculations on physics. He suggested that the heavenly bodies were ignited clouds; that all things were originally mud, because fossils of sea-creatures are found inland; and that the sea will dry up, and then the process will be reversed. He also attacked the immoral gods of Homer, stating that there was one single deity, which was 'in no way like men in body or in thought', but 'shaking all things by the thought of his mind'. Later Greek historians treated Xenophanes as the first ELEATIC, because of the superficial resemblance between his one god (which according to ARISTOTLE was coextensive with the world) and the Being of PARMENIDES. Xenophanes certainly stated that positive philosophical certainty lay out of men's reach: 'seeming is wrought over all things'. See also PRE-SOCRATICS.

Z

Zeno of Citium (c.333–262 BC) Greek philosopher, founder of STOICISM, which was so named from the Painted Stoa (colonnade) where he taught. He came to Athens from Cyprus in 312–11, attended the lectures of Polemo, head of the ACADEMY, studied dialectic under Stilpo and Diodorus of the Megaric School, but was most strongly influenced by Crates the CYNIC. The immense literary output and authority of CHRYSIPPUS, the third head of the School, has made it difficult to penetrate to Zeno. But the fundamental doctrines and the outline of the system are certainly due to him. His philosophy proceeded from the Cynic base of the self-sufficiency of virtue, but he incorporated much from other sources, such as SOCRATES (probably through the works of ANTISTHENES) and the Peripatetic development of ETHICS. (I.G.K.)

Zeno of Elea Greek philosopher and follower of PARMENIDES, who flourished in Greece c.450 BC. He defended Parmenides' doctrine of single motionless Being by arguing that plurality and motion entailed logically contradictory consequences. Fragment 3 gives a typical argument against plurality. '(a) If there are many, there must be just as many as there are and neither more nor less; but if they are as many as they are, they must be limited. (b) If there are many, existing things are infinite; for there are always other things between the things that are, and again others between those; thus the things that are are unlimited.' One of his arguments against motion ran as follows: it is impossible to cross the stadium, for you must first reach half-way across, and before that quarter-way across, and so *ad infinitum*; thus the distance is infinite. This and his other arguments ('Achilles and the tortoise', 'the flying arrow', and 'the moving rows') all assumed that space could be divided into portions which could be correlated with portions of time. The PYTHAGOREANS believed that things were composed of discontinuous units, and many scholars think that Zeno was attacking their kind of plurality in particular. His arguments seemed, nevertheless, to be valid against other pluralistic systems in general, though in fact many of them were fallacious. See also ELEATICS and PRE-SOCRATICS. (G.S.K.)